Frank C. Darling

The Westernization of Asia
A Comparative Political Analysis

G. K. Hall & Co., Boston, Massachusetts

Schenkman Publishing Company, Cambridge, Massachusetts

Technical art by Andrew G. Somogyi

Copyright 1979 by Frank C. Darling

Library of Congress Cataloging in Publication Data

Darling, Frank C
    The westernization of Asia.

    Includes bibliographical references and index.
    1. Asia—Politics and government.   2. Asia—Social conditions.
    3. Asia—History. 4. Comparative government. I. Title.
JQ5.D36   1979   950   78-20873
ISBN 0-8161-9005-4

This publication is printed on permanent/durable acid-free paper
MANUFACTURED IN THE UNITED STATES OF AMERICA

To Ann

and to our daughters,

Diane, Heather, and Beth.

Contents

Tables

Figures

Preface

The primary purpose of this book is to meet a growing need for a comparative analysis of the politics and history of the entire region of Asia. It is designed primarily for an academic audience interested in the historical development of modern Asian societies. It presents new approaches to the historical background of contemporary political systems and should also be of significant interest to scholars working in the expanding field of empirical theory and methodology. Since Western influences have shaped important aspects of the international relations of Asian societies, this work should likewise be of considerable value to government officials involved in the process of formulating and implementing foreign policy. The book presents new information and one hopes new insights into Asian politics and history which should be of considerable usefulness to informed laymen genuinely concerned about Asian affairs.

A study of this kind seems especially relevant as both Western and Asian nations cope with the rapidly changing international and domestic environments in the last quarter of the twentieth century. The retrenchment of American military presence in Asia and the increasing multipolarity of international power in the region are causing each nation, noncommunist and communist alike, to rely more on its internal human and physical resources for security and economic progress. In this process, each Asian nation is looking more closely at its own past and seeking a better understanding of the combination of indigenous and foreign historical influences which have shaped its political life. Westerners likewise who will continue to exert certain important roles in the affairs of Asian nations should know how the political systems were founded and developed.

This study has evolved from a growing interest and curiosity in Asian politics and history over a period of about thirty-five years. It has benefited from almost seven years in residence and travel in the Asia and Pacific region; two years in the United States Navy during World War II, three years as a visiting lecturer in the Faculty of Political Science at

Chulalongkorn University in Bangkok from 1953 to 1956, one year as a Fulbright professor in the Philippines from 1965 to 1966, and six months as a researcher in Thailand in the Southeast Asia Fellowship Program sponsored by the Association for Asian Studies and the Ford Foundation during 1976. In addition, I have traveled for briefer periods of time in other countries in Asia.

My analysis of the Western impact in Asia has been aided by personal interviews and conversations in the region with prominent Asian, European, and American scholars. These persons include Phya Anuman Rajadhon, Rong Syamananda, Prince Wan Waithayakon, Luang Sithsayamakan, and W. A. R. Wood in Thailand; Mary Hollnsteiner, Father John J. Carroll, Father de la Costa, Jose Abueva, and Remigo E. Agpalo in the Philippines; U Hla Myint and John S. Furnivall in Burma; Wang Gungwu and Unku Abdul Aziz in Malaysia; and Soedjatmoko in Indonesia. My analysis of the Westernization of other Asian societies such as China, Japan, and India has been assisted by the courses I have taught on the government and politics of these countries for about fifteen years.

The research in this study has also been helped by advice and consultation in the United States with numerous American scholars specializing in Asian affairs. These experienced "Asia hands" have been of much assistance since any author of a comparative analysis of the entire Asian region must rely heavily on other country specialists for important historical information and political interpretations. In this regard I am especially grateful to several political scientists and historians who have read my original manuscript and made many useful recommendations for its improvement. These persons are Lucian Pye and Myron Weiner of the Massachusetts Institute of Technology, John Cady of Ohio University, Clark Neher of Northern Illinois University, and John Wilson and Clifton Phillips of DePauw University.

I am also grateful to DePauw University for a grant to assist in the typing and duplicating expenses involved in preparing this manuscript for publication.

I do, of course, assume full responsibility for the data and interpretations contained in this study.

Greencastle, Indiana   FRANK C. DARLING

Introduction

One of the most complex and fascinating phenomena in the evolution of men and nations is the interaction of different civilizations and cultures. These cross-societal, historical movements inevitably involve the adaption, augmentation, diminution, and rejection of specific foreign values and modes of behavior by the people of any particular "recipient" society. The long-run impact of this assimilative process varies according to the important factor of timing which affects the intensity of the external influences and the strength of the indigenous culture. It varies according to significant geographical factors, especially the physical access of one society to another. It likewise varies according to the types of persons or linkages conveying their own civilization to a foreign land.

The impact of Western culture on the highly diversified societies of Asia constitutes one of the most significant interactions between different civilizations in human history. Beginning in the final years of the fifteenth century and increasing in scope and vigor into the twentieth century, Western influences imparted a stimulus which permanently altered the purpose and functions of virtually all societies in Asia. An understanding of this external impact and the diversified effects it transmitted is crucial to an understanding of the formation of the modern nation-states in the region. A better knowledge of the origin and nature of Western influences is also vital in understanding the government and politics of each Asian society.

Yet in spite of the extensive Western role in the development of contemporary Asian societies, very few scholars, Asian or Western, have sought to analyze and compare the broad forces and movements involved in this important historical process. In 1934 Hans Kohn published a small study entitled *Orient and Occident* which assessed in relatively brief form some of the significant cultural, social, economic, and political problems caused by the increasing contacts between Western and Asian nations after World War I.[1] In the preface to this book, Professor Kohn warned of the increasing challenges confronting the West because of the widespread disruptions in Asia wrought by the inroads of Western civilization:

> The unrest and the spirit of activity of Western Europe and North America have conquered the world. This Europeanization of mankind, a spiritual victory of the dynamic civilization of the West over the static civilization of the East, turns politically and economically against the West and its hegemony which was based on the exclusive mastership of its civilization.[2]

It is also noteworthy that Professor Kohn included a bibliography at the end of his short book which cited ten other publications dealing with Western influences in Asia. Yet only three of these works dealt with broad elements of the Western impact in the entire region. These works were Meredith Townsend, *Asia and Europe* (London, 1901); Arminius Vambery, *Western Culture in Eastern Lands* (London, 1906); Sir Valentine Chirol, *The Occident and the Orient* (Chicago, 1924).

One of the major paradoxes of modern scholarship on Asian affairs is that fewer books have been written on the impact of Western civilization in Asia by either Asian or Western authors since World War II than before. A very useful study was written in 1953 by Maurice Zinkin entitled *Asia and the West* which analyzed some of the important political and economic developments in the region following the drastic changes caused by World War II.[3] At the same time an Asian point of view on the role of Western influences in the entire region was vividly portrayed by K. M. Panikkar in his book, *Asia and Western Dominance*.[4] Panikkar's work dealt with many broad aspects of the Western influences in Asia from 1498 to 1945 as well as with the effects of Western civilization in specific Asian countries. It likewise depicted many of the early frustrations and antipathies felt by Asian thinkers toward the impact of Western culture on their societies just after they had received their independence from Western domination.

Perhaps the major paradox of modern scholarship on Asian affairs is that the most scholarly work on the interactions between Asia and the West deals not with the impact of Western civilization on Asian societies, but with the converse, namely, the role of Asian cultures and ideas in the formation of European societies. This work is the masterful two-volume study published in 1965 by Donald Lach, *Asia in the Making of Europe*.[5] Nothing approaching the quality of the scholarly research devoted to this seminal study has been accomplished in analyzing the much greater role of Western culture and ideas in the formation of Asian societies.

Actually, the deficiency of scholarly literature on Western influences in

Asia is not as serious or as blatant as indicated above. In considerable degree it has been caused by the highly diversified characteristics of the societies in Asia and the highly diversified influences imposed by Western nations in Asia. Modern scholarship has accordingly focused largely on specific Western influences in specific Asian countries. The micro-level research in many of these studies is of very high quality and many of these works will be used in this study on the Westernization of Asia. These scholarly publications include detailed descriptions of the role of Western explorers, diplomats, advisers, missionaries, scholars, entrepreneurs, and educators in particular Asian societies. They also consist of historical accounts of the reaction of specific Asian people and groups to the fermentation and changes induced by specific Western influences.

In some degree, this book seeks to update and broaden the earlier efforts of other authors such as Hans Kohn, Maurice Zinkin, and K. M. Panikkar by studying salient historical factors involved in the Western impact of the entire region of Asia. Equally important, it seeks to present different methods of analyzing historical data which can provide a more thorough and accurate understanding of the evolution of Asian political systems. It likewise endeavors to make a fuller use of the rich laboratory of Asian history in making new comparisons and new assessments of the early development of Asian polities.

My study recognizes that many elements of history are *sui generis*. The development of a specific catenation of human events in any society tends to be unique to a particular configuration of forces and circumstances. Seldom, if ever, would the interaction of these events occur precisely in the same manner or same sequence within a different society. Yet some elements of history in disparate societies such as those in Asia do have certain common characteristics which can be classified and analyzed in some degree to obtain a more precise understanding of different modes of social and political behavior. This approach, I believe, can give additional meaning to the expanding literature on political development and political modernization which urgently needs some theoretical foundations relating history to the processes of change taking place in Asia and in other non-Western regions.[6] This endeavor may succeed in rectifying in some degree the deficiency cited by Professor Samuel Huntington that "the comparative history approach is weak in theory."[7]

This work is based on the assumption that the basic social unit or organization in comparative historical analysis is not the rise and fall of civilizations nor the whole of the human race nor the isolated individual, but the *polity*. It is, I believe, the aggregate of people organized in a political context whether as a village, feudal state, kingdom, or empire which provides the coalescence and common identity necessary for pursuing collective objectives and goals. It is the polity, in brief, which gives purpose and direction to the organized human community. And it is the development of the polity which requires careful study and explanation to obtain an understanding of the various elements of contemporary political systems. According to one historian, the body politic is the "elemental entity in history":

> It is here, amongst bodies politic or polities, that one finds rise and fall, growth and decay, florescence and subsidence; polities are the "moving parts" of history.... A polity, no matter what its form, has the cohesion to act as an entity in history and thereby acquire a destiny, a track record, a trajectory through time. The individual persons who make up a polity are consciously aware that together they have this common destiny, this common trajectory. Within limits (physical, economic, demographic, psychological) the members of a polity do in fact direct its actions and formulate its aspirations. Thus it becomes a meta-bionic organism: a seeming living thing. And within the purview of the variables which the members of the polity can control, it does act like a living being: indeed like a *human* being, for human minds are the source of its lifelike quality.[8]

The basic methodology used in this study will be the analysis of what I will call *historical inputs.* These inputs are not conceived of in the highly structured form of demands and supports from various types of political groups as advocated by Professor David Easton.[9] Nor are they the politically-oriented communication actions of "input" structures such as interest groups and political parties as defined by Professors Gabriel Almond and G. Bingham Powell, Jr.[10] Instead historical inputs are conceptualized here in a more generalized form as historical influences, forces, or conditions which emerge and persist over a period of time. Specifically, historical inputs are conceived as the *interrelated values, modes of behavior,* and *institutions* which originate, survive, decay, or merge with new historical inputs as an organized polity passes through successive stages of history. Other commonly employed terms for various aspects of historical inputs are usages, customs, mores, traditions, folkways, heritages, and legacies.

Unlike most historians who relate historical data in a time-oriented causal manner, the political scientist, I believe, must pursue the explanation of evolving political systems by isolating *discrete* and *politically-relevant* aspects of historical inputs and comparing these historical influences in some kind of organized method of analysis. My approach will consequently endeavor to identify *political* values, modes of behavior, and institutions in various stages of political history, and, as effectively as possible, to classify and assess them. I will also apply a systematic analysis to the historical processes by which these politically relevant historical inputs are induced and changed. In many places the data and analysis of Asian history and politics are somewhat generalized and fragmented, a quality which may make them appear cursory and incomplete to some historians. Also, the study is not a rigorous "scientific" work with elaborate statistics and quantitative data seeking some kind of exact measurement of historical inputs, a characteristic which may make it seem somewhat imprecise to behaviorally-oriented social scientists. Instead it is very likely a work in some kind of "middle-range" theory attempting to explain relevant factors in distinctive phases of political history, and to compare their accumulated roles in shaping the values, behavior, and institutions of the political systems of contemporary Asian societies. A unique aspect of the study is the continual effort to analyze politically relevant historical inputs in the context of their total human and geographical environment. By using several new methods, it seeks to present a broad environmental or ecological assessment of political behavior. It strives, in brief, to portray the "big picture" of government and politics.

The phases of political history through which historical inputs in Asian societies have developed are the traditional society, the Western impact, and the indigenous response to the Western impact.[11] This book will accordingly be divided into three parts and a conclusion. Each part is devoted to a description and comparative analysis of historical inputs and the processes shaping them in a specific phase of Asian political history. Part One will cover the genesis and evolution of politically relevant historical inputs during the time of the traditional societies in Asia. I will use the term *traditional historical inputs* to designate the specific values, modes of behavior, and institutions generated by these traditional societies. Part Two will cover the period of the Western impact in Asia, and the term *Western historical inputs* will be used to denote the values, behavior, and institutions induced by specific Western influences. Part Three will analyze the indigenous response in Asian societies to the Western impact, and the term *fusional historical inputs* will be employed to designate the values, modes of behavior, and institutions caused by the amalgamation of traditional and Western historical factors. The conclusion will include a brief explanation of longitudinal political analysis which will relate the classifications and assessments used in my study to a broader and more accurate understanding of the historical background of contemporary Asian polities. The final pages will likewise relate my method of analysis to the important field of political development as well as to area studies which urgently need a more effective means of utilizing historical data.

In the concluding segments of the book I will differentiate between Westernization and modernization in the development of the national societies in Asia. I define Westernization as the broad interaction between indigenous values and behavior and the external influences from either Western colonial powers or Western national powers exercising partial control over Asian societies through the imposition of "unequal treaties." This historical process persisted until Asian societies achieved their national independence or complete national sovereignty which terminated the political domination previously exercised by one or more Western powers. Except for Japan, the time of ending the influences of Westernization was just after World War II.

Modernization, on the other hand, overlaps readily with the processes of Westernization, and many preindependence influences from Western nations continued in the postindependence period, some with a markedly expanding effect. Yet the external influences in the postindependence period have come from numerous external sources, including many nations located outside Western Europe or North America as well as from public, international organizations such as the United Nations and private, international actors such as multinational corporations. My study consists largely of a detailed analysis of the Westernization of Asia; it deals in a more general manner with the increasingly complex and multifaceted influences of modernization in Asia. Yet an understanding of Westernization is vital to an understanding of modernization, and it is toward this goal that this book is devoted.

PART ONE
THE TRADITIONAL SOCIETY

The Traditional Society

Before engaging in an analysis of the Westernization of Asia, we must describe and assess in some depth the politically relevant characteristics of the traditional societies in the region prior to the impact of Western influences. An understanding of the governments and politics of pre-Western Asia is important for a number of reasons. One reason is the enormous diversity of the traditional societies in Asia and the great differences in the cultural, religious, and political systems which affected their ability to resist or to assimilate various Western values and institutions. Another reason is the great diversity of geographic locations relative to the major areas of Western penetration which heavily shaped the intensity and characteristics of the Western impact. Very important were the different class structures in traditional Asian societies which were in various stages of unity or disarray when Western intrusions began to exert an influence. These differences in class structure, in turn, induced wide differences in the capacity of the traditional rulers to maintain control over their territories. It is important, in brief, to begin this study with a survey of the relative strengths and weaknesses of the traditional historical inputs in pre-Western Asian societies so I can later explain with reasonable accuracy the role of specific Western influences in the development of the modernizing national societies in the region.

The traditional society in Asia comprised collective groupings of people living and working with common patterns of behavior that were shaped by particular beliefs and customs. The economy was based on agriculture. The shared cultural behavior was transmitted from generation to generation which provided an unbroken channel of continuity with the past. The value-systems and personal interrelationships made these societies something more than a mere aggregate or collection of people. They made the traditional society a community organized for a purpose.

A few traditional societies in Asia emerged from early sedentary cultures such as the Bronze Age culture in the Yellow River valley in northern China and the ancient Indus Valley civilization in northwestern India. Most traditional societies in the region, however, were formed by large-scale migrations across land or sea by people seeking new territory, resources, security, or power. In time each traditional society developed one or more "cradles of civilization" from which its own distinctive culture emerged.

In Part One I will be concerned with traditional societies in Asia from the time of their origin to the period between the sixteenth and nineteenth centuries (A.D.) when they began their encounter with the West. The analysis will focus specifically on the characteristics of politically relevant traditional historical inputs just before they began the process of reacting to values and institutions of Western civilization. My purpose has been well described by an eminent historian who has stated that "the first step in understanding a modern society is to understand the heritage of traditional institutions as they existed in a relatively stable form on the eve of the impact of modern knowledge."[1]

An explanation of traditional historical inputs at the very end of the pre-Western era can be accomplished by analyzing the interrelated *cultural systems, class structures,* and *societal structures* of the traditional society.

I. CULTURAL SYSTEM

The cultural system consisted of the subsystem of the traditional society which produced and sustained primary values, beliefs, attitudes, and motivations. It comprised the primordial orientations which imparted an intensely personalistic and parochial quality to the society. It was the collective normative pattern induced by basic social forces such as the family, language, customs, and orthodox religion or doctrine. A major function of the cultural system was the transmission of traditional values and institutions to oncoming generations, a function which closely interlinked the present with the past. The cultural system also blended the entire society with the polity; it generated social and political roles which were undifferentiated and diffuse.

The cultural systems of traditional societies in Asia provide one of the most effective bases for classifying and analyzing the formation of politically relevant traditional historical inputs. A useful method of classification is to depict these cultural systems according to their relative orientation toward sacred or secular objects. I will consequently use a two-fold classification of *sacred-oriented* and *secular-oriented* cultural systems.

Sacred-Oriented Cultural Systems: Religion constituted the dominant social force of the sacred-oriented cultural systems. An intense affinity toward an otherworldly deity or spirit induced social and political behavior shaping what Professor Donald Smith has labeled "religio-political systems" in which religion provided the traditional society with a "common framework of meaning and experience."[2] This type of cultural system developed in the regions which today comprise South and Southeast Asia, excluding portions of the territory of Vietnam. The analysis in Chapter One will deal with four cultural systems in this region: (1) the *Hindu* cultural system embodied in most traditional societies in the Indian subcontinent which also exerted significant influences on traditional societies in Ceylon and Southeast Asia (excluding much of Vietnam), (2) the *Theravada Buddhist* cultural system in Ceylon, Burma, Thailand, Laos, and Cambodia which also exerted important religious influences in traditional societies in portions of Indonesia; (3) the *Islamic* cultural system in traditional societies in scattered portions of the Indian subcontinent as well as in Malaya, Indonesia, and parts of the southern Philippines; and (4) the *atomized animist* cultural system in the island archipelago which was organized into a single social and political entity for the first time by the Spanish in the sixteenth century and called the Philippines.[3]

Secular-Oriented Cultural Systems: A worldly and pragmatic orientation induced the basic social and political norms of the secular-oriented cultural systems. The predominant collective attitude in these societies was focused on mundane and earthly objects. Social relationships and political authority were defined in a secular doctrine or value system. These cultural systems were not devoid of sacred or religious influences during their pre-Western historical development, but by the sixteenth to nineteenth centuries most of these influences were either declining or exerting a minor social and political impact. Secular-oriented cultural systems emerged in the traditional societies of the region which today comprises East Asia, including much of the territory of Vietnam. The analysis in Chapter Two will cover two cultural systems in this classification: (1) the *Confucian* cultural system in the traditional societies in China, Korea, and Vietnam; and (2) the *Japanized Confucian* cultural system in the traditional society in Japan.[4]

II. CLASS STRUCTURE

The class structure of traditional societies in Asia constitutes a second method of analyzing the formation of traditional historical inputs. Class structures in all pre-Western societies in the region were hierarchical and stratified. All had subjugated classes or castes. All class structures were closely related to values embodied in the cultural systems. The class structures can consequently be classified in a manner similar to the classification of the cultural systems.

Sacred-Oriented Class Structures: The stratification of sacred-oriented class structures was designed to perpetuate the religion embodied in the cultural system. It accorded high social status to religious leaders and relegated low social status to classes engaged in mundane roles. Sacred-oriented class structures comprise important traditional historical inputs in the Hindu, Theravada Buddhist, Islamic, and atomized animist cultural systems.

Secular-Oriented Class Structures: The stratified hierarchy of secular-oriented class structures was essentially the converse of sacred-oriented class structures. Their purpose was to preserve the secular philosophy or doctrine and the orthodox social order. Secular-oriented class structures accordingly upheld the highest social status to persons engaged in the combination of scholarly and administrative roles and a lower social status to classes performing more earthy and less prestigious roles. Significant traditional historical inputs were created and developed by this type of class structure in the Confucian and Japanized Confucian cultural systems.

III. SOCIETAL STRUCTURE

The organizational configuration of geographic jurisdictions in the traditional society constituted the societal structure. It consisted of two levels of social and political authority. An "upper," "central," or "urban" level exercised jurisdiction over the entire geographical area of the traditional society, including one or more semiautonomous provincial areas and numerous virtually autonomous villages. A "lower," "local," or "rural" level existed in each village community. The noted anthropologist, Robert Redfield, has described these upper and lower levels as follows:

> At the bottom the series of units consists of people in personal and traditional relationship to another; there kinship and neighborhood are the prevailing connections. At the top of the series are people in more impersonal and formal institutional relationship to one another. As a system of hierarchically arranged social relations, a peasant society is two connecting halves. . . .[5]

Redfield labeled these two disparate and interrelated levels as the "great tradition" and the "little tradition."[6] A similar analysis of pre-Western societies by Professor Gideon Sjoberg referred to these two levels as a "feudal society" and a "folk society."[7]

The great tradition consisted of the complex combination of personal loyalties and impersonal values by which the central political elite of a traditional society maintained effective administrative control over vast territories and peoples. This type of societal structure often contained people of different cultures, but it also included the bulk of the population of the dominant culture of the traditional society. Usually the great tradition was called an "empire" and its ruler was recognized as an "emperor." It exercised control through semi-independent provincial administrators who remained under the jurisdiction of the central political elite, but who often enjoyed considerable autonomy in managing local affairs. The great tradition exercised a form of political rule which created an image of eminent power, grandeur, and unity that was transmitted to succeeding generations over a wide geographic territory. Figure I shows the societal structure of the great tradition.

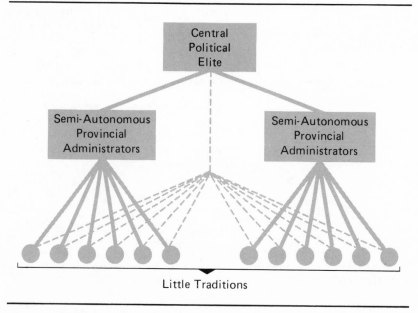

Fig. I.   The societal structure of the great tradition. The broken lines depict the relatively tenuous relationships between the central political elite and the little traditions in the rural villages.

I will use the term "middle tradition" to designate a societal structure which controlled only a portion of the territory with people of a similar culture. This type of traditional society was not an administrative sub-unit or provincial area of a larger great tradition, although it often ruled over a part of the territory of a former great tradition. The middle tradition had its own independent political elite which exercised effective administrative control over territories of vastly different sizes. Some middle traditions such as those in Malaya and pre-Meiji Japan were very small; other middle traditions such as those in the Indian subcontinent were quite large. Middle traditions were usually called "kingdoms," "princely states," or "feudal states." At times they became subordinate administrative regions of a larger traditional society when they lost their independence and were absorbed militarily by a great tradition. At other times they broke away from a deteriorating great tradition and asserted their own political autonomy. Figure II shows the societal structure of the middle tradition.[8]

In addition to the analysis of traditional historical inputs induced by the cultural systems, class structures, and societal structures of the traditional society, Part One will include an analysis of the linkages from the external environment which influenced the development of the traditional society. Part One will also include an assessment of the influence of significant terminal factors on the traditional society just prior to the Western impact.

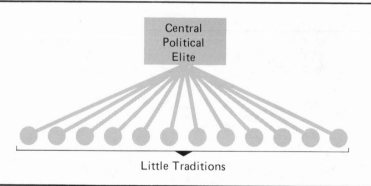

Fig. II.   The societal structure of the middle tradition.

Chapter 1

Sacred-Oriented Traditional Societies

The basic purpose of this chapter is to analyze and describe politically relevant traditional historical inputs induced by the four sacred-oriented traditional societies in Asia. I will not elaborate in detail the values, modes of behavior, and institutions of these pre-Western polities. Instead, my goal is to enumerate and conceptualize salient elements of these early historical influences so their relative strengths and weaknesses can be assessed prior to an analysis of the significant changes caused by the Western impact.

HINDU TRADITIONAL SOCIETY

I. *Politically Relevant Values of the Hindu Cultural System*

A. *Religious Idealism—Political Apathy:* The Hindu cultural system generated one of the most abstract orientations of religious thought in the annals of mankind.[1] Its cosmological views were so transcendental that its concepts of ultimate reality were virtually impossible to perceive or define. Yet in spite of numerous doctrinal nuances, its basic religious truth was the absorption of the individual soul into the Absolute through the achievement of purified and elevated thought. Hindu precepts were bolstered by a theological monism in which all religious knowledge was deemed to be a single unified entity. All cultural and secular pluralism was consequently to be subordinated to the vague maxims of this universal doctrine. The religious idealism induced by these intensely otherworldly views created a deep-seated disdain for mundane affairs. It caused political apathy and precluded the evolution of a body of accepted theory regarding political authority. It engendered numerous ambivalent behavioral norms, including the renunciation of material goods while justifying the acquisition of wealth for certain castes and certain stages of personal life. Its lofty religious ideals also produced an element of dogmatism, self-righteousness, sanctimoniousness, and pietism in Hindu culture.

B. *Religious Eclecticism — Psychological Pluralism:* In sharp contrast to the absolute and universal doctrine promoting religious idealism, the Hindu cultural system also spawned a vast variety of religious beliefs and practices. The highly abstruse religious principles encouraged a powerful tendency toward diverse forms of concrete worship ranging from elements of primitive animism to polytheism. The practice of Hinduism consequently deviated markedly from adherence to a single sacred doctrine. Each individual was free to develop his own religious persuasions and choose his own form of religious worship and behavior. This custom promoted the evolution of numerous religious sects which likewise espoused their own eclectic religious doctrines and practices.[2] Organizational unity among these sects was relatively weak; new doctrinal changes occurred readily causing the splintering and formation of new sects. This religious eclecticism engendered a high degree of psychological pluralism. It contributed an element of curiosity, tolerance, forbearance, and moderation to Hindu culture. It encouraged a receptivity to new ideas suitable for assimilation with established doctrines. It likewise fostered the usage of consensus-building among divergent individual or group viewpoints on fundamental principles while leaving considerable flexibility in concrete practice.

C. *Fatalism — Historical Determinism:* The belief that the evolution of worldly events is determined by forces beyond human control was and is one of the most deeply engrained values in Hindu culture. This precept was derived from a combination of pre-Hindu animism and the widely accepted Hindu doctrine of the cycle of rebirth in which *karma,* or the law of cause and effect, determined the rebirth of each individual according to the moral effects of his deeds in this life. Theoretically each individual has the choice of achieving a significant advancement in the next life by the performance of good works in his present existence.[3] Yet the concept of this life as only one of a long series of previous lives, and only a brief single step in a lengthy cycle of future lives, inspired little individual initiative to improve the secular environment. In effect the law of *karma* discouraged the individual from elevating his earthly status. It induced a sense of passivity and resignation. The fatalism molding individual life was expanded to the forces of history. To Hindu thought, history is illusory and of minor significance. Historical events, like the cycle of rebirth, are determined by powers largely beyond man's control.

II. Politically Relevant Values, Modes of Behavior, and Institutions of the Hindu Class Structure

A. *Caste System*: Rigid and sacred-oriented values in the Hindu cultural system induced tenacious and pervasive influences on the Hindu class structure.[4] Yet these influences were most significant in social and political relationships between specific groups in India rather than within these groups. According to Hindu religious texts, the caste system consisted of four distinct castes or *varnas:* Brahman, Ksatriyas, Vaisyas, and Sudra which Kothari states correspond to "the four functions of knowledge, defense, wealth, and labor."[5] A lowly "scheduled caste" of untouchables or *harijans* were often segregated from the recognized castes due to Hindu beliefs about their "impure" origin and demeaning economic roles. In practice these four castes never existed as hierarchical classifications of persons in specific roles over large areas of Hindu culture. Instead the castes consisted of *jatis* or endogamous social groups usually composed of persons with a common racial origin and type of employment. The gradual absorption of new social groups into the Hindu cultural system throughout much of India's turbulent pre-Western history produced thousands of castes or jatis often inhabiting a particular geographic area. Each caste or jati had its own social and political leadership roles based on age and patriarchal custom. Each caste excluded outsiders through strict rules regarding diet, marriage, religious beliefs, and rules of morality. The intense "in-group" orientation caused by the caste system has been ably described by Vincent Smith as follows: "The essential duty of the member of a caste is to follow the custom of the group, more particularly in relation to diet or marriage. Violation of the rules on those subjects, if detected, usually involves unpleasant and costly social expiation and may result in expulsion from the caste, which means social ruin and grave inconvenience. . . . It is almost impossible for a Hindu to regard himself otherwise than as a member of some particular caste, or species of Hindu mankind."[6] Most jatis, however, did assume some connection with a particular caste or varna sanctioned by Hindu sacred teachings. The legendary four-tiered caste structure did therefore exert some influence as entire jatis often moved up to a higher caste and acquired increased social status and prestige. A significant traditional historical input consequently induced by the caste system was intense fragmentation and differentiation between the caste groups and a strong cohesion and unity within each caste group.

B. *Law*: The Hindu legal system comprised a total body of criminal and civil law which governed every aspect of human life. It was based on the sacred doctrine of *dharma* embodying religious obligations and duty. It was also interrelated with the caste system; its norms prescribed punishments according to caste status. Hindu law and the caste system generated both unifying and fragmenting tendencies in traditional societies. In the absence of a cohesive priestly class, the legal system supplied the most significant consolidating influence. By bolstering the caste system it provided what Donald Smith has called an "all-pervasive principle on which social life evolved."[7] Established legal norms in the caste system also served as a conservative social and political force and contributed to stability in the traditional societies. Dharma and law enabled the caste to serve as what Professor Eisenstadt has labeled the "group referent" or unifying element which "was wider than that of any ascriptive and territorial group."[8] The legal system facilitated the process of strengthening mutual social bonds by legitimizing common patterns of sacred and secular behavior. It instilled an "activist" emphasis in individual conduct to conform to accepted moral and religious behavior. Yet the failure to apply the concept of dharma in universal terms combined with the weak corporate concept of ecclesiastical organization contributed greatly to social and political fragmentation in Hindu traditional societies. Each caste had its own dharma and legal standards. Each caste conceived of itself as a self-contained entity and evolved its own sub-culture. No attempt was made to assimilate "outsiders" by seeking converts or absorbing minorities. These pluralistic applications of law engendered particularism and exclusiveness. In practice they strengthened the intricate web of family and kinship ties which provided a primary source of personal identity and social security. They contributed to a local-oriented social and political culture devoid of a concept of a larger impersonal community beyond the confines of familiar personal relationships.

C. *Personal Political Rule — Authoritarianism*: The intense religious orientation of the Hindu class structure and the absence of an accepted body of secular political theory promoted authoritarian rule.[9] The concept of absolute kingship was bolstered by the idea of *devaraja* or "god-king"; the centralized political order was considered to be a secular manifestation of the unified cosmological order. The legal system upheld the ideal of a benevolent sovereign, yet the lack of specific limitations on political authority facilitated the unrestricted practice of acquiring, maintaining, and expanding political power. The caste system fostered authoritarianism by creating a sense of deference and obedience, and by justifying harsh punishments by political authorities to offenders of the law. The absence of a body of secular political theory also encouraged personal political rule. Impersonal political institutionalization remained extremely weak. The quality of political rule depended essentially on the individual capabilities of the ruling sovereign. Political leadership was frequently surrounded with an element of personal "mysticism" or "charisma" which bestowed additional influence and authority. At the same time political leadership depended heavily on an intricate and shifting web of personal ambitions and loyalties.

D. *Separation of Religion and Politics*: The concept of dharma and the Hindu caste system induced the separation of religion and politics. Each caste was sanctioned by religious law to perform its own prescribed duties. The priestly class composed essentially of members from the Brahman caste monopolized religious roles. The ruling sovereign consisting usually of a military leader exercised secular authority as well as the body of religious law with its requirement for all believers to fulfill the performance of their traditional duties. The management of secular affairs was accordingly conducted by a distinct ruling group separate from religious jurisdiction. No concept was ever developed in Hindu law or the caste system by which political authority could be challenged by the priestly class.

III. Politically Relevant Institutions of the Hindu Societal Structure

A. *Great Tradition*: The great tradition of the Hindu traditional society induced an image of relatively brief and temporary acquisitions of unified political power over large territories. India as a unified or coherent "nation" did not exist until the time of the Western impact. Major great traditions erected by Hindu rulers in this region consisted of the Mauryan Empire (322–185 B.C.) founded by Chandragupta Maurya and the Gupta Empire (320–510 A.D.) founded by Chandragupta I. Two other empires which exercised some unity over sizeable geographic areas and created memories of a Hindu great tradition were the Vijayanagar Empire which fought Moslem invaders prior to the establishment of the Mogul Empire (1556–1707), and the Marathas Empire which emerged in central India after the demise of Mogul power. The Mauryan and Gupta great traditions induced the strongest memories of early Hindu power and influence. These periods of imperial political unity were remembered as classical periods of Hindu culture. During these times religious and philosophical teachings flourished. Outbursts of creativity made major advances in art, architecture, music, and literature. Hindu cultural influences were spread to nearby societies in Ceylon, "Further India" (mainland Southeast Asia), and Sumatra, Java, and Bali.

B. *Middle Tradition*: The middle tradition constituted the predominant form of political territorial organization in the Hindu traditional society. Except for the few brief great traditions, the political history of the Indian sub-continent prior to the Western impact consisted essentially of the rise and fall of provincial kingdoms reigning over regional territories. Notable middle traditions included the Kingdoms of the Andhras, Chalukyas, Rashtrakutas, Hoysalas, Yadavas, Bahmani, and Rajputs. These middle traditions were based on diverse ethnic, cultural, or linguistic groups which generated distinct provincial identities and loyalties. They imparted to succeeding generations a horizontal and heterogeneous political pattern of communalism and particularism. Hierarchical political rolès within each princely state were shaped by the central political elite which exercised control over rural villages outside the provincial capital. Land owners often resided at the provincial centers where they exercised considerable political power due to their control over rural village communities. Middle traditions had their own civil bureaucracy and military forces, as well as an active merchant class. A special type of middle tradition developed in strategic coastal regions which I will call an "enclave tradition." These small entrepot states were also ruled by their own political and social elites who sought to remain autonomous from nearby great traditions or middle traditions. Examples of enclave traditions in Indian traditional society were Karachi, Bombay, Cochin, Trivandrum, Karikal, and Madras. They achieved relatively high levels of economic prosperity due to their pivotal commercial role in the exchange of goods between internal and foreign markets.

C. *Little Tradition*: The collective life embodied in rural villages scattered across the landscape of the Indian subcontinent comprised the little tradition. These rustic communities were called *gaon* in Hindi- and Urdu-speaking areas. They contained the vast majority of the population. They displayed no significant differentiation between the cultural, social, economic, and political spheres. Each form of human activity was closely interlinked in daily routine behavior. The "local" culture embraced a syncretic religious orientation consisting of numerous superstitions and rituals derived from a primitive animism and a few elements of the "higher" Hindu sacred doctrine. The peasants understood little of the lofty beliefs and principles propounded by the Brahman priestly caste. Religion oriented their thought toward the "other-worldly" and provided a psychological channel to escape the harshness and uncertainties of daily life.

The village society in the little tradition consisted of an intricate web of personal relationships centered on family and primary kinship groups. The accepted patterns of behavior stressed affection, harmony, and conformity. They sought to avoid conflict and shame. Intimate personal contacts tended to reduce social inequalities and fostered a relatively homogeneous community. Modest economic differences caused limited social stratification between free landowning peasants, several categories of indebted peasants, and propertyless peasant laborers. Yet all village inhabitants considered themselves as part of an integrated social fabric. Intimate personal contacts gave each individual a sense of identity. A unified cultural outlook governed their daily lives and provided the dominant restraint on deviant behavior. Professor Lucian Pye has commented on this traditional ethical and moral force as follows: "In the main, custom ruled; the government did not have to police the people, for they ceaselessly policed each other."[10]

The little tradition possessed no explicit political consciousness. It had no sense of individualism nor any concept of popular participation in the decisions of the urban political elites. The peasants habitually regarded the "public" affairs of the upper castes as beyond their comprehension and concern. They viewed higher political authority as an inherently evil institution whose primary functions were the collection of taxes, making war, and glorifying the ruling dynasty. They expected few if any services in return. Pye has stated that "those who belonged outside the realm of government might feel that they had been mistreated with respect to particular acts, but they never felt that they had either legitimate rights or valid claims on government."[11] Yet each peasant did feel an intricate part of his own village community. He expected to participate in some degree in local affairs concerned with his own welfare and prosperity. The only political institutionalization of the little tradition consisted of a small council of village elders called the *panchayat* which managed the collective affairs of the community according to traditional norms. These positions of village leadership tended to be filled by the more efficient and prosperous members of the community who usually owned larger plots of land than the average peasant.[12] Yet the panchayat received very few demands from the village society which governed itself largely by custom. The primary function of village leadership was to maintain security and order within the community.

Solitary villages inhabited by primitive aborigines or tribesmen existed in isolated territories of the Indian subcontinent. These people have been called the "remote peasants" by Redfield.[13] They include the Santals and Hos in Bihar, the Mizo, Nagas, and Kukis in Assam, and the Daflas, Abors, and Mishmis in the northeastern areas. These small aboriginal groups fiercely resisted attempts by central or provincial authorities or by nearby village communities to assimilate them into the dominant culture of the traditional society. They thereby received no influences from the great tradition or middle tradition. Their own little tradition remained completely detached from the mainstream of the traditional society.

THERAVADA BUDDHIST TRADITIONAL SOCIETY

1. *Politically Relevant Values of the Theravada Buddhist Cultural System*

A. *Religious Progressivism — Political Apathy*: The religious teachings of Theravada Buddhism included some of the same universal doctrines of Hinduism such as "karma," the insubstantiality of the secular world, and the renunciation of material things.[14] Yet Theravada Buddhism was less abstract and less transcendental than most teachings of Hinduism. It was much more concerned with the religious progress and development of its adherents by placing great emphasis on individual voluntarism for the purpose of spiritual and moral advancement. The basic doctrine of this offshoot of Hinduism upheld that the inherent suffering of life was caused by human desires which tied the individual to the cycle of rebirth. Suffering would cease and Nirvana be achieved only by purifying the individual ego and eventually extinguishing its innate desires through the practice of moral virtues outlined in the Noble Eight-fold Path. In daily practice individual merit for a better future life could also be acquired by a prescribed ritualism which included the worship of Buddha and his relics, daily respect and support for the order of Buddhist monks (*the Sangha*), and assistance in the construction of Buddhist temples. The other-worldly orientation of Theravada Buddhism was consequently less intense than that of Hinduism. It induced political apathy by a detachment rather than a disdain for secular affairs. It also produced its own forms of gentleness, tolerance, and moderation.

B. *Religious Eclecticism — Psychological Pluralism*: Like the Hindu cultural system, Theravada Buddhism fostered an eclectic and assimilative tendency to adapt new religious doctrines to established precepts and customs. Pluralist proclivities were also induced by the lack of a single scriptural authority and the encouragement of individual inquiry regarding doctrinal interpretation and significance. The spread of Buddhism gradually led to a division of the Theravada (or Hinayana) school in southern Asia and the Mahayana school in northern Asia, and several sects of monks upholding modest doctrinal differences emerged in each Buddhist cultural system.[15] This religious and psychological pluralism was further intensified by a variety of animist beliefs and practices regarding the propitiation of numerous local gods and spirits. Yet Theravada Buddhist cultural systems never splintered into the highly diversified religious orientations of the Indian sub-continent. Instead, they promoted a relatively uniform mode of religious and secular behavior.

C. *Fatalism — Historical Determinism:* The precept that the evolution of secular affairs is shaped by forces beyond human control was essentially the same in Theravada Buddhism as in Hinduism. Yet this specific cultural influence was less intense. More emphasis was placed on individual choice and self-reliance despite the doctrine of "karma." History was taken more seriously. Yet no stress was placed by Theravada Buddhist cultural systems on social reform or social justice. Social or political development was not a significant religious concern. There was no doctrinal authority for individual efforts to improve the secular environment.

II. *Politically Relevant Values, Modes of Behavior, and Institutions of the Theravada Buddhist Class Structure*

A. *Hierarchical Class Structure:* The doctrines of Theravada Buddhism prescribed no stratified class structure. Instead they rejected the caste system of Hinduism and upheld a vague egalitarian norm. The emphasis on voluntary individual religious development induced different responses in traditional societies which adopted Theravada Buddhism as the dominant religion. Most elements of the hierarchical class structures of the pre-Buddhist era were retained, yet the impact of the teachings of the Buddha made them less rigid and less stratified. The strongly Hinduized class structures of Ceylon and Cambodia consequently experienced less liberalization from the impact of Theravada Buddhism than the more loosely structured class systems in Burma, Thailand, and Laos.

The *sovereign ruler* at the apex of the Theravada Buddhist class structure (usually called a king) consisted of a successful military and administrative leader or one of his scions. The power of the king was supported by the Hindu concept of *devaraja* which imparted a strong religious sanction to royal authority. The king served as the defender of the Buddhist religion while at the same time he exercised Hindu law. He served as the major patron of the Sangha. He appointed the top leaders of the Buddhist hierarchy, enforced discipline in the Sangha, and called religious councils for the purpose of reaffirming and reinterpreting the sacred doctrine. The Sangha exerted an important indirect political influence in legitimizing royal authority and in promoting peace and stability throughout the kingdom. While the Buddhist religious order was independent of political authority in doctrinal interpretation, it depended on the ruling sovereign for financial support, high-level appointments, and disciplinary action, a relationship which made it subordinate to secular jurisdiction. Below the king and the Sangha were the *royalty* consisting of blood relatives of the ruling sovereign and the *nobility* comprising commoners who received various official ranks and status for distinguished service to the realm. Intermixed with the top ruling elite was an *administrative class* which performed official duties such as the collection of taxes and the construction of public works. The vast majority of the population consisted of *peasants,* most of whom owned their own land and who were required to perform *corvee* labor intermittently for public works projects ordered by the king. At the bottom of the class structure were *outcastes* consisting largely of slaves. Most of these persons were prisoners of war, debt slaves, or persons born into slavery.

The hierarchical class structure of the Theravada Buddhist traditional society constituted a system designed to maintain the elevated status of the king and the Sangha, and to preserve the order and stability of the royal domain. This sacred-oriented social order generated a tradition of deference and obedience to higher class authority. Persons "above" were sanctioned by religion and custom to rule; persons "below" were expected to obey. The division of classes caused a sense of parochialism and exclusiveness. It strengthened family and kinship loyalties which provided the dominant source of personal identity and security. Like its counterpart in the Indian sub-continent, the Theravada Buddhist class structure also failed to assimilate minority groups. Yet this separation was not as harsh or inflexible as in Hindu traditional societies; it was caused primarily by an attitude of detachment and indifference rather than a sense of hostility and distrust toward outsiders.

B. *The Sangha*: In addition to its role in the hierarchical class structure, the Sangha bequeathed one of the most powerful unifying influences to successive generations. In many ways the Buddhist religious order performed the same integrative role in Theravada Buddhist polities as the law performed in Hindu polities. It supplied the dominant cohesive social force and served a significant indirect function in preserving the hierarchical class structure. The Buddhist monks exercised no coercive power based on any single scriptural authority or body of sacred law. Instead the Sangha was unified by a common devotion to the teachings of Buddha and the detailed code of discipline upheld by the ecclesiastical hierarchy. The Sangha served as the major acculturating medium in communicating a conventional religious orientation throughout the traditional society. It produced the bulk of the literature, primarily religious literature, and it disseminated a uniform religious tradition through direct participation in the monastic schools, temple ceremonies, and holy pilgrimages.[16]

C. *Personal Political Rule — Authoritarianism*: A highly personalized authoritarian rule was induced in Theravada Buddhist polities as in the Indian sub-continent by the adoption of the *devaraja* concept of political power. Popular deference to a highly centralized political authority was also promoted by the hierarchical class structure and the legitimization of political rule by the Sangha. Authoritarian political rule engendered by Theravada Buddhism theoretically exceeded that of Hinduism due to the subordinate status of the Sangha which was unable to check the exercise of political power. The hierarchical religious order inculcated attitudes of submission and obedience in Buddhist monks just as the hierarchical class structure induced similar attitudes in the lay population. Political institutionalization remained extremely weak. The quality of government depended almost entirely on the personal administrative abilities of the absolute ruling sovereign.

D. *Separation of Religion and Politics*: In Theravada Buddhist class structures the king cooperated intimately with the ecclesiastical hierarchy, while the hierarchy legitimized and buttressed the political authority of the king. Professor W. Howard Wriggins has stated: "In the Buddhist tradition the ruler promoted the Way of Piety, nurtured the Sangha, and was himself guided by the precepts of the Sangha and the Buddha's Way. Church and state were closely knit."[17] Yet in practice the division and subordination of the Sangha from secular authority engendered the separation of religion and politics. The performance of religious and political functions was filled by distinct and independent roles. Buddhist doctrines sanctioned no religious authority to challenge the conduct of political affairs. This institutional and structural value was bolstered by the Buddhist concept of the irrelevance of political action to individual religious development and the achievement of Nirvana. The Sangha accordingly confined its teachings and advice to other-worldly matters.

III. *Politically Relevant Institutions of the*
Theravada Buddhist Societal Structure

A. *Great Tradition*: The great traditions of Theravada Buddhist polities
generated images of grandeur and power for relatively lengthy periods of
time. These kingdoms tended to be more durable than Hindu great traditions because of the integrative forces of Theravada Buddhism and the
imposition of a unified political rule over smaller geographical territories. The most enduring and pervasive memories of historical greatness
of Theravada Buddhist great traditions were induced by the Kingdom of
Pagan, Toungoo Dynasty, and Alaungpaya Dynasty in Burma, the Kingdoms of Sukhothai, Ayudhya, and Bangkok in Thailand, the Chenla and
Khmer Empires in Cambodia, the Kingdom of Lan Chang in Laos, and
the Sailendra and Srivijaya Empires in Sumatra and surrounding territories. The most notable image of a Theravada Buddhist great tradition
in Ceylon was fostered by the brief kingdom established by Parakrma
Bahu the Great during the twelfth century. Some of these great traditions, such as the Kingdom of Pagan, the Kingdom of Sukhothai, and
the Chenla Empire were remembered for celebrated cultural achievements in their genesis and formative stages. Other great traditions such
as the Toungoo and Alaungpaya Dynasties, the Kingdoms of Ayudhya
and Bangkok, and the Khmer Empire engendered distinctive reputations
from their consolidation and expansionist phases.

B. *Middle Tradition*: The middle traditions of Theravada Buddhist polities tended to experience a precarious existence due to their relatively
small territorial size and their vulnerability to domination by nearby
great traditions. At times they exercised considerable autonomy; often
they were absorbed into powerful empires or kingdoms. Some of these
middle traditions, such as the Mon kingdom of Pegu and the Tamil kingdom in Ceylon comprised ethnic, cultural, and linguistic groups distinct
from the dominant population. The historical images of these middle
kingdoms consequently induced powerful divisive and separatist tendencies. Other middle traditions, such as the three princely states in Laos
and the kingdom of Chiengmai in Thailand, consisted of people of a
common racial stock or a sub-group racially and culturally similar to the
dominant population. These territorial subdivisions of cognate populations engendered lesser centrifugal forces than alien middle traditions,
yet they also imparted a collective proclivity toward localism and provincialism to succeeding generations.

C. *Little Tradition*: Like the villages of the Indian subcontinent, the little traditions of Theravada Buddhist traditional societies contained the bulk of the population. This small societal structure was called *gama* in Sinhalese Ceylon, *ywa* in Burma, *mu ban* or *moung* in Thailand and Laos, and *phum* in Cambodia. Most social patterns of behavior in these rustic village communities were similar to those of Hindu little traditions. Their cultural life was dominated by an admixture of animism and selected elements of the "higher" Buddhist religion. Family and kinship loyalties were extremely powerful. Each peasant derived his individual identity and purpose from the collective life of the village. Like the Hindu little tradition, local political institutionalization in the Theravada Buddhist traditional societies consisted almost entirely of a small council of village elders, often aided by a village headman. These leadership roles were filled by the more efficient and capable male members of the community who were selected by an informal consensus of adult males in the village. Their major function was to promote harmony and order within the community.

Remote peasants in Theravada Buddhist traditional societies consisted of aboriginal tribesmen or small nomadic mountain groups. They included the Vedda in Ceylon, the Stieng, Phnong, and Por in Cambodia, the Yao, Meo, Ho, Akha, Lisu, and Semang in Thailand and Laos, and the Palaungs and Was in Burma. As in the Indian subcontinent these isolated village communities resisted efforts to assimilate them into nearby great, middle, or little traditions. They remained detached from the loosely organized societal structures of the traditional society.

ISLAMIC TRADITIONAL SOCIETY

I. *Politically Relevant Values of the Islamic Cultural System*

A. *Religious Dogmatism — Political Egalitarianism*: Islam promoted an intense dogmatism by its rigorous monotheistic, "this-worldly" orientation.[18] In sharp contrast to the religious tenets of Hinduism and Buddhism, the teachings of Mohammed upheld the reality of the secular world as an important element of God's creation. Each individual human being possessed an eternal soul, yet his life on earth had significance and it should be rigidly patterned according to sacred norms. Religious dogmatism was also caused by the fundamental belief that the Koran contained the eternal and perfect truth and that Mohammed was Allah's final prophet. No religious councils or institutions were established for subsequent revelation or reinterpretation of the holy word.

Islamic law fostered doctrinal purity by imposing an all-embracing sacred authority over every aspect of daily life. It sanctioned no separation between religious and secular affairs. Political, economic, and social relationships were carefully prescribed to preserve and promote the Islamic faith. Islamic traditional societies tended to exclude non-believers; they often discriminated against unorthodox views. Yet in spite of this doctrinal uniformity, Islam fostered political egalitarianism theoretically based on the spiritual equality of all true believers. In practice class hierarchies existed in different Moslem traditional societies. Yet all Moslems were equal in the eyes of God and Islamic law. The holy teachings provided no theory of clericalism or priesthood. A primary principle of Islamic political theory upheld legitimacy for political rulers exercising both religious and secular authority over a brotherhood of equal believers.

B. *Religious Eclecticism — Psychological Pluralism*: In spite of the intense dogmatism induced by Islam, the teachings of the Prophet were modified in varying degrees as this proselyting religious movement spread eastward from the Middle East to the Indian subcontinent and Southeast Asia.[19] Islamic traditional societies in Asia, like Hindu and Theravada Buddhist traditional societies, embodied an eclectic array of religious beliefs and modes of behavior. Pluralist tendencies in the spread of Islam were caused by both internal and external factors. Splits were encouraged within the Moslem movement because of the absence of an officially ordained clergy and the lack of a formal ecclesiastical structure. The *ulama* or Islamic legal scholars never achieved the role of a separate autonomous religious order capable of exercising a unifying influence. As Islam spread, the ulama remained under the authority of a diversity of political rulers, thereby precluding the possibility of maintaining doctrinal homogeneity. Internal schisms were also caused by doctrinal fragmentation into several "schools" of Islamic thought. Qadaritism and Mu'tazilitism, for example, upheld varying degrees of freedom and efficacy of the human will; Ash'arism advocated a combination of Mu'tazilitism and orthodoxy. Sufism combined different forms of mysticism with Islamic worship. Additional factionalism occurred with the formation of the large Sunni and Shi'ite sects which fostered subsequent divisions of numerous smaller sects.

External factors causing religious eclecticism and psychological pluralism assumed major significance as Islam embraced diverse racial and linguistic groups inhabiting an entire subcontinent and a vast island archipelago. In this fusion of Islam with different indigenous cultures, doctrinal purity tended to vary directly with the passage of time and

the realm, wage *jihad* or holy war against rebellious non-Moslems, or suppress internal disorder and unorthodoxy.

The *ulama* were the religious and legal scholars who ranked below the upper ruling classes. Unlike the Sangha in Theravada Buddhist cultural systems, the ulama lacked a corporate concept of a unified clerical role. Egalitarian norms inhibited the formation of a separate and elevated priestly class. The Moslem scholars had their own integrated and stratified ecclesiastical order, yet it was organized and supported as part of the judicial system by the sultan. The ulama received their religious and legal training at educational institutions provided by the state. Their promotions in the clerical hierarchy required the sanction of the sultan. They received considerable social prestige from the populace for their religious devotion and learning, yet they were not revered or worshipped. Their major function was to teach the Islamic religion and assist in the administration of Islamic law.

In contrast to the Hindu and Theravada Buddhist cultural systems, *merchants* and *artisans* enjoyed a relatively high social status in Islamic sacred-oriented class structures. The teachings of the Prophet contained no religious precepts directly supporting economic roles in the social hierarchy, yet they embodied no conflict between religious values and the accumulation of material wealth. In practice considerable emphasis was placed on commerce and entrepreneurship in Islamic cultural systems. Mohammed himself was a successful merchant and he used the money of his wife (a wealthy widow) to promote his new religion. The tradesmen and craftsmen of these traditional societies have been labeled "the old middle class" by Professor John Kautsky.[21] They assumed varying degrees of specialization and often acquired considerable wealth and influence. They resided in the urban centers of great traditions and middle traditions, and they depended entirely on the sultan and higher classes for protection and markets. *Peasants* at a lower level of the Islamic class structure comprised the large majority of subjects. Peasants lived in the little traditions of rural villages and provided the manual labor for agricultural production. *Infidels* or non-Moslems were tolerated and accommodated by many Islamic cultural systems, especially in Southeast Asia. Different religious communities were permitted to maintain their religious identity and forms of worship, yet they were expected to recognize the supreme political authority of the sultan. According to Donald Smith, infidels were considered "second-class subjects."[22] At the bottom of the Islamic class structure, a class of *slaves* consisting of war captives and suppressed minorities performed various social and economic roles considered degrading and "immoral" by members of higher social classes.

B. *Law*: The Islamic legal system, like that of Hindu cultural systems, embraced a total body of law regulating every aspect of human life. The law or *shari'ah* was based on the Koran and the Sunnah which contained Mohammed's specific written prescriptions for orthodox behavior. It constituted the basic cohesive force of Islamic traditional societies. The law embodied all religious, ethical, and legal norms. It contained detailed descriptions of religious duties and forms of worship as well as an elaborate body of jurisprudence covering marriage, divorce, burial, and family inheritance. The shari'ah combined all aspects of criminal and civil law. It sanctioned the religious and political authority of the sultan and prescribed the educational and judicial roles of the ulama. The pervasive effect of Islamic law was to interlace every daily act with religious value and significance.

C. *Personal Political Rule — Authoritarianism*: The dogmatism of Islam and the supreme religious and secular authority vested in the sultanate fostered authoritarian political rule. Absolutist political behavior was likewise bolstered by the all-embracing norms of the Koran and Islamic law which regulated every aspect of daily conduct. As the "vice-regent of Allah," the sultan exercised God's will and sovereignty over the members of lower classes; no ecclesiastical or political institutions nor any sacred values limited his pervasive authority. The sultan's political power received additional religious sanction by the fourth "pillar" of Islamic faith prescribed in the Koran upholding the sacred obligation to pay taxes and give alms for the maintenance of a Muslim society. Since the broad holy commandments of Mohammed provided only vague guidance to political leadership, the power of the sultanate in practice was augmented by the requirement to supplement religious law with secular laws and decrees. In the Indian subcontinent and Southeast Asia, the absolutist political rule of the sultan in Islamic traditional societies was further strengthened by assimilation with the preceding Hindu concept of *devaraja* (god-king) and the tradition of a highly centralized political system as a secular manifestation of the unitary cosmological order. Authoritarianism was combined with a powerful personalist ethos at the top of the Islamic class structure due to the fluid class mobility and egalitarian religious and social norms. At times the acquisition of the supreme political power vested in the sultanate was achieved by hereditary succession; at other times the incumbent was a non-royal person selected by influential members of the aristocracy and military leadership on the basis of administrative and military skills as well as individual merit. Yet the acquisition and maintenance of dominant political power always required a demonstrated personal ability in political maneuver, deception, and intrigue. As in the sacred-oriented Hindu class structures, political authority in Islamic traditional societies was broadly institutionalized; yet the characteristics of the actual exercise of political power were essentially dependent on the personality and individual capabilities of the ruling sultan. In assessing the absolute and personal power of Moslem political leadership in India, Vincent Smith has stated that "the merits of government depended mainly on the character of the supreme ruler."[23]

D. *Fusion of Religion and Politics*: Islamic cultural systems and class structures, unlike their Hindu and Theravada Buddhist counterparts, embodied a fusion of religion and politics. As a total way of life, Islam eschewed any separation between sacred and secular values and institutions. All institutions, including the state, were religious. Secular laws and decrees regulating all aspects of the entire society were based on the Koran and holy law. Religious and political structures were fused in the role of the sultanate. His supreme religious and political authority was to be used in governing secular affairs in such a manner as to preserve the purity of Islamic doctrine and forms of worship as well as to suppress religious unorthodoxy.

III. *Politically Relevant Institutions of the Islamic Societal Structure*

A. *Great Tradition*: The only Islamic great tradition in Asia was the Mogul Empire (1556–1707) which imposed a unified political system over sizeable portions of the Indian subcontinent. The memory induced by this immense societal structure was heavily weighted with the assertion of Moslem power over Hindu power since a large majority of the subjects of the Mogul emperors were Hindu. The relatively brief period of the Mogul great tradition was also remembered for the most notable administrative and artistic achievements of Islamic traditional societies in Asia. Mogul rulers utilized an efficient decentralized administrative organization in which local districts (*sarkar*) were vested with carefully regulated authority to maintain law and order, to try criminal cases, and to collect taxes. Under Akbar, the most gifted of the Mogul rulers, the empire flourished through the practice of religious tolerance between Moslems and Hindus. The Mogul great tradition gradually declined following the death of Akbar since his successors were less capable in providing political and administrative leadership. The revival of religious intolerance and abortive military ventures again caused political fragmentation in the Indian sub-continent. Thereafter the influence of the Mogul empire consisted chiefly of its administrative systems which were retained by subsequent rulers, and its artistic achievements, notably new modes of poetry and historical writing influenced by Persia. Its most enduring artistic feats, however, were the construction of world-renowned architectural structures including the Shalimar gardens in Lahore and Kashmir, the mosques at Lahore and Delhi, Humayun's tomb in Delhi, and Fatehpur Sikri and the Taj Mahal in Agra.

B. *Middle Tradition*: The Islamic middle tradition, like its counterpart in Hindu traditional societies, was the most common form of societal structure established by Moslem political rulers. Stable political authority was maintained only over relatively small geographic regions. Islamic middle traditions in the Indian subcontinent included the Sultanate of Delhi, the Moslem kingdoms of Bengal, Jaunpur, Malwa, Gujarat, Khandesh, and Kashmir, and the Deccan Sultanates of Berar, Ahmadnagar, Bijapur, Bidar, and Golkonda. In Indonesia only two middle traditions, the Sultanate of Djokjakarta and the Sultanate of Surabaja, exercised political rule over sizeable coastal and internal territories. The most common form of Islamic societal structure in Indonesia and Malaya was the enclave tradition or small entrepot states along river deltas or coastal areas. The most notable Moslem enclave tradition in this area was Malacca which developed into a powerful trading center and dominated sea-faring trade in the Straits of Malacca for about a century prior to its capture by the Portuguese in 1511. Adjoining Islamic middle (and enclave) traditions embraced a common religious and secular value-system. Yet they induced a traditional historical input of regionalism and provincialism due to their diverse ethnic, cultural, and linguistic populations and the competing political and economic interests of their ruling elites.

C. *Little Tradition*: Like rural villages in Hindu and Theravada Buddhist traditional societies, the little traditions of Islamic societal structures constituted the vast majority of the population. Moslem little traditions were called *gaon* in Urdu-speaking regions in the Indus River valley and *kampong* in Malaya and Indonesia. Many patterns of social behavior in these undifferentiated village communities were essentially similar to those in Hindu and Theravada Buddhist little traditions. Family and kinship ties were very strong. Geographic distances and a particularistic localism inhibited the imposition of religious and political authority from nearby great or middle traditions. The Islamic little tradition was largely autonomous from centralized political control; its reli-

gious orientation was primarily animist. Like little traditions in Theravada Buddhist societal structures, it had limited local political institutionalization in a single headman consisting of a competent and trusted
male leader of the village. In Malaya and Indonesia this position was
called *ketua kampong*. The inability of Moslem rulers at higher levels of
the traditional society to erect a uniform cultural system in rural areas
augmented the role of these rustic village leaders; it made orthodox Islam
essentially an urban phenomena.

The remote peasants in Islamic traditional societies consisted largely of
aboriginal tribes inhabiting isolated mountain villages in peninsular and
island territories in Southeast Asia. These tribal groups included the
Semang, Sakai, and Jakun in Malaya and the Menangkabau, Bataks,
Atjehnese, Dayaks, Bugi, Mangkasaras, and Papuans in Sumatra, Java,
Borneo, and eastern islands of Indonesia. These remote peasants, as in
Hindu and Theravada Buddhist societal structures, remained aloof from
Islamic middle or little traditions.

ATOMIZED ANIMIST TRADITIONAL SOCIETY

I. *Politically Relevant Religious Values of
the Atomized Animist Cultural System*

A. *Eclectic Spiritism — Political Apathy*: The pre-Western cultural life
in the island territories which today comprise the central and northern
regions of the Philippines was unique among the cultural systems of
Asia. Here the immigrating Malay village communities remained
detached from permanent and penetrating exposures to the "higher"
religions or secular cultural doctrines emanating from great and middle
traditions on the Asian mainland. They developed no great or middle
traditions of their own. Their cultural values were derived entirely from
primitive belief-systems of small autonomous rural societies scattered
along the coastal lowlands of the archipelago.[24] Some of its pristine
animism was peculiar to early Malay village culture; some was common
to rural communities in all Asian traditional societies. Animist values
embraced an eclectic spiritism characterized by an irrational addiction to
the unknown and an elaborate array of superstitions, fables, and
notions. Animist thought and worship involved crude elements of idola-
try, demonology, astrology, and mysticism. It embodied nature-worship
and ancestor-worship. It contained an intricate pattern of spiritualistic
beliefs regarding the continued existence of disembodied spirits of
deceased persons capable of imparting either beneficial or invidious in-

fluences to living beings and the surrounding environment. The major political significance of these diverse forms of animism and spiritism was the mystical capacity theoretically vested in the supreme community leader to intercede invisible good and evil spirits (*anitos*) in order to maximize beneficence and to minimize adversity. This precept enhanced the "religious" and political authority of the village leader and encouraged apathy and deference among the village members. It imparted a touch of theocracy by providing a modicum of "priestliness" to the village headman. In modest degree it abetted charismatic leadership.

B. *Kinship Communalism — Familial Personalism*: The autonomous village communities of pre-hispanic Philippines consisted of highly integrated and extended family groupings. These kinship communal societies were called *baranguays,* named after the large outrigger canoes which transported entire extended families to these islands from Indonesia and Malaya. Settled communities in the islands continued to develop from the original family grouping. The extended family and the community were undifferentiated; family ties and communal ties were combined. Personal behavior conformed to the customary norms of the community. Professor Onofre Corpuz has stated: "Interpersonal or social relations in such a community tended to be informal, and government was based on kinship rule and custom, rather than on enacted law and administrative regulation. Moreover, the values governing social relations and individual behavior were the values of the kinship group."[25] Strong communal loyalties emerged from the common need for physical security and economic survival. Each village community cultivated its own communal land. Each community defended itself and its lands from hostile attack. From this kinship communalism developed one of the most intense family-oriented value systems in Asia. The extended family structure constituted a very durable institution in all Asian traditional societies, yet in the pre-Spanish Philippine cultural system the family and the local community totally monopolized personal loyalties since familial and communal relationships were not shaped in any degree by the abstract values of a higher religion. In other Asian traditional societies, religious values were susceptible to modest change caused by doctrinal sectarianism and/or reinterpretation. Religious values were also frequently compromised by the practical needs of daily secular life. In pre-Western Philippines personal obligations to family-communal groupings were not mitigated in any manner by supplementary or conflicting obligations to a higher religious authority, political ruler, law, or institution. The absence of a higher religion consequently caused family relationships to be formed only by the rigorous pragmatic exigencies of custom and survival. In effect, the individual person in the atomized animist cultural system possessed an identity which had social significance only as part of a family and community.

C. *Village Fatalism*: Animist beliefs induced a form of village fatalism. This rustic determinism envisioned secular developments as inevitable circumstances largely beyond man's control. Social and natural adversities were silently accepted as intermittent afflictions caused by inimical indwelling spirits in the surrounding environment. Professor William McCord has declared:

> Indeed, no one who has experienced village life can overlook the way in which fatalism reinforces the village's inertia... This conviction that existence cannot be altered by passing events has a foundation in the hard realities of village existence. If one is always under the command of fickle nature, life may seem to change superficially, but actually one cannot escape the round of seasons, the cycle of drought and flood, the threat of locusts or plague.[26]

Village fatalism in the atomized animist cultural system was not supplemented by the predestinarianism of any higher religious doctrine of historical determinism as in the Hindu, Theravada Buddhist, and Islamic cultural systems. The baranguays had no higher religion nor any conscious sense of history. Each autonomous village community exercised impressive self-reliance in its endeavor to cope with the immediate physical environment. Yet village welfare was considered to be heavily determined by numerous unseen and uncontrollable forces and dangers.

II. *Politically Relevant Values, Modes of Behavior, and Institutions of the Atomized Animist Class Structure*

A. *Hierarchical Village Structure*: The stratified class structure of pre-Spanish Philippine village communities was based partially on animist beliefs. This rural social order, however, was shaped largely by custom. The village leader was the *datu* who exercised customary and personal authority over the community.[27] This supreme social position was achieved through hereditary succession. As mentioned previously, it embodied a modest religious element in the mystical capacity to intercede surrounding indwelling spirits to enhance the welfare and safety of the community. This simple "sacred" role was unencumbered due to the absence of any competing priestly class. The datu was assisted and advised by a small group of village *elders* who likewise received their favored social status through hereditary succession. The majority of the baranguay consisted of *free peasants* who owned their own homes and cultivated communal lands. At the bottom of the village hierarchy was a modest yet well-regulated class of *serfs* and *slaves*.

B. *Personal Communal Rule — Authoritarianism*: The primitive village class structure outlined above intensified personalist and authoritarian orientations in the atomized animist cultural system. The military and administrative leadership exercised by the datu engendered a sense of loyalty and obedience in the members of the village community. Professor Jean Grossholz has stated: "In the barangay community a good leader was a strong, brave man who embodied the old traditions and preferably had benevolent ancestors, and a good citizen was a loyal follower who lived up to the obligations of his community and family status."[28] The quality of communal leadership, in turn, was entirely a function of the datu's personal capabilities.

III. *Politically Relevant Institutions of the
Atomized Animist Societal Structure*

A. *Great Tradition*: No great tradition exercised political or social authority in the atomized animist cultural system. Intermittent contacts were made in the archipelago by the Indonesian great traditions of Srivijaya and Majapahit, and occasional trading vessels came to Luzon and the central islands from mainland China. Yet no great tradition existed in this unique societal structure.

B. *Middle Tradition*: No middle tradition likewise exercised any political or social authority in the atomized animist cultural system. Several attempts were made to form baranguay confederations prior to Spanish colonial rule, yet none of these loose decentralized structures exercised effective control over autonomous village communities, and they endured for very brief periods of time.[29] Only Sulu and some coastal areas in Mindanao were incorporated into Islamic middle traditions during the fifteenth and sixteenth centuries. No middle tradition existed elsewhere in this pre-Western societal structure.

C. *Little Tradition*: The little tradition was the only organized social entity in the atomized animist traditional society prior to the Western impact. These small undifferentiated social and political systems contained an extended family grouping which included some 30–100 nuclear families. The largest baranguays contained little more than 2000 persons. These tiny independent communal societies scattered over extensive island territories caused intense particularism and localism in this distinctive societal structure. In spite of common Malay racial characteristics, the atomized animist traditional society contained highly fragmented and pluralist behavioral patterns. The autonomous little traditions in prehispanic Philippines were highly diversified in custom and language.

The remote peasants in the atomized animist cultural system were aboriginal negroid pygmies who were pushed into interior regions by the early Malay immigrants. Thereafter these primitive nomadic tribal people (*aeta*) moved to more isolated jungle and mountainous areas. As in other Asian societal structures, they remained detached from the Malay little traditions.

SUMMARY

Table I comprises a summary of politically relevant traditional historical inputs induced by the four sacred-oriented traditional societies in Asia. Table II is added to compare the Hindu caste system and the hierarchical class structures in the other traditional societies.

Table I. *Summary of politically relevant traditional historical inputs induced by the cultural systems, class structures, and societal structures of the sacred-oriented traditional societies in Asia.*

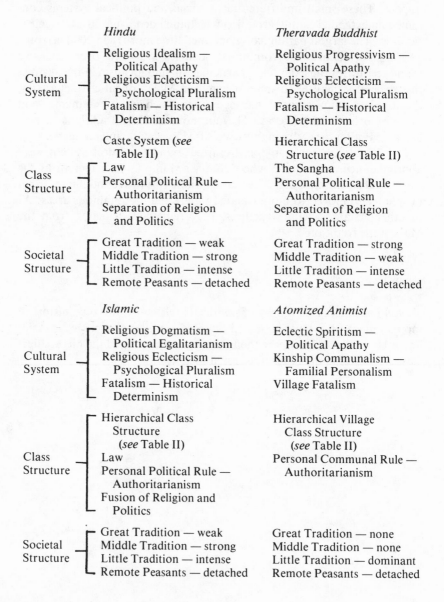

	Hindu	*Theravada Buddhist*
Cultural System	Religious Idealism — Political Apathy Religious Eclecticism — Psychological Pluralism Fatalism — Historical Determinism	Religious Progressivism — Political Apathy Religious Eclecticism — Psychological Pluralism Fatalism — Historical Determinism
Class Structure	Caste System (*see* Table II) Law Personal Political Rule — Authoritarianism Separation of Religion and Politics	Hierarchical Class Structure (*see* Table II) The Sangha Personal Political Rule — Authoritarianism Separation of Religion and Politics
Societal Structure	Great Tradition — weak Middle Tradition — strong Little Tradition — intense Remote Peasants — detached	Great Tradition — strong Middle Tradition — weak Little Tradition — intense Remote Peasants — detached

	Islamic	*Atomized Animist*
Cultural System	Religious Dogmatism — Political Egalitarianism Religious Eclecticism — Psychological Pluralism Fatalism — Historical Determinism	Eclectic Spiritism — Political Apathy Kinship Communalism — Familial Personalism Village Fatalism
Class Structure	Hierarchical Class Structure (*see* Table II) Law Personal Political Rule — Authoritarianism Fusion of Religion and Politics	Hierarchical Village Class Structure (*see* Table II) Personal Communal Rule — Authoritarianism
Societal Structure	Great Tradition — weak Middle Tradition — strong Little Tradition — intense Remote Peasants — detached	Great Tradition — none Middle Tradition — none Little Tradition — dominant Remote Peasants — detached

Table II. *A comparison of the Hindu caste system and the hierarchical class structures of other sacred-oriented traditional societies in Asia.*

Hindu (Legendary)*	Theravada Buddhist	Islamic	Atomized Animist
Priests (Brahman)	King	Sultan	Datu
Warriors (Kshatriyas)	Priests (Sangha)	Aristocracy	Village Elders
Merchants (Vaisyas)	Royalty — Nobility	Administrative Class	Peasants
Workers — Peasants	Administrative Class	Military Class	Serfs — Slaves
(Shudra)	Peasants	Religious Scholars	
Untouchables	Outcastes — Slaves	Ulama	
		Merchants — Artisans	
		Peasants	
		Infidels	
		Slaves	

*The hierarchical structure within the castes or jatis of India in practice was actually based on age and patriarchal custom. The legendary four-tiered caste system, however, did exert important differentiating influences in relationships between separate castes.

Chapter 2

Secular-Oriented Traditional Societies

The purpose of this chapter is similar to Chapter One; it delineates in brief form the traditional historical inputs generated by the cultural systems, class structures, and societal structures of the secular-oriented traditional societies in Asia. The chief goal is to depict the politically-relevant values, modes of behavior, and institutions of the Confucian traditional society in China, Korea, and Vietnam and the Japanized Confucian traditional society in Japan which were shaped extensively by a secular doctrine.

CONFUCIAN TRADITIONAL SOCIETY

I. *Politically Relevant Values of the Confucian Cultural System*

A. *Doctrinal Idealism — Political Pragmatism*: Confucian values induced a powerful secular orientation which formed the basis of social and political norms.[1] In contrast to the sacred-oriented cultural systems based on the abstract precepts of Hinduism and Theravada Buddhism, the Confucian social order was intensely "this-worldly." Though it did contain an element of proper respect for heaven, nature, and ancestors, and tolerated a diversity of animist beliefs and superstitions, Confucian thought conceived of man essentially as a product of his immediate secular and cultural environment. In spite of some religious trappings including temples, ritualism, and a small "priestly" class, it comprised a humanist philosophy focusing primarily on man's relationship to man. It supplied no ontological basis for any ecclesiastical order explaining man's relationship to some other-worldly deity or future life. It upheld an inherent goodness in human nature and sought the supreme societal goal embodied in *li* or the harmony achieved by the proper conduct of each person fulfilling his allotted role in the community. Confucianism also contained a doctrine of inequality prescribing a natural hierarchy of superior-inferior relationships in which each person was under someone else's authority. It stressed duties rather than rights; its chief virtues were obedience, contentment, order, stability, moderation, patience, and restraint.

The political pragmatism of the Confucian cultural system was derived from its all-embracing ethical code. Like Islam, it sought to govern every aspect of personal life. According to Professors Reischauer and Fairbank, the Confucian concept of politics was that "government is basically an ethical problem."[2] Moral customs, not formal laws, largely enforced the norms of Confucian society. The preservation of this unique ethical culture came from a political leadership based on moral example upholding the image of a society ruled by a small elite of virtuous and superior men. The Confucian cultural system possessed no corporate "state" or formal "government" as conceived in the West. It was absolutist in theory, yet it actually exercised a small role in the affairs of the society. Its major political functions were defense, public works, and taxation. It relied little on external coercive authority. Social and political norms were enforced by extra-governmental institutions such as the family, clan, and village leadership. Confucian theory merged with Confucian practice when virtuous leaders and morally-instructed followers adhered to their proper roles in society. This fundamental usage was aptly stated in the maxim: "Let the ruler be a ruler and the subject a subject: let the father be a father and the son a son."

The idealism and pragmatism of Confucian values received some alteration in the contiguous cultural systems in Korea and Vietnam.[3] Social and political norms were affected by a higher degree of volatility in Korean culture and a stronger hereditary and personalistic orientation. Confucian values in Vietnam were modified by a more militant and expansionist tradition as well as a centralized imperial authority bolstered more by military leadership than a Confucian-trained bureaucracy.

Doctrinal idealism and political pragmatism in the Confucian cultural system in China, Korea, and Vietnam were influenced in some degree by several religious influences which imparted distinct traditional historical inputs. A native Taoism developed alongside Confucianism after the second century A.D. which sought to detach thought away from turbulent worldly affairs to an uninhibited form of self-expression.[4] Taoism soon spread from the scholarly class to the peasants where it caused diverse forms of individual escapism at times of trouble and adversity. Mahayana Buddhism was the only foreign cultural influence assimilated by the Confucian cultural system in China prior to the Western impact. The spread of this "greater Vehicle" School of Buddhism from India began after the fourth and fifth centuries A.D. and quickly met a deep spiritual yearning among Chinese people of all classes. It subsequently had a widespread influence in Korea and Vietnam. The idealistic teachings of Buddhism, however, were given a distinctly secular and pragmatic mold in these Confucian-oriented traditional societies. Relatively little emphasis was placed on the rigorous mental discipline and individual asceticism required in the original teachings of Buddha. Instead, Mahayana Buddhism had a strong humanist bent stressing charity, good works, love, and compassion.

The mixture of idealism and pragmatism in the Confucian cultural system in China, Korea, and Vietnam was likewise influenced by the political doctrine of legalism inaugurated by Emperor Shi Huang-ti early in the Ch'in dynasty (221–206 B.C.).[5] Based on a pessimistic view of human nature, this traditional historical input envisioned man capable of proper social conduct only when governed by Hobbesean-type autocracy employing severe laws and harsh punishments. The primary purpose of the state was the augmentation of its power and wealth. Law was based primarily on edicts issued by the ruler to maintain an orderly and obedient society. In pre-Western China the legalist concepts embracing an activist state clashed with Confucianist moral values which relied on decentralized enforcement of ethical customs and norms. Yet the legalist emphasis on a broad impersonal legal-administrative system was more in accord with the political needs of imperial rule in China than the ideal extended family and village tradition of Confucianism. Legalism met the frequent need for a powerful centralized state capable of maintaining some form of political unity among the massive and widespread rural populace.

B. *Doctrinal Dogmatism — Cultural Ethnocentrism*: The adoption of Confucianism in China, Korea, and Vietnam induced a rigid value system and an inflexible orthodox creed. The formation of Confucian cultural systems quickly developed an official ideology which eschewed innovation and unconventional attitudes and respected only accepted traditions and behavior. The moderation of Confucian idealism and pragmatism was thereby intermixed with tendencies toward arrogance, intolerance, harshness, and self-righteousness. Change was legitimized only when it evolved from within the Confucian social order. Doctrinal dogmatism was strongly bolstered by the reactionary attitude of the scholarly-bureaucratic class which monopolized the educational process and deprived the society of new and competing ideas. The examination system by which aspiring scholars were admitted to this privileged administrative elite served to ingrain Confucian orthodoxy in all aspects of the social culture. Competence in the Confucian classics as the sole criteria for official appointment interlinked the small educated minority and the ruling class which served as the model for the entire society.

Cultural ethnocentrism was induced by a strong sense of history espoused by the scholarly-bureaucratic class. This intellectual administrative group painstakingly recorded the events and achievements of their society and became one of the most history-prone ruling classes in the world by their obsession in managing contemporary affairs according to the written annals of the past. Official scholars oriented thought toward an idyllic classical period which in turn obviated the search for new knowledge suitable to the current needs of the society. One source has declared:

> Most of the Confucian scholar bureaucrats knew very little about branches of knowledge other than the classics... Their minds were often so hypnotized by the classics that they really believed everything in the pre-Ch'in era to be a golden example fit for incorporation in the everyday life of their times. Many such obstinate classical scholars attained high government positions; their cultivated ignorance cost the government dear in population and prestige.[6]

A cultural superiority complex was likewise induced in the Chinese traditional society by the inequality incorporated in the Confucian imperial system which envisioned the Middle Kingdom as "the center of the universe," the Chinese emperor as "the Son of Heaven," and Chinese civilization as the paragon of collective human behavior to be imitated by inferior alien societies. Ethnocentric tendencies were somewhat less apparent in Korea and Vietnam which recognized the "superiority" of Chinese culture. Yet Korean society derived considerable satisfaction and pride by serving as the channel for transmitting many elements of Chinese culture, including Confucian values and institutions, to Japan. Vietnam, like imperial China, exercised intermittent suzerainty over adjoining Cham, Laotian, and Khmer kingdoms which were administered as vassal states and recognized as culturally "inferior."

C. *Fatalism — Historical Determinism*: As in the sacred-oriented cultural systems in South and Southeast Asia, Confucian values tended to support the view that the evolution of human affairs was largely beyond man's control. Yet this common Oriental precept in China, Korea, and Vietnam was bolstered by the belief that adversities occurred in human societies because of mundane actions and powers rather than some unseen spiritual forces such as karma, the predetermination of

Allah, or the destinism of animism. Fatalism in Confucian cultural systems was based heavily on the pervasive secularism which closely linked human fortunes to the vagaries of the immediate physical and social environment. The attitude that the development of human affairs is beyond man's control was further strengthened by the strong proclivity to rely on written historical records of previous natural and human adversities as an explanation of current events. A fatalistic tendency also received considerable reinforcement from an aspect of Taoism upholding a doctrine of inaction and quietism, which generated a widespread sense of futility in seeking improvement in the human environment by individual effort and ambition. These strains of determinism in Confucian thought hampered consistent action toward social or political reform.

II. *Politically Relevant Values, Modes of Behavior, and Institutions of the Confucian Class Structure*

A. *Hierarchical Class Structure*: The secular-oriented class structure of the Confucian cultural system was designed to promote and preserve the orthodox doctrine. In its social and political context this significant traditional historical input contained some major contradictions between theory and practice. It provided stability but prevented change. It upheld the ideal of social mobility based on personal merit, yet the requirements for upward social movement engendered a rigid and conservative stratification which favored the wellborn. The class structure likewise provided the highest social prestige to learned persons directly concerned with the articulation and preservation of the official doctrine, and it afforded the lowest social status to merchant and laboring classes performing mundane roles. Yet at times of crisis the upper social classes often exerted little influence on the outcome of important political developments while top leadership roles were exercised by skillful military commanders emerging from the lower levels of the class structure.

At the top of the Confucian hierarchical class structure, the *emperor* exercised a "divine right" to rule derived from his theoretical role as the representative of heaven and his possession of the "mandate of heaven."[7] Although Confucian values ascribed most duties to the lower social classes, they did uphold the obligation of the "good" ruler to exercise a wise and benevolent rule for his subjects and to refrain from despotic excesses. Succession to the imperial throne was based on hereditary status, usually according to male primogeniture. Surrounding the emperor was a small *court aristocracy* which also maintained itself largely by hereditary succession and assisted in the centralized administration of the imperial system.

The limited but widespread administration of imperial authority was vested in the *scholarly-bureaucratic class* which overlapped extensively with the landed gentry. This unique elite of civil servants was the primary force which preserved the Confucian cultural system through successive dynasties and maintained the social and cultural unity of the traditional society. As mentioned previously, recruitment into the scholarly-bureaucratic class was achieved entirely by an examination system based on competence in the Confucian classics rather than practical knowledge or skills. In theory the examination system opened recruitment into the official administrative class to persons of all social classes. Yet with few exceptions only the sons of wealthy landowners could afford the lengthy classical training required to pass the rigorous entrance examinations. Admission to this privileged administrative order began a life-long career in an elaborate official hierarchy with its own distinctive dress, ritual, and mode of behavior. The entire recruiting and promotion system of the scholarly-bureaucratic class made government service the ideal occupation in the Confucian class structure as well as the most promising means for the acquisition of personal prestige and wealth.

The *peasants* ranked just below the scholarly-bureaucratic class in social prestige, and they were customarily respected as the backbone of the Confucian class structure and the cultivators of the basic human necessity of food. Yet the peasants derived few privileges or rights from this theoretical "middle" social status. They were heavily taxed by the emperor and the landed gentry, and they relied largely on village autonomy, administrative inertia, and official aloofness to reduce political oppression. Under the peasants was a small *artisan class* of skilled urban workers who were organized into *hui* or guilds and recruited and trained in a special apprentice system. Near the bottom of the Confucian class structure was an urban class of *merchants* who engaged in a variety of entrepreneurial activities and often acquired considerable wealth. Yet the orthodox doctrine viewed merchants as an "unproductive" class seeking the socially disapproved goal of personal profit and gain. Private economic activity was usually regulated and heavily taxed by imperial rulers.

Slavery was abolished early in the Chinese traditional society, although a subordinate class of *landless farm workers* and *domestic servants* evolved which performed menial physical tasks and received low social status.

As in the case of doctrinal values, the orthodox Confucian class structure underwent several notable changes in Korea and Vietnam. Class lines were more rigid in Korea than in China and even less class mobility was achieved by the examination system. Social status was determined more by birth and less by personal merit. In some degree a more personalistic class structure was maintained in Korea due to the fact that Confucianism did not spread to Korea until after the establishment of the Yi dynasty in 1392.[8] The traditional Korean class structure also had more extensive kinship ties than in the more limited extended family system in China and there were closer familial relationships between the Confucian-trained scholarly-bureaucratic class and the landed gentry. At the bottom of the Korean class structure was a large "lowborn" class (ch'onmin) which included sizeable numbers of private and government-owned slaves. Class lines were less rigid in Vietnam than in China due to the frequency of warfare and a more active role of military leadership at the top of the traditional class structure. In contrast to the Confucian traditional society in China which tended to assimilate certain racial minorities with its all-embracing culture, the Vietnamese class structure sought to eliminate surrounding alien groups and it relegated the few surviving war captives to a degraded social status of serfdom or slavery. Factionalism within the ruling elite was more common in both Korea and Vietnam than in China and tended to undermine the stability of the bureaucracy.

B. *Family*: In the Confucian class structure, the family, not the individual, comprised the basic social and political unit. Familial relationships were more explicitly prescribed by the Confucian doctrine than in any other traditional society in Asia. In many respects the family constituted a small-scale "state." Max Weber labelled the Chinese traditional society as a "familistic state."[9] The nuclear family served as the dominant acculturating institution which instilled particularistic attitudes in each of its members toward oneself, the extended family, the village community, the province, the entire civilized society, the Emperor, and the universe. Filial piety and ancestor worship designed to preserve the family system were venerated pillars of the secular-oriented Confucian class structure. According to a mode of collective responsibility (*pao-chia*) each member of a family or group of families was responsible for the behavior of other members, a form of behavior which intermittently induced collective pride and achievement as well as collective embarrassment and shame. The family structure, like the class structure, was based on inequality and hierarchical concepts. It was dominated by the father and the status of each member was determined by prescribed relationships based on sex and age. Among the five doctrinal social relationships between ruler and subject, father and son, husband and wife, elder brother and younger brother, and friend and friend, three relationships were involved with "proper" behavior within the family. The family structure, like the class structure, also subordinated the individual. It provided stability and resisted change. Combined with the influence exerted by the widespread scholarly-bureaucratic class, it aided in preserving the Confucian cultural system over a period of many centuries.

C. *Personal Political Rule — Authoritarianism*: The quality of imperial authority in Confucian class structures, as in other Asian traditional societies, was a function of the personal abilities of the ruling sovereign. Confucian societies were governed by men, not by law; they were administered by persons theoretically exemplifying the ethical virtues of the official doctrine rather than the impersonal sanctions of formalized statutes. The intensely personalistic orientation of Confucian polities was largely responsible for the dynastic cycle by which the founder and early rulers of a new dynasty exercised popular and effective authority while the quality of imperial rule progressively deteriorated due to the declining competence and vigor of successive scions of the original ruling family. Eventually the entire dynasty was overthrown by the rise of new capable rulers leading a popular revolt. The authoritarian behavior which pervaded Confucian class structures was derived largely from deep-seated doctrinal values of inequality and social stratification. Imperial power was strengthened by the attitudes of superiority and privilege in the upper classes and the virtues of contentment and obedience instilled in the lower classes. Authoritarian rule was further bolstered by the legalist doctrine with its stress on an activist state designed to augment centralized political power capable of maintaining stability and order.

Authoritarian personal rule within each dynasty tended to increase with the passage of time. Successive rulers became increasingly despotic and imposed larger burdens on their subjects in an effort to halt the decline of their diminishing political control. Yet more than any other Asian traditional society, the Confucian class structure provided some institutional and impersonal checks on oppressive imperial rule. The "mandate of heaven" supplied a measure of justice and efficiency by upholding the "divine right" to rule only so long as the ruling sovereign provided a reasonably benevolent and proper administration. A theory of revolution early incorporated in Confucian political behavior upheld the right of opposition leaders and disgruntled segments of the populace to rebel whenever the existing imperial authority had "lost" the mandate of heaven because of excessive human or natural adversities. One source has defined this precept as follows:

As it developed from the time of Chou, the theory held that only virtuous rulers could retain the *t'ien ming* (Mandate of Heaven). Those who had lost the mandate to rule had neither the moral superiority to stave off, nor the right to suppress, rebellion. This doctrine emerged clearly in Confucian political thought and, later, as an important check on the absolute power of the Emperor.[10]

Another limitation on imperial authority was the ubiquitous institutionalized influence of the scholarly-bureaucratic class seeking to preserve the orthodox behavior of the Confucian class structure. This administrative elite served as a buffer between the emperor and the lower social classes. The Confucian-trained civil servants were closely tied to the landed gentry which, like the emperor, also exploited the peasants and lower social classes. Yet their role as guardians of the official doctrine often mitigated the harshness of imperial rule.

D. *Fusion of Doctrine and Politics*: Confucian values and class structure embraced a fusion of doctrine and politics. Like Islam, Confucianism defined a total way of life. All institutions, policy, and social behavior were derived directly from the orthodox ideology. No separation existed between doctrinal values and political authority. Politics was inextricably interlinked with moral precepts. Political virtues were merely a subordinate aspect of ethical virtues. The fusion of doctrinal and political values and structures was institutionalized essentially in the supreme societal roles of the emperor and the scholarly-bureaucratic class. The dominant political authority of both upper classes was derived from their theoretically superior exemplification of Confucian morality. This union of political and philosophical roles involved an element of what might be called a "secularized theocracy." The propagation of the official value system and the exercise of political power were combined in a single ruling group. The preservation of the Confucian class structure depended preeminently on the maintenance of the privileged roles of this ethically-based governing elite.

III. *Politically Relevant Institutions of the Confucian Societal Structure*

A. *Great Tradition*: The great traditions of Confucian traditional societies induced images of political power and grandeur over sizeable areas for relatively long periods of time. These traditional historical inputs varied somewhat in China, Korea, and Vietnam. The great tradition in

China for many centuries was widely recognized, internally and externally, as one of the most renowned and impressive empires in world history. Chinese societal prestige rested on its own self-created "superior" culture and its dominant suzerain role over surrounding vassal states.[11] Widespread respect for the Chinese great tradition was also derived from the durability of its society which remained essentially intact in spite of the rise and fall of some fourteen dynasties between the Hsia dynasty (ca. 2205–1766 B.C.) and the Ch'ing dynasty (1644–1912 A.D.). Some dynasties, such as the Chou, Ch'in, Han, and Tang, were recognized for special contributions to Chinese culture, yet in time all dynasties were considered as integral parts of a vast imperial system which survived for more than 3000 years. The construction of many imposing architectural structures and public works by successive rulers added tangible evidence of strength and eminence to the Chinese great tradition.

The great tradition in Korea possessed less vigor and honor than its counterpart in China since it was heavily influenced by a foreign (Chinese) great tradition. Also, it had existed for a shorter period of time, and its authority extended over a much smaller geographical territory. Yet several dynasties of the Korean traditional society made notable achievements which generated memories of a powerful and prestigious great tradition. This traditional historical input began with the Koguryo rulers who asserted Korean independence from China during the second century B.C. and began the expansion of indigenous control over the Korean peninsula.[12] Similar images of societal advancements were induced by the Silla rulers who unified the entire peninsula in the seventh century A.D. and ushered in a "golden age" in art, architecture, and religion. The Yi dynasty (1392–1910) received societal recognition for its adoption of Confucian political institutions and its survival as the longest dynastic cycle of any Confucian traditional society.

The Vietnamese great tradition was somewhat less impressive than the great traditions of China and Korea in its geographic coverage and the duration of dynastic rule. Yet Vietnamese rulers induced a heritage of power and fame by important accomplishments in the development of their traditional society. This traditional historical input assumed major significance with the military victory and political independence from China in A.D. 939.[13] It received added strength from the imperial system established during the fifteenth century by the Le dynasty which ousted Chinese intruders, expanded Vietnamese power to the south, and won decisive military victories over the Champa, Khmer, and Laotian kingdoms. The Nguyen dynasty inaugurated by Emperor Gia Long in 1802 maintained the power and prestige of the Vietnamese great tradition by imposing imperial authority from the Chinese border to the Gulf of Siam and by introducing a "golden age" in art and learning.

B. *Middle Tradition*: Theoretically a middle tradition did not exist in Confucian traditional societies. The great tradition contained numerous provincial administrative units in its highly decentralized political system, but it rigorously eschewed independent provincial power. The development of autonomous provincial authority was hampered by a common secular doctrine and written script. Cultural and political unity was bolstered by the scholarly-bureaucratic class maintained by a common recruitment system, a system of rotating administrative appointments, and the investigative jurisdiction of the censorate. Yet middle traditions did emerge in Confucian traditional societies when the authority of the central political elite was fragmented and weak. At these times some middle traditions developed as autonomous focal points of political authority. They exercised effective political power and introduced an element of provincialism in Confucian traditional societies. Examples of middle traditions in China were the Southern Dynasties (Sung, Ch'i, Liang Chen) from 420–589 A.D., the Northern Dynasties (Northern Wei, Western Wei, Eastern Wei, Northern Ch'i, Northern Chou) from 386–581 A.D., and the Five Dynasties (Later Liang, Later T'ang, Later Tsin, Later Han, Later Chou) from 907–960 A.D.

These periods of political fragmentation in China aided in the development of powerful provincial centers. Internal disunion also engendered a powerful cultural division between the more placid Mandarin-speaking majority in northern and central China and the more volatile linguistic minorities in the southern provinces. The emergence of middle traditions in the Korean traditional society was affected by the intense factional disputes within successive ruling dynasties which often surpassed the divisions of administrative authority over provincial territories. Yet provincial orientations did emerge during the long Yi dynasty in administrative centers such as Pusan, Taejon, Kwangju, and Pyongyang. The dominant tendency toward a middle tradition, however, was the general and implicit division between the people in the northern and southern provinces. Middle traditions were more common in the feudal-like controversies and internecine warfare which often fragmented the Vietnamese traditional society prior to the Western impact. By the nineteenth century the major division in Vietnam was the bifurcated political loyalties between the northern Tonkinese people centered around the powerful Trinh family in Hanoi and the central and southern Annamese people surrounding the Nguyen ruling family in Hue.

C. *Little Tradition*: As in the sacred-oriented traditional societies of South and Southeast Asia, the little traditions of Confucian traditional societies contained the bulk of the population. These lowest levels of the societal structure were called *ts'un* in China, *mau'ul* in Korea, and *làng* in Vietnam. They were largely autonomous from the political authority of the great or middle traditions in China; they possessed less autonomy from imperial rule in Korea and Vietnam due to the smaller geographic territory. As elsewhere in Asia, the intense personalistic and familial orientation of the little traditions in Confucian traditional societies was the primary source of particularistic values and relationships. These village communities embodied a unique blending of rural animism and the "higher" Confucian doctrine. The official secular ideology exerted a greater influence in the little traditions than the "higher" religion exerted in their counterparts in sacred-oriented traditional societies (excluding the Islamic) since Confucian modes of behavior such as filial piety and ancestor worship prescribed specific social prerogatives and obligations at the village level. Confucian values likewise defined the concentric relationships between individuals, families, clans, and village associations in the little tradition and the imperial authority of the great tradition. Village government was exercised by a village headman and a small group of village elders chosen informally by leading members of the village community. Primary administrative duties were to maintain order, to assist in general welfare, and to represent the village in intermittent dealings with the lowest level of the official bureaucracy.

Aboriginal tribes or remote peasants inhabited relatively isolated areas adjacent to the Chinese and Vietnamese traditional societies. On the northern, western, and southern borders of the Chinese traditional society were scattered tribal communities including Mongolian, Turkic, Tadzhik, Tibetan, Tibeto-Burman, Thai, and Miao-Yao. On the western border of the Vietnamese traditional society were mountain tribes of Meo, Thai, Miao-Yai, and Mon. These remote peasants sought to remain detached from nearby Confucian traditional societies. As mentioned previously, the Chinese great tradition at times endeavored to assimilate some of the surrounding non-Chinese tribal groups. In contrast, the Vietnamese great tradition tended to eliminate or enslave nearby tribal peoples.

JAPANIZED CONFUCIAN TRADITIONAL SOCIETY

I. *Politically Relevant Values of the Japanized Confucian Cultural System*

A. *Doctrinal Eclecticism — Political Pragmatism*: Political thought in pre-Western Japan consisted of a highly diversified mixture of beliefs and values which oriented political behavior toward secular and earthly affairs.[14] Yet as the Confucian cultural systems, some politically relevant values in Japan were shaped by religious influences. Generally, these religious elements were stronger in Japan than in the Confucian cultural systems. Political precepts were selectively incorporated into the Japanized Confucian cultural system through an eclectic process involving both indigenous and foreign sources. Foremost among native concepts was the emperor myth upholding a unique belief-pattern about the "divine" descent of the first imperial ruler which imparted to an unbroken line of successors a "divine" legitimacy to reign over the Japanese people. The institution of the emperor was closely interlinked with the Japanese society and state. He was perceived by his subjects as the benevolent father of his island populace which in turn was envisioned as one vast "family" or "household." The concept of *kokutai* (usually translated as "national polity") was closely tied to the emperor myth. It defined the Japanese state, like the emperor himself, as divine and eternal. It claimed that Japanese society comprised a superior race possessing a divine mission to spread its culture to lesser societies. The collective island community was to be preserved at all costs; the individual was always subordinate to the welfare of the Japanese state. Shinto (usually translated as "the way of the gods") constituted the "national cult" and was intimately related to the emperor myth and kokutai. This indigenous mythology embodied a mixture of primitive nature worship, animism, and shamanism. It supported the precepts concerning the divine ancestry of the imperial family and it sanctified the "sacredness" of Japanese soil. *Shinto* also enhanced the divine right of imperial authority and it intensified the collectivist orientation in the Japanese traditional society.

A native military tradition glorified martial virtues contained in its own ethical code or standards of chivalry (*bushido*).[15] This moral doctrine venerating obedience, self-denial, austerity, and honor gradually embraced the entire island society. Japanese military values justified the intermittent use of armed power to pursue political goals and engendered unpredictable behavior oscillating between docility and violence. An indigenous convention of hereditary authority eschewed the use of a merit system and stressed intense loyalty to members of the same family and ancestry. Heredity was the primary foundation of social and political authority. It served as the fundamental basis of personal rights and supported an inflexible hierarchical class structure. A unique system of "dual government" combined the titular and symbolic role of the emperor with the actual control of political power by a ruling military elite.

Various forms of Buddhism induced diverse traditional historical inputs in pre-Western Japan. This foreign influence, derived from India (via China and Korea), produced some of the same political effects as in the Theravada Buddhist traditional societies in South and Southeast Asia. These included the desire for individual spiritual advancement toward other-worldly goals which promoted a widespread apathy in personal behavior and enhanced authoritarianism in political behavior. Yet the Japanese applied major modifications to Buddhist precepts to meet their own individual and collective needs. Buddhism assumed a more positive and mundane orientation in Japan than in South and Southeast Asia. It served more as an outlet for emotional and aesthetic expression than as a rigid code of religious or ethical conduct.[16] Buddhism bolstered the emperor myth among some Japanese who believed the emperor was a reincarnation of Buddha. As it competed with the Confucian-oriented imperial court, Buddhism likewise abetted feudalism by promoting the formation of autonomous landed estates protected by their own military garrisons.

The most significant external influence, however, was Confucian elements first adapted by early Taika rulers to primitive Japanese culture between the sixth and eighth centuries A.D. Confucian values later became dominant in the Japanese traditional society during the Tokugawa era (1603–1868).[17] The adoption of selected aspects of Confucianism during these two historical periods was part of a massive acculturation diffusion which affected virtually every aspect of Japanese culture, including its art, literature, scholarship, script, customs, and behavior. On both occasions Chinese Confucian values and institutions were assimilated voluntarily by the Japanese. This external influence was imparted by example, not coercion. The pervasiveness of Confucian influence in pre-Western Japan, combined with distinct indigenous values and modes of behavior, is the major reason I have labelled it a Japanized Confucian traditional society.

Confucianism in Japan induced many similar traditional historical inputs as in the Confucian traditional societies in China, Korea, and Vietnam. These values and modes of behavior included filial piety, ancestor worship, inequality, contentment, obedience, and harmony. The Japanized Confucian cultural system likewise maintained a strong pragmatic and humanist orientation as well as the orthodox precept of government by a morally superior elite. Confucian political values were used by the early Tokugawa rulers to promote stability and order in their pursuit of a secluded island utopia. At the same time Confucianism was modified by Japanese political rulers to meet particular indigenous needs. These changes were much more extensive than in Korea and Vietnam, and they resulted in a traditional society fundamentally different than the Chinese model. The system of hereditary authority in the Japanized Confucian cultural system precluded the adoption of a unified scholarly-bureaucratic class recruited by open competitive examinations in the Confucian classics. Social and political status was determined by birth, not merit. Hereditary rights determined imperial succession and caused an unbroken lineage from the ruling emperor to the original descendant of the legendary sun-goddess. The Japanized Confucian cultural system contained no mandate of heaven as the basis for imperial authority nor any impersonal theory of revolution to remove an ineffective royal ruler. Pre-Western Japan never established any semblance of centralized political or administrative authority. Instead a system of dual government combined the symbolic power of the emperor and the actual exercise of political power by a dominant military leader. The Confucianism of the Tokugawa rulers was also supplied with a metaphysical and cosmological bent to compete with Buddhism and a new importation of Chinese Taoism.

The variegated doctrinal sources of the Japanized Confucian cultural system produced several additional forms of political pragmatism. A consensus approach to decision-making required the development of fundamental agreement among all involved parties before undertaking social or political action.[18] This collective disposition eschewed decisive leadership or "majority rule" which could entail embarrassment and shame for the "minority party." It enhanced the use of consultation, compromise, and a distinctive form of "government by committee." The eclectic tradition combined with the isolation of an island society induced a very important traditional historical input comprising an openminded propensity to learn and borrow selectively from foreign cultures. This innovative spirit and the geopolitical luxury of adapting external influences without coercion instilled a willingness to change. It mitigated the growth of a superiority complex and aroused a sense of curiosity. It engendered an achievement motivation and directed thought toward the future as well as the past. This two-fold time-oriented disposition contrasted sharply with the Confucian cultural systems in China, Korea, and Vietnam which were oriented solely toward the past. It generated its own form of progressive conservatism which deeply revered tradition and at the same time readily accepted new changes.

B. *Doctrinal Dogmatism — Racial Ethnocentrism*: While the doctrinal diversity of the Japanized Confucian cultural system induced multifarious social norms, it also possessed an intense proclivity toward social conformity and uniform behavior. Once the assimilation of indigenous and foreign influences was completed, new hybrid standards of conduct became the basis for a rigid orthodoxy which permitted little opportunity for individual expression.[19] This value-pattern produced propensities toward intolerance, fanaticism, cruelty, and self-righteousness. Doctrinal dogmatism became especially powerful during the Tokugawa period. A high population density and crowded living conditions promoted an inflexible adherence to detailed rules of personal behavior. This tendency was also enhanced by the self-discipline of the military tradition. Yet in contrast to the doctrinal dogmatism interlinked with Confucian cultural pride in China, Korea, and Vietnam, doctrinal dogmatism in pre-Western Japan was closely tied to racial ethnocentrism. This phyletic convention embodied a "we-they" syndrome upholding a view of the world as divided sharply into Japanese and non-Japanese societies. In spite of an eclectic predisposition, it espoused an indomitable determination to conform only to indigenous social norms. This self-centered racism was reinforced by isolation and an insular mentality. Sir George Sansom has stated:

> It will be seen that the civilization of Japan was formed in comparative seclusion, and this has given it a very special character. Its many foreign elements were borrowed in such circumstances that they could not overcome a stubborn indigenous character, and even until modern times Japanese life has preserved much of its earliest native quality. No nation has been more ready to consider new teaching, and yet none has been more tenacious of its own tradition.[20]

The absence of direct contact with foreigners over a period of several centuries produced a homogeneous race and a homogeneous racially-oriented culture. Racial self-consciousness was abetted by a fear of inferiority and a collective dread of being overawed by the nearby "superior" culture and power of China. Racial egotism was likewise induced by a strong sense of history and a widespread awareness of the long period of isolated detachment which made the Japanese people feel they were distinct and unique.

C. *Fatalism — Historical Determinism*: As in all traditional societies in Asia, the Japanized Confucian cultural system contained a deep-seated fatalism and widespread belief that secular affairs were largely beyond man's control. This precept was derived partially from the Confucian element in Japanese culture. Fatalist tendencies were also engendered by indigenous values. The emperor myth and kokutai linked the societal leadership and the populace in a common destiny over which human effort could exert little if any influence. *Shinto* tended to overwhelm the individual with the view that life was determined by inexorable forces of imperial authority, ancestry, and nature. Personal initiative was also hampered by the system of hereditary authority which determined social status solely by birth. The desire to elevate social and economic conditions was discouraged by the absence of class mobility or social advancement based on merit. In assessing the Tokugawa period Professor Reischauer has declared:

> With such a feudal background, it was natural that Tokugawa ethics became phrased largely in terms of specific obligations — obligations to feudal lord, to parents, to family, and, perhaps most important of all, to oneself, in the sense that one must properly play the role assigned to one by fate in a society of hereditary status.[21]

Social and political thought in pre-Western Japan consequently embraced a sense of resignation and passiveness. The fatalism shaping individual life was likewise assumed to be determinant in the broad forces of history. Like the Confucian traditional societies in China, Korea, and Vietnam, the Japanese were very historically conscious. They produced their own detailed written accounts of the adversities inflicted in their physical and human environment. They were well aware of the uncertainties caused in a land ravaged more severely than the Asian mainland by hurricanes, floods, earthquakes, and droughts. Pre-Western Japan consequently adhered to its own fatalistic beliefs that secular affairs were shaped by powerful natural and societal forces beyond human control.

II. *Politically Relevant Values, Modes of Behavior, and Institutions of the Japanized Confucian Class Structure*

A. *Hierarchical Class Structure*: The social norms of diverse doctrines shaped the hierarchical secular-oriented class structure of pre-Western Japan. Social stratification was induced by the emperor myth and kokutai which prescribed an exalted status to the person symbolizing imperial authority and a subordinate role for the broad masses of the populace. The shamanism and imperial veneration embodied in *Shinto* further elevated the personage of the emperor and the ruling elites sanctioned by his imperial power. The military tradition engendered a high social status for the military class, and the system of hereditary authority reinforced sharp lines of class stratification. The Confucian doctrine of inequality and its strong emphasis on stability and order also exerted a significant influence in molding the rigid class structure of Tokugawa Japan. Confucian norms bestowed the most exalted social stature on persons directly concerned with the articulation and preservation of the official doctrine, and it provided the lowest social prestige to classes engaged in mundane roles. However, unlike the Confucian class structures in China, Korea, and Vietnam, the Japanized Confucian class structure placed the military class, not the scholarly-bureaucratic class, in a position of high social and political influence. It was based essentially on practical skills rather than classical knowledge. It was more effective in social engineering and more capable of adjusting to externally induced change.

The *emperor* at the apex of the Japanized Confucian class structure symbolized the imperial authority derived from the unbroken hereditary lineage dating from the legendary origin of Japanese society. All political and administrative power emanated from the royal sovereign. Yet in practice the emperor exercised no effective political authority. Aided by a loyal court nobility and surrounded by an elaborate court ritualism, he provided legitimacy to powerful political leaders who actually conducted the functions of government in his name. The major role of the emperor was consequently to preserve the purity of imperial ancestry and to provide a symbolic link to the past.

The *shogun* was the dominant political ruler who actually exercised sovereign civil and military power. As already explained, his authority was sanctioned by the emperor. Sansom has described this unique form of shared powers or "dual government" by stating that "the Emperor was an absolute monarch in theory, the Shogun was an absolute ruler in practice."[22] While the emperor preserved the appearance that government was benevolent and moral, the shogun actually administered the political affairs of the society. During the Tokugawa period the shogun directly controlled his own domain comprising approximately one-fourth of the territory of Japan from his administrative headquarters (*bakufu*) in Edo (Tokyo). He also imposed a carefully regulated system of indirect rule (often called "centralized feudalism") over some 270 feudal lords. The shogun was superior in authority and prestige to these feudal lords due to his predominant military power and his prerogatives legitimized by the emperor.

The *daimyo* or feudal lords under the shogun were the rulers of small semi-autonomous states which comprised 73% of Japanese territory during the Tokugawa era. These feudal leaders exercised virtually supreme authority over the people within their domain (*han*). Yet their political power was greatly circumscribed by a system of centralized checks and controls imposed by the shogun. Previous to the Tokugawa period the daimyo exercised considerable military authority in defending their domain, yet just prior to the Western impact they were little more than local administrators. Directly under the daimyo were the *samurai* or professional military caste with its own hierarchy, martial code, and methods of hereditary recruitment.[23] The primary function of the samurai was to protect their feudal lord and his domain. The traditional warrior class assumed that it had the prime responsibility for the security and prosperity of their feudal state. For their loyalty and services they received a retaining fee or stipend from their daimyo. Early in the Tokugawa period the samurai enjoyed a high social status due to their martial skills and exemplary behavior, yet the absence of internal warfare during the long period prior to the Western impact largely reduced this military elite to a useless and unproductive class.

Below the upper levels of the Japanized Confucian class structure were the orthodox elements of the secular-oriented Confucian class hierarchy. *Peasants* had a somewhat lower social status in pre-Western Japan than in the Confucian class structures in China, Korea, and Vietnam. Peasants were heavily taxed by their daimyo and kept perpetually at a subsistence economic level. The inflexible class structure and the total lack of social mobility kept them oriented toward the rigorous pursuit of sustenance and survival. An *artisan class* which produced handcrafted household and artistic goods resided in provincial towns and a few large cities. A *merchant class* likewise dwelt in urban areas and engaged in small-scale entrepreneurial enterprises. According to Confucian norms, the merchants in pre-Western Japan were considered an unproductive class concerned solely with personal profit and gain. Their commercial activities were stringently regulated by the shogun. Yet some merchants acquired considerable wealth and obtained some prestige through financial loans or intermarriage with higher social classes. A small class of outcastes (*eta*) performed "degrading" roles such as butchery and leather production. A modest class of *slaves* occupied the lowest level of the hierarchical class structure.

B. *Hereditary Authority*: The system of hereditary authority in pre-Western Japan comprised the primary matrix of the secular-oriented class structure.[24] This traditional historical input pervaded all levels of the stratified class structure, and it provided the same integrative force as the law in Hindu and Islamic class structures, the Sangha in Theravada Buddhist class structures, and the family in Confucian class structures. The Japanese tradition of hereditary authority derived some of its strength from Confucian values and modes of behavior. Filial piety and ancestor worship bolstered familial loyalties and relationships. The Confucian doctrine of inequality and related hierarchical concepts engendered a durable family structure and orientation. Yet the major elements of the system of hereditary authority in the Japanized Confucian class structure were indigenous. Unlike the Confucian class structure in China, the Japanese never moved toward some impersonal standards or concepts of authority based on individual merit and ability. They never relinquished in any degree the primitive attitude of transmitting political power or personal rights on any basis other than familial inheritance. While the Japanese family was smaller than its counterpart in China and its relationships vis-à-vis the state were weaker, the Japanese traditional society retained a tenacious adherence to the concept of authority based solely on heredity. This social norm provided the fundamental ingredient of the unmitigated hierarchical class structure. It gave primacy to age and sex. It reduced competition for traditional political roles and stabilized the process of political succession. It likewise hampered political and social change, and intermittently it aided in producing widespread social unrest and instability.

C. *Personal Political Rule — Authoritarianism*: The quality of political rule in the Japanized Confucian class structure, as elsewhere in Asia, depended on the personal capacities of the ruling leader. Yet this personalized mode of political rule was somewhat less intense than in other Asian traditional societies due to the higher degree of structured behavior and political institutionalization. The legitimacy provided by the unbroken hereditary lineage of imperial authority extended a historic and impersonal approbation to the political power exercised by the shogun. It obviated the evolution of a highly personalized rule or "dynastic cycle" in pre-Western Japanese political behavior. The feudal pattern of government and the tradition of hereditary authority likewise engendered an extensive legal system which protected personal rights and mitigated arbitrary political rule. Authoritarianism was caused by diverse doctrinal norms and modes of behavior. The inequality perpetuated by Confucianism and the apathy produced by Buddhism strengthened elitist political rule. Political authority was reinforced by the indigenous military tradition which bolstered the power of the shogun and daimyo. According to Professor John Whitney Hall:

> The primacy of authority over the freedom of action of all persons and groups was one of the outstanding features of the Tokugawa political system. The emphasis on authority derived in

large part from the attitudes of the military class, which traditionally exacted unquestioning obedience. It derived also from
the overwhelming force possessed by the military authorities.[25]

Authoritarianism was abetted during the Tokugawa era by an all pervasive monism which justified extensive political control over "private"
affairs and the moral conduct of all imperial subjects. Submission to
higher authority was also facilitated by the intense self-discipline in Japanese culture.

D. *Fusion of Doctrine and Politics*: Diverse norms induced the fusion of
doctrine and politics in the Japanized Confucian traditional society. The
amalgamation of several value-patterns embraced a total way of life and
prescribed all accepted institutions and morality. The emperor myth,
kokutai, and *Shinto* interlinked politics with orthodox precepts and
behavior. Confucian influence subordinated political virtues to ethical
virtues. Sansom has declared that "in both China and Japan the secular
authority has traditionally regarded it as its duty to promote ethical
teaching, so that in both countries political and moral philosophy are
combined in one doctrine."[26] The linkage between doctrine and politics
was further intensified by the ubiquitous military tradition and the system of hereditary authority which extended to the imperial family, the
shogunate, and all elements of the hierarchical class structure. The
supreme social and political roles of the emperor and the shogun institutionalized the fusion of doctrinal norms and political authority. The
superior status of these separate and overlapping elements of "dual
government" provided the sources of legitimacy and the actual exercise
of political power. The shogunate obtained the specific prerogative to
espouse and maintain the orthodox ideology. As in the Confucian class
structure, this union of doctrinal and political roles involved a degree of
"secularized theocracy." The articulation of official norms and the exercise of political authority were vested in a single role. The maintenance of
the hierarchical secular-oriented class structure in pre-Western Japan
depended essentially on the preservation of the dominant role of this
doctrinally-based political authority.

III. *Politically Relevant Institutions of the
Japanized Confucian Societal Structure*

A. *Great Tradition*: The great tradition of the Japanized Confucian
societal structure consisted largely of the collective achievements accom-

plished by the relatively centralized political system prior to the beginning of the Kamakura Period (1185 A.D.) and by the increasingly centralized political power exercised by the Tokugawa Shogunate (1603–1868). The loyalties and memories induced by this unique great tradition were also deeply affected by differences between theory and practice. The Japanese perceived of the emperor as the living symbol of a long unbroken hereditary lineage vesting a "divine right" in imperial authority. They also assumed the emperor to be the titular "Head" and benevolent "Father" of the Japanese race comprising a single "family" and "household." Yet for almost eight centuries the Japanese people were aware that their society was a fragmented feudal system and political power was actually exercised by the shogun and subordinate daimyo. The great tradition of impressive achievements by the leaders of a unified society was consequently a latent aspiration, not a concrete reality. It produced a modest doctrinal loyalty to imperial authority and an intense personal loyalty to local feudal leaders and the family. At the same time both elements involved in the great tradition were widely recognized as the source of specific contributions to Japanese traditional society. In their separate and overlapping spheres the emperor and the shogun inspired the view of the Japanese people as a distinct island race possessing a vaguely conceived mission to spread its influence elsewhere in Asia. Some recognition of societal grandeur was accorded to the impressive architectural structures and imperial ceremony at the traditional capitals of Nara and Kyoto. Similar pride was aroused toward the shogun and his imposing fortress at Edo. Some sense of collective achievement was likewise engendered by the ornate Buddhist temples and shrines located at important religious centers throughout the country.

B. *Middle Tradition:* The middle tradition constituted the dominant political institution of the Japanized Confucian societal structure. Political power was exercised by the feudal state which comprised the intermediate political entity between the dualistic authority of the great tradition and the little tradition in rural villages. During the Tokugawa period there were approximately 270 middle traditions exercising varying degrees of autonomy from the centralized power of the shogun.[27] Approximately 175 feudal states were governed by "inner daimyo" who had supported the first shogun, Tokugawa Ieyasu, from the beginning of his struggle to quell civil strife and "unify" the country. These rulers of the middle traditions received special favors from the shogun but they were more closely controlled by his centralized authority. About 90 feudal states were headed by "outer daimyo" who received fewer favors from the shogun but enjoyed greater local autonomy. The authority of each feudal state was bolstered by samurai warriors employed by the ruling daimyo. All roles within the civil and military elites of each feudal state were filled by hereditary succession. A few middle traditions acquired some regional predominance, including Shimonoseki, Kagoshima, Nagoya, and Mito. The evolution of an "enclave tradition" exercising considerable local autonomy in sea-going commerce and trade occurred at Nagasaki. All middle traditions in pre-Western Japan tended to disperse political loyalties and hamper development toward a unified nation-state. While the actual exercise of political power became increasingly centralized, the form of political power remained feudal. The middle tradition likewise engendered a powerful system of feudal law as the basis of personal rights and obligations. It required the maintenance of the military class to defend the territory of each feudal state from nearby threats. It accordingly reinforced the elevated status of the samurai caste in the hierarchical class structure.

C. *Little Tradition*: The little tradition of pre-Western Japan was represented in the villages, or *mura,* which contained the vast majority of the population. These lowest levels of the societal structure enjoyed less autonomy than the little tradition elsewhere in Asia due to their close proximity to the centers of political authority in the relatively small territories of quasi-autonomous feudal states. Yet the autonomy of rural village communities gradually increased during the Tokugawa period as the daimyo transferred the samurai class from the countryside to fortified towns and delegated the administration of rural affairs to village headmen. Within each little tradition a village headman (*nanushi*) was selected by a representative of the daimyo to manage village affairs and represent the village in dealings with higher administrative authorities. The village headman was assisted by a village assembly made up of prominent large landowners. As in the Chinese little tradition, a system of social and political control was instituted whereby ten village families were collectively accountable for numerous obligations including the payment of taxes and proper social behavior. The little tradition of pre-Western Japan, as in other Asian societal structures, comprised the primary source of ascriptive and particularistic values and modes of behavior. It combined orthodox social norms with a rural animism. It enforced many of the personal rights and obligations derived from feudal law and the system of hereditary authority.

The only aboriginal tribes or "remote peasants" in the Japanized Confucian societal structure were the *Ainu* who inhabited the northeastern territories of Honshu when large-scale contact was made by immigrating

Japanese. These primitive tribal people resisted the expansion of Japanese society. Yet a combined process of conquest and assimilation by Japanese great, middle, and little traditions gradually removed the Ainu tribesmen to the northern island of Hokkaido and virtually eliminated this single minority group in the island society.

SUMMARY

Table III comprises a summary of politically relevant traditional historical inputs induced by the two types of secular-oriented traditional societies in Asia. Table IV is included to compare the hierarchical class structures of the Confucian and Japanized Confucian traditional societies.

Table III. Summary of politically relevant traditional historical inputs induced by the cultural systems, class structures, and societal structures of the secular-oriented traditional societies in Asia.

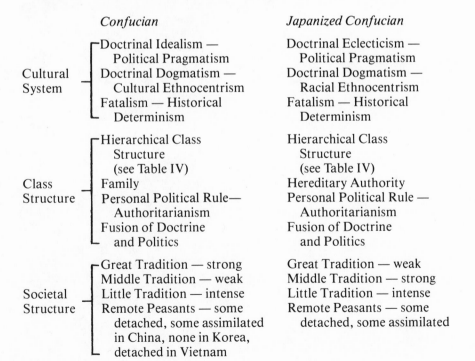

	Confucian	*Japanized Confucian*
Cultural System	Doctrinal Idealism — Political Pragmatism Doctrinal Dogmatism — Cultural Ethnocentrism Fatalism — Historical Determinism	Doctrinal Eclecticism — Political Pragmatism Doctrinal Dogmatism — Racial Ethnocentrism Fatalism — Historical Determinism
Class Structure	Hierarchical Class Structure (see Table IV) Family Personal Political Rule— Authoritarianism Fusion of Doctrine and Politics	Hierarchical Class Structure (see Table IV) Hereditary Authority Personal Political Rule — Authoritarianism Fusion of Doctrine and Politics
Societal Structure	Great Tradition — strong Middle Tradition — weak Little Tradition — intense Remote Peasants — some detached, some assimilated in China, none in Korea, detached in Vietnam	Great Tradition — weak Middle Tradition — strong Little Tradition — intense Remote Peasants — some detached, some assimilated

Table IV. A comparison of the hierarchical class structures of the secular-oriented traditional societies in Asia.

Confucian	*Japanized Confucian*
Emperor	Emperor
Scholarly-Bureaucratic Class	Shogun
Peasants	Feudal Lords (daimyo)
Artisan Class	Military Caste (samurai)
Merchant Class	Peasants
	Artisan Class
	Merchant Class
	Outcastes (eta)
	Slaves

Chapter 3

The External Environment and Linkages

The politics of the traditional society was not shaped solely by the indigenous cultural system, class structure, and societal structure. Politics was also affected by the extra-societal environment. Some additional method of analysis is consequently needed to delineate and compare the role of external influences on internal political phenomena. A suitable model for this purpose can clarify and add precision to the analysis of the genesis, development, modification, or demise of traditional historical inputs. It can lend further insights into the transfer of values, modes of behavior, and institutions from one traditional society to another. It can provide additional variables which are important in comparative political history.

The aggregated role of external influences transmitted by one society to another society has often been referred to as an "impact." The large shaded arrow in Figure III shows this relationship in the form of the impact of Society A on Society B.

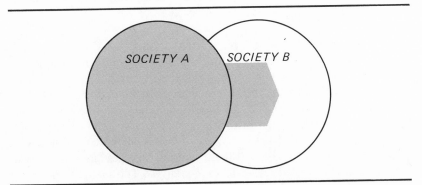

Fig. III. The impact of Society A *on Society* B.

Examples of this cross-societal phenomenon implicit in the analysis of traditional historical inputs in Chapter One and Chapter Two were the expansion of Hindu and Islamic religious influences in Southeast Asia and the transmission of Chinese Confucian influences to Korea, Vietnam, and Japan.

This common mode of explanation by both political scientists and historians is useful, but it is much too broad and oversimplified for accurate political analysis. The external impact, in fact, did not induce changes in all sectors of the recipient society. The Hindu and Islamic impacts in traditional societies in Southeast Asia and the Chinese Confucian impact in Korea, Vietnam, and Japan actually touched only limited and specific areas of the lesser developed societies. A more exact form of analysis of the external impact on these recipient societies is needed to isolate specific influences or linkages embodied in the general external impact and to assess political changes caused by each external linkage. The several linear arrows in Figure IV show this relationship in the form of specific linkages from Society A to Society B.

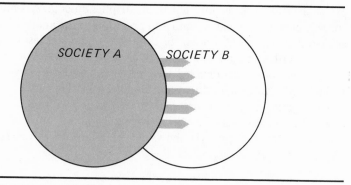

Fig. IV. Specific linkages from Society A *to Society* B.

These cross-societal linkages have been defined by Professor James Rosenau as "any recurrent sequence of behavior that originates in one system and is reacted to in another."[1] The terms "exchanges," "penetrations," and "influences" are often used to denote this inter-societal phenomenon. In this study these external linkages can be viewed as another source of traditional historical inputs in a specific society which shaped its indigenous values, modes of behavior, and institutions. A total and systematic analysis of these external linkages and their internal reactions can be labeled *macro-linkage-analysis*. This methodology seeks to understand the political role of foreigners (or what Rosenau calls "non-members") in the development of the indigenous "penetrated political system."[2] It endeavors to incorporate all relevant external and internal factors in an effort to obtain a total environmental or ecological view of political behavior. As cited in the Introduction, this methodology is an early attempt to pursue the "big picture" of politics.

EXTERNAL LINKAGES IN ASIAN TRADITIONAL SOCIETIES

I. *Military Invasions*: Military invasions comprised one of the most significant external penetrations in the traditional society. These linkages created or shaped many of the great and middle traditions in the Indian sub-continent beginning with the Aryan incursions in the fifteenth century B.C.[3] Successive waves of Persians, Afghans, Greeks, Turks, Arabs, and other racial groups poured through the northern mountain passes until about 1700 A.D. These military invasions aided in the formation of the Mauryan, Gupta, Mogul, and Marathas empires. They were also involved in the development of middle traditions such as the Kingdoms of the Andras, Chalukyas, Rashtrakutas, Hoysalas, Yadavas, Bahmani, and Rajputs. Military intrusions increased ethnic pluralism in all of these traditional societies. They likewise served to spread the "higher" religions of Buddhism (under Asoka) and Islam (after the twelfth century A.D.) to various regions of the sub-continent.[4] Mass migrations accompanied by military action also formed many great and middle traditions in Southeast Asia. The formation of the Burmese, Thai, and Vietnamese traditional societies occurred through mass migrations from their original homelands in southern China into the sparsely populated territories to the south after the ninth century A.D.[5] Sumatran and Javanese societies in Indonesia erected imposing great traditions during this same era by large-scale invasions in the archipelago and adjoining territories.

Great and middle traditions in China, Korea, and Vietnam were involved in relatively fewer military invasions than the societies in South and Southeast Asia. Large areas in China were intermittently attacked by Tartars, Mongols, and Manchus, and armed intrusions were instrumental in the establishment of the two non-Chinese dynasties (Yuan and Ching).[6] Yet foreign invaders in China imparted fewer cultural influences than their counterparts in South and Southeast Asia due to the immensity of the indigenous population and the intense doctrinal conformity induced by the Chinese cultural system. Even when China was ruled by alien emperors, the Confucian cultural system remained essentially intact. Korea was subjected to several military invasions from China, but it suffered no permanent loss of territory. Vietnam experienced a larger number of military intrusions from its northern neighbor during its long struggle for independence, yet these invasions served the dual role of strengthening a distinct Vietnamese culture and at the same time shaping that culture by a single foreign influence.[7] In contrast, Japan was not touched by any external military power until the American occupation at the end of World War II. The Confucian societies in East Asia consequently experienced fewer cultural infusions from foreign "non-members" than the traditional societies in the southern region. This factor contributed to a relatively high level of racial and cultural homogeneity within these traditional societies.

Military invasions exerted a significant effect on the indigenous cultural system and class structure of threatened traditional societies. External armed attacks strengthened collective values of the orthodox religion or doctrine which in turn augmented a sense of common identity and purpose. This tendency was facilitated by the fusion of religion or doctrine and politics in Islamic and Confucian traditional societies; it was hampered by the separation of religion and politics in Hindu and Theravada Buddhist traditional societies. Military aggression caused the exercise of expanded authoritarian rule by the sovereign ruler of the endangered traditional society and tested his personal political skills in defending the territory of his realm. It likewise intensified the centralization of the great or middle tradition under attack and increased the involvement of the sovereign ruler in the affairs of semi-isolated rural villages. External intrusions enhanced the role of the indigenous military class engaged in defensive actions against the enemy. This condition exerted a greater societal upheaval in Confucian traditional societies where the military had a low social status than in the Hindu, Islamic, and Japanized Confucian traditional societies where the military enjoyed high social status. Military hostilities tended to reinforce the stratification of the hierarchical class structure in the common effort to maintain internal stability and order. Emergency warfare conditions justified the demands of the sovereign ruler for increased loyalty and sacrifices from subordinate classes.

II. *Foreign Missionaries*: Foreign missionaries constituted a second linkage between the external environment and the traditional society. Religious emissaries carried new values and new modes of behavior from Hindu traditional societies in India to many parts of Southeast Asia.[8] The earliest conveyers of this "higher" religion were Brahman priests and members of the Kshatriyas military caste who spread their own cultural influences during the first millenium of the Christian era. Often these high-caste missionaries accompanied Hindu merchants and traders in their commercial missions to "Further India." Their contacts with traditional societies in Southeast Asia were confined to upper levels of the indigenous class structure which readily accepted the Brahman doctrines bolstering their favored political and religious roles. Local rulers were likewise conducive to Hindu religious influences since they did not entail the adoption of a total alien way of life but provided a sophisticated religious orientation adaptable to the local cultural system.[9] The transmission of Hindu values to these indigenous upper classes included a high degree of psychological pluralism, a legal system based on the doctrine of *dharma,* and the idea of *devaraja* or god-king. Following the decline of Hinduism around 1000 A.D., these foreign influences were overlaid with new infusions of Buddhism or Islam, yet many Hindu influences remained.

Buddhist monks emanating from India and Ceylon spread another "higher" religion over local forms of animism and Hinduism in traditional societies in Southeast Asia. The rejection of the rigid Hindu caste system and a more practical religious orientation embodied in the teachings of the Buddha appealed to broader social groups than the upper-class religion of the Brahmans. Buddhist monks moving northward from India also carried their teachings to China from 200 to 800 A.D. and imparted the only foreign cultural influence in the Middle Kingdom prior to the Western impact.[10] As previously explained, the original teachings of Buddhism were altered in the process of expansion in China and they emerged largely in the modified form of Mahayana Buddhism. Mahayana Buddhism thereafter was conveyed to Korea by Chinese monks, largely during the T'ang dynasty (618–907 A.D.).[11] During this same period Korean monks carried the Chinese form of Buddhism to the islands of Japan.

In a similar manner of peaceful penetration, Islamic missionaries brought the teachings of the Koran to Malaya and Indonesia after the twelfth century A.D.[12] These religious teachers often accompanied Moslem traders coming from the Gujerat and Malabar coasts in southern India. More learned Islamic scholars subsequently came to Southeast Asia from Egypt and Mecca. The relative simplicity of Islam combined with the practice of mass conversions enabled it to spread more extensively and rapidly than Hinduism or Buddhism. The new religion expanded the use of the Persian script and implanted Islamic law. It promoted the fusion of religion and politics. Yet Islam also underwent significant changes in its encounter with indigenous cultural systems in Southeast Asia. Moslems in Malaya and Indonesia preserved a relatively high status for women and retained many local beliefs, including animism and ancestor veneration. They constructed their mosques more like Hindu and Buddhist pagodas than the imposing minaret-studded religious structures of the Middle East.

Foreign missionaries created the eclectic religious orientations of the great and middle traditions in Southeast Asia. Foreign Buddhist monks also generated a new religious orientation in China, Korea, Vietnam, and Japan that competed intermittently with the indigenous cultural systems based on Confucianism, Taoism, or Shinto. In varying degrees this distinct method of external penetration provided the doctrinal norms by which the local priestly class promoted a common cultural bond within the traditional society. Itinerant indigenous priests traveling throughout the realm brought elements of the "higher" religions imparted by foreign missionaries to the little traditions in rural villages. They reinforced the legitimacy of the dynastic ruler and strengthened rural loyalties toward the central political authority. The orthodox religious teachings enabled the priestly class to serve as a major internal linkage between the upper, intermediate, and local levels of the society. According to Eisenstadt:

> They [the priestly class] were the great potential allies of the ruling elites in the latter's endeavors to remain identified with the political and cultural systems and their symbols. Further, they usually were the chief connecting links between the local traditions of the vast strata of the population and the "Great Tradition" of the cultural and political centers.[13]

III. *Foreign Traders*: The activities of foreign traders served as another form of external penetration into the traditional society. From pre-Christian times modest quantities of goods were transported over land routes from the Middle East to India and China, although the most significant trading routes were by sea. With few exceptions the early traders were private entrepreneurs engaged in small-scale commercial operations. Within Asia, their trading ventures emanated from strategically located ports in India, Malaya, Sumatra, Java, China, and Japan. From these coastal centers some goods were conveyed inland. As mentioned previously, Indian merchants accompanied Hindu and Islamic missionaries in a combined expansion of religion and commerce in Southeast Asia. Chinese trading vessels actively plied the coastal waters of the South China Sea from the early Christian era. Until the seventeenth century, Japanese warrior-traders (*wako*) operated as pirates and plundered seafaring vessels and unguarded towns along the coasts of China and Southeast Asia.

Foreign traders imparted a major impact on coastal enclave traditions. These sea-oriented states detached from a great tradition participated much more actively in external commercial activities than in the affairs of internal traditional societies. Foreign traders consequently exerted relatively minor political influences on great or middle traditions in the interior. Professor Murphey has stated: "The great cities [of pre-Western Asia], and indeed nearly all of the important urban centers, were inland, related to internal rather than external concerns."[14] The limited contact between external trade and internal traditional societies was confined primarily to the indigenous merchant class. Foreign traders supplied these local entrepreneurs with luxury goods in the form of gold, silks, ivory, pearls, and aromatic woods which were purchased largely by the upper social classes. They also provided spices for the preservation of food.[15] At times, foreign traders paid special taxes to the ruling sovereign for protection and trading privileges. Improvements in the quality of imported goods intermittently generated new technical skills among the local artisan class. With few exceptions the social and political influence of foreign traders was severely limited due to the low level of economic development. In Confucian and Japanized Confucian traditional societies this specialized external penetration was further reduced by the low prestige of commercial enterprises.

IV. *Tribute Missions*: The tribute missions between a powerful great tradition (suzerain) and nearby subordinate great or middle traditions (vassals) constituted another external linkage. These missions consisted of periodic journeys by officials of the vassal society to the royal court of the suzerain society. Tribute bearers presented gifts to the suzerain ruler and performed prescribed ceremonial rituals symbolizing the cultural and political superiority of the suzerain society.[16] In return, the visiting tribute mission received gifts from the suzerain ruler in recognition of their ruler's loyalty and his acknowledged inferior status. This hierarchical pattern of traditional "diplomacy" involved no formal treaties; it constituted a pattern of inter-societal behavior based on custom and usage rather than contract or law. In practice the long distances between the suzerain society and vassal societies and the primitive methods of transportation enabled the rulers of vassal societies to govern their internal affairs with relatively little interference by the suzerain power. The tribute system originated in the interrelationships between the Chinese emperor and sovereign rulers in Korea and Southeast Asia from the early Han dynasty to the early twentieth century.[17] A similar system was employed by the Thai kings at Ayudhya and Bangkok in their relations with Laos, Cambodia and Malay rulers prior to the imposition of Western colonial rule. Tribute missions from nearby vassal societies were likewise received by the rulers of the Srivijaya and Majapahit empires in Sumatra and Java from the seventh until the sixteenth centuries.[18]

The tribute system exerted a unique political influence in both the suzerain society and the vassal society. In the suzerain society it enhanced collective values in the cultural system and added prestige to the sovereign ruler, especially in the area near the royal capital where local inhabitants could witness the arrival of foreign tribute missions. Periodic visits by tribute bearers acknowledging the superiority of China, for example, strengthened doctrinal dogmatism and cultural ethnocentrism. They abetted the superiority complex deeply ingrained in the Chinese Confucian value-system. Professor Harold Hinton has stated:

> It soothed the cultural pride of the Chinese to see those they regarded as barbarians coming to the imperial capital to acknowledge a largely nominal suzerainty of the Chinese Emperor over their own rulers. For this euphoria the Chinese paid the barbarians well with rich gifts and empty titles and occasionally with more valuable protection against foreign and domestic enemies.[19]

Tribute missions also imposed certain requirements on the political authority exercised by the ruler of the suzerain society. It generated the need for current information on the internal affairs of vassal societies as well as sufficient resources to maintain some semblance of inter-societal order and security. It created the demand for certain specialized administrative roles in the "foreign office" of the sovereign ruler.

In the vassal society the external source of protection and security provided by the tribute system often reduced the need for large military forces. The suzerain ruler served as an additional source of legitimacy to the ruler of the vassal society since the failure to gain recognition by a tribute mission often resulted in intervention by suzerain authorities to restore the "rightful" local ruler to the throne. The tribute system likewise encouraged a modest trade between the suzerain society and the vassal society since merchants were permitted to accompany tribute bearers between both royal capitals. The system also served as an additional channel of cultural diffusion among the upper classes of the vassal society since personal exposure to a "superior" culture caused some returning officials to adopt selected modes of behavior observed abroad. This practice enabled a few Chinese Confucian influences to spread to the royal courts of several great traditions in Southeast Asia, although these external influences were minor compared to the more pervasive and flexible Hindu influences. The tribute missions to China from Korea and Vietnam played a much larger role in transmitting Confucianism to these vassal societies due to the absence of a competing "higher" foreign cultural penetration.

V. *Indigenous Returnees*: Indigenous persons returning from foreign travels constituted a significant means of transmitting external influences to the traditional society. Their numbers were small, but their internal impact was often deep and extensive. The tribute bearers of a vassal society, already cited, exerted a modest penetration of this kind. More important were local religious leaders returning from study and meditation at major religious centers in foreign lands. Until the tenth century A.D. religious leaders came from Southeast Asia to study under Hindu teachers at Banaras, Amarnath, Nasik, and Allahabad. The famous Chinese monk, Fa-hsien, studied Buddhism in Indian in 399 A.D. before spreading it in his own society.[20] Early in the Ayudhya era many Thai priests received direct exposure to the teachings of Theravada Buddhism in Ceylon. Korean priests studied Mahayana Buddhism in China before carrying it to their own country and Japan.[21] Japanese priests, on the other hand, traveled directly to the source of Mahayana Buddhism in China rather than to the Korean peninsula from where it originally entered their own society. Moslem scholars from Malaya and Indonesia studied the Koran at Mecca and other Islamic centers of learning in the Middle East before undertaking religious proselyting in their own societies. The acceptance of indigenous returnees by their own people and their familiarity with local beliefs and behavior enabled them to exert a unique role in disseminating orthodox religious teachings. Landon has stated: "The most effective missionaries are indigenous persons who have gone abroad and have been thoroughly indoctrinated and who then return home to affect their home communities."[22] The influence of indigenous returnees intensified the earlier impact of foreign missionaries. Often they distributed sacred writings which they had translated into local languages. Frequently they became ardent defenders of religious purity, and with more justification than foreign missionaries they denounced the "corruption" of orthodox teachings by the infusion of local customs and practices. In other cases indigenous returnees facilitated the blending of foreign "higher" religions with the local culture.

VI. *Political Exiles:* Political exiles constituted an external influence in some traditional societies. Often these persons were members of the upper class disfavored by the sovereign ruler who had left their own society voluntarily, by official request, or due to physical threats. Some political exiles were unsuccessful contenders for the throne who fled to a foreign territory rather than suffer death or imprisonment from a newly-ensconced ruler. Political exiles exerted two types of political influences. One group abandoned political activities once they found refuge in a foreign land and remained in exile for the rest of their lives. Some of these permanent expatriates served as additional conveyers of their own culture to the societies where they resided. Chinese political exiles in Korea, for example, assisted in strengthening Confucian values and modes of behavior in the adjoining "Hermit Kingdom" over a period of many centuries. The second group of political exiles, however, retained the hope of returning to positions of power in their own homeland. These persons often posed a constant threat to the sovereign ruler in their native traditional society. At times, they plotted in collusion with sympathetic factions at the royal court of the sovereign ruler. This type of political exile was more common in the intersocietal power struggles between the kingdoms of Burma, Thailand, Laos, Cambodia, and Vietnam prior to the Western impact.[23]

VII. *Foreign Communities:* Foreign communities comprised a final form of external penetration into the traditional society. These communities consisted of a distinct foreign "presence" caused by immigrants assuming permanent residence after entering the society peacefully. Foreign communities were of several types. Some foreign communities such as the small Chinese coastal villages in Southeast Asia prior to the Western impact remained detached from the adjoining traditional society and exerted no significant social or political influences.[24] More important were the foreign communities which resided at the center of great, middle, or enclave traditions. Many of these foreign communities engaged in commerce and trade. Chinese communities in Vietnam served this role at Hue, Hanoi, and Saigon, in Siam at Ayudhya, Lopburi, and Chiengmai, and in coastal enclaves in Malaya and Indonesia.[25] Often the Chinese formed the dominant portion of the merchant and artisan class in the traditional society. This foreign presence either prevented or hampered the development of an indigenous merchant "middle class" engaging in economic activity. It added a racial dimension to social tensions between the indigenous upper classes and local entreprenurial enterprises. A third type of foreign community consisted of small numbers of religious refugees who posed no threat to the indigenous rulers and performed certain social roles. The Parsis who adhered to Zoroastrianism and fled Muslim persecution in Persia during the seventh and eighth centuries A.D. entered traditional societies along the west coast of India where they became a progressive and competent commercial class.[26] A Japanese community composed of Roman Catholic refugees from early Tokugawa rule resided at Ayudhya during the seventeenth century and served faithfully as palace guards for the Thai king.[27] The most important foreign communities, however, were those which served as permanent centers of religious influence and supplemented the efforts of foreign missionaries in spreading a foreign "higher" religion. The resident Hindu communities at the royal courts in Southeast Asia from approximately 100 to 1000 A.D. served this significant cultural role. Hindu values and modes of behavior were transmitted by admitting indigenous rulers into the Kshatriyas caste through ceremonies performed by resident Brahman priests. Hindu influences were reinforced by intermarriage between upper caste Hindus and the daughters of local rulers. Indigenous artists imitated Hindu models in sculpture, literature, and architecture. Local names were Sanskritized. These foreign penetrations induced a more rigid class structure and a more exalted social and political role for the indigenous ruler.

Chapter 4

Terminal Analysis of Traditional Historical Inputs

The analysis of politically relevant traditional historical inputs and the external linkages shaping them does not by itself provide a complete explanation of the politics of the traditional society as it came to an end and encountered the Western impact. Certain conclusive conditions or what I will call *terminal factors* imparted special influences on the values, modes of behavior, and institutions of Asian traditional societies in their final stages. These terminal factors are also important historical variables in comparative political analysis. They make it possible to assess important aspects of the traditional society in their "end-state." They provide a necessary conceptual tool in explaining fundamental changes in traditional historical inputs as they reached a significant chronological "turning point" and became exposed to a vastly different source of external influences. The methodology used in applying terminal factors to the traditional society at the time of the Western impact I will call *terminal analysis.*

The terminal factors affecting the traditional society are the following:

1. THE DEGREE OF ADAPTABILITY OF THE TRADITIONAL CULTURAL SYSTEM TO FOREIGN-INDUCED CHANGE

This variable might also be characterized as the degree of resiliency, tolerance, flexibility, eclecticism, or response-capacity of the cultural system of the traditional society to external influences. It was shaped in some degree by the interactions between traditional societies prior to the Western impact.

A first step in analyzing this very important terminal factor is to designate the type of indigenous cultural system and to assess its propensity toward foreign-induced change. Traditional cultural systems embracing a value of religious or doctrinal dogmatism tended to exhibit a low degree of adaptability and a high degree of resistance to foreign influences. Conversely, traditional cultural systems upholding a value of religious or doctrinal eclecticism exhibited a high degree of adaptability and a low degree of resistance to externally-induced change. Professor David Apter has analyzed the degree of adaptability and resistance to foreign influences in African traditional societies by positing a dichotimized typology of an "instrumental" value-system which is pragmatic, fragmentary, and secularly-oriented and relatively responsive to external change, and a "consummatory" value-system which is intensely religious, cosmologically-oriented, and deeply hostile to external change.[1] This method of analysis must be modified somewhat in applying these concepts to Asian traditional societies. Yet generally the Confucian and Islamic cultural systems contained a high level of dogmatic and "consummatory" values, while the Japanized Confucian and most Theravada Buddhist cultural systems had a high level of eclectic and "instrumental" values. The Hindu cultural systems in India combined elements of both types of these values.

A second step in analyzing the degree of adaptability or resistance to foreign-induced change is to specify the types of external linkages in each traditional society and to assess the effect of these foreign influences on the indigenous cultural system. Table V shows the specific types of external linkages in Asian traditional societies.

The response of the indigenous cultural system to these pre-Western external linkages varied considerably. Some external linkages were rejected outright and served mainly to reinforce indigenous values, modes of behavior, and institutions. Other external linkages "got through" and imparted major transformations to the indigenous cultural system. Some external linkages did both; they transmitted some foreign influences and strengthened some indigenous elements of the traditional society.

A third step in this analysis is to designate the source or sources of the external linkages in the traditional society. The name of the foreign traditional society can be used for this purpose when it served as the dominant and primary source of external linkages to another traditional society. Thus, Korea, Vietnam, and Japan were "Confucian-China-penetrated" traditional societies. Ceylon, Burma, Thailand, Laos, and Cambodia were "Hindu-penetrated" traditional societies. When the traditional society received significant external linkages from two or more foreign traditional societies it can be called a "mixed-penetrated" traditional

Table V. Types of external linkages in Asian traditional societies. The atomized animist traditional society in pre-hispanic Philippines is excluded since it was unaffected by external linkages.

Hindu	Theravada Buddhist and Islamic
Military invasions	Military invasions
Foreign traders	Foreign missionaries
Foreign communities	Foreign traders
	Tribute missions (only in Southeast Asia)
	Indigenous returnees
	Foreign communities

Confucian	Japanized Confucian
Military invasions	Foreign missionaries
Foreign missionaries	Foreign traders
Foreign traders	Indigenous returnees (prior to Tokugawa era)
Tribute missions	
Indigenous returnees	

society. The Islamic traditional societies in Southeast Asia (Malaya and Indonesia) were examples of "mixed-penetrated" traditional societies which received major foreign influences from Hindu, Theravada Buddhist, and Islamic sources. Generally, the "Confucian-China-penetrated" traditional societies absorbed a high degree of "consummatory" doctrinal dogmatism into their cultural systems which reinforced the propensity to resist subsequent foreign-induced change. Conversely, the "Hindu-penetrated" traditional societies adopted an "instrumental" eclecticism in their cultural systems which facilitated the gradual assimilation of subsequent external influences. "Mixed-penetrated" traditional societies imbibed varying foreign elements of "consummatory" dogmatism and "instrumental" eclecticism.

This method of analysis makes it possible to compare the cultural systems of the traditional societies in Asia in a high-low continuum showing the degree of adaptability or resistance to foreign-induced change. This continuum is shown in Figure V.[2]

Thus, the Hindu and Hindu-penetrated cultural systems tended to be the most highly adaptable and least resistant to foreign-induced change. The mixed-penetrated cultural systems combining Hindu, Theravada Buddhist, and Islamic external linkages were somewhat less adaptable

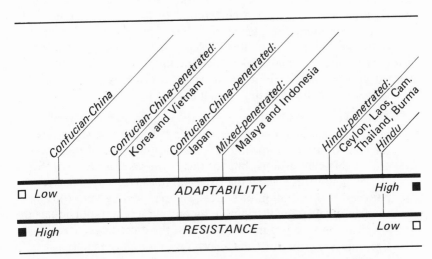

Fig. V. High-low continuum showing the degree of adaptability or resistance of Asian cultural systems to foreign-induced change.

and more resistant to foreign influences. The Confucian-China-penetrated cultural systems in Japan, Vietnam, and Korea were respectively less adaptable and more resistant to foreign change. The Confucian Chinese cultural system itself was the least adaptable and the most resistant to external influences.

2. THE DEGREE OF COHESIVENESS WITHIN THE HIERARCHICAL CLASS STRUCTURE OF THE GREAT TRADITION OR MIDDLE TRADITION

This variable was determined primarily by the personal capacity of the ruling sovereign to maintain a unified and stabilized authority at the top of the class structure and to prevent dysfunctional centrifugal forces within the upper social and political strata. This endeavor sharply divided the small ruling elite from other elements of the traditional class structure. It also strained prescribed modes of behavior among certain members of the ruling class. Some individuals and groups within the governing hierarchy did not passively accept the policies pursued by the traditional ruler. Competing factions at the center sought to advance and protect their own interests. The struggles between the ruler and these early "interest groups" and the conflicts between the contending groups themselves constituted most of the "politics" of the traditional society. This phenomenon has often been referred to as "palace politics." It consisted of the interactions between "circles" and "cliques" governed in part by their ascriptive political roles, but also influenced in some degree by strong personal leaders and, at times, certain achievement-oriented groups. This contest for power was often extremely intense. Professor John Kautsky has described it as follows:

> The stakes are evidently high, for the conflict can be a very bitter one in which much, even life, is risked. These stakes are the control of governmental offices, not on behalf of the interests of different groups, but for their own sake. Such a conflict, too, is politics, for while the issues do not involve alternative patterns of distribution of scarce resources among major groups, they do involve the distribution among cliques and individuals of what are, in wholly agrarian societies, the exceedingly scarce "resources" of prestige, high social position, and material wealth.[3]

Many clashes were caused by undifferentiated and undefined political roles within the upper ruling elite. Most positions of power and prestige depended on the personal choices of the sovereign ruler. Disagreements and jealousies among the recipients of these royal appointments continually affected the shifting loyalties among contending factions. Disunity was also induced by antithetical tendencies between traditional and rationalizing political groups. Ascriptive and achievement-oriented roles within these groups tended to undermine each other. In the long run, the traditional roles prevailed. Important political institutions never became fully rationalized. Instead they were constantly penetrated and weakened by ascriptive loyalties.

The degree of cohesiveness within the hierarchical class structure of the great or middle traditions affected the extent to which the values, modes of behavior, and institutions of the traditional society were exposed to the Western impact. A high-cohesive authority at the center of the traditional class structure possessed a relatively strong capacity to maintain effective control over the traditional society and to resist encroachments by Western powers. An example of a high-cohesive traditional leadership was the Chakkri dynasty in Thailand which maintained sufficient unity within the ruling elite throughout the nineteenth century to resist repeated incursions by Western nations and to retain effective control over most of the original territory of the traditional society. A low-cohesive traditional leadership conversely possessed a relatively weak capacity to maintain effective control over the traditional society and to resist Western influences. Low-cohesive traditional political elites were the most likely to succumb to Western colonial rule or to a status of inferior treatment by Western powers. Examples of low-cohesive traditional rulers were the Mogul dynasty in India, the Konbang dynasty in Burma, the Ching (Manchu) dynasty in China, and the Tokugawa leadership in Japan.

The degree of cohesiveness within the traditional ruling elite also affected the level of satisfaction or discontent within the entire traditional class structure. This factor in turn influenced the specific social and political groups most resistant or susceptible to change at the time of the Western impact. The subordinate political role of Hindus in pre-British India, for example, caused upper elements within this religious group to respond more favorably to most Western influences than the recently dominant Moslems. Merchants and artisans in low prestigious roles in the Confucian class structures in China, Korea, and Vietnam were generally more eager for Western commerce and technology than the upper level members of the scholarly bureaucratic class. The disgruntled lower samurai in Tokugawa Japan were more anxious for Western modernization than the relatively satisfied shogun, daimyo, and upper samurai.

3. THE DEGREE OF COHESIVENESS BETWEEN THE GREAT, MIDDLE, AND LITTLE TRADITIONS OF THE SOCIETAL STRUCTURE

This variable overlapped in some degree with the previous terminal factor, i.e. the degree of cohesiveness within the hierarchical class structure of the great or middle traditions. The degree of effective centralized control over the territories of the great or middle traditions was always a function of the degree of unity within the ruling political elite. Yet other traditional historical factors also influenced the degree of cohesiveness between the center of the societal structure and its geographic sub-units. The most significant historical factors were relevant values embodied in the cultural system and class structure, and the composition of the population inhabiting the great, middle, and little traditions. These factors can be used to construct a high-low continuum suitable for comparing the degree of cohesiveness of the traditional societies in Asia. This continuum is shown in Figure VI.

High-cohesive societal structures tended to have a secular-oriented cultural system, a secular-oriented class structure embodying an important role for the bureaucracy, and a fusion of doctrine and politics. These societal structures invariably were characterized by a great tradition

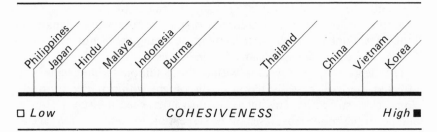

Fig. VI. High-low continuum comparing the degree of cohesiveness of the societal structures of Asian traditional societies.

which embraced most or all of the territory and people of the traditional society. They also had a relatively homogeneous population residing in little traditions which were accessible to the political authorities in the great or middle traditions. "Remote peasants" were either non-existent or few in number, docile, and gradually being assimilated. These societal structures were relatively stable and offered significant resistance to the Western impact. The most highly cohesive societal structures in Asia were the Confucian traditional societies of Korea, Vietnam, and China.

Low-cohesive societal structures tended to have a sacred-oriented cultural system, a sacred-oriented class structure with a significant social role for a clerical class and the military, and a separation of religion and politics. They were characterized by the absence or infrequency of a great tradition, numerous and powerful middle traditions (usually ruling over relatively small territories), and a heterogeneous population. Some little traditions often had considerable independence of political authorities at the center of the middle traditions, and sizeable numbers of unassimilated "remote peasants" inhabited inaccessible territories on the fringes of the traditional society. These societal structures were relatively fragile and offered weak resistance to the Western impact. The least cohesive societal structures in Asia were the atomized animist traditional society in pre-hispanic Philippines, the fragmented traditional society in Japan, and the Hindu traditional societies in the Indian sub-continent. Somewhat more cohesive were the Theravada Buddhist and Islamic traditional societies in South and Southeast Asia.

4. THE GEOGRAPHIC FACTORS OF THE TRADITIONAL SOCIETY RELATIVE
TO THE PURPOSE AND SCOPE OF THE WESTERN IMPACT

Several geographic factors affected the initial phases of the Western
impact and shaped the final historical inputs of the traditional society.
They constitute specific forces of time, space, and nature over which the
political leadership of the traditional society had little or no control.
These factors are strategic location, the physical size of the territory, the
physical characteristics of the boundaries, topography, natural
resources, and climate.

Strategic Location: Traditional societies physically located near the
major areas of Western power were either dominated or significantly
modified by the Western impact. Conversely, traditional societies whose
territories were distant from the major centers of Western expansion
were less affected by oncoming Western influences. Except for the early
maritime explorations of the Spanish which came across the Pacific
Ocean, the major areas of Western penetration in Asia were the Indian
Ocean, the South China Sea, the East China Sea, and Russian Siberia.
The role of the strategic location in the demise or alteration of the traditional society by the Western impact can be measured and compared by a
high-low continuum showing the degree of exposure of the traditional
society to these specific sea and land channels of Western power. A high-
low continuum comparing the degree of exposure of traditional societies
in Asia to the Western impact is shown in Figure VII.

This continuum shows that the strategic location of most traditional
societies in South and Southeast Asia induced a high exposure to

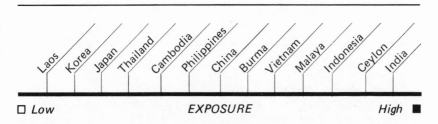

□ *Low*   *EXPOSURE*   *High* ■

*Fig. VII. High-low continuum comparing the degree of exposure to
Western power caused by the strategic location of Asian traditional
societies.*

Western penetration, a factor which contributed to the imposition of Western colonial rule in this area. The continuum likewise shows the lesser exposure of traditional societies in East and Northeast Asia to the Western impact, a factor which assisted these traditional societies in evading Western colonial rule and in mitigating many Western influences.

Physical Size of the Territory: The physical size of the territory affected the degree of "survival capacity" of the traditional society. Traditional societies with large territories possessed a relatively high degree of survival capacity since they posed greater geographic obstacles to military conquest by Western nations. Conversely, traditional societies with small territories were easily overrun by Western powers. A high-low continuum comparing the degree of survival capacity caused by the physical size of the traditional societies in Asia is shown in Figure VIII.

Figure VIII shows the high survival capacity of the traditional society in China caused by its vast physical size. This geographic factor assisted Chinese leaders in evading Western colonial rule, although it did not prevent large coastal territories from becoming divided into spheres of influence by the Western powers. The extensive physical size of the Indian sub-continent caused British colonial rule to spread in a gradual, piece-meal process, and it enabled many traditional rulers in small "princely states" (middle traditions) to retain certain powers through treaties with Great Britain in a system of "indirect" colonial rule. The large territory of the Indonesian archipelago confined effective Dutch colonial administration to Java and Sumatra until the early twentieth century. Yet small traditional societies were relatively easy to conquer by

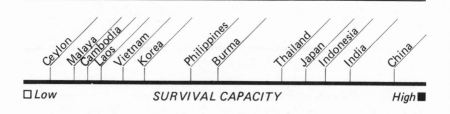

Fig. VIII. High-low continuum comparing the degree of survival capacity caused by the physical size of Asian traditional societies.

the Western colonial powers. This geographic factor facilitated the establishment of Western colonial rule in Ceylon, Malaya, Laos, Cambodia, Vietnam, Burma, and the Philippines.

Physical Characteristics of the Boundaries: The physical characteristics of the boundaries of the traditional society also influenced its survival capacity and shaped its final stages. Since all Western penetrations in Asia except that of Tzarist Russia came by sea, only the boundaries of land-locked traditional societies such as Laos, Tibet, and Nepal contributed to a high survival capacity and imposed significant obstacles to Western encroachments. The survival capacity of all other Asian traditional societies was significantly reduced by their direct physical exposure to Western maritime power. This geographic factor facilitated maximum Western influences in the territories near the coastal boundaries of these traditional societies. It caused lesser Western influences in areas more remote from adjoining bodies of water or inland waterways. The special case of the land boundary between Tzarist Russia and Asia served to confine Russian influences essentially to infringements and modifications of several elements in the final stages of the Chinese, Mongolian, and Korean traditional societies along their northern borders.

Topography: The configuration of the internal territory and terrain of the traditional society likewise affected the survival capacity of the traditional society and some of its components in its final stages. The presence of imposing internal barriers such as mountain ranges, swamps, jungles, etc., served to discourage or delay the spread of Western influences and to prolong many traditional historical inputs. Conversely, the absence of internal geographic obstacles facilitated Western encroachments in the traditional society.

Natural Resources: The real or imagined presence of natural resources in the traditional society suitable for profitable exploitation augmented the intensity of Western expansion and power. The production of valuable spices in the Molucca and Sunda islands was a primary factor causing the aggressive trading enterprises of the Portuguese, Dutch, and British during the sixteenth and seventeenth centuries.[4] Subsequently, the presence or potential of commercially valuable food products and raw materials in any traditional society made it a major target of Western expansion, especially during the initial stages of European industrialization. The presence of abundant fertile soil and extensive mineral deposits in India made it the chief goal of early British colonial policy in Asia which in turn hastened the destruction of many Hindu and Islamic traditional societies in the Indian subcontinent. The presence of a suitable soil for food and rubber production in Java and Sumatra accelerated the spread of Dutch colonial rule and the decline of the traditional society. The presence of tin and rubber in Malaya attracted British exploitation during the latter part of the nineteenth century which caused a major alteration of Malayan traditional society.[5]

Climate: The climate influenced the final stages of the traditional society by either attracting or repelling Western expansion. Favorable climatic conditions by Western standards often served as the equivalent of an additional natural resource which contributed to the development of profitable food products and raw materials. This factor attracted Western penetration in parts of India, Burma, Vietnam, Sumatra, Java, China, and Japan. Conversely, an unfavorable climate tended to discourage habitation by Western nationals and to reduce commercial exploitation by Western commercial enterprises. This geographic factor minimized Western influences in central India, central Malaya, Borneo, and New Guinea.

5. THE DURATION OF THE TRADITIONAL SOCIETY AS A CONTINUOUSLY ORGANIZED COMMUNITY INHABITING ESSENTIALLY THE SAME GEOGRAPHIC AREA, AND THE DURATION OF DISCRETE TRADITIONAL HISTORICAL FACTORS

In most cases this terminal factor is difficult to measure with a high degree of accuracy since historical documentation on the exact chronological "beginning" of a traditional society and its constituent parts is meager, unreliable, or controversial. A similar difficulty is confronted, although in a somewhat reduced degree, in assessing the precise date when the traditional society and specific traditional historical factors were "terminated." Yet some effort must be made to analyze and measure the duration of the traditional society and its specific parts as accurately as possible since they acquired dignity, strength, and tenacity in some proportion to the passage of time. A lengthy time-span of the traditional society and discrete traditional historical factors induced a strong sense of antiquity and grandeur in the collective consciousness of its leaders and people which generated a corresponding strong resistance to change. A short time-span of the traditional society and its constituent parts induced a weaker sense of "time-honored" legacies and a weaker resistance to change.

The measurement of the duration of the traditional society and specific traditional historical inputs involves a vastly complex and detailed process. Only a few salient aspects of measuring this important terminal factor can be outlined here.

The duration of the traditional society itself may be measured with some degree of accuracy by selecting the approximate date of its most reliably documented origin and the approximate date of its initial major encounter with Western influences.[6] The selection of these dates determines the duration of the traditional society in number of years. Table VI shows a comparison of the approximate date of the origin of traditional societies in Asia, the somewhat more reliable date of their initial major encounter with the Western impact, and their duration in number of years.[7]

Table VI shows the extensive period of more than four millennia which imparted strength and stature to traditional societies in India and China and made them highly resistant to foreign-induced change. It reveals the somewhat shorter time-spans of approximately two millennia for the traditional societies in Korea and Vietnam. The table likewise depicts the

Table VI. A comparison of the approximate dates of origin and the initial major encounter with the Western impact, and the duration in years of Asian traditional societies.

Traditional Society	Approximate date of origin	Approximate date of initial major encounter with the Western impact*	Duration in years
India	2500 B.C.	1757 A.D.	4257
China	2205 B.C.	1825 A.D.	4030
Vietnam	257 B.C.	1859 A.D.	2116
Korea	57 B.C.	1850 A.D.	1907
Ceylon	500 A.D.	1815 A.D.	1315
Cambodia	550 A.D.	1865 A.D.	1315
Japan	552 A.D.	1854 A.D.	1302
Indonesia	650 A.D.	1623 A.D.	973
Burma	1044 A.D.	1824 A.D.	780
Thailand	1238 A.D.	1855 A.D.	617
Laos	1353 A.D.	1893 A.D.	540
Malaya	1403 A.D.	1786 A.D.	383

*The dates cited here are generally those of the initial major encounter of the territorial periphery of the traditional society with the Western impact. Numerous encroachments by Western influences occurred at subsequent dates within the territory claimed by the rulers of the traditional society.

relatively recent origin and much shorter durations of most traditional societies in Southeast Asia which made them less "time-honored" and more malleable when confronted by Western influences.[8]

The measurement of the duration of the traditional society alone is of only partial value in terminal analysis. Equally important is the measurement of the duration of discrete traditional historical inputs in the cultural system, class structures, and societal structures. This more detailed assessment is of major importance in analyzing the interactions between specific elements of the traditional society and the diverse influences comprising the Western impact.

The duration of discrete values in the cultural system of the traditional society can be measured with some degree of accuracy by selecting their approximate dates of origin and the dates of their initial major encounter with the Western impact. Table VII shows these dates and the duration in years of specific values in several Asian cultural systems. Table VII also shows some interesting and useful comparisons in the duration of discrete values of several cultural systems in Asia. The table reveals that values such as religious idealism-political apathy and religious eclecticism-psychological pluralism in Hindu cultural systems and doctrinal idealism-political pragmatism in the Chinese Confucian cultural system were very lengthy "time-honored" traditional historical inputs. Specific values in the Theravada Buddhist cultural system in Thailand and the Islamic cultural system in Indonesia were of considerably briefer duration and strength. Table VII also shows some major differences in the duration of specific values *within* a single cultural system. In the Islamic cultural system in Indonesia, for example, the value of religious eclecticism-psychological pluralism had a relatively long duration of 973 years, while the value of religious dogmatism-political egalitarianism had a very brief duration of 173 years. Within the Chinese Confucian cultural system the value of doctrinal idealism-political pragmatism was much longer and more tenacious than doctrinal dogmatism-cultural ethnocentrism. Doctrinal eclecticism-political pragmatism which emerged early in the Japanized Confucian cultural system had a much longer time-span and greater strength than doctrinal dogmatism-racial ethnocentrism which evolved mostly after the beginning of the Tokugawa period.

The duration of discrete traditional historical inputs in the hierarchical class structures of the traditional society can also be measured by selecting their approximate dates of origin and the dates of their initial major encounter with the Western impact. Table VIII shows these dates and the duration in years of specific politically relevant classes or roles in several Asian class structures.

Table VII. A comparison of the approximate dates of origin of discrete cultural values, the approximate dates of their initial major encounter with the Western impact, and their duration in years.

Cultural System	Value	Approximate date of origin	Approximate date of initial major encounter with the Western impact	Duration in years
Hindu	Religious Idealism — Political Apathy	1500 B.C.	1757 A.D.	3257
	Religious Eclecticism — Psychological Pluralism	2500 B.C.	1757 A.D.	4257
Theravada Buddhist (Thailand)	Religious Progressivism — Political Apathy	1250 A.D.	1855 A.D.	605
	Religious Eclecticism — Psychological Pluralism	1350 A.D.	1855 A.D.	505
	Religious Dogmatism — Political Egalitarianism	1450 A.D.	1623 A.D.	173
Islamic (Indonesia)	Religious Eclecticism — Psychological Pluralism	650 A.D.	1623 A.D.	973
	Doctrinal Idealism — Political Pragmatism	600 B.C.	1825 A.D.	2425
Confucian (China)	Doctrinal Dogmatism — Cultural Ethnocentrism	618 A.D.	1825 A.D.	1207
	Doctrinal Eclecticism — Political Pragmatism	600 A.D	1854 A.D.	1254
Japanized Confucian	Doctrinal Dogmatism — Racial Ethnocentrism	1600 A.D.	1854 A.D.	254

Table VIII shows some notable similarities and differences of specific classes and roles in several Asian class structures. The duration of some of these traditional historical factors in a single class structure was essentially equal. This condition prevailed with the priestly and warrior castes in the Hindu class structure, the king and the separation of civil and military roles in the Thai class structure, and the sultan, patih, and ulama in the Indonesian class structure. The duration of other traditional historical inputs within a single class structure varied considerably. The role of the emperor in the Chinese Confucian class structure was about 2046 years old at the time of its initial major encounter with the Western

Table VIII. A comparison of the approximate dates of origin of specific classes or roles in several Asian class structures, the approximate dates of their initial major encounter with the Western impact, and their duration in years.

Class Structure	Specific Class or Role	Approximate date of origin	Approximate date of initial major encounter with the Western impact	Duration in years
Hindu	Priests (Brahman)	1200 B.C.	1757 A.D.	2957
	Warriors (Kshatriyas)	1200 B.C.	1757 A.D.	2957
Theravada Buddhist (Thailand)	King	1238 A.D.	1855 A.D.	617
	Separate Civil and Military Roles	1450 A.D.	1855 A.D.	405
Islamic (Indonesia)	Sultan	1475 A.D.	1623 A.D.	148
	Patih (Chief Minister)	1300 A.D.	1623 A.D.	323
	Ulama	1400 A.D.	1623 A.D.	223
Confucian (China)	Emperor	221 B.C.	1825 A.D.	2046
	Scholarly-Bureaucratic Class	589 A.D.	1825 A.D.	1236
Japanized Confucian	Emperor	300 A.D.	1854 A.D.	1554
	Shogun	1192 A.D.	1854 A.D.	662
	Daimyo	1500 A.D.	1854 A.D.	354
	Samurai	1185 A.D.	1854 A.D.	669

impact and approximately 800 years older than the scholarly-bureaucratic class. The role of the emperor was also the most "time-honored" traditional historical input in the Japanized Confucian class structure. It antedated the daimyo class by about 1200 years, and the shogunate by almost 900 years at the time of its initial major encounter with the Western impact.

The measurement of the duration of discrete traditional historical inputs in the traditional societal structure involves only the measurement of the duration of great and middle traditions. The widespread illiteracy outside the small educated elite at the center of great and middle traditions precluded a knowledge of history or past "grandeur" in the little traditions or among the remote peasants.

The measurement of the duration of specific traditional historical inputs in traditional societal structures requires two separate methods. The first method is the measurement of the duration of great or middle traditions which were intact at the time of the Western impact. Table IX shows these measurements for three great traditions in Asia. Table X shows similar measurements for four middle traditions which were intact at the time of the Western impact.

Table IX shows the great strength acquired by the great tradition in Confucian China due to its long duration of 2046 years prior to the Western impact. The somewhat lesser power of the great tradition in Japan was caused by its slightly shorter duration of 1554 years, and the more modest tenacity of the Thai great tradition was engendered by a smaller time-span of 617 years prior to its contact with Western powers. Table X also reveals the very brief duration of four middle traditions in Asia which embodied minor endurance at the time of the Western impact.

The second method is the measurement of the strength contained in the collective "memory" of great or middle traditions which were not intact at the time of the Western impact. This assessment can be achieved with some degree of accuracy by measuring the durations of defunct great or middle traditions, and the duration between their demise and the date the subsequent traditional society made its initial major encounter with the Western impact. Generally, a lengthy duration of a defunct great

Table IX. A comparison of the approximate dates of origin of three Asian great traditions, the approximate dates of their initial major encounter with the Western impact, and their duration in years.

Great Tradition	Approximate date of origin	Approximate date of initial major encounter with the Western impact	Duration in years.
Confucian China	221 B.C.	1825 A.D.	2046
Japanized Confucian	300 A.D.	1854 A.D.	1554
Thailand	1238 A.D.	1855 A.D.	617

Table X. A comparison of the approximate dates of origin of four Asian middle traditions, the approximate dates of their initial major encounters with the Western impact, and their duration in years.

Middle Tradition	Approximate date of origin	Approximate date of initial major encounter with the Western impact	Duration in years
Marathas Kingdom (India)	1707 A.D.	1790 A.D.	83
Mataram (Indonesia)	1582 A.D.	1755 A.D.	173
Malacca (Malaya)	1400 A.D.	1500 A.D.	100
Kingdom of Luang Prabang (Laos)	1707 A.D.	1893 A.D.	186

or middle tradition tended to instill a strong memory of former grandeur and power, yet a lengthy duration between the demise of a defunct great or middle tradition and the encounter of subsequent traditional societies with the Western impact tended to reduce the strength of its memory and legacy. Table XI shows these measurements for several defunct great traditions in Asia.

Table XI reveals some important comparisons in the diverse strength of traditional historical inputs induced by defunct great traditions in Asia. The two former Hindu great traditions in India (Mauryan and Gupta) exerted only modest potency in 1757 A.D., partially due to their rather brief durations, but largely due to the long periods between their demise and the Western impact. The legacy of the defunct Mogul Empire, conversely, imparted only modest strength from its brief duration, yet it induced great influence due to the very short time-span between its demise and the Western impact. The defunct Srivijaya Empire centered in Sumatra transmitted a considerable historical heritage due to its lengthy duration of 548 years, although its influence was greatly reduced by the long time span of 401 years between its disintegration and the Western impact. The more recent Majapahit Empire based in Java survived for a lesser period of time, yet it imparted a significant influence due to the relatively short period of 170 years between its demise and the beginning of Dutch colonial rule. Similar measurements for several defunct middle traditions in Asia are shown in Table XII.

Table XI. A comparison of the duration in years of defunct great traditions in Asia, and the duration in years between their demise and the date of the initial major encounter of subsequent traditional societies with the Western impact.

Defunct Great Tradition	Duration in years	Approximate date of initial major encounter of subsequent traditional societies with the Western impact	Duration in years between the demise of the defunct great tradition and the date of the initial major encounter of subsequent traditional societies with the Western impact
Mauryan Empire 332-185 B.C.	147	1757 A.D.	1942
Gupta Empire 320-510 A.D.	190	1757 A.D.	1247
Mogul Empire 1556-1707 A.D.	151	1757 A.D.	50
Srivijaya Empire 674-1222 A.D.	548	1623 A.D.	401
Majapahit Empire 1222-1453 A.D.	231	1623 A.D.	170

Table XII shows some aspects of the diverse provincial and regional influences induced by defunct Asian middle traditions. The Kingdom of Chalukyas imparted certain pluralistic legacies due to its relatively long duration of 617 years, yet this influence was mitigated by the almost equally long time-span of 590 years between its demise and the Western impact. The Kingdom of Gujerat survived for a much briefer period of time, yet it transmitted considerable influence due to the short duration of 120 years between its cessation and the beginning of British colonial rule. The Shan Kingdom in northern Burma which lasted for only 66 years and disintegrated some 460 years prior to the Western impact exerted much less historical influence than the Mon Kingdom at Pegu which survived for 470 years and disappeared only 67 years before the coming of Western influences. The Koguryo Kingdom in Korea existed much longer than the small feudal states during the period of Sixteen

Table XII. A comparison of the duration in years of defunct middle traditions in Asia, and the duration in years between their demise and the date of the initial major encounter of subsequent traditional societies with the Western impact.

Defunct Middle Tradition	Duration in years	Approximate date of initial major encounter of subsequent traditional societies with the Western impact	Duration in years between the demise of the defunct middle tradition and the date of the initial major encounter of subsequent traditional societies with the Western impact
Kingdom of Chalukyas (India) 550-1167 A.D.	617	1757 A.D.	590
Kingdom of Gujerat (India) 1411-1537 A.D.	126	1757 A.D.	120
Mon Kingdom (Pegu, Burma) 1287-1757 A.D.	470	1824 A.D.	67
Shan Kingdom (Burma) 1298-1364 A.D.	66	1824 A.D.	460
Koguryo Kingdom (Korea) 37 B.C.-668 A.D.	705	1850 A.D.	1182
Sixteen Kingdoms (China) 304-439 A.D.	135	1825 A.D.	1386

Kingdoms in China, yet the extremely lengthy period of more than a millenium between the demise of both of these middle traditions and the Western impact was a significant factor in the low level of provincialism and regionalism in these two Confucian societal structures.

A final aspect in the analysis of the duration of the traditional society and discrete traditional historical inputs is the measurement of the duration of pre-Western external linkages which influenced the traditional society and its cultural system, class structure, and societal structure. This assessment also involves the measurement of the duration between the final stages of many pre-Western external linkages and the beginning of the Western impact. In some respects these general chronological calculations are more complex and more precarious than the measurement of the time-spans which shaped other traditional historical factors. Historical documentation on the incidence of many pre-Western foreign influences is very meager and imprecise. Yet some effort must be made to appraise the duration of external linkages in the traditional society since the impact imparted by these pre-Western foreign influences tended to increase with the passage of time and to decrease in proportion to the duration between their final stages and the beginning of the Western impact. The duration of pre-Western external linkages also affected the degree of assimilation between foreign and indigenous elements within the traditional society.

Generally, a lengthy duration of a pre-Western external linkage tended to augment the degree of assimilation between external and internal values, modes of behavior, and institutions. Conversely, a short duration of a pre-Western external linkage tended to maintain a high degree of diversity between foreign and indigenous values, modes of behavior, and institutions. In some cases pre-Western external linkages were intact at the time of the Western impact, a factor which tended to maximize their social and political influence. Table XIII shows the duration of specific external linkages in three Asian traditional societies, and the duration between their final stages and the beginning of the Western impact.

Table XIII. A comparison of the duration in years of specific external linkages in three traditional societies in Asia, and the duration between their final stages and the beginning of the Western impact.

Pre-Western External Linkages	Duration in years	Duration in years between the final stages of the pre-Western external linkages and the beginning of the Western impact
HINDU *(Indian sub-continent— Beginning of Western impact: 1757 A.D.)*		
Military Invasions:		
Aryan (1500-500 B.C.)	1000	2257
Hellenic and Central Asian (180 B.C.-200 A.D.)	380	1557
Ephthalite (500-528 A.D.)	28	1229

Table XIII cont'd.

Pre-Western External Linkages	Duration in years	Duration in years between the final stages of the pre-Western external linkages and the beginning of the Western impact
HINDU, *cont'd.*		
Moslem (1175-1340 A.D.)	165	417
Foreign Traders:		
Persian and Central Asian (0-500 A.D.)	500	1257
Arab (900 A.D.-)	857*	0 (intact)
Foreign Communities:		
Arab (900 A.D.-)	857*	0 (intact)

THERAVADA BUDDHIST
(Thailand — Beginning of Western impact: 1855 A.D.)

Military Invasions:		
Burmese (1530-1810 A.D.)	280	45
Cambodian (1353-1812 A.D.)	459	43
Foreign Missionaries:		
Cambodian (1375-1450 A.D.)	75	405

Table XIII cont'd.

Pre-Western External Linkages	Duration in years	Duration in years between the final stages of the pre-Western external linkages and the beginning of the Western impact

THERAVADA BUDDHIST, *cont'd.*

Foreign
Traders:

Chinese (1500 A.D.-)	355*	0 (intact)

Tribute
Missions:

To China (1371-1888 A.D.)	517	33†
From Cambodia (1432-1867 A.D.)	435	12†
From Laos 1828-1893 A.D.)	65	38†

Indigenous
Returnees:

From Ceylon (1753-1758 A.D.)	5	97

Foreign
Communities:

Chinese (1300 A.D.-)	555*	0 (intact)
Malay (1450 A.D.-)	405*	0 (intact)

Table XIII cont'd.

Pre-Western External Linkages	Duration in years	Duration in years between the final stages of the pre-Western external linkages and the beginning of the Western impact
CONFUCIAN CHINA— *(Beginning of Western impact: 1825 A.D.)*		
Military Invasions:		
Hsiung-nu (300 B.C.-222 A.D.)	522	1603
Turkic, proto-Mongol, Tibetan (304-589 A.D.)	285	1236
Khitan, Tangut, Mongol (905-1279 A.D.)	372	546
Manchu (1620-1644 A.D.)	24	181
Foreign Missionaries: (Buddhist)		
From India (175-600 A.D.)	425	1225
Tribute Missions:		
From Korea (1369-1895 A.D.)	526	70†
From Southeast Asia (1371-1890 A.D.)	519	65†

Table XIII cont'd.

Pre-Western External Linkages	Duration in years	Duration in years between the final stages of the pre-Western external linkages and the beginning of the Western impact
CONFUCIAN CHINA, *cont'd.*		
Indigenous Returnees:		
From India (Buddhist) (385-750 A.D.)	365	1075
From Southeast Asia and Indian Ocean (maritime expeditions) (1405-1431 A.D.)	26	394

*This figure is the duration in years from the *origin* of this pre-Western external linkage and the beginning of the Western impact, a figure whose significance is reinforced due to the fact that this foreign influence was intact and flourishing at the time of the Western impact.

†This figure is the duration in years this pre-Western external linkage survived *after* the beginning of the Western impact.

Table XIII shows some useful measurements of the duration of pre-Western external linkages which shaped important traditional historical inputs. The table also reveals significant comparisons in the durations between the final stages of pre-Western external linkages and the beginning of the Western impact. The long duration of 1000 years of Aryan invasions into Hindu traditional societies in the Indian sub-continent, and the much longer time-span of 2257 years between the end of these foreign incursions and the beginning of British colonial rule were major factors promoting a high degree of assimilation between Aryan and Dravidian peoples in the evolution of a reasonably coherent Hinduized culture. In contrast, the short duration of 165 years of Moslem invasions in India and the brief period of 417 years between the last major Moslem invasion and the beginning of British colonial rule were significant factors maintaining a high degree of diversity between Hindu and Moslem communities in the sub-continent. In the Thai traditional society the relatively long period of Burmese invasions (280 years) and the longer period of Cambodian invasions (459 years) induced a traditional historical input of intense hostility toward these two adjoining societies. Also, the short durations between the final stages of these foreign military invasions (45 years and 43 years respectively) and the beginning of the Western impact were significant factors in the relatively high degree of centralized political and military power in the Thai traditional society in the mid-nineteenth century.

In the Confucian Chinese traditional society the lengthy periods of pre-Manchu military invasions were important factors inducing frequent unification and defensive measures by Chinese imperial rulers in the northern territories. The Manchu invasion of 24 years which implanted a foreign dynasty in power after 1644, and the relatively long period of 181 years from the beginning of this dynasty and the beginning of the Western impact were significant factors inducing an increasing anti-Manchu sentiment in China and a declining power in the traditional political leadership during the nineteenth century. The Western impact in China would have confronted much greater resistance if it had occurred during a Chinese dynasty or at an earlier period in the Manchu dynastic cycle. The relatively lengthy duration of Buddhist foreign missionaries (425 years) and Buddhist indigenous returnees (365 years) in Confucian China were important factors in the widespread effect of this foreign religious influence. Yet the lengthy time-spans between the termination of these pre-Western external linkages and the beginning of the Western impact contributed to weak Buddhist influences in the Chinese traditional society by the early nineteenth century. Conversely, the long duration of more than five centuries of tribute missions to China from Korea and Southeast Asia tended to reinforce the strength of the superiority complex in the Chinese traditional cultural system.

PART TWO
THE WESTERN IMPACT

The Western Impact

The diverse array of Western values, modes of behavior, and institutions imposed on traditional societies in Asia from the fifteenth century to the end of Western political domination constituted the Western impact. As mentioned previously, these historical influences will be called *Western historical inputs.*[1] They comprised vitally important elements in the formation of new values, modes of behavior, and institutions in the development of modern Asian societies. They likewise constitute significant historical variables in comparative political analysis.

The initial extension of Western power into Asia occurred during the decline of the medieval church in Europe and the rise of secular national rulers. The imposition of Western historical influences comprised a staggered, piece-meal process, and involved numerous unforeseen events and consequences. Each Western nation pursued its own foreign policy according to its particular national interests, a policy which often changed with the passage of time and the emergence of new demands and new conditions in both the Western and Asian societies. Western influences in Asia also changed with new developments and new rivalries within the Western community of nations.

The substance of the Western impact consisted of a vast complex of diverse ingredients, many of which originated outside the geographic territory of Western Europe. Professor Karl Deutsch has claimed that Western civilization embodies numerous elements derived from the Graeco-Roman tradition, the Celtic, Teutonic, and Slavic barbarian cultures, the Semiticized and Orientalized influences contained in Judaism and Christianity, the impact of Arab culture, the influences of Mongol and Chinese cultures, and, finally, the impact of the "Amerindianization" of this Western-Arabic-Mongolian civilization as it expanded to North and South America.[2] Deutsch has declared:

> What we call today Western civilization is in a very real sense a
> World civilization, not merely in what it brought to other coun-

tries, but also very significantly in what it received from them. Perhaps its "Western" peculiarities lie, then, not only in its ability to originate, but also in its ability to innovate, that is, to learn actively from others. All these traits of creativity and of the ability to learn are present in all great civilizations of the world, and the West here, too, has perhaps gone faster and farther on a road traveled to some extent by all.[3]

The expansion of Western civilization to the traditional societies of Asia rested on a distinct dynamism and sense of curiosity. Sir George Sansom has traced this unique "outreach" behavior to early Greek culture. He has stated:

> Onward from the days of the Aegean city states it [the Western ethos] continues to manifest the restless energy that impelled Hellenic culture to expand, to reach out to other lands and peoples. There are dark and silent intervals, and sometimes the Hellenic spirit seems to be in danger of extinction; but it reasserts itself and continues to exert upon the Eastern as well as the Western World an influence that cannot be permanently resisted. The intrusion of this disruptive, challenging element into the sequestered and conservative life of Asia must be a dominant theme in the modern history of any Asiatic state.[4]

Western vigor and drive was often combined with a commercial incentive derived in part from a reaction to the economic deprivation and narrow cultural outlook of the Middle Ages. In effect, the Western impact was usually a mixture of the quest for knowledge, adventure, profit, and power. In some cases it also sought to spread the Christian religion. It was not the first historical example of widespread cultural diffusion as the expansion of Greek, Roman, Confucian, Hindu, and Islamic cultures took place over large territories in earlier times. Yet the Western impact was the only cultural diffusion from a distinct and relatively small geographic region to the entire world. Also, the Western impact is the only cultural expansion which has retained its vigor and élan. With increasing intensity since the sixteenth century, its influence has become more extensive and intense.

The "disruptive, challenging element" of Western civilization began to flourish at a crucial time in the interrelationships between Europe and Asia. Prior to the sixteenth century, the flow of influences had been largely from East to West.[5] Asian cultures exhibited an intense pride and a sense of superiority; Western people were diffident and insecure. Asia sought little from the West while Europe borrowed certain elements of

Oriental art and literature. Yet during the early 1500's the expansive Western spirit began to reverse this process, and European influences began to penetrate Asian societies at an ever-increasing pace. Within a century the initiative rested almost entirely with the West. European nations were becoming more unified and consolidated while many Oriental societies became increasingly fragmented. The people of the West began exhibiting a sense of self-confidence and hope while Asian cultures adhered to conservatism and orthodoxy. Western civilization was becoming secular and activist while Oriental cultures held firmly to traditional values and institutions. Perhaps most important, the West began launching into the age of science and the quest for the mastery over the forces of nature; the East remained steeped in time-honored superstitions and fatalism.

The Western impact in Asia took two major forms: (1) the colonization of virtually all societies in South and Southeast Asia, and (2) the establishment of "unequal" treaties in societies such as China, Japan, and Thailand which retained a precarious sovereignty until the twentieth century. Western historical inputs were also imparted in two distinct and overlapping chronological phases. The first phase took place from the early pioneering explorations of the Portuguese and Spanish around 1500 until the end of the Napoleonic wars in 1815. During this era Western contacts in Asia were confined to a few strategic coastal areas (except Spanish rule in the Philippines and British rule in northern India). Few Western influences were extended to the interior of the traditional societies. What has been called the "fortress system" first utilized by the Portuguese served as the model for other European powers. According to Professor Brian Harrison:

> In several respects Portugal laid down the pattern of future
> European rule in Asia. In the sequence of steps by which she
> normally approached her objectives—a sequence which may be
> expressed by the formula: voyage, factory, fortress—she was fol-
> lowed by her European successors. In the essential basis of her
> rule—the fortress system—her example was again followed.
> European rule in Asia remained a fortress system, in principle,
> down to the nineteenth century.[6]

The second phase of spreading Western historical inputs in Asia occurred during the rapid expansion of industrialization in Western societies from the early nineteenth century until the aftermath of World War II. This period has been called the era of "imperialism." It started with the conclusion of the Napoleonic wars which ushered in a century of relative peace in the relations between European nations and provided the opportunity to expand Western domination to economically under-developed societies in Asia, Africa, and the Middle East. The drive for economic development in Europe encouraged more widespread and intensive expansion in these non-Western regions than during the first phase of the Western impact. Initial Western influences confined in most cases to coastal territories were extended to the interiors of the traditional societies often resulting in the establishment of colonial rule. Also, Western influences exerted during the first phase by small maritime nations in Western Europe were supplemented by influences imparted by Western continental powers such as the United States, Germany, and Russia (the Soviet Union after 1918) as well as the partially Westernized society of Japan.

The analysis of the Western impact in Part Two will consist of five chapters. Chapter Five will present a model of the *colonization process* suitable for analyzing politically relevant Western historical inputs imparted to the Asian colonized societies. Chapter Six will present a model of the *unequal treaty process* suitable for analyzing Western historical inputs transmitted to the semi-independent Asian societies. Chapter Seven and Chapter Eight comprise a second application of *macro-linkage-analysis* which will assess the political influences imparted by specific Western linkages in both the colonization process and the unequal treaty process. Chapter Seven will cover the *governmental linkages* involved in both processes; Chapter Eight will cover the *nongovernmental linkages* engaged in both types of Western impact. Chapter Nine will present a second application of *terminal analysis* assessing the role of important terminal factors in shaping Western historical inputs just prior to the achievement of national independence or complete national sovereignty by Asian societies.

Chapter 5

The Colonization Process

The pattern of governmental and nongovernmental linkages between the Western colonial powers and their colonized societies in Asia constituted the colonization process. It involved the following variables: (1) the expansionist factors in the Western colonial power, (2) the concept of colonial rule, (3) the political and administrative structures maintaining colonial rule, and (4) the economic and social policies in the colony. Figure IX shows the structure of this process between the Western colonial power and the Asian colonized society.

EXPANSIONIST FACTORS

All Western colonial powers extended their influences to non-Western regions due to the general expansive impetus of Western civilization already cited. Yet specific factors within each Western colonial power precipitated and guided the movement beyond its national boundaries to distant unknown lands. While the colonization process involved numerous interrelated historical forces within the society of the Western colonial power, primary factors often caused its initial external expansion and acquisition of overseas colonies. This particular mode of expansion in turn affected specific groups and interests in the Western colonial power, and it induced a distinct variety of Western historical inputs in the Asian colonized society. It influenced the degree of differentiation of the colonization process as well as its intensity, stability, and duration. This historical factor likewise affected the geographic scope of each Western colonial power and it shaped other variables in the colonization process.

The primary factors which characterized each form of Western expansion consisted of the *types of aggrandizement* in each Western colonial power and the *types of timing* of each Western impact.

Types of Aggrandizement

The basic aggrandizement by Western colonial powers engaged in

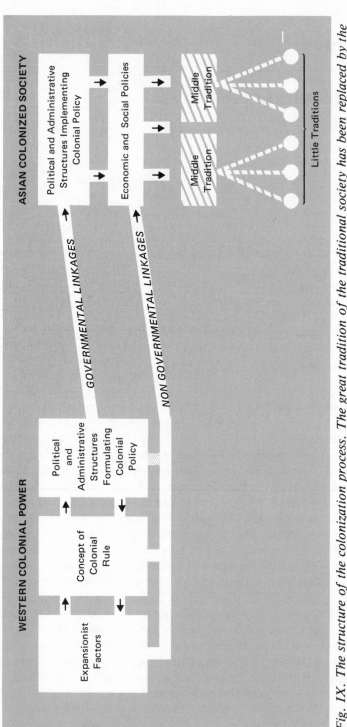

Fig. IX. The structure of the colonization process. The great tradition of the traditional society has been replaced by the political and administrative structures implementing colonial rule. The middle tradition was also destroyed as an autonomous political entity by the imposition of Western colonial rule, yet it often retained a social and cultural identity.

expanding their control to Asian traditional societies consisted of four types: (1) *dynastic,* (2) *economic,* (3) *ideological,* and (4) *tutelary.*

Dynastic aggrandizement: This occurred with the assumption of dominant political power by a royal sovereign seeking to extend the influence of his domain to Asian territories. This mode of expansion prevailed in the colonization processes of Portugal, Spain, France (until the Third Republic), Germany (under Kaiser William II), and Tzarist Russia (from about 1850 to 1917).[1] The augmentation of dynastic power by each of these Western nations was due to the personal ambition of the sovereign ruler or his support to influential persons at the royal court seeking overseas expansion. Dynastic aggrandizement was intensely personal, and the colonization process was generally conducted in the name of the sovereign ruler. It placed great emphasis on the advancement of national pride, prestige, and glory. It was characterized by a highly centralized control of the colonial system and a low level of differentiation. It involved few groups outside the royal court and achieved relatively little domestic support.

Dynastic aggrandizement by Portugal was motivated largely by the support of King Manoel to overseas explorers such as Vasco da Gama and Afonso d'Albuquerque.[2] The participation of additional groups in the Portuguese colonization process occurred with the crusading mission of the Roman Catholic Church and the exploits of a rising merchant class aided by the maritime skills developed by Prince Henry the Navigator and the capacity to construct seaworthy vessels suitable for accommodating large numbers of men on long ocean voyages.[3] Spanish aggrandizement followed a similar pattern, although in expanding beyond the feudal concept of wealth based on land, the Spanish commercial class sought a new form of capital by investing in the more profitable enterprises in the New World, rather than in Asia. French expansion prior to the Napoleonic Wars consisted primarily of a few grandiose schemes promoted by ambitious persons supported by the king, including Colbert, de Chaumont, and Dupleix. Dynastic aggrandizement by France took its most vigorous form during the reign of Napoleon III which was combined with a crusading religious zeal and a renewed military rivalry with Great Britain. The assumption of power by Kaiser William II in Germany in 1890 was perhaps the best example of dynastic aggrandizement. The dismissal of Bismarck and his "no colonial" policy opened the way for Germany to pursue a "new course" and obtain colonial territories in Africa and Asia.[4] This policy involved the proponents of German naval power and a portion of the commercial class seeking outlets for the surplus of consumer goods resulting from the government-sponsored industrialization program. Russian expansion in Asia prior to the nineteenth century involved only a few fur traders, the establishment of several penal colonies, and minor geographic exploration of the northern Pacific. Dynastic aggrandizement took place after 1850 with the policy of Tzar Nicolas II to acquire a Russian sphere of influence in China in addition to the consolidation of Russian power in Siberia and the Maritime Provinces.[5] The contiguity of Russian territory to China, Korea, and Japan likewise caused Russian aggrandizement in Asia to expand by land rather than by sea, the method used by all other Western colonial powers.

The intensity of dynastic aggrandizement tended to be vigorous during its early stages which resulted in the sudden acquisition of extensive colonial territories. Within a few years Portugal constructed coastal factories and fortresses over a territory stretching from the coasts of India to the islands of Japan. At the same time Spain promptly established control over the Philippines (as well as the bulk of the region soon called "Latin America"). Rapid seizure of Asian territories was similarly accomplished by dynastic rulers in France, Germany, and Russia once they decided to pursue a policy of expansion.

Yet the stability and duration of the colonization process established by dynastic aggrandizement was precarious and uncertain. The continuity of these forms of colonial rule depended entirely on the personal ability of the dynastic ruler and the vagaries of shifting political influences at the royal court. The policy of expansion and the conduct of colonial policy could be drastically altered or suddenly terminated according to the changing fortunes of the ruling dynasty. Thus, Portuguese colonial rule in Asia declined rapidly after the union of the royal families in Portugal and Spain in 1580. Spanish rule in the Philippines was intermittently affected by struggles between conservative and liberal factions at the royal court. The French "empire" in India erected by Dupleix which challenged the emerging power of the British during the 1750's suddenly collapsed due to the lack of support from Paris.[6] Erratic shifts in the colonial policies of Germany and Russia were likewise caused by the changing personal goals of the sovereign ruler and the maneuvers of "palace politics" in Berlin and Moscow. The overthrow of the Hollenzollern dynasty in 1918 resulted in the immediate loss of all German colonies to other colonial powers; the demise of the Romanov dynasty in 1917 jeopardized Russian territories in the Far East for several years, although they were eventually restored under Moscow's control by the new leaders of the Soviet Union.

Economic Aggrandizement: This took place when the propensity to expand and acquire overseas colonies was motivated primarily by the desire to promote the rapid economic development of the Western colonial power. This kind of expansion typified the colonization processes of the Netherlands and Great Britain. Powerful economic interests also influenced the colonial systems of Portugal and Spain, but these two Iberian powers relied much more extensively on dynastic support for external expansion. The royal families in Holland and Great Britain were involved in the establishment of overseas colonies, but their role was subordinate to rising industrial and commercial groups. This mode of expansion was more impersonal and more institutionalized than dynastic aggrandizement. It involved more groups outside official government circles, and throughout most of its duration, it enjoyed considerable popular support in the society of the Western colonial power.

Economic aggrandizement by the Netherlands was induced by the necessity to develop a profitable foreign trade in order to protect the independence of the newly-unified country after its separation from Spain. This move was precipitated by the imposition of exorbitant prices in the spice trade at the port of Lisbon. Protestant merchants at Dutch ports comprised the dominant group seeking new methods and channels to compete with this external economic threat.[7] Other groups involved in overseas expansion were the shipping interests which made new advances in naval construction and military weapons, and the Calvinist churches which inculcated a sense of thrift, discipline, and industry in Dutch culture. Economic aggrandizement by Great Britain was likewise motivated by the requirement for a growing foreign trade to promote domestic economic development. This movement became imperative after the imposition of exorbitant prices in the spice trade by the Dutch. The dominant expansive force in Great Britain consisted of emerging industrial and commercial groups, which, like their competitors in the Netherlands, needed a flourishing overseas trade to contend with foreign rivals as well as to strengthen democratic political institutions in their conflict with the king. After 1815 other groups became increasingly involved in external expansion, including the growing laboring and clerical classes who soon developed a vested interest in the success of the colonization process.

The intensity of economic aggrandizement was generally at a high level during its early and intermediate stages when strong expectations for rapid economic development based on the exploitation of colonial territories prevailed in the Western colonial power. Only in the final stages was the intensity of economic expansion moderated in some degree by non-economic factors (such as education, public health, social welfare, etc. in the Asian colonized societies.) The intensity was shaped by economic forces in the Western colonial power which in turn influenced the acquisition of additional colonial territories. Thus, the growing market for new food products such as tea, coffee, and sugar, or the expanding demand for new raw materials such as rubber, tin, and oil, caused Holland and Great Britain to extend their control into accessible and untouched colonial territories. The intensity of economic aggrandizement was also closely related to geographic and economic conditions in the domestic territory of the Western colonial power. The intensity was consistently high in the Netherlands due to its small territory and vulnerable geopolitical location. A modest agricultural base and a dense and growing population made a lucrative foreign trade imperative. Unlike other Western colonial powers, the Netherlands could not shift to new domestic resources with successive advances in science and technology. These internal conditions induced a colonial system characterized by a rapid and vigorous colonial enterprise. Its primary purpose was the advancement of Dutch wealth and prosperity. The intensity of economic expansion was somewhat less in Great Britain due to its larger domestic territory and a more favorable geopolitical location detached from the European continent. Some important resources were available internally to promote economic modernization. The insular geographic location precluded the need for a large standing army and provided the opportunity to create a superior navy and merchant fleet which further assisted overseas expansion. The intensity of British economic aggrandizement increased markedly after 1815 with the establishment of world-wide commercial interests and the hastened drive toward large-scale industrialization which required large imports of food products and raw materials from overseas colonies.[8] This development accelerated the speed of British expansion and at the same time caused more differentiation among British colonial systems. India became a major source of a vast variety of raw materials for British industry and remained the most profitable of the British colonies. Ceylon and Malaya were developed to produce valuable mineral and food products while also serving as important military bases. Burma quickly became a primary source of surplus food for Great Britain and British colonies in Asia as well as a buffer zone against French expansion from Indochina.

Economic aggrandizement maintained a more stable colonial rule than dynastic aggrandizement. Changes in the colonization process were caused largely by changes affecting the entire economy of the Western colonial power. These changes were relatively gradual and predictable. They differed markedly from the erratic and unpredictable changes in the colonial rule established by Western dynastic rulers. This condition is a major reason for the long duration of Dutch and British colonial domination in Asia. Only during the final stages with the rise of nationalism and the adversities caused by World War II did the colonization process become unstable.

Ideological Aggrandizement: This consisted of the extension of Western national power into colonial territories by an expansionist regime pursuing the goals of an abstract messianic doctrine. This method of expansion in its clearest form was used by Imperialist Japan and the Soviet Union.[9] It involved the application of intense expansionist actions guided by a conviction of historical inevitability. At times it promoted a fanaticism and ruthlessness which "justified" the wanton destruction of human lives and property to attain its objectives. Theoretically, it embodied the entire population of the colonial power which provided collective support for the expansionist values espoused by the ideology.

Japan pursued ideological aggrandizement from the late 1930's until the end of World War II. Its earlier expansion to Formosa and Korea was of a much milder variety which imitated many features of economic aggrandizement used by Great Britain and the Netherlands. Yet the assumption of political power by military leaders after 1932 led increasingly to a unique form of militarism and imperialism.[10] The "new order" derived internal support from traditional historical inputs such as the emperor myth, *kokutai, bushido,* doctrinal dogmatism, racial ethnocentrism, and historical determinism. It sought the total elimination of Western influences from Asia, and it upheld the obligation of Japan to bring the fruits of modern technology to the economically underdeveloped societies in the region. This racist ideology motivated the Japanese conquest of Southeast Asia and portions of China, and led to war with the United States and the European colonial powers.[11] It affected all Japanese people, but it most directly involved the armed forces, business, industry, and the bureaucracy.

Ideological aggrandizement by the Soviet Union did not seek the physical conquest of colonial territories in Asia; instead it consisted of establishing communist parties in Asian societies to provide a foundation for the future expansion of its universal revolutionary doctrine.[12] Soviet ideological aggrandizement also sought to weaken the capitalist societies of the Western colonial powers by threatening their control in the Asian colonies. The promotion of the elaborate Marxist-Leninist ideology by Moscow theoretically involved the entire Russian population; in practice it primarily affected the Communist Party of the Soviet Union, especially its overseas bureaus.

The intensity of ideological aggrandizement, like that of dynastic aggrandizement, was high during its early stages. Thereafter the intensity depended on the interaction of the ideology with concrete contingencies. The intensity of Japanese expansion was extremely vigorous during the early months of World War II, but thereafter it varied with changing circumstances in the military conflict against the Allied powers. Soviet ideological aggrandizement also was at a high level immediately following the Bolshevik revolution and the pursuit for Trotsky's goal of "world communism." Yet external conditions soon caused a downgrading of the goal for a world-wide proletarian revolution and the adoption of Stalin's policy to build "socialism in one country." The stability and duration of ideological aggrandizement likewise resembled that of dynastic aggrandizement. Changes in the colonization process depended on shifting political forces within the ruling expansionist regime; the termination of the colonization process occurred with the overthrow of the ruling regime. Japanese colonial rule in Southeast Asia following its initial successes witnessed numerous unpredictable changes caused by frequent shifts within the ruling regime. Japanese colonial rule was liquidated when this regime was removed in the military defeat by the United States. Soviet ideological penetration in Asia was also influenced by the uncertain struggle for power within the Soviet ruling elite and the erratic policy changes using Asian communist parties to promote Russian national interests. Soviet ideological aggrandizement, unlike that of Japan, has not been removed from Asia. It has not sought the establishment of colonial territories, but it has assisted in varying degrees the establishment of communist regimes in North Korea, Communist China, and North Vietnam. It likewise continues to promote its ideology among communist parties in virtually all non-communist Asian societies.

Tutelary Aggrandizement: This consisted of the acquisition of colonial territories for the primary purpose of instructing the indigenous people in selected elements of the culture of the Western colonial power. This form of expansion was utilized by Spain and the United States in the Philippines, and by France in Indochina after the formation of the Third Republic. Aspects of tutelary aggrandizement were also used by Great Britain during the final stages of its colonial rule in India, Burma, Ceylon, and Malaya, and a special form of tutelary aggrandizement accompanied Japan's Greater East Asia Co-Prosperity Sphere. In its purest form, this method of expansion comprised a desire to spread a part of the "way of life" in the Western colonial power to its colonized subjects. Its goal was allegedly altruistic, yet it inherently involved a sense of cultural superiority. Like economic aggrandizement, it was highly impersonal and institutionalized.

Tutelary aggrandizement by Spain in the Philippines took place following the rapid decline of its expansionist vigor in Asia resulting from the intense competition with Portugal and the concentration of Spanish colonization in Latin America.[13] Spanish economic activity in the Philippines remained at a low level until the very end of Spanish colonial rule, and for over two centuries the only contact between Madrid and its Asian colony was confined to the single annual voyage of the Manila Galleon from Acapulco, Mexico. Yet the Spanish in the Philippines turned promptly to the field of religious proselytism and exerted more cultural influence on the indigenous people than any other European power during the first phase of the Western impact. Spanish missionary zeal came from the national policy to oppose Protestantism and Islam, and from Papal support to bring Christianity to the pagan peoples of Asia and the Americas. This movement primarily involved the overseas Roman Catholic missions in Spain who were the first Westerners to spread colonial rule to the interior of an Asian traditional society.

American tutelary aggrandizement in the Philippines occurred with the eruption of a fervid jingoism in the United States at the turn of the twentieth century during the first major American encounter with the international community since the early history of the republic. This move resulted also from broadening American strategic interests in the Pacific, the desire to imitate the European colonial powers, and a diplomatic accident in the settlement of the Spanish-American War. In practice American colonial policy confined its tutelary role to the formation of indigenous democratic political institutions modeled after those in the United States which in turn involved the establishment of a supplementary American-oriented educational system. The colonization process of the United States tended to be erratic and constrained due to the domestic clash between expansionism and isolationism. It was the only Western colonial system whose avowed purpose at the outset was its own liquidation. Tutelary aggrandizement by France replaced dynastic aggrandizement following the demise of the Second Empire. The leaders of the Third Republic gradually became susceptible to appeals for the extension of French power and influence to Asian territories after the defeat by Germany in the Franco-Prussian War and increasing rivalry with Great Britain.[14] Prominent spokesmen such as de Lagree, Garnier, and de Genouilly upheld a renewal of French expansion as necessary to preserve French prestige throughout the world and to prevent another decline of French national power. The dominant motivation became *mission civilisatrice* involving the quest to spread French culture to colonial peoples. This goal in Asia caused France to acquire Cochin China, Annam, Tonkin, Cambodia, and Laos, which in 1887 were collectively administered as French Indochina. A high level of tutelary aggrandizement, however, was applied only in Cochin China, Annam, and Tonkin; a very mild form of economic aggrandizement was used in Cambodia and Laos. The major groups participating in the French colonization process included the navy, educational institutions, geographical societies, commercial interests, and overseas Roman Catholic missions. French tutelary aggrandizement induced much deeper intrusions into the lives of the people in Cochin China, Annam, and Tonkin than did the Spanish or American colonial rule in the Philippines. The French sought to impart their entire culture to the indigenous populace, whereas the Spanish confined their tutelary efforts primarily to spreading their religion, and the Americans sought mainly to transfer their own form of political democracy.

Like other types of aggrandizement, the intensity of tutelary aggrandizement was strong in its early stages. Yet it tended to be relatively moderate, and, once established, it sought no additional territory. Its continuity and stability were affected by competition with other subsequent goals of the Western colonial power and intermittent changes in colonial administration. The tutelary activities by Spanish priests in the Philippines were subject to changing policies of the Spanish colonial administration which varied from the application of more humanitarian methods following the bitter domestic and foreign reaction to Spanish atrocities to native people in Latin America to the expulsion of the independent-minded Jesuit religious order from the archipelago. The tutelary goals of American colonial rule in the Philippines also vacillated as the United States government confronted new domestic problems and made frequent changes in colonial administrators. The *mission civilisatrice* in Indochina (primarily Vietnam) was likewise affected by numerous changes in colonial administration, but it remained generally stable and coherent due to the consistent desire to provide broad and effective channels for spreading French culture. The termination of tutelary aggrandizement involved much ambiguity since it was impossible to determine when the colonial subjects had "learned" enough of the "way of life" of the Western colonial power. This goal could obviously never be fully achieved since the Asian colonized society had a cultural system, class structure, and modified societal structure of its own. Even the small indigenous classes most thoroughly exposed to the Western impact displayed an admixture of Western and Oriental behavior. Thus, the termination of tutelary aggrandizement was caused by more mundane considerations such as the immediate economic and political interests of the Western colonial power.

Types of Timing

The types of timing by each Western impact comprise the second expansionist factor. An analysis of this factor is important since the type of aggrandizement by itself did not determine the expansion of the Western colonial powers. The type of aggrandizement must also be assessed within the context of time.

One aspect of the timing of the Western impact has already been analyzed in Chapter Four dealing with terminal analysis.[15] This analysis in varying degrees involved the timing of the Western impact relative to the degree of adaptability of the traditional cultural system to foreign-induced change, the degree of cohesiveness within the hierarchical class structure of the great tradition and/or middle tradition, the degree of cohesiveness between the great, middle, and little traditions of the societal structure, the geographic factors of the traditional society relative to the purpose and scope of the Western impact, and the duration of the traditional society as a continuously organized community inhabiting essentially the same geographic area, and the duration of discrete traditional historical inputs.

The consideration of the timing of the Western impact relative to the traditional society must be supplemented by analysis in a second dimension, namely, the timing of each Western impact in relation to other Western impacts. This factor influenced the expansive capacity of each Western colonial power which was affected by the degree of competition from other Western powers at the time of a new Western impact. The timing of the interactions between contending Western colonial powers shaped the geographic scope of each Western impact as well as the other variables of the colonization process.

Two types of timing occurred in the interactions between the Western colonial powers: (1) *unilateral-monopolistic timing,* and (2) *multilateral-competitive timing.*

Unilateral-Monopolistic Timing: Such timing took place when a Western colonial power enjoyed a "head-start" and expanded its influence and control to overseas colonial territories without any significant competition from other Western powers. The expansion occurred during a "power vacuum" and the Western colonial power essentially monopolized the application of Western influences to Asian traditional societies. The extension of the Western impact was limited only by the available resources and voluntary restraints of the Western colonial power. Maximum power could be exerted by the Western "first-comer" against traditional societies which had to rely on their own internal resources and could not appeal to other Western colonial powers for assistance.

Unilateral-monopolistic timing took place in Asia during the expansion of Portugal, Spain, Holland, and Great Britain. The rapid and resourceful thrust of overseas exploration and territorial conquest by Portuguese dynastic aggrandizement at the end of the fifteenth century gave Portugal the opportunity to establish commercial and naval outposts at strategic coastal areas in Asia before the arrival of any other Western power. Minor competition came temporarily from the Spanish who entered Asia from the opposite side of the world and briefly challenged Portuguese supremacy in the southwest Pacific islands. Yet the Papal division of colonial territories in the New World and in Asia between the two Iberian maritime powers combined with the defeat of Spanish intrusions into the Moluccas by local rulers and the Portuguese, caused Spain to confine its colonial rule in Asia to the Philippines and to concentrate its major colonial enterprises in Latin America. The absence of Western competitors enabled Portugal to monopolize the lucrative spice trade and other commerce in Asia for almost a century. Yet the fragile structure of the Portuguese colonial system based on small scattered coastal outposts facilitated its overthrow by the Netherlands early in the seventeenth century.[16]

Early Dutch colonial expansion likewise enjoyed the advantages of unilateral-monopolistic timing since it coincided with the decline of Portuguese national power. The Dutch built a more extensive colonial system and monopolized the Oriental trade for many decades. Yet the Netherlands, unlike Portugal, acquired a firm geographic base in the East Indies (mainly Java) from which it supported commercial operations in other areas. The Dutch monopoly was reduced by the rising naval power of Great Britain during the latter part of the eighteenth century, and Dutch control of its territorial base was threatened temporarily by the British occupation of Java during the final years of the Napoleonic war. However, a treaty negotiated in 1824 with Great Britain recognized Dutch sovereignty over the island territories of Indonesia. The unilateral-monopolistic timing which shaped Dutch colonial rule resulted in one of the major paradoxes of the Western impact in Asia. It enabled a small European nation which exercised minor international influence to acquire the second most valuable colony in all of Asia[17] and *the* most valuable colony in Southeast Asia. The absence of other Western powers in the region (except Great Britain) for several decades after the end of the Napoleonic period created the opportunity to establish this unique form of colonial rule.

Perhaps the best example of unilateral-monopolistic timing took place in the unprecedented expansion by Great Britain into Asian territories following its victory over France in 1815. Prior to this time British expansion in the region had been delayed due to domestic political turmoil and the concentration of British colonial enterprise in North America. British traders had been unable to compete with the Dutch in the East Indies trade and they were forced to withdraw to less profitable outposts in the Red Sea, the Persian Gulf, and the Indian coast. Yet, like the Netherlands, Great Britain established a firm geographic base in these territories which enabled the rapid extension of British power following the weakening of Holland and France during the Napoleonic wars. The British victory in Europe provided the opportunity to expand into a vast power vacuum extending throughout most of Asia. The only opposition to the expansion of British influence came from local traditional societies, most of which were declining in power. For several decades this condition gave Great Britain the option to follow the example of Portugal and Holland and establish a monopoly of Western influence in the entire region. British troops had occupied Manila from 1762 to 1764 and British administrators had controlled Java from 1811 to 1816. Just after the Napoleonic wars, British power was sufficient to remove Spanish rule from the Philippines and Dutch rule from Java. The British likewise could have readily ousted the few French missionaries from Indochina. Yet these expansive moves were beyond British interests or comprehension at the time. Great Britain itself had been weakened after the loss of its colonies in North America and the long bitter war against France. Instead of attempting to monopolize Western rule in Asia, the British extended their power from the territory already under their control. From India and Ceylon they expanded their colonial rule to Burma, Malaya, and North Borneo. They likewise exerted significant influences in the early Westernization of Thailand, China, and Japan.

Multilateral-Competitive Timing: This timing occurred when the extension of a new Western impact confronted opposition from one or more competing Western powers. A power vacuum no longer existed in territories subject to colonization. No longer could a single Western power monopolize the application of Western influences over vast areas containing sizeable traditional societies of significant ethnic diversity. The expansive capacity of a new Western impact was a function of its interaction with competing Western powers. A new extension of Western power often resulted in increased rivalry among Western colonial powers which in turn tended to reduce the thrust of a new Western impact into a traditional society. A new Western impact also faced the likelihood that the ruler of a threatened traditional society would obtain assistance from other Western colonial powers. The fear of competing Western involvement was often a major reason for removing the ruler of the traditional society and establishing colonial rule.

Multilateral-competitive timing took place in Asia in the expansion of Spain and France during the first phase of the Western impact and with the expansion of all Western colonial powers except Great Britain during the second phase. The extension of Spanish power to Asia in the early sixteenth century immediately confronted the opposition of Portugal and confined Spanish colonial influence to religious tutelage in the limited area of the Philippines. A similar form of timing by France in the seventeenth century caused French expansion to confront the growing power of Great Britain. The timing of this competition with a major Western rival caused the French to dissipate their limited resources in a fruitless attempt to expel the British rather than to obtain a secure territorial base for future expansion. French expansion in the nineteenth century was likewise characterized by multilateral-competitive timing which involved a confrontation with British and Dutch colonial rule already established in South and Southeast Asia. Yet opposition from these Western competitors was less intense than during the earlier period and they did not block the French acquisition of territories in Indochina. The early extension of Russian power to Asia was affected by many elements of unilateral-monopolistic timing since it confronted no competition from other Western colonial powers and it readily established Russian control in Siberia and the Maritime Provinces. Yet the policy to carve out a Russian sphere of influence in Manchuria and adjoining territories in northern China during the nineteenth century was influenced by multilateral-competitive timing. Russian expansion into this area was opposed by determined Western competitors, first by Great Britain and France, and later by Japan.

Tutelary aggrandizement by the United States in the Philippines was deeply affected by multilateral-competitive timing, not in seeking an extension of American power beyond the archipelago, but in rationalizing its acquisition. A major purpose justifying American expansion was to prevent the islands from falling under the control of Germany, Japan, or other Western colonial powers. This form of timing also contributed to the tutelary role of the United States in promoting training in self-government and promising national independence which the Americans hoped would serve as a model to the European colonial powers. One of the best examples of multilateral-competitive timing occurred in the expansion of Germany to Asia at the end of the nineteenth century. By this time the most suitable colonial territories had already been acquired, and Germany was forced to take less desirable areas such as northeastern New Guinea (Papua) and the Marshall, Caroline, and Mariana island groups in the Pacific. The Germans also obtained their own small sphere of influence in the Shantung peninsula in China. Attempts at further expansion were blocked by Russia, Great Britain, Japan, and the United States. The status of Germany as a "latecomer" deprived the Kaiser of sufficient national prestige and contributed to increased rivalry among the Western colonial powers. Multilateral-competitive timing likewise confined early Japanese expansion to the relatively small and unprotected territories of Formosa and Korea. During the early months of World War II, Japanese expansion enjoyed some aspects of unilateral-monopolistic timing when a power vacuum existed in Asia due to the involvement of Great Britain, France, and the Netherlands with Nazi aggression in Europe.[18] The abortive Greater East Asia Co-Prosperity Sphere was a design to establish a Japanese monopoly in the region. Yet the sudden military advances of Japanese power into Southeast Asia soon confronted the obstacles imposed by multilateral competitive timing since it precipitated a major war with the United States and the European colonial powers.

CONCEPTS OF COLONIAL RULE

The prevailing idea among each of the Western colonial powers regarding their role in the colonial territories comprised the concept of colonial rule. This value or "theory"' emerged from a consensus within the political leadership of the Western colonial power and the groups involved in the colonization process. It was influenced by both expansionist factors (types of aggrandizement and types of timing). The concept of colonial rule changed somewhat with the passage of time, but, once established, its major assumptions remained remarkably consistent and intact. It also shaped other variables in the colonization process.

The concept of colonial rule shared by all Western colonial powers during the first phase of the Western impact was mercantilism. This economic doctrine upheld the goal of exploiting the resources of the colonial territories for the primary purpose of enhancing the wealth of the "mother country." It was most ardently articulated in Western societies pursuing some combination of dynastic and economic aggrandizement such as Portugal, the Netherlands, and Great Britain.[19] It supported the idea of a unified political and economic system maximizing monetary income by extensive government control. Its implementation abroad involved the accumulation of bullion, a favorable balance of trade, and the establishment of foreign trading monopolies.

During the second phase of the Western impact, the concept of colonial rule became more differentiated and nationalistic. Each Western colonial power espoused a distinct viewpoint of its role among the people inhabiting its own colonized societies. These variegated concepts reflected the diversity of interests pursued by the Western colonial powers. In most cases they were formulated by a more explicit and conscious process than during the first phase of the Western impact, and they became more clearly articulated as each colonization process developed.

The concepts of Western colonial rule were of three types: (1) *inferential,* (2) *eclectic-pragmatic,* and (3) *unitary-doctrinaire.*

Inferential Concept of Colonial Rule: The inferential concept of colonial rule was largely undeclared and implied. It involved little formulation of a coherent and conscious policy guiding the implementation of colonial rule. It gave little if any consideration to the impact of Western historical inputs on the indigenous people; its dominant assumptions were directed solely toward the interests of the Western colonial power. It emerged as an unspoken by-product of dynastic aggrandizement. In practice it promoted a rigid and inflexible colonization process, and it included no provisions for its eventual termination. Each colonial system based on an inferential concept of colonial rule was abruptly and totally destroyed by adversities inflicted on the political leadership of the Western colonial power.

Inferential concepts of colonial rule in Asia were involved in the colonization processes of Spain, Germany, and Russia. Shortly after its establishment, Spanish colonial rule in the Philippines relied on relatively little conscious conceptualization or justification. The Philippines were detached from the mainstream of Spanish colonial interests in Latin America, and the only official concern was the maintenance of Spanish rule to promote the spread of Roman Catholicism which was supported modestly until the nineteenth century by the Pope and the Spanish king. German dynastic aggrandizement at the end of the nineteenth century likewise induced little thought regarding the influence of a new Western impact on the people in its modest colonial territories. The German concept of colonialism was based essentially on the Kaiser's quest for national grandeur, widespread recognition as a major world power, and an intense rivalry with Great Britain. The core idea of German colonial rule was voiced by the German philosopher, Treitschke, who stated: "People from older states, who have been disciplined, go out and found new states ... Every virile people has established colonial power."[20] Russian dynastic aggrandizement at the same time sought a similar goal. The idea supporting the establishment of a Russian sphere of influence in

Manchuria and northern China was based on the desire of the Tzar to expand his domain and enhance his personal and national prestige. Professor Dallin has stated:

> It was axiomatic that the goal of Russian foreign policy was aggrandizement of Russia. No explanation was needed and the "ideology" of the policy could not be rationally explained. The aim was to enhance the grandeur of the empire, add to its glamour, and increase the glory of the Russian monarch... It was the tsar's duty and responsibility to work for the everlasting glory of Russia, for her continuous expansion, and toward making her superior in strength to other nations.[21]

Eclectic-Pragmatic Concept of Colonial Rule: This consisted of an explicit and formulated idea which evolved through an inductive process and included a consensus of the secular interests of the groups participating in the colonization process. It contained some elements of the inferential concept of colonial rule in also seeking the expansion of Western national power and prestige and in its basic assumptions oriented toward the interests of the Western colonial power. Yet the eclectic-pragmatic concept of colonial rule went much further in rationalizing the structures and policies employed in dealing with the indigenous people. It consciously recognized the cultural differences between the society of the Western colonial power and the people inhabiting the colony. It likewise perceived that the Western impact would disrupt many aspects of the life of the indigenous people, and it did not presume that all local customs and values should be changed. It opposed the transfer of a totally new way of life; instead it justified a partial intervention of the colonized society in pursuing the specific and limited goals of the Western colonial power. This concept of colonial rule was activist and at the same time it was indifferent to much of the indigenous response. It was reformist and also tolerant of numerous local differences. It upheld a flexible approach to the implementation of colonial rule and provided for new responses to changing conditions in both the society of the Western colonial power and in the colony. In varying degrees it recognized the need to plan for the termination of colonial rule.

The eclectic-pragmatic concept of colonial rule was used in the economic aggrandizement of Great Britain and the Netherlands and in the tutelary aggrandizement of the United States. This concept in British colonial rule evolved from a consensus among administrators, industrialists, traders, and scholars who upheld the inherent diversity of the races and cultures of the world. This view recognized the social and cultural differences among British colonial subjects and it sought to preserve these differences as much as possible. It supported the formation of various forms of colonial rule suitable for the particular needs of each colonized society. It justified an enlightened paternalism exercised by a friendly but separate association with the colonial people. It included some elements of assimilation of British culture by specific indigenous groups. When defending his views during the debate over the adoption of English as the language of instruction in Indian educational institutions, Lord Macaulay illustrated this idea by advocating the emergence of an Indian elite which would be "Indian in blood and colour, but English in taste, in opinion, in morals and in intellect."[22] A few British thinkers also dimly foresaw the time when the indigenous people living under British colonial rule would absorb certain Western political values and demand self-government. In practice the British concept of colonial rule displayed a genius for "muddling through" by a mixture of actions involving economic exploitation, social association, cultural assimilation, and a vague promise of eventual national independence.

The concept of colonial rule of the Netherlands has been labeled "cultural relativism."[23] It was formulated primarily by administrators and commercial interests, and like the British view, it recognized the deep differences between Western and Asian cultures. Yet the intense economic motivation supporting Dutch colonial rule and the influence of Calvinism made this division much more rigid and bifurcated than in the British colonies. According to Professor Lucian Pye:

> For the Dutch there were essentially two respectable worlds, that
> of traditional Indonesian culture and that of the Europeans . . .
> in the Dutch scheme there were only the standards that went
> with these two worlds; there was no room for the transitional
> man, the man who sought to become Westernized without neces-
> sarily losing all of his traditional values.[24]

In a colonial system of "like over like," both Dutch administrators and Indonesian traditional rulers were conceived as the possessors of significant yet separate functions. In theory their roles were equal, yet in practice the Dutch role was superior. The forms of the traditional society were retained, but the centralization of Dutch colonial rule transferred all effective decision-making power to Dutch authority. This concept induced a much higher level of paternalism than in the British colonies, which in turn generated the idea that the survival and continuity of Indonesian society depended on Dutch guidance and control. In contrast to the tolerance and flexibility in the British concept of colonial rule, the Dutch provided no rationale for the indigenous person who was part traditional and part Western. Dutch colonial rule consequently excluded all but a few of the indigenous people from a broad and unrestricted exposure to Western culture and some sense of individual self-confidence and dignity. After World War I a few Dutch spokesmen reluctantly voiced the need for eventually granting self-government to the Indonesian people. Yet until the very end, powerful economic interests in this valuable colony opposed genuine moves toward Indonesian independence.

The American concept of colonial rule was the most formulated and articulated view of the role of a Western colonial power in any Asian colonized society. This intensely eclectic-pragmatic concept emerged from the erratic interaction between the American tradition of anti-colonialism and the nationalistic fervor attending the initial emergence of the United States as a major world power. It was defined by the leaders of both American political parties in the executive and legislative branches. It was based on the obligation to promote conditions in the Philippines as rapidly as possible which would facilitate the abolition of colonial rule. It conceived of the training of indigenous political leaders suitable for the maintenance of a democratic society. Like Great Britain and the Netherlands, the United States recognized the major differences between Western and Oriental cultures, an awareness which promoted the effort to preserve Philippine mores and customs that did not interfere with orderly progress toward rapid political development. This view was codified in the original instructions to the first American commission assigned to the archipelago. A portion of these instructions stated:

> In all the forms of government and administrative provisions which they are authorized to prescribe the commission should bear in mind that the government which they are establishing is designed not for our satisfaction, or for the expression of our theoretical views, but for the happiness, peace, and prosperity of the people of the Philippine Islands, and the measures adopted should be made to conform to their customs, their habits and even their prejudices, to the fullest extent consistent with the accomplishment of the indispensable requisites of just effective government.[25]

The Wilsonian concept of national self-determination promulgated at the end of World War I further strengthened the idea of a rapid transfer of sovereignty to the Philippines. The flexibility induced by the American concept of colonial rule aided this trend in the first voluntary termination of Western colonial rule in an Asian colonized society.

Unitary-Doctrinaire Concept of Colonial Rule: This rule comprised an explicit and formulated view derived deductively from an expansionist doctrine upholding the formation of a homogeneous and unified colonial system. This concept envisioned the spread of the doctrine according to preconceived plans implemented by the central political authority of the Western colonial power. It also included certain elements of the inferential concept of colonial rule in seeking the augmentation of Western power and prestige, and in its fundamental suppositions directed toward the interests of the Western colonial power. Yet the unitary-doctrinaire concept of colonial rule embodied the most intense and dynamic vision of the role of an "advanced" Western power in altering the lives of the people in its colony. It upheld a "universalist" view of mankind and an "ideological" mission by the Western colonial power. It conceded the existence of cultural and social differences between the society of the Western colonial power and the indigenous people, but it sought to exploit, reduce, or destroy these differences rather than to preserve or strengthen them. Its core value was that all peoples, Western and Asian alike, could embrace the common doctrine and share its benefits and modes of behavior. Unlike the eclectic-pragmatic concept of colonial rule, it sought to transfer a total alien way of life to the local people and it justified an unlimited intervention in their society and culture. It was activist and intolerant of indigenous differences. It was reformist and it pursued widespread conformity to its values.

The unitary-doctrinaire concept of colonial rule likewise induced a rigid and inflexible form of colonial rule, which in practice made some modifications for local cultural variations. Yet these conditions were only to be temporarily tolerated until the doctrine had become stronger and its uniformity more deeply implanted in the indigenous culture. Like the inferential concept of colonial rule, it provided no rationale for the termination of Western colonial rule. Instead its espousal of inherently superior doctrinal values generated militant opposition to ending the colonization process. This attitude was caused by the belief that termination would deprive the indigenous people of continual exposure to the doctrine and the enjoyment of its rewards. Consequently, this concept of colonial rule was antithetical to the emergence of the idea of self-government and national self-determination.

The unitary-doctrinaire concept of colonial rule was used in the tutelary aggrandizement of France and in the ideological aggrandizement of Japan and the Soviet Union. The French concept of *mission civilisatrice* envisioned the direct extension of French culture to Asian (and African) societies with no major modifications for local conditions. This principle rested on a distinct "universalist" view of human society and the powerful assimilative capacity of French culture. The French approach to colonial rule has been ably described by Professor Rupert Emerson. In comparing it to the British concept, he has stated:

> The fundamental French appreciation of the nature of the colonial problem is clearly distinguished from that of the British whose tendency is to assume that peoples are properly distinct and separate.... The roots of the differences in the two positions are to be sought in the British conviction that there are many breeds of men, each destined to develop along its own lines and the contrary French belief in the ultimate oneness of mankind. It has fitted the French genius in the past to assume that the people of their colonies could become Frenchmen and to aim at their integration into the homogeneous society of a single Greater France revolving around Paris. The British on the other hand, work toward the creation of a looser Commonwealth made up of diverse and independent peoples.... the French, more rationalist-universalist in outlook, find it natural that their colonial wards should aspire to be Frenchmen, while the British, culturally pluralistic and seeing their pattern of life as something peculiar to themselves, almost resent the thought that another people might enter into it, and, indeed have the gravest doubt that it can really be done. To the British, a man who has so far departed from his own is a natural object of suspicion; to the French he is a man who has seen the light.[26]

The French realized that their limited numbers in colonized societies made it impossible to impart their culture to the entire indigenous population so they concentrated their cultural diffusion on the traditional elite. In considerable degree this small select group was expected to become "brown Frenchmen." From this privileged class the French assumed that some benefits of their culture would filter down to the lower levels of the indigenous class structure. This concept of cultural assimilation was implemented most effectively in Asia in colonial territories under direct French control such as Vietnam. In colonies of lesser importance such as Laos and Cambodia, the French adopted aspects of the British version of association which sought the more limited objective of establishing stable and harmonious relationships with the indigenous people and preserving certain elements of their own culture. Yet the French concept of association did not preclude the transfer of some French influences through cooperation and example. In Indochina the

French gave no thought to granting national independence to their colonies until they were confronted with widespread nationalist opposition and the possibility of a complete communist takeover. The idea of self-government was abhorrent to ardent exponents of *mission civilisatrice* since the severance of political ties with metropolitan France would deprive the local people of continuing their full exposure to French culture.

The unitary-doctrinaire concept of colonial rule utilized by Japan emerged from a "pan-Asian" movement following World War I which culminated in the Greater East Asia Co-Prosperity Sphere in 1940 designed to "liberate" Asia from Western influences. The Japanese view was less "universalist" than the French *mission civilisatrice*. It conceived of the world as divided into several regional spheres of influence each dominated by a single major power. It upheld the vision of a new structure of power in Asia involving the replacement of the former Confucianist system centered around Imperial China and the existing Western colonies with a new sphere of influence based on the superior technology and military power of Japan. This idea supported the military conquest of Southeast Asia and the dissemination of certain elements of Japanese culture to the indigenous people. Japan recognized the cultural differences among these diverse societies, yet these differences were used to enhance and strengthen Japanese imperial control. After the tide of the military conflict in World War II favored the Allied powers, the Japanese granted varying degrees of "independence" to several Southeast Asian societies to gain their support in opposing the return of the Western powers. Yet a firm centralized control from Tokyo over the entire region was maintained. According to Professor Cady:

> The various peoples of Southeast Asia would exercise varying degrees of autonomy but would all be assimilated to the Japanese Empire as vassal political and economic units. Western prestige must be completely discredited, and Japan would emerge as "the leader, the protector, and the light of Asia."[27]

The mode of colonial control espoused by the Soviet Union after 1918 was an excellent example of the unitary-doctrinaire concept of colonial rule. Unlike other concepts of Western colonial rule, it did not perceive the immediate physical control over distant colonial territories and peoples. A centralized totalitarian authority in Moscow promoted a genuinely "universalist" revolutionary doctrine based on Marxist-Leninist ideology. It envisioned an eventual world-wide classless society dominated by proletarian rule, and it contained a powerful "anti-imperialist" appeal in its mission to destroy Western capitalism. It sought to interlace

Marxism-Leninism with the idea of national self-determination, an idea espoused by Soviet leaders only in non-communist societies to intensify anti-Western sentiment and promote conditions favorable to the future expansion of communism. This dual concept of nationalism-communism enabled the Soviet Union to exploit anti-colonial resentment and promote the formation of indigenous communist parties in all Asian societies by the 1930's. This idea also contributed to an ideological environment conducive to extensive penetrations by the Soviet Union in newly-independent national societies in Asia after World War II.

POLITICAL AND ADMINISTRATIVE STRUCTURES MAINTAINING COLONIAL RULE

These structures maintaining colonial rule consisted of the specialized governmental institutions and modes of behavior created by the Western colonial powers to achieve their goals in the colonized societies. These structures were the organized channels of authority through which the concept of colonial rule was implemented. They were shaped by other variables in the colonization process, and they influenced the specific governmental and non-governmental linkages between the Western colonial power and the Asian colonized society. They existed at two levels: (1) the structures in the Western colonial power engaged essentially in the formulation of colonial policy; (2) the structures in the colonized society concerned primarily with the implementation of colonial policy. Some overlap occurred in the interrelationships between these two organizational levels since certain roles within the structures in the Western colonial power exercised influence on the implementation of colonial policy, and some roles in the structures within the colonized society exerted varying degrees of influence in the formulation of colonial policy. The political and administrative structures in the Western colonial power were directly susceptible to political influences emanating from within its own society, whereas the structures in the colony were susceptible to political pressures from both the society of the Western colonial power and the colonized society. The structures in the colonies maintained a form of direct or indirect colonial rule or a combination of both. Direct colonial rule involved the implementation of colonial policy entirely by officials of the Western colonial power without any division of authority with indigenous traditional rulers. Indirect colonial rule consisted of a division of authority between a resident "adviser" of the Western colonial power and an indigenous traditional ruler (usually the ruler of a former middle tradition).

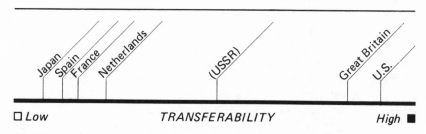

Fig. X. *High-low continuum showing the degree of transferability of political and administrative structures maintaining Western rule in Asian colonized societies.*

The political and administrative structures maintaining colonial rule were of two types: (1) *high-transferable,* and (2) *low-transferable.* A high-low continuum showing these two types of political and administrative structures maintaining Western colonial rule in Asia is shown in Figure X.

High-Transferable Political and Administrative Structures Maintaining Colonial Rule: This consisted of structures at both levels which were designed at some time during the period of colonial rule to transfer sovereignty from the Western colonial power to the Asian colonized society. These types of structures imparted some of the most significant Western historical inputs in the formation of new national societies. They sought to transmit some understanding of Western forms of government to Asian leaders and peoples. Western control over the political and administrative structures in the colony was envisioned as temporary, and Western policy-makers made institutional and role changes to provide for the liquidation of colonial rule. The Western colonial power assumed an "outer-directed" orientation and took genuine measures to transfer its own political and administrative skills to sizeable numbers of indigenous people. This attitude evolved from a dual response to a growing propensity within the society of the Western colonial power to grant independence to colonized peoples and to increasing demands for self-government from nationalists in the colony. It likewise confronted the moral issue raised by the imposition of foreign rule over alien populations for an extended period of time, and it recognized the limited ability of the Western colonial power to maintain a stable rule as larger numbers of indigenous people acquired a sense of nationalism.

High-transferable political and administrative structures were employed to implement the eclectic-pragmatic concepts of colonial rule of the United States and Great Britain. A unique form of this type of structure was used in the unitary-doctrinaire approach to colonial rule by the Soviet Union.

The best example of high-transferable political and administrative structures maintaining colonial rule occurred in the colonization process established by the United States in the Philippines.[28] As previously mentioned, the preconceived purpose of this colonial system was to train Filipinos in self-government and to grant national independence at the earliest possible date. The political and administrative structures in the United States consisted of the existing executive and legislative branches which became more democratic during this period but underwent no major structural changes themselves. These increasingly representative institutions of the American national government provided an accessible and effective channel for implementing widely supported demands for change in the American colonization process. The political and administrative structures established in the Philippines consisted of a highly centralized and direct form of colonial rule whose purpose was to create new political institutions and modes of behavior modeled on the American constitutional system of bicameralism and the separation of powers. Successive changes in transferring authority to these new structures were made in compliance with executive orders issued by the President of the United States and legislation passed by the United States Congress. Qualified Filipinos were rapidly incorporated into these structures, at first in an independent judiciary and later in representative legislative bodies. Actions proposed by members of the Filipino nationalist movement who filled the roles in these institutions were often balked and rejected by American colonial authorities, but the nationalist movement was never suppressed. The dominant issue with the colonial power was the timing of national independence, not its justification.

High-transferable political and administrative structures used by Great Britain also transmitted important political institutions and modes of behavior to indigenous persons in British colonies, although in Asia this process was generally conducted with less speed and less consistent enthusiasm than in American colonial rule in the Philippines.[29] The decision-making structures in Great Britain consisted of the highly centralized parliamentary machinery which underwent significant institutional and political changes during the long period of British colonial rule. The changes which affected the transferability of British political and administrative influences to the colonies included the declining power of the House of Lords, the rising influence of the House of Commons, the moderation of the Conservative Party, and the growth of the Labour Party. The formation of more representative political institutions and the inclusion of new classes in the British electorate provided increasingly effective channels for broadly supported changes in colonial policy. The high-transferable capacity of British political and administrative structures in the colonies was usually confined to the territories under direct colonial rule (British India, Ceylon, Burma, and the Federated States of Malaya), whereas relatively few political and administrative skills were transferred in territories under indirect colonial rule (Indian princely states, the Unfederated States of Malaya, the North Borneo territories). In the territories under direct colonial rule, the British used the "council system" in transferring political and administrative structures to indigenous control. Through Cabinet orders and legislation passed by Parliament, British colonial authorities created executive and legislative councils at the central and provincial levels of the colonial system. Participation by indigenous persons gradually increased in these councils which were intermittently expanded in size and changed from an appointed to an elected membership. Useful political experience was also imparted as their role was partially altered from advisory to supervisory functions. In contrast to American colonial rule in the Philippines, the British were more concerned with training efficient bureaucracies than in developing democratic political institutions. This objective was promoted by an exceptionally qualified career colonial service which required high administrative performance by both British and indigenous personnel. The British delayed the development of local courts and legislatures much longer than the Americans, and they waited in transferring executive-administrative authority to local political leaders until just prior to World War II. British colonial authorities took more rigorous action in restraining the nationalist movements in their colonies than their American counterparts in the Philippines, and they imprisoned nationalist leaders when their actions threatened the stability of their colonial rule. Yet the nationalist movements in British colonies were never consistently suppressed. Their major issue with the colonial power increasingly involved the timing of national independence, not its justification.

A special type of high-transferable political and administrative structure was used by the Soviet Union in extending its influence to Western colonies in Asia. The purpose of this structure was not to transfer a broad array of political and administrative skills from a Western colonial power to a colonized society moving toward national independence. Instead it sought to transmit Lenin's model of a communist party to a small indigenous group dedicated to the seizure of political power, either from a Western colonial power or a newly-independent national society. Training in the use of this highly specialized revolutionary apparatus accompanied Soviet-sponsored tutelage in Marxist-Leninist doctrine. From the Soviet view-point, this high-transferable political and administrative structure was to bring about the formation of a communist government in an Asian society which in some degree would be subordinate to Moscow. The Soviet leaders established the Communist International (Comintern) to transfer their ideology and revolutionary skills to non-communist societies. A special department within the Comintern, the Eastern Secretariat, supervised communist activities in China, Japan, Korea, India, Indonesia, and other Asian colonies.[30] The Comintern administered its operations throughout the Asian region from its Far Eastern Office, the Dalburo, located in Shanghai. It utilized two methods in transferring communist organizations to Asian societies: (1) it sent Russian or other foreign communist advisers to assist the formation of indigenous communist parties; (2) it brought Asian communists to the Soviet Union or third countries for advanced political indoctrination and training. The Comintern was abolished by the Soviet Union during World War II to appease the Western allies, but its activities were quickly revived by other Soviet governmental structures following the Japanese surrender.

Low-Transferable Political and Administrative Structures Maintaining Colonial Rule: Structures of this sort were operative at both levels which made no conscious or sustained effort to transfer sovereignty to the Asian colonized society. Western governmental structures in the colony were assumed to be permanent, and they took no concrete action to prepare for their own liquidation. The Western colonial power maintained an "inner-directed" orientation and opposed appeals from the colonized society for national independence. This attitude was based on the immediate interests of influential leaders and groups within the Western colonial power who essentially ignored both the long-range moral implications of imposing foreign rule on an alien population and the practical problems of maintaining a stable colonial system as increasing numbers of indigenous persons became influenced by a sense of nationalism. Within the structures of the Western colonial power various political leaders and factions intermittently voiced the need to transfer sovereignty to the colonized society, but these forces were never able to obtain sufficient influence to gain control of the political and administrative structures at both levels and put their proposals into practice.

Low-transferable political and administrative structures were used in the inferential colonial rule of Spain, in the eclectic-pragmatic colonial rule of the Netherlands, and in the unitary-doctrinaire colonial rule of France and Japan.[31]

The intensely religious colonial rule established by Spain induced low-transferable political and administrative structures in the Philippines. The political structures in Spain controlling colonial policy remained highly centralized and authoritarian except during brief liberalizing periods in the nineteenth century. No attempt was made by Spanish colonial authorities in the archipelago to transmit administrative skills to Filipinos. The Spanish did impose significant administrative responsibilities on early *datus* as their villagers were forcibly relocated in new towns (*pueblos*) in a centralized colonial system.[32] The datus were renamed *cabeza* and retained their leadership role over their own *barangays* in each pueblo. Their position remained hereditary, and they were given the responsibility of collecting taxes and organizing public labor. The cabezas of each pueblo were known collectively as the *principalia*, or leading citizens, and one of these town leaders served as the *gobernador-cillo*, or "little governor." Although there was much intermarriage between the Spanish and the leading local families, the Spanish colonial authorities never gave political prestige or administrative stature to the principalia. Yet these indigenous leaders played an important "middleman" role between the Spanish colonial administration and the Filipino population. They retained considerable respect from their own people, and near the end of Spanish colonial rule they began to emerge as the dominant economic and social class.

The political and administrative structures maintaining Dutch colonial rule remained at a low level of transferability due to the intense economic orientation of the Dutch colonial system and the fear of a drastic decline in Dutch prosperity in the event the Indonesian colony achieved independence. The structures in the Netherlands formulating colonial policy became increasingly democratic throughout the nineteenth century, although they remained more rigid and resistant to change than political and administrative structures in Great Britain and the United States. The personal influence of the Dutch monarchy on colonial policy was terminated after 1848, and the control over colonial affairs was concentrated in the parliamentary bodies, the Cabinet and the States General, which supervised the administration of the Colonial Department. The rise of the Liberal Party after 1860 increased demands for reforms in the colonial policy in Indonesia, yet these demands were significantly reduced after the Liberal Party achieved control of the government and other proposals to liberalize the colonial system were effectively blocked by conservatives in the Colonial Department.[33] The Dutch made no attempt to transfer modern governmental skills to indigenous leaders whose primary role was to supervise the acquisition of export crops and to collect taxes. After 1903 the Dutch established a system of local and provincial councils similar to those in British colonies, and in 1916 they created the *Volksraad* (Peoples' Council) consisting of elected and appointed representatives to provide a channel for both Dutch and indigenous public opinion throughout the archipelago.[34] Yet these structures remained largely symbolic and advisory; they transferred no significant Western values and modes of behavior to indigenous leaders. Just prior to World War II Dutch officials held 94% of the major positions in the colonial bureaucracy and they comprised 58% of the personnel in the entire administrative service.

The ethos of *mission civilisatrice* likewise induced low transferable political and administrative structures in the French colonization process.[35] The structures in France, like those in Holland, became more democratic during the Third and Fourth Republics, but their instability and the frequent changes in top-level policy-makers hampered the implementation of consistent colonial policies. In addition to the Cabinet and the National Assembly, a cumbersome hierarchy of advisory bodies, chambers of commerce and agriculture, and geographical societies shaped colonial policy. Their objective was to enhance the quality and utility of the colonial system, rather than to plan for its eventual liquidation. In contrast, the formation of the socialist and communist parties in France early in the twentieth century aroused growing demands for the termination of French colonial rule and national independence for French colonies. To placate this move, the French government adopted the unique practice among the Western colonial powers of providing token representation in both houses of their national legislature for delegates from French colonies who participated at the periphery of the legislative process and in the election of the President of France. This highly decentralized and splintered process enhanced the role of the permanent bureaucracy in the Ministry of Colonies in Paris which remained unsympathetic to major reforms in the colonial system.

The political and administrative structures in Indochina imposed a complex system of direct and indirect colonial rule which transferred few important governmental skills to indigenous persons. The Governor-General of Indochina administered colonial policy through an elaborate organization which included a Lieutenant-Governor, *chefs du province,* lower administrative personnel in Cochin China, and three *Resident*

Superieur in Annam and Tonkin, Cambodia, and Laos. A system of advisory councils was established at most levels of the administrative system similar to that in British and Dutch colonies. Yet attempts to transfer political authority to the small number of indigenous persons on these councils were hampered by the rapid turnover of incumbents in the position of Governor-General. Twenty-three persons filled this top-level post from 1892 to 1930. As in France, this instability increased the influence of professional colonial administrators who opposed reforms of the colonial system. The councils never achieved more than consultative status, and their recommendations were always subject to veto by French colonial authorities. Nationalist spokesmen in all Indochina territories were suppressed, and nationalist leaders were imprisoned, exiled, and, in some cases, executed. Some moves toward self-government in Vietnam were under consideration just after World War II, but these deliberations quickly collapsed with the outbreak of violence between the French and the communist-led Viet Minh. No significant political reforms were initiated in Cambodia or Laos until just prior to their independence in 1953. French administrative structures also undertook only token measures to transfer modern managerial skills to indigenous persons. A few Vietnamese mandarins were retained in high administrative posts in Annam and Tonkin to preserve the appearance of shared authority with the traditional rulers, but all important administrative roles were filled by the French. Only after 1911 were small numbers of Vietnamese employed at the lowest levels of the colonial bureaucracy. In Cambodia and in the southern provinces of Laos, the French likewise dominated the administrative hierarchy, although some Vietnamese were used in low level administrative roles in these adjoining colonies. No modern administrative skills were provided to Cambodian or Laotian personnel.

The transferability of Japanese political and administrative structures was more complex and inconsistent than in the Western colonial systems in spite of the highly articulated goal advocating the steady expansion of Japanese power. These structures tended toward low transferability in Korea and Taiwan, and inadvertently assumed certain forms of high transferability in several Southeast Asian colonies (especially Burma and Indonesia).[36] This fragmented process was caused in considerable degree by the fluid and competitive interrelationships in the Japanese political system among aristocratic, military, industrial, bureaucratic, and parliamentary cliques. The Diet effectively administered colonial policy only during the brief parliamentary period of the 1920's, yet its efforts were directed toward internal political reforms rather than changes in the colonial system. The administrative structures in the colonies created after the acquisition of Taiwan and Korea at the turn of the twentieth century and extended to Southeast Asia in the military conquest of World War II consisted of a complex system of military and civilian spheres of authority, which, like the French colonial system, was further complicated by the frequent rotation of top-level administrative personnel. Japanese governmental structures in Taiwan and Korea imposed a system of direct colonial rule and transferred minor administrative skills in low-level roles. In Korea the Japanese established advisory councils at various levels of the administrative hierarchy similar to those in British, French, and Dutch colonies, but the few Koreans appointed to these councils exercised no political power.[37]

Japanese political and administrative structures in Southeast Asia during World War II exercised various forms of indirect colonial rule. Thailand was placed under a Japanese military occupation, but the Thai government was granted virtually complete autonomy over internal affairs. The French colonial system in Indochina was likewise subject to the supervisory authority of a Japanese military commander, yet it retained actual control over internal affairs until the final six months of the war (in marked deviation from Japan's alleged goal of "Asia for the Asiatics"). Elsewhere in the region the Japanese initiated reforms through political and administrative structures created by the former Western colonial powers, not for the purpose of advancing genuine self-government, but to manipulate anti-Western nationalist sentiment and promote a "new order" loyal to Japan. In colonies such as Burma and the Philippines where considerable political and administrative skills had been transferred by the Western colonial powers, the Japanese pursued this objective by granting "independence" in 1943, although effective supervisory control was retained by Japan. In Indonesia the Japanese released prominent nationalist leaders from imprisonment and placed them in leadership roles in an indigenous political organization known as *Putera*. Brief but significant political experience was acquired by Sukarno and other Indonesian nationalists as the Japanese made additional promises and undertook concrete moves toward some form of independence.[38] No administrative skills were transferred by the Japanese in Thailand or Indochina, but in British and Dutch colonies they initiated significant administrative reforms to supplement their anti-Western propaganda programs. In Burma and Indonesia the Japanese employed sizeable numbers of indigenous persons in top and middle level posts which had been denied them by the Western colonial powers. These administrative changes, like the political reforms, were more symbolic than substantive since native administrators exercised limited authority under key Japanese "advisers," yet by the end of the war many indigenous personnel had acquired considerable administrative experience.

ECONOMIC AND SOCIAL POLICIES IN THE COLONY

These policies consisted of concrete actions by the Western colonial power to pursue specific goals envisioned by the concept of colonial rule. These policies were of primary importance to the Western colonial power since they determined many benefits derived from the entire colonization process. They were also of major significance in imparting Western historical inputs in the Asian colonized society and in the formation of a new domestic environment. They introduced new values and new modes of behavior in utilizing physical and human resources. They comprised a concrete manifestation of the secular orientation of the newly-emerging scientific culture of the West seeking to expand man's mastery over the forces of nature. These policies influenced the degree of Western penetration and its effect on different groups and territories in the colony. They likewise shaped the emergence of more differentiated subsystems in an evolving transitional society.

The economic and social policies in the colony were of two types: (1) *high-transformative,* and (2) *low-transformative.* A high-transformative economic or social policy comprised actions which achieved major alterations in the Asian colonized society. A low-transformative policy comprised actions which caused little or no change in the colony. The economic policy consisted of the specific actions designed to exploit the physical and human resources in the colony in the endeavor to enrich the economy of the Western colonial power, although this policy often involved increased economic benefits to certain indigenous groups within the colonized society. Many economic actions caused the construction of permanent fixtures in the territory of the colony (such as the construction of ports, highways, bridges, etc.). The social policy was designed to establish new social standards and new modes of social behavior among certain groups in the indigenous population. Many elements of this policy likewise produced physical facilities which became fixed assets on the soil of the colonized territory (such as universities, schools, hospitals, etc.).

Some indication of the variety of impacts imparted by the two types of policies can be seen on a limited basis in analyzing briefly the diversity of Western influences during the mercantilist phase of the early Western impact. The Portuguese applied a high-transformative economic policy and a low-transformative social policy. The sudden removal of their scattered commercial enclaves at the end of the sixteenth century prevented them from imparting any significant permanent influences in the formation of a new environment in Asian traditional societies. The Spanish in the Philippines applied a low-transformative economic policy and a high-transformative social policy in the form of religious proselytizing. The high-transformative social policy imparted the most significant impact in promoting the spread of Roman Catholicism in the Philippine archipelago. The Dutch and the British followed the example of the Portuguese in using a high-transformative economic policy and a low-transformative social policy, although near the end of this period the British began providing modest public support to education and abolishing "inhumane" religious customs such as *suttee* (widow-burning) in India. Yet the Dutch and the British, unlike the Portuguese, imparted a lasting impact due to a more intensive application of their economic policy and their control of a sizeable geographic base.

Economic Policies: The economic policies of the Western colonial powers became more diverse after 1815, and more differentiation occurred in the transformative impact of these policies. A high-transformative economic policy was generated largely by the drive for industrialization by Western colonial powers from a relatively small territorial base and the need to rely heavily on the colonized society for raw materials and markets in accelerating domestic economic development. A high-transformative economic policy was used by Great Britain in all of its Asian colonized societies, by the Netherlands in Indonesia, by France in Vietnam, and by Japan in Korea and Taiwan. A low-transformative economic policy was caused by a minor demand in the Western colonial power for raw materials in the Asian colonized society and the absence of profitable markets for manufactured goods. A low-transformative economic policy was implemented by Spain and the United States in the Philippines, France in Cambodia and Laos, and Japan in Southeast Asia. A high-low continuum showing these two types of economic policies used by Western colonial powers in Asian colonized societies is shown in Figure XI.

The colonization process of Great Britain adhered consistently to a "liberal" free-trade policy designed to extract the maximum profit from the unrestricted flow of goods and services into the channels of international commerce. This policy upheld a limited governmental role and aimed primarily at creating an environment conducive to the production and distribution of goods and services through private enterprise. The functions of the political and administrative structures consisted essentially of maintaining law and order, providing a sound currency, and offering suitable tax incentives to encourage the investment of Western and local capital. The government also provided the infrastructure on which a privately-oriented economy could thrive. These additional functions included the construction of ports, railroads, highways, water-

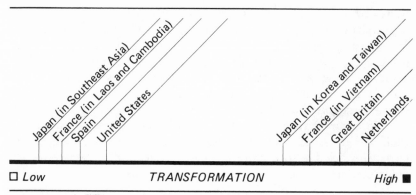

Fig. XI. High-low continuum showing the degree of transformation induced by the economic policies of Western colonial powers in Asian colonized societies.

control projects, and research facilities. This high-transformative economic policy induced massive infusions of British capital in colonial economic development, yet it involved relatively small numbers of British administrative and commercial personnel residing permanently in the colony. At the same time it caused the mass migration of cheap labor from densely populated to sparsely populated societies within Asia. It facilitated the movement of many thousands of Indian workers to Ceylon, Burma, and Malaya, and Chinese workers to Southeast Asia. Economic development promoted by British capital and trade provided opportunities for many of these immigrants to enter new forms of employment such as the professions, commerce, and skilled trades.

The high-transformative economic policy of the Netherlands involved a much more active governmental role than the British free trade policy. It also required a much larger number of its own administrative and commercial personnel residing permanently in the colony. The policy of the Dutch likewise was changed according to new political and economic developments in Dutch society. From 1830 until the 1860's the Dutch imposed the Culture System which required peasant cultivators in Java to plant one-fifth of their land in export crops designated by the Dutch colonial authorities.[39] The village chiefs were given the responsibility for delivering these cash crops which were marketed by the official trading monopoly. Special regulations were designed to provide tax-exemption on the land and restrictions on the labor performed in the cultivation of these crops. Yet in practice these regulations were abused by Dutch officials who obtained enormous profits from this exploitative system. The economic policy was changed after 1870 to the Liberal Policy designed to expand economic exploitation by private entrepreneurs and to reduce the role of government-owned commercial organizations.[40] Official restrictions on many sectors of the economy were removed and incentives were provided to encourage the investment of private capital. The Dutch again took measures to protect the native population, primarily in the enactment of a law prohibiting the sale of land to non-Indonesians. The Liberal Policy combined with the opening of the Suez Canal caused extensive economic change. The development of sugar cultivation in Java and the production of oil, tin, coal, and other minerals in the Outer Islands promoted the construction of ports, highways, railroads, communications, and inter-island shipping services by the government. This high-transformative economic policy also caused large capital investment by other industrializing nations, including the United States, Great Britain, Germany, and Japan.[41] It provided special favors to Chinese immigrants who entered the colony in increasing numbers and found employment in the colonial bureaucracy and commercial enterprises. By 1940 the Chinese minority comprised 2,000,000 persons and it dominated the retail trade.

The high-transformative economic policy of the French in Vietnam adhered essentially to a neo-mercantilist concept seeking the exploitation of the resources of the colonial territory, not for the outmoded practice of accumulating bullion, but to enhance the wealth of public and private groups in France through the use of government-controlled commercial monopolies.[42] After 1900 French entrepreneurs in Vietnam were required to promote rapid economic development as the central authorities in Paris curtailed public expenditures to pay for the deficits incurred by the colonial administration. In the drive for economic self-sufficiency, the French quickly dominated the mining and manufacturing enterprises in northern Vietnam and played a large role in the production and processing of rice, sugar, tobacco, tea, and rubber in the southern provinces.[43] They monopolized several retail markets and imposed high tariffs on non-French imports including those which did not compete with French goods without providing any reciprocal advantages to Vietnamese products in French domestic markets. This economic policy was intensified after World War I when the stability of the Indochinese piaster and the depreciation of the French franc caused a flood of new investment to colonial economic development. As in the British and Dutch colonies, the French colonial administration constructed the infrastructure necessary for the expansion of modern economic enterprises. This policy provided employment for large numbers of permanent French residents in Vietnam, although the proportion of commercial personnel was much less than the number of Western civil servants in the British and Dutch colonies.[44] The high-transformative economic policy of the French likewise caused the rapid influx of Chinese immigrants who settled largely in Cochin China where they quickly dominated the rice and retail trades.

The Japanese applied a high-transformative economic policy in Korea and Taiwan, which, like that of the Netherlands in Indonesia, utilized a large governmental role in promoting major economic change. It also involved large numbers of Japanese administrative and commercial personnel residing permanently in these two colonies. In addition, the Japanese government transshipped Japanese peasants to promote agricultural development in southern Korea and it facilitated the development of mining, forestry, and light industry by Japanese corporations in the northern provinces. In Taiwan the Japanese likewise promoted agricultural development and established light industry. In both colonies, the colonial administration constructed a modern infrastructure, including ports, railroads, and communications.

A low-transformative economic policy was administered by Spain in the Philippines due to the vast distances involved in the galleon trade and the highly profitable ventures in more accessible Spanish colonies in Latin America (until the early nineteenth century). Spanish economic activity in the Philippines was confined largely to the establishment of a *hacienda* system which produced export commodities to support the costs of the colonial administration and a widespread church domination of productive rice lands in the provincial areas.

The low-transformative economic policy of the United States in the Philippines was caused by the lack of incentive for large-scale investment in the colonial economy and the competition of Philippine products with agricultural commodities produced in the United States.[45] The Americans in the Philippines, like the French in Vietnam, applied a neo-mercantilist policy, not for the purpose of exploiting its resources for the economic development of the United States, but in creating a virtual monopoly for American commercial interests operating in the colony. A bilateral trade relationship was established regulating the exchange of goods between the two countries. Duties were imposed on external goods which competed with American manufactured products, and a free market was provided in the United States for Philippine agricultural products. The Philippine economy became almost totally dependent on the United States, and by the 1930's the American economy was consuming 75% of the Philippine exports and providing 85% of its imports. This low-transformative economic policy maintained much of the economic system inherited from the Spanish. American policy provided expanded incentives for increasing the production and processing of a few food exports, but the structure of the Philippine agrarian economy remained essentially unchanged. American colonial administrators broke up the extensive land holdings of the Roman Catholic church, but these were not widely distributed to landless peasants.[46] In effect, the United States took little effective action to resolve the serious problem of land alienation and absentee landlordism in the archipelago. American colonial authorities constructed a modern infrastructure, although this technological advancement was undertaken primarily for administrative rather than economic purposes. American policy encouraged an influx of Chinese immigrants who played a major role in the wholesale and retail trades as well as in the financing of rice and lumber production. American policy also facilitated the immigration of a small Japanese community which settled largely in the Davao area.[47]

The status of Cambodia and Laos as buffer states between Thailand and British Burma and the valuable French colony in Vietnam caused an exceedingly low transformative economic policy in these two sparsely populated societies.[48] The French took no major actions to promote their economic development. In Cambodia the French made a modest investment in rubber and tin production and they constructed a railroad and highway system linking this territory to Cochin China. In the landlocked society of Laos the French engaged in no significant economic enterprises except for a minor mining operation in the southern provinces. The colonial administration made a small highway system to assist in administration and defense. A modest influx of Chinese and Vietnamese immigrants in both colonies caused their commerce to become dominated by small-scale alien entrepreneurs.

Japan also implemented a low-transformative economic policy in Southeast Asia during World War II despite the vast natural resources of this region. Japanese economic policy was subordinate to the social policy seeking to extricate Western cultural influences. Many natural resources, even in wealthy territories such as Indonesia and Malaya, were not immediately essential to Japanese military power which relied more on other sources (such as Korea and Manchuria) that were nearer to the Japanese islands and were already integrated into Japanese wartime production. A few strategic products such as tin, rubber, oil, and rice were exported from Southeast Asia to Japan during the early months of the war, but these transshipments were gradually reduced due to increasing losses of merchant vessels caused by the war. Japan constructed no permanent infrastructure in the region. Instead it reversed the economic development of the region which had been achieved by the Western colonial powers.

Social Policies: A high-transformative social policy was induced by a high priority to social measures in pursuing the goals of the colonial system. This type of policy was used in the colonial systems of Great Britain throughout Asia, France in Vietnam, Spain and the United States in the Philippines, and Japan in Korea, Taiwan, and Southeast Asia. A low-transformative social policy, conversely, was caused by a low priority to social actions in supporting the goals of the colonial system. This type of policy was used in the colonial systems of the Netherlands in Indonesia and France in Laos and Cambodia. A high-low continuum depicting these two types of social policies used by Western colonial powers in Asian colonized societies is shown in Figure XII.

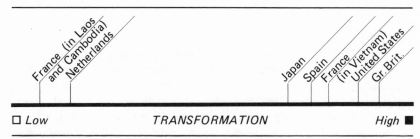

☐ *Low*   *TRANSFORMATION*   *High* ■

Fig. XII. High-low continuum depicting the degree of transformation induced by the social policies of Western colonial powers in Asian colonized societies.

The high-transformative social policy of Great Britain in its Asian colonies was designed essentially to assist in maintaining political stability and promoting economic development. Education comprised the dominant element of this policy which sought to supply sufficient numbers of trained indigenous personnel for administrative and commercial roles. The "filtration" policy was adopted early in the nineteenth century in India, which, according to Sir Percival Griffiths, was "one of the turning points of Indian history" and "opened the floodgates to European thought and literature and subjected the best brains of India, from their childhood onwards, to the powerful influence of English liberal and scientific thought."[49] This policy with minor modifications was applied in other British colonies. It sought to impart a Western education to a small indigenous elite which was expected to spread Western values and modes of behavior to broader segments of the local population. It downgraded the traditional educational system and the use of classical languages. It led to the establishment of a Westernized three-level educational system consisting of a large number of primary schools in accessible rural villages, a small number of secondary schools in urban centers, and one or a few colleges and universities in major metropolitan areas. These educational institutions received varying degrees of support from the British colonial authorities ranging from direct supervision of public schools to government grants to a wide variety of private schools. After World War I the British provided increasing vocational training at both the secondary and college levels to meet the growing need for qualified technical and clerical personnel. In addition, British social policy included public health facilities, famine relief, labor legislation, workmen's compensation, unemployment benefits, and public housing. To maintain the primary goals of political stability and economic development, the British used their social policy to bestow certain favors on specific majority and minority groups, including the Sikhs and Gurkhas in India, the Sinhalese in Ceylon, the Malays in Malaya, and the Karens in Burma. Yet British colonial authorities refrained from long-term efforts to manipulate educational opportunities and curriculum or social welfare programs for the purpose of suppressing nationalism and perpetuating British colonial rule.

The high-transformative social policy of France in Vietnam was designed primarily to promote the broad goal of spreading French culture to the indigenous population. This policy imparted a more universalistic value-system than the administrative and economic-oriented social policy of Great Britain. It was also much more politicized than the British social policy. The dominant element of this policy was the formation of a French-oriented educational system which supplemented and overshadowed the vernacular schools spreading classical knowledge. The French, like the British, endeavored to extend their educational program to a small indigenous elite with the expectation that French values and behavior would disseminate gradually to other groups in the colonized society. The French colonial administration created a school system which relied almost entirely on the French language.[50] The Vietnamese language was taught only through a romanized script devised by French missionaries. The French educational system was meager in size compared to that established in British colonies, and it was constructed almost entirely in urban areas. The colonial administration provided little support to primary schools and it established only fourteen secondary schools and one university (Hanoi). The French attempted to restrict admission to the University of Hanoi and the high quality secondary schools to Vietnamese students thoroughly versed in the French language and overtly sympathetic to French colonial rule. When anti-colonial agitation erupted after World War I, the French intermittently closed the university and secondary schools, and they altered the curriculum from liberal arts to technical subject matter to discourage the spread of nationalism. French social policy in Vietnam involved few actions besides education. The colonial authorities constructed modest health and sanitation facilities, yet they provided no social welfare services as did the British during the final years of their colonial rule. The high-transformative social policy of the French was buttressed by the Roman Catholic church which was closely interlinked with the French-supported educational system and served to intensify the assimilative capacity of *mission civilisatrice*. The church provided an additional channel for educated Vietnamese to demonstrate their adoption of an important aspect of French culture.

The high-transformative social policy applied by Spain in the Philippines consisted almost entirely of its religious proselyting endeavors. Spanish priests accompanied Spanish troops and colonial administrators in the formation of a unified colonial system. Until the end of Spanish rule, ecclesiastical administration supplemented civil administration. In most rural areas the Spanish clergy were the sole authorities of the colonial order. Within less than a century most Filipinos living in Luzon and the Visayan Islands embraced at least the ceremonial trappings of Spanish Catholicism. While aiding the administration and efficiency of a centralized colonial system, the Spanish priests at times mitigated the harshness imposed by civil authorities on the indigenous populace.

The United States likewise implemented a high-transformative social policy in the Philippines. Yet in sharp contrast to the Spanish social policy, it consisted largely of a widespread dual-purpose program of secular education designed to transmit democratic values and behavior to a mass electorate and to train an indigenous elite in the use of democratic political institutions. Both aspects of this educational policy were considered necessary to the proper functioning of the democratic system the United States was seeking to transplant.[51] The major element of the policy involved the formation of a compulsory primary education system in Manila and most provincial towns. During the first two decades of American colonial rule large numbers of American teachers were sent to the archipelago to teach in the schools constructed in these areas. At higher levels the American colonial authorities did much less to promote public education. The secondary schools, colleges, and universities remained largely under private control, although the colonial administration exerted varying degrees of influence in orienting the curriculum of these schools toward the dissemination of democratic values. The colonial administration established the University of the Philippines in

Manila as the first public institution of higher education and eventually added several branches of the university outside Luzon.[52] By 1922 more than one million Filipino students were attending public schools, an unprecedented educational achievement by any Western colonial power in Asia. The avowed purpose of the American-sponsored educational policy to provide political tutelage necessary for the liquidation of colonial rule precluded the use of educational curriculum or administration to perpetuate colonial rule or to oppose the evolution of nationalism. In addition to the massive educational program, the high-transformative social policy of the United States involved the establishment of health and sanitation facilities, including the construction of modern water and sewage systems and new hospitals and medical dispensaries.

Japan applied a high-transformative social policy to achieve varied purposes in different regions. In Korea and Taiwan, the Japanese established a modest educational system designed primarily for indoctrinating indigenous youth with loyalty toward the Japanese imperial system. This policy also imparted low-level administrative and technical skills as well as widespread use of the Japanese language. In Korea the Japanese made a determined effort to weaken the indigenous culture by prohibiting the use of the Korean language in schools and commerce. In Southeast Asia the high-transformative social policy was conducted for the purpose of erasing Western cultural influences and disseminating new standards of social behavior. As in Korea, this policy involved the manipulation of languages. The public use of the English language was curtailed, and the use of Japanese and indigenous languages was expanded. By the time of the Japanese surrender, the use of Burmese, Tagalog, and Indonesian languages was widespread throughout their respective societies. Japanese social policy also entailed the utilization of indigenous religions to weaken Western influences and to strengthen Japanese rule. Japanese colonial authorities supported the teaching of Buddhism in Burma and Thailand and assisted the expansion of Islam in Malaya and Indonesia. This policy likewise involved special treatment to alien immigrant groups useful in augmenting Japanese influence and power. Japanese colonial administrators favored the Indian minorities in Malaya and Burma and induced many local Indians to join the Indian Independence League and the Indian National Army for a planned military invasion of British colonial territory in India.[53] The Chinese minorities in all Southeast Asian societies were harassed and terrorized by the Japanese.

The low-transformative social policy of the Netherlands in Indonesia was induced by the desire of the Dutch colonial authorities to interfere as little as possible with non-economic elements in the colonized society for the purpose of maximizing economic benefits. Following World War I this policy also included concrete actions to prevent the emergence of a national identity and a sense of nationalism among the indigenous people. The Ethical Policy promoted by reformist groups in Holland after 1900 to provide certain social benefits to the Indonesian populace was strongly opposed by colonial authorities and private Dutch entrepreneurs in the archipelago. Only a minor portion of this new policy was effectively implemented. A modest primary educational system enrolled 227,000 students by 1913, a number which increased to 2,300,000 by 1940 (in a colonized society of approximately 80,000,000 people). Secondary schools enrolled 2% of these students and graduated only 800 students each year. The Dutch established several universities after 1920 yet these institutions of higher education were confined to the technical fields of engineering, law, and medicine, and their total annual attendance averaged 1100 students, including a large portion of Chinese. A modest liberal education program was started in 1940. The Dutch, like the Japanese, manipulated the teaching of languages to maintain the colonial system. They often discouraged the use of the Dutch language to reduce indigenous exposure to Western intellectual and cultural influences, and they restricted the use of the Indonesian language to prevent the emergence of a national lingua franca. Instead the Dutch encouraged linguistic pluralism. They prohibited the use of the term "Indonesian" by the indigenous people.

The low transformative social policy of France in Cambodia and Laos involved the least disruptive action by any Western colonial power in Asia. Traditional education through monastic schools in both societies continued uninterrupted throughout the period of French colonial rule. A few secondary schools were established by the French in provincial cities in both colonies, although qualified students from upper class families usually attended secondary schools and the university in Vietnam. A few members of the traditional elite in both societies received advanced education in France.

SUMMARY

The impact of Western colonial powers in Asian colonized societies was highly differentiated and multifaceted. There were numerous and significant differences between the colonization processes of the Western colonial powers, and there were important differences within the colonization processes maintained by a single Western colonial power. Table XIV comprises a summary comparing the diverse intensity of specific Western influences in the Western colonies in Asia. The Western colonial powers are ranked according to the assessment in Chapter Five of their political, administrative, economic, and social impacts.

Table XIV. A comparison of the intensity of political, administrative, economic, and social impacts in the Western colonies in Asia.

Western Colonial Power	Political	Administrative	Economic	Social
1. Great Britain	high	high	high	high
2. United States	high	high	low	high
3. Japan in Southeast Asia	high	high	low	high
4. France in Vietnam	low	low	high	high
5. Japan in Korea and Taiwan	low	low	high	high
6. Netherlands	low	low	high	low
7. Spain	low	low	low	high
8. France in Cambodia and Laos	low	low	low	low

Chapter 6

The Unequal Treaty Process

The pattern of governmental and nongovernmental linkages between Western nations and Asian societies based on treaties upholding extraterritoriality and special tariff privileges constituted the unequal treaty process. This unique international interrelationship was established in China, Japan, and Thailand at a time when these societies were too weak to resist certain aspects of Western expansion, yet they possessed sufficient capacity to prevent the imposition of Western colonial rule.[1] The unequal treaties required them to conduct some of their relations with Western nations on an inferior basis and other relations on a basis of national equality. They created a system in which these Asian societies exercised sovereignty over limited sectors of their internal affairs until the process was abolished by the negotiation of new treaties with each Western nation. In effect, the unequal treaties imposed a semi-independent status on China, Japan, and Thailand.

The unequal treaty process, like the colonization process, imparted a variety of influences which shaped the transmission of Western historical inputs in these three Asian societies. It involved the following variables: (1) the expansionist factors in the Western nation, (2) the goals of Western foreign policy, (3) the political and administrative structures conducting Western foreign policy, (4) the Western official mission inside the semi-independent Asian society. Figure XIII shows the relationships between these variables in the Western nation and the semi-independent Asian society.

EXPANSIONIST FACTORS

Western nations extended their power and influence through the unequal treaty process due to the expansive Western ethos already cited in the initial analysis of the Western impact. Yet specific factors again motivated each Western national power in its impact on the semi-independent Asian societies.

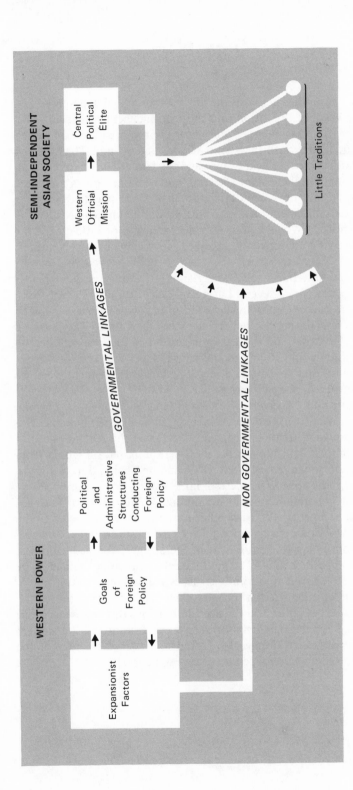

Fig. XIII. The structure of the unequal treaty process. The central political elite of the great tradition was in power during the early stages of this process. In the final stages the central political elite of a modernizing nation-state was governing. The former semi-autonomous provincial administrators in China and Thailand were abolished as were the former middle tradiitions in Japan.

Economic aggrandizement was the most common and widespread factor inducing Western expansion into the semi-independent Asian societies. The drive for raw materials and markets promoted the penetration of British and Dutch influences into China, Japan, and Thailand.[2] A similar aggrandizement caused France and the United States to seek economic advantages in these same societies, and economic goals promoted Japanese expansion into China after the turn of the twentieth century. Economic aggrandizement on a lesser scale induced a much broader and more differentiated Western impact in the extension of influences from numerous Western nations not involved in Asian colonial ventures. These nations included Austria-Hungary, Belgium, Sweden, Norway, Portugal, Denmark, Italy, and Switzerland.[3] In China unequal treaties were also negotiated with several Latin American countries such as Peru, Brazil, and Mexico. Dynastic aggrandizement was used on a much smaller scale and during a much briefer period of time. The personal ambition of the Kaiser and the Tzar was the prime factor extending the power of Germany and Russia to the semi-independent Asian societies for a short duration. Tutelary and ideological aggrandizement were not involved in the unequal treaty process.

The type of timing of diverse Western influences through the unequal treaty process was confined in every case to multilateral-competitive timing. The unequal treaties occurred only during the second phase of the Western impact. (In most cases they were imposed on China from 1842 to 1943; on Japan from 1858 to 1899; and on Thailand from 1855 to 1927.) During this historical period no Western power enjoyed the advantages of unilateral-monopolistic timing. Western nations both cooperated and competed with each other in the societies subjected to the unequal treaties. Competition among the Western powers did not involve the acquisition of large territories as in the struggle for new colonies. Instead the competition caused by multilateral-competitive timing largely entailed contention over rights and privileges granted by the government of the semi-independent Asian societies. This type of timing caused the establishment of "spheres of influence" in portions of Chinese territory and the loss of sizeable Thai territories to Great Britain and France. Yet multilateral-competitive timing also served to preserve portions of the sovereignty in these semi-independent Asian societies.

GOALS OF WESTERN FOREIGN POLICY

The goals of foreign policy of the Western nations consisted of the broad objectives pursued through the unequal treaties. They served the same essential purpose as the concept of colonial rule in the colonization process. They guided and rationalized specific actions by each Western nation in the semi-independent Asian societies. These goals evolved from the expansionist factors and they shaped other variables in the unequal treaty process.

Two types of foreign policy goals guided the actions of the Western powers in the unequal treaty process: (1) *commercially-oriented,* and (2) *strategically-oriented.*

A *commercially-oriented foreign policy goal* was pursued for the primary purpose of gaining economic advantage and maximizing trade. This goal was sought by all Western nations, large and small. It was more actively pursued by the major Western powers motivated by economic aggrandizement such as Great Britain and France which established commercial and trade relations in all three semi-independent Asian societies. Profitable commercial enterprises were also promoted on a more limited basis by economic interests in the United States, Japan, and small Western nations. Commercial goals likewise emerged from the dynastic aggrandizement of Germany and Russia, although they guided the foreign policies of these major European powers on a lesser scale than in the Western nations expanding their influences primarily by economic motivation. Commercially-oriented foreign policy goals combined with multilateral-competitive timing were the prime factors causing the formation of "spheres of influence" in China by all major Western powers except the United States.[4]

A *strategically-oriented foreign policy goal* was pursued only by major Western powers for political and military purposes rather than economic advantage. This type of goal was applied in the semi-independent Asian societies to protect the indigenous or colonial territory of a major Western power. This goal invariably overlapped with the pursuit of commercially-oriented goals. A strategically-oriented foreign policy goal was applied by Tzarist Russia in obtaining a sphere of influence in Manchuria and northern China to protect Russian territories in Siberia and the maritime provinces from Chinese or Japanese aggression. Japan pursued a similar goal in Korea just prior to the imposition of colonial rule to erect a buffer state between its own territory and the threat of military aggression from China and Russia. Great Britain and France were guided by strategically-oriented foreign policy goals in establishing Thailand as a buffer state between their colonial territories in Burma and Indochina.

The inclusion of provisions for extraterritoriality and special trading privileges in the unequal treaties constituted the method of achieving both types of foreign policy goals by all Western nations. Extraterritoriality has been defined by one scholar as "the extension of jurisdiction beyond the borders of the state. It embodies certain rights, privileges, and immunities which are enjoyed by the citizens, subjects, or proteges of one state within the boundaries of another, and which exempt them from local territorial jurisdiction and place them under the laws and judicial administration of their own state."[5] In brief, the principle of extraterritoriality enabled the Western nations to entend their judicial authority to their own nationals living in specified areas in the three semi-independent Asian societies. In Europe and the Middle East this diplomatic practice had been used by Western nations for many centuries where it was based on custom and usage; in Asia it was based on written treaties and enforced by Western diplomatic and military power. It was essentially a judicial concept, yet it had profound philosophical, social, and political implications. It served as a concrete manifestation of the vast gulf between the values and institutions of Western and Asian civilizations. It signified that the Western nations considered their own political and legal systems to be superior to those in Asia, and it caused the semi-independent Asian societies to relinquish their sovereignty in this specific realm of their foreign relations. At the same time, extraterritoriality largely confined Western penetration in these societies to the treaty ports and other limited areas where Western citizens were protected by their own laws and courts. With few exceptions it hampered the movement by Western nationals into the interior of the semi-independent Asian societies.

Special trading privileges for Western nations supplemented the provisions for extraterritoriality. The governments of the semi-independent Asian societies were required to relinquish their jurisdiction over specific aspects of their foreign trade. These privileges included the imposition of fixed tariffs (five per cent ad valorem in China and Japan; three per cent ad valorem in Thailand), the opening of numerous treaty ports (China and Japan), the opening of inland waterways to Western commerce (China), and the granting of leased territorial concessions at treaty ports (China) where Western nationals could reside, construct commercial installations, and conduct trade outside the jurisdiction of the local government.

POLITICAL AND ADMINISTRATIVE STRUCTURES CONDUCTING FOREIGN POLICY

The political and administrative structures conducting foreign policy consisted of the executive, legislative, and judicial institutions in the Western nations formulating and implementing diplomatic relations. In the major Western powers these structures tended to overlap with the specialized governmental institutions maintaining colonial rule. Yet the unequal treaty process involved these structures in a different type of impact than the colonization process. It caused a variety of new relationships between the executive and legislative structures in the extension of extraterritorial authority. Great Britain, for example, protected British nationals residing in China, Japan, and Thailand under the authority of the Crown, rather than Parliament.[6] The United States placed American citizens under the authority of Congress, rather than the President. France assisted its nationals by a specially organized extraterritorial judicial system established by the cabinet and the national legislature. The democratization of the legislative structures in most Western nations, as in the colonization process, caused some demands for reforms in the unequal treaty process as well as occasional requests for its termination. These proposals, however, were much less intense than the demands in Western democracies such as Great Britain and the United States seeking the abolition of colonial rule.

The unequal treaty process involved new roles for the judicial structures and the diplomatic and military services of the Western nations. Western court systems were modified and expanded to provide extraterritorial jurisdiction to Western nationals residing in the semi-independent Asian societies, especially in China. Great Britain increased the judicial authority of the Privy Council and established a Chief Justice in Hong Kong and His Britannic Majesty's Supreme Court for China in Shanghai.[7] The United States Supreme Court intermittently issued decisions regarding extraterritorial jurisdiction over American citizens, and Congress created a special appellate structure, the United States Court for China. Similar geographic extensions of judicial authority in China were made by France and Japan. Other Western nations relied on consular courts within their own diplomatic missions to administer extraterritorial jurisdiction to their citizens. The unequal treaty process likewise caused all Western nations, large and small, to enlarge their foreign offices and diplomatic services to handle the expanding political and commercial relations with the semi-independent Asian societies. The major Western powers were required to expand their armed services, especially their naval forces, to support their increasing interests and commitments with the occasional use of "gunboat diplomacy."

THE WESTERN OFFICIAL MISSION INSIDE THE SEMI-INDEPENDENT ASIAN SOCIETY

The Western official mission inside the semi-independent Asian society consisted of the diplomatic service, the consular courts, and the leased concessions (in China) through which the unequal treaty provisions were implemented and enforced. This official mission served as the primary channel for Western national influences in the semi-independent Asian societies. It was similar to the political and administrative structures implementing colonial rule in the colonization process, although it interacted with the indigenous population on a much smaller scale and it exerted a direct impact largely in the capital and treaty ports of the semi-independent Asian societies. Also, the official mission was involved in the pursuit of flexible and unpredictable goals of foreign policy, rather than the implementation of the more stable and formulated economic and social policies of colonial rule.

The diplomatic service consisted of an embassy or legation at the capital of the semi-independent Asian societies authorized by treaty to conduct political relations with the indigenous government. It also included the consular missions at treaty ports providing official services to their own citizens. The diplomatic service supervised and coordinated the other structures of the Western official mission. The consular courts were specialized institutions within the diplomatic and consular missions which involved Western officials in a judicial capacity exercising the provisions of extraterritoriality for their own citizens. In this role Western officials applied their own system of law to their own nationals accused of civil and criminal offenses in the semi-independent Asian societies. In addition to the consular courts, the provisions of extraterritoriality in China were expanded to include the presence of Western judicial officials in "mixed" courts and "mixed" cases at trials in Chinese courts.[8] From 1896 until 1911 this practice was augmented in the International Mixed Court at Shanghai which tried Chinese defendants in the international settlement under Chinese civil and criminal law. The leased concessions comprised the Western territorial settlements established at treaty ports in China. These Western enclaves were established by treaty and their occupants remained outside the jurisdiction of the Chinese government. Each Western concession imposed its own laws on all residents living within its authorized territory.[9]

The Western official missions inside the semi-independent Asian societies were of two types: (1) *high-demonstrative,* and (2) *low-demonstrative.* The high-demonstrative Western official missions imparted the most intensive impact in the form of values, modes of behavior, and institutions, not as in the colonization process through direct actions imposed on colonized subjects, but through indirect interrelationships with a semi-sovereign populace caused by personal contacts, persuasion, threats, and "demonstration effect." This type of

Western official mission imparted its influences through large diplomatic installations at the capitals of the semi-independent Asian societies and through their consular offices at numerous treaty ports. They likewise promoted and protected significant nongovernmental linkages consisting of large numbers of their own nationals engaged in advisory positions in the indigenous government and in trade and missionary enterprises. Their political and legal institutions served as models for indigenous political and legal modernization. They supported their unequal treaty privileges with the intermittent use or threat of military power. The low-demonstrative Western official missions extended a minor penetration to the semi-independent Asian societies. The number of their nationals affected by the Western official missions was relatively small, and they applied no military power of their own in enforcing the unequal treaties. Instead they relied on the diplomatic and military power supporting the high-demonstrative Western official missions.

The high-demonstrative official missions with only two exceptions were those of the major Western powers, Great Britain, France, and the United States.[10] Japan maintained a high-demonstrative official mission in China from 1896 until the 1930's. The low-demonstrative official missions tended to be those of the relatively small European and Latin American nations. A high-low continuum depicting the degree of demonstration effect caused by Western official missions in the semi-independent Asian societies is shown in Figure XIV.

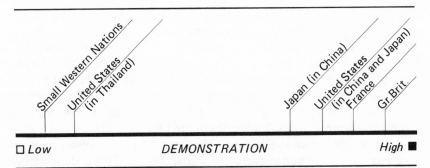

□ Low   DEMONSTRATION   High ■

Fig. XIV. High-low continuum depicting the degree of demonstration effect caused by Western official missions in semi-independent Asian societies.

The official missions of Great Britain imparted the most significant high-demonstrative impact through the unequal treaty process, just as British colonial rule in South and Southeast Asia exerted the most widespread Western impact through the colonization process. The British played the dominant role in opening China to Western diplomatic and commercial penetration and in negotiating the first unequal treaty at Nanking in 1842.[11] This treaty and subsequent diplomatic and military actions enabled Great Britain to establish a large embassy in Peking and consular offices at sixteen treaty ports. These official missions facilitated the major British role in opening the vast Yangtze River to foreign commerce. They enabled Great Britain to be the first Western nation to obtain the right for their citizens to travel to the interior of China, and the first to require the Chinese government to conduct its diplomatic relations through a modernized Ministry of Foreign Affairs (*Tsungli Yamen*) rather than the traditional Bureau of Dependencies. The British official mission provided military advisers to the beleaguered Manchu dynasty during the Taiping Rebellion and technical advisers at various levels in the Chinese administration. The official mission of Great Britain also played a significant role in terminating the isolation of Tokugawa Japan, although the United States assumed the leadership in negotiating the first unequal treaty and opening Japan to Western intercourse. The dramatic achievements of British military power in China during the middle of the nineteenth century encouraged an end to Japanese isolationism and facilitated the expansion of Western penetration in Japan.[12] Great Britain quickly followed the American diplomatic breakthrough and established an embassy at Edo (Tokyo) and consular offices at Shimoda, Hakodate, and other treaty ports. Through these official missions the British maintained extensive trade and cultural relations with Japan. Great Britain provided naval vessels for the modernization of the Japanese fleet and British technicians served as advisers in newly-created Japanese industries. The official missions of Great Britain likewise assumed the dominant role in spreading early Western influences in Thailand. A British diplomatic mission negotiated the first unequal treaty at Bangkok in 1855 which facilitated the establishment of extensive trade and cultural relations.[13] The large British presence promoted the employment of numerous British advisers by the Thai government to assist in the early administrative and technological modernization of the kingdom.[14]

The high-demonstrative official missions of France tended to emulate the behavior of Great Britain in the unequal treaty process. In none of the three semi-independent Asian societies did the French become the major Western influence, yet they established sizeable diplomatic missions at the capitals and maintained consular offices at authorized treaty posts. The official mission of France cooperated with those of Great Britain and the United States in reorganizing the Chinese Customs Service in the 1850's, and French troops joined the British-led military expedition to Peking (1858-1860) which further broadened Western penetration through the unequal treaty process. The French official mission took the lead in expanding Western cultural influences in China by obtaining extraterritorial privileges for foreign missionaries working in the interior of the country.[15] This development soon extended extraterritorial rights to Chinese Christians. The French official mission in Japan, like that of Great Britain, exerted considerable influence in promoting the end of isolationism and in serving as the channel for trade and cultural relations. The French provided military advisers during the final years of the Tokugawa regime, and the Napoleonic code served as a model in the modernization of Japanese law.[16] The French official mission in Thailand exerted a minor influence until the 1890's when a combination of diplomatic and military actions enabled France to transfer sizeable Thai territories to Cambodia and Laos and establish the Thai kingdom as a buffer state between French colonial territory in Indochina and British colonial territory in Burma.[17] Thereafter the French official mission in Thailand assumed a high-demonstrative role. The Franco-Thai treaty of 1893 extended extraterritorial rights to French Asian subjects (Vietnamese, Cambodian, and Laotian) living in Thailand, and French consulates in the Thai kingdom provided extraterritorial privileges to large numbers of Chinese immigrants (*resortissants*).[18] The French official mission likewise facilitated the employment of French advisers in the Thai government, and many elements of French law were borrowed in the modernization of the Thai legal system.[19]

The official mission of the United States in China exerted a high-demonstrative effect through the unequal treaty process, more by its diplomatic role and protection of missionary activities than through extensive trade and commercial relations. The conduct of this official mission was unique among Western nations in China in its unpredictable vacillation between American national interest and American idealism. It joined the official missions of Great Britain and France in the 1850's in reorganizing the Chinese Customs Service, yet it took no part in the British and French military attack on Peking. It cooperated with the British in legalizing opium traffic and it participated with other major Western powers in suppressing the Boxer Rebellion, yet it refrained from carving out a sphere of influence or maintaining leased concessions at Chinese treaty ports. After 1900 it provided significant diplomatic support to the Chinese government through the Open Door policy. The

American official mission promoted a further extension of Western missionary activities by the Treaty of Wanghia which broadened extraterritorial privileges to include the right of foreigners to buy Chinese books and employ Chinese teachers.[20] The American official mission likewise facilitated the emigration of large numbers of Chinese laborers to railroad construction projects in the United States where most remained as permanent residents. In Japan the official mission of the United States exerted a high-demonstrative effect much like the British and French official missions in China and Thailand. The American official mission promoted the establishment of extensive trade and cultural relations. It encouraged the employment of American advisers in new government ministries and American technicians in new industries. It also promoted the use of American school teachers in the modernization of the Japanese educational system.[21] The American official mission facilitated the emigration of many Japanese workers to Hawaii and the west coast of the United States where many stayed as permanent residents. The American official mission in Thailand imparted a low-demonstrative effect, primarily through its diplomatic influence and assistance to missionary enterprises. This mission served as a channel for American anti-colonial sentiment which assisted the quest of Thailand for national equality and unrestricted sovereignty. It was the first Western diplomatic mission to be elevated from a consulate to a legation, and it assisted the negotiations following the Versailles peace conference through which the United States assumed the lead in abolishing the unequal treaties.[22] The American mission facilitated the employment of American advisers by the Thai government who were instrumental in eventually negotiating new treaties with all Western nations on the basis of complete national equality.[23]

The Japanese high-demonstrative official mission in China was established by the Treaty of Shimonoseki in 1895 following the Sino-Japanese War. The extraterritorial rights granted to Japan by the weak Manchu dynasty enabled this official mission to assert Japanese national equality in the international community and gain recognition of Japan as a major world power. It likewise served as the channel through which the most aggressive foreign penetration was extended into China during the first half of the twentieth century. In many respects Japan strengthened the unequal treaty process at a time when its vigor was declining among the Western nations. The Japanese official mission was the first to obtain the new extraterritorial privilege of constructing industrial and manufacturing enterprises at Chinese treaty ports.[24] This achievement encouraged further expansion of Japanese commercial interests and territorial designs in the interior of China, a movement that was blocked largely by the United States until the 1930's. The official mission of Japan likewise exerted a unique effect in demonstrating to the Chinese the new-found capabilities accruing a non-Western nation adopting Western science and technology.

The low-demonstrative official missions of less powerful Western nations were invariably established after the negotiation of the first unequal treaties in the three semi-independent Asian societies by one of the major Western powers. On a more limited scale their behavior tended to emulate the high-demonstrative official missions. The official mission of the Netherlands exerted a modest yet special influence in Japan due to its unique experience as the only Western nation permitted to trade in Japan during the long isolationist policy of the Tokugawa era. During the early years of the Western impact, the Dutch mission played an important communicative role between the high-demonstrative official missions of the major Western powers and the Japanese rulers. It likewise provided information and knowledge about the Western world to the emerging indigenous intellectual class, including numerous Japanese "Dutch" scholars.[25] The low-demonstrative official missions of Denmark, Belgium, Italy, Portugal, and Spain were the first to conduct negotiations with the Chinese Nationalist government in 1930 for the purpose of relinquishing their extraterritorial rights and abolishing their unequal treaties in China.[26] The official mission of Denmark in Bangkok facilitated the employment of Danish military advisers by the Thai government at the end of the nineteenth century in the development of a modern army and navy.[27]

SUMMARY

The impact of Western nations in the unequal treaty process tended to be less extensive and less differentiated than the impacts imparted through the colonization process. Yet the Western impacts in the three semi-independent Asian societies were diversified in some degree. There were likewise some significant differences in the impacts imparted by a single Western nation. Table XV comprises a summary comparing the diverse intensity of specific Western impacts in the unequal treaty process. The Western nations are ranked according to the assessment in Chapter Six of their demonstrative effect in the semi-independent Asian societies.

Table XV. A comparison of the intensity of demonstrative impacts imparted by Western nations in the unequal treaty process in the semi-independent Asian societies.

Western Nation	China	Japan	Thailand
1. Great Britain	high	high	high
2. France	high	low	high
3. United States	high	high	low
4. Japan	high	——	(no unequal treaty)
5. Small Western Nations	low	low	low

Chapter 7

Governmental Linkages

The colonization process and the unequal treaty process constituted different forms of external impacts on Asian societies.[1] The analyses of these impacts in Chapters Five and Six provided many useful classifications and comparisons in assessing specific elements of these complex intersocietal relationships. Yet the methodology presented in the two preceding chapters is not sufficient by itself in providing precise explanations of the politically relevant values, modes of behavior, and institutions transmitted by Western nations to Asia. The high-transferable political and administrative structures of Great Britain, for example, actually touched only limited sectors of India, Ceylon, Burma, and Malaya. The high-transformative economic and social policies of Western colonial powers induced changes only in certain areas of their colonized societies. The same phenomenon occurred in the high-demonstrative Western official missions involved in the unequal treaty process.

A more detailed and structured approach is consequently needed to isolate specific external linkages involved in the transmission of Western historical inputs to Asian societies. As in the analysis of the diverse external influences imparted to the pre-Western traditional societies, this endeavor will use a broadened form of *macro-linkage-analysis.*[2] This methodology can again be applied in explaining the political roles of foreigners or "non-members" in a "penetrated" society and in providing a pattern of historical variables necessary in comparative political analysis. Again it attempts to combine external and internal factors relevant to political analysis to obtain a complete environmental or ecological view of political behavior. Again it pursues the "big picture" of politics.

The level of analysis of the external linkages in this important historical period will be modified from the first application of macro-linkage-analysis which combined a description of each external linkage with an assessment of the reaction it induced in the traditional society.[3] The primary focus here will be only on the first aspect of the Western external linkages, namely their role in imparting new politically relevant historical inputs to the indigenous Asian societies. This methodology is necessary since the Western external linkages in both the colonization process and the unequal treaty process were much more numerous, complex, and differentiated than the external linkages in the traditional society during the pre-Western era. Western external linkages involved a much larger role by governmental structures in both the Western nations and the Asian societies. They possessed the capacity to affect more indigenous people and to reach a more widespread geographic territory. They also penetrated more deeply into specific sectors of the indigenous society within a relatively short period of time.

The second aspect of the political role of Western external linkages which comprised the individual and collective reactions to the Western impact in Asian societies will be analyzed in considerable depth in Part Three dealing with the indigenous response.

The application of macro-linkage-analysis in Chapter Seven will assess the Western historical inputs imparted by governmental linkages. This analysis will be divided into three classifications: (1) governmental linkages involved in the colonization process; (2) governmental linkages involved in the unequal treaty process; and (3) the governmental linkage (political agents) involved in both forms of external impact. Chapter Eight will deal with politically relevant Western historical inputs transmitted to Asian societies by non-governmental linkages. These classifications in both chapters are made with the understanding that there was considerable overlapping between the influences transmitted by some governmental linkages and some non-governmental linkages. The analysis will also include assessments of the phenomena of "shared influence" in which similar values, modes of behavior, and institutions were imparted and reinforced by more than one type of Western external linkage.

GOVERNMENTAL LINKAGES INVOLVED IN THE COLONIZATION PROCESS

The governmental linkages involved in the colonization process were *Western colonial administrators, Western resident advisers,* and *Western colonial military forces.* Numerous Western historical inputs were transmitted by these external linkages in virtually all Western colonial systems. The transmission of additional Western values, modes of behavior, and institutions by specific forms of Western colonial rule was a function of the degree of transferability of their political and administrative structures.

WESTERN COLONIAL ADMINISTRATORS

Western colonial administrators comprised a linkage which imparted some of the most extensive and differentiated influences of the entire Western impact. One of the most significant Western historical inputs transmitted by this external linkage was the *concept of the nation-state.* The transfer of this Western framework of political organization served as the foundation on which a new kind of political authority in the colonized society was constructed. This "modern" institution had emerged in Western Europe following the French revolution.[4] It was an achievement of the rising European middle class based on a spreading sense of rationalism and a dynamic commercial spirit. The transmission of this unique concept was the most widespread "shared influence" extended to Asian colonized societies by all Western linkages. Yet the basic values and institutions of the nation-state were most vividly personified and demonstrated by the hierarchy of civil servants administering the official colonial policy. Explicitly and implicitly they depicted the idea of the Western nation-state as the combination of a fixed "national" territory, a populace united by a common pattern of "national" loyalties, and a sovereign political authority administering a common body of "national" law. The colonial bureaucracy likewise revealed the nation-state as the fundamental political norm used to justify and rationalize the pursuit of common societal goals. They showed the dominant role of "the national interest."

Western colonial administrators transmitted the concept of the nation-state by initiating the overlapping developmental processes of state-building and nation-building.[5] The function of state-building involved the prompt, conscious, and direct effort to construct a single impersonal corporate authority over the colonial territory and indigenous peoples of diverse races, religions, languages, and customs. It consisted of the creation of a state-colony, a *Gesellschaft,* a political, legal, and universalistic structure. This achievement was accomplished by the imposition of a unified legal, administrative, and monetary system. It likewise required the establishment of fixed geographic boundaries surrounding the colonial territory. Western colonial administrators formed specialized administrative agencies and military forces to regulate the movement of people across these formally established boundaries. They directed indigenous loyalties toward the sovereignty of the Western colonial power (the British Crown, the United States Constitution, etc.), and they required oaths of allegiance to these sources of authority from local persons employed in the service of the colonial system. They upheld the status of "subject" to indigenous persons and bestowed on them a common "nationality." They provided specific "national" documentation, rights, and obligations to the small numbers of colonial subjects who traveled outside the colonized territory. With few exceptions, the Western colonial administrators were the first political rulers to establish a stable and unified state over the territory and people of the colonial society.

Western colonial administrators started the process of nation-building subsequent to that of state-building. They served as one pole of a complex "love-hate" interrelationship with a small indigenous elite seeking both an individual and collective sense of "national" identity. They thereby induced the formation of a state-nation, a *Gemeinschaft,* a psychological, cultural, and particularistic grouping among local persons held together by shared loyalties.[6] Western colonial civil servants exerted this specific influence gradually, indirectly, and usually, unintentionally. They abetted a nationalizing socialization process by displaying their own brand of nationalism depicted in their dedication, obedience, and personal sacrifices in the service of the "mother country." In several cases they strengthened this influence by incorporating the name of the Western colonial power in the "national" identification of the colonized society. Examples of this practice in Asia were the creation of *British* India, *French* Indochina, and the *Dutch* (or *Netherlands*) East Indies. The colonial bureaucracy also fomented a national consciousness by undertaking the task of "social mobilization" and "national integration" in organizing physical and human resources to pursue the official goals of the colonial policy.[7]

The process of state-building was advanced farther by Western colonial administrators than the process of nation-building. Yet neither process was completed during the period of Western colonial rule. The effective jurisdiction of the state was confined in most cases to strategic geographic boundaries, coastal areas, cities, and provincial regions containing important natural resources. Vast rural territories containing large segments of the indigenous population were never incorporated into the authority of the state. In effect, the Western colonial bureaucracies created what Professors Rejai and Enloe have labeled "skeletal states" or partially organized "frameworks for political decision-making."[8] The expansion of a genuine sense of nationalism caused by Western colonial administrators was even more restricted than the expansion of the authority of the state. With few exceptions, effective nation-building was limited to the initial interactions among a relatively small number of Westernized, urban-based indigenous leaders.

In spite of these limitations, Western colonial bureaucracies exhibited the greatly augmented political capacity of the nation-state to produce an increasingly organized and controlled secular environment. They vividly revealed the newly-discovered ability of Western science and technology to master many forces of nature. This new political capability accomplished official tasks far beyond the meager functions of the Asian traditional society. In addition to the maintenance of an unprecedented level of external and internal security, Western colonial administrators produced an environment conducive to rapid economic and social development, including the construction of modern infrastructure, the founding of Western-style educational institutions, and the reduction of ancient scourges such as famine, disease, and high infant mortality. They created a permanent need for a strong centralized political system and efficient administrative structures to perform essential governmental services and maintain a stable rule over a large geographic territory. They generated a new political entity in which the "urban" political elite had to be the "national" political elite. They established a model and a precedent which precluded future indigenous political leaders from reverting to the weak political system and the inefficient administrative structures of the traditional society. In transmitting the concept of the nation-state and in launching the processes of nation-building and state-building, the Western colonial administrators exhibited values, institutions, and modes of behavior in the period of a few decades which had required many centuries to achieve in Western societies. They artificially telescoped the fruitage of a long and turbulent historical process; they were unable to portray the full and heavy price exacted for many achievements of the Western nation-state.

Another historical input imparted by Western colonial administrators was the *concept of progress*. This value applied in the secular realm induced one of the most profound alterations in the colonized society. It overlapped with the achievement orientation embodied in the idea of the nation-state; it also comprised one of the most extensive "shared influences" with other Western linkages. In penetrating the colonized society with the concept of progress, the Western colonial bureaucracy portrayed the teleological view implanted in Western culture by the ancient Greeks that individual and collective life is motivated in some degree by a purpose, design, or goal. They likewise demonstrated some of the Western religious values derived from early Judeo-Christian teachings and intensified by the Reformation and the Renaissance that man and society are motivated by a "higher" spiritual law and a sense of compassion imparting some form of "upward" change in secular affairs. This norm engendered a need for an "advancement" toward a predetermined objective. It produced a desire for a series of purposeful actions seeking to "get ahead." It originated a pursuit for a gradual "development," an "elevation," or an "uplift" in mundane standards of living. It clashed severely with ascriptive loyalties and intensified achievement consciousness. It caused a perpetual dissatisfaction with the *status quo* and engendered cultural secularization. It created a technological viewpoint conducive to the multiplication of the works of man through the application of general scientific laws to the solution of specific concrete problems. Western colonial civil servants spread this idea by the formation of an orderly and controlled environment which made economic and social "improvements" possible through successive stages or degrees. The result was the diffusion of permanent and guided change.

A third historical input imparted by Western colonial administrators was *the concept of equality*. This fundamental value of Western political and legal theory was derived from the ancient Stoic doctrine upholding that in spite of numerous physical and personal differences, all men are of equal dignity and worth and should enjoy the rights of equal treatment by society. Influenced by subsequent Western thinkers such as John Locke and the Protestant Reformers, the idea developed in the political realm that all men have the right to equality before the law and government authorities have a primary responsibility in promoting equality of opportunity. The concept of equality was broadened from a focus on individual rights to an inherent right of sovereign nations by international lawyers such as Hugo Grotius. Both levels of equality were more an ideal than a reality in the domestic affairs and international relations among Western nations themselves, yet it was a norm by which governments and societies in the West increasingly measured their motives and actions.

Much of the style and conduct of colonial administrators in the colonization process in Asia depicted gross inequality. The entire justification for Western colonial rule was the assumed superiority of Western civilization over inferior Asian cultures. This attitude was strengthened by the tendency to recruit colonial administrators from the upper classes in Western societies who tended to assume a superior or paternalistic attitude toward the "lower" classes in Asia. Yet within the colonial systems this specific governmental linkage transmitted certain elements of the idea and practice of equality. Recruitment into the colonial administration by Westerners was usually accomplished by open and competitive examinations, and promotion in the colonial administrative hierarchy was based on the universalistic standards of merit and achievement, rather than particularistic criteria of social status and ascription. The regulations of Western administrative and legal systems in the colonization process were usually applied equally to individual indigenous persons of different social classes and ranks. Colonial administrators made varying attempts to prevent excessive abuses to specific indigenous groups and to reduce traditional barriers to equal opportunity.

Another historical input imparted by Western colonial administrators was *the expansion of cultural pluralism.* This intensified mode of behavior simultaneously counteracted some of the unifying forces generated by the colonial bureaucracy in state-building and nation-building. The addition of a new level of social heterogeneity was caused by several administrative actions. The formation of a single colonized society within a large territorial base automatically produced a more diversified population. The imposition of fragmented patterns of direct and indirect colonial rule subjected the indigenous populace to a variety of Western influences. These influences tended toward maximum effect in areas under direct colonial rule and minimal effect in areas under indirect colonial rule. By direct administrative action and by creating an environment conducive to rapid economic development, Western colonial bureaucracies caused an influx of transient and permanently-domiciled regional aliens into the colonized societies (with the exception of India and Korea). Western colonial administrators also facilitated the mobility of these regional aliens into economic roles either as skilled or unskilled artisans or as small-scale entrepreneurs. They likewise caused a new dimension of pluralism by the use of "divide and rule" administrative tactics. This policy consisted of applying special favors or sanctions to distinct ethnic groups to intensify divisions in indigenous movements seeking undesirable alterations in colonial policies or structures. This practice was most commonly and openly used in the eclectic-pragmatic colonial systems of Great Britain and Holland against nationalist movements in the twentieth century, although it was also applied in the unitary-doctrinaire systems hastily organized by Imperialist Japan in Southeast Asia during World War II.

The creation of state-nations with more pluralistic populations by Western colonial administrators resulted in the formation of two types of societies. A *dominant-ethnic society* consisted of a colonized society containing a single dominant ethnic group and one or more smaller ethnic minorities. The smaller ethnic minorities were clearly subordinate and inferior in size and potential influence compared to the dominant ethnic group. Examples of dominant-ethnic societies were Burma, Ceylon, Indonesia, Vietnam, Cambodia, and Korea in which Burmans, Sinhalese, Javanese, Vietnamese, Khmers, and Koreans respectively comprised a large majority of the indigenous populations. In these societies Western colonial administrators created social conditions in which the emerging nationalist movement and leadership came largely from the dominant ethnic group, and major schismatic tendencies developed within some of the smaller ethnic minorities during the final stages of colonial rule. A *consensual-ethnic society* consisted of a colonized society lacking a dominant ethnic group and containing two or more ethnic groups none of which comprised a significant majority of the population. Examples of consensual-ethnic societies are India, Pakistan, Malaya, Laos, and the Philippines.[9] In most of these societies a single ethnic group (such as the Aryans in India, the Bengalis in Pakistan, the Malays in Malaya, and the Lao-Thai in Laos) comprised a slight majority of the population. Yet other ethnic groups constituted minorities of considerable size and influence, and their combined population tended to balance that of the "slight-majority" ethnic group. In these societies Western colonial bureaucracies created social conditions in which the emerging nationalist movement and leadership came from two or more ethnic groups. The success of the nationalist cause required some form of social and political consensus among the leaders of the major ethnic groups. These conditions created a situation in which a single ethnic group confronted major internal opposition if or when it attempted to dominate the nationalist movement.

Another historical input induced by Western colonial administrators was the formation of *modern urbanization*. Professor Rhoads Murphey has defined the cities in Asia created by the Western impact as the "transplants of the new urban-commercial-industrial order" which "acted as both the spearheads and the catalysts of Asia's modernization."[10] Western colonial bureaucracies fomented the growth of these urban areas by two methods:. (1) by establishing capital cities, and (2) by promoting the growth of commercial cities. They performed the first role by constructing administrative facilities and official residences on a common site suitable for the effective government of the colonized society. These hubs of Western officialdom were invariably located on territory separate from the locus of the deposed great tradition, a practice which tended to reduce traditional loyalties and symbolized the formation of a new source of political and administrative power.[11] Capital cities were also founded near coastal or deltaic regions to facilitate official communications and administrative support from the "mother country" by means of sea transportation. Western colonial administrators accomplished the second method of city-building by establishing an environment and specialized administrative services conducive to the development of private commercial enterprise. Most commercial cities were also established near coastal areas to facilitate the expansion of industry and sea-borne trade. In many cases the capital city and the major commercial city were located on the same geographical site. Only in large colonial societies such as India, Indochina, and Indonesia were sizeable commercial cities founded away from the colonial capital.

In contrast to the religious or philosophical orientation of the great tradition, both types of modern cities created by Western colonial administrators became fountainheads of achievement-consciousness and cultural secularization. In contrast to the ceremonial and cultural roles of pre-Western "urban" centers, they directed thought toward the augmented political capacity of the Western nation-state and the flow of goods and services between internal sources and external markets. They focused attention toward the future, rather than the past. They engendered a "cosmopolitan" personality feeding on ideas and opinions from numerous external sources. In constructing these modern cities, the Western colonial bureaucracies added another and unique dimension of social pluralism. Urbanization served as a powerful magnet attracting external migration by regional aliens and internal migration by achievement-oriented subjects. In a relatively small geographic area these diversified migrants lived and worked in close proximity with each other. Some moved into specialized professional roles and formed the nucleus of a fledgling middle class. The Western-created cities inculcated these developing "national" elites with the vigor and potential of Western ideas and methods. They became the foci of social, economic, and political fermentation dispersing new concepts, opinions, and issues into an embryonic "mobile" society.[12] They served as training schools in indigenous nationalism and facilitated organization-building by the local nationalist movement. By establishing an environment suitable for the growth of metropolitan concentrations of unprecedented size, Western colonial civil servants also caused an unforeseen and unwanted by-product in the creation of vast urban slums. This trend witnessed a denigration of human life which contrasted sharply with genuine improvements and progressive influences imparted by this same linkage and other Western linkages through different functions. In discussing this "soul-destroying" influence by British colonial rule, Griffiths has stated:

> No European, estimating the impact of Britain on India, is entitled to ignore the unspeakable degradation of the life of the poor in the great modern Indian cities, and in India, as in Europe, the thoughtful observer must often wonder if the price paid for progress has been too high.[13]

A new historical input induced by Western colonial administrators was the transmission of a *Western language* to the colonized society. The thrust of this "primary instrument of social communication" was a function of the degree of transformation in the colonial social policy.[14] It exerted a maximum effect in the high-transformative social policies of

Great Britain, France (in Vietnam), the United States, and Japan; it exerted a minimal effect in the low-transformative social policies of Holland and France (in Laos and Cambodia). Within each colonized society, the process of spreading a Western language by Western colonial administrators was likewise one of the most widespread "shared influences" with other Western linkages. With few exceptions this role was confined primarily to urban areas. Western colonial civil servants tended to ignore indigenous languages thereby causing local persons with whom they dealt to learn the language of the Western colonial power. They required an understanding of this language as a prerequisite for employment in low-level administrative roles. In brief, they supplied the inducement to achievement-oriented subjects to master the Western *lingua franca* of law, administration, science, technology and commerce.

Western colonial officials also initiated *"humanitarian" reforms* and abolished certain indigenous customs which clashed with basic Western values. Some of these reforms were directly involved in the process of imposing a unified system of law and administration, including famine relief, the elimination of rural banditry, and the gradual abolition of slavery. Other reforms were implemented by Western colonial bureaucracies which depicted in some degree the desire of Western governments to elevate human life and dignity by means beyond the fundamental functions of providing defense and maintaining internal law and order. This elimination of local "inhumane" practices provided an early example of public support for "the general welfare." Western colonial administrators started this trend by reducing "barbarous" customs such as physical torture and the maltreatment of women and children.[15] They stopped specific "backward" religious usages such as *suttee* in India and ordeal by fire in Hinduized societies in Southeast Asia. In making these reforms, Western colonial officials established another precedent for future indigenous political leaders which tended to discourage the revival of these traditional customs following national independence.

Another historical input made by all Western colonial administrators was the establishment of *Western-oriented institutions of higher education*. These specialized structures launched the process of constructing an integrated and modern educational system in the colonized society. In their early stages, they were designed to assist the official goals of colonial policy. Spanish authorities aided in establishing the University of Santo Tomas in Manila early in the seventeenth century to provide higher education for Spanish youths residing in the Philippines, many of whom subsequently served in the colonial administration. Lord Wellesley, the Governor-General of the British East India Company, founded Haileybury College in 1806 to train personnel for the Indian Civil Service. Lord

Hastings started a Moslem college at Calcutta to promote cooperation between Moslems and Hindus. British officials also established the University of Rangoon in 1921 to provide education for a new and articulate youthful elite. American colonial administrators founded the first public institution of higher education in the Philippines by starting the University of the Philippines in 1908 to elevate economic and social standards and develop a democratic political system.[16] French colonial officials established the University of Hanoi to assist the spread of French culture, and Dutch colonial administrators started educational institutions in law, medicine, and technology to aid their economically-oriented colonial system. In spite of their original intentions, Western colonial bureaucracies added a highly diffused channel of Western values and behavioral patterns in establishing these institutions of higher education. These state-created universities became one of the most significant "modernizing" structures in the colonized society and they functioned as an important source of a new "national" culture. They supplied a unique medium dispensing achievement consciousness and a fertile breeding ground promoting indigenous nationalism. Their location in large metropolitan areas enhanced the urbanization process in attracting students from surrounding areas. They imparted the highest standards and instruction in spreading the language of the Western colonial power. Their academic curriculum and requirements served as a model to public and private secondary schools in the colonized society.

An important historical input generated by all Western colonial administrators was to serve as the major tangible *symbol of the "superiority" of Western culture.* This function was caused by specific concrete manifestations such as the construction of modern office buildings, lavish official residences, and exclusive recreational facilities. It was likewise induced by various modes of "snobbish" personal behavior and a sense of dominance over the indigenous society. This tendency was the most intense in the economic-oriented colonial systems of Great Britain and Holland; it was less intense in the tutelary colonial systems of France and the United States. Yet all Western colonial bureaucracies were characterized in some degree by a sense of "the white man's burden," an attitude made apparent to many indigenous persons by the Western display of self-confidence and determination even when confronting major administrative and technical problems. This posture of superiority implicitly imparted an element of inequality which clashed with the egalitarian concepts and behavioral patterns transmitted through other influences exerted by Western colonial civil servants. This symbolic relationship changed markedly after World War I with the decline of self-confidence and self-esteem among the Western colonial powers. Thereafter many Western colonial administrators in the high-transferable political and administrative structures openly voiced respect for the indigenous Asian cultures and expressed support for the accelerating movement toward national independence. Western colonial administrators in the low-transferable political and administrative structures sought to preserve their former dominant stature, and they continued to oppose reforms toward national independence. Yet their symbolism of superiority over colonial subject likewise tended to decline.

A final historical input imparted by all Western colonial administrators comprised the *promotion or performance of scholarly research* on various aspects of the indigenous society. Western colonial officials exercised this specific role in several ways. They promoted scholarly research within the colonized territory by providing the necessary security for professional Western scholars to conduct archeological and anthropological studies at the centers of former great traditions such as Orissa and Rajputana in India, Anuradhapura in Ceylon, Angkor in Cambodia, Borobudr in Java, and Pagan in Burma. In other cases the promotion of scholarship on Asian cultures by Western colonial administrators involved the formation of specialized research institutions, the most notable of which was the *École Francaise d'Extreme-Orient* established in Hanoi by Paul Doumer, the Governor-General of Indochina from 1897 to 1902.[17] Numerous Western colonial administrators wrote personal memoirs on their experiences and travels in the colonized society which often included official explanations and justifications of the existing colonial policy. A few Western colonial officials themselves engaged in serious pioneering research. The British were the most productive in imparting this influence. Thomas Stamford Raffles, the British governor of Java from 1811 to 1816, wrote *The History of Java* (1830) which was one of the first scholarly studies in this field in a Western language.[18] John Crawfurd, Raffles' deputy, wrote several significant books on Indonesia and other nearby societies, including a three-volume *History of the Indian Archipelago* (1820). These and other writings by Western colonial administrators assisted in arousing a deeper interest and curiosity in Asian cultures within the society of the Western colonial power, especially among professional scholars, as well as among a small and growing number of indigenous persons in the Asian colonized society. In addition to providing an expanding body of knowledge on cultural, social, and administrative affairs, Western colonial administrators did much to promote scientific research in new areas of interest such as tropical agriculture and medicine.

As stated previously, Western colonial administrators comprised an external linkage which imparted additional historical inputs in the colonized society according to the degree of transferability of their political and administrative structures. In Asia the most significant differentiation occurred between the high-transferable political and administrative structures of Great Britain (in territories under direct colonial rule) and the United States, and the low-transferable political and administrative structures of France, Holland, and Japan (in Korea and Taiwan).[19]

In high-transferable political and administrative structures, Western colonial administrators also served as the makers of a *rationalized indigenous bureaucracy*. They constituted the specific Western linkage building the "steel frame" of trained local personnel capable of administering the functions of a modern nation-state. These Western colonial bureaucracies created and transferred to indigenous control the modernizing governmental structures oriented more toward state-building than nation-building. They intensified the distribution of achievement values in the administrative realm. They supplied the model of an official administrative apparatus guided by the broad purpose of serving the general public welfare and theoretically deriving its ultimate authority from the sovereign will of an entire national populace. They established the precedent of civil servants administering a bureaucracy upholding impersonal, specific, and equal rights for all citizens.

The high-transferable political and administrative structures of Great Britain performed the specific role of administration-building more effectively than those of the United States. In contrast to the Americans, the British colonial administrators were more concerned with transferring bureaucratic efficiency than political skills.[20] They accomplished this task by maintaining the same educational and performance standards for indigenous personnel as for British personnel. Colonial subjects were admitted to high-level administrative positions only after passing open competitive examinations and gaining promotion according to universalistic criteria of merit and achievement. This slow and gradual process frustrated indigenous nationalists and intensified anti-Western sentiment. Yet it enabled British colonial officials to bequeath a qualified indigenous civil service and widespread respect for modern systems of administration and justice. American colonial officials in the Philippines engaged in indigenous bureaucracy-building at a faster pace than the British.[21] They placed less emphasis on the transfer of administrative efficiency and imposed a shorter training period for local personnel. They encouraged more political involvement in the performance of administrative functions than in British-created bureaucracies. In spite of these differences of emphasis, American colonial civil servants imparted many similar administrative values as the British.

Western colonial administrators in the low-transferable political and administrative structures of France, Holland, and Japan created highly rationalized and integrated bureaucratic organizations, yet they transferred few administrative skills to indigenous personnel. They confined state-building to Western administrative control and restricted indigenous experience in performing the bureaucratic functions of a modern nation-state. They transmitted little more than rudimentary administrative training to scattered groupings of low-level indigenous personnel, and they minimized the spread of achievement values in the administrative realm. This failure exacerbated hostility within the indigenous nationalist movement as knowledge of reforms by British and American colonial administrators slowly spread in these colonized societies.

A second historical input transmitted by Western colonial administrators in high-transferable political and administrative structures was the values and institutions of *constitutional democracy*. This specific influence was not imparted by the broad, direct, and planned methods used in administration-building since Western colonial officials could not themselves participate in indigenous politics. Only a portion of this democracy-building role was accomplished by the direct and preconceived action of supervising periodic free elections for an expanding indigenous electorate and creating legislative bodies to provide a forum for elected indigenous representatives. British colonial bureaucracies performed this role in implementing electoral and legislative reforms in India, Burma, Ceylon, Malaya, and Singapore from the Morley-Minto Reforms in 1909 until these colonial societies were granted independence after World War II. American colonial civil servants exerted a similar influence in the Philippines from the first indigenous elections held in 1907 until the creation of the Commonwealth in 1935. In addition to this direct process of making electoral systems and legislative bodies, these Western colonial administrators also created a framework and maintained an environment in which important supplementary modes of democratic behavior were formed and nourished. In the final stages of colonial rule, they articulated the democratic ideology and praised indigenous progress in democratic practices. They enforced special laws providing civil rights for colonial subjects, including the freedom of speech and freedom of the press which facilitated the spread of democratic values and behavior.[22]

The entire process of implanting constitutional democracy was oriented more toward nation-building than state-building. It opened wider channels for the indigenous nationalist movement to engage overtly in the initial steps of social mobilization and national integration. It stressed achievement values in the political realm which greatly intensified the fervor of indigenous nationalism. Western colonial administrators in these high-transferable political and administrative structures also generated overt interest articulation by recognizing, assisting, and restraining various racial, religious, economic, and social groups. They induced overt interest aggregation by recognizing and legitimizing the nationalist movement, usually composed of diverse coalitions and political parties. They abetted the evolution of experienced modernizing civilian elites by recognizing elected leaders of the nationalist movement as the spokesmen of a newly-emerging "national" society. They added to the political stature of these indigenous leadership groups by alternately opposing some of their demands and yielding to others. In brief, they caused both the personal sacrifices and the political achievements which elevated many indigenous leaders to "national" prominence. In the final stages of the colonial system, these Western colonial administrators provided policy-making experience in both executive and administrative roles to these emerging political elites.

The high-transferable political and administrative structures of the United States performed the role of imparting constitutional democracy more effectively than those of Great Britain. American colonial officials started earlier than their British counterparts in holding free elections for large electorates and in yielding to the demands of indigenous nationalists. They admitted the indigenous political elite more rapidly into high policy-making positions and they created a more conducive environment in which a democratic political system was formed and developed. In spite of these different methods, both types of Western colonial administrators transferred many similar democratic values and modes of behavior.

Western colonial administrators in the low-transferable political and administrative structures prevented the development of constitutional democracy. Dutch colonial officials in Indonesia held elections among a small propertied electorate for seats in the Volksraad after World War I, but this advisory colonial legislature primarily represented elected representatives of Dutch private interests and appointed indigenous representatives sympathetic to the continuation of Dutch colonial rule. French and Japanese colonial bureaucracies held no genuinely representative elections in their colonial systems, and they provided only token representation by indigenous sympathizers on a few advisory councils. In contrast to the favorable democratic environment produced by British and American colonial administrators, these low-transferable political and administrative structures purposely discouraged and suppressed the spread of democratic values and behavior. They enforced specific laws designed to restrict nationalist sentiment and imposed severe punishments for violations by colonial nationalists. They thereby precluded initial overt attempts by indigenous leaders to engage in nation-building and social mobilization. They obviated overt interest articulation by indigenous groups or overt interest aggregation by the indigenous nationalist movement and political parties. They imparted a negative and hostile orientation to indigenous nationalism which directed local nationalist groups toward covert political action inside the colonized society and both overt and covert political activity in exile. They likewise produced the personal sacrifices and martyrdom which enhanced the political stature of many indigenous nationalist leaders after national independence.

Another historical influence made by Western colonial administrators in high-transferable political and administrative structures was to induce increasingly *differentiated and specialized sub-systems* in the colonized society. They generated more of what Professors Almond and Powell have called "subsystem autonomy."[23] They imparted this important historical input by creating an increasing number of differentiated and specialized roles among the indigenous populace. These Western colonial bureaucracies formed a highly autonomous and specialized political and administrative system which was gradually transferred to indigenous control. They likewise developed an environment in which other differentiated sub-systems were able to emerge and grow. Directly and indirectly they aided the establishment of significant secondary structures such as educational systems and voluntary associations in expanding urban areas which induced a more autonomous sphere of secularized social activity. They also created an environment conducive for the development of a private and multi-faceted economic system. The increasing specialization of new roles among the growing private sector caused increasing autonomy and differentiation in the economic realm. In brief, Western colonial administrators in the high-transferable political and administrative structures provided the foundation on which a new type of national society began to emerge consisting of increasing specialization and differentiation among its political, economic, social, and cultural sub-systems.

Western colonial administrators in the low-transferable political and administrative structures generated relatively little differentiation and specialization among the sub-systems of their colonized societies. They induced relatively minor "subsystem autonomy." Instead they purposely hampered the development of private economic and social sectors which could have involved increasing numbers of colonial subjects. They exerted a centralized political control over the indigenous populace and maintained an integrated authority over all significant economic and social activities. They created few structures outside the political and administrative system through which colonial subjects could develop autonomous or specialized roles. In effect, the Western colonial bureaucracies with low-transferable political and administrative structures retained a "modernized" form of those elements of the defunct great tradition of the pre-Western society in which the political, economic, social, and cultural sub-systems were essentially undifferentiated and fused.

An additional historical input involving Western colonial administrators in high-transferable political and administrative structures was their role as the major tangible *target of the emerging nationalist movement.* This specific influence was closely related to the indigenous hostility caused by Western colonial bureaucracies serving as symbols of the superiority of Western culture. This role became increasingly significant following the decline of Western self-confidence after World War I.[24] The expanding indigenous nationalist organizations directed their broad efforts toward the termination of all aspects of Western domination, yet their primary goal was to obtain control of the political and administrative system created by the Western colonial administrators. These Western colonial civil servants thereby became the chief focal point of the growing indigenous opposition to Western colonial rule. Their power and privileges served to agitate and unify the diverse groups within the nationalist movement.[25] Their presence indicated that the Western colonial system was still operating and intact. In the eyes of the local nationalists only the removal of these Western colonial administrators from the territory of the colonized society would symbolize the achievement of national independence. In this role the British and American colonial administrators might be called "targets of reform" since they intermittently yielded to the demands of nationalist leaders for increasing indigenous influence over the political and administrative system. These reforms merely whetted the appetite of the nationalist movement for more and broader reforms. At times British and American colonial civil servants caused increasing anti-colonial hostility and stronger nationalist sentiment by balking and delaying the process of transferring political authority to indigenous leaders. Yet they never permanently suppressed the nationalist movement. In spite of much contention and unrest within the local nationalist organizations, they encouraged the development of a relatively moderate form of indigenous nationalism which pursued the achievement of national independence primarily by overt, gradual, and nonviolent means.

The Western colonial administrators of the low-transferable political and administrative structures served the same role as targets of the emerging nationalist movement. Yet they might be called "targets of revolution.'' The Dutch, French, and Japanese officials in these colonial systems implemented no important reforms when confronted by demands from indigenous nationalist leaders for a larger voice in the administration of colonial policy. In varying degrees they realized that even the most modest political reforms would merely open the floodgate for new demands seeking broader changes and the eventual achievement of national independence. Instead they maintained an implacable opposition to indigenous nationalism and suppressed its outcroppings by secret informants, incarceration, harsh physical punishment, and occasional police or military action. The reaction of many local nationalists toward these stringent and unbending targets of revolution promoted the development of a militant form of indigenous nationalism which found no other channel in the pursuit of national independence except through covert, revolutionary, and violent means. In brief, the Western colonial administrators of the low-transferable political and administrative structures by their policy and example indirectly served as mentors of intrigue, subversion, and/or guerrilla warfare to the indigenous nationalist movement.

WESTERN RESIDENT ADVISERS

Western resident advisers constituted an external linkage which imparted limited and specific influences in territories (usually middle traditions of the traditional society) administered by indirect colonial rule. These specialized colonial officials and their small professional staffs performed a combined diplomatic-administrative role in implementing colonial policy in societies usually of lesser economic and strategic importance located adjacent to the colonized society. This unique form of external influence and control was used by Great Britain through treaties negotiated with traditional rulers in more than five hundred Princely States in India and the five Unfederated States in Malaya.[26] France imposed a somewhat similar relationship by establishing a *resident superieur* in Cambodia and Laos after these two Indochinese territories became protectorates at the end of the nineteenth century. The primary function of the Western resident adviser was to provide for the defense of the territory and to maintain internal security. In some cases he also assisted in promoting limited economic development. According to the legal formalities, the Western resident adviser was supposed to ''advise'' the traditional rulers in the administration of these secular affairs; in practice he controlled the administration of these partially-colonized territories. The indigenous ruler, however, retained his traditional authority over cultural, religious, and social affairs. He was provided with a regular monetary stipend from the Western colonial power for his cooperation and loyalty. In many cases this financial income was larger and more consistent than the resources available to the traditional ruler prior to the imposition of indirect colonial rule.

The Western resident advisers imparted several historical inputs similar to those extended by the Western colonial administrators. They promoted a higher degree of cultural pluralism in the emerging national societies (except Cambodia) by inducing a greatly reduced pattern of Western influences compared to the modernizing trends in the adjoining territory under direct colonial rule. They assisted in preserving traditionalism as well as many cultural differences among disparate ethnic and linguistic groups. The Western resident adviser also aided in imparting a Western language to the traditional ruler and most members of the ruling class. His pre-eminent administrative position likewise caused him to serve as a symbol of the "superiority" of Western capability in the management of secular affairs.

The major distinctive influence of the Western resident adviser was to serve as a *model of modernization* to the traditional ruler and the ruling class of the territory administered by indirect colonial rule. This specific Western influence abolished the effective political power of the traditional ruling class and made its position dependent on the Western colonial power. Yet the security and order provided by Western colonial rule supplied the opportunity for some members of this small indigenous elite to attain a deep exposure to Western modernization and culture. In some cases certain members of the traditional ruling class acquired a more extensive and variegated insight into Western civilization than many people living under direct colonial rule. The symbolic authority and personal example of the Western resident adviser aroused their interest in Western modernization and encouraged the effort to obtain a Western education, usually first at intermediate schools in the nearby colonized society and thereafter at universities in the Western colonial power. The regularized subsidy granted to the traditional rulers under the system of indirect colonial rule provided the means to finance this higher education.

In performing this role the Western resident adviser assisted in the individual development of some of the major nationalist leaders in South and Southeast Asia. Many upper-class Indians from the princely states obtained their intermediate education in British India and their professional training at universities in Great Britain. Mahatma Gandhi's father and grandfather were traditional rulers in the Kathiawar princely states, and Gandhi attended a British high school at Rajkot and obtained a law degree through a matriculation course at London University.[27] Jawaharlal Nehru was born in Allahabad in British India, yet his parents were the descendants of a prosperous Brahmin family from the princely state of Kashmir which had migrated to northern India during the early phase of British colonial rule. Nehru received his early education from English tutors and governesses and he obtained professional training in law and natural science at Harrow and Cambridge in England. A similar trend occurred among the traditional rulers and their scions in Malaya, Laos, and Cambodia. The father of Tengku Abdul Rahman was the Sultan of the unfederated state of Kedah, and the Tengku received his middle education at a British high school in Alor Star and a law degree from Cambridge. King Sisavang Vong of Luang Prabang received a year's education in Paris early in the twentieth century and started the practice of sending male members of the Laotian royal and upper-class families to intermediate French schools in Vietnam and to universities in France for advanced professional training, usually in law or engineering. Both Prince Souvanna Phouma and Prince Souphanouvong obtained engineering degrees from French universities. Prince Norodom Sihanouk likewise was educated at a French lycée in Saigon and he made frequent observation trips to metropolitan France.

The Western resident advisers, in brief, exerted a modest but potentially significant influence in initiating the process of developing some of the most notable nationalist figures in Asia. They assisted in the formation of future leaders whose lives were influenced by an admixture of traditional and Western values and whose political careers sought to extend to their own people what they considered the best elements in the two cultures. Their chief goal was the achievement of national independence, a value which grew in intensity from their early exposure to modernization through contacts with the Western resident adviser and the advances he implemented through indirect colonial rule.

A second historical influence of the Western resident adviser was to strengthen *the non-political functions of the traditional ruler and to bolster traditionalism among the rural populace.* This historical input contrasted markedly with the first role of facilitating deep exposure to Western modernization for some members of the indigenous ruling families. This linkage served specifically to enhance the traditional institution of indigenous rulership. It was caused by the augmented capacity of the Western-administered system of indirect colonial rule, the Western security forces which reduced threats from external and internal rivals, and the steady financial income from the Western colonial power. These Western-sponsored services relieved the traditional ruler of his former political and administrative responsibilities, reduced the taxes he was required to extract from his own people, and, in most cases, eliminated the intermittent need to recruit young male villagers for military service. This new role enabled the traditional ruler to devote virtually his full time to religious and cultural affairs. In this endeavor he was able to strengthen numerous court and ceremonial functions which previously had been neglected or only partially fulfilled. He was able to assume certain religious roles which formerly had been delegated to the priestly class. He was able to utilize these new social powers to forge closer personal and institutional bonds with larger numbers of his own people. These new opportunities generated a growing desire to retain a cultural identity separate from the modernizing behavior induced by Western influences in the nearby colonized society. In exercising this role, the Western resident adviser in effect assisted in shielding traditional values and behavior from competing Western influences. He indirectly hampered the extension of other Western linkages into the semi-colonized society, and he impeded changes capable of leading toward political, economic, and social modernization. When the territories administered by Western resident advisers were incorporated into new national societies at the time of national independence, they were relatively untouched by the Western impact. They comprised some of the most traditional areas of the new nation-state.

WESTERN COLONIAL MILITARY FORCES

Western colonial military forces exerted their influences in two historical phases. They were first used in establishing either direct or indirect colonial rule. This action involved the direct application of Western military power against indigenous military forces and/or against the military forces of a competing Western colonial power.[28] In this phase both the ground and naval forces of the Western colonial power played important roles, with naval forces often exercising a decisive influence in the final outcome. The ground forces tended to exert a temporary influence over a widespread geographic area since they were deployed wherever organized resistance to the imposition of colonial rule occurred. The second phase involved the use of Western colonial military forces to maintain the colonial system after it was established. In this role these military forces supplied the coercive power which supported the roles of the colonial administrators and resident advisers. They largely comprised a security mission designed to preserve internal order and to discourage external threats.

In the second phase, Western colonial ground forces exercised the dominant military influence in shaping indigenous behavior. Western colonial powers continued to maintain sizeable naval forces, but they were seldom seen by the local populace and with few exceptions their role was not apparent to most of the indigenous population. The ground forces exerted their influences largely at strategic locations in the territory of the colonized society where they were permanently stationed, primarily near major administrative and commercial cities, ports, railroad centers, and sensitive border areas.[29]

The specialized historical inputs transmitted by Western colonial military forces tended to overlap with certain influences imparted by the Western colonial administrators. One of their major roles was to strengthen the concept of the nation-state and enhance its institutionalization by providing the coercive instrument necessary for the effective functioning of the legal and administrative systems of the colonized society. Their use or the threat of their use bolstered the process of state-building and delayed the process of nation-building. The colonial military forces supplied the power base for the colonial administrators which obviated the need for developing a common national consensus among diverse indigenous groups until the final stages of colonial rule or after national independence. They illustrated vividly that a modern nation-state and a modernized political and administrative system required a rationalized and professional body of trained military forces.

Western colonial military forces assisted in conveying the concept of progress by serving as a model of modern science and military technology. Their military achievements during both phases of the colonial system displayed the superiority of Western military power over traditional weapons and tactics. In the early period of establishing colonial rule, they exerted a powerful demonstration effect by their conquest of the sea and the overthrow of many great and middle traditions with relatively small military forces. The Portuguese initiated this influence early in the sixteenth century by constructing sea-worthy vessels capable of accommodating large numbers of men for long ocean voyages, and by developing "the ship carrying cannon" with a longer range and better accuracy than the weapons of their enemies.[30] This combination of navigational skills and modern sea power enabled the Portuguese to establish their first colonial outpost on the coast of India and command the Indian Ocean for almost a century. Similar feats were achieved by Western colonial military forces on land. In 1746 a force of 230 French troops and 700 Indian mercenaries defending the port city of Madras routed an attacking force of more than 10,000 troops of the Nawab of the Carnatic by the adroit use of maneuver and modern artillery power. According to Griffiths, "This action had an electric effect. It made the military reputation of the French in the Carnatic forthwith and inculcated in the minds of Indian commanders a wholesome respect for European arms and discipline.''[31] This influence was further strengthened after the famous Battle of Plassey in 1757 in which a small contingent of British troops commanded by Robert Clive defeated the larger military forces of the Nawab Siraj-ud-daulah which ended French influence in India and launched Great Britain on the path of building several colonial systems in South and Southeast Asia.

The demonstration effect of the superiority of Western military power was continued by the colonial military forces in the performance of their security mission after the colonial systems were established. One method of exhibiting the efficacy of Western science and military technology was the elimination of challenging internal insurgencies such as the British suppression of the Sepoy Mutiny in India in 1857 and the Saya San rebellion in Burma in 1931–2, the success of American army units in quelling the armed insurrection of the Moros in the southern Philippines in 1917–8, and in the Dutch crushing of the Communist-led revolt in Java in 1926–7. In addition to these relatively rare overt applications of Western military power, the colonial military forces exerted their role as a model of modern military technology on a more widespread and frequent basis by the use of military parades, land maneuvers, and naval port calls.

Additional linkages of the Western colonial military forces, like those of the colonial administrators, were a function of the degree of transferability of political and administrative structures. The most significant differentiation in Asia occurred between the high-transferable military structures of Great Britain (in British India, Ceylon, and Malaya) and the United States, and the low-transferable military structures of Holland, France, and Japan (in Korea and Taiwan). The Japanese utilized a special type of high-transferable military structure in several countries of Southeast Asia during World War II.

The high-transferable military structures of Great Britain and the United States served as the architects of a *modernized indigenous military force*. These Western colonial military services imparted this important influence by engaging in a training mission similar to that of the colonial administrators, although in the case of Great Britain the transfer of military roles to indigenous personnel was made more gradually and cautiously than the transfer of administrative roles. Both types of high-transferable military structures performed this training role by incorporating large numbers of indigenous personnel into the colonial military forces and transmitting a Western language to many local officers. Great Britain provided military training by maintaining an army structure in which all top officers were British and a sizeable and expanding portion of middle-level officers were recruited from the local population. Qualified indigenous personnel were commissioned as officers only after many years of military experience usually combined with advanced professional training at Sandhurst. A similar procedure was used in creating a small navy and air force in each colonial system after World War I. The vast majority of enlisted men in all British colonial military forces were recruited from indigenous "martial" races. The British used relatively few of their own nationals as enlisted troops in maintaining their colonial rule.

The training role of American military forces in the Philippines was largely delayed until the formation of the Commonwealth in 1935, not because the United States feared the possibility of a local armed uprising against the colonial system, but due to the maintenance of sizeable American army, navy, and air force units in the archipelago to discourage external threats.[32] This condition was also maintained because of the prevailing American attitude that large indigenous military forces might be inimical to the development of constitutional democracy. The establishment of the Commonwealth and the growing threat of war after the mid-1930's urged the United States to accelerate the transfer of military roles to Filipinos.[33] This process was performed in a manner similar to that used by British colonial military forces. The Philippine Army was created by the first Commonwealth government and placed under the command of Lt. General Douglas MacArthur. The Philippine Scouts was set up as a separate but integral part of the United States Army largely officered by Americans with Filipinos comprising all enlisted ranks. American army units formed and trained the Philippine Constabulary, a semi-military force designed to maintain internal security which was largely officered by Filipinos. Philippine personnel also served in the Asiatic Squadron of the United States Navy, usually in the enlisted ranks. Many officers in the Philippine Scouts and Philippine Constabulary were graduates of West Point; a few Filipino naval officers received advanced professional training at Annapolis.

The low-transferable military structures of the Netherlands, France, and Japan engaged in little or no transfer of military roles to indigenous personnel, primarily due to the justifiable fear of armed action against the colonial system. The Dutch in Indonesia relied entirely on their own nationals in all ranks of the colonial military forces. The only exception was the provision of modest military training to a few thousand trusted Christians in Amboina just prior to World War II. The French in Indochina likewise utilized their own nationals to fill almost all ranks of the colonial military forces, and until World War II they refrained from giving military training and equipment to sizeable numbers of indigenous personnel. After the outbreak of open warfare against the Communist-led Viet Minh the French colonial military forces trained non-Communist Vietnamese officers (usually Roman Catholics) as well as an expanding enlisted ground force which until national independence was usually commanded by French officers. This military training provided an important socializing influence on a small indigenous officer corps which assumed a significant political role after national independence. Many of these military leaders contributed to the political power of Ngo Dinh Diem just after the termination of French colonial rule, and top-ranking Vietnamese officers such as Nguyen Van Thieu and Nguyen Cao Ky assumed powerful political roles after the overthrow of Diem in 1963. Japan adhered to a similar policy in refraining from transferring military roles to indigenous persons in Taiwan and Korea, although the Japanese trained a small Korean military force during World War II.[34] As in Vietnam, this military training imparted a socializing influence to a small group of Korean military officers who played an important political role in supporting the Syngman Rhee regime after 1948 and in assuming key political positions in the military-dominated governments after 1960. The most notable Korean military leader trained by the Japanese who subsequently assumed a powerful political role is Park Chung Hee. Also during World War II, the Japanese performed the role of high-transferable military structures by creating and equipping new "nationalist" military forces in Burma and Indonesia to support their policy of manipulating indigenous nationalism against the former Western colonial powers and to promote local sentiment favorable to the goals of the Greater East Asia Co-Prosperity Sphere.

A second historical input caused by high-transferable military structures was the *expansion of cultural pluralism* within the colonized society. This specific linkage involved the use of "divide and rule" tactics in bestowing special favors and benefits on the particular indigenous ethnic groups who provided the bulk of the locally recruited officers and troops for the colonial military forces. This external influence was exercised only by the high-transferable military structure of Great Britain in India and Burma; the United States did not recruit Filipino military personnel on the basis of racial or ethnic origin.[35] The British colonial military forces intensified pluralism by purposely selecting their indigenous military personnel from the local "martial" races. These ethnic groups consisted of minority groups possessing traditional grievances against the larger "non-martial" groups in the colonized society. According to Professor Frank Trager, "The general troops and military police [in India and Burma] were recruited from among the ethnic minorities so as to insure better protection against the untrusted majority.''[36] The British provided special administrative favors to the provincial areas inhabited by these minority groups in recognition of their contribution to the colonial military forces and the preservation of order in the colonial system. In India the martial races included the Sikhs, Gurkhas, Rajputs, Jats, Punjabi Muslims, Baluchis, and Dogras; in Burma they consisted largely of the Karens, Chins, and Kachins, as well as a sizeable force of Indian military personnel. In Malaya the British also strengthened cultural pluralism, but they imparted this influence by recruiting indigenous military personnel solely among the Malays who comprised the majority ethnic group and were fearful of domination by the economic skills of the large Chinese minority.[37] The use of martial races in occasional police actions against non-martial ethnic groups augmented many traditional hostilities and intensified communal loyalties.

The low-transferable military structures of Holland and France also imparted divisive influences in their colonial systems, although they generated a much lower level of pluralism which occurred only under emergency conditions near the end of colonial rule. This influence largely involved the formation of a schism between the dominant population and a small indigenous group favored by the colonial military forces on the basis of their status as Christian converts. The Dutch caused this relatively insignificant split by arming the small Protestant minority in Amboina. The French induced a potentially important fragmentation within Vietnamese society by transferring military roles at the officer level in the army and air force largely to Vietnamese Roman Catholics.

GOVERNMENTAL LINKAGES INVOLVED IN THE UNEQUAL TREATY PROCESS

The governmental linkages involved in the unequal treaty process were *Western diplomats, Western national military forces,* and *Western advisers.* The Western historical inputs transmitted by these external linkages were imparted largely by the major Western powers.

Western Diplomats

The external linkage formed by Western diplomats in the unequal treaty process corresponded in some aspects with the penetration of the Western colonial administrators in the colonization process. The Western diplomats, like the colonial administrators, comprised the chief official channel implementing the policies of their own government. The influence of Western diplomacy, however, was much more limited than that of

Western colonial authority since the indigenous political system was not abolished and many goals pursued by Western nations through the unequal treaty process depended on the performance of local rulers. In administering the foreign policy of their government, Western diplomats and their official staffs engaged in the dual role of dealing on an equal basis with the indigenous political elite in some aspects of diplomatic relations and on a superior-inferior basis in enforcing the special privileges of the unequal treaties. The direct influence of Western diplomats in this unique international relationship was confined primarily to the indigenous ruling class since Western diplomatic officials had little personal contact with the local populace. Their impact was imparted almost entirely in urban areas since they exercised their influence through an embassy (or legation) located at the national capital of the semi-independent Asian society and at consular offices (and leased concessions in China) in treaty ports.

Some historical inputs exerted by Western diplomats were similar to the influences imparted by Western colonial administrators. They conveyed the Western concept of the nation-state with its value system upholding a fixed "national" territory, a population unified by common "national" loyalties, and a sovereign political authority administering a common body of "national" law. Yet unlike the colonial administrators who directly engaged in the formation of many prerequisites for nationhood, the Western diplomats indirectly transmitted this concept through official contacts and negotiations with indigenous rulers and through their judicial role in administering extraterritorial authority in the consular courts. In the conduct of official diplomacy they demonstrated the idea of the nation-state by exposing the local government to some of the basic principles and practices of international law, including territorial sovereignty, diplomatic immunity, and most-favored nation treatment. In their judicial capacity they illustrated some of the legal rights and benefits derived from the possession of Western national citizenship. Local rulers soon realized that the jurisdiction of unified and corporate Western nation-states possessed sufficient power and resources to uphold these rights granted to their citizens under the unequal treaties.

Western diplomats also initiated the overlapping developmental processes of state-building and nation-building. They aided the process of state-building by imposing on the indigenous ruling class the requirement to create and maintain sufficient administrative and legal structures for the conduct of normal diplomatic and commercial relations with other nations. They required the establishment of unified and impersonal corporate structures over the recognized territory of the society with sufficient capacity to uphold the treaty commitments made with the

Western powers and to protect Western nationals residing at authorized locations. In two of the semi-independent Asian societies, Western diplomats exerted an important influence in the formation of national boundaries. British, French, and Russian diplomats played a significant role in the settlement of most of the present national borders of the People's Republic of China; British and French diplomats exerted a similar role in establishing all present national boundaries of Thailand. This influence was obviated in the case of Japan due to its insular location and the early termination of its unequal treaties.

Like the Western colonial administrators, Western diplomats exercised an influence in the process of nation-building. Yet unlike the delayed development of a national consciousness in the colonial systems, the process of nation-building in the semi-independent Asian societies began simultaneously with the process of state-building. Instead of inducing a new "national" identity among diverse indigenous leaders and groups as in the colonized societies, the interference of Western diplomats in the unequal treaty process served to prod the indigenous ruling class into arousing traditional loyalties and racial pride among its own people. In this capacity Western diplomats served as a catalyst which united certain local cultural forces in the early pursuit for a national community.[38] Western diplomatic officials indirectly abetted the creation of a national consciousness by encouraging the local political elite to attain a higher level of "social mobilization" and "national integration" over its human and physical resources. This popular movement was important to prevent further infringements by the Western powers on the tenuous "national" sovereignty. In effect, Western diplomats fomented a more balanced approach to the dual processes of state-building and nation-building in the semi-independent societies in Asia than Western colonial administrators induced in the colonized societies. By the twentieth century the leaders in Japan and Thailand had established effective state institutions and a growing nationalist sentiment within their national boundaries. In China an imbalance between a more advanced nation-building process and a less developed state-building process was caused by the ineptitude of the Manchu dynasty prior to 1912 and extensive foreign interference until after World War II.

Western diplomats also imparted the concept of progress. This influence was partially achieved in the overt display of administering more efficient governmental structures than the indigenous rulers. It was likewise transmitted by the assumption underlying the unequal treaties which implied the superiority of many aspects of Western culture. The extraterritorial rights protected by Western diplomats illustrated the need for indigenous rulers to improve their own administrative and judicial systems so as to comply with Western standards. The imposition of these special privileges for Western nationals was increasingly galling to the local government, but it served as a painful reminder that its judicial and legal system was inferior to those in the West, and many internal improvements would be required before the unequal treaties could be terminated. The idea of progress was intensified by the understanding that Western diplomats would recommend the abolition of extraterritoriality to their governments when the inferior local conditions were rectified. This progressive influence aided in the dissemination of achievement values and cultural secularization in urban areas. In these locations this trend generated a dissatisfaction among certain indigenous groups with the *status quo* and engendered a propensity toward change. Western diplomats at consular offices in treaty ports strengthened this movement by promoting an environment which caused an expanding flow of commerce from the interior of the society into the channels of international trade.

Like the colonial administrators, the diplomats of Western nations on the surface demonstrated little of the Western concept of equality. The entire unequal treaty process was based on the assumption that Western judicial systems were superior to Asian legal customs. Yet in some aspects, Western diplomats did convey certain egalitarian influences. In handling extraterritorial cases they exerted a modest demonstration effect by applying their own systems of law to their nationals on the basis of individual equality. The gradual mitigation of some of the restrictions imposed by the unequal treaty process as indigenous judicial systems incorporated higher Western standards exposed Chinese, Japanese, and Thai people to more of the rights they would eventually enjoy in an international system upholding the principle of national equality. The concept of national equality was likewise strengthened by numerous diplomatic usages, including arbitration, mediation, immunity, and most-favored-nation treatment.

In promoting an environment conducive to the growth of modern urbanization, Western diplomats aided in fostering *a geographical and functional division between the national capital of the semi-independent Asian society serving as a political and administrative center and other local cities chiefly engaged in commerce and trade.* Western embassies (or legations) at the national capital constituted a reminder to the indigenous rulers of Western encroachments on their society. While these Western diplomatic missions induced certain administrative reforms, they also caused the local political elites to retain many elements of traditionalism. On the other hand, Western consular offices at the treaty ports assisted in promoting a rapid expansion of commerce and trade. In many cases they played a role favorable to the creation of entirely new cities inhabited by increasing numbers of indigenous transients seeking new employment and better economic opportunities. In these new coastal cities traditionalism was less intense than at the national capital. Western diplomats helped them become the most modernized urban centers in the semi-independent society.

In China, the national capital at Peking witnessed some modernizing innovations caused by the unequal treaty process, yet it was preserved by the ruling regime as a major center of Chinese culture and tradition. The Western consular offices at treaty ports such as Shanghai, Dairen, Tsing-tao, and Canton, on the other hand, facilitated an environment in which these distant coastal cities were developed as the major centers of Chinese urbanization and modernization. In Japan this influence of Western diplomats was modified somewhat since Tokyo had been recently reestablished as a new national capital and it also became a lead-ing commercial center. Yet traditionalism remained stronger in Tokyo than in other modernizing coastal cities such as Yokahama, Osaka, and Kobe. In Thailand the influence of Western diplomats aided in the growth of Bangkok as both the national capital and the major commer-cial center. Yet even here a modest geographic separation and a large functional differentiation occurred between the Thai ruling class which maintained political and administrative power at the royal palace and government ministries, and the Chinese merchants who dominated sev-eral major commercial areas within the confines of the Thai national capital.

Western diplomats, like Western colonial administrators, transmitted a Western language. They also tended to avoid learning indigenous lan-guages thereby requiring increasing numbers of persons in the local government dealing with Western diplomatic missions to learn a Western language. In the initial stages of the unequal treaty process this need was often obviated by conducting diplomatic negotiations through a few local or foreign bilingual interpreters. Yet in time the mastery of certain Western languages became a prerequisite for effective diplomacy by the indigenous government. This need became especially important to illus-trate the local adoption of many elements of Western culture and assist the quest to abolish the unequal treaties. This task involved the mastery of only the languages of the high-demonstrative diplomatic missions of the major Western powers. In all three semi-independent Asian societies, English and French became the Western languages of international diplo-macy and trade, although for a brief time German and Russian were used in some areas of China. The English and French languages consequently became major channels exposing the urban areas of these societies to the advances of modern Western civilization. Western officials of the diverse low-demonstrative diplomatic missions aided this linguistic and acculturation process since they also were required to use English or French in their dealings with the indigenous government.

Western diplomats likewise served as the official tangible symbols of the "superiority" of Western culture in the semi-independent societies. The presence and extraterritorial authority of Western diplomats depicted the wide differences between Western and Asian cultures. This system based on Western supremacy was a sharp reversal of the pre-Western intersocietal relations in two of the semi-independent Asian societies. For many centuries China had maintained a superior attitude and role in dealing with adjacent non-Chinese societies. Thailand likewise, had considered itself a vassal state of imperial China, yet it had maintained a position of superiority at various times over smaller adjoining kingdoms in Laos, Cambodia, and Malaya.

The historical input generated by Western diplomats as symbols of the superiority of Western culture were closely related to the role of serving as a major tangible target of the emerging nationalist movement. Western diplomatic missions directly exerted this specific influence in the early stages of the growth of nationalism in the semi-independent Asian societies by provoking hostile actions against their installations and personnel. Yet modernizing leaders of the indigenous nationalist movement quickly realized that their long-range goals would not be fulfilled by the physical removal of Western diplomats from their society, but in abolishing the unequal treaties through the use of negotiation. Emerging nationalist leaders wanted a diplomatic relationship in which Western diplomats would conduct official business only on the basis of national equality, rather than the superior-inferior relationship of extraterritoriality. The presence and authority of Western diplomats caused indigenous nationalists to pursue this goal by first overthrowing their own traditional ruling elite in order to establish a new modernizing state and eventually deal with Western diplomacy from a position of strength. They could then achieve their goal of terminating the unequal treaties.

This indirect role of Western diplomats in aiding the growth of nationalism was seen most clearly in Japan and China. The initial policy of the fledgling Japanese nationalist movement in the 1850's and 1860's following the negotiation of the unequal treaties with Western powers consisted briefly of the reactionary and militant effort to "expel the (Western) barbarians." When this endeavor failed because of the military power supporting Western diplomacy, the nationalists switched to a "revere the emperor" policy in an effort to remove the Tokugawa Shogunate and establish a strong modernizing state capable of developing Japan and dealing with Western nations on a powerful and equal basis.[39] This role of Western diplomats was likewise seen in the move of the nationalist movement in China to overthrow the Manchu dynasty in the Taiping Rebellion in the 1850's and 1860's, in the abolition of the traditional Confucian system in 1912, and in the "unification" of China under the Kuomintang in 1928. As in Japan, the Chinese nationalists were seeking sufficient national unity and power to deal with Western nations on a more equal basis to abolish the unequal treaties. The slow evolution of nationalism in Thailand largely precluded this role of Western diplomacy since the unequal treaties were largely removed during the time of the absolute monarchy. Yet a chief goal of the small group of Westernized civilian and military officials who overthrew the absolute monarchy in 1932 was to reduce the favored economic status which had been achieved by Europeans (and Chinese) through the unequal treaties.[40]

Western diplomats, like Western colonial administrators, promoted and produced some significant published writings and scholarly research on the semi-independent Asian societies. They facilitated the admission, travel, and protection of professional Western scholars in the indigenous society for the purpose of conducting a broad array of archeological, linguistic, historical, and cultural studies. They also wrote books themselves which supplemented the published works of earlier Western explorers and diplomatic officials involved in the initial phases of the Western impact in Asia.[41] During the unequal treaty process a few Western diplomats with scholarly inclinations expanded this influence. Thomas T. Meadows, an official Interpreter in the British Consulate in Canton, wrote two books entitled, *Desulatory Notes on the Government and People of China* (1847) and *The Chinese and Their Rebellions* (1856), which contained extensive (and still useful) information and analysis of Chinese philosophy, ethics, law, and administration as well as a detailed account of early Western influences in China. Sir Ernest Satow, the Secretary of the British Legation in Tokyo, wrote *A Diplomat in Japan* (1921) which included a historical record of Western influences in Japan during the latter half of the nineteenth century. Western diplomats in Thailand who published useful scholarly works included W. A. R. Wood, the British Consul in Chiengmai, whose book, *A History of Siam* (1924), still comprises the only general English-language history of Thailand from its early origins to the end of the eighteenth century, and John G. D. Campbell, whose book, *Siam in the Twentieth Century: Being the Experiences and Impressions of a British Official* (1902) assessed some of the changes made during the two previous decades by King Chulalongkorn. These and other studies produced by Western diplomats induced an influence similar to the published writings of Western colonial administrators. They served to expose the West and a few indigenous persons to a broader understanding of the semi-independent societies. In some cases they comprised a pioneering effort to obtain new knowledge on various aspects of the local culture. In every case they constituted the initial studies of the Western impact on the semi-independent societies.[42]

The most distinctive historical input imparted by Western diplomats in the unequal treaty process was to serve as a *model and mentor of political and administrative modernization*. This comprised the major state-building role of the Western diplomatic missions. It consisted of the complementary task of supplying some of the examples, information, and guidance needed by the local government to comply with the requirements imposed by Western diplomacy under the unequal treaties.

Western diplomats initiated this role by requiring the reform of the indigenous bureaucracy, primarily in the functions closely related to diplomacy and international trade. In addition to the example of their own administrative structures and the provision of information on their own bureaucratic methods, Western diplomats assisted this reform by supplying their own nationals as advisers to the indigenous government. British diplomats required China to conduct its diplomacy through a Ministry of Foreign Affairs organized according to Western standards instead of the traditional Bureau of Dependencies. In the early phases of this change, the British diplomatic mission in Peking provided its own advisers to assist in establishing a modern bureaucratic organization capable of administering the provisions of the unequal treaties affecting British nationals. British, French, and American diplomats utilized a similar procedure in providing their own advisers in the establishment of the Chinese Customs Service capable of administering the special tariff restrictions imposed on China. The Western diplomatic missions of the major Western powers assisted in inducing similar reforms in the administration of foreign affairs and commerce in Japan and Thailand. They indirectly aided in generating broader administrative reforms in all three semi-independent societies since the modernized administration of diplomacy and international trade served as a model for subsequent reforms in other branches of the indigenous bureaucracy.

Western diplomats likewise facilitated *the reform of the indigenous legal system*. They imparted this influence by several means. In the normal conduct of their diplomatic function, they depicted a revolutionary change to the indigenous political elite in the management of human and legal relations. Their role in administering the Western system of international law between sovereign nations served as a model in imparting the need for an internal legal system capable of managing relations between persons and corporate institutions with predictable order and efficiency.[43] Western diplomats exposed the local government to the modern capacities of legal systems constructed on universalistic norms in contrast to the traditional legal system utilizing particularistic values based on custom and usage. In some degree they exhibited the crucial advantages derived from the rule of law over the rule of men. They showed that the Western legal system, like its technological counterpart, could be utilized to manage and change human relationships, often within a relatively short period of time, for the purpose of gaining more control over secular and mundane affairs.

The normal activity of Western diplomatic missions also aided in exposing the urban areas of the semi-independent Asian societies to some basic Western political concepts. In administering many treaty provisions such as extraterritoriality, most favored nation treatment, and diplomatic immunity, Western diplomats helped to convey the concept of both individual and national equality. They denied many aspects of this fundamental Western value to the indigenous government and society, yet they illustrated many of its practical applications to local observers in treating their own nationals impartially in the judicial courts of the consular missions, in demanding equal privileges granted by treaty to other Western nations, and in insisting on the same immunities from local restrictions for their own diplomatic personnel as their governments were providing all foreign diplomatic personnel in the capitals of Western nations. The idea of individual property rights was imparted by the example of Western diplomatic missions upholding the special privileges of their nationals to acquire land, goods, and monies under a system of law. The idea of individual civil rights was illustrated in the treaty provisions administered by Western diplomats protecting their own nationals from arbitrary treatment by local authorities. Western diplomatic missions assisted in transmitting this vital concept in which the individual is provided with legal restraints against the state, and his personal freedoms are defined and protected under an impersonal legal system.

Western diplomats likewise served as *a channel of information on their own political and legal systems.* They supplied the indigenous government with copies of their own constitutions, legal codes, statute books, court decisions, etc., which provided detailed data on the concepts and practices of legal systems in the West. Some of these foreign-supplied legal models were directly copied by the local government; many served as samples which were modified and adapted to traditional behavior in the formation of a new legal order. French diplomatic missions were the most influential in imparting this specific Western influence as the Napoleonic code was used as a model in modernizing the legal systems in Japan and Thailand.[44] All Western diplomats engaged in this practice with the implied understanding that the indigenous government would utilize the information on their own political and legal systems to improve the local legal system and eventually achieve adequate standards to terminate the unequal treaties.

Western National Military Forces

Like Western colonial military forces, the national military forces of the Western powers exerted their influences during two phases in the unequal treaty process. They first applied military power or threatened its use in making initial encroachments against the semi-independent Asian societies and obtaining the special treaty rights of extraterritoriality and fixed tariffs. This action involved the use of Western naval and ground forces in China, and the use of naval power alone in Japan. Neither form of military power was applied in Thailand since the threat of Western military forces from adjoining colonial territories was sufficient to encourage King Mongkut to negotiate the unequal treaties. The second phase occurred after the unequal treaties were established. During this later period Western national military forces consisted almost entirely of naval forces. The only notable exception to this deployment of Western military power was the stationing of small numbers of British and French troops in the port cities and leased concessions in China. These nearby military forces and the threat of their use against the semi-independent societies supplied the coercive power supporting Western diplomacy in the administration of the unequal treaties. Their essential purpose was to symbolize the superiority of Western power, to protect Western nationals residing in the semi-independent society, and to resist violations of the special treaty rights by the indigenous government. The intermittent use of Western naval vessels to fulfill this role resulted in the concrete action popularly referred to as "gunboat diplomacy."

One of the specific historical inputs imparted by Western national military forces was to strengthen the concept of the nation-state within the semi-independent Asian societies. In some degree these Western military forces supplemented the role of Western diplomats in transmitting this distinct Western value and institution. Their relatively infrequent use and limited display in the semi-independent societies caused their impact to be much less than that of the Western colonial military forces in the colonized societies. Yet their presence or threat aided in promoting the processes of state-building and nation-building. The adversities caused by their occasional interference in internal affairs intensified demands within the indigenous government to build a modern administrative system and develop a unified national consciousness.[45] The symbolic display of Western national military forces strengthened the desire of the local political elite for increased military power to cope with Western military forces in the context of international diplomacy rather than the inferior status imposed by the unequal treaties. Western national military forces, in brief, augmented the domestic demand for a completely sovereign and independent nation-state. They also imparted the important lesson of *Realpolitik* that the diplomacy of a modern nation-state must be supported in some degree by the use or credible threat of military power.

A second historical input induced by Western national military forces was to serve as a *model of modern science and military technology* to the indigenous government and society. Like the Western colonial military forces, the national military forces displayed the superiority of Western military weapons and techniques over indigenous military forces. Their demonstration effect was limited since they exerted their direct influence almost entirely by naval vessels operating in coastal waters. They were rarely observed or experienced by the inhabitants of the semi-independent societies. Their only significant role in Japan during the second phase of the unequal treaty process was to make occasional port calls. Only once were Western naval vessels used to bolster Western diplomacy in Thailand, and this move in 1893 was more involved in the struggle between Great Britain and France to establish Thailand as a buffer site than in rectifying violations of the unequal treaties by the Thai government.[46] Only in China did gunboat diplomacy exert an intermittent influence. Western naval vessels were maintained at all treaty ports and they patrolled approximately 1500 miles of the Yangtze River. Also, China was the only semi-independent Asian society in the second phase of the unequal treaty process which witnessed direct military action by sizeable numbers of Western ground forces in the suppression of the Boxer Rebellion. Yet these modest and relatively infrequent exhibitions of Western military power sufficiently impressed the indigenous government with the superiority of Western military capabilities. Local rulers quickly imitated Western military methods and obtained similar types of military weapons. Western national military forces served as models in the creation of new national armies capable of defending the entire territory of the semi-independent societies. They strengthened this influence on several occasions by providing training to newly-formed indigenous military forces who purchased modern weapons and equipment from their own armament industry.

Western Contracted Advisers

Western contracted advisers consisted of the relatively small number of Western nationals employed in an advisory capacity by the governments of the semi-independent Asian societies. The classification of Western persons comprising this specific linkage is somewhat different from other governmental linkages of the unequal treaty process. Their "official" capacities varied considerably, and many did not serve as representatives of their own governments. The Western advisers who served essentially in a governmental linkage were those employed by the governments of the semi-independent societies at the explicit or implicit request of Western diplomatic missions. This practice was most common in the early stages of the unequal treaty process in China and Thailand when Western diplomats began undertaking major actions to promote the modernization of specific branches of the indigenous bureaucracy. In a somewhat reduced official capacity were the few Western advisers who had formerly served as diplomats and had befriended the government of the semi-independent society. These advisers served in this role after leaving their own diplomatic service. Americans included in this unique category were Anson Burlinggame and John W. Foster who served as advisers to the government of China, and Francis B. Sayre who served as an adviser to Thailand.[47] Other Western advisers were private Western nationals employed by the governments of the semi-independent societies, usually through a written contract for a specific assignment and a fixed period of time. These advisers worked as temporary employees for the indigenous regime and took no directions from their own government.

At their specialized places of employment within the indigenous government structure, Western contracted advisers imparted several "shared influences" with Western diplomats. Their recognized competence assisted in conveying the concept of progress through their performance of a "modern" administrative function. The contracted adviser likewise assisted in transmitting the concept of individual equality by assisting improvements in the protection of individual rights in the evolving domestic legal systems. He also aided in strengthening the important idea of national equality by utilizing the channels of international law on behalf of the Asian government employing his specialized services and achieving a wider international recognition of its rights as an equal sovereign nation. The adviser aided in imparting a Western language to a specific coterie of indigenous administrative officials which broadened their exposure to Western knowledge and culture. He served as a tangible symbol of the "superiority" of Western culture since the entire assumption underlying his employment was based on his role as a representative of an advanced political and technological culture. Following the initial stages of the unequal treaty process, the Western contracted adviser became a tangible target of indigenous nationalists who were envious of his influential position and who sought the removal of all Western advisers from advisory posts in the government lest they strengthen the unpopular impositions of the unequal treaties and cause new infringements on the nation's sovereignty. A few advisers published their personal memoirs or engaged in modest writing. Their books and articles did not usually consist of scholarly research on the indigenous society, but they provided useful information and insights on the early Western impact in the semi-independent societies.[48]

The most specialized historical influence of Western contracted advisers was to serve as makers of a modern and rationalized bureaucracy. This external role supplemented the demonstration effect induced by Western diplomatic missions and it enabled trained Western specialists to play a direct role in creating or improving many administrative structures in the indigenous government. Western advisers in Japan exerted a relatively modest role in developing a rationalized bureaucracy due to the modernizing propensity and competence of the Meiji leaders. In China they exercised a variety of influences in different branches of the bureaucracy, although their most significant influence was in the administration of the customs service. In Thailand they imparted an influence in virtually every ministry and department of the reorganized administration made by King Chulalongkorn in 1892.

Western contracted advisers performed these state-building roles by several methods. Although they were allegedly employed to advise indigenous officials, they actually assumed control of their administrative organizations in many cases due to the policy of their own government, their personal zeal, or the apathy of indigenous officials. In some cases their original advisory role within a single ministry or department was broadened so their modernizing influence could be extended to other branches of the government. In Thailand the role of the first Adviser to the Ministry of Foreign Affairs (a Belgian) was subsequently elevated to the rank of General Adviser with an advisory authority expanded to all branches of the government. The most widespread influence of the Western contracted advisers was to perform a training function by transmitting knowledge and skills to indigenous officials who eventually acquired the qualifications to replace the Western advisers. The governments of Japan and Thailand were especially effective in utilizing this procedure. They gradually reduced the employment of Western advisers as their own administrative personnel obtained the proficiency to manage new roles in a modern rationalized bureaucracy.

GOVERNMENTAL LINKAGE INVOLVED IN BOTH EXTERNAL IMPACTS

The only governmental linkage involved in both the colonization and unequal treaty processes was political agents. This unique form of external influence was employed on a broad scale by the government of the Soviet Union after 1918 which utilized an ideological type of aggrandizement and a modified unitary-doctrinaire concept of colonial rule. The Soviet government used Russian communist agents only in China where Gregory Voitinsky and other Russian Comintern cadre were sent by Lenin to assist in the formation of the Chinese Communist Party during the early 1920's.[49] The Kremlin also sent European communists such as Pavel Mif to aid the fledgling Communist Party in China. Elsewhere in Asia it utilized both European and American communists to promote the establishment of indigenous communist parties. These political agents included the Dutch communist, Hendrik Sneevliet (*alias* Maring), who played a major role in organizing the Indonesian Communist Party in Java in 1920, and the British communist, Charles Ashleigh, who made an abortive attempt to assist in the formation of the Communist Party of India in 1922.[50] The Soviet government likewise dispatched five Comintern agents from its Far Eastern Bureau in Shanghai to Singapore during the late 1920's to organize the Nanyang (Southseas) Communist Party, which developed into the Malayan Communist Party in 1931. The Soviet-inspired Southeast Asia Youth Conference in Calcutta in February 1948 (sponsored by the World Federation of Democratic Youth and the International Union of Students) was attended by the Australian communist, Lawrence Sharkey, who traveled to Singapore shortly thereafter and urged the Malayan Communist Party to launch an insurgency against British colonial rule.[51] The Soviet government also used Asian communists such as Ho Chi Minh from Vietnam and Tan Malaka from Indonesia to aid in the formation of communist parties in Southeast Asia. Yet the major influence of these two Asian communist leaders was the establishment of a communist party in their own emerging national societies. Their political influence was consequently exerted more in the role of an indigenous returnee (which will be discussed in Chapter Eight on non-governmental linkages) than as a governmental linkage.

The dominant Western historical input implanted by Soviet political agents in Asia was the *Communist ideology and organizational techniques*. These covert foreign infiltrators sought to exploit the growing nationalist sentiment among indigenous radicals, primarily urban intellectuals and labor leaders, who were seeking the rapid termination of Western domination and the acquisition of political power. They likewise portrayed the Soviet Union as the model for all communist revolutionaries seeking the abolition of inequality and poverty in non-Western societies allegedly caused by Western capitalism and imperialism. Communist political agents in India, Indonesia, and China also assisted in linking the newly-established indigenous communist party to the global Comintern apparatus controlled by the government of the Soviet Union. In contrast to "home-grown" communist parties elsewhere in Asia which remained detached from the Comintern and continued to exploit the nationalist issue, these Soviet-controlled communist parties became the only indigenous political groups subservient to a foreign government. They thereby lost credibility from indigenous nationalist leaders. They also suffered intermittent reversals as political directives from the Kremlin oscillated from a rigid adherence to Marxist doctrine to non-ideological appeals to support Russian national interests.

Communist political agents likewise increased *ideological pluralism* within the colonized and semi-independent Asian societies. By aiding the formation of Marxist conspiratorial parties, they indirectly fomented varying degrees of anti-communism among competing political groups who shared certain Marxist economic and social goals but opposed the establishment of a totalitarian state and subservience to the Soviet Union. Communist political agents also served as targets of Western colonial administrators in colonized societies and of the indigenous police in semi-independent societies. Their presence was used by Dutch colonial authorities as additional justification for imposing severe suppressive measures against all indigenous dissidents in Indonesia during the 1920's and 1930's. Among some British colonial administrators, the clandestine operations of foreign communist agents in colonized territories were used to rationalize delays in political reforms leading toward national independence. The intermittent infiltration of foreign communist agents in China was used by the Chinese Nationalist regime to justify increasing police-state suppression of political dissidents and the expansion of authoritarian rule.

SUMMARY

Governmental linkages involved in the colonization process and in the unequal treaty process transmitted numerous and diverse Western values, modes of behavior, and institutions. Table XVI comprises a summary comparing these Western historical inputs imparted by specific governmental linkages.

Table XVI. *A comparison of Western historical inputs imparted by specific governmental linkages.*

WESTERN GOVERNMENTAL LINKAGES

Western Historical Inputs	Colonial Admini- strators	Resident Advisers	Colonial Military Forces	Diplomats	National Military Forces	Contracted Advisers	Political Agents
1. Concept of the nation-state	X		X	X	X		
2. Concept of progress	X		X	X		X	
3. Concept of equality	X			X		X	
4. Expansion of cultural pluralism	X	X	X				
5. Modern urbanization	X			X			
6. Western language	X	X		X		X	
7. Humanitarian reforms	X						
8. Western-oriented institutions of higher education	X						
9. Symbol of the "superiority" of Western culture	X	X		X		X	
10. Promotion or performance of scholarly research	X			X		X	
11. Rationalized indigenous bureaucracy	X			X		X	
12. Constitutional democracy	X*						
13. Increased sub-system differentiation	X						
14. Target of the emerging nationalist movement	X			X			
15. Model of modernization			X		X		
16. Modernized indigenous military forces			X		X		
17. Communist ideology and techniques							X
18. Expansion of ideological pluralism							X

*This specific Western historical input was transmitted only by British or American colonial administrators.

Chapter 8

Nongovernmental Linkages

The nongovernmental linkages involved in both the colonization process and the unequal treaty process consisted of persons employed in private and nonofficial roles. These linkages were *Western entrepreneurs, Western missionaries, Western scholars, indigenous returnees, Eurasians,* and *foreign communities.* In varying degrees the complex array of Western historical inputs imparted by these specific external penetrations was dependent on many roles performed by Western governmental linkages. Some of the values, modes of behavior, and institutions transmitted by these nongovernmental linkages overlapped with Western official influences. The most important nongovernmental linkages were those involved in the high-transformative economic and social policies in the colonization process or those supported by high-demonstrative Western official missions in the unequal treaty process.

WESTERN ENTREPRENEURS

Western entrepreneurs consisted of private Western capitalists, bankers, merchants, traders, and businessmen who exerted an expanding influence in almost all Asian societies after the establishment of the formal governmental structures involved in the colonization process and the unequal treaty process. This nongovernmental linkage was increasingly effective during the second phase of the Western impact from the end of the Napoleonic Wars until the aftermath of World War II. Unlike earlier Western traders in Asia whose economic influence was largely confined to a few coastal areas and consisted almost entirely of small-scale commercial operations, the later Western entrepreneurs engaged in extensive capital investment for the purpose of large-scale industrial production and the manufacture of cheap consumer goods for world markets.[1] They induced major economic changes inside the Western colonial systems where a cooperative administration and political stability provided a widespread opportunity to exploit natural resources and reach a large domestic market. The penetration of Western entrepreneurs in the semi-independent societies also exerted significant internal economic influences, yet it touched fewer indigenous people and its direct role was largely confined to coastal cities.

Western entrepreneurs tended to strengthen several influences imparted by Western governmental linkages. One of these "shared influences" was to bolster the Western concept of the nation-state. This function was accomplished by various actions involved in the formation of an emerging national economy. Western capitalists performed this role in the colonial systems by constructing modern transportation and communication systems as well as portions of the physical infrastructure which unified some elements of the colonial economy. Directly or indirectly they induced a similar influence in the semi-independent societies by encouraging the indigenous governments to construct these basic physical facilities for economic modernization. Western entrepreneurs, often in cooperation with Western colonial administrators or Western diplomats, also assisted in shaping a national economic outlook, first in their own minds, and later in the minds of influential indigenous persons. Their disjointed exploitation of local natural resources caused a reaction among local nationalists who gradually absorbed the viewpoint of a colonial or national economy. The scattered and diverse economic operations by specific groups of Western entrepreneurs generated a demand among indigenous critics for a unified control over all internal economic activities for the purpose of benefiting the local population, rather than Western interests. They induced a growing understanding of the primacy of politics over economics. In effect, Western entrepreneurs made the achievement of an independent or completely sovereign nation-state one of the prime goals of the indigenous nationalist movement. According to Professor Rupert Emerson:

> Imperial Western economic systems worked in a variety of ways to stimulate the nationalism of the peoples on whom they impinged. In the ordinary course of events they did not create national economies overseas in the sense of encouraging a full-scale division of labor and internal diversification of products and markets. They did foster some consciousness of unity by domination. A sense of being exploited and victimized was associated with the penetration of an underdeveloped area by an advanced Western economy.[2]

Western entrepreneurs transmitted the concept of progress in the economic realm by demonstrating the "Protestant Ethic" and what Professor David McClelland has called "the Achievement Motive" (or "n Achievement").[3] Within the colonized and semi-independent societies Western businessmen exemplified the spreading bourgeoise values in Western culture which upheld a sense of inner self-fulfillment (or "salvation" according to Weber) by the acquisition of a continual augmentation of material goods. They depicted a basic norm of capitalism in the pursuit of increasing wealth as an end in itself. They showed the progressive thrust motivating much of the industrial and commercial revolutions in the West, and they introduced successive changes in Asian societies derived from the use of Western science and technology to the potential attainment of greater human prosperity and comfort. Western capitalists involved in both the colonization and unequal treaty processes served as the representatives of this new systematic pattern of economic behavior. They illustrated the application of discipline, industry, thrift, saving, and investment in the quest of producing and merchandising useful material goods for personal profit. They promoted cultural secularization by pursuing a more rationalized utilization of human and physical resources as a prerequisite for a more progressive and advanced society.

The formation of a *higher degree of cultural pluralism* in the smaller Asian societies was caused by Western entrepreneurs who created plural economies.[4] The imposition of large-scale Westernized economic operations over traditional subsistence economies generated the need for an intermediate level of economic activity in the form of commerce and skilled and unskilled labor which indigenous peasants were unwilling to perform. Western capitalists thereby induced the economic stimulus which caused the migration of regional aliens to fill this need. As mentioned previously, Chinese migrants in varying numbers entered every society in Southeast Asia; Indian migrants entered the British colonies in Ceylon, Burma, and Malaya; Vietnamese migrants moved to Laos and Cambodia. Western entrepreneurs thereby aided in creating sharp divisions of labor between these alien minorities and the indigenous majority. Previous grievances caused by religious and cultural differences between the small foreign communities and the local populace prior to the Western impact were intensified by new and separate economic roles among the much larger numbers of migrant aliens. The social unrest engendered by this Western-sponsored pluralism was most volatile in urban areas where Western nationals, regional aliens, and indigenous persons lived and worked in close proximity.

Additional social fragmentation also occurred as Western entrepreneurs involved a growing portion of the indigenous population in commercial agriculture at favorable rural locations while large numbers of local inhabitants continued to work in subsistence agriculture. These specialized labor-intensive economic activities caused significant splits within the indigenous majority as seen in the modern economic innovations adopted by coastal or deltaic villagers in Ceylon, Burma, Thailand, and Vietnam who produced rice for the export trade in contrast to villagers of the same racial or ethnic composition in more inaccessible areas who continued to produce food by traditional methods. This division within the indigenous majority caused additional economic and social schisms as the population in modernized sectors increased rapidly while population density in areas of subsistence agriculture remained essentially unchanged. In other cases, large-scale rural agriculture fostered by Western capitalists caused increased migrations of regional aliens who added another economic dimension to cultural pluralism. Examples of this practice were the employment of thousands of Indian workers on tea plantations in Ceylon and rubber plantations in Malaya. The social friction caused by the coincidence of cultural pluralism with economic pluralism became more acute as the concept of a unified colonial or national economy developed and the indigenous nationalist movement sought independence or complete sovereignty over a centralized nation-state.

One of the most important historical inputs transmitted by Western capitalists to Asian societies was modern urbanization. The creation of Westernized commercial centers broadened the secularization of economic activity and intensified achievement values in the economic realm. According to Professor Rhoads Murphey, these metropolitan areas became and still remain "predominantly an economic phenomenon . . . with overwhelmingly economic functions."[5] Virtually all Western and local entrepreneurs resided in urban areas created by Western economic change. It was largely in these concentrations of modern economic activity where Western entrepreneurs displayed the spirit of capitalism which made them the dominant channels for economic modernization. The commercial cities of Asia from Karachi to Tokyo became showcases for the bourgeoise élan of Western merchants, exporters, importers, bankers, and insurance agents who increasingly oriented the indigenous economy into the channels of international trade and distributed cheap foreign imports to an expanding local market. Within a short time after their founding, many of these modern hubs of industry and trade rivaled the political and administrative authority of the capital cities. Shanghai soon wielded more influence in Chinese society than Peking; Bombay, Calcutta, and Madras after 1911 exercised more influence in many aspects of Indian society than New Delhi. In the smaller uniurban societies such as Burma, Thailand and the Philippines, some of the competition between politics and commerce imparted a corrupting influence on governmental functions subjected to the surrounding expansion of material wealth.

With few exceptions, the physical facilities and mass products of Western entrepreneurs served as concrete manifestations of the economic "superiority" of Western civilization. Modern office buildings, industrial factories, mining enterprises, and agricultural methods conveyed a deep and widespread recognition of the enormous capabilities of Western technological skills. The manufacture and sale of cheap consumer goods was the first time in history that a sizeable and expanding portion of the indigenous population could obtain some manufactured products which could make their lives more healthy and productive. Millions of local urban dwellers and rural villagers with few earthly belongings were soon able to obtain some factory-made textiles and metal wares instead of depending entirely on the hand-woven cloth and earthen household goods of the traditional economy. The availability of mass-produced Western goods gradually convinced Asians of all social strata that they were confronted by a much more advanced economic and technological order. According to Sansom:

> When one considers the various forms of intercourse between nations, it appears that trade relations, which are usually thought of as nothing but the exchange of things, are in fact those which exercise the greatest influence, especially between countries separated by long distances. Attempts to impose ideas by means of religious missions or books or other means of persuasion seem to have less effect than the objects of trade, which are silent but convincing. . . . The influence of ideas is at any rate slow to operate and almost invariably evokes a resistance that is not met with by — let us take for example — guns, tobacco, potatoes, watches, and clocks in Asia or silks, gums, and spices in Europe. These are accepted at first without qualm and often with alacrity, and it is only after a lapse of time that their true influence becomes apparent, for better or for worse.[6]

The most distinct historical input imparted by Western entrepreneurs was the formation of an *indigenous modernizing entrepreneurial class.* Like Western governmental linkages, Western businessmen also assisted in training and inducting their own local counterparts into an emerging modernizing society. As the apostles of modern capitalism, they imparted their managerial skills to a new business class which no longer produced or sold a few hand-made necessities or luxury goods for a traditional society, but now engaged in the production or distribution of manufactured goods for mass markets. This important influence was conveyed in several ways. The presence of Western entrepreneurs required local entrepreneurs to learn a Western language. Like most Western officials, Western businessmen did not usually learn indigenous languages. They thereby required some competence in their own language for local businessmen seeking to succeed in commerce and trade. Western entrepreneurs likewise employed small numbers of indigenous persons or regional aliens in their own business organizations which provided some training and experience in the performance of modern managerial roles. British capitalists in India transferred entrepreneurial skills with considerable speed through the Managing Agency system by which British firms provided the initial risk capital for specific ventures that gradually attracted Indian investors after they became profitable.[7] This monopolistic practice was widely criticized, but it served as a catalyst for the development of the Indian-owned textile industry and the Tata iron and steel works. Most important, Western businessmen promoted the formation of the largest number of local entrepreneurs by establishing an economic environment in both the colonial and semi-independent societies which required numerous small-scale commercial enterprises, many of which were family-operated and depended directly or indirectly on large Western firms.

A specialized form of Western entrepreneurial influence was the establishment of the first mass media in the form of *modern newspapers*. Examples of early Asian presses started in major cities by Western editors include *The Times of India, Rangoon Gazette, Bangkok Calendar, Straits Times (Malaya),* and *The Manila Times*. The purpose of these early Western newspapers, like that of Western industry and commerce, was to make a profit. This was achieved by supplying the small Western community with current information on international and domestic affairs. Much of the local news concerned commerce and trade. In some cases these Western newspapers increased their earnings by publishing a variety of cheap pamphlets and books on subjects of interest to the local Western community. Yet the political and social impact of these initial shapers of public opinion quickly outpaced their economic significance. They soon served as models for locally-owned newspapers publishing similar information in local languages for a much larger readership.

The content of the first vernacular newspapers consisted largely of translations of the Western language press. Yet local editors soon began disseminating information specifically related to the social and political interests of their own audiences. The growth of both Western and local newspapers soon created the need for a genuinely "modern" person to understand at least one Western language as well as one or more local languages. These newspapers broadened and intensified the exposure of their readers to Western culture and advancements. They also spread new ideas to a variety of urban groups and indigenous political leaders. Some vernacular newspapers reached small scattered audiences in the more accessible villages where a literate person could read their contents to illiterate peasants. An early vernacular publication in Malaya, for example, cited twenty-six specific roles of modern newspapers, including "the light of the mind, the talisman of the thoughts, the mirror of events, the servant of the wise, the prompter of the forgetful, a guide to those who stray, a prop to the weak, the guardian of the community, and the forum for all discussion."[8]

In addition to their role as the makers of a local modern entrepreneurial class, Western capitalists also created an *urban and rural proletariat*. At industrial plants, rural plantations, and mines, they employed sizeable numbers of local persons in a variety of skilled and unskilled roles. As the economic system became increasingly differentiated, the local labor force, like the local entrepreneurial class, experienced increasing specialization. Western capitalists aided this diffraction by promoting the development of vocational training, not by directly establishing technical schools themselves, but by generating the need for local low-cost skilled labor. In some cases the employment of local workers by Western firms hastened the growth of the local entrepreneurial class. The completion of construction projects financed by Western capital caused many unemployed workers, especially regional aliens, to move into more lucrative and less arduous employment in small self-owned enterprises.

A special economic influence was imparted by Western entrepreneurs in colonial systems with high-transferable political and administrative structures (i.e. India, Ceylon, Burma, Malaya, and the Philippines) and in the small semi-independent society of Thailand with high-demonstrative Western diplomatic missions. In these societies, Western capitalists induced *an increasingly autonomous economic system.*[9] They created a privately-owned economic sector and increasingly separated it from the guidance and control of political authority. In addition, Western entrepreneurs also induced increasing specialization and differentiation within the economic system. Their roles aided in the delineation of an agricultural sector containing both commercial and subsistence elements, and a commercial sector consisting of diverse enterprises involved in the sale and distribution of an expanding variety of goods. Different elements of each economic sector were foreign or locally operated and owned. In effect, Western entrepreneurs caused increasing differentiation within an increasingly autonomous economic system which itself was an important subsystem of a new modernizing society.

Western entrepreneurs likewise served as *latent targets of the indige-nous nationalist movement.* This specific historical input was closely related to their role in conveying the idea of the nation-state. Western businessmen did not serve as the same tangible nationalist target as governmental linkages composed of Western colonial administrators or Western diplomats. Yet the widespread disruptions caused by the perva-sive influences of Western-sponsored economic change served to inten-sify indigenous hostility and opposition to Western colonial rule or the unequal treaties. While most indigenous nationalist leaders recognized the numerous technological advances made by Western capitalists, they were usually more conscious of apparent economic dislocations as well as the sharp economic contrasts between the small prosperous Western minority and the masses of indigenous people living in newly-discovered "poverty."[10] Western entrepreneurs were blamed by indigenous nationalists for exacerbating many traditional problems and adding a host of new problems as many economic advances were largely counter-productive due to population increases. In colonial systems with high-transferable political and administrative structures, Western corpora-tions intermittently became manifest targets of indigenous nationalists as the latter used them to illustrate their growing opposition to the con-tinuation of Western colonial rule. Gandhi utilized this practice in orga-nizing a strike against British indigo plantations in Bihar province in 1917.[11] Western firms were also targets of labor strikes organized by nationalist leaders in Burma and the Philippines. In the semi-independent societies, especially China and Thailand, Western business organizations likewise served as symbols of hostility used by nationalist leaders seeking to place them under indigenous political control.

WESTERN MISSIONARIES

Western missionaries consisted of proselytizing members of Christian churches who traveled to Asian societies seeking to convert heathen peo-ples to their religion.[12] They were itinerant representatives of the reli-gious fervor which emerged in the West following the demise of papal authority at the end of the medieval period. Their logistical support came from governmental agencies or religious bodies in Western nations pro-moting the propagation of Christianity to the entire non-Western world. Unlike other Western linkages, the Christian missionaries sought inti-mate and direct contacts with people of all social strata within the indige-nous society. Also unlike other Western linkages, many missionaries spent their entire lives in the indigenous society. Usually they mastered its language and understood much of its culture. Their behavior was often observed over a period of many years by some local persons with whom they developed deep and close friendships.

The historical inputs imparted by Western missionaries came in two phases. The first phase was dominated by Roman Catholics who relied almost entirely on their personal ability and skills in understanding the local culture and ingratiating themselves with local rulers. In this endeavor they received little or no effective assistance from their own governments.[13] The work of the Italian Jesuit, Matteo Ricci, who founded the Christian mission in China, symbolized this early practice. He claimed the success of spreading Christianity depended not on converting a few local persons, but in gaining a respected status at the top levels of the Chinese class structure.[14] At first Ricci and his fellow missionaries dressed and acted like Buddhist monks until they learned that the Confucian intelligentsia enjoyed a higher status in Chinese society. Thereafter they accordingly altered their attire and behavior to conform to that of this influential scholarly elite. Ricci also studied the Confucian classics, performed the kowtow and other obeisant court ceremonies, and sided with Confucianists in their struggles with the Buddhists. He sought to blend elements of Christianity with Confucianism, most notably the concept of love with the rites of ancestor worship.[15] Other Jesuit missionaries followed a similar policy in India and Japan. In addition to these theological compromises, the early Roman Catholic missionaries sought to combine their proselytizing efforts among the local masses with ambitious attempts to gain influence (including converts) among the ruling class. Jesuits argued the virtues of Christianity at the Mogul court of Emperor Akbar, and Francis Xavier went to Japan with the high hope of converting the Emperor. The Jesuits sought to expand their influence at the Imperial court in Peking, and French missionaries in Thailand in 1688 sought to convert King Narai to the Roman Catholic faith. All Western missionary activity during this first phase depended on the cooperation of a sympathetic or indifferent indigenous ruler. When suspicion of Western religious intrusion developed during this period, Western missionaries were suppressed or expelled from the local society.

The second phase of Western missionary influence began in the early nineteenth century. It consisted largely of a movement led by American and British Protestants, although significant missionary activity was also conducted by activist Roman Catholic orders from France, Italy, the United States, and other Western nations. This phase occurred simultaneously with the spread of the Industrial Revolution. The proselyting endeavor tended to be more militant and aggressive than during the first phase.[16] Its intensity varied among Asian societies. In the colonized societies it was a function of the type of aggrandizement which established colonial rule. Missionary influences were the most intensive under tutelary colonial rule (i.e., Spanish and American rule in the Philippines, and French rule in Vietnam); they imparted a more marginal influence in the colonization processes motivated by economic aggrandizement (i.e., British rule in India, Burma, Ceylon, and Malaya, and Dutch rule in Indonesia). In the semi-independent societies, Western missionaries were most influential in China and Thailand where their special privileges lasted for a long duration; they exerted relatively minor long-run influence in Japan where the unequal treaties were quickly terminated. However, in every case the position of Western missionaries was much more secure and institutionalized than during the first phase. They enjoyed Western police or diplomatic protection and no longer were dependent on the personal favor of a local ruler. No longer did they need to attempt to adapt their proselyting efforts to the indigenous religion or culture. Unlike other Western linkages which largely represented upper-class groups of Western societies (colonial administrators, diplomats, advisers, and entrepreneurs), the Western missionaries conveyed much of the value-system embraced by the broad middle and lower classes of their own society. They formed one of the early genuine "people-to-people" programs between distant and diverse cultures. According to Panikkar:

> Indeed, it might be appropriately said that while political aggrandizement was the work of governments and groups, and commerce the interest of organized capital, mission work was the effort of the people of the West to bring home to the masses of Asia their view of the values of life.[17]

Like other Western linkages, the missionaries generated new historical inputs in the form of new values, institutions, and modes of behavior, and they helped shape other Western historical inputs. They assisted in conveying the Western concept of the nation-state. In some cases they imparted this shared influence by openly combining their religious fervor with the nationalistic goals of colonial or foreign policy. Yet in most cases they transmitted the concept of the nation-state implicitly and indirectly. They exemplified the Western nation-state, rather than articulating it. In all cases the missionaries advanced an understanding of this modern Western political institution through their reliance on police or diplomatic protection provided by Western colonial administrators or Western diplomatic missions. The impact of the concept of the nation-state was expanded after World War I when a rising spirit of nationalism and a declining sense of Western confidence caused the missionaries to transfer more clerical roles to indigenous Christians. "National" Christian churches were created and native Christians were appointed to important positions in the church hierarchy. The idea of the nation-state in colonized societies was further bolstered by Western missionaries who began to advocate the cause of indigenous nationalism. In most cases they were the first Westerners to propose the transfer of national sovereignty to indigenous control. In the semi-independent societies of China and Thailand, a small minority of missionaries were the first Westerners to advocate openly the abolition of extraterritoriality.[18]

The transmission of the concept of progress comprised one of the most pervasive historical inputs involving the Western missionaries. This impact at the doctrinal level was imparted by early evangelical workers, primarily among Protestant denominations, who, unlike the initial Roman Catholic missions openly and unabashedly denounced the "backward" values of the indigenous religions and cultures. They preached a gospel urging receptive hearts and minds to adhere to the Christian doctrine as "the way, the truth, and the life." Evangelical Christianity thereby induced a propensity to change, to improve, to transform one's entire life and mental outlook. On a different but related level, it imitated many aspects of the impact of Western entrepreneurs in depicting the dynamism and aggressiveness of the spreading scientific culture in the West.

The concept of progress conveyed by Western missionaries, however, exerted its most profound influences in the secular realm. The meager fruitage of evangelical Christianity caused most Western missions after 1870 to emphasize the practice, rather than the preaching, of the Christian doctrine. The primary focus became "good works" and "this-worldly" reform, a move which coincided with a contemporary stress on the "social gospel" in the United States and Great Britain.[19] While this fermenting impetus was one of the most widespread shared influences among all Western linkages, the basic Western concept of progress was transferred in its purest form by the Western missionaries. Within the newly emerging societies in Asia, it constituted the core idea of modernization in which the quest for human improvement became a conscious, rational, and permanent goal. For the first time in Asian history, secular change and development were conceived as worthy purposes in themselves. This catalyst induced what Professor Robert Bellah has defined as "an increase in learning capacity" and an augmentation in "the possibility of rational conscious choice of ends."[20] This distinctly Western value quickly spread from the small bands of Western missionaries to expanding coteries of local Westernized individuals, primarily in the urban areas. Relatively few of these indigenous persons were formally converted to Christianity, yet their behavior was subtly and radically altered by this revolutionary Christian norm. The propensity to change and improve at the secular level generated a sense of rationality, inquisitiveness, and independent thought. It spawned the idea of the dignity of labor. The consequent thrust toward modernization formed the psychological and political base for liberalism and socialism which quickly established deep roots in both the colonial and semi-independent societies. These secular ideologies evolved separately from the organized Christian movement, yet their source was inextricably intertwined with the worldly influences of the Western missionaries.

Christian missionaries likewise expanded the idea of secular progress by direct participation in administrative and social affairs. They promoted reforms in many colonial systems by persuading colonial administrators to require additional changes in indigenous behavior beyond minimal "humanitarian" requirements for law and order. In the semi-independent societies of China and Thailand they accomplished lesser but similar innovations by example and protest. In both types of Asian societies they exerted varying influences in the reduction or abolition of slavery, child marriage, polygamy, footbinding, corporal punishment, torture, the mistreatment of women, and customary indignities imposed on lower castes or classes. They also engaged in famine relief, and constructed modern hospitals, medical clinics, orphanages, and leper colonies. At times they promoted basic modifications of Western colonial policy. The most notable example of this influence was the role of Dutch missionaries in the adoption of the "Ethical Policy" in Indonesia after 1900.[21] Western missionaries assisted administrative modernization in China and Thailand by serving as government advisers. Near the end of the nineteenth century a Protestant missionary was appointed by the Chinese government as the first President of Peking University to initiate a Western-oriented curriculum. At the same time King Chulalongkorn in Thailand appointed Protestant missionaries to the posts of Superintendent of a new government school and Dean of the Royal Medical College. In the special case of the Philippines, Roman Catholic missionaries caused similar progressive changes by active participation in local administration and social improvements.

Another significant historical input induced by Western missionaries was the creation of important Western-oriented institutions of modern education. This specific influence comprised the dominant impact of many Christian missions following the widespread attraction of Western education and the gradual expansion of educational enrollment to indigenous non-Christians. In the colonized societies the Western missionaries were the originators of modern educational systems combining primary, secondary, and university institutions into some kind of coherent academic program and serving a distinct function in an organized and modernizing society. They created the first primary schools utilizing a secular curriculum detached from religious and political authority. These private primary schools were outnumbered by public primary schools established by colonial administrators after the beginning of the twentieth century, and the influence of Christian missionaries overlapped in some degree with larger numbers of Western educators employed in the public schools by the colonial bureaucracy. Yet the Christian missionaries with few exceptions retained a pre-eminent pedagogical influence as their private schools maintained high academic standards and they continued to enroll some of the most talented students, including many from upper-class indigenous families.

The influence of Western missionaries at higher levels of education in the colonization process was a function of the degree of transferability of the political and administrative structures. In the British and American colonies with high-transferable political and administrative structures, the private secondary schools and universities founded by Christian missions were either the first higher educational institutions established in the society or they outnumbered the few schools and colleges founded by early colonial administrators. Until the twentieth century they constituted the major or sole channel within the colonized society to a modern Western education. While these institutions served many goals of official colonial policy, they also promoted the acculturation and development of broadly educated individuals. They provided the advanced secular academic training which enabled an educated indigenous elite to fill an increasing variety of professional and technical roles. In the Dutch, French, and Japanese colonial systems with low-transferable political and administrative structures, the restrictive colonial policy either hampered or prevented the development of private institutions of higher education by Western missionaries. With minor exceptions, the relatively few significant colleges and universities in these colonized societies were established and controlled by colonial administrators. Their essential purpose was to serve as a symbol of "reform" to placate indigenous nationalist sentiment and to train a few indigenous persons for low-level administrative or technical roles in the colonial bureaucracy.

In the semi-independent societies of Japan, China, and Thailand, the Western missionaries tended to exert more confined and fragmented educational influences. Their major common impact was to assist in arousing a widespread thirst for modern Western education. In Japan where Christian missions operated for only three decades under the protection of extraterritoriality, their role was the least significant of the three semi-independent societies. The modern education system erected after the Meiji restoration was created essentially by Japanese initiative, although Western educational advisers were employed by the Japanese government and the Christian missions exerted a significant specific influence in promoting the education of women at the secondary and university levels. The educational influence of Western missionaries in Thailand was somewhat more extensive and diffuse than in Japan. Christian missions founded the first primary schools and several of the early secondary schools. Their proposal to establish a private university was rejected by the Thai government, and official leadership assumed the primary responsibility for establishing a modern educational system, including the two public universities (Chulalongkorn and Thammasat) constructed prior to World War II. As in Japan, the educational influence of Western missionaries overlapped in some degree with professional Western educators employed as advisers by the Thai government during the early stages of educational development. Among the semi-independent societies, Western missionaries imparted their largest educational influence in China. Their primary schools were the most numerous and widespread educational institutions at this lower level until the Chinese government adopted the policy of supporting public primary schools on a sizeable scale in the 1930's. Secondary schools and universities founded by Christian missions likewise served as the major channel for Western values and behavior which exceeded the more restricted influences of Western governmental linkages. Even after the Chinese government imposed various controls over private educational institutions at all levels, the Christian secondary schools and universities continued to be leading educational models and pedagogical innovators.[22]

In both the colonial and semi-independent societies, the universities founded by Western missionaries exerted some of the most profound psychological, social, and political influences imparted by any Western linkage. While several of the traditional societies in Asia had intermittently maintained significant centers of classical or religious studies, they had never established any educational body comparable to the Western university which had evolved in Europe from the medieval era. The imposing title of these institutions of higher education, derived from the Latin word "universitas," signified their status as an autonomous corporation with a separate identity and an independent role from the surrounding society. They had earlier constituted a self-perpetuating meeting place for serious scholars. Their essential intellectual purpose was the pursuit of knowledge and truth. By the nineteenth and twentieth centuries, they had evolved into "permanent institutions of learning" comprising specific collections of buildings, a fixed number of students, faculty, and administrators, a prescribed curriculum and examination system, and some kind of diploma or degree.[23]

Yet the process of transferring this distinct Western institution into an Asian environment produced a markedly different effect. The provision of a partial and indirect exposure to the broad currents of Western culture induced a severe and disrupting fermentation in the minds of many inquisitive indigenous students. It generated conflicting and antithetical tendencies combining disparate elements of both Western and Asian cultures. It produced a secularizing influence in the intellectual realm and oriented thought toward mundane and practical affairs.[24] The Western universities established by the Christian missions particularly symbolized the idea of equality of opportunity, and they made higher education the key channel for upward social mobility. In the realm of politics, they served as blending centers for Western concepts, especially the ideas of progress and the nation-state. They performed both nation-building and state-building roles by fostering shared values and experiences among a uniformly educated Christian or Christian-influenced elite seeking self-government over the territory of the colonial society or complete sovereignty over the affairs of the semi-independent society. The Western university likewise aroused a near-frantic effort among the newly-emerging indigenous elite to catch up with the modernizing nations of the West, a mood which gave these Western-created educational institutions an aura of emergency and immediacy.

Christian missionaries bolstered provincial loyalties in many Asian societies by devoting proselyting and humanitarian endeavors among communal groups physically detached from competing secular influences in the capital and commercial cities. In contrast to the initial efforts of the early Roman Catholic missionaries who sought to convert the political leaders of traditional Asian societies, the Western missionaries during the second phase of the Western impact sought initially to bring Christianity to the broad masses inhabiting the rural villages (little traditions) of Asia. This policy was symbolized in some degree by the name, China Inland Mission, used by the large British Protestant organization founded in 1866.[25] A "rural" approach likewise strengthened a provincial identity among progressive Christian and Christian-influenced groups in such places as Travancore in southern India, the Karen territory in Burma, Chiengmai in northern Thailand, the island of Amboina in eastern Indonesia, and the southern island of Kyushu in Japan. In rural areas Western missionaries also worked among unassimilated hill tribes isolated or relatively untouched by major indigenous religions. Regardless of the enormous physical and cultural hardships involved in this endeavor, many Christian missions attempted to bring their religion to the backward villages of these "remote peasants."

In spite of the merits of the early rural approach, Western missionaries increasingly strengthened their evangelical and secular efforts in urban areas where they won many of their most notable successes. They gradually discovered that the most promising milieu for spreading Christianity and Christian influences was the modernizing cities where sizeable numbers of transient persons removed from family and traditional ties were experiencing deep psychological problems and thereby susceptible to the message of a new religion. Western missionaries exacerbated pluralistic forces within the urban centers by creating and strengthening Christian minorities whose ranks included lower class or underprivileged groups such as the untouchables and Shudra caste in India, regional aliens (Chinese and Indians) in Southeast Asia, the working class in Japan, and entrepreneurs in China. This divisive influence was enhanced by the schools, universities, hospitals, and administrative centers of the Christian missions which tended to be located in the modernizing cities.

Western missionaries imparted their most distinct historical input by promoting *the value of religious freedom* in both colonial and semi-independent societies. Religious toleration had been practiced previously in various Asian traditional societies, and many early Roman Catholic missionaries enjoyed much religious freedom at traditional royal courts from India to China and Japan. This privilege, however, depended entirely on the personal disposition of the traditional ruler. Whenever he decided that Christian missionary activity constituted a threat to his kingdom, he promptly removed this external influence from his domain. During the second phase of Christian endeavor in Asia, the Western missions accordingly sought to end the arbitrary practice of religious freedom and establish it as a basic civil right protected by governmental authority.

This specific influence was most effective in the economic and tutelary colonial systems maintained by Protestant colonial powers (Great Britain, Netherlands, and the United States) where Christian missionaries actively utilized the rights of religious freedom established by law. This value evolved more slowly in the tutelary colonies maintained by Roman Catholic colonial powers (France and Spain) which aborted or hampered proselyting and secular activities by Protestant missionaries until their final stages. In all colonized societies the Western missionaries were influential in obtaining special legislation and court action which further enhanced the legal status of indigenous Christians regarding inheritances and family relationships.

In the semi-independent societies of Japan and Thailand, the Western missionaries assisted religious freedom by persuading the traditional ruler to uphold this important civil right as a means to convince Western governments of sufficient indigenous legal reform to justify the abolition of extraterritoriality. Pressure and protests from Western missionaries caused the Japanese government in 1873 to rescind an official order forbidding the propagation of Christianity and to issue a decree providing for religious toleration.[26] Following the execution of two Thai Christians in 1869 by the Prince of Chiengmai, Protestant missionaries in Thailand succeeded in obtaining an "Edict of Religious Toleration" from King Chulalongkorn, a portion of which stated: "That there is nothing in the laws and customs of Siam, nor in its foreign treaties, to throw any restriction on the religious worship and service of any one."[27] Western missionaries in China displayed an extended form of religious freedom which gained temporary success, but never succeeded in implanting this basic Western value in Chinese culture. They utilized extraterritoriality to extend Western diplomatic protection to Chinese Christians, yet the intermittent use of gunboat diplomacy to enforce these special treaty privileges made the Christian missions heavily dependent on foreign military power. The idea of religious freedom consequently failed to gain deep roots in the emerging Chinese society.

Like some other Western linkages, the Western missionaries served as targets of the emerging nationalist movement. In the minds of indigenous nationalist leaders, especially non-Christian leaders, the Christian missions were considered responsible for many social and cultural disruptions experienced by the newly emerging society. This supicion and opposition to Western missionary activity in colonized societies was usually latent and rarely overt. Yet the presence of Christian missions strengthened the desire of nationalist leaders to gain national independence as soon as possible in order to impose restrictions on this external religious influence. Among the semi-independent societies only in China did Western missionaries serve as manifest targets of xenophobia and emergent nationalism. The intimate association between Western missionaries and Western diplomatic power caused the Christian missions to serve as volatile points of friction which generated hostility into the surrounding Chinese society. Frequent tension aided in strengthening a sense of racial and patriotic pride which encouraged acts of violence against missionary personnel and property. An example of this anomic tendency was the expanding anti-Western sentiment which culminated in the Boxer Rebellion in 1900, an action directed initially against Western missionaries but which sought to remove all Western influences from China.

Western missionaries published books on many Asian societies which supplemented the scholarly research accomplished by other Western linkages. Like other Western writers, some of these studies consisted of personal memoirs, and in the case of the missionaries, they often contained a distinct religious bias. Yet many writings by Christian missionaries contributed significantly to the knowledge of Asian societies among Westerners and the indigenous educated class. With few exceptions these published works were based on long and intimate personal experience in the local society, and they provided important insights into the early interactions between the impact of Christianity and Western secular influences on different Asian cultures. James Legge, a British missionary in China during the 1850's and 1860's, for example, translated eight volumes of Chinese classics into the English language and supplemented this work with detailed commentaries.[28] Samuel Wells Williams, an American missionary, wrote a general introduction to Chinese civilization entitled *The Middle Kingdom* in 1848. An Italian missionary, Father Vincentius Sangermano, lived in Burma from 1782 to 1808 and wrote a book entitled *Description of the Burmese Empire* which was translated into English in 1833 and influenced Western writers in this British colony throughout the nineteenth century.[29] One of the most permanent and far-reaching scholarly influences achieved by Western missionaries in Asia was the intensive linguistic studies conducted by the French Roman Catholic missionary, Alexandre de Rhodes, who romanized the Vietnamese script into *quoc-ngu* during the seventeenth century and facilitated its adoption by the entire Vietnamese society.[30]

The combined effect of Western missionaries, like that of several other Western linkages, induced a movement toward a higher level of sub-system autonomy. This impact was most advanced in the British and American colonial systems where Protestant influences upheld the separation of church and state and a pragmatic tradition upheld the value of higher education administered by various decentralized public and private authorities. One of the distinctive roles of Christian missionaries in these Anglo-Saxon colonial systems was manifested in promoting an increasingly differentiated religious sphere separate from the political and economic systems. The missionaries likewise engendered a specialized educational system seeking autonomy from political authority. This development was much less advanced in the Dutch and French colonies, although modest tendencies toward more autonomous religious and educational sub-systems was achieved during their final stages. In spite of the minor differentiation in these two colonial systems, the Christian missionaries in many cases had raised the issue of more autonomy and decentralization in religious and educational affairs. Relatively little sub-system autonomy in religion and education was promoted by Christian missionaries in the three semi-independent societies of China, Japan, and Thailand.

Western scholars consisted of academic specialists who conducted archeological, anthropological, linguistic, historical, and social research on Asian societies. This penetration overlapped in some degree with the part-time scholarship performed by other Western linkages. Yet the studies conducted by these full-time professional scholars exerted a distinct impact since their primary purpose was to explore the sources of early Asian civilizations and uncover new reliable knowledge on the development of their religions, languages, and cultures. This particular influence was imparted largely in colonized societies where classical studies of former great traditions and middle traditions had long been dormant, and where intensive research by Western scholars was facilitated by the security and freedom of movement provided by cooperative colonial administrators. An example of this specialized penetration was Sir William Jones, one of the leading British Orientalists in India, whose historical research identified the Emperor Chandragupta with the Sandrokottus of Greek historians thereby establishing a fixed chronological point for comparisons of Asian and Western civilizations. Jones also founded the Bengal Asiatic Society in Calcutta which became a leading center of Sanskrit studies.[31] Other British scholars deciphered the inscriptions on Asoka's pillars and uncovered a vast amount of Buddhist literature. French scholars at the Ecole Francaise d'Extreme Orient in Hanoi performed some of the most sophisticated studies by Western scholars in Asia. They discovered and restored ancient Khmer architectural structures, most notably the temples at Angkor Wat and Angkor Thom. They likewise deciphered the records of the early Khmer ruling class which revealed the former extension of Khmer power and its impressive cultural influences.[32] They engaged in similar studies on a smaller scale among architectural and cultural relics of former Vietnamese, Laotian, and Cham dynasties. Early in the twentieth century, Dutch scholars conducted systematic studies of the Srivijaya, Sailendra, and Majapahit empires in Indonesia. Western scholars exerted relatively little influence in the semi-independent societies where a Confucian tradition had maintained classical studies over a period of many centuries or where security and mobility for Western scholars were inadequate.

The most distinct historical input induced by Western scholars in the colonization process was to provide *prestige to the indigenous culture* by making it an object of intensive research. The meticulous efforts of Western scholars to discover the values and institutions of former traditional societies gave them dignity and worth. Western scholars comprised the only Western linkage emphasizing the pre-Western accomplishments of the indigenous society. They were the only Western influence seeking to preserve the traditional culture, and they were the only Western penetration opposing the broad aggressive thrust of Western modernization and change. This unique role indirectly exerted a profound influence on indigenous nationalism. By uncovering knowledge of former grandeur and power in defunct great and middle traditions, Western scholars assisted in alleviating the individual and collective identity crisis among many members of the indigenous educated class by providing a passage to the roots of their own culture. Western scholars strengthened the process of nation-building by revealing many aspects of a common pre-Western historical experience. The expanding understanding of their own cultural heritage gave Asian nationalists a desperately needed sense of self-confidence in their confrontations with Western colonial rule.[33] The trauma produced by the impressive capabilities of Western science and technology was moderated in some degree by the comprehension of the duration, richness, and tenacity of the indigenous culture. This knowledge generated some sense of equality with Western colonial powers; in several cases it induced a feeling of superiority toward the West. These diverse psychological and political forces caused by Western scholarship likewise supplied an additional impetus to the indigenous nationalist movement in the semi-independent societies. A good example was the scholarly work of many Western officials and missionaries in Thailand which uncovered new knowledge of the achievements of the Sukhothai and Ayudhya periods and thereby strengthened a sense of nationalism.

The role of Western scholarship simultaneously imparted a counterbalancing influence by increasing cultural pluralism. In contrast to the centripetal forces induced by Western scholarship on early traditional societies, the knowledge of ancient cultural heritages often revealed historical grievances among different ethnic groups. An understanding of previous communal conflicts served to intensify certain ethnic, provincial, and religious prejudices.[34] The formation of deeper schisms between diverse communal groups was further strengthened by the revival of classical languages initiated by Western philologists. Western-sponsored studies of Pali, Sanskrit, and Urdu intermittently exacerbated religious conflicts between Hindus and Moslems in India. Similar Western research promoted provincial loyalties in Java and Sumatra in Indonesia, and it aroused animosity toward the Khmer minority in Vietnam and the Vietnamese minority in Cambodia. These fragmenting forces tended to mitigate some of the fervor and unity of the indigenous nationalist movement.

INDIGENOUS RETURNEES

Indigenous returnees consisted of indigenous inhabitants of colonized or semi-independent societies who resumed residence in their own societies after a period of residence, observation, travel, or study abroad, usually in the West.[35] This linkage began on a small scale during the early stages of the colonization and unequal treaty processes, and it assumed a significant political role largely during the twentieth century. The number of indigenous returnees was infinitesimally small compared to the total population of the colonized or semi-independent societies, yet this unique influence deeply affected the expanding movement toward modernization since it comprised the transmission of Western ideas and modes of behavior by an indigenous, not a Western, linkage. As in the traditional societies, the propagation of external values by foreign-traveled indigenous leaders aided in the legitimization and acceptance of these values within the colonized and semi-independent societies.[36]

Indigenous returnees in colonized societies consisted largely of young upper-class males whose families could afford the long periods of travel and residence abroad. With few exceptions these persons were private individuals who had received an advanced education at a university in the society of the Western colonial power. A smaller number of indigenous returnees were indigenous Christians, usually from lower social classes, returning from religious training at theological institutions in the West. A special group of indigenous returnees consisted of 50,000 Vietnamese manual laborers returning from France after World War I.[37]

The impact of Western culture on indigenous returnees educated in the West tended to be much deeper than the indirect influence of higher education obtained solely within the colonized society. Education in the West involved the mastery of a Western language and the acculturation of Western values through direct personal contact with a Western society. The absorption of many elements of Western culture was enhanced by the complete physical detachment from the colonized society and the ability to partake actively in many liberties and opportunities enjoyed in Western societies. Liberal and egalitarian behavioral patterns adopted in the West assumed major and revolutionary significance when these privileges were denied to indigenous returnees after their return to the colonized society.

Indigenous returnees in the semi-independent societies were more diversified than their counterparts in colonized societies. Some indigenous returnees were government officials returning from study and observation tours in the West. These persons included Prince Ito Hirobumi and a sizeable number of Japanese government officials,

Generalissimo Chiang Kai-shek and a large array of Chinese government officials, and King Wachirawut, King Prajadhipok, and numerous high-ranking Thai administrators. The largest category of indigenous returnees in the semi-independent societies, however, as in the colonized societies, consisted of private upper-class males who were recipients of government scholarships or whose families financed their education and travel in the West. Both types of indigenous returnees imparted more dif-ferentiated Western national influences than indigenous returnees in colonized societies since the former had more freedom of choice in traveling and studying in the West. They were not educated or exposed solely to the society of one Western power. Instead they returned from several Western societies, often with the encouragement of their govern-ment which sought to avoid excessive reliance or favoritism in any single Western nation. Indigenous returnees in Japan, for example, included lawyers and administrators trained primarily in Germany, and techni-cians educated largely in the United States and Great Britain. Indigenous returnees in China came mostly from the United States and Japan, although small numbers had studied in Great Britain, France, and Ger-many. Indigenous returnees in Thailand were divided essentially on a civilian-military basis; most civilians had studied law and technology in Great Britain and France; military officers had received their advanced military training in France, Denmark, Germany, or Russia.

The major Western historical input transmitted by indigenous returnees was to strengthen the concept of the nation-state and to advance the processes of nation-building and state-building. Indigenous returnees in the colonized societies fostered nation-building by serving as articulate spokesmen and agitators for the cause of national self-determination which they had learned in Western societies. They tended to envision most clearly the potential of their own society as a unified nation-state possessing common political values and institutions as the advanced sovereign nation-states they had observed in the West. Accord-ing to Professor Rupert Emerson:

> Since it was an age of nationalism in the West the achievement
> and maintenance of national unity and independence were cen-
> tral themes of the literature, history, and political tradition to
> which they [the indigenous returnees] were exposed. The praise
> of freedom and equality, and of the patriots who fought for
> national honor and integrity were basic assumptions of their new
> intellectual milieu.... The academic fare which was laid before
> them and the climate of ideas and expectations in which they
> came to live formulated for them their own grievances and

aspirations and pointed the paths they might follow.[38]

The experience of study and travel in the West also gave a sense of national identity and common purpose to indigenous returnees from diverse ethnic or provincial backgrounds within the colonized society. Many indigenous returnees also relinquished communal and particularistic loyalties by participation in nationalist student organizations at universities in the West.[39] Some obtained stronger nationalist convictions through their contacts with subjects from other non-Western colonies studying or traveling in the society of the Western colonial power.

Many indigenous returnees who had received an advanced education in the West assumed leading roles in the nationalist movement after their return to the colonized society. These persons tended to oppose extremist elements within the nationalist movement and to espouse a *moderate form of nationalism* seeking the termination of Western colonial rule by gradual and non-violent reform. Their ability to attain the dominant leadership role in the nationalist movement was a function of the prestige derived from their education in the West and the transferability of the political and administrative structures of the Western colonial power. The high-transferable political and administrative structures of Great Britain in India enabled moderate Western-educated nationalist leaders such as Gandhi and Nehru to achieve dominant leadership roles in the Indian National Congress. Similar structures exerted a comparable influence for D. S. Senanayake in Ceylon, Ba Maw in Burma, and Tengku Abdul Rahman in Malaya. Low-transferable political and administrative structures maintained by France in Vietnam were a major factor preventing moderate leaders such as Bui Quang-chieu and Pham Quynh from gaining a dominant role in the nationalist movement.[40] Instead the French colonial structures indirectly enhanced the influence of Ho Chi Minh whose personal experience in the West involved no formal education and consisted primarily of the adoption of revolutionary ideas and tactics through his contacts with the French Communist Party and his political training in the Soviet Union. The low-transferable political and administrative structures of the Dutch in Indonesia were likewise an important factor in reducing the political influence of moderate indigenous returnees, such as Mohammed Hatta who had been educated in the Netherlands, and in strengthening the extremist nationalism of Sukarno, who had not traveled or studied in the West and whose higher education consisted of technical training received at the Bandung engineering college.[41]

Indigenous returnees imparted a more limited influence on the process of nation-building in the semi-independent societies of Japan and Thai-

land where the political leadership was not foreign and where the government was already implementing policies designed to enhance a widespread consciousness of national identity and national unity. Nationalism espoused by government officials and most private nationals returning from the West was directed primarily against further Western
encroachments on national sovereignty. The major internal effect of this
form of nationalism was to promote authoritarianism by increasing the
demand for political centralization and administrative efficiency, both of
which were considered necessary to enhance modernization and to augment national power against external Western threats. Only in China
among the semi-independent societies did indigenous returnees perform
a major nation-building role. This influence was initially exerted during
the period of Manchu rule prior to 1912 when Western-educated Chinese
returnees such as Dr. Sun Yat-sen espoused national self-determination
against the alien Ch'ing dynasty. After the overthrow of Manchu political domination, Chinese returnees, as in Japan and Thailand, sought
positively to advance a sense of national identity in order to bolster
national unity and to reduce foreign infringements on national
sovereignty.

The influence of indigenous returnees in the process of state-building
consisted of diverse specialized roles which strengthened the impersonal
administrative and legal systems generated by the Western impact. In the
colonized societies this specific linkage was constituted largely of
Western-educated indigenous returnees who obtained administrative and
technical roles in the colonial bureaucracy. State-building was also
enhanced by small numbers of indigenous returnees serving as private
lawyers. This penetration in the colonies with high-transferable political
and administrative structures did not assume significant proportions
until the period after World War I. In colonies with low-transferable
political and administrative structures, modest state-building by indigenous returnees did not occur until the period just prior to national independence. The common educational experience of indigenous returnees
in the society of the Western colonial power assisted unity and efficiency
in the emerging administrative and legal systems in both types of colonized societies.

Indigenous returnees in the semi-independent societies exerted larger
state-building roles than their counterparts in the colonized societies.
Their Western education was utilized at higher levels during the early
stages of constructing modern administrative and legal systems due to
the urgent need for indigenous expertise in forming a unified modern
state and in dealing effectively with the Western powers. Although the
indigenous returnees in the semi-independent societies tended to exert a

more significant state-building role than indigenous returnees in the colonial systems, their diverse educational backgrounds in numerous Western nations imparted a fragmenting influence among the emerging state structures. Their role was consequently instrumental in the formation of more differentiated administrative and legal systems.

In both the colonized and semi-independent societies, indigenous returnees also assisted in transmitting *liberal and leftist political ideologies* which in varying degrees complemented the concept of the nation-state. These ideologies were liberalism, socialism, and communism. They were conveyed almost entirely by indigenous returnees in private capacities. Their most fertile breeding ground was in Great Britain and France after 1900 where a tradition of political freedom in a period of fermentation and rapid change facilitated exposure to a vast array of political thinkers ranging from John Stuart Mill and Harold Laski to Karl Marx and V. I. Lenin.[42] Some indigenous returnees susceptible to the ideologies espoused by liberal and radical groups in these Western democracies strengthened their revolutionary orientation with formal political training in the Soviet Union before returning to their own societies. Indigenous returnees who played important roles in transmitting Western leftist ideologies included Chou En-lai, the son of a prosperous Chinese mandarin family, who received a high school education in Paris and exerted a moderating influence among contending factions within the Chinese Communist Party after 1928; M. N. Roy, an Indian revolutionary who traveled in Europe, the United States and Mexico, assisted in establishing Communist training programs in the Soviet Union during the early 1920's, and later assisted in the organization of the communist parties in China and India; and Dr. N. M. Parara, the son of a prestigious Ceylonese family who was educated at the London School of Economics and helped establish the Marxist-oriented Lanka Sama Samaja Party in Ceylon in 1935.

Throughout the period of the Western impact some indigenous returnees resumed residence in their own societies after periods of travel, study, or observation in other non-Western societies, usually in the nearby region. Many of these returnees were religionists maintaining an external linkage which had originated during the period of the traditional society. The most significant influence of this kind in Asia consisted of Moslem devotees returning to India and Southeast Asia after the pilgrimage to Mecca, Medina, and other Islamic holy places in the Middle East. Their major internal role was in maintaining the vigor of Islam and in transmitting Modern Islamic Thought (after 1900).[43] Similar pre-Western linkages which had spread Hinduism, Buddhism, and Confucianism in the region were reduced to insignificant proportions during the Western impact. Other indigenous returnees in this category consisted of transient nationalists who expanded their goals and organizations after observing nationalist movements and national achievements in nearby regional societies. This linkage comprised Vietnamese nationalists returning from contacts with the Chinese nationalist organization of Sun Yat-sen, as well as Burmese and Indonesian nationalists returning from observations of the Indian National Congress in British India.

The intensity of the Western historical input imparted by indigenous returnees was a function of the following three factors:

1. *The Type of Foreign Exposure:* Higher education imparted the maximum impact on indigenous returnees from Western societies. The study of law and the social sciences caused a deeper acculturating influence than the study of science or technology. A legal training generated the largest political influence since it provided indigenous returnees with numerous insights into the basic religious and philosophical values of Western culture, and it examined fundamental questions regarding the Western approach to justice and human dignity. The inculcation of these Western values induced intensive aspirations for their application to colonized or semi-independent societies. Different exposures in the West by indigenous returnees were also influenced in some cases by supplementary travel and residence in more than one Western society. The nationalist fervor of Gandhi, for example, was sharpened by his personal experiences with racial discrimination in the Union of South Africa after his legal training in Great Britain.[44] The nationalism and socialism of Ho Chi Minh were made more radical and revolutionary by his political training in the Soviet Union following his travels and observations in France.[45] Yet the nationalist aspirations of most indigenous returnees, including Nehru, Senanayake, Ba Maw, Tengku Abdul Rahman, Pridi Phanomyong, and Mohammed Hatta were shaped primarily by personal exposure in a single Western society. Brief observation tours in the West, usually by government officials from the semi-independent societies, tended to exert the least impact on indigenous returnees. These persons were invariably impressed with technological and social advances in Western societies, but they achieved little if any meaningful understanding of the underlying scientific and political orientation of Western societies causing these forms of modern progress.

Different influences were likewise exerted by diverse exposures among indigenous returnees from non-Western societies. A larger impact was made by Moslem adherents who studied religion under learned Islamic scholars in the Middle East than Moslem laymen who undertook the pilgrimage to Mecca and Medina. A stronger effect was transmitted to nationalists in Southeast Asia who had direct personal contact with leading nationalist figures in other Asian societies than to those who merely saw some of the overt signs of nationalist movements in nearby societies.

2. *The Timing of Exposure to Foreign Societies:* The impact of Western political values and institutions on indigenous returnees was less intense in the period prior to World War I than in the period between the two world wars. During the earlier period the influence of Western ideas on indigenous returnees was muted due to the sense of confidence and contentment in the West, and the general assumption that Western power in non-Western regions would remain dominant and unchallenged. The impact of Western ideas on indigenous returnees markedly increased during the 1920's and 1930's when a widespread sense of doubt and uncertainty in Western societies was combined with increasing support for national self-determination in Europe and America. This expanding appeal of eventual national independence for Asian colonies in the West augmented nationalist aspirations among Asian indigenous returnees. An example of the influence of timing on indigenous returnees was seen in the relatively moderate nationalism of British-educated leaders of the Indian National Congress prior to World War I, and the militant nationalism of similarly educated leaders who assisted Gandhi after 1920. Different timing of exposure by indigenous returnees in regional non-Western societies also produced diverse effects. Indonesian nationalists, for example, were more influenced by their observations in India after 1937 when Congress leaders had obtained considerable power from the British at the provincial level than by their contacts in India during the early 1920's when widespread nationalist agitation by the Congress was in its early stages. Vietnamese nationalists likewise were more impressed by their personal contacts with the Chinese nationalist movement early in the twentieth century when it was opposing Manchu rule and Western encroachments, than during the 1930's when the Kuomintang had become a highly centralized and conservative regime.

3. *The Timing of the Return of Indigenous Returnees to Their Own Society:* The coincidence of the return of indigenous returnees with an increase of nationalist sentiment in the colonized or semi-independent societies tended to augment their influence. Prior to World War I the muted nationalism in colonized societies caused most indigenous returnees to remain apolitical and to ape Western residents. After World War I more indigenous returnees were strongly politicized and militantly opposed to Western colonial rule.[46] The significance of this factor was seen in the timing of the assumption of leading nationalist roles by Gandhi and Nehru between the two world wars when popular agitation was increasing against British colonial rule, a condition which enabled both men to emerge as the dominant nationalist leaders in India. The

timing of the return of indigenous returnees was also important in semi-independent societies. Indigenous returnees in China strengthened the nationalist organization of Sun Yat-sen and Chiang Kai-shek in the struggles against domestic warlords and foreign encroachments just after World War I, whereas indigenous returnees became some of the most severe critics of the Kuomintang after 1935 when it became repressive and reactionary. Indigenous returnees in Thailand assumed increasing influence during the late 1920's just as the country was adversely affected by a severe economic depression and the traditional respect for the absolute monarchy was declining due to the weak personality of King Prajadhipok. The confluence of these forces was significant in the overthrow of the absolute monarchy in June 1932.

EURASIANS

Eurasians were the offspring of conjugal relationships between Westerners and Asians, between Eurasians and Asians, or between Eurasians themselves.[47] This particular Western linkage induced several Western historical inputs only in colonized societies. It tended to wield an influence much larger than its relatively small size due to the fluency of Eurasians in the language of the Western colonial power, their easier access to Western education, and their natural acculturation into many aspects of Western culture. Yet in spite of the common label, "Eurasian," this class constituted an extremely complex and differentiated grouping of mixed racial personalities, torn often between Western and Asian cultures and usually sensitive about their origin and identity.[48] Most first-generation Eurasians were the children of a Western father and an Asian mother who adhered strongly to Western culture. Subsequent generations of Eurasians tended to be less oriented toward Western values and behavior and many sought to assimilate into the indigenous culture. Large numbers of Eurasians experienced travel, residence, or study in the West, and thereby received many of the same influences (already discussed) affecting indigenous returnees. In some cases, the racial consciousness among Eurasians who became indigenous returnees was more intensified and articulated than among indigenous persons.

The evolution of a Eurasian class created another minority with distinct racial and cultural characteristics which augmented cultural pluralism in the colonized society. This group was called "Anglo-Indian" in British India, "Anglo-Burman" in Burma, "burgher" in Ceylon, and "mestizo" in the Philippines. Its size and degree of Western orientation was a function of the timing of the expansion by the Western colonial power and its concept of colonial rule. Early Western colonials in Asia were required to intermarry in large numbers with indigenous women since few Western women assumed residence in the colonized society. During later stages of the colonization process less interracial marriage occurred among Westerners in the governmental linkages (colonial administrators, resident advisers, and colonial military officers) since larger numbers of Western women took up residence in the colonized society. Considerable interracial marriage continued, however, between non-governmental persons such as Western entrepreneurs and indigenous women. Also, the Eurasian class tended to be larger in colonized societies ruled by Roman Catholic colonial powers (Portugal, Spain, and France) since their colonial personnel were inclined to minimize the racial differences of indigenous women with the expectation that they would adopt their Western language, religion, and culture. The expansion of the Eurasian class in colonized societies ruled by Protestant colonial powers (Great Britain, Holland, and the United States) was limited by an attitude stressing the racial and cultural differences of indigenous women which posed a significant barrier to interracial marriage.

The political influence of Eurasians in the colonization process was a function of the degree of transferability of the political and administrative structures of the Western colonial power. In the high-transferable administrative structures of Great Britain and the United States, Eurasians exerted a significant role in the colonial bureaucracy. This influence was the most prevalent among first and second generation Eurasians whose personal orientation remained strongly attached to Western culture. These persons were able to pass civil service examinations in sizeable numbers due to their command of the English language and their knowledge of Western society and behavior. Some Eurasians in high-transferable administrative structures attained top-level civil service positions, including important posts in the police and military services. In the high-transferable political structures of the two English-speaking colonial powers, many Eurasians exerted important influences in the nationalist movement and the process of political reform.[49] This influence was more common among Eurasians psychologically detached from their original Western ancestry and whose personal orientation was directed primarily toward the indigenous society. The Eurasians in the Philippines exerted the maximum political influence among the colonized societies by dominating the Nacionalista Party from its formation in 1907 until national independence in 1946. In Singapore, Eurasians were likewise active in the movement toward self-government. David Marshall was the first Chief Minister of Singapore during its semi-autonomous status, and Sir George Oehlers was the first Speaker of the Singapore

Legislative Assembly. In India, Burma, and Ceylon, Eurasians played a peripheral role in the movement toward national independence by campaigning for the small number of special seats allotted to their class in the legislative councils established by successive political reforms.[50] In the low-transferable administrative structures of the Netherlands and France, Eurasians, like most indigenous persons, filled only minor roles in the colonial bureaucracy. In the low-transferable political structures of these two continental European powers, Eurasians also exerted no influence in the nationalist movement or political reforms.

These factors during the colonization process affected the role of Eurasians at the time of national independence. In the high-transferable political and administrative structures of Great Britain and the United States, many Eurasians were able to attain sufficient influence which tied them to the indigenous society and promoted an opportunity for continual service after national independence. A few Eurasians sought permanent residence in the society of the former Western colonial power, yet sizeable numbers remained in the newly-independent society after the termination of colonial rule. In the low-transferable political and administrative structures of the Netherlands and France, few Eurasians were able to attain influential roles in the civil service or in the nationalist movement prior to the end of colonial rule. In these colonized societies the Eurasians tended to be distrusted by the newly emerging political elites since they were considered sympathetic to the continuation of colonial rule. The majority of Eurasians in Indonesia and Indochina (especially Vietnam) consequently sought permanent residence in Holland or France after the achievement of national independence.

FOREIGN COMMUNITIES

Foreign communities consisted of foreign residents whose collective modes of behavior and life styles within the colonized or semi-independent societies transmitted certain Western historical inputs in addition to those imparted by each specific external linkage.[51] These foreign "presences" were much larger and more differentiated during the Western impact than their counterparts in the pre-Western era of the traditional society.[52] They comprised a Western community which was a totally new phenomenon in the indigenous society, and one or more regional alien communities which often antedated the Western community yet assumed new forms and influences during the Western impact. The Western and regional alien communities were themselves diversified among long-term residents and transient persons who remained in the indigenous society for relatively brief durations. Both types of foreign communities often occupied specific geographic areas within the capital or commercial cities where the vast majority of foreign residents were domiciled. The dominant Western presence was located in such areas as Forbes Park in Manila, Bangkapi in Bangkok, Menteng in Batavia (Djakarta), and Diplomatic Enclave in New Delhi. Chinese residents predominated in urban sections such as Cholon (adjoining Saigon), Sampeng in Bangkok, and Glodok in Djakarta. The influences exerted by the foreign communities emanated largely from these specific metropolitan areas.

The Western community assisted in transmitting various forms of the Western concept of progress by incorporating new social practices and behavior into the colonized or semi-independent societies. The Western community promoted modern urbanization by providing employment for sizeable numbers of servants, drivers, and maintenance personnel in the capital or commercial cities. In these metropolitan areas, Westerners utilized their own styles of colonial architecture and city planning. Their presence added another element of cultural pluralism. In colonized societies, the Western community was relatively homogeneous since it consisted almost entirely of citizens of the Western colonial power; in semi-independent societies, the Western community was more heterogeneous since it comprised diverse groups of Western nationals.[53] The Western presence likewise served as a tangible symbol of the "superiority" of Western culture since virtually all Western residents sought to maintain or increase the living standards they were accustomed to in the West. In relatively large numbers they resided in commodious homes with creature comforts and indigenous servant help in a life style which was surpassed only by the most wealthy and prominent members of the indigenous upper class. This practice, combined with the establishment of exclusive hotels, sports clubs, and other social facilities, created an inferior status for indigenous persons, a condition which aroused increasing anti-Western sentiment, especially among Western-educated indigenous returnees. The Western communities also served as targets of the nationalist movements. The superior life style of Western residents became a symbol of Western dominance and instilled a sense of envy and resentment in the minds of nationalist leaders.[54] In British and American colonies with high-transferable political and administrative structures, the entire Western communities, like the Western colonial administrators, served as targets of moderate reform which strengthened indigenous attitudes seeking national independence. In the French and Dutch colonized societies with low-transferable political and administrative structures, the Western communities became targets of violence during the final struggles for national independence. In the semi-independent society of China, the Western communities in the leased concessions likewise served as targets of nationalist hostility and agitation during the long struggle for complete national sovereignty.

Regional alien communities also transmitted several Western historical inputs to the indigenous society. The pre-Western religious or commercial roles of these foreign communities were drastically altered by the Western impact.[55] Regional alien communities became much larger than before, and they tended to outnumber the relatively small Western community. They depicted a hybrid life style showing varying degrees of Western technological achievement and a cultural pattern generally familiar to the indigenous population. Prosperous members of regional alien communities in some cases acquired luxurious life styles which equaled or surpassed those of the Western community.

To the indigenous society the regional alien communities displayed the Western concept of progress by pursuing higher living standards and the continual acquisition of material goods as a permanent economic and social goal. As a collective group they embodied achievement consciousness. They demonstrated to the indigenous population that many aspects of Western commerce and technology could be mastered by non-Western people. They increased cultural pluralism, largely in the urban areas. Like Western communities, they tended to be exclusive and clannish, although increasing numbers of regional aliens began to intermarry and assimilate in the indigenous society after the second or third generation.[56] Their restrictive social behavior combined with their influential economic roles made them targets of the indigenous nationalist movement as Western dominance began to decline. Their conspicuous economic prosperity at the time of national independence made them prominent targets of indigenous nationalist leaders seeking to reduce their preeminent economic roles.

INTERLINKAGE AND INTRALINKAGE POLITICAL BEHAVIOR

A final step in macro-linkage-analysis of Western linkages is the consideration of interlinkage and intralinkage political behavior. Interlinkage political behavior consisted of political interactions *between* certain external linkages involved in the colonization and unequal treaty processes. Intralinkage political behavior consisted of political interactions *within* these external linkages. While the diverse Western groups comprising each linkage adhered generally to the broad goals of colonial or foreign policy in both processes, they disagreed at times over policy implementation which affected their own specific interests. These groups consequently engaged in certain forms of "politics" in seeking modifications in colonial or foreign policy. This phenomenon occurred most frequently and openly in Western colonial systems with high-transferable political and administrative structures. In these societies, contending Western linkages exerted an additional demonstration effect of "modern" political behavior to indigenous persons which depicted a conflict of interests over diverse economic and social goals. Interlinkage and intralinkage political behavior occurred on a more reduced scale in colonial systems with low-transferable political and administrative structures since Western linkages in these systems maintained a higher degree of unity, and foreign disputes over colonial policy were more concealed from the indigenous society. In the unequal treaty process there was also relatively little "open" politics between and within Western linkages as most Westerners retained a strong vested interest in preserving their special treaty privileges.

In the colonized societies interlinkage political behavior occurred most commonly in contending relationships between Western colonial administrators and Western entrepreneurs. In performing their role of maintaining stable and efficient colonial rule, Western colonial bureaucracies did not serve as direct and immediate instruments of Western private enterprise. In varying degrees they assumed some responsibility for the general welfare of colonial subjects, and they often opposed political demands from Western commercial interests. According to Professor Emerson:

> It would be a misreading of the picture to see a complete identification of private Western enterprise and of government because, in fact, their outlooks and interests not infrequently diverged considerably. Colonial governments developed from the beginning a range of functions and concerns of their own — they were, after all, *governments* and not commercial companies. The colonial civil services liked to regard themselves as the protectors of the peoples they governed and not as the instruments of private economic interests.[57]

At the same time, Western entrepreneurs in the colonized societies were able through the articulation of their interests to colonial administrators as well as to the national legislature of the Western society to engage in profitable economic exploitation and to obtain an expansion of public services, including police protection, vocational training, agricultural research facilities, and sanitation programs. Some of these political interactions were institutionalized by the election or appointment of Western entrepreneurs to executive and legislative councils within the colonial systems. In these "advisory" councils, Western commercial interests demonstrated the influences of "group politics," especially in the British and American high-transferable political and administrative structures where they were increasingly observed by expanding numbers of elected and appointed indigenous representatives.[58]

Some interlinkage political behavior likewise occurred in the conflicting goals of Western colonial administrators and Western missionaries. The dominant contention in this relationship tended to be the divergent interests of colonial bureaucracies seeking order and stability within the colonized society and Western missionaries promoting the propagation of Christianity which in some areas fostered hostility and unrest. After the Sepoy mutiny in India, for example, British colonial administrators restricted the evangelical efforts of Christian missionaries among certain indigenous religious groups, and they provided indigenous religious leaders to serve the religious needs of Hindu, Moslem, and Sikh enlisted men in the Indian Army. Dutch colonial administrators in Indonesia likewise placed numerous restrictions on the proselyting work of Christian missionaries. They promoted political stability by facilitating the travel of Moslem teachers from the Middle East to Java and Sumatra in order to assist in spreading Islam. Western missionaries, however, were not totally helpless at the hands of Western colonial bureaucracies. As cited earlier, British missionaries in India were influential in obtaining humanitarian reforms in colonial policy which provided public assistance to underprivileged castes and groups. Dutch missionaries in Indonesia were instrumental in the adoption of the Ethical Policy after 1900 which provided more public welfare to indigenous people. Occasionally a major change in official colonial policy caused numerous Western groups in non-governmental linkages to combine their political influence in opposing new actions by colonial administrators. This form of political action occurred in India during the 1880's when non-official British citizens throughout the subcontinent organized "defense leagues" and collectively agitated against the Ilbert Bill pending in Parliament which would place British and Indian magistrates on an equal status and empower Indian magistrates to try British subjects.[59]

Within the linkage of Western colonial administrators, the most common form of intralinkage political behavior was the different approaches between conservative and liberal civil servants in promoting reforms leading toward national independence. In India this conflict was seen in the divergent views and actions among British factions within the Indian Civil Service as the British government negotiated the "Round Table" talks with Gandhi and Congress leaders after 1930 which eventually led to the Government of India Act of 1935 granting limited powers to indigenous political leaders and defining for the first time the conditions necessary for national independence.[60] Similar differences occurred among young Dutch colonial administrators in Indonesia after 1900 who vigorously pushed the Ethical Policy and the more cautious senior colonial officials who succumbed to conservative pressures of Dutch entrepreneurs after 1917. Intralinkage political behavior was also seen in the Philippines where the Democratic colonial administration of Francis B. Harrison from 1913 to 1921 facilitated a rapid transfer of political and administrative roles to Filipinos, and the Republican colonial administration of General Leonard Wood from 1921 to 1927 which slowed the process of transferring power to indigenous political leaders.[61] Intralinkage political behavior among Western entrepreneurs was witnessed in the conflicting influences on colonial policy exerted by diverse economic and commercial interests, including mining corporations, plantation owners, bankers, insurance companies, etc. The best example of intralinkage political behavior among Western scholars was the conflict in the 1830's between the British Orientalists who sought to preserve Indian traditional culture and the British modernists who advocated the "filtration" theory for colonial educational policy.

One of the most significant Western historical inputs generated by interlinkage and intralinkage political behavior in both the colonial and semi-independent societies was a stronger concept of the nation-state. This impact was imparted as indigenous nationalist leaders observed changes in Western colonial or foreign policy caused by political interactions among contending Western groups. These local leaders were soon aware that Western colonial or foreign policy was not implacable; with sufficient pressure they realized it could be changed. After watching successful changes generated by the "politics" of conflicting Western linkages in their own societies, they increasingly sought to make some changes themselves. Unlike the contending Western groups, however, the dominant goal of indigenous nationalists was not merely to change the substance of Western colonial policy or the unequal treaties, but to abolish these forms of external control.

Interlinkage and intralinkage political behavior in the high-transferable political and administrative structures in British and American colonies also transferred considerable skills in constitutional democracy to specific indigenous economic and social groups. Like competing Western groups, they sought to advance their own particular interests by articulating demands and exerting pressure on governmental authorities. Many of their specific goals were subordinated during the common quest for national independence, yet their observations of this form of Western political behavior provided the experience by which they were able to pursue these goals after national independence. Interlinkage and intra-linkage political behavior likewise assisted in providing some substantive issues and controversy to the constitutional reforms initiated by British and American colonial administrators. The increasingly democratic behavior induced by these reforms in turn caused greater differentiation and specialization within the emerging political and economic systems of British and American colonized societies.

SUMMARY

Nongovernmental linkages involved in the colonization process and the unequal treaty process imparted many differentiated Western historical inputs to Asian societies. Most of the Western values, modes of behavior, and institutions transmitted by these private and nonofficial linkages reinforced similar historical inputs caused by governmental linkages. They therefore comprised "shared" historical influences imparted by other Western linkages. A few historical inputs transmitted by non-governmental linkages were distinct and unique. Table XVII comprises a summary comparing these two types of historical inputs made by specific nongovernmental linkages and the specialized inputs imparted by inter-linkage and intralinkage political behavior.

Table XVII. A comparison of Western historical inputs imparted by specifi non-governmental linkages and by interlinkage and intralinkage politica behavior.

WESTERN NON-GOVERNMENTAL LINKAGES

Shared Western Historical Inputs	Entre-preneurs	Mission-aries	Scholars	Indigenous Returnees	Eurasians	Foreign Communi-ties	Interlinkage and Intralinkage Political Behavior
1. Concept of the nation-state	X	X	X	X			X
2. Concept of progress	X	X		X		X	X
3. Concept of equality		X		X	X		X
4. Expansion of cultural pluralism	X	X	X		X	X	
5. Modern urbanization	X					X	
6. Western language	X	X				X	
7. Humanitarian reforms		X					
8. Western-oriented institutions of higher education		X					
9. Symbol of the "superiority" of Western culture						X	
10. Promotion or performance of scholarly research		X	X			X	
11. Rationalized indigenous bureaucracy				X	X		
12. Constitutional democracy							X
13. Increased sub-system autonomy	X	X					
14. Target of the emerging nationalist movement	X	X					
Distinct Western Historical Inputs							
1. Modernizing indigenous entrepreneurial class	X						
2. Modern newspapers	X						
3. Urban and rural proletariat		X					
4. Religious freedom			X				
5. Prestige to the indigenous culture			X				
6. Moderate nationalism				X	X		
7. Liberal and leftist ideologies			X	X	X	X	

Chapter 9

Terminal Analysis of Western Historical Inputs

As in the final analysis of traditional historical inputs, the application of politically relevant terminal factors is also required in assessing the final changes in the values, modes of behavior, and institutions induced by the Western impact. Again this specialized methodology is needed to provide additional historical variables in comparative political analysis. This terminal analysis will supply supplementary criteria or standards capable of measuring the modifications of Western historical inputs as Asian societies achieved national independence or complete national sovereignty.

The terminal factors which affected the final stages of Western historical inputs in Asian societies are the following:

1. *The Duration of Western Linkages Involved in the Colonization Process or the Unequal Treaty Process:* This factor must be assessed for each Western external linkage, not only for the commonly cited duration of Western colonial administrators.[1] As in the duration of the external linkages which shaped traditional historical inputs, the influences of each Western linkage tended to increase with the passage of time.[2] A lengthy duration by colonial administrators augmented their role in transmitting important Western historical inputs such as the concept of the nation-state, the concept of progress, modern urbanization, a Western language, and Western-oriented institutions of higher education. A shorter duration tended to reduce the intensity of these differentiated Western historical inputs. Table XVIII comprises a comparison of the approximate dates of the origin of disparate Western linkages and their duration in years in Asian colonized societies. The dates of achieving national independence are shown in parentheses under the name of each colonized society. The approximate or exact dates of the origin of each Western linkage are shown in parentheses in the table under the duration of each linkage measured in years. The time-span of colonial administrators and military forces cited in this table is determined from the date these linkages exercised effective political control over the entire territory of the colonized society. In several cases, these durations must be augmented

Table XVIII. A comparison of the approximate or exact dates of origin of Western linkages in Asian colonized societies and their duration in years.

ASIAN COLONIZED SOCIETIES

WESTERN LINKAGES	India-Pakistan (1947)	Ceylon (1948)	Burma (1948)	Malaya (1957)	Philip-Pines (1946)	Indonesia (1949)	Vietnam (1954)	Cambodia (1953)	Laos (1953)
Colonial Administrators and Military Forces	90 (1857)*	127 (1815)	63 (1885)	67 (1890)	48 (1898)**	150 (1799)***	67 (1887)	88 (1856)	57 (1896
Political Agents	25 (1922)	—	—	—	—	29 (1920)	32 (1922)	—	—
Entrepreneurs	90 (1857)*	123 (1825)	123 (1825)	67 (1890)	41 (1905)	249 (1700)	64 (1890)	53 (1900)	
Missionaries	122 (1825)	98 (1850)	98 (1850)	57 (1900)	45 (1901)**	99 (1850)	179 (1775)	—	—
Scholars	117 (1830)	108 (1840)	68 (1880)	—	45 (1901)	69 (1880)	74 (1880)	63 (1890)	—
Indigenous Returnees	57 (1890)	68 (1880)	28 (1920)	47 (1910)	36 (1910)	29 (1920)	34 (1920)	33 (1920)	33 (1920
Eurasians	67 (1880)	58 (1890)	48 (1900)	37 (1920)	45 (1901)	49 (1900)	34 (1920)	—	—
Foreign Communities	180 (1767)	298 (1650)	78 (1870)	446 (1511)	381 (1565)	199 (1750)	64 (1890)	88 (1865)	57 (1896

*British colonial administrators and military forces and British entrepreneurs actually began the colonization process in India about 1767 under the semi-official authority of the British East India Company. The date 1857 is cited in this table as the time when British colonial rule in India was directly controlled by the British government in London.

**These figures depict the date and duration of American colonial and military authority and American missionaries in the Philippines. The duration of Spanish colonial rule and Spanish missionaries was 333 years extending from 1565 to 1898.

***Dutch colonial administrators and military forces began the colonization process in Indonesia during the seventeenth century under the semi-official authority of the Dutch East India Company. The date 1799 is cited in this table as the time when Dutch colonial rule in Indonesia was directly controlled by the Dutch government in The Hague.

for certain geographic areas since colonial administrative and military authority was extended over these territories prior to these dates. In Burma, for example, British colonial administrators and military forces first established a tenuous control in the Irrawaddy delta region in 1826. This control was expanded to the central area in 1852. British colonial authority was finally exercised over the entire Burmese territory in 1886.

Similar piecemeal expansion of territorial control was made in the colonization process in Malaya, Indonesia, and Vietnam. The dates cited in Table XVIII for most nongovernmental linkages are estimated from the time they assumed social and political significance.

Table XIX shows the approximate dates of the origin of different Western linkages in the semi-independent societies in Asia and their duration in years. The dates of achieving complete national sovereignty by the termination of the unequal treaties with Western nations are shown in parentheses under the names of each semi-independent society. As in Table XVIII the dates cited for most nongovernmental linkages are estimated from the time they assumed some social and political importance.

Table XIX. A comparison of the approximate dates of origin of Western linkages in semi-independent Asian societies and their duration in years.

SEMI-INDEPENDENT ASIAN SOCIETIES

WESTERN LINKAGES	China (1943)	Japan (1898)	Thailand (1937)
Diplomats	99 (1844)	44 (1854)	82 (1855)
National Military Forces	104 (1839)	58 (1840)	44 (1893)
Contracted Advisers	83 (1860)	28 (1870)	72 (1855)
Political Agents	22 (1921)	—	—
Entrepreneurs	123 (1825)	43 (1855)	72 (1855)
Missionaries	93 (1870)	28	109 (1828)
Scholars	73 (1870)	—	—
Indigenous Returnees	63 (1880)	23 (1875)	47 (1890)

The preceding comparisons of the duration of specific Western linkages in the colonized and semi-independent societies of Asia show that
the longest influences were exerted by colonial administrators, colonial
military forces, diplomats, and national military forces among the
governmental linkages, and by entrepreneurs and missionaries among
the nongovernmental linkages. The Western historical inputs generated
by these external penetrations therefore induced the most significant
changes. Important and challenging in the analysis of this terminal factor
is the comparative influence of the duration of traditional historical
inputs most of which extended over many centuries, and the duration of
Western historical inputs which lasted over much briefer periods of time.
The value of religious eclecticism-psychological pluralism in the Hindu
cultural system, for example, endured for 4257 years, and the value of
doctrinal idealism-political pragmatism in the Confucian cultural system
in China lasted for 2425 years.[3] In sharp contrast was the concept of the
nation-state and the concept of progress imparted by Western colonial
administrators for only 90 years in India and by Western diplomats for a
mere 99 years in China. Yet the relatively short durations of most
Western historical inputs induced more significant influences in Asian
societies than many traditional historical inputs which had spanned
many centuries. The quantitative assessment of this terminal factor
involving the duration of disparate Western linkages must consequently
be combined with the qualitative analysis presented in Part Three dealing
with the various responses of Asian societies to diverse Western historical
inputs.

2. *The Size of Each Western Linkage in the Colonization Process:*[4]
The size refers to the number of Western nationals comprising each specific Western linkage at the crucial period when colonial rule began coming to an end. This factor was shaped by the concept of colonial rule and
the degree of transferability of Western political and administrative
structures. The eclectic-pragmatic colonial rule and high-transferable
political and administrative structures in the colonized societies governed
by Great Britain and the United States induced sizeable nongovernmental linkages and relatively small governmental linkages. The eclectic-
pragmatic concept of colonial rule of the Netherlands combined with
low-transferable political and administrative structures produced both
sizeable governmental and nongovernmental linkages. The unitary-
doctrinaire colonial rule of France and Japan and their low-transferable
political and administrative structures produced large governmental linkages and relatively small nongovernmental linkages. These factors
affected the process of transferring national independence to indigenous
control and the form of nationalism espoused by indigenous leaders dur-

ing the final period of colonial rule.

The process of transferring independence proceeded relatively smoothly in the colonized societies with sizeable nongovernmental linkages and small governmental linkages. It proceeded with considerable turbulence and resistance in the colonized societies with large governmental linkages and small nongovernmental linkages. Large governmental linkages, primarily colonial administrators, opposed the move toward national independence since they were totally dependent on their own governments for employment, and the termination of colonial rule with few exceptions meant the end of a desirable and prestigious official career.[5] Their only alternative was an uncertain future in their own Western society, a society which was surprisingly remote and strange to many of these persons who had spent much or all of their lives in the colonized society. Large non-governmental linkages, on the other hand, especially entrepreneurs and missionaries, were more willing to accommodate themselves to the emerging national society. They had a vested interest in the indigenous society in the form of property and a clientele which they wanted to preserve. They tended to exhibit some doubts about their future prospects in a society governed by inexperienced indigenous leaders, yet they maintained considerable hope that they would continue to operate effectively in the period of national independence.

The relative size of Western linkages tended to reinforce these contrasting viewpoints. Within large Western linkages the attitudes seeking the continuation of colonial rule were strengthened. The feeling that numerous Western nationals wanted to preserve their position in the colonized society bolstered the collective opinion that this sizeable group could not be removed and replaced. Within small Western linkages the prevailing attitude was to accept the "inevitable" and seek accommodation with an emerging indigenous government. The relatively few number of Western nationals in these groups felt there was little or nothing they could do to affect the movement toward national independence.

3. *The Size, Economic Role, and Duration of Regional Alien Communities:*[6] The size of regional alien communities affected nationalist attitudes within the indigenous political leadership as colonial rule entered its final stages. Large regional alien communities, like large Western governmental linkages, tended to favor the continuation of Western colonial rule. In most cases the economic and social status of these groups had improved considerably during the Western colonization process, and they felt their interests would suffer in an independent national society. Small regional alien groups, conversely, tended to accept national independence as inevitable and exhibited few overt signs

of resisting the movement toward national independence. The economic role of regional aliens varied from entrepreneurs to skilled and unskilled labor. The economic role of regional alien communities also was influenced by the passage of time.[7] A long duration of regional aliens in the society caused a large proportion of these persons to be engaged in entrepreneurial roles. A short duration of this foreign group caused a large proportion to be employed in skilled and unskilled laboring roles. The relatively long duration of Chinese communities in Burma, Indonesia, and the Philippines prior to national independence, for example, resulted in a preponderance of entrepreneurial roles among these regional alien groups. The relatively short duration of many Chinese aliens in Malaya and Singapore before national independence caused large numbers of these persons to be employed in laboring roles.

4. *The Degree of Harshness of the Western Colonization Process or the Unequal Treaty Process:* The assessment of this important terminal factor is complicated by the fact that virtually all influences imparted by Western linkages in colonized and semi-independent societies in Asia involved some degree of harshness and severity for indigenous people throughout the period of the Western impact. Yet some attempt must be made to measure as accurately as possible the degree of harshness imposed by Western domination since it affected the transfer of many Western values, modes of behavior, and institutions to the emerging national society. This terminal factor was of special significance in shaping the ideas and behavior of indigenous nationalist leaders. Figure XV comprises a high-low continuum showing the degree of harshness imposed by Western nations in the colonization process and the unequal treaty process in Asia.

Like the size of Western linkages, the degree of harshness in the colonization process was influenced by the concept of colonial rule and the degree of transferability of political and administrative structures. The eclectic-pragmatic concept of colonial rule and high-transferable political and administrative structures of the United States involved the least degree of harshness on the indigenous society in the colonial system in the Philippines. American colonial administrators delayed many reforms advocated by Filipino nationalist leaders seeking a rapid transfer of national independence, yet they did not impose incarceration or physical punishment in resisting the demands of indigenous nationalist leaders. A similar concept of colonial rule and high-transferable political and administrative structures of Great Britain likewise entailed minor restrictions on leaders of indigenous nationalist movements in the colonial systems in Ceylon, Burma, and Malaya. The degree of harshness of British

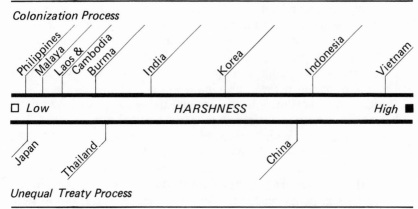

Fig. XV. *High-low continuum comparing the degree of harshness imposed by Western nations in the colonization process and the unequal treaty process in Asia.*

colonial rule was somewhat more intense in India where British administrative and military authorities intermittently applied physical force and incarceration in suppressing Indian nationalist leaders until the rapid transfer of national independence following World War II.

The eclectic-pragmatic colonial rule and low-transferable political and administrative structures of the Netherlands in Indonesia produced a considerably higher degree of harshness than in the American or British colonial systems. Prior to World War I the Dutch used corporal punishment, including floggings and executions, to suppress nationalist sentiment. Between the two world wars they reduced these methods of physical punishment, yet they continued to impose long prison terms on nationalist agitators.[8] The unitary-doctrinaire concept of colonial rule and low-transferable political and administrative structures of France and Japan induced the highest degree of harshness in the colonized societies in Vietnam and Korea. Limited French influences and minor manifestations of nationalist sentiment in Laos and Cambodia involved relatively few suppressive measures in these two sparsely populated colonized societies. Yet French colonial authorities imposed severe physical punishment, including long prison terms, torture, and executions, on Vietnamese nationalist agitators until just prior to World War II.[9] Similar coercive measures and the use of military power were applied by the

French in an effort to suppress the Viet Minh communist-nationalist movement after 1946. The harshness of Japanese colonial rule in Korea was usually muted and subtle since Japan relied essentially on indirect controls through economic and educational measures to retain control of the indigenous people. With few exceptions Korean nationalists were overtly active only in foreign countries. Yet Japanese colonial authorities did use strong and ruthless suppressive action against several overt exhibitions of nationalist sentiment in the Korean colonized society.[10]

The degree of harshness in the unequal treaty process exerted more indirect and intermittent influences than in the colonization process. This terminal factor in the semi-independent societies was affected by the goals of foreign policy of the Western powers. Although there was some overlapping, a commercially-oriented foreign policy tended to restrain the severity of Western suppressive measures, while a strategically-oriented foreign policy tended to increase them. In effect, the Western powers undertook stronger actions in the semi-independent societies in protecting their territorial interests and upholding their political stature as major world powers than in promoting commercial interests for their own nationals. The degree of harshness was least significant in Japan where Western powers sought an expansion of trade after the Meiji Restoration and gradually recognized Japan as a major power in the Asia and Pacific region. The Western powers accordingly relied solely on diplomacy to administer their unequal treaties in Japan until they were abolished in 1898. The harshness of the unequal treaty process was somewhat more intense in Thailand where conflicting strategic goals of Great Britain and France involved the use of diplomacy and military power to uphold their special treaty privileges as well as to obtain additional territorial concessions. This practice ended in 1909 when the last territory was detached from Thailand, and the two European powers relied entirely on diplomacy in administering the unequal treaties until they were completely terminated in 1937. The degree of harshness in the unequal treaty process was most severe in China where bitter clashes between the strategic policies of the Western powers and Japan caused major diplomatic and military intrusions in Chinese internal affairs. These disruptive external influences continued until the unequal treaties were abolished during and after World War II.

5. *The Degree of Military Violence in the Final Stages of the Colonization Process or Unequal Treaty Process:* The degree of military violence involved in this terminal factor consisted of the intensity of military action and destruction between the Western colonial powers and Imperialist Japan during World War II, and between Western colonial powers and indigenous insurgents just prior to national independence. Fig-

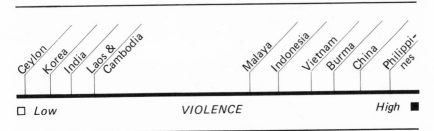

Fig. XVI. High-low continuum showing the degree of military violence during the final stages of the colonization process or the unequal treaty process in Asia.

ure XVI comprises a high-low continuum depicting the degree of military violence in the final stages of the colonization process or the unequal treaty process in Asia.

No military violence occurred in the termination of the colonization process in Ceylon, and relatively little military destruction took place in the final stages of the colonial systems in Korea, India, Laos, and Cambodia. A higher degree of military activity occurred in the final stages of colonial rule elsewhere in Asia and in the unequal treaty process in China. Extensive military actions were undertaken by Japanese troops in China, the Philippines, Burma, and Malaya early in World War II, and large-scale military violence took place in most of these same societies by Allied and indigenous military forces near the end of the war. Additional military action was used in the British campaign against Communist insurgents in Malaya shortly after World War II, and guerrilla warfare was waged by indigenous insurgent forces in Vietnam and Indonesia to oppose the reimposition of Western colonial rule.

6. *The Psychological, Political, and Economic Effect of World War II on the Attitude of Western Colonial Powers Toward Granting National Independence to Colonized Societies:* This terminal factor was influenced by the role of Western colonial powers in the military hostilities against the Axis powers, and it shaped post-war considerations regarding the issue of national independence for the colonized societies. A major role by a Western colonial power in the military defeat of the Axis alliance generated a sense of self-confidence and national esteem in its government and populace. It enhanced its national prestige at a time of crucial realignments in the power structure of international society. It reduced a desire to demonstrate national power by reimposing colonial

rule over pre-war colonized societies. These conditions combined with the post-war global appeal for a stable peace and more individual and collective freedom tended to encourage the granting of national independence by Western colonial powers. This action in turn enhanced the status of the diplomatic mission of the former Western colonial power in the newly-independent national society, and in some cases it facilitated the stationing of modest Western military forces in the territory of the former colony. A peaceful transfer of national independence likewise preserved a favorable image of nongovernmental linkages which continued to operate in a generally friendly indigenous environment.

Conversely, military defeat and/or military occupation of a Western colonial power by the Axis alliance induced a sense of national frustration and uncertainty in the early post-war era. The restructuring of international power caused an intense desire within these Western societies to restore pre-war national prestige. Wartime damage, either physical or psychological, engendered an urgent need to revive the national economy and reassert national power. These conditions encouraged the restoration of colonial rule and strengthened resistance to granting national independence. The desire to repair the setbacks of the war and to regain national esteem tended to ignore the upsurge of post-war idealism stressing peace and freedom for colonized societies. This action damaged the stature of the diplomatic mission of the former Western colonial power after national independence was achieved and it encouraged the removal of all Western military forces from the former colony. It also tarnished the reputation of nongovernmental linkages which were either removed from the newly-independent national society or operated in a generally hostile environment. This phenomena was seen in the impact of World War II on all Western colonial powers in Asia.[11]

The emergence of the United States as a major victor in the war against the Axis powers facilitated the prompt transfer of national independence to the Philippines, and it enabled the United States to become the first Western colonial power to grant national independence to an Asian colonized society. While the United States had previously taken significant steps toward Philippine independence, this final action was encouraged by the wartime demonstration of American national power in successfully waging large-scale military campaigns on two fronts and bringing about the Japanese surrender by the use of atomic weapons. American national territory was untouched by wartime destruction, and the post-war future appeared promising and bright. The United States was quickly recognized as a new superpower in the structure of international politics. It exerted a leading role in the formation of the United Nations, and it extended considerable economic assistance for the rehabilitation of numerous war-torn countries.

Great Britain also emerged as a victor in the military conflict against the Axis powers, and it likewise began the process of granting national independence to its colonies in Asia. These moves were made with the same basic motivation as that of the United States, although at a somewhat slower pace. The termination of British colonial rule was facilitated by the demonstration of British power in waging war against Nazi Germany for the longest period of any Allied nation and in its contribution to Allied victories in North Africa, Europe, and Burma. Unlike the United States, however, the post-war status of Great Britain was hampered by extensive damage from German bombing and a slow economic recovery. The British played a significant role in the formation of the United Nations, but they no longer exerted their pre-war role as a major power. This impending decline of British influence and prestige caused some political leaders, such as Winston Churchill, to advocate the restoration of British colonial rule in Asia. Yet the dominant national attitude was reflected in the electoral victory of the Labour Party in July 1945 which resulted in prompt parliamentary action to grant national independence to British colonies in Asia.

The occupation of the Netherlands by Nazi Germany and the extensive wartime damage inflicted on Dutch cities were significant factors encouraging the Dutch to seek the restoration of their colonial rule in Indonesia. The Dutch were not concerned with the revival of their national power or national prestige for the purpose of asserting a major role in international politics; they only wanted sufficient national power to reestablish control over their profitable Southeast Asian colony. In considerable degree they pursued the same economic-oriented colonial policy after 1945 seeking the acquisition of important raw materials in Indonesia to rebuild their war-damaged economy as they had done after 1815 in using their profitable trade in Indonesia to recover from the wartime occupation by Napoleonic France.[12] This attitude encouraged Dutch military action against the hastily formed Republic of Indonesia from 1945 to 1949 until pressures from Western and non-aligned powers through the United Nations and bilateral diplomatic channels forced the Netherlands to grant national independence to its former Asian colony.

The sudden and humiliating defeat of France by Nazi Germany early in World War II was likewise an important factor which promoted the policy to restore French colonial rule in Indochina in the post-war era. The French wanted to regain control over the resources of these Asian colonies to assist in the physical rehabilitation of France. More important, the French were seeking desperately to restore their national prestige after five years of Vichy rule and German occupation, and to regain international recognition of their pre-war status as a major Western power. The minor French role in the defeat of the Axis alliance encouraged a prompt reassertion of French administrative authority over liberated colonies in Asia (and North Africa) to demonstrate French national power.[13] This attitude encouraged military action against the nationalist-communist movement in Vietnam from 1946 to 1954 when a combination of French political instability, French military ineptitude, and international pressures forced the government in Paris to grant national independence to Laos, Cambodia, a communist state in North Vietnam, and a non-communist state in South Vietnam.

The terminal factors affecting Western historical inputs imparted distinctive and unique influences as Asian societies entered a new historical era. The focus in this chapter has been only on the final conditions affecting *Western* values, modes of behavior, and institutions during this important period of political development. The impact of these same terminal factors in shaping the *indigenous role* in the political systems of these newly-emerging national societies will be explained in Chapter Sixteen dealing with the terminal analysis of fusional historical factors.

Part Three
The Indigenous Response

The Indigenous Response

The indigenous response consisted of the reaction and replication of the indigenous people to the Western impact.[1] It comprised the internal effect and local initiatives caused by the stimuli of external Western influences. Unlike the indigenous response to foreign influences in the pre-Western era, the indigenous response to the Western impact involved sharp and major changes with the past. No longer were foreign values and foreign institutions gradually absorbed by indigenous leaders and people in the process of maintaining an essentially unchanged traditional society. Instead the indigenous response to Western civilization unleashed new forces and new influences which led eventually to the formation of markedly different types of societies.

The indigenous response occurred simultaneously with the Western impact, but was distinct from it. In the Orient it comprised what Panikkar has termed "the renaissance of Asia."[2] This very important historical process, however, is much easier to envision conceptually than empirically since many aspects of the interaction between traditional and Western influences were closely intertwined. The separation of the indigenous response from the Western impact for comparative political analysis consequently has many shortcomings as much of the development of new historical inputs cannot be neatly classified into "Western" and "indigenous" categories. Some aspects of this difficulty have already been encountered in Part Two of this study. Two specific examples of the close relationship between important Western and indigenous influences were indigenous returnees and Eurasians.[3]

Yet the effort must be made to isolate and analyze as accurately as possible the complex process of the acculturation and adoption of new values, modes of behavior, and institutions by Asian people, individually and collectively, during the time of the Western impact. The residue or "end-product" of this historical intercultural amalgamation produced the foundation of new national societies which achieved their independence at the conclusion of the colonization process or the unequal treaty process. In effect, a detailed and systematic study of the indigenous response is necessary in explaining and measuring the relative strength of the diverse political elements involved in the formation of these newly-independent societies. This effort will help elaborate the evolution of what Joungwon Kim has labeled "the predevelopmental system."[4]

The analysis of the indigenous response in Part Three will focus on the interaction between traditional historical inputs and Western historical inputs which engendered what I will call *fusional historical inputs.* This methodology will seek to isolate and interpret what the indigenous people did in the political realm during the Western impact just as the analysis in Part II sought to classify and assess the numerous and diverse political influences transmitted by Western linkages during this important historical period. Fusional historical inputs were the complex admixture of traditional and Western values, modes of behavior, and institutions produced by indigenous people in their quest for an end to Western domination. They were the amalgamated, synthetic and composite elements of new national societies which evolved until the time of achieving national independence. These fused historical inputs are crucial ingredients in the emergence of what is commonly referred to as "transitional" societies. They are consequently involved in the widely studied field of comparative politics of non-Western nations which has sought to explain "traditional" and "modern" phenomena for almost two decades, and has been an important influence in the behavioral movement in political science.[5]

A few fusional historical inputs were common to all societies in Asia. All of these politically relevant historical influences were closely interrelated. Firstly, the indigenous response was largely an *urban response.* The impact of Western culture mainly affected indigenous persons at the central and upper levels of the former great traditions or middle traditions of the traditional society. Some technological innovations made by the Western impact, such as new transportation facilities and some commercial enterprises, affected a relatively small number of rural villagers, but with very few exceptions the major psychological, social, and political response to Western historical inputs occurred in the cities of these newly-emerging societies.[6] The vast majority of indigenous people living in the little traditions in rural areas remained less touched by Western values and influences.

Another widespread fusional historical input was the quest for modern nationhood utilizing the Western-induced ideology of *nationalism.* Almost from the beginning of the colonization process or the unequal treaty process thinking Asians wanted to achieve a modern form of national identity and an end of Western domination.[7] This widely shared attitude was based on a mixture of cultural, racial, linguistic, and religious or doctrinal values, yet its most essential characteristic was the common historical experience seeking national freedom from Western rule. It involved the growing desire to attain a mastery of the physical and social environment produced by the impact of Western science and technology. This attitude opposed the revival of the societal structure and many norms of the traditional society, but it did not reject all traditional values and customs, and it upheld the desirability of preserving and strengthening many indigenous modes of behavior. Yet newly-emerging Asian leaders were dedicated to the formation of modern national societies modeled after those in the West and using the scientific and technological methods of the West. The adoption of this Western value was one of the clearest forms of imitative behavior in the indigenous response.

A third fusional historical input experienced throughout Asia was *the rapid increase in population.* In most societies this new phenomena was the natural increase in population caused by the orderly and controlled environments produced by the Western powers.[8] In some societies important population increases were also caused by the migration of regional aliens, such as the movement of Chinese migrants to Southeast Asia, Indian migrants to Burma and Malaya, and Vietnamese migrants to Cambodia and Laos. Everywhere the innovation of modern sanitation and the diminution in the loss of life due to efficient administrative systems generated a large decrease in the death rate of these societies. This factor combined with an unchanged birth rate resulted in a sudden and dramatic increase in the number of inhabitants residing in each society in what has been widely labeled "the population explosion." This new demographic influence caused numerous social changes including an increase in family size, a larger number of older people, an increased population density in some rural areas, and a rapid population growth in urban centers. Implicitly and subtly this process which enabled more people to live longer engendered a greater respect for human life and eroded in some degree the fatalistic orientation deeply imbedded in all Asian cultures. At the same time the rapid population increase induced countervailing tendencies by causing greater poverty, intensified pressure on the land, and a growing demand in many societies for a new system of land reform.

Cultural secularization comprised a final fusional historical input which became increasingly intense in all Asian societies. This pervasive influence oriented indigenous leaders and people to rational and empirical approaches to concrete problems. According to Almond and Powell:

The secularization of culture is the processes whereby traditional orientations and attitudes give way to more dynamic decision-making processes involving the gathering of information, the laying out of alternative courses of action, the selection of a course of action from among these possible courses, and the means whereby one tests whether or not a given course of action is producing the consequences which were intended.[9]

Cultural secularization clashed most severely with the values and institutions of the sacred-oriented traditional societies in South and Southeast Asia, and it began the process of separating religion from the resolution of mundane social and political problems. Conversely, cultural secularization tended to intensify some of the pragmatic behavior of the secular-oriented traditional societies in East Asia, yet this influence likewise began to separate many norms and modes of traditional behavior from the adoption of modern administrative and technological changes. In both types of societies the new Western-induced secularization seeking rational solutions to political and economic problems directed thought from the traditional focus on the past to the improvement of life in the future.

These few common fusional historical inputs among the societies of Asia were exceptional; most aspects of the indigenous response in this vast and populous region varied greatly. Just as the Western impact consisted of highly diversified and variegated stimuli, so did the indigenous response to this impact comprise a highly diversified and variegated reaction. Within each society occurred an amazing variety of responses to Western historical inputs. Some indigenous individuals and groups sought to assimilate, absorb, imitate, or accommodate specific Western influences; other indigenous elements endeavored to resist, reject, vilify, or distort these same Western values and behavior. Almost always there were significant overlappings between these two seemingly opposing tendencies. The complexity of this cross-societal diffusion was compounded by the fact that not all elements of the traditional society clashed with Western values and influences. Some traditional customs and institutions were seriously weakened or destroyed by the Western impact, but other traditional behavior was strengthened and enhanced. Many social and political elements became an interesting blending of traditional and Western characteristics. Politically relevant elements of these fusional historical inputs will be analyzed in Part Three. They are the amalgamated composites which shaped the evolving process of secularized political change. They are, in brief, the mixture of the old and the new which comprised the various parts of the emerging political systems and moved the societies of Asia into the era of modernization.

This phenomena creates the need for a model capable of analyzing the broad array of differentiated fusional historical inputs and for classifying the new types of societies and political systems in Asia. Such a model must be suitable for clarifying and measuring in some degree the autonomy of the political systems in these newly-emerging nations. It should also be capable of explaining the degree of differentiation and specialization within the evolving polities. I will accordingly use a model adapted from the systems analysis approach of David Easton and the structural-functional theory of Gabriel Almond.[10] This model conceives of the political system of a modern national society as the specialized sub-system converting demands and supports (political inputs) generated in the domestic and foreign environments into official governmental policies (political outputs). As defined by Easton, "the political system is the most inclusive system of behavior in a society for the authoritative allocation of values."[11] As perceived by Almond, the political system consists of "all the interactions which affect the use or threat of use of ligitimate physical coercion."[12] The function of the political system, in brief, involves the positive response of the society to the challenges of its environment and the mobilization of its resources for the achievement of selected common goals. This function is performed by the legitimate, corporate, and coercive sub-system which protects and regulates the society as it seeks collectively desired objectives.

Figure XVII shows the relationships between traditional, Western, and fusional historical inputs in the formation of a modernizing society, its domestic environment, and the political system.

In this figure the political system is depicted as three interrelated processes. The *normative process* constitutes the embodiment, production, modification, and refinement of political values, standards, and norms caused by the interaction between an abstract *political ideology* (largely derived from foreign sources) and the indigenous *political culture*. The political ideology consists of the structure of ethical criteria which shapes the assimilation of basic political ideas and principles with the political culture comprising politically relevant attitudes, beliefs, skills, and customs of a specific society.[13] In brief, the political ideology is the value-producing element of the normative process; the political culture is the collective psychological orientation toward political behavior. The normative process legitimizes the passage of new ideas and new demands as they interact with the political process and the governmental process.

The *political process* consists of the process of communicating politically relevant information and opinions in the society, articulating particular political demands among specific groups, aggregating broad

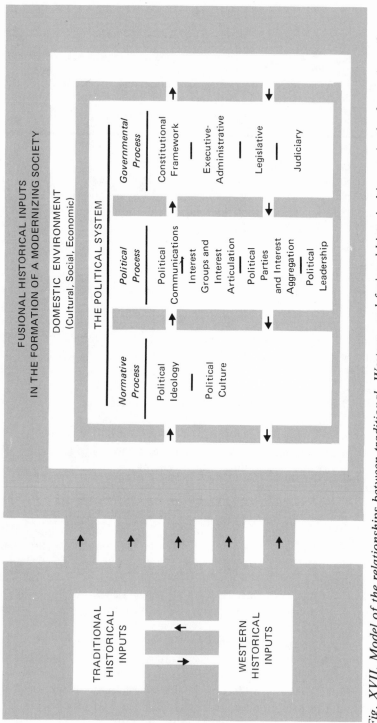

Fig. XVII. Model of the relationships between traditional, Western, and fusional historical inputs in the formation of a modernizing society, its domestic environment, and the political system.

political support among individuals and organizations, and selecting specific programs and policies by political elites. The political process thereby includes *political communication, interest groups and interest articulation, political parties and interest aggregation, and political leadership.*[14] This process takes place both outside and inside the formal organs of government, although it is essentially an extra-official process.

The *governmental process* is the process of modifying, legitimizing, and implementing the outputs or official actions induced by political inputs from the normative and political processes. The governmental process takes place largely within the formal institutions of government, *executive-administrative, legislative,* and *judiciary,* and it is often structured in some degree by a *constitutional framework.* The outputs take the form of economic, social, and foreign policies providing benefits and favors to selected groups both within the society and in the foreign community. This process is the part of the political system which remained entirely or largely under Western control during the colonization process or was legally subordinate in specific areas to Western powers in the unequal treaty process. The complete control of the governmental process was the major goal of nationalist leaders and organizations in Asia seeking the termination of Western domination.

Part Three will consist of an analysis of the six types of political systems produced by the Western impact in Asia. These types are the *quasi-democracies* (India, Pakistan, Ceylon, Burma, Malaya, the Philippines), the *bureaucratic polities* (Nationalist China, Japan, Thailand), the *truncated totalitarian polities* (Communist China, North Korea, North Vietnam), the *truncated authoritarian polities* (South Korea, South Vietnam), the *hybrid polity* (Indonesia), and the *dynastic polities* (Cambodia, Laos). This part of the study will conclude with an analysis of relevant terminal factors which shaped politically relevant fusional historical inputs just prior to national independence or the achievement of complete national sovereignty.

As cited in the Introduction, my study consists essentially of a detailed political analysis of the broad historical process which I have defined as the Westernization of Asian societies up to the time of the termination of Western colonial rule or Western extraterritorial controls.[15] The more recent process of modernization which overlaps considerably with the process of Westernization and which began promptly in most Asian nations with the post-independence era will be explained in a very brief and general manner in the Conclusion. This short discussion of political development of independent national societies in Asia will logically follow an explanation of longitudinal historical analysis which will give some useful concluding insights into the relationships between traditional, Western, and fusional historical inputs in the pre-independence period and post-independence government and politics.

Chapter 10

The Quasi-Democracies

Six of the seventeen emerging national societies in Asia developed into quasi-democracies during the indigenous response. Many traditional authoritarian elements remained strong in these evolving nation-states, and democratic values and institutions rested lightly on the thought and behavior of their people at the time of national independence. In most cases the struggle for independence had touched only a small number of indigenous political activists, and a vast majority of the local populace was completely untouched by the gradual transfer of political power from Western to indigenous control.

Yet many fusional historical inputs in these six developing societies oriented their political systems closer to Western democratic standards than in any other type of emerging society in Asia. There are several significant reasons for this phenomena. Some traditional influences in these six societies enhanced the development of democratic values and behavior. Certain aspects of their sacred-oriented cultural systems and class structures contributed to a sense of tolerance and moderation in the new political culture. The traditional society possessed a highly assimilative and eclectic capacity as well as a high degree of adaptability to foreign-induced change. It embodied an instrumental ethos which urged indigenous leaders and groups to elevate social and economic standards throughout the new national society. The evolving political style was increasingly rational and achievement-oriented.

All of the quasi-democracies had sizeable ethnic groups which also promoted a sense of flexibility and accommodation in the new national politics. This type of polity evolved in what I have called *consensual-ethnic societies* (India, Pakistan, Malaya, the Philippines) containing two or more ethnic groups none of which comprised a significant majority of the population, or it developed from *dominant-ethnic societies* (Ceylon, Burma) containing a single dominant ethnic group with sizeable ethnic minorities.[1] The presence of large numbers of regional aliens (Arabs, Indians, Chinese) induced cultural and social pluralism which likewise promoted certain accommodative political behavior in all of the quasi-democracies except India.

The major force shaping the political systems of the quasi-democracies, however, was their common pattern of Western influences. All of these polities were made by the high-transferable political and administrative structures and the high-transformative social policies of British or American colonial rule. All had experienced a relatively low degree of harshness in the colonization process. All were affected by the high degree of self-confidence of the Western colonial powers after World War II and their readiness to grant national independence to their Asian colonies. The quasi-democracies were likewise shaped by the relatively small-sized governmental linkages in the colonization process which contributed to an indigenous rationalized bureaucracy and indigenous democratic institutions engaging in the processes of state-building and nation-building. The emerging political systems were also influenced by deep penetrations of large-sized non-governmental linkages, including Western entrepreneurs, Western missionaries, Western scholars, indigenous returnees, Eurasians, and foreign communities.

DOMESTIC ENVIRONMENT

There was relatively little uniformity in the fusional historical inputs caused by the cultural, social, and economic changes in the quasi-democracies during the indigenous response. Yet some common elements did evolve in the amalgamation of traditional and Western influences which contributed in varying degrees to a democratic orientation and behavior. One of these elements was the movement toward a much greater diversity of religious values and behavior which somewhat paradoxically encouraged religious toleration and social harmony. The eclectic and experimentive ethos motivating much of Anglo-American colonial policy served to reinforce many elements of the religious eclecticism embodied in the Hindu, Theravada Buddhist, Islamic, and atomized animist cultural systems which assisted this trend. Western values of progress, equality, and individualism also contributed to a stronger "this-worldly" outlook. Especially important was the effect of Western science and technology in arousing more rapid changes among the indigenous urban populace toward pragmatism and secularization.

Some orthodox religious groups in the quasi-democracies responded negatively to the cultural influences imparted by Great Britain or the United States, and they sought to retain the purity of their traditional doctrines. A few indigenous persons reacted at the opposite extreme and imitated Western behavior with little if any blending of the local culture.[2] The indigenous group which exerted the most significant influence in moving these societies toward some democratic practices, however, was the new modernizing elite which sought to combine what it considered to be worthy elements of both the traditional religion and Western culture. This group quickly became an important fusional historical input. It sought to preserve many traditional values which did not conflict with the adoption of Western scientific and social innovations.[3] It became a class of "nominal" adherents of the indigenous religion who continued to observe traditional rituals and remained in symbolic contact with the broad masses of the indigenous populace. Yet it adopted much of the inner spirit of Western culture, especially the achievement ethic and the expectation of higher material standards.

This secularizing trend increasingly detached the emerging nationalist leaders from the limited vision of their own people. It influenced the new elite to cooperate with the colonial rulers and pursue independence through a gradual and reformist process. In India it included Hindu leaders such as Raja Rammohan Roy, M. G. Ranade, G. K. Gokhale, Mahatma Gandhi, and Jawaharlal Nehru. Important Moslem leaders in the sub-continent were Sir Syed Ahmad Khan, Mazhar-ul-Huq, Syed Hasan, and Mohammad Ali Jinnah. Other moderate nationalists in South and Southeast Asia were Sir James Peiris, Sir D. B. Jayatilaka, and D. S. Senanayake in Ceylon; U May Oung and U Thein Maung in Burma; Dato Onn bin Ja'afar, Tengku Abdul Rahman, and Tun Razak in Malaya; and Jose Rizal, Sergio Osmena, and Manuel Quezon in the Philippines. An aspect of the unique admixture of traditional and Western proclivities among these political leaders was well described by Nehru. He said:

> India was in my blood and there was much in her that instinctively thrilled me. And yet I approached her almost as an alien critic, full of dislike for the present as well as for many of the relics of the past that I saw. To some extent I came to her via the West and looked at her as a friendly Westerner might have done. I was eager and anxious to change her outlook and appearance and give her the garb of modernity. And yet doubts arose within me. Did I know India, I who presumed to scrap much of her past heritage? There was a great deal that had to be scrapped, that must be scrapped; but surely India could not have been what she undoubtedly was, and could not have continued a cultured existence for thousands of years, if she had not possessed something very vital and enduring, something that was worth while.[4]

This widespread view among Asian nationalist leaders combining traditional and Western affinities aroused an intense desire to "catch-up" with the West which in turn imparted a powerful progressive thrust to the government and politics of the evolving national society.

Another significant fusional historical input which emerged in all of the quasi-democracies during the indigenous response was the development of a three-tiered linguistic pattern. The politics of these six emerging national societies was deeply affected by: (1) the English language, (2) a "national" language, and (3) one or more languages of minority ethnic groups. Guy Hunter has labeled this triad as the "international language," the "dominant indigenous" language, and the "minority languages."[5]

The English language in the quasi-democracies quickly became a *sine qua non* for membership in the new indigenous elite and employment in the colonial bureaucracy and Western business enterprises. English was also the language of modern education. It was one of the major factors separating the modernizing leadership from the vast rural population. Due to the fact that its use was never restricted or manipulated for political purposes by British or American colonial rulers, English became a rapidly expanding means of communication. It played a crucial integrating role by providing a common media to indigenous leaders of diverse ethnic groups with mutually unintelligible languages. It became the language of the nationalist movement and provided a common exposure to the knowledge of the Western world. Direct intellectual contact with Western models of political and economic development in Great Britain, France, the United States, and the Soviet Union induced a growing demand for political reforms. The English language likewise imparted some unifying effect as the language of a nascent international regionalism. It provided a common communication linkage to nationalist movements in other Asian societies seeking the termination of Western colonial rule. This exposure to similar experiences bolstered indigenous nationalism with a sense of participation in a broad international movement against Western domination.

At the same time, the English language generated significant fragmentary forces within the political systems of these emerging national societies. The expanding political consciousness aroused by the spread of the English language combined with a common means of communication enabled the leaders of diverse indigenous groups to articulate their differences as well as their mutual interests. The Western language aroused powerful "sub-national" loyalties and generated a strong desire to preserve particular ethnic cultures and languages. The spoken and written English word, in brief, served as a catalyst which intensified cultural pluralism; it contributed to new social and political issues related to linguistic pluralism.

The educational system in this kind of polity comprised one of the major instruments of social and political change. It produced a deepening indigenous reaction to the scientific ethos of Western civilization, and it aroused a strong recognition by Asian thinkers that the acquisition of Western education and knowledge was the key to mastering the essentials of modernization. This attitude was typified by D. S. Sarma, a leading Indian scholar, who stated:

> Already there were new forces working silently towards a great Renaissance which came into full vigour in the early years of the present [twentieth] century. The most important of these forces is, of course, the spread of English education, which broke the intellectual isolation of the Indian mind and brought it into contact with Western science, literature, and history. The result of this was a great mental expansion similar to that which the European nations experienced at the revival of Classical Learning in the fifteenth and sixteenth centuries. A new world of ideas revealed itself to the wondering gaze of our young students in schools and colleges. In place of the extravagant mythical geography, legendary history and pseudo-science with which they had been acquainted, came sober and correct ideas about the configuration of the earth, the rise and fall of nations and the unalterable laws of Nature.[6]

The indigenous response caused by education was in considerable degree a function of traditional cultural values, traditional class status, and colonial social policy. An indigenous person acculturated with a high degree of religious eclecticism, psychological pluralism, and a separation of religion and politics tended to respond rapidly and enthusiastically to a Western education as a means for individual advancement. These relatively progressive individuals were most numerous among Hindus in India and Buddhists in Ceylon and Burma. Conversely, indigenous persons imbued with a high degree of religious dogmatism and a fusion of religion and politics were more likely to respond slowly and haltingly to Western education. These more conservative individuals were most numerous among Moslems in India and Malaya. Access to Western education at the highest levels was also most readily available to indigenous persons in the upper classes of the traditional class structure such as Brahman and Kshatriyas castes in India, the nobility and administrative classes in Ceylon, Burma, and Malaya, and the *illustrados* in the Philippines. Restricted access to Western education at lower levels was available to persons of the lower classes. What Professor Coleman has called the "unevenness in the impact of education" was also caused by the social policy of the Western colonial power.[7] The British contributed to this "unevenness" in Malaya, for example, by establishing public educational institutions only for the Malay upper class and providing few government-supported educational opportunities for Chinese and Indians. The heavy stress on education to support the political tutelary goals of American colonial policy in the Philippines likewise favored the small upper class which had the means to enroll in the University of the Philippines or good private colleges and universities established by Americans.

One of the most significant indigenous responses in the educational systems started in the quasi-democracies was the evolution of a distinct group of intellectuals serving as perennial critics of the emerging political system and expressing dissenting views in a free political environment.[8] These persons were the local thinkers most deeply affected by the "love-hate" reaction to Western knowledge, and they served as important amalgamators of traditional and Western values. Their attempt to preserve worthy aspects of the indigenous culture was strongest in territories under direct colonial rule where the penetration of Western influences was the most intense. Regarding the response of leading Indian intellectuals to Western ideas, Professor Stephen Hay has posited the hypothesis that "the greater the threat from the West to their sense of cultural and political integrity, the greater their psychological need to hold on to an idealized conception of the East as a counterweight to Western power and influence."[9] This reaction bolstered the widely-acclaimed "renaissance" in these newly-emerging national societies; it also aroused a more limited provincial "renaissance" which contributed to parochialism and communalism. Western education likewise aided in the evolution of a pluralistic political elite consisting of a coalition of political leaders from major ethnic groups. Western education also provided these indigenous leaders with both the need and the means for establishing a constitutional framework capable of allocating specific segments of governmental authority and preserving the institutions for individual freedom started under Western colonial rule.

Politically relevant changes caused by the indigenous response in the emerging economies of the quasi-democracies are difficult to assess. A vast majority of the indigenous population was not directly touched by Western economic enterprises, and the bulk of the local people remained attached to traditional economic roles. Some scholars have accordingly given a low rating to the economic aspects of the indigenous response during the colonization process. Professor Rupert Emerson has declared:

Economic forces are involved in the development of nations and
nationalism in a bewildering variety of ways. Such forces loom
peculiarly large — perhaps even deceptively large — in an imperialist setting where the drive for material gain has been so
strong on one side and the resentment against exploitation so
bitter on the other. Yet, whatever else nations may be, they are
not inherently consolidated economic entities nor the resultant of
economic processes. Although economic elements in many
respects have been of central importance in rousing national consciousness, they have played only an incidental role in the
shaping of the nations themselves.[10]

This assessment is reinforced in some degree by the fact that the indigenous response in the plural economies created by British or American
colonial rule consisted largely of scattered and diverse indigenous participation in economic roles created by Western exporting enterprises.
There was little coherency among these fragmented economic operations
designed solely for Western profit.

At the same time these Western export enterprises conducted their
operations within a single colonial or "national" administrative framework which provided some semblance of an economic "system" in the
newly-emerging society. The indigenous response in the economic realm
likewise imparted several common influences in the six quasi-
democracies. It supplied much of the stimulus for the expansion of modern urban areas and modern educational institutions. In modest degree it
also strengthened democratic values and behavior. It contributed to the
formation of diverse political ideologies and a pluralistic political culture. It provided the membership for the interest groups and political
parties which developed in the relatively free political environment maintained by British or American colonial rule. It also assisted the movement toward the establishment of a popularly elected legislature and
independent courts.

The primary areas in the new economies of the quasi-democracies
where these modest liberalizing trends occurred were commercial agriculture, commerce, and the processing industry.

Commercial agriculture became an important factor in the new plural
economies due to the response of increasing numbers of rural peasants
who quickly adapted to the production of cash crops involved in the
growing export trade. This "peasant response" was caused in large measure by the demonstration effect of Western commercial enterprises. It
has been described as follows:

It was a swift and massive response, a great change made easy
precisely because it required so little change in peasant practices
and economic values. Growing familiar crops like rice and coco-
nuts, or new crops like rubber and tea, whose market value had
been demonstrated by European plantations, was a natural
extension of the peasants' established subsistence agriculture.[11]

This particular indigenous response contributed to the formation of an
increasingly stratified three-tiered rural class structure. At the top of this
new class hierarchy was a landlord class composed of large traditional
landowners who adopted modern agricultural methods to produce food
and other commodities for profit. A much larger group in this rural elite
was an indigenous class of new landlords whose thrift and efficiency
enabled them to acquire larger amounts of land, either from newly-
developed land or the foreclosure of unpaid debts by small independent
landowners.[12] At the second level was a class of small indigenous landowners who quickly mastered the methods of producing cash crops and
began to enjoy some improvements in their standards of living. Yet the
rural villagers in this class operated in a precarious economic environment. Their solvency was continually dependent on the uncertain balance
between their fluctuating income derived from export crops and high
short-term interest rates. At the bottom of the rural class structure was a
class of indigenous tenant peasants and rural workers. Some persons in
this landless class were new migrants, but increasingly it consisted of
dispossessed small landowners.

The size and composition of these rural classes varied considerably in
the commercial agricultural sectors of the six quasi-democracies. Yet they
imparted some similar political influences. They participated in the
expanding awareness of a new *national* economy and society. They increased the demand for a larger governmental role in economic modernization in the form of land reclamation, flood control, transportation
services, marketing facilities, etc. The major effect, however, was the
increasing disparity of wealth between the three rural classes which
assumed special political significance when it involved severe economic
controls by indigenous or regional alien landlords over landless peasants.
This condition invariably produced rural unrest. During the 1930's it
fomented peasant uprisings against Indian landlords in Burma and
against the indigenous landlord class in the Philippines.[13] These violent
outbreaks were not directed against the Western colonial power, yet these
and similar rural grievances were used by the leaders of the nationalist
movement in urban areas to intensify their demands for independence
from Western economic exploitation.

The indigenous response in the commercial sectors of the quasi-democracies consisted essentially of an expansion of an achievement-oriented commercial class. The spreading participation by local persons in this sector resulted in the formation of two different types of "middle class" roles. The first type was the development of an indigenous commercial class composed of members of the traditional class structure who already possessed certain entrepreneurial skills. This kind of response occurred in India among the *vaisyas* or traditional merchant castes who moved into new commercial roles created by British colonial rule.[14] A somewhat similar response was made by some traditional upper-class members in Ceylon and the Philippines. The second type of commercial response was the acquisition of commercial roles by regional aliens (largely Chinese and Indians) which has been cited previously in this study. This response occurred on a massive scale in Burma and Malaya and on a small scale in Ceylon and the Philippines.

Each type of commercial response produced different forms of political influences. The indigenous commercial class in India, Ceylon, and the Philippines remained in the mainstream of the expanding nationalist movement. Its members often differed with specific views and policies espoused by prominent nationalist leaders, but they generally supported the nationalist cause. Some persons in this class saw the possibility of greater commercial opportunities in the era of national independence. Very important, the indigenous commercial class began making direct demands on the emerging political leadership to advance its own interests during the final years of Western colonial rule and in the coming era of national independence. The new commercial class, in brief, began to operate as an economic-oriented interest group in an emerging democratic political system.

In contrast, the regional alien commercial class was detached from the indigenous nationalist movement and it became increasingly apprehensive of its status and wealth in the post-independence period. At times it appeared sympathetic with efforts of the Western colonial power to delay the transfer of national sovereignty to indigenous control. It intermittently responded with its own forms of economic and cultural nationalism. This foreign commercial class consequently became a major target of the indigenous nationalist movement.[15] As independence became inevitable, it reacted with efforts to establish indirect and subtle financial links with the emerging political elite for protection and influence. Its wealthy members became targets of extortion practices by aspiring indigenous politicians. The presence of this regional alien commercial class thereby contributed a major corrupting influence both inside and outside the political system as the new society achieved independence.

The most important element in the indigenous response in the industrial sector was the formation of a laboring class employed in both the Western-owned and locally-owned processing industries.[16] This new wage-earning class consisted of indigenous laborers in India and both indigenous and regional alien laborers in Ceylon, Burma, Malaya, and the Philippines. The relatively few workers employed in locally-owned industries usually maintained a personal and dependent relationship with their employers and tended to remain politically docile. Yet the sizeable numbers of workers employed in Western-owned industries operated on a more impersonal and contractual basis. They were consequently more susceptible to early organizational efforts and methods of collective bargaining. This development often led to the formation of labor unions. Disputes over wages and working conditions between local workers and Western industrialists in turn provided another source of grievances to the leaders of the nationalist movement and further reinforced their protests against Western economic domination. These early labor unions likewise began to operate on a modest scale as interest groups seeking favorable governmental policies.

THE POLITICAL SYSTEM

The indigenous response in the emerging political systems of the six quasi-democracies was greatly influenced by the requirement to eliminate an entire system of Western political control in order to attain the status of a sovereign nation-state. This effort involved the need to create a new form of indigenous political rule caused by the Western-induced hiatus *between* the era of the traditional society and the period of national independence.[17] The new polity, in turn, eventually exercised sovereignty over a highly diversified national society comprising the territories and peoples of numerous pre-Western traditional societies. While there were many significant differences between the political systems of the six societies evolving from British or American colonial rule, the indigenous response produced many similar characteristics in a normative process containing important democratic and progressive values, a political process shaped by diversity and pluralism, and a governmental process utilizing elements of constitutionalism and the rule of law.

Normative Process

As mentioned previously, the dominant concept in the political ideology of the six quasi-democracies was nationalism. It comprised a fusional historical input combining an intense indigenous cultural pride and the Western ideas of national equality and national self-determination.[18] Yet in this kind of developing polity, the nationalist ideology was mellowed by the assimilation of specific democratic values from the Anglo-American political tradition such as popular sovereignty, limited government, and majority rule. Nationalism was the most widely shared political norm in the new society, and it was embraced by virtually the entire politically-conscious indigenous population. Nationalist sentiment developed first among indigenous persons inhabiting areas where Western colonial rule had been implanted the longest or where it was the most intense.[19] These territories were Bengal and Maharashtra in India, the coastal lowlands in Ceylon, the Irrawaddy delta in Burma, the western lowlands in Malaya, and central Luzon in the Philippines. Nationalism remained largely an urban phenomenon in the indigenous response, although it reached sporadically into some rural areas. It initiated the process of nation-building among the indigenous populace prior to significant indigenous participation in the process of state-building.

Nationalist ideology assumed several forms, each of which engendered its own impetus for change. In this kind of normative process, it included conservative, militant, and moderate forms. In addition it had its own distinct forms of idealistic nationalism and ethnic nationalism. These diverse ideologies contained different perceptions of the nature and purpose of the emerging nation-state. Yet they were not mutually exclusive. Most indigenous nationalists espoused the attitudes and viewpoints of several forms of nationalism depending on the time and circumstances.

Conservative nationalism sought the removal of Western colonial rule for the purpose of restoring real or imagined glory of former great or middle traditions. It also sought to reassert traditional religious teachings. In India it stressed Hindu virtues including a religious entity known as *Bharat* which allegedly embraced the entire sub-continent in pre-Western times. A similar kind of nationalism in the territories which became West Pakistan sought to restore some aspects of the Mughal Empire and Islamic doctrine; in East Pakistan it reaffirmed Bengali grandeur and early sacred precepts. Ceylonese (Sinhalese) nationalism in the early twentieth century was aroused partially by a revival of Buddhism intermixed with a temperance movement. A brief outburst of conservative nationalism in Burma caused the Saya San rebellion in the early 1930's which sought to revive the status and religious trappings of the traditional monarchy. The traditionalist *Kaum Tua* movement in Malaya shortly after 1900 espoused a form of Islamic resurgence combined with technological modernization. Even in the Philippines where historical research has failed to uncover a pre-Western middle or great tradition, a conservative nationalism advocated by Bonifacio and other leaders of the *Katipunan* claimed the existence of an integrated religious state with a flourishing culture and trade prior to the Spanish. These forms of conservative nationalism were usually strongest in the early stages of the indigenous response and tended to mellow from increasing contact with the moderate policies and high transferable political and administrative structures of Western colonial rule. Their major role was to provide much of the symbolism but little of the substance of the indigenous nationalist movement.

A form of militant nationalism in this kind of political system was based on a harsh *anti-colonialist* reaction toward the highly visible and widespread presence of Western colonial rule. This "radical" ideological element tended to overlap with the religious motivation embodied in conservative nationalism. Yet it was greatly (and silently) impressed with the accomplishments of Western technology. It was a complex admixture of a xenophobia and a grudging admiration directed toward the Western colonial power. This form of anti-colonialist nationalism wanted the emerging national society to appear Western but it wanted to do things "its own way." It desired the fruits of Western modernization without the substance of Western civilization. According to Professor Daniel Lerner:

> The hatred sown by anti-colonialism is harvested in the rejection
> of every appearance of foreign tutelage. Wanted are modern
> institutions but not modern ideologies, modern power but not
> modern purposes, modern wealth but not modern wisdom,
> modern commodities but not modern cant.[20]

The exponents of militant nationalism tended to be intellectuals from the middle or lower urban classes who were educated entirely within the colonized society. These outspoken dissidents always remained a minority in the indigenous nationalist movement, yet they supplied a sense of urgency and haste to pre-independence nationalism. They increased pressure on moderate nationalists to push harder against the resistance and delaying tactics of the Western colonial power. At the same time they aroused hostility among different ethnic and religious groups. Militant Hindu nationalists in India incited a bitter reaction among Muslims. A similar kind of nationalism in Ceylon caused tension between Sinhalese and Tamils. Communal friction was also caused by militant nationalists in Burma and Malaya. The intensity of these fragmenting forces was a function of the indigenous response to the reforms made by the Western colonial power in the transition to national independence. Ethnic fragmentation caused by militant nationalism was stronger in India and

Burma where British reforms toward national independence were considered by indigenous nationalists as meager and inadequate; ethnic tension and militant nationalism were weaker in Ceylon, Malaya, and the Philippines where the process of transferring sovereignty to indigenous control by the Western colonial power won wide popular approval.

Moderate nationalism consisted of a reformist and gradualist response to Western colonial rule which sought national independence by peaceful and negotiated means. It was a fusional historical input imbued with both the substantive and procedural values of Western constitutional democracy which were used to prod the Western colonial rulers in the pursuit for national freedom. It was the predominant form of nationalism in the political ideology and it provided the most progressive and future-oriented thrust to the emerging political system. This form of nationalism was pragmatic and secular.[21] It placed heavy emphasis on balancing the quest for national independence with a recognition of individual rights and group interests in domestic affairs. It also upheld the need to retain good relations with the Western colonial power in the period after national independence to preserve the mutual good-will developed during the indigenous response and to continue the processes of economic and social modernization.

Moderate nationalists leading the indigenous nationalist movement consisted largely of members of the urban upper class, including a number of intellectuals educated in the West (i.e., indigenous returnees). Implicit in the leadership role of this new political elite was the effort to eliminate Western colonial rule without jeopardizing its own favored status in the upper levels of the transitional class structure of the emerging national society. Moderate nationalism, in brief, wanted to broaden the channels of political participation in the new political system, but it was opposed to excessive popular involvement that might lead to a major social restratification. Jawaharlal Nehru depicted this view of moderate nationalism in India when he stated: "The Indian national movement is obviously not a labor or proletarian movement. It is a bourgeoise movement, as its very name implies, and its objective so far has been, not a change of the social order, but political independence."[22]

A distinctive element in the nationalist ideology of the six quasi-democracies was an idealistic nationalism caused by a moral reaction to Western colonial rule. This form of nationalism was strongest in the emerging polities of India, Pakistan, Ceylon, and Burma which attained independence from Great Britain shortly after World War II. It claimed that Western colonial rule was morally wrong and that national independence was achieved largely through the combined moral repugnance in the Western colonial power against this form of foreign domination and the morality embodied in the indigenous nationalist movement.[23] Idealistic nationalism likewise assumed in some degree that since Western colonialism was morally wrong the victims of Western colonial rule were somehow morally right. This reaction reinforced the idealism of some nationalist leaders in these societies and caused them to ignore many mundane factors involved in the achievement of national independence. It overlooked the important role of the Axis powers in weakening British colonial rule in Asia which hastened the transfer of national sovereignty to indigenous control. It caused some naivete in the new political leadership and directed its attention away from important pragmatic problems. This response created the impression that national progress in the post-independence era could be achieved by idealistic slogans and rhetoric rather than by careful planning and hard work.

One of the most unique elements in the ideology of this kind of political system was an ethnic nationalism caused by the inclusion of diverse ethnic groups in the territory of the newly-emerging national society. Ethnic nationalism (or sub-nationalism) was a fusional historical input combining an indigenous ethnic culture and the Western concept of the nation-state. The effort to establish some form of ethnic nationalism at the time of independence resulted in several different indigenous reactions. One was secession and armed rebellion against the newly-independent indigenous government. This type of action was rare and was undertaken only by Karen "nationalists" in southern Burma.[24] The most widespread response was the effort of an accommodative ethnic culture to attain maximum autonomy from the central government in some form of federalism. This move was made by Shan leaders in Burma and many leaders of ethnic-linguistic communities in India. Another kind of reaction by ethnic nationalists was the endeavor to gain an influential role in the top leadership of the dominant political party assuming control of the newly-independent national society. This effort was made by Tamil leaders in the United National Party in Ceylon and by leaders of diverse linguistic and island groups in the Nacionalista Party in the Philippines.

Constitutional democracy was another element in the political ideology of the emerging national society. As previously discussed, it comprised the values of Anglo-American liberalism such as freedom, equality, popular sovereignty, majority rule, and limited government which were assimilated largely by moderate nationalists. While constitutional democracy was a distinctly Western mode of behavior, it also received much strength from the eclecticism, tolerance, and "instrumental" qualities of many traditional historical inputs in these societies. Yet the adoption of Western democracy by the indigenous political elite was one of the most significant conscious breaks with the past. The authoritarianism of former great or middle traditions was an aspect of the pre-Western period eschewed by the new nationalist leaders. According to Professor Emerson, the emerging political elite viewed constitutional democracy as "a superior form of government."[25] This elevated precept, in turn, imparted a powerful progressive dynamism to the emerging political ideology. It instilled a strong determination in the minds of the nationalist leaders to prove to themselves, to the Western colonial power, and to the world that they too could master this "advanced" form of government. It aroused an urgent desire to make further necessary changes in the newly-independent society to preserve the same kind of democratic polity as in modern Western nations.

This response was unique in Asia. Nationalist leaders elsewhere in the region gave lip-service to this form of government, but only in the six quasi-democracies evolving from Anglo-American colonial rule did some of the substance and form of Western liberalism get implanted by the time of national independence. This borrowed political doctrine was not merely intended in these societies to provide a symbol of national independence or a part of the trappings of political modernization. Instead it comprised a complex but respected decision-making process accepted by indigenous leaders to govern the affairs of the newly-independent national society.

In addition to nationalism and constitutional democracy, the political ideology contained several doctrines related to the role of the government in managing economic affairs. These doctrines were capitalism, socialism, and communism which assumed a unique form due to the relatively free political environment maintained by the Western colonial power.

Capitalism became the predominant economic doctrine in the political ideology where two conditions prevailed: (1) the traditional class structure had included a significant role for a merchant class and traditional religious values did not eschew the acquisition of material wealth; and (2) the indigenous political leadership directly benefited from a capitalist-oriented economy and it perceived the economic policies of the Western colonial power as essentially beneficial to the emerging national society. At the time of national independence this phenomena prevailed in Pakistan, Ceylon, Malaya, and the Philippines. Private enterprise was also embraced by a considerable number of indigenous persons in India and Burma, but by the time of national independence it was a declining influence. As elsewhere in Asia, capitalism was less explicit as an ideology and it developed with little doctrinal guidance from the economic activities of indigenous entrepreneurs copying the behavior of Western capitalists. Its emphasis on private initiative and a limited governmental role in economic affairs was largely assimilated subconsciously. Although it upheld some separation between politics and economics, the capitalist ideology in this kind of emerging society served to integrate many aspects of the political and economic systems. It linked the political elite and wealthy landowners in Pakistan, Ceylon, and the Philippines. In Malaya a "division of labor" was agreed on by the Malay political elite and the Chinese commercial class just prior to independence to promote maximum economic benefits to both communal groups through a free enterprise economy.[26]

Socialism became the most salient economic doctrine in the political ideology where the following conditions prevailed: (1) a priestly class had held a high status in the traditional class structure and traditional religious values opposed the acquisition of material wealth; (2) the indigenous political leadership perceived Western capitalism as an exploitative economic order which had inflicted numerous adversities on the indigenous population; and (3) the urban classes had extensive exposure to socialist and Marxist thought through the influence of indigenous returnees, local universities, Communist political agents, and Western educators of socialist or Marxist persuasion. These conditions made socialism a significant influence in the political ideology in India and Burma.[27] It was adopted by some indigenous persons in Pakistan, Ceylon, Malaya, and the Philippines, but it was relatively weak. Socialist doctrine was closely tied to moderate nationalism in India and Burma, and it provided another progressive impetus to the emerging political system by seeking indigenous control over private enterprise (foreign and domestic) and the formation of a welfare state in addition to the achievement of national independence. The process of constructing a new social and economic order, however, was to be achieved gradually and without violence.

Communism became a part of the political ideology largely through an extremist and militant reaction caused by the pervasive and direct exposure to Western colonial rule. It was also bolstered by certain elements of militant nationalism. Marxist idealism blended with some idealistic values in the traditional cultural system and it held a special attraction for intellectuals intensely repulsed by Western and indigenous capitalism. Marxist theory likewise gained strength from its "scientific" analysis of historical change which appealed to indigenous leaders suffering from a variety of psychological and cultural shocks caused by the Western impact.[28] The communist ideology produced what Professor Harry Benda has called the "revolutionary intellectual" who broke with the socialists over the use of violent means to achieve a major economic and social restructuring of the new society.[29] Revolutionary intellectuals comprised the bulk of the membership of the indigenous communist party, although they succeeded in spreading a simplified version of Marxism to a few labor unions.[30] The spread of Marxist doctrine in this kind of political system was made possible through the indifference or tolerance of the British or American colonial rulers who did not suppress the emergence of these radical and revolutionary organizations. Yet in spite of the widespread abject poverty and many justifiable grievances caused by Western colonial rule, communism gained very few adherents among the local populace. Moderate nationalism and constitutional democracy remained the predominant elements of the political ideology and received the support of the largest number of followers. The failure to attract a sizeable following, however, did not deter the small indigenous communist party from becoming increasingly violent as the Western colonial powers began their final preparations to grant national independence. In India, Burma, Malaya, and the Philippines, communist cadre began moving in growing numbers from urban centers to rural areas to wage an armed insurgency against the newly-independent indigenous government.

One of the most distinctive aspects of the political system in the six quasi-democracies was a political culture formed by the interaction of the abstract democratic ideology transmitted by British or American colonial rule with indigenous patterns of behavior in a culturally heterogeneous society. This amalgamation imparted a progressive ethos and a desire for modernization in the leadership of different ethnic groups. It likewise induced the crucial requirement for some form of consensus among these divergent elites regarding the enormous problems confronting the emerging nation-state. The result was a political culture which was highly pluralistic. It contained an accommodative quality in an increasingly fluid political environment, and it was a chief factor shaping a pluralistic political process and a constitutional governmental process.

This kind of political culture developed largely from the political actions of the leaders of different ethnic groups as they pursued the goal of national independence. This new pattern of political behavior was essentially detached from the rank and file memberships of these various groups. Cooperation among the pluralistic indigenous leadership was promoted by the common use of the English language, an acceptance of Western democratic methods, and a shared experience in the struggle for independent nationhood. The new political behavior was also based on a consensus among these leaders to preserve the cultural identity of their respective ethnic groups and share political authority among themselves rather than to pursue some kind of integrated and homogeneous "national" culture. Professor Pye has called this phenomena a "fragmented" political culture in which the new political leadership was influenced by a sense of newness and insecurity, a conflict between traditional and modern values, and a resentment toward colonial rule.[31]

The stability of these fragmented or pluralistic political cultures was affected by the number and relative size of the various ethnic groups. Professors Rabushka and Shepsle have posited four types of political cultures: dominant minority, dominant majority, balanced competition, and fragmentation.[32] Among the six quasi-democracies, the least stable political culture was the dominant minority type in which a minority ethnic group began to acquire dominant political power. This kind of political culture developed in the indigenous response in Pakistan where West Pakistanis (largely Punjabis and Pathans) dominated the army, civil service, and political leadership of the new national society, yet they comprised only 42% of the total population. A more stable pluralistic political culture was the balanced competition type between two sizeable ethnic groups with relatively equal influence. This kind of "equilibrium" behavior evolved between Malays and Chinese in Malaya. A higher degree of stability occurred in a dominant majority political culture in which a single ethnic group comprised a large majority of the population and acquired a dominant political position. This type emerged in Burma and Ceylon. The most stable political culture was the fragmentation type consisting of numerous minority groups which were forced to cooperate at a high degree in order to maintain unity and accommodation in a new national society. This phenomena occurred in India and the Philippines.

A bargaining characteristic in this type of pluralistic political culture developed from the dual interrelationships between the leaders of different ethnic groups and between these leaders and their own followers. The first form of political behavior which created the requirement for a degree of cooperation and consensus within the emerging political leadership has already been discussed. The second form of bargaining political behavior requires some elaboration. It was caused by increasing popular participation in the election of indigenous representatives to the legislative bodies established by the Western colonial power. This behavior was both progressive and elitist. It sought to advance the emerging national society toward higher economic and social standards, and it developed a two-level power relationship involving a small urban and secular leadership and a vast rural and traditional populace. In varying degrees this kind of political culture was engaged in a "revolution from above" in which a Westernized national elite began the effort to bring more of its own people into the processes of modernization and change. This condition existed in the political behavior of new nationalist elites in virtually all emerging societies in Asia.

Yet the political culture was unique in the six quasi-democracies because it was greatly influenced at the highest level by the values and institutions of constitutional democracy. The assimilation of Western concepts such as popular sovereignty, representative government, the rule of law, and majority rule imposed the obligation on the new national elites to bring the broad masses of people into some meaningful role in the procedures of democratic decision-making. Indigenous political leaders upheld a markedly superior attitude toward the largely illiterate and impoverished peasants they represented, but their political behavior was influenced by the need to appeal to these rural people who intermittently cast their ballots for their elected representatives.

The bargaining political culture which emerged from this new political practice consisted of the complex web of personal loyalties and mutual obligations between the elected leaders and their followers.[33] It came from the promises and expectations of the democratic electoral campaigns supervised by the Western colonial power. A large majority of people remained "parochials" in this kind of political culture and were largely disinterested in the affairs of the emerging political system.[34] Yet a growing number of "subjects" who were affected by government policies entered into an informal bargaining relationship with their elected political leaders. Most significant was the relatively large number of "participants" who actively engaged in the articulation of demands and expected some benefits from government authorities. Some of this participation was bureaucratic participation by indigenous persons who joined the civil service of the Western colonial power, yet the predominant form of participation was political participation which consisted largely of participation in the nationalist movement. In some cases it also consisted of some participation in organized protests, electoral campaigns, and legislative lobbying to advance specific interests. This form of political participation in the bargaining political culture caused the roles of elected political leaders to become diffuse and multi-functional.[35]. The representatives of different groups served as educators of their own people on general issues affecting national and local affairs. They also served as arbitrators between competing factions among their own followers. They likewise served as political brokers between the demands of their own constituents and the policies of the national political leadership. They were required, in brief, to become skillful in the art of compromise and accommodation in dealing with their own supporters as well as with the leaders of other groups.

Political Process

The political process was the behavioral aspect of the indigenous response to the democratic political ideology imparted by the Western colonial power. It had an elitist quality which confined most indigenous political activity to a relatively small group of "national" political leaders. Yet the continual expansion of popular participation in the emerging political system caused an increasing fragmentation in the communication and articulation of indigenous political interests. This pluralizing tendency affected the efforts of the nationalist leadership to aggregate these different interests into a coherent nationalist movement. This characteristic, in turn, helped shape the new governmental process which legitimized and reinforced many of the pluralistic forces in the emerging national society.

Political communication in this kind of polity consisted of the dissemination of political information and opinion through both modern and traditional channels. In considerable degree these different modes of transmitting political news overlapped and penetrated each other. They also involved a "two-step flow of communications" between "opinion leaders" and a large uneducated audience.[36] Yet political communication in the six national societies emerging from British or American colonial rule was unique. Increasing indigenous political participation and the free political environment maintained by the Western colonial powers made the indigenous role in the dissemination of political news and persuasion the most extensive and differentiated of any society in Asia. It likewise had a distinctive two-way interaction between the emerging political leadership seeking support for the nationalist movement and the people responding with some form of "feedback" to these new political leaders.

The indigenous role in modern channels of political communication consisted mostly of indigenous-owned newspapers and indigenous participation in institutions of higher education. These methods of spreading political ideas and views were actively used in political campaigns for the elected representatives established by the Western colonial power, and they served an important integrative and centralizing function in the quest for national independence.[37] At the same time the indigenous role in modern channels of political communication induced many pluralistic forces, some of which were temporarily submerged in the nationalist movement. In large degree political communication interlinked the bargaining ethos of the pluralistic political culture with the new political process. The most significant modern media contributing to pluralistic politics was the vernacular language press which provided political information to specific ethnic groups and assisted in arousing ethnic nationalism. The variegated institutions of higher education also contributed to increasing diversity in the flow of political news and opinion. Intellectuals were especially important in this kind of political communication since their mutual resentment toward Western colonial rule and their intense nationalism promoted the dissemination of a wide variety of views on domestic and foreign issues. A new factor in the fragmentation of political communication was indigenous participation in commerce and industry which generated a growing array of economic interests and added another dimension of pluralism. Some of the most powerful pluralistic influences were caused by traditional channels of communication which distributed political information to increasing portions of the rural populace. The role of rumor and personal contacts in disseminating political news through a few educated rural leaders and the vast illiterate village population imparted some of the strongest centrifugal forces in the emerging political system.

The development of an indigenous role in interest groups and interest articulation was largely a by-product of the nationalist movement. In fact, the political organization which eventually assumed the leading role in the nationalist movement started as an interest group composed of moderate Western-educated reformers articulating an early demand for national independence.[38] As national consciousness grew, some groups and individuals became increasingly aware of more specific economic and social interests. The free political environment maintained by the Western colonial power facilitated this trend, and interest articulation in this kind of political system became the most intensive and differentiated of any emerging society in Asia. In some degree this development added another pluralistic influence in the new national society. At the same time, interest groups and interest articulation were relatively diffuse and weak by Western standards. The form of these inchoate interest groups often resembled their counterparts in the West, but they exerted a markedly different political role. Professor Lucian Pye has stated that these groups "tend to adopt diffuse orientations that cover all phases of life in much the same manner as the political parties and cliques. It is the rare association that represents a limited and functionally specific interest."[39] In describing the role of interest groups in Ceylon, Professor Howard Wriggins has declared:

> The pattern of interest groups is not well defined and their concerns
> are not expressed in a stable manner. A group will become active
> as its emotions are stirred, interests challenged, or competition
> for leadership brings on a temporary increase of activity.[40]

In addition to their highly generalized political focus, interest groups during the indigenous response had different degrees of autonomy from larger political organizations. Only a few interest groups were completely independent; most were organizationally linked to a larger political party. Few interest groups sought to influence public policy by shaping legislation; most endeavored to promote their interests by direct and personal contacts with the colonial civil service.

Anomic interest articulation occurred in the form of "spontaneous penetrations" in the political system and in various kinds of violent protest.[41] Examples were the civil disobedience campaigns waged by Gandhi in India during the 1920's, the university student strike in Burma in 1920, the communal riots in Ceylon in 1915, and the peasant uprisings in the Philippines during the 1930's. Non-associational interest groups were also active in articulating political demands on an intermittent basis. These semi-organized groups tended to express their demands only when confronted by a particular need or issue. They included tribal, untouchable, and peasant groups in India, Chinese and Indian associations in Burma and Malaya, religious organizations in Ceylon, and the landlords and the Roman Catholic Church in the Philippines. The most significant interest groups were associational interest groups which were usually based in urban areas and shaped by direct exposure to Western economic enterprises. Indigenous business organizations were the best organized and the most autonomous interest groups. Indigenous chambers of commerce were established in each of these six emerging societies as well as some specifically functional groups such as the Bombay Millowners Association in India, the Low Country Products Association in Ceylon, and the Confederation of Sugar Planters in the Philippines. Other types of associational interest groups were trade unions, student organizations, community associations, and a few peasant organizations.

The type and intensity of the demands articulated by these new interest groups varied greatly. Many demands depicted intense indigenous frustrations against Western colonial rule or against competing indigenous groups. They tended to seek increased indigenous participation in the political and administrative structures established by the Western colonial power more than to influence economic and social policies. Yet this form of interest articulation served an important educational role. It served to strengthen many indigenous political groups and it provided skills in attempting to shape public policy through organized political action.

The institution of the political party consisting of a coalition or aggregation of diverse individuals and groups seeking control of formal government offices was entirely a Western political usage. This political institution was not transmitted to Asian societies by any Western governmental or non-governmental linkage. Instead it was a fusional historical input resulting from the effort by Asian political leaders to imitate or modify the roles of a Western-style political party in their own emerging national society. Political parties emerged in these societies, according to Professors LaPalombara and Weiner, "whenever the activities of a political system reach a certain degree of complexity, or whenever the notion of political power comes to include the idea that the mass public must participate or be controlled."[42] The formation of political parties was greatly influenced by the Western concept of popular sovereignty which sought to use the appearance of popular support as a basis for political legitimacy.

The development of political parties in this kind of political system resulted in the evolution of a dominant party system. This pattern of party behavior by the time of national independence consisted of one large and broadly based political party and one or more small political parties. The dominant political parties were the Indian National Congress in India, the Moslem League in Pakistan, the United National Party in Ceylon, the Anti-Fascist Peoples Freedom League in Burma, the Alliance in Malaya, and the Nacionalista Party in the Philippines. Some small parties cooperated with these dominant parties in the common pursuit for national independence, but as the post-independence era began they broke away and became "opposition" parties.[43] The most prominent of these emerging opposition parties were left-wing socialist and communist parties and right-wing religious-based parties which had been allowed with few exceptions to operate openly by the Western colonial power.[44] They had a limited popular appeal and were organized on a relatively small political base. Yet they began the post-independence period as important organized critics of the dominant party controlling the newly-independent national government.

The dominant political party achieved its preeminent role from its capacity to aggregate virtually all organized indigenous groups into a sufficiently unified nationalist movement. Its leadership consisted of Western-educated moderates from the upper and middle classes who began occupying key positions in the political structures transferred by the Western colonial power.[45] In upholding the democratic values and behavior borrowed from the West, the dominant party exhibited no inclination at the time of independence to suppress the small political parties. At the same time, it showed no desire to share political power with them.

While the dominant political party had played a vital role in promoting unity and cooperation in the nationalist movement it was itself a highly pluralistic organization. It consisted more of an aggregation of leaders of diverse economic and ethnic groups than a mass following of the members of these groups. The Indian National Congress, for example, comprised mostly Hindu political leaders as well as leaders of other religious groups and left, center, and rightist factions. The Moslem League consisted mostly of landlords, merchants, journalist, professionals, and civil servants. The leaders of the United National Party were upper class Sinhalese, wealthy Ceylon Tamils, and the leaders of major Buddhist organizations. The Anti-Fascist Peoples Freedom League included the Thakin group and the leaders of the communist, socialist, and Marxist political parties. The Alliance included the leadership of the United Malay Nationalist Organization, the Malayan Chinese Association, and the Malayan Indian Congress. The Nacionalista Party aggregated the heads of prominent families from Luzon and the Visayan Islands.

The dominant political party system was one of the most highly developed elements in these emerging polities, and it bolstered political stability and democratic institutions at the time of national independence. In varying degrees these political parties had acquired important experience in organization and electoral techniques and in seeking political power. They had passed through what LaPalombara and Weiner have called the necessary "crises" in political party formation, namely "legitimacy, integration, and participation."[46] The most significant factor in this mode of political development was the formation of the dominant political party as the only indigenous party organized on a nation-wide scale and possessing widespread legitimacy and prestige from its role in achieving national independence. The strength of the dominant party at this crucial time was also enhanced by the lack of a unified political opposition. In comparison with other parties, the dominant party was a relatively moderate political organization seeking gradual domestic changes rather than a major social restratification. As it entered the era of national independence, its own ranks became one of the most important centers for political debate and decision-making.

Political leadership consists of the important variable in the political process which makes the final decisions among numerous demands and alternatives before they are legitimized into formal laws. It consists of the small ruling elite which exerts the dominant influence on the policies managed by the governmental process. The sources of political leadership, according to an eminent scholar, "lie in the vast pools of human energy known as wants, needs, aspirations, and expectations."[47] In this kind of emerging polity, it was both an independent and a dependent variable. The new political elite was an integral part of the dominant political party; it was likewise separated from this expanding political coalition. The top political leaders in all six quasi-democracies were Western-educated civilian politicians, most of whom had been lawyers, journalists, or educators. These men were the prime mentors of the indigenous nationalist movement and they served as the leading spokesmen for the pursuit of modernization under indigenous, rather than Western, control.

The political leadership in these emerging democracies was elitist and oligarchical. It was also highly pluralistic. While one or two highly prestigious leaders were dominant in the new political elites, other national figures also exerted varying degrees of influence. Besides Gandhi and Nehru, important political leaders in India were Vallabhbhai Patel, Subhash Chandra Bose, Rajendra Prasad, G. B. Pant, and Satyanarayan Sinha. While Jinnah dominated the leadership of the Moslem League prior to Pakistani independence, his role was supplemented by that of Mohammed Iqbal, Liaquat Ali Khan, Aziz Ahmad, and Khwaja Nazimuddin. The powerful role of D. S. Senayake in the United National Party in Ceylon was supplemented by that of John Kotelawala, S. W. R. D. Bandaranaike, and G. G. Polonambalam. In Burma, the political influence of Dr. Ba Maw and Aung San was shared with that of U Ba Hliang, U Nu, Than Thun, Ne Win, Thein Pe, and Kyaw Nyein. In addition to the Tengku, political leadership in Malaya included Tun Razak, Dato Syed Ja'afar Albar, and Dr. Lim Chong Eu. Just prior to independence in the Philippines important political roles were played by Manuel Roxas, Claro Recto, Jose Laurel, Gil Puyat, and Elpidio Quirino in addition to Manual Quezon and Sergio Osmena.

Each of the men in these pluralistic elites acquired prestige and power from their own role in the struggle for national independence. A few such as Gandhi and Nehru acquired considerable charisma from their many personal sacrifices in opposing British colonial rule. Most other leaders received less prestige where the transfer of sovereignty to indigenous control was completely gradual and non-violent. Pluralism within the emerging political leadership reinforced the tendency toward moderation in the policies of the first independent indigenous government. It discouraged a temptation toward excessive personal power or the establishment of authoritarian rule. It helped preserve an element of democratic behavior at the top level of the indigenous political leadership in the difficult early stages of the post-independent era.

Governmental Process

As already cited, the governmental process consists of the official institutions and structures of the political system which legitimize and implement specific policies for the society. In the final stages of Western domination this process in the six quasi-democracies in Asia was defined in some degree by a constitutional framework which allocated limited authority to specific branches and offices of the government. Like the Western usage of the political party, constitutionalism in these emerging national societies comprised a fusional historical input combining both traditional and Western influences. In most cases the written constitutions were made by combined bodies of Western colonial administrators and indigenous political leaders. Some traditional values and modes of behavior were incorporated in these constitutions which deviated markedly from Western democratic norms. These elements included the primacy of society over the individual, and special legal and voting rights for members of "privileged" ethnic groups. Yet the indigenous assimilation of a limited form of government allocating certain defined powers to specific official offices and branches contained the highest degree of genuine constitutionalism in any emerging national society in Asia. It comprised a dual response of increasing indigenous political participation in the official formulation of public policy as well as increasing indigenous administrative participation in the implementation of public policy. Very important, it enabled a growing number of indigenous people to accelerate the process of state-building which had been previously dominated by Western colonial administrators and had lagged behind the more advanced stages of nation-building.

The indigenous role varied considerably in drafting the written documents which established the official structures and procedures of this type of governmental process. Indigenous political leaders in the five British colonized societies largely exerted a consultative role while the actual drafting of the constitution was done by royal commissions established by the British Parliament. Indigenous participation was the least in the adoption of the Government of India Act of 1935 which was produced by British officials with only modest consideration of constitutional proposals favored by Indian nationalists. The indigenous role was larger in Ceylon, Burma, and Malaya where the new nationalist leadership exerted more influence in shaping official governmental institutions. Indigenous participation was the largest in the Philippines where the drafting of the constitution was done entirely by Filipino political leaders with only the three requirements for a representative form of government, a bill of rights, and a provision for religious freedom imposed by the United States government.[48]

These indigenous roles in constitution-making facilitated the transfer of the particular form of constitutionalism of the Western colonial power. The constitutions in the five national societies emerging from British colonial rule established a parliamentary system with a union of executive and legislative powers and an independent judiciary. The constitutional framework in the Philippines institutionalized a presidential system and a separation of executive, legislative, and judicial powers. The territorial allocation of governmental powers, however, did not follow any consistent pattern of borrowing from the Western colonial power. Instead the division of powers between the central government and local governments was adapted to meet particular indigenous needs. A federal system was established in India, Pakistan, and Malaya, while a unitary system was formed in Ceylon, Burma, and the Philippines. These constitutional frameworks indicated in considerable degree that the indigenous political leadership in the national societies emerging from British colonial rule expected to rely more on their political role at the head of the dominant political party than on their constitutional role as members of the Cabinet to provide strong executive leadership in the difficult post-independence era. Filipino political leaders, on the other hand, expected to rely more on the extensive Presidential powers in the constitution to exert a strong executive role than on their position as leaders of the majority political party.

Indigenous participation in executive roles involved the smallest number of persons in the entire governmental process due to the retention of executive authority by the Western colonial power until the very end of colonial rule. Yet this modest participation was extremely important in maintaining a constitutional form of government as national sovereignty passed from Western to indigenous control. The transmission of executive powers to indigenous political leaders was accomplished by two methods, (1) *consultative* and (2) *functional*. The *consultative method* consisted of the appointment of prominent indigenous persons to executive councils by top-level Western colonial administrators for the purpose of providing some channel for local "public opinion" in the administration of colonial affairs. In a few cases the indigenous role went beyond mere consultation and assumed certain restraining influences over colonial executive authority, especially some aspects of the collection of local taxes. This approach was first adopted in India by the Morley-Minto Reforms of 1909 which placed one appointed Indian on the Viceroy's executive council and one appointed Indian on the Governor's council in each provincial government.[49] This channel of indigenous consultation was expanded modestly in India by subsequent constitutional reforms. Similar roles were established for indigenous persons in the executive councils in Ceylon, Burma, and Malaya. Indigenous consultation in the American colonial system in the Philippines began with the appointment of three Filipino leaders to the Governor-General's commission in 1901.[50] While these consultative roles in each evolving governmental process were modest, they provided an exposure for indigenous politicians to the problems of modern civil administration. They also increased indigenous self-confidence in using Western methods of government and intensified the local desire for national independence.

The *functional method* consisted of the transfer of executive authority over specific ministries, departments, and bureaus from Western control to elected indigenous leaders. This exercise of executive power by indigenous politicians was first achieved in India, Ceylon, and Burma through the system of "dyarchy" which retained certain "reserved" functions (defense, police, finance) under British control, but placed specific "transferred" functions (education, health, agriculture) under indigenous ministers.[51] A similar though less structured policy of transferring specific executive functions to indigenous political leaders was employed in the American colonial system in the Philippines. Though limited in the number of persons, this method of indigenous participation in the exercise of executive authority was one of the most important elements in the entire indigenous response. It comprised valuable political and administrative experience for indigenous political leaders during an important "learning process" under Western guidance and tutelage. The gradual reduction of Western colonial control over specific executive functions also transferred to indigenous political leadership the need for competency and responsibility in the execution of public policy.

The largest indigenous participation in the governmental process of the six emerging quasi-democracies occurred in the colonial civil service. This official element of the indigenous response also took place over the longest period of time. Indigenous persons were early employed in low-level clerical and maintenance roles by Western colonial administrators, but the spread of nationalism and modern education at the turn of the twentieth century provided the means for indigenous personnel to enter middle and high level administrative positions in steadily increasing numbers. As mentioned in Part Two, British colonial administrators placed great stress on maintaining high standards of professional ability and integrity for both British and indigenous civil servants.[52] This policy restricted indigenous participation in important administrative posts until the 1930's since relatively few indigenous applicants were able to pass the difficult competitive examinations required for employment in the colonial bureaucracy. Yet by the time of national independence, highly qualified indigenous personnel comprised a sizeable portion of top-level civil administrators. The prestigious Indian Civil Service, for example, employed 992 officers in 1892 of which only 21 were Indian.[53]

Yet by 1935 approximately one-third of the officers in the I.C.S. were indigenous.[54] Similar expansion of indigenous participation in the civil service occurred in other British colonies, although this employment in Ceylon and Burma included a number of regional aliens, mostly Indians. The pace of indigenization of the colonial bureaucracy in the Philippines moved more rapidly than in the British colonies due to the absence of an American colonial tradition comparable to that of the British and the rapid turnover of American administrative personnel caused by inadequate incentives.[55] During the intense Filipinization of the colonial bureaucracy from 1913 to 1921, the proportion of American personnel declined from 29% to 4%.[56] In 1936 when the Philippine Commonwealth was created only a few American administrators were employed in educational and technical posts.

Indigenous participation in the armed forces of these emerging polities also developed in a gradual manner, although relatively few indigenous personnel were admitted to the officer ranks prior to national independence. Also, a disproportionate number of indigenous enlisted men in the British colonial systems were members of favored ethnic minorities known as "martial races." In the transfer of national sovereignty an important factor contributing to the maintenance of a constitutional governmental process was the assertion of the principle of civilian supremacy by the elected indigenous leadership and the establishment of civilian supervision over the new national armed forces. This trend was enhanced by the professional attitude of the small indigenous officer corps which at that time opposed military involvement in politics and confined the use of the armed forces to national defense.

In spite of the different Western approaches to indigenous participation in the colonial civil and military services, they created one of the most important elements of the indigenous response. The formation of an experienced corps of indigenous administrators provided an extremely valuable instrument in coping with the difficult problems of early national independence. It enabled these emerging societies to supply basic public services by their own trained personnel as experienced Western colonial administrators withdrew. Yet the combined establishment of indigenous executive authority and indigenous administrative capacity initiated the complex political conflict which has affected all modernizing societies, namely the conflict between political leaders and career bureaucrats over the formulation and implementation of public policy.[57] While this struggle between indigenous political and administrative leaders was largely submerged during the final stages of Western colonial rule, it began to manifest itself at the time of national independence. Indigenous politicians quickly began to interfere in the decisions of the allegedly non-political civil service to promote their own political goals. This penetration was resisted in varying degrees by career administrators who wanted to retain the expertise and impartiality of the national bureaucracy. Political intervention in the civil service tended to be less pervasive in the national societies emerging from British colonial rule than in the American colonial system in the Philippines due to higher standards of honesty and professional ability transmitted during the Western impact.

In spite of these differences, the governmental process in each of these developing societies was deeply affected by the competing perspectives of elected politicians and career administrators. A complex pattern of behavior began to emerge which responded to diverse interests and personalities in the government and in the society. One source has called these political and administrative elites "the bureaucratic-politics group" which in a modern society utilizes "the pluralistic concept of power" and embraces the idea "that power in modern society is diffuse, that advanced societies are characterized by complex and highly differentiated organizations, and that power is dispensed in response to the diversification of interests."[58] This political-administrative conflict was at a low level in this kind of political system at the time of national independence. Yet its early emergence indicated the initial stages of a power struggle which was to become more diversified and more intense as the processes of modernization continued in these new national societies.

The legislatures in this type of governmental process were the official institutions created by the Western colonial power which symbolized in largest degree that a democratic form of government had been established. Like other elements in this constitutional-oriented political system, the legislative bodies combined both modern and traditional modes of behavior. They were modeled after the national legislature of the Western colonial power and shaped to provide some representation for the diverse parties, groups, and leaders in the emerging society. Quasi-bicameral legislatures were created in the British colonial systems which included a popularly-elected lower house vested by the constitution with the dominant legislative role. Most members of the Cabinet held seats in these lower chambers. The upper houses were either fully or partially elected and designed primarily as advisory bodies with certain delaying powers. These upper legislative bodies also provided some representation to distinguished citizens, special groups, and designated territorial units of local government inhabited largely by a single ethnic minority. Their legislative role, however, was minimal. The Chamber of Nationalities in Burma, for example, represented three states and gave an exaggerated number of seats to the Shans, Kachins, and Karens.[59] Yet the decisions of this upper house on ordinary legislation could be overridden at anytime by the membership of the larger lower house, and it could delay financial legislation for only 21 days. The 58-member Senate in Malaya had 32 seats appointed by the Paramount Ruler which gave some representation to Eurasians, aborigines, and rubber and tin producers.[60] However, this upper legislative body possessed only meager delaying powers over both ordinary and financial legislation. The only genuine bicameral legislature in Asia was established in the Philippines. It was modeled after the United States Congress, and the approval of both the 24-member Senate and the 104-member House of Representatives was required to pass legislation. The election of Senators from the nation at large for six year terms gave the upper house a powerful institutionalized role in checking the executive branch. The presiding officers of both chambers were especially influential in the legislative process.

These legislative bodies were the only official institutions filled with elected indigenous representatives. They were the only governmental structures which had some "grass-roots" support and reflected in some degree the diverse interests of the emerging society. Very important, they were the major legal bodies where many compromises between nationalist leaders and the leaders of various factions and groups were settled and incorporated into law. Yet these pre-independence legislatures had numerous weaknesses as training grounds in making legislation. They were often used more as a channel to appeal to nationalist sentiment and demand the prompt termination of Western colonial rule than to deliberate on pending bills. In the British colonial systems the legislatures were distinctly weak in imposing effective limits on executive authority. As indigenous political leaders assumed greater powers during the final stages of colonial rule, the legislature largely became an official and legal facade for the policies of the dominant political party. Parliamentary checks on indigenous executive authority such as the question-and-answer period and the vote of no-confidence were virtually meaningless in a legislative chamber containing an overwhelming membership from a dominant political party. The national legislature in India, Pakistan, Ceylon, Burma, and Malaya consequently became more of a forum for the leaders of the dominant political party to announce and defend new government policies than a deliberative law-making institution. This subordinate role of the legislature assisted in keeping the locus of decision-making activity within the top level of the dominant political party. Only in the Philippines was the legislature a significant official body in the formulation of public policy.[61] The intense bargaining political culture and the highly fluid political process served to enhance the role of the Philippine Congress in checking executive power and in exerting a significant role in modifying and legitimizing legislation.

The judiciary in this type of governmental process was largely independent of executive and legislative authority, and by the time of national independence it was the official institution which enjoyed the largest respect and prestige from the indigenous populace. It was recognized primarily as the governmental institution designed to protect civil rights and to serve as some kind of check on both executive and legislative power. It was likewise seen as the official branch of government which most clearly symbolized the change from the traditional "rule of men" to the modern system of the "rule of law."[62] The high professional standards required for appointment to the judiciary delayed sizeable indigenous participation until the later stages of Western colonial rule. This requirement also confined this participation almost entirely to indigenous returnees trained at leading law schools in the Western colonial power. One of the major elements of the indigenous response was the increasing use of modern legal codes by indigenous persons in resolving civil and criminal disputes and in establishing governmental standards in the expanding commercial and industrial sectors. A significant achievement of indigenous judicial experts was the incorporation of relevant elements of traditional custom and traditional religious law into a coherent legal system for the entire emerging society. As some decline began to occur in the efficiency and integrity of executive-administrative offices and legislative bodies at the time of national independence, a growing number of indigenous persons looked to the judiciary as the final protector of civil rights and the final defender of constitutional government. Yet this respect for the indigenous judiciary was tempered in some degree by the tendency of most judges to uphold a strong conservative economic and social policy and to oppose many governmental actions seeking to reduce the enormous maldistribution of economic wealth.

The outputs or official policies administered by indigenous participants in the constitutional governmental process were involved almost entirely with domestic affairs. This tendency was caused by the overt and moderate nationalist movement which had publicized many adverse conditions within the society allegedly caused by Western colonial rule. The strong attachment toward domestic policy was also engendered by the political and administrative experience acquired by many indigenous persons in official domestic programs prior to national independence. The values in this kind of political system likewise placed a high priority on internal economic development, a priority whose implementation was largely determined by the emerging political leadership. Domestic economic policy in India and Burma where political leaders were strongly socialistic quickly required the need for government planning and the establishment of a welfare state. Economic advancement in Pakistan, Ceylon, Malaya, and the Philippines where the political leadership was essentially conservative was pursued largely by government assistance to private enterprise. Social policies in education, public health, labor relations, and social welfare which had been initiated by the Western colonial power were promptly adopted and in some cases expanded by the indigenous political leadership. A unique challenge in domestic policy was the need for adequate governmental machinery under indigenous control to protect civil rights, a need which had been relatively well fulfilled by the Western colonial power.

Unlike domestic policy, indigenous experience in foreign affairs was virtually non-existent due to the retention of this function by the Western colonial power until the day of national independence. With few exceptions indigenous participation in foreign policy was consequently speculative and intentional rather than practical and experienced.[63] It comprised a formative stage of policy probings which had several common characteristics in each of the six quasi-democracies. The political leadership exhibited a strong desire to retain friendly relations with the former Western colonial power in order to preserve the good-will generated during the Western impact and the indigenous response, and to continue the processes of economic and social modernization through future trade and cultural relations.[64] At the same time it depicted Western colonialism as an "evil" system which in turn aroused suspicion and fear of the revival of Western domination in new and subtle forms. It also entertained a degree of apprehension in joining the international community at a time of increasing tension between the Western and communist blocs. This uncertainty induced an urgent desire to gain global recognition of national independence through membership in the United Nations.

More diversified attitudes shaping foreign policy developed from a blending of specific traditional and Western historical inputs. Some orientations toward a policy of non-alignment in India evolved from the revival of traditional religious idealism and Gandhian morality used in the quest for national independence. A similar policy took shape in Burma from a growing strain of Buddhist pacificism and the widespread abhorence of the wanton destruction on Burmese soil caused by foreign military campaigns during World War II. A somewhat militant foreign policy developed in Pakistan due to the emergence of some aspects of religious dogmatism and an intense fear of India. A relatively "pro-American" foreign policy was formed in the Philippines due to the mutually amicable relations of the colonial period and the joint military actions of Americans and Filipinos against the Japanese wartime occupation. An effort to appear sympathetic with newly-independent and non-aligned nations in Asia was made by Ceylon and Malaysia, although both of these emerging societies sought to preserve close relations with Great Britain because of a relatively good colonial experience and extensive trade relations. Some of these inchoate foreign policy factors were altered as they began to interact with the "realities" of international politics in the post-independence era. Yet many of these forces remained intact as these new nations began to assert their sovereignty and pursue their own interests in a rapidly changing world community.

Chapter 11

The Bureaucratic Polities

The interaction between traditional and Western historical inputs in the three semi-independent societies in Asia caused an indigenous response which produced the type of political system labeled in this study a bureaucratic polity. The term *bureaucratic polity* has been used by Professor Fred Riggs in describing and analyzing the political system in Thailand.[1] This type of political system is dominated by a ruling elite composed of career government officials (civilian and military), while "extrabureaucratic" elements such as political parties, interest groups, public opinion, etc., exert a minor role. It is likewise a polity shaped by Western historical influences which "unconsciously produced an imbalanced pattern of development, one in which the rate of differentiation of structures within the bureaucracy has proceeded more rapidly than the compensatory growth of co-ordinating institutions outside the bureaucracy which could assure a high level of performance by these new, functionally specialized units."[2] It is my thesis that the indigenous response in Nationalist China and Japan during the unequal treaty process likewise resulted in the formation of a bureaucratic polity.

Some traditional historical inputs in these three semi-independent societies had certain common characteristics which oriented them toward this authoritarian type of political system. Each was a *dominant-ethnic society* with no sizeable ethnic minorities within its geographical borders, a condition which reduced the need for accommodation and compromise among competing interests and groups. Each had a pre-Western cultural system containing values based on an orthodox doctrine or religion which promoted conformity and collective harmony. The traditional class structure was hierarchical, and each had a strong legacy of autocratic rule. Each placed primary emphasis on the community; there was no traditional heritage supporting individual rights or limited government.

Yet there were many differences between politically relevant traditional historical inputs in the secular-oriented traditional societies in

Confucian China and Japan and the sacred-oriented traditional society in Thailand. Many of these political elements were as distinct and unique as the highly diversified traditional elements in the six national societies emerging from British or American colonial rule. Thus, traditional factors alone did not constitute the major force which produced the bureaucratic polities.

The dominant influence which did induce this type of political system in Nationalist China, Japan, and Thailand was the indigenous response to the unequal treaty process imposed by the Western powers, especially the high-demonstrative impact exerted by Great Britain, France, and the United States. The common pattern of fusional historical inputs emerging from this impact was caused by a different array of governmental and non-governmental linkages than in the colonization process. The indigenous response was even more confined in the urban areas within the three semi-independent societies, and it aroused a different and reduced type of political participation than in the six quasi-democracies. Very important, the indigenous response in its early stages consisted of an attempt to resist Western encroachments by military power and diplomatic action. When this effort failed and the unequal treaties were imposed, the indigenous leadership in each semi-independent society sought thereafter to retain the maximum autonomy by adopting selected elements of Western culture. Each elite upheld what early Chinese reformers called a policy of "self-strengthening" which advocated mastery over the physical and human environment through the use of Western science and technology and thereby preventing further incursions by the Western powers.[3] This policy produced a deep social and psychological cleavage in each of the semi-independent societies between a small political elite eager to adopt certain Western innovations and governmental institutions and a massive conservative populace attached to traditional values and behavior. Unlike the indigenous response in the six colonized societies in South and Southeast Asia, this policy caused Nationalist China, Japan, and Thailand to engage in the process of state-building and nation-building simultaneously throughout the entire period of the Western impact.

DOMESTIC ENVIRONMENT

As in the six quasi-democracies, the cultural, social, and economic changes in the three semi-independent societies produced a vast variety of politically relevant fusional historical inputs during the indigenous response. Yet some common developments also occurred. Some of these similar inputs strengthened the movement toward an authoritarian bureaucratic polity. One input was the dogged tenacity of traditional cultural values due to the limited geographic scope of the Western impact. The restricted coverage of Western diplomatic missions in the capital cities and leased concessions (in China) as well as the limited contacts of many non-governmental linkages enabled the vast majority of the indigenous populace to remain untouched by direct Western influences. In rural villages, orthodox attitudes and behavior remained very strong. There was more blending of traditional attitudes with Western culture in the urban areas, but here also the animosity toward Western extraterritoriality and the unbroken link with the pre-Western traditional society served to bolster many traditional values and institutions. A powerful disposition toward authoritarianism consequently continued essentially intact.

Western languages in the three semi-independent societies did not impart the same integrating and pluralizing effect as they did in the six emerging quasi-democracies. There was increasing use of a Western language, usually English, by the small indigenous urban elite, yet a single indigenous language continued to exert a powerful socializing role. The spoken national language, already used by all or an overwhelming majority of the population, faced no competition from minority languages. The written national language was gradually taught to increasing numbers of indigenous people which minimized some Western influences and preserved national customs and behavior. Chinese and Thai linguists, for example, developed their own translations of Western technical and social terms; Japanese language experts adapted their own words to the needs of the modern scientific and technological era. Also, the introduction of a Western language in Nationalist China, Japan, and Thailand did not separate the new political elites from the broad rural population as it did in the six national societies emerging from British or American colonial rule. Instead these societies preserved the dignity and the primacy of their own nation-wide means of spoken and written communication. This condition enabled the new political leadership to speak directly to the bulk of the national population. It aided the political elite in maintaining a strong centralized control over successive stages of economic and social modernization.

The educational systems in the three emerging bureaucratic polities comprised a combination of traditional and Western approaches which induced many social and political changes. This new instrument of mass learning developed differently in Nationalist China, Japan, and Thailand, yet in each society it contributed to stronger centralized administrative controls.

Modern education exerted the greatest political influence in Japan where a French-styled three-tiered school system comprising eight universities, 256 middle schools, and 53,760 elementary schools was established by the Fundamental Code of Education in 1872.[4] Within one year 28% of the Japanese children were attending elementary schools, and by the end of the unequal treaty process in 1898 more than 90% of the nation's youth were participating in a nation-wide compulsory education program. A fourth element of the Japanese educational system was a government-sponsored program sending qualified students to institutions of higher learning in Europe or the United States.

A much smaller political influence was made by modern education in China where only a few public school programs were started by indigenous leaders prior to 1949. An elementary educational system was launched during the final years of the Manchu dynasty, but it enrolled only 1,600,000 children comprising less than 2% of the school-age population.[5] A few vocational and technical schools were also erected at this time by Chinese initiative. Yet the major channel of modern education for Chinese youth until the establishment of a few universities by the Nationalist regime after 1928 was foreign education in Europe, the United States, or Japan, or the secondary schools and universities in China established by Christian missionaries.

The most meager political impact from modern education among the three semi-independent societies occurred in Thailand where official apathy and indifference delayed public school construction until after the overthrow of the absolute monarchy in 1932. Only a few primary schools were started in Bangkok and several provinces by the central government during the unequal treaty process, and a few specialized schools were constructed in the national capital for training civil servants, lawyers, and doctors. Chulalongkorn University was established in 1915 and it remained the only indigenous institution of higher education until the University of Moral and Political Science was founded by Pridi Phanomyong in 1933. As in China, the major channel of advanced education for Thai youth was a government-sponsored program in Europe or America which began in 1897 and provided a Western university education for an increasing number of royalty and commoners.[6]

The modernizing educational systems in the three semi-independent societies contributed to the development of a bureaucratic polity in several ways. Most important, it provided specialized training to the expanding ranks of administrative personnel employed in the various ministries and departments of the national bureaucracy. Modern education also strengthened collective values and behavior in the new political ideology and the new political culture. In Japan, the educational policy had a strong utilitarian orientation, and after the early 1890's it was used by the government to promote a military-sponsored program stressing uniformity and national regimentation.[7] The reduction of the individualistic curriculum imparted by early American educational influences and the adoption of a state-oriented program inspired by German pedagogical theory led to the reassertion of the traditional concept that education should be used for moral training and the benefit of society. Mori Arinori, a Minister of Education, stated: "In the administration of all schools, it must be kept in mind, that what is done is not for the sake of the pupils but for the sake of the country."[8] On a more modest scale the much smaller modernizing educational system in China likewise provided the specialized skills and knowledge needed in the expanding ranks of the government bureaucracy. The Chinese schools also abetted the spread of anti-foreign sentiment after World War I which aided the rise of the Nationalist regime (and the Communist Party). Modern education in Thailand served almost entirely in providing the central government with the skilled personnel required in the administrative reforms started in 1892 by King Chulalongkorn.[9]

It is important to note that the modern educational system in the three semi-independent societies also generated a small but growing number of intellectuals outside the bureaucracy or at its periphery who advocated democratic and constitutional reforms. These "extrabureaucratic" voices imparted a variety of liberalizing influences seeking some form of popular controls over the emerging bureaucratic polity. Yet in none of these societies did they gain a powerful political role. Beginning in the 1880's in Japan, these early "liberals" became some of the most articulate proponents of a genuine parliamentary form of government. After the formation of the first cabinet under the Meiji constitution in 1889, they continued to serve as critics of the government and its massive bureaucracy. Intellectuals in China, bolstered by the traditional respect for scholars and their Western-acquired knowledge, also exerted a growing non-official role after 1928. They strongly supported the Nationalist regime in the struggle against Imperial Japan, but they became its most outspoken opponents when Chiang Kai-shek placed higher priority on the suppression of indigenous communists than on waging a unified national campaign against the Japanese. Many Chinese intellectuals became a "third force" between the Nationalists and the Communists after 1941.[10] Modern education in Thailand was likewise a key factor in the evolution of a small group of intellectuals who provided the ideological motivation in the overthrow of the absolute monarchy.[11] Yet unlike China and Japan, these intellectuals were civilians employed in various posts of the national bureaucracy. Their "revolution" was waged from *within* the bureaucratic polity. The successful removal of the absolute monarchy was made possible by the cooperation of a sympathetic group of Western-trained army officers.

The economies of the three semi-independent societies remained largely agricultural during the unequal treaty process, a condition which preserved many traditional values and modes of behavior. Yet the modernizing sectors of the economic systems in Nationalist China, Japan, and Thailand comprised important fusional historical inputs, some of which prodded the emerging national society toward democracy while others strengthened the development of a bureaucratic polity.

Agriculture in the three semi-independent societies contained both subsistence and commercial sectors, and the relative size and direction of these two sectors depicted in considerable degree the rate of economic modernization. The subsistence sector in Japan began to decline during the unequal treaty process, while the commercial sector rapidly expanded, largely by labor-intensive rather than capital-intensive methods. This change in Japanese agriculture was encouraged by the population increase on a small island-nation with limited areas of arable soil. The increasingly precarious ratio between population and food production contributed to the intense outward thrust of the entire Japanese economy after 1868 and an aggressive economic-oriented foreign policy by the 1890's. Agricultural land was heavily taxed by the Meiji leaders to finance industrial (and military) expansion, and peasants were kept at extremely low income levels.[12] Since most early industrial workers came from rural areas, the intense poverty in both agricultural sectors kept wages depressed for urban labor. Increasing numbers of peasants were dispossessed of their land during this period, and an expanding tenant and rural laboring class emerged.[13] These adverse developments among rural land owners and underprivileged peasants were instrumental in the early formation of interest groups and political parties in the 1880's. The strong official reaction against these "extrabureaucratic" organizations also contributed to the development of a bureaucratic polity.

Agriculture in China and Thailand changed much less drastically in structure and scope than in Japan during the unequal treaty process. The subsistence sector in these two societies remained very large. A small commercial sector in Chinese agricultural production was devoted almost entirely to domestic needs. Like Japan, the increasing population pressure on limited areas of arable land in China resulted in intense and spreading alienation in many rural areas. This development was accompanied by the concentration of larger landholdings in the hands of fewer landlords and a rising proportion of tenant and landless peasants, a condition which made many parts of the countryside ripe for insurgency and revolution.[14] Wisespread poverty in rural areas contributed to low wages and exploitative working conditions among the small numbers of Chinese urban laborers. The growing desire of the Nationalist leaders to modernize agricultural production after 1928 bolstered the trend toward more centralized and efficient administrative controls, a move which aided the formation of a larger and more specialized bureaucracy.

A rapidly expanding commercial sector developed in Thailand after 1855 due to increasing foreign demand for rice, tin, teak, and rubber. The growing channels of foreign trade brought large quantities of foreign currency into what Professor Ingram has called an "exchange economy," and by the end of the unequal treaty process Thailand had become one of the major rice exporters in the world.[15] This modernizing commercial sector became a major source of government revenue and enabled the central government to finance new technological and administrative advances.[16] In sharp contrast to Japan and China, Thailand had a small population and large areas of uncultivated arable land capable of absorbing the rural population increase during the period of the unequal treaties. Thai peasants consequently remained untouched by many adversities in the early process of economic modernization, and the rural areas in the kingdom experienced no significant social unrest. Yet a disproportionate increase in national wealth derived from commercial agriculture went to Western exporting firms and Chinese middlemen which aroused increasing hostility from a growing Thai urban class. This condition caused the Thai government to impose additional restrictions on Western and Chinese commercial activity and to establish several government-owned industries. Both steps further bolstered the authority of the emerging bureaucratic polity.

The commercial sectors in the economic systems of the three semi-independent societies consisted largely of the distribution and sale of Western-made consumer goods imported under the restrictions imposed by the unequal treaties. Commerce likewise included the export of raw materials such as silk, rice, and minerals to Western and other foreign markets. Commercial activity in Japan remained under indigenous control and it quickly assumed a growing role in the modernizing economy. This rapid expansion was due to the significant commercialization of the economy prior to the Meiji restoration as well as the economic impact of the West.[17] By the 1890's increasing quantities of Japanese-made consumer goods were entering the domestic economy and seeking foreign markets, especially in China. The close relationship between Japanese commercial development and Japanese foreign trade was a major factor promoting an aggressive foreign policy and a strong central government at the end of the unequal treaty process.

Commercial activity in China developed much more slowly than in Japan during this period due to official and private inertia and the traditional low status of the merchant class. Western commercial organizations in the Chinese treaty ports aided in overcoming this obstacle by serving as "training centers" for indigenous entrepreneurs and an attractive area for Chinese investment. The political and economic stability in these Western treaty ports enabled an increasing number of Chinese businessmen to establish flourishing commercial enterprises. The desire of the Nationalist regime to channel this commercial activity on the periphery of the mainland into broader elements of national economic development after 1928 aided in the evolution of a larger and more efficient administrative system.

Unlike Japan and China, the commerce in Thailand was largely foreign-owned due to the religious and cultural disdain of the Thai people for entrepreneurship. Large Western corporations exerted a major influence in the modest commercial development of the kingdom through the exporting of rice and a few raw materials and the importing of Western-made consumer goods. Chinese immigrants in Thailand established small family-operated enterprises and dominated commercial activities such as rice-milling, rice distribution, and retail trade. An expanding bureaucracy dominated by the Thai gradually exercised numerous controls over this alien commerce and extracted a growing portion of national income.

Modern industrialization comprised a fusional historical input which depended on a favorable combination of traditional attitudes and modernizing resources. These included competent entrepreneurship and an access to raw materials. In Japan this process was hampered in its early stages by a lack of natural resources (except for modest deposits of coal), but the urgent desire to break out of the rigid isolationism of the pre-Meiji era, and an increasing access to raw materials in foreign lands enabled the Japanese to give their industrialization effort a uniquely dynamic and outward thrust. In the 1880's the government began the construction of heavy industries in iron and steel making, ship-building, armaments, etc., many of which served as "model plants" and were subsequently sold at low prices to private corporations.[18] This policy contributed to the rapid expansion of the *zaibatsu* and the concentration of large industrial, commercial, and financial enterprises in a few hands.[19] It added to the evolution of a sizeable urban working class which constituted approximately 18% of the total population by the end of the unequal treaty process. In 1898 the Japanese people had achieved only modest industrialization by Western standards, but they had undergone the basic psychological and political changes which oriented their economy on a path which soon equalled or surpassed the industrial development of many major Western nations. The rapidly expanding urban population on a shrinking resource base made the economic system increasingly dependent on foreign sources for food and raw materials, a condition which also contributed to an aggressive and expansionist foreign policy in the early twentieth century. This powerful economic force abetted the evolution of a more specialized and centralized bureaucracy and a strong authoritarian rule.

China, in contrast to Japan, possessed vast natural resources which compared favorably with those of many Western industrialized nations.[20] Yet the lack of skillful political leadership and economic stability throughout most of the unequal treaty process seriously hampered modern industrialization. Modest indigenous industrial activity occurred in textiles and a few consumer goods in Shanghai and several other treaty ports, and industrial growth managed to expand by 5% per year between 1912 and 1949.[21] Yet China's industrialization was one of the lowest among the large countries in the world, and its per capita gross national product in 1949 was approximately $50.[22] Most industrial development was done by foreigners. Sizeable iron and coal industries were developed by the British in northern China, and even larger industrial enterprises were established by the Japanese in Manchuria. Industrialization in effect had only minimal influence on the emerging national society in China, although it did produce a small urban working class living on extremely low wages. One of its major roles was to arouse a growing desire among Chinese nationalists for a strong central government capable of reducing the high proportion of foreign industry and promoting a larger sector of domestic industry, an attitude which added further impetus to the formation of a bureaucratic polity.

Thailand, like China, had several valuable natural resources, but it made little industrial progress during the unequal treaty process. The bulk of the modest industrialization which did occur in the production of tin, teak, and rubber was undertaken by foreign interests.[23] The government built a few factories for the production of sugar, cement, and tobacco during World War I, and government monopolies were established in some industries such as trucking and forestry.[24] This modest but growing consumer-oriented industry created only a small urban working class in Bangkok, but it did add large numbers of government employees to the expanding bureaucracy.

THE POLITICAL SYSTEM

The evolution of fusional historical inputs in the indigenous response of the three semi-independent societies was heavily shaped by the need to remove partial Western controls in order to regain complete national sovereignty. The indigenous reaction which formed the bureaucratic polities in Nationalist China, Japan, and Thailand was also influenced by the fact that indigenous leaders continued to administer most governmental functions in the unbroken historical link between the traditional society and total national independence. Unlike the six quasi-democracies emerging from British or American colonial rule, they experienced no gap of total Western domination between their traditional and sovereign national status.[25] They were not required to remove a complete form of Western rule.

Yet the struggle to terminate the unequal treaties was nonetheless intense and severe. It was characterized by a greater emphasis in making rapid and extensive internal reforms than in opposing external Western controls. Both efforts were obviously made by the indigenous elite, but the former received top priority. In fact, it was the elevation of domestic governmental functions (primarily legal and administrative) to Western standards which resulted in the termination of this unique form of Western domination. Advances in these governmental functions soon led to reforms in many non-governmental roles. In this process the political system quickly became the most powerful and autonomous sub-system of the emerging national society, and it soon extended its authority into many new areas of human affairs. Its normative process, like that in the six quasi-democracies, embodied many progressive and nationalistic concepts. Yet the political process was much more rigid and elitist, and the governmental process was dominated by executive authority and a massive official bureaucracy.

Normative Process

As in the six evolving quasi-democracies in South and Southeast Asia, the dominant political ideology in the three bureaucratic polities was nationalism. This fusional historical input aroused a desire to break with the past and at the same time to preserve certain "time-honored" elements of the traditional society. In its early stages it was a "protest movement [and] largely negative, signifying a reaction against foreign domination."[26] One political scientist has defined this kind of nationalism as "a state of mind ... an idea, an idée-force, which fills man's brain and heart with new thoughts and new sentiments, and drives him to translate his consciousness into deeds of organized action."[27] No major "ethnic nationalism" or sub-national nationalism evolved in this type of polity. The new political ideology demanded the rapid formation of a modern nation-state; the emerging nation-state in turn fostered stronger forms of nationalism. The processes of nation-building and state-building occurred simultaneously and reinforced each other. A Gemeinschaft and a Gesellschaft evolved in tandem during the entire unequal treaty process.

Like the six political systems emerging under British or American colonial rule, the normative process also included conservative, moderate, and militant forms of nationalism. Yet in the three bureaucratic polities conservative nationalism, rather than moderate nationalism, became the dominant type. This form of nationalism upheld the goal of restoring much of the grandeur and prestige of former great traditions. This attitude built on a sense of cultural pride, and in its own strange way it imparted a progressive impetus to the entire political system. It eschewed any attempt to move backward and revive defunct great traditions, yet it urgently desired a collective sense of satisfaction and self-confidence emanating from memories of former greatness. It was a form of nationalism which was deeply aggravated by the sense of inferiority imposed by the West, and it sought to attain a status of international equality as soon as possible. Conservative nationalism in China has been described by Fairbank as "the inherited pride of culture or 'culturalism' [that] has inspired a new cultural nationalism which may in the future outdo the merely political nationalisms that originated in Europe."[28] Reischauer has referred to this phenomenon in Japan as follows:

> A national sense of inferiority might also be associated with the early appearance of nationalism in Japan. . . . This early rise of nationalism was partly the result of the clear-cut geographic and linguistic delimitations of Japan, which have set it apart as a separate country ever since early days. . . . Whatever isolation may have had to do with the early rise of Japanese nationalism, there can be no doubt that nationalism deserves a large share of the credit for Japan's recent Cinderella success story.[29]

Conservative nationalism in Thailand involved the preservation of the traditional loyalty to the king, religion, and nation; at the same time it sought to promote Western-style change. Wilson has stated:

> Thai nationalism is for the most part unmilitant. Its historical background is the long diplomatic struggle to maintain indepen-

dence.... Because of this history, Thai nationalism is different from other Southeast Asian nationalisms. Culturally, it is not nativist but assimilative. Politically, it is not revolutionary but conservative, often taking the form of appeals for peace and tranquility for the sake of the nation. An important theme of this nationalism is the idea that Thailand is one of the "civilized" nations, is "up to date," has the ability to handle its own affairs, and is the equal of any nation, to which is added a strong element of anti-Chinese sentiment.[30]

A moderate form of nationalism in the three semi-independent societies consisted of a restrained national loyalty which fostered cooperation with other nation-states and intermittently upheld a somewhat benevolent attitude toward the indigenous populace. This milder kind of nationalism eschewed a narrow ethnocentrism in the conduct of foreign policy and promoted occasional respect for individual and group rights in domestic affairs. It was shaped by the absence of a colonial experience and the less onerous struggle of regaining national sovereignty under the unequal treaties than in obtaining national independence from Western colonial rule. It justified close and continual contacts with major Western powers in order to maintain the inflow of modern science and technology. It contained an implicit respect for concrete military and economic factors in the quest for complete national sovereignty which engendered a more pragmatic and less moralistic form of nationalism than in the six quasi-democracies emerging under British or American colonial rule.

The third kind of nationalism was a militant variety which emerged in Nationalist China, Japan, and Thailand during the unequal treaty process from a growing sense of racial superiority and xenophobia. This radical value-system and behavior contributed to an aggressive foreign policy and more regulated governmental control over the indigenous populace. It fed on a harsh racist reaction to the humiliation experienced in the subordinate status imposed by Western extraterritoriality. A form of racial nationalism erupted in China during violent outbreaks such as the Boxer Rebellion and the May Fourth Movement.[31] Racial nationalism was espoused by the founder of Nationalist China, Dr. Sun Yat-sen, as a necessary political force to help China in its "divine mission" to fight Western imperialism and help "wronged races." Sun likewise advocated racial nationalism as the matrix required to unify the traditional masses of rural China depicted as a "sheet of loose sand."[32] Racial nationalism was an important fusional historical input in the Nationalist Chinese regime when it fled to Taiwan in 1949 vowing that someday a "return to the mainland" would restore "one China" under its own rule.

A type of militant nationalism based on the emperor myth, *kokutai,* and *Shinto* began to emerge in the normative process in Japan after 1890. This extremist attitude developed from a latent sense of racial superiority which became stronger during the rapid technological progress in the 1870's and 1880's. A form of "cultural nationalism" combining "Eastern morals and Western science" led to a reactionary movement incorporating many martial values and modes of behavior following Japan's military victory over China in 1894–5.[33] As the unequal treaties ended in 1898, this element of Japanese nationalism was directed increasingly against Western opposition to Japan's expansion in Asia. Militant nationalism was less intense in Thailand, yet it assumed a unique racist quality from the efforts of King Wachirawut to unify the Thai people behind his colorful and dynamic leadership from 1910 to 1925. The king himself became an avid propagandist, and under a pseudonym he wrote numerous articles praising "the Thai country, the Thai nation, the Thai people, the Thai virtues, etc."[34] This early form of militant Thai nationalism was directed largely at the local Chinese minority. It assumed a broader and more vehement form just after the termination of the unequal treaties in 1937 in the irredentist policies aimed at the "lost provinces" in French Indochina and the internal social regimentation promoted by Premier Phibun Songkhram.

In addition to the three types of nationalism, the political ideology in this kind of normative process included constitutional democracy, capitalism, socialism, and communism.[35] Like nationalism these Western political ideologies intermixed with traditional historical inputs yet they were espoused by relatively small numbers of modernizing persons largely outside the ruling elite and the official bureaucracy.

The threat of augmented foreign intervention combined with the intense domestic effort to push economic and administrative reforms created an unfavorable environment for the evolution of genuine democracy. The political leadership sought almost continually to preserve its own power to maintain order and security in a time of rapid social change. It tolerated little or no dissent. Occasionally some members of the ruling elite voiced lip service to the ideal of constitutional government, but they used this distinctly Western ideology only as a respectable facade over their highly centralized rule. This phenomenon occurred when Ito Hirobumi and a few trusted aides publicly voiced support for Japan's movement toward constitutional democracy during the 1880's while they drafted the Meiji constitution which retained a powerful authoritarian system. Constitutional democracy was the highly publicized final goal in Sun Yat-sen's three-stage revolutionary strategy, yet it was never incorporated into the political system developed by the

Chinese Nationalists. Pridi Phanomyong and his co-conspirators in Thailand praised constitutionalism while overthrowing the absolute monarchy and forming a new type of oligarchical rule. The primary value in the normative process in all three semi-independent societies continued to be authoritarianism. Constitutional democracy symbolized the progressive intentions of the political system, but it did not guide its processes and behavior. According to Professor Emerson:

> Although the Western influence has normally been less direct in states which retained their independence [such as China, Japan, and Thailand], their leaders, like those in the colonies, have had the world prestige of democracy thrust upon them. Even where the people have been denied any significant share in power, old-style autocracy has not infrequently seen fit to parade itself in the outward areas of democratic institutions and may also, like the colonial nationalists, have found it politically expedient to seek a measure of popular support in the effort to throw off alien encroachment and win international favor.[36]

Capitalism was a fusional historical input comprising a much less explicit "ideology" than other elements of the normative process. It emerged with little or no planning or justification from indigenous participation in the commercial, industrial, or financial enterprises induced by the Western impact. Many of its major advocates were achievement-oriented members of the pre-Western commercial class exhibiting a new and unique form of "rugged individualism." In China capitalism was confined mostly to a few indigenous industrialists and numerous small-scale commercial entrepreneurs. In Japan its most salient manifestation was the monopoly capitalism utilized by the *zaibatsu*. In Thailand capitalism was subconsciously employed almost entirely by Chinese entrepreneurs.

Socialism in various forms was advocated during the indigenous response in the three semi-independent societies by some intellectuals, labor leaders and minority spokesmen in an effort to obtain a redistribution of wealth and to reduce economic and social inequality. It was bitterly opposed by the ruling elite which sought maximum use of the nation's resources to promote economic and military power rather than individual well-being.[37] This Western leveling value-system consequently was a sensitive source of friction between the political leadership and opposition groups throughout the unequal treaty process. While some social and economic reforms were implemented by the governments in Nationalist China, Japan, and Thailand, the socialist ideology was never accepted by the top political leadership.

Communism did not develop in Japan during the indigenous response prior to 1898. In China and Thailand this alien Western ideology which gained world-wide attention after the Bolshevik seizure of power in Russia was militantly suppressed by the ruling regime throughout the indigenous response. The totalitarian value-system of Marxism-Leninism was seen in official eyes in both of these countries as a radical departure from the values and behavior of the traditional cultural system. A small indigenous communist organization did emerge in Thailand during the 1930's, but it always operated in a clandestine manner and in a hostile environment.[38] Communism survived in China in insurgent form due largely to the military intervention of Japan after 1937 and the political skills of Mao Tse-tung in building a revolutionary party on a peasant rather than a proletarian base.[39] Communism in China also gained considerable strength from its admixture with certain aspects of Confucianism which promoted government by a moral and intellectual elite, and the "mandate" to overthrow a corrupt ruling regime by the use of violence.

The most significant quality of the political culture in the normative process in the three semi-independent societies consisted of the attitudes, sentiments, and behavior which confined the actual exercise of political power to a small number of people actively seeking to modernize the emerging national society, regain complete sovereignty, and achieve equality with the West. This kind of political culture consequently was both progressive and elitist. It comprised a bifurcated pattern of behavior between a vast rural and tradition-bound populace and a small but growing number of modernizing urban dwellers. It comprised the relationships within a secular and ambitious political leadership waging a "revolution from above" to bring its own traditional countrymen into the modern era. Political culture in Nationalist China, Japan, and Thailand during the indigenous response embodied a preponderant majority of what Almond and Powell have called "parochials" or persons "who manifest little or no awareness of the national political systems."[40] It contained a small number of "subjects" living usually in urban areas who were oriented toward the political system and affected by many governmental policies, but who made no effort to initiate political inputs. The political culture had a modest number of "participants" or individuals consciously engaging in articulating demands and making decisions. Yet the major form of "participant" behavior in this kind of normative process was a *bureaucratic* participation, either in the civil service or the armed forces, rather than participation in making political demands through electoral campaigns, interest groups, legislative lobbying, etc. It was this significant characteristic of the political culture in the three semi-independent societies which generated a large specialized administrative system. It likewise contributed to an elitist political process seeking to expand the capacity of the political system in order to regain complete national sovereignty from Western extraterritorial controls.

Political Process

The political process in this kind of political system was the result of an indigenous response seeking sufficient change to terminate the unequal treaties, but at the same time avoiding change which could become sufficiently disruptive to threaten the power of the makers of change. The political process consequently assumed a highly elitist quality which restricted governmental decision-making authority to very few powerful leaders. Yet it gradually involved some political influences exerted by a small number of disparate individuals and groups outside the official ruling elite. The new national politics, in brief, was characterized essentially by a new political leadership wielding the dominant authority and growing coteries of political aspirants who frequently challenged that authority. The vast masses of rural peasants beyond these two levels of political activity remained apathetic and inert. In varying degrees both types of activists at the top of the political process were advocates of conservative nationalism and constitutional democracy; both elements were likewise affected by the emerging governmental process which greatly enhanced the capacity of the ruling elite and the bureaucracy to maintain themselves in power.

Political communication in this kind of political process, like that in the six national societies emerging under Anglo-American colonial rule, was confined largely to urban areas. In addition to the traditional and modern channels of the communication systems, political information and opinions were conveyed through the transportation system, universities in the educational system, commerce, industry, and finance. The flow of political ideas through these diverse means during the unequal treaty process was closely related to the competitive tendencies between the ruling elite and its small but growing political opposition. Early mass media such as the press and subsequently the radio (in China and Thailand) was used by the political leadership to announce and defend official policies promoting modernization. The press was used as the major channel by the small number of political opponents to criticize the ruling elite.

Institutions of higher education likewise served as conduits of political information contributing to these competing levels of political activity. At times all these channels of political communication were subjected to government censorship or control. The Chinese Nationalists used Peking University and the Whampoa Military Academy to convey their ideas and defend their policies, while other universities, usually Christian missionary universities, frequently disseminated anti-government views.[41] Tokyo Imperial University served increasingly as a center for advancing the goals of the Meiji leaders, while political activists at several lesser universities promoted dissenting opinions.[42] The medical faculty and civil service schools in Bangkok were centers of loyalty to the Thai absolute monarchy, yet the law faculty at Chulalongkorn University was used by Pridi Phanomyong and a few followers to spread anti-royalist sentiment which led to the establishment of a constitutional monarchy. These channels of political communication distributed many similar values such as progress and equality which strengthened the nationalist ideology. Political communication also induced larger participation in politics and consequently assisted in gaining adherents for constitutional democracy. Yet greater efforts to broaden political participation for the purpose of challenging the ruling elite resulted in renewed efforts by the ruling elite to bolster and preserve its own power. Political communication consequently enhanced a unique type of elitist political process.

Interest articulation and interest groups in the three semi-independent societies were less differentiated than in the six emerging quasi-democracies analyzed in Chapter Ten. Some protest groups were organized which assumed a massive and revolutionary scale such as the Taiping Rebellion in China and the Saigo uprising in Japan. Yet the predominant form of interest articulation occurred in the organization of what Almond and Powell have labeled "associational" and "non-associational" interest groups largely seeking economic goals.[43] These types of interest groups were organized on a modest scale in China and Japan. No interest groups of this kind were formed during the indigenous response in Thailand. The only interest groups which exerted political significance in China and Japan were those which retained close personal and financial ties with the ruling regime. These included wealthy industrialists and landlords in China and the *zaibatsu* in Japan. Interest groups which tended to oppose the government, such as labor unions and peasant organizations, were consistently weak. The most significant interest articulation in this kind of emerging political system was that produced by powerful factions within the ruling elite. These factions included the Whampoa clique, the CC clique, and the intellectuals in China, the bureaucracy *(kambatsu)* in Japan, and civilian and military factions in Thailand. This modern form of "palace politics" contributed further to an elitist form of political rule.

The development of political parties in the three bureaucratic polities occurred only in the final stages of the indigenous response. It comprised an effort by political leaders inside and outside the ruling elite to organize diverse individuals and groups into a political organization capable of maintaining themselves in power or getting themselves in key official positions. The only political parties which achieved any significant influence were upper "middle class" parties oriented primarily toward economic goals. These political parties tended to oppose government policies and cause the ruling elite to counter-organize with the formation of its own political party. This practice promoted a unique dominant party system. In Japan the Liberal Party *(Jiyuto)* formed in 1881 represented rural landlords, and the Constitutional Progressive Party *(Rikken Kaishinto)* organized the following year represented large financial interests. A government party called the Constitutional Imperialist Party *(Rikken Teiseito)* was established at the same time. The dissolution of these political parties in 1885 was followed by the revival of opposition bourgeoise parties after the first national elections in 1889. By the end of the unequal treaties in 1898 the opposition parties had again forced the ruling regime to organize its own political party and set up the first party-based cabinet.[44] The dominant political party in China was the *Kuomintang* organized by Sun Yat-sen along Leninist lines for the purpose of defeating the warlords and unifying the national society. After 1928 the KMT was used by Chiang Kai-shek as a power base in his struggles against the Chinese communists, Japanese invaders, and Western powers. A few small political parties led by Western-educated intellectuals attracted some popular support in Chinese urban centers during the 1930's and after World War II, but they possessed no military power which was a *sine qua non* in the political struggle during the final stages of the indigenous response. The organization of civilian and military leaders in Thailand which overthrew the absolute monarchy in 1932 used the label of the "People's Party" (or "The Promoters"). However, the new ruling elite abolished all political parties in the early period of the constitutional monarchy claiming that the Thai kingdom was not ready for this kind of modern political organization.

Political parties in all three semi-independent societies were greatly limited by internal divisions, personal rivalries, and corruption. They were alien institutions which tended to fragment the body politic and they operated almost continually on an extremely narrow political base. They clashed constantly with the traditional value upholding the fusion of politics and doctrine in Nationalist China and Japan, and the traditional loyalty to king, country, and religion in Thailand. The effort to organize these political parties consequently ran counter to the tendency of the ruling elite to achieve "total" aggregation or mobilization among all persons and groups in the newly-emerging national society. This all-embracing effort in turn served to strengthen the political leadership at the expense of the political parties.

As in the six quasi-democracies in South and Southeast Asia, the political leadership in the three bureaucratic polities was the most significant fusional historical input in the emerging political process. The strenuous demands imposed by the unequal treaties in Nationalist China, Japan, and Thailand required the development of a markedly different type of political elite than in the pre-Western traditional society. The need for efficiency and speed in resisting further Western encroachments and the urgent desire to regain complete sovereignty greatly enhanced the authority of the new modernizing political leadership. During the indigenous response this ruling elite consisted of three types of leaders: (1) civilian politicians, (2) civilian technocrats, and (3) military politicians.

The civilian politicians were the early "nationalist" activists among the disgruntled classes during the final years of the traditional society. They were the first to protest the inability of the last traditional ruler to cope with the infringements and adversities imposed by the Western powers. They were also the first to recognize the urgent need to adopt Western technology in order to resist the West. In addition to these early perceptions, the original "founding fathers" possessed the ability to organize a revolutionary movement capable of overthrowing the traditional elite and overcoming "counter-revolutionary" efforts to displace them.

In China the civilian politicians included Dr. Sun Yat-sen and other civilian leaders who aided in the early organized opposition to the Manchu dynasty. Most of these new national leaders were from merchant or scholarly families who had acquired some degree of modern education. According to Professor Fairbank, "they were typically 'alienated intellectuals,' whose modern education pulled them out of the traditional society, restless misfits who found careers as full-time professional politicians and military or party organizers."[45] In forming the Kuomintang in 1912, this group sought to combine traditional and Western ideas in a new revolutionary strategy designed to achieve complete independence and sovereignty. The civilian politicians in Japan were the Sat-Cho leaders from the lower samurai class which overthrew the Tokugawa Shogunate and retained political power throughout the Meiji restoration. In contrast to the individual style of civilian political leadership in China, the Japanese ruling elite comprised a collective form of leadership. It included Ito Hirobumi, Yamagata Aritomo, Kido Koin, Inoue Kaoru, Okuma Shigenobu, Iwakura Tomomi, and Sanjo Santetome. It has been described by Hane as a group of men who "were patriotic individuals possessed of a strong sense of public responsibility, dedication, energy, and vision. Their leadership was collective, that is, no single person emerged as a strong man, and they ruled in accordance with the time-honored tradition of collective leadership and consensus politics."[46] Civilian politicians developed late in the indigenous response in Thailand due largely to important modernization reforms initiated by the absolute monarchy and the lack of widespread economic and social alienation. Civilian leadership consisted of Pridi Phanomyong and a small group of European-educated followers who provided the ideology and motivation for overthrowing the absolute monarchy in 1932. These persons were likewise from a small frustrated "middle class" seeking the end of the *ancien regime* in order to accelerate the political and economic progress of the Thai kingdom.

Civilian technocrats were usually from the same personal background and experience as the civilian politicians. They tended to come from upper classes during the final years of the traditional society, and they were persons who had acquired considerable professional training either at home or abroad. They were strongly nationalistic and anxious for modernization and change. Yet unlike the civilian politicians, they tended to lack strong political ambitions. Their primary concern was the need for a stable and efficient government as a means for promoting administrative and technological advances. The civilian technocrats remained subservient to the top civilian politicians. They comprised the chief administrative and technical officials whose expertise was sorely needed to implement programs for economic and social progress.

Military politicians consisted of high-ranking military officers who acquired increasing degrees of political influence and power during the indigenous response. These military leaders represented what Almond and Powell have labeled an "institutional" interest group articulating its own interest or the interests of other groups from *within* the formal organization of the government.[47] Military politicians were secular and progressive. They had their own perceptions of nationalism and national goals. They moved into positions of political power either held or claimed by civilian politicians, and they became a dominant or significant political force by the end of the unequal treaties. This acquisition of political power by military officers occurred by default in Nationalist China, by gradualism in Japan, and by opportunism in Thailand.

As the dominant military politician in Nationalist China, Chiang Kai-shek expanded his power following the death of Sun Yat-sen by leading the resistance against the Chinese communists, the Japanese invaders, and the remnants of Western imperialism.[48] In one of the major paradoxes in Asian politics, Chiang and other rightist military politicians in Nationalist China were mortally weakened and forced to flee to Taiwan due in considerable degree to the military defeats and political demoralization caused by rightist military politicians in Imperial Japan. Japanese military politicians, in turn, gained enormous national stature and popularity following the Sino-Japanese war which brought international recognition of Japan as a major world power. By 1898 they had emerged as a distinct political clique (*gumbatsu*) which espoused its own militant and expansive brand of Japanese nationalism.[49] These military politicians were not yet in positions of dominant power, but they were gaining influence and exerting a larger role in the political process. Military politicians in Thailand exerted a relatively moderate role under the leadership of Colonel Bahol Phonphayuhasena following the abolition of the absolute monarchy in June 1932.[50] Yet when Bahol retired in 1938 due to poor health, his successor, Colonel Phibun Songkhram, initiated a new style of political leadership which soon began promoting its own form of Thai militarism and irrendentism.[51]

The emergence of military politicians at the top of the political process was one of the most salient fusional historical inputs in the three emerging bureaucratic polities. It was one of the most far-reaching influences engendered by the indigenous response. The new military politicians comprised a *nouveau* elite which had worked its way up from the peasant class and exerted a political role which tended to be ruthless and unrestrained. They aided in spreading military values and behavior into larger segments of the new national society. They abetted an extremist form of militant nationalism which contributed to international tension and internal regimentation. These military leaders were the first in Asia to reveal the phenomena which has occurred frequently in the region and other non-Western areas since World War II, namely the assumption of political power by indigenous military leaders whenever civilian politicians have proved incapable of providing stable and progressive leadership at a time of rapid social change.

Governmental Process

The formation of the governmental process in the three bureaucratic polities was greatly influenced by the Western concepts of progress and the nation-state. It was a fusional historical input caused by the internal administrative reforms required for the termination of the unequal treaties and the achievement of complete national sovereignty. As previously mentioned, this kind of indigenous response occurred first in the realm of legal and administrative reforms (especially customs, finance, and transportation) to meet the requirements for abolishing extraterritoriality and the fixed tariffs imposed by the West. Yet the impetus for improvement quickly induced similar reforms in almost all administrative departments and agencies. The endeavor to establish a modern, rationalized bureaucracy was likewise closely related to the new political culture in which a powerful and progressive elite began to wage a "revolution from above" in order to achieve rapid and sweeping changes. The formal governmental institutions created by the ruling elite were a significant part of this unique form of "revolution." They constituted the administrative arm or instrument used by the ruling regime to implement its designs for national defense and economic modernization. The indigenous persons involved in the new bureaucratic structures constituted the major form of "political participation" seeking to build a new national society and opposing further infringements by the Western powers.

The governmental process in Nationalist China, Japan, and Thailand was legitimized by written constitutions which in effect justified the formation of a powerful centralized state rather than allocating limited authority to specific official organs. Unlike the six quasi-democracies in South and Southeast Asia, the constitutions in the three bureaucratic polities served largely as an official facade for an elitist political process, although they appeared to be imbued with Western liberal democracy. They all resulted from considerable experimentation with "provisional" governmental institutions established immediately after the overthrow of the final traditional ruler. They were all written in the final stages of the unequal treaties. They provided a slightly larger arena for the political struggles between the ruling elite and its opposition, yet they served primarily as symbols of national modernization and were promulgated to hasten the abolition of Western extraterritoriality.

The introductory portions of the 1947 constitution of the Republic of China, the 1889 (Meiji) constitution of the Empire of Japan, and the 1932 permanent constitution in Thailand contained numerous provisions upholding important civil rights for the citizens of these societies. These privileges included the freedom of speech, religion, and assembly, equality before the law, and the right to own private property. Most of these rights, however, were legal rights rather than constitutional rights, and they could be altered at any time by law. Their role was likewise qualified by numerous provisions emphasizing the duties of citizens, including the obligation to pay taxes, to serve in the armed forces, and to respect the law.

Yet the essence of these written documents was contained in the provisions for a powerful executive authority which in effect dominated all formal governmental organs. The organs institutionalizing executive authority were the major official structures used by the ruling elite to legitimize and exercise its pre-eminent power. This sweeping executive-administrative role was achieved in the presidential-type constitutional framework in Nationalist China by the provisions defining broad and general powers for the President of the Republic. These powers gave the President direct control over all administrative ministries and also provided him with extensive appointive powers in managing the affairs of other branches of government. The President was both the chief of state and the chief of government. His executive power was reinforced by the legal authority to appoint the members of the Executive Yuan defined in the constitution as "the highest administrative organ of the State." Executive dominance was legalized in the quasi-parliamentary constitution in Japan by vesting the source of national sovereignty in the Emperor, rather than the people, and by providing the Emperor with vast and loosely defined powers. The actual authority to exercise these broad powers in turn was given to the cabinet or "Ministers of State" who "shall give their advice to the Emperor, and be responsible for it." Specific authority for cabinet members to exercise the Emperor's extensive powers came from the brief provision of Article 55 which stated: "All Laws, Imperial Ordinances and Imperial Rescripts of whatever kind, that relate to the affairs of the State, require the countersignature of a Minister of State." Similar provisions in the quasi-parliamentary constitution in Thailand vested all legislative, executive, and judicial powers in the King and provided the cabinet or "Council of Ministers" with dominant legal authority to exercise these basic powers. Section 46 of the Thai constitution stated: "The Council of Ministers is charged with the duty of conducting the government of the State."

Below the top executive organs were the major ministries and departments of the government managed by civilian technocrats, and, in some cases, by high-ranking military officers. Many of these specialized bureaucratic organizations acquired a high level of professional competence during the unequal treaties, especially the ministries dealing with diplomacy, the armed forces, finance, foreign trade, transportation, and communications. By the time of complete national sovereignty these large administrative structures of the governmental process contained an experienced civil service. Yet this notable development in bureaucratic skills was largely "outer-directed." It was induced by the intense desire to ward off an external threat and satisfy treaty obligations imposed by foreign powers. It largely precluded the type of political development which had occurred in Western nations in the simultaneous evolution of political parties and a genuine national legislature. Most politics in this kind of governmental process consequently took place within the executive-administrative organs rather than outside them. The result was a mode of political behavior often referred to as "bureaucratic politics." In some degree it was an extended and modernized form of the traditional "palace politics." It has been described very adequately by Professor Townsend as follows:

> The first condition of bureaucratic politics is that the protagonists must themselves be officials, the more highly placed the better, who reject or conceal any large-scale organizational backing, although they may claim to speak in general terms of popular support for their proposals. Interests lacking influential official spokesmen are in effect denied expression except at the lowest level. Secondly, political struggle itself is carried on by maneuvering within the bureaucratic hierarchy, in which questions of rank and personal influence become all important. The objective is not to gain support from the largest number of colleagues — which may help but which runs the risk of punishment for "factionalism" — but rather to get a favorable decision from the authoritative office for the case in question. Secrecy and gossip, friendship and enmities, decision expressed in changes of personnel, and small coalitions competing for the favor of superiors are, then, the stuff of bureaucratic politics.[52]

The governmental process also included a legislative branch which provided a modest channel for the articulation of demands by the "opposition," but in effect this "representative" institution did little to limit or check the dominant executive authority exercised by the ruling elite. Executive pre-eminence was maintained by the establishment of weak legislative bodies in these constitutional frameworks, and by filling many of the seats in these deliberative chambers with members sympathetic to the ruling regime. This practice was accomplished in Nationalist China by the constitutional provisions which restricted the sessions of the Legislative Yüan to two three-month periods a year, the prohibition "to increase expenditures listed in the budget presented by the Executive Yüan," and the procedures outlined in Article 57 by which cabinet officials in the Executive Yüan could require a two-thirds majority in the legislature to resolve a piece of controversial legislation. The most significant form of executive control, however, was the election of loyal members of the Kuomintang in the Legislative Yüan both on the mainland and on Taiwan. The Meiji leaders in Japan preserved their powerful executive-administrative authority by creating a bicameral legislature with an upper house appointed by the Emperor (i.e. the cabinet) and a lower house elected by a limited propertied electorate. Executive dominance was reinforced by limiting the sessions of the Diet to three months a year, extensive executive veto authority over pending legislation, and the imperial authority to dissolve the lower house at any time. The political power of the ruling elite was further enhanced by appointing members of the royal family, the nobility, and leading entrepreneurial families to the upper house to check the influence of the more democratic lower house. The preservation of executive dominance in Thailand was achieved by the unique constitutional device of establishing a period of ten years in which the membership of the unicameral Assembly of People's Representatives was to be equally divided into "first category" members elected by the people and "second category" members appointed by the King (i.e., the cabinet). The military-directed leadership which put this constitution into practice after 1932 was confronted for several years with modest opposition from some elected members in the national legislature, but this trend was effectively checked by the appointment of large numbers of military officers as second category members.[53]

The judiciary in this kind of governmental process was likewise subordinate to executive authority. A highly centralized court system was established in each of the emerging bureaucratic polities with jurisdiction over civil, criminal, and administrative cases. The constitutions stated that the judicial branch was to be "independent" in dispensing justice, yet in practice the structures and procedures of the courts were heavily regulated by law and served essentially an administrative role. Judges were appointed by executive authority from a small pool of trained legalists whose education and outlook was primarily concerned with protecting the welfare of the state, rather than the rights of the individual. At no time during the unequal treaties, did the judiciary in Nationalist China, Japan, or Thailand serve as an effective check or limitation on executive authority.

Unlike the six quasi-democracies, the outputs or official government policies in this kind of political system were highly developed in *both* foreign and domestic affairs. The conduct of foreign policy was characterized by a strong respect for the role of military power and a vigilance toward shifting configurations in the international balance of power. A sophisticated brand of diplomacy emerged from the successful effort to abolish the unequal treaties with nations more powerful and more experienced in international politics. The new diplomacy embodied a high degree of self-confidence and a willingness to join international organizations, military alliances, etc., to advance important national interests. The formulation of foreign policy was likewise affected by a respect for the major tenets of international law, especially the rights and privileges of national sovereignty.

Domestic policies in the three bureaucratic polities were also well developed which enhanced the power of the emerging nation-state. Ministries and departments engaged in the maintenance of internal security and economic modernization were reasonably well staffed and experienced by the end of the unequal treaties. Yet few domestic policies were directed at the improvement of living standards for the broad masses of people. Government programs concerned with public health, labor relations, social security, social welfare, etc., were either non-existent or meagerly funded. A notable exception was in the field of education, although the new national educational systems were directed primarily at improving the security and development of the nation rather than the intellectual advancement of individuals. The widespread absence of individualism in turn aided in strengthening the dominant political role of the ruling elite and the bureaucracy.

Chapter 12

The Truncated Totalitarian Polities:

Three truncated totalitarian polities emerged in Asia from a highly unique admixture of traditional and Western historical inputs.[1] Some common traditional influences contributed significantly to the formation of these highly centralized and tightly disciplined political systems. A secular-oriented Confucian cultural system provided an ideological foundation suitable for the creation of an all-embracing moral and political order. Other pre-Western values enhanced this development, including a doctrinal idealism, a doctrinal dogmatism, a political pragmatism, a cultural ethnocentrism, and a "mandate" to overthrow a corrupt and oppressive ruling regime.[2] The secular-oriented class structure of the traditional society likewise left a legacy which aided the emergence of a totalitarian system led by a pragmatic-intellectual elite and administered by a uniformly-trained bureaucratic cadre. Each communist regime was further bolstered by the memories of former great traditions which had exhibited grandeur and power for extensive periods of time. The drive for national unity and total territorial control was assisted by the absence or weakness of middle traditions or feudal states during the pre-Western era and the time-honored goal of preserving a unified and homogeneous culture. Each of the new totalitarian polities in Asia consequently comprised a *dominant-ethnic society* consisting largely of a single racial and linguistic community with a widespread conformity in social behavior. Except for relatively small numbers of Manchus, Mongols, Tibetans, Turks, and mountain tribesmen along some of the remote borders of Communist China, and the small numbers of Meo and Thai tribesmen in North Vietnam, none of these new communist societies contained sizeable ethnic minorities, a factor which enhanced the spread of an orthodox party doctrine and uniform revolutionary behavior.

A considerable diversity of Western historical inputs also influenced the development of these three totalitarian polities. Communist China emerged in response to foreign influences, largely Japanese, generated during the final two decades of an unequal treaty process caused by both economic and strategic factors which lasted a total of 99 years. The political system in North Korea was molded in considerable degree by the economic aggrandizement motivating Japanese colonial rule which endured for the much smaller time period of 35 years. The polity in North Vietnam was deeply affected by the tutelary form of colonial rule imposed by France for an intermediate period of 67 years.

Yet in spite of these differences in the form and duration of the Western impact, several common Western historical influences contributed significantly to the establishment of truncated totalitarian societies in Communist China, North Korea, and North Vietnam. One of the most significant was nationalism which provided the initial value-system for the early communist movements in each of these societies. Another similar Western input was cultural secularization which accelerated the erosion of traditional values and behavior, and intensified the psychological trauma and frustrations among small radical groups which formed the nucleus of the communist movements in each of these three national societies. One of the most important common Western influences in the formation of these totalitarian polities was the high degree of harshness in the unequal treaty process in China and in the colonization processes in Korea and Vietnam.[3] This factor aroused a similar harshness and brutality in the indigenous response. Likewise was the violence and disruption caused by the major Western powers and Imperial Japan in and around these three societies at the end of World War II an important common factor which enhanced the political goals of indigenous communist organizations. In many respects the unexpected internal developments caused either directly or indirectly by major military operations in the final phases of this global war were the prime catalysts which led to the creation of the three truncated totalitarian polities.

Among the most salient common characteristics in the development of the three communist polities were those embodied in the indigenous response which produced the most similar types of political systems in Asia. The historical time frames during which each of these totalitarian societies emerged are the most distinct and precise in the political history of the entire region. The years 1918–1921 clearly mark the beginning of the combination of indigenous and Western historical inputs which eventually produced these highly regimented nation-states. The communist movement in China developed from the militant nationalism which gained strength after the May Fourth Movement in 1919.[4] Communist organizations in Korea emerged from a similar intense nationalist reaction which first erupted in the March First Movement during the same year.[5] A communist apparatus surfaced in Vietnam at a somewhat later date (in the late 1920's), yet the emergence of Vietnamese communist leaders and party organizations in Europe, the Soviet Union, and China also began during the years immediately following the end of World War I.[6]

In effect, each communist polity in Asia developed from an extremist and militant reaction to Western intervention which split off from the more moderate nationalist movements that had existed in each of these societies prior to World War I. In the case of China, a simple patriotic response in varying forms had been underway since the Taiping Rebellion in the mid-nineteenth century. It rapidly gained strength and direction in Sun Yat-sen's nationalist movement following the overthrow of the Manchu dynasty in 1912. Similar anti-foreign reactions had emerged in Korea and Vietnam, although for shorter periods of time. Yet the communist-oriented reactions which started in China, Korea, and Vietnam just after World War I were based on a revolutionary fervor among small Marxist-Leninist groups seeking not only the end of foreign rule, but also the termination of various forms of internal "capitalism" or "feudalism" imposed by indigenous propertied classes. At times the communist response overlapped with the nationalist response, and on several occasions they formed a "united front." However, the primary ideological and political goal of the communist organizations was to broaden the on-going nationalist revolution into an economic and social revolution which would liberate the society from both foreign domination and the domestic "old order."

Another important common element in the indigenous response shaping the communist political systems in China, Korea, and Japan was what I will label the "exiled revolution." This unique form of "revolution" was conducted almost entirely by indigenous communist organizations operating from foreign countries or from remote rural territories inside the society. With the passage of time the exiled revolution developed a combined political, military, and subversive capacity to wage an ideological warfare against both local and foreign opponents.[7] The extensive use of foreign exile or exile in remote rural areas was required by the severe suppression of indigenous dissidents in Korea and Vietnam by Japanese and French colonial rule and by the similarly brutal suppression of communist organizations in China by the Chinese Nationalists and Japanese occupation troops.

The exiled revolution in China assumed a somewhat different geopolitical form from that in Korea and Vietnam. The exiled revolution in China took place from rural bases established first by Mao Tse-tung, Chu Teh, and other communist leaders in Kiangsi, Hunan, and Fukien provinces in the south, and later by these and other communist leaders in

Shensi, Shansi, Kansu, Hopei, Shantung, and other provinces in the north.[8] The immense physical size of Chinese national territory and the rugged terrain in many interior areas provided the relatively secure sanctuaries from which this exiled revolution was fought. The exiled revolution in Korea and Vietnam, in contrast, was conducted and supported largely from nearby foreign territories. The Korean exiled revolution was waged entirely from foreign countries due to the rigid control maintained by Japanese security forces over all Korean territory until the sudden Japanese surrender in August 1945. The sources of this foreign-based revolution were Japan, Shanghai, Manchuria, and the Maritime Provinces of the Soviet Union.[9] The locations of the exiled revolution in Vietnam were a function of time. They were almost entirely in foreign countries prior to World War II; thereafter they assumed both an internal and an external dimension. Before 1941 the Vietnamese communist revolution was supported from France, the Soviet Union, China, and Thailand.[10] In the period after November 1946 the exiled revolution in Vietnam was waged largely from insurgent bases in the rugged terrain of several northern provinces adjoining the Chinese border.[11]

Yet in spite of these geopolitical differences, the role of the exiled revolution in shaping the three truncated communist societies was essentially the same. The absence of communist control over all or most of the indigenous population during the final stages of colonial rule or foreign military occupation combined with the power vacuum created by the sudden collapse of the international power structure in Asia at the end of World War II gave an enormous advantage to the highly disciplined and militarily-skilled organizations of exiled communist leaders bent on seizing political power. In sharp contrast to the indigenous response of the six quasi-democracies emerging from Anglo-American colonial rule in South and Southeast Asia and of the three bureaucratic polities emerging from the unequal treaty process in Nationalist China, Japan, and Thailand which had engaged in varying degrees of state-building and nation-building, the indigenous response in the three truncated totalitarian societies was involved almost entirely in party-building and revolution-building. The creation of each communist polity depended heavily on the most dynamic, militant, and aggressive indigenous reaction anywhere in Asia. Also, the acquisition of power by communist leaders in these new totalitarian societies, much more than anywhere else in the region, was enhanced by the nature and timing of numerous unexpected "accidents" in the global and regional international environment which caused much sheer "good luck."

DOMESTIC ENVIRONMENT

As previously cited many values of the Confucian cultural system in China, Korea, and Vietnam assisted the communist-directed indigenous response. Two traditional norms were of special significance in aiding the small communist party elites to gain adherents and maintain relatively cohesive party organizations in spite of many obstacles and reversals. The traditional idea of cultural ethnocentrism was one of these values. This pre-Western norm experienced a gradual transformation as it encountered Western cultural influences, and by the 1920's and 1930's it had engendered a psychological reaction highly favorable to the acceptance of a new technological and social order.[12] By this time a growing number of indigenous persons, including many rural villagers, were aware that the Confucian culture was rapidly declining and it would never revive in its traditional forms. An important and somewhat paradoxical development in this cultural malaise was an intense desire to preserve a distinctly racial and native quality in the adoption of a new life-style and mode of behavior. In many ways the fermentation caused by the interaction of traditional and Western cultures reinforced a tendency to assert an indigenous component in the evolution of a new modernizing culture. The Chinese had responded with a similar ethnocentrism in the aftermath of the Mongol conquest during the thirteenth century.[13] The Korean people had reacted similarly to intermittent cultural infusions from China with a strong desire to retain a distinctly Korean quality in the assimilation of Confucianism.[14] The capacity of the Vietnamese people to preserve many national characteristics while absorbing numerous elements of Chinese culture is well known and widely documented.[15] During the second and third decades of the twentieth century a similar native pride again emerged in these three societies seeking the preservation of some aspects of the indigenous culture as it was increasingly subjected to the Western impact. The combination of a renewed sense of cultural ethnocentrism at a time when the traditional culture was decaying produced the often cited phenomena in non-Western societies of being "poor" and "subjugated" but "proud." This tendency further strengthened an indigenous demand for an end to foreign intervention and the pursuit of political, economic, and social changes under a native leadership. It likewise meant that new national leaders could expect widespread support from their own people.

The emerging cultural patriotism and the growing desire for indigenous-led cultural change affected both the nationalist and communist organizations in China, Korea, and Vietnam. It undoubtedly touched a much larger number of followers in the nationalist movement and strengthened their resolve to retain certain elements of the indigenous culture. Yet the stronger fervor and more intense dynamism in the communist organizations gave a special thrust to this combination of native pride and a demand for progress. The new form of cultural ethnocentrism became a popular theme of the communist leaders, and enabled them to appear as "national" spokesmen for a much larger segment of the indigenous population than they actually represented. It likewise gave them the opportunity to give their own direction and emphasis to the formation of a new national culture. It made it possible, in brief, for the communist revolutions to add a cultural dimension in their ideological quest for a "new" nation and a "new" social order. Mao Tse-tung illustrated this tendency in his well-known essay, "On New Democracy." He stated:

> For many years we Communists have struggled not only for China's political and economic revolution but also for her cultural revolution; all this aims at building up a new society and new state for the Chinese nation. In that new society and new state there will be not only new politics and a new economy but also a new culture. That is to say, we want not only to change a politically oppressed and economically exploited China into a politically free and economically prosperous China, but also to change a China which has been ignorant and backward under the rule of the old culture into a China that will be enlightened and progressive under the rule of a new culture. In a word, we want to build up a new China. To build up a new culture of the Chinese nation is our aim in the cultural sphere.[16]

The broad emphasis on a "total" revolution by communist leaders in all three societies assisted them in preempting a sizeable portion of the nationalist response to foreign intervention. In China and Korea, the communists continued to face intense competition from the nationalist movements. Yet in Vietnam the stress on sweeping economic, social, and cultural changes with a distinct native quality by Ho Chi Minh and his fledgling communist organization enabled them to virtually capture the nationalist movement, an achievement greatly facilitated by the relentless suppression of non-communist nationalists by French colonial authorities.

A second Confucian cultural value which enhanced the communist-led indigenous response was the fusion of doctrine and politics.[17] The remnants of this traditional behavior fostered the spread of the Marxist-Leninist doctrine linking the communist party leadership, the communist party organization, and the indigenous population to a massive historical and dialectial change. While the communist party elites in all three societies tended to despise Confucianism, they cleverly utilized the pre-Western cultural bond uniting political authority to an all-embracing ethical and social order. They constructed a new orthodoxy on the traditional organic and harmonious relationships uniting the individual, the family, the clan, and the province to the entire society. On this basis they gradually broadened the communist revolution into a "people's" revolution. In this transformation, they successfully created the image of an intimate bond between themselves and the broad masses of people in spite of the fact that the communist elites in these emerging totalitarian societies were more detached from the populace they were seeking to "liberate" than in any other indigenous response in Asia. This blending of local and foreign behavior combined with the potency of the new cultural ethnocentrism gave added strength to the communist organizations.

Only a portion of the modernizing educational institutions in China, Korea, and Vietnam aided the communist-oriented indigenous response, but this portion was extremely important. At the highest levels it provided the psychological milieu in which militant and radical nationalism was converted into communism. It produced the small but growing body of embittered intellectuals who gave up Western liberalism for Marxism-Leninism. This reaction was the strongest in China where leading universities such as the University of Peking operated with some detachment from the government and society, especially during the crucial formative years of the communist movement after World War I. Communist adherents also emerged at institutions of higher education established by colonial administrators and indigenous educators in Korea and Vietnam, but they were less numerous than in China due to the stringent security measures imposed by the colonial regimes. The communist organizations in Korea and Vietnam depended heavily on party leaders educated or trained abroad.

The partially isolated atmosphere at universities and other schools attended by indigenous nationals gave early social thinkers an opportunity to examine what appeared to them to be relevant aspects of contending foreign ideologies. It gave them a choice in selecting the goals and methods they wanted their societies to follow. It enabled these partially westernized intellectuals to grasp some of the "messianic" and "cosmic" elements of Marxist-Leninist doctrine, and it gradually caused many of them to relinquish completely their receding attachments to Western freedom and individualism.[18] The spread of communist proclivities at these learning centers was facilitated in considerable degree by the traditional tutor-disciple relationship of the Confucian system which made it possible for a few leading Marxist thinkers to shape the political views of a wide body of devoted followers. The universities also became the haven for small Marxist study groups which supplied much of the leadership of the early communist parties.[19] They bolstered the elitist approach of the communist-directed indigenous response by arousing an intense desire among communist adherents to lead the entire society in a total revolution against foreign and local opponents.

Economic modernization in these three societies, as elsewhere in Asia, brought numerous changes which benefited foreigners and a small indigenous upper class much more than the broad masses of rural villagers and a small growing class of urban workers. The grievances caused by this rapid transformation added enormously to native resentment against foreign capitalism which in turn reinforced nationalist sentiment and the quest for an end to foreign economic exploitation. Yet to the communist parties in China, Korea, and Vietnam, the economic changes initiated by foreign enterprises played a much greater political role than they did for the more moderate nationalists. Grievances induced by modernizing economic changes became a prime target in the ideological struggle against capitalism and an important *raison d'etre* for the communist-led revolution. The communist parties gave special attention to disruptive alterations in the traditional class structure and to the widening gaps in wealth, status, and influence in a new class structure.

Economic modernization in parts of China combined with more efficient administrative and legal capacities produced by the unequal treaty process produced a smaller and more affluent landlord class and a much larger tenant and landless peasant class. Statistics on the extent of landholdings during this period in China are few and controversial, but the spread of peasant unrest in many areas was widely recognized. Professor Townsend has described this condition as follows: "High rates of tenancy and the presence of a few large landowners were obvious sources of peasant dissatisfaction and obvious targets for reformers and revolutionaries, although neither was a condition typical of all China."[20] Similar changes occurred in Korea and Vietnam which induced even greater rural discontent since they involved a landlord class consisting of both foreign and native landowners. In Korea, the proportion of landless peasants increased from 37.7% in 1918 to 55.7% in 1938.[21] By 1942 only 4% of the landowners possessed 40.2% of all rice land, with a sizeable majority of Koreans in this landlord class. According to Professor Henderson: "Gaps of wealth and poverty widened, and there was a steady creation of a rural proletariat... this caused resentment and the emigration of hundreds of thousands to Manchuria and Japan."[22] In Vietnam, large landholdings occurred almost entirely in the southern provinces of Cochin China. By 1938 some 6300 large landowners in this

French-annexed territory owned almost 50% of all cultivated rice land.[23] As in Korea, most of the large landlords were indigenous, yet in this colonized society the French landowners possessed approximately 12% of all arable land. A peasant class of small landowners owned only 15% of the cultivated land, and below them was a large tenant class comprising 50% of the entire rural population. There were only 50 large landowners in Annam and about 500 in Tonkin, yet the living conditions of Vietnamese peasants in these protectorates were often worse than in Cochinchina due to the rapid population increase and the small expansion of cultivated land. In addition to large French holdings in rice lands, French landowners possessed virtually all of the rubber plantations established in Vietnam after 1906, and many thousands of Vietnamese workers were employed on these plantations under extremely adverse conditions through a system of forced labor.[24] The indigenous response to these French-sponsored economic innovations has been described by Professor Buttinger as follows:

> The land policies of the French in Vietnam, even more than the
> taxes and monopolies they introduced, explain fully why the
> hostility of the rural masses toward the colonial regime was
> never overcome. The time would come, as some foresaw long be-
> fore World War I, when France would have to pay a heavy price
> for the errors and misbehavior of her *colons* and administrators
> in Indochina. It is safe to say that if the French had chosen a
> less disastrous approach to the land question and employed all
> available means for eliminating rural poverty, the Communist
> movement of Vietnam would never have gained its extraordinary
> strength.[25]

Grievances caused by economic modernization in urban areas were also exploited by the communists. Many Marxists predictions which had been invalidated in Western industrialized societies appeared relevant to communist leaders as additional wealth and influence were acquired by a small entreprenurial class and increasing misery was experienced by an expanding urban proletariat. In China the industrial working class grew from small numbers in the nineteenth century to approximately 2,000,000 workers by 1925.[26] Most of this laboring class worked in the mining, transportation, textile and rice-milling industries in Shanghai, Wuhan, Tientsin, Canton, and the northeastern provinces. This new proletariat was mostly apolitical until the May Fourth Movement in 1919 when small-scale demonstrations and strikes against foreign enterprises occurred in some major Chinese cities. It was in this disgruntled urban working class where the Chinese communist party first gained a few members outside the institutions of higher education.

Industrial development occurred much more slowly in Korea and it did not exert a significant effect on the indigenous people until after 1931 when Japanese expansion in Manchuria made Korea an important communication and transportation center as well as a source of raw materials. Korean workers were employed in both mining and industrial enterprises established by the Japanese, and by the end of World War II they numbered 733,000.[27] Unlike China, labor organizations were forbidden in Korea, and discrimination by Japanese industrialists combined with arduous working conditions aroused deep discontent in the emerging Korean proletariat. Henderson has stated: "This agitated [Korean] populace had a wide variety of new needs and a new potential to engage in political movements. Atomized and anxious with the collapse of even such associations as existed in 1945, many Korean workers became comparatively easy prey to politics in the form of Communist organization."[28] The industrial working class was even smaller in Vietnam, although the unique economic policies imposed by the French colonial authorities did much to create a widespread proletarian consciousness. The number of Vietnamese workers employed in industry, mining, and rubber plantations by the 1930's has been estimated at 220,000 persons, but this figure included only Vietnamese workers in French-owned enterprises and did not include fairly large numbers of Vietnamese employed in Chinese commercial organizations.[29] Much more important is the fact that the highly mobile system of forced labor used by the French caused most Vietnamese laborers to work in industrial enterprises for only short periods of time before returning to their rural villages. Through this system it is estimated that several million Vietnamese workers were exposed to a style of Western capitalism which involved extremely brutal and humiliating conditions. In explaining the impact of this aspect of French colonial rule on Vietnamese society, Buttinger has declared:

> Although the [Vietnamese] working class, as a result of the denial of industry, remained small, the nature of colonial capitalism spread the negative effects of modern labor exploitation over an exceptionally vast number of people. It thus prepared not only the people in factories, mines, and towns, but also those in thousands of villages, for the days when revolutionary leaders would seek to win the support of the masses.[30]

Thus, in many ways the widening gaps and growing frustrations in the emerging class structures in all three societies seemed to verify aspects of Marxist doctrine regarding an economically-motivated class struggle and an "inevitable" downfall of capitalism.

THE POLITICAL SYSTEM

Politically relevant fusional historical inputs in the political systems of the three truncated totalitarian societies were formed by two awewome and staggering goals: 1) to remove foreign domination from native soil, and 2) to abolish the "decadent" behavior and class structures of the traditional indigenous culture. The first goal involved the end of a total system of foreign colonial rule in Korea and Vietnam; it involved the slightly lesser task of removing a system of partial foreign controls in the unequal treaty process in China. In either case both objectives were by far the most ambitious and demanding purposes embodied in the indigenous response anywhere in Asia. They were especially demanding since they consisted of a totally new type of political and social revolution. While the communist revolutions were assisted by some elements of the traditional culture, they comprised an effort to establish a completely new society. Nothing like them had previously existed on the territory of the former traditional society. Unlike the indigenous reactions which produced the six quasi-democracies and the three bureaucratic polities as already cited, they had no historical links to the past. Instead they denied much of the morality and utility of the past. Their quest for power was guided by the future-oriented vision supplied by a foreign ideology and the model of a single foreign nation (the Soviet Union). This struggle induced a normative process with a dynamic and revolutionary political ideology and a fluid and action-oriented political culture. The formation of the three truncated totalitarian polities likewise depended on a political process utilizing a distinctive organizational structure capable of seizing the unique opportunities provided by an unstable and rapidly changing international environment in the aftermath of a major global war. With only modest exceptions in China and Vietnam, the exiled communist revolutions had little or no governmental process until just before their formation as sovereign nation-states. They remained essentially revolutionary parties motivated by a revolutionary ideology until almost the very end of their struggle for national independence.

Normative Process

The political ideology motivating the communist revolutions in China, Korea, and Vietnam contained several diverse elements, including nationalism, communism, democracy, and socialism. Each of these value-systems caused considerable overlapping and conflict among the political norms in non-totalitarian societies elsewhere in Asia, yet in the three emerging totalitarian polities they were combined in a manner which made them the most homogeneous and rigid normative pattern of any political system in the region.

Militant nationalism was the only form of nationalism in the communist-oriented indigenous response. Moderate or conservative nationalism which developed in the six quasi-democracies and the three bureaucratic polities was absent. In some respects militant nationalism in China, Korea, and Vietnam was not unlike that in other Asian societies emerging from Western domination. It consisted essentially of a harsh anti-foreign reaction based on racial and cultural pride. It was impelled by the intense frustration and indignation among small groups of urban intellectuals and students who resented the continual subjugation of their societies by foreign powers.

Yet militant nationalism in the three totalitarian societies was also different from that elsewhere in Asia. Instead of developing over a period of many years from numerous provocations by Western influences, it erupted abruptly just after World War I when large numbers of indigenous nationalists almost overnight became deeply disillusioned with the failure of the Western powers to express sympathy with their national problems or take actions favorable to their national interests. These sudden outbursts of militant opposition to foreign intervention thereby inherited a portion of the legacy left by earlier resistance movements against foreign domination, such as the Boxer rebellion in China, the Tonghak rebellion in Korea, and the Can Vuong resistance movement in Vietnam. Perhaps most significant, militant nationalism in other Asian societies was the most extreme form of nationalism shared by only a small minority of followers within a much broader nationalist movement. In contrast, militant nationalism in China, Korea, and Vietnam was the sole form of nationalism on which other political values, especially those of Marxism-Leninism, were added. In effect, militant nationalism in the communist indigenous response was only the first element of a political ideology which included other revolutionary ideas and concepts.

Peasant nationalism was a variant of militant nationalism in the political ideology of the three communist revolutions.[31] It was a distinctly unique fusional historical input among the emerging polities in Asia. Only in the territories controlled by the communist-oriented indigenous response did sizeable numbers of rural peasants manifest some cognizance of nationhood and a willingness to participate actively in organized resistance against foreign domination. This form of nationalism emerged from the reaction against the severity of the unequal treaty process in China or the harshness of the colonization process in Korea and Vietnam. Peasant nationalism in China became the basic element in the political ideology of Mao Tse-tung after 1927 when he sought to transfer the communist revolution from the urban proletariat to the rural peasantry. It did not, however, gain widespread influence until Mao and his followers had consolidated their power in Shensi province after the Long March in 1935 and Japanese military forces began their invasion of northern China two years later. The atrocities meted out by Japanese army troops in the countryside quickly politized the traditionally apathetic rural populace and forced large numbers of Chinese peasants to seek security with the Chinese communist guerrilla forces. For the first time in history these peasants thought of themselves as members of a nation seeking to liberate itself from foreign rule. With only a modest attachment to the values of Confucianism, they were also susceptible to other norms of the communist revolution. Peasant nationalism and communism were thereby joined. The Chinese communist leaders gained the most significant political base in their quest for power. Chalmers Johnson has described this development as follows:

> Before the Japanese invasion the Chinese peasantry was indifferent to "Chinese" politics, being wholly absorbed in local affairs. The war totally destroyed the traditional rural social order and sensitized the Chinese peasantry to a new spectrum of possible associations, identities, and purposes. Foremost among the new political concepts were those of "China" and "Chinese nationality." ... During the war, the peasants began to hear and use such terms as Han-chien (Chinese traitor), *wei-chun* (bogus army, i.e. the puppet forces), *wan-chun* (reactionary army, i.e. the KMT forces as seen by Yenan), and *Jih-k'ou* (Japanese bandits). The intrusion of these terms into the peasant's vocabulary signified the spread of a force that hitherto was prevalent only among the intelligentsia and city-bred people — namely, nationalism.[32]

The suppression of indigenous nationalism which usually prevailed in urban areas of Korea and Vietnam caused the communist leadership in these colonized societies to promote peasant nationalism as a continual and permanent tactic. It did not spread rapidly in response to a foreign military invasion as in China. Yet it was only in remote rural territories in or near these two societies where security measures were either non-existent or sufficiently weak that this rustic form of nationhood could gain sizeable numbers of followers. Peasant nationalism in the Korean communist revolution was established almost entirely among Korean peasants inhabiting the border provinces in Manchuria where Japanese control was absent and Chinese authority was minimal. One source estimates that ten per cent of the adult Korean population in Manchuria was either communist or pro-communist by 1930.[33] The revolutionary potential of peasant nationalism in Vietnam was first shown in the formation of the Nghe-Tinh soviets in 1930 and the bitter peasant revolts against French colonial rule which took almost an entire year to pacify.[34] The growing national consciousness among Vietnamese peasants was also a crucial factor after the outbreak of open warfare between French colonial forces and Ho Chi Minh's "Government-in-the-Bush" in November 1946.[35]

The core of the political ideology of the three exiled communist revolutions consisted of the ideas and principles of Marx and Lenin. These radical value-systems transmitted by Cominterm agents, indigenous returnees, and the model of the Bolshevik revolution greatly reinforced the xenophobia and urgency among militant nationalists. They gave a philosophical legitimacy to both militant and peasant nationalism which provided a sense of direction and purpose to these revolutionary organizations and directed them toward all segments of the indigenous population, including the broad masses of poor peasants. Marxism-Leninism, however, was not received as a single uniform doctrine by revolutionary thinkers in China, Korea, and Vietnam, especially in the early stages of the communist-oriented indigenous response. The theoretical precepts of Marx exerted a different influence on communist leaders from the more practical teachings of Lenin.

In many respects Marxist thought alone imparted an influence on the normative process of the communist revolutions similar to that in other modernizing polities in Asia. In China, Korea, and Vietnam, as in all modernizing agricultural societies in the region, Marx's analysis and criticism of industrial capitalism in the West was largely irrelevant. Much of Marxism was likewise in conflict with traditional values and behavior. The class struggle was at variance with the time-honored norm of social harmony. The key role of economics clashed with the traditional emphasis on culture. The primacy of the industrial working class deviated markedly from the low status of the artisan in the traditional class structure. Yet to all Asians embittered by the adversities of Western domination, the spirit of Marxism much more than its letter provided the vision of a world-wide historical change alleviating the sufferings of underprivileged people living under the yoke of foreign capitalism. The humanitarian and emotional content of Marx came across just as strongly as the sweeping utopian view of a classless society and the end of an oppressive state. Also important were the contradictions of capitalism and the predictions of its imminent downfall. Marx's anti-capitalist diatribe won special appeal throughout Asia since it was a scathing attack against Western capitalism from within the West. It was something more than another condemnation of Western oppression by another Asian.

Pure Marxism, however, had a distinctive impact on the communist revolutions in China, Korea, and Vietnam. In some degree the assimilation of Marxist precepts into indigenous thought in these three societies was facilitated by certain aspects of the traditional cultural system.[36] Marx's heavy stress on materialism and his atheistic tone encountered no major opposition from indigenous religious values as occurred in the sacred-oriented societies in South and Southeast Asia. The intensely secular outlook of Marx blended readily with the "this-worldly" orientation of traditional Confucianism. Marx also provided some justification for the use of violence in the struggle against capitalism which was much more relevant in the three communist revolutions reacting to harsh forms of foreign oppression than in the six quasi-democracies or the three bureaucratic polities gradually gaining independence from less severe types of Western domination through reform and negotiation. Marx's "scientific" analysis of historical determinism likewise gave the exiled communist revolutions a sense of hope and expectation which in turn generated enormous perseverance and staying power in the arduous pursuit of their ideological goals. Very important was the totality and universal application of Marxist doctrine which aroused a special appeal in these Confucianist societies. Embittered nationalists suffering from an individual and collective identity crisis were searching for a new ideology to replace the outmoded traditional doctrine. They were probing for a completely new *Weltanschauung* or "way of life." They did not perceive of the individualistic, experimentive, and gradualist approach of Western liberalism as a suitable replacement. Instead many found an alternative in Marxism. Duiker has described this transformation in Vietnam as follows:

> The decline of Confucianism in the cities left an emotional and intellectual void in the minds of patriotic intellectuals, and many obviously found Marxist doctrine an attractive modern alternative to the discredited Sino-Vietnamese tradition. As an intricate and sophisticated philosophy, with a universal dogma and a comprehensive explanation of history that was optimistic, scientific, impregnated with moral fervor, and staunchly anti-imperialist, Marxism could be accepted without great difficulty as a modern equivalent of Confucianism.[37]

Leninism also had a theoretical component which won a wide appeal in Asia. This was his principle of anti-imperialism as "the highest stage of capitalism," a concept which "explained" the historical and economic factors which caused the first successful communist revolution to occur in a backward agricultural nation rather than in a modern industrialized society. This element of Lenin's doctrine, in sharp contrast to much of Marxism, was eminently germane to political thinkers in Asia. It greatly reinforced the universalistic and messianic vision originally created by Marx of an impending collapse of capitalism and the liberation of suppressed peoples and classes from the burdens of foreign imperialism. As cited later by Ho Chi Minh, the teachings of Lenin had a magnetic appeal to militant Asian nationalists because he was the first leader in the West to consider seriously "the colonial question."[38] Lenin was also the first communist leader to link the world-wide communist movement to the peasants of non-Western societies. In his famous *Thesis on the National and Colonial Questions,* the Russian leader declared:

> It is of special importance to support the peasant movements in backward countries against the landowners and all feudal survivals; above all we must strive as far as possible to give the peasant movement a revolutionary character, to organize the peasants and all the exploited into the soviets, and thus bring about the closest possible union between the Communist proletariat of Western Europe and the revolutionary peasant movement of the east and of the colonial and subject countries.[39]

In effect, Leninism broadened the anti-capitalism of Marx to a form of anti-imperialism which had an immediate meaning to numerous Asian dissidents.

Yet the bulk of Leninist doctrine contained a highly practical orientation which was ideally suited for the particular needs of the exiled communist revolutions in China, Korea, and Vietnam. Intermixed with the indigenous demand for drastic revolutionary change, this applied element of Lenin's thought helped in forming a powerful fusional historical input. Of major importance was Lenin's concept of the communist party which supplied the specific political weapon for small groups of militant revolutionaries in these three societies fighting against harsh forms of foreign domination and control. The idea of a tightly-knit clandestine organization pursuing a common ideological goal was well suited for the tasks of coping with the severe counter-measures frequently taken by domestic and foreign opponents. Lenin's principle of democratic centralism combined with a highly stratified party organization greatly enhanced the unity and discipline of the communist party organization.

The role of the communist party also supplied an important element of timing in revolutionary development which was lacking in Marxism. As the vanguard of the proletariat, the communist party was seen as the crucial organizational instrument which would hasten the historical processes outlined by Marx and accelerate the changes leading to the downfall of capitalism. Lenin's innovation of a revolutionary communist party thereby precluded the lengthy waiting period for the forces of dialectical materialism to produce the economic and social conditions favorable for the overthrow of capitalist societies.

Lenin, much more than Marx, also justified the use of violence against the declining imperialist order. Lenin went beyond Marx's vague call to the "workers of all countries" and actually organized a world-wide communist movement. In doing this he linked the communist revolutions in China, Korea, and Vietnam to the Comintern in the Soviet Union. This organizational connection quickly led to important practical benefits for the struggling communist parties in these three societies in the form of ideological training, political tutelage, money, and new clandestine skills.

The concept of democracy in the three exiled revolutions did not have the same meaning as it did in the West or in other Asian societies emerging from Western influence and control. The word "democracy" was extensively used in the writings of communist leaders in China, Korea, and Vietnam, yet it referred to a political movement which included all classes willing to cooperate with the communists in a united struggle against foreign and domestic opponents. These cooperative classes usually included the proletariat, the peasants, and some elements of the indigenous bourgeoise. It excluded "anti-democratic" classes such as imperialists, feudalists, and revisionists. This version of democracy was used at various times to justify the formation of "united fronts" with non-communist parties and groups as a necessary expedient to oppose new forms of foreign oppression. The "democratic revolution" was thereby depicted as the first stage in the communist revolution against imperialism.[40]

The idea of socialism was essentially the same as that used by communist leaders in the Soviet Union. It had no meaningful relationship to the type of socialism in non-totalitarian societies seeking a broader distribution of wealth through governmental intervention by parliamentary means. Instead socialism in the communist-oriented indigenous response was the initial stage of communism after the overthrow of the former capitalist system. It was a justification for a "socialist revolution" against the remnants of capitalism under a new dictatorship by the communist party.[41]

The political ideology of the three communist revolutions, in brief, consisted of several elements which were mutually reinforcing. These elements were important fusional historical inputs formed by an admixture of indigenous and foreign influences. The indigenous forces of militant nationalism and peasant nationalism were greatly strengthened by the doctrine of Marxism-Leninism derived mostly from the Soviet Union, and the entire revolutionary ideology was given considerable respectability by the universally prestigious concepts of democracy and socialism. The final composite on the eve of national independence was the most vigorous and aggressive value-system in the normative process of any nation in Asia. The intense dogmatism and self-confidence inspired by the ideology more than compensated for the relatively short duration of the communist-oriented indigenous response and its deficiency in deep historical roots. The formation of a communist-dominated independent nation prompty induced a new normative goal in the form of "national liberation" or eventual political control over the truncated territory of the adjoining or nearby non-communist society.

The political culture which constituted the second part of the normative process in the three exiled communist revolutions was a highly fluid and action-oriented form of political behavior. It was a political culture shaped entirely by the requirement to wage and win an ideologically-motivated warfare largely from remote rural territories. As in the six quasi-democracies and the three bureaucratic polities in Asia, it was a highly elitist political culture, although the separation between the political leadership and their rank and file followers was much wider due to the use of a tightly organized and disciplined party structure. More than elsewhere in Asia the prevailing political style was molded by a "revolution from above." There were also other important differences. The absence of ethnic minorities or autonomous political parties and groups precluded the need for compromise or a bargaining quality in the emerging political culture. The absence of a formal governmental apparatus obviated the inevitable bureaucratic conflicts between politicians and administrators or the competition in top-level decision-making between civilians and the military. Instead there were no sharp divisions between "participants," "subjects," and "parochials" in the communist political culture since the dominant form of participant behavior during the indigenous response was *revolutionary* participation.[42]

The political culture in the exiled communist revolutions was also characterized by a disposition toward tentative conciliation, persuasion, and intrigue when confronting obstacles from a position of weakness; it was likewise a form of political behavior with a propensity toward violence and ruthlessness when confronting obstacles from a position of strength. In essence, the political culture was highly opportunistic. In many respects it comprised a revival of a former Oriental political style or what might be called a "neo-Byzantinism" which had been embedded in the Russian political tradition since the time of the Mongol invasions and the "Tartar yoke." This form of political behavior reflected the prevailing "realpolitik" in the traditionally autocratic regimes in Eastern and Southern Europe rather than the gradual liberalizing movement toward limited and parliamentary government which followed the Renaissance and the Reformation in Western Europe. According to an eminent Russian historian, this pattern of political attitudes

> was built upon the principle of unquestioning submission of the individual to the group, first to the clan and through the clan to the whole state. . . . It led to the system of universal service to the state which all without differentiation were forced to give. . . . All classes of society were made a definite part of the state organization. Taken together, these ideas amount to a peculiar system of state socialism. . . . The Mongolians also introduced a new view regarding the power of the prince. The power of the Khan was one of merciless strength. It was autocratic; submission to it was unqualified. . . . When the last threads of Tartar control were broken by Moscow, the dukes of Moscow openly regarded themselves as absolute monarchs and considered their people completely subject to their will. All lands within the boundaries of the state were claimed by the duke to be devoted to the interests of the state.[43]

In some degree the Comintern agents sent by Lenin and Stalin to assist the fledgling communist parties in China, Korea, and Vietnam, such as Voitinsky, Mif, Manuilsky, and Shumaitsky, were consequently bringing back to the region an extremely rigid and absolutist mode of political behavior which had originated in the region and, in contrast to the political ideology, did have some deep historical roots.[44]

Political Process

The political process in the communist-oriented indigenous response was intimately related to the normative process. Overt behavioral patterns were produced by the urgent desire to attain the goals of the revolutionary ideology. These patterns included a system of political communications in the formative stages of the revolution consisting of written articles and essays by various party thinkers followed by the dissemination of party doctrine and regulations through the centralized channels of the communist party structure. The most significant element in the political process, however, was the communist party organization itself which maintained a high level of unity within the revolution and served as the crucial instrument of the communist elites seeking the total acquisition of political power.

The political communications in the early stages of the three communist revolutions took the form of published articles and essays by communist writers which reached relatively small numbers of urban people. With few exceptions, this media supplemented the role of institutions of higher education in disseminating communist ideas and doctrine. Often these publications were used to wage intra-party debates over various interpretations of communist ideology and its application to existing social conditions. Often they were suppressed by counter-measures taken by indigenous or foreign security officials. The early impact of Mao Tse-tung on the Chinese Communist Party was made through the use of political essays appearing in a left-wing student newspaper called the *Hsiang Chiang Review* which he edited in Hunan province in 1919.[45] Several years later Mao wrote a pamphlet entitled "An Analysis of the Different Classes of Chinese Society" which contained an appeal for a "radical land policy and vigorous organization of the peasantry" in opposition to the "Right opportunist policy" of a leading communist writer, Ch'en Tu-hsiu.[46] Political pamphlets were likewise used in a more restricted and covert manner in the early years of the communist movement in Korea. After 1920 Korean communists in Shanghai, Irkutsk, and inside Korea began disseminating communist ideas through published articles and essays.[47] In the Korean enclaves in Manchuria, Kim Il-song and several comrades undertook a similar task by publishing a journal called *Bolshevik* in 1930.[48] The major writer spreading Marxist-Leninist doctrine in the Vietnamese communist movement was Ho Chi Minh whose essay "French Colonization on Trial" became what Sacks has labeled a "landmark" in the development of the totalitarian society in North Vietnam.[49]

A second form of political communication in the communist-oriented indigenous response occurred after the formation of the communist party and the consolidation of dominant power within the party by a single leader. Thereafter the communist party itself became the primary channel of political information and opinion in furthering the goals of the exiled communist revolution. This channel disseminated in written and oral form the party doctrine as elaborated in major political writings by the top party leader. Mao's form of communism as stated in major published works such as "On Protracted War," "On New Democracy," and "On Coalition Government," became a major theme of the information channels linking the expanding organizational structure of the Chinese Communist Party. A similar trend took place in the political communication of the Vietnamese Communist Party where Ho Chi Minh's essay, "French Colonialism on Trial," and other writings such as "The Path Which Led Me to Leninism" and "The U.S.S.R. and the Colonial Peoples" were disseminated through party channels. Political communication in the scattered Korean communist parties in China, the Soviet Union, and inside Korea relied on overtly or covertly produced pamphlets and printed materials until the Japanese surrender when Soviet assistance in the establishment of communist-controlled radio and telecommunication facilities were instrumental in the emergence of Kim Il-song as the dominant leader of the new communist state formed in North Korea.

In theory, interest articulation and the formation of interest groups in the three emerging communist polities should have involved only one economic and social class: the proletariat. In practice, the small proletarian class in these societies played a minor role in the communist revolution. The dominant groups consisted of disgruntled intellectuals who quickly developed into professional revolutionaries and disgruntled peasants who served as the "shock troops" of the revolution. These two groups comprised the upper and lower levels of the highly disciplined communist party organization. No autonomous interest groups developed in this type of political system. No independent interest articulation evolved from any specific class. The only articulation of different views and policy demands took place among contending factions within the top levels of the communist party. At times this factionalism was ideological as seen in the major doctrinal differences between Li Li-san and the Returned Students in China who adhered to the orthodox urban-based party line of the Soviet Union, and Mao Tse-tung who pursued a new rural-based strategy. More often the factionalism within each communist revolution was personal. This phenomena was especially prevalent in the numerous Korean communist parties and groups both inside and outside Korean territory. Lesser degrees of personal factionalism occurred in the Vietnamese communist movement. These forms of factionalism, however, were gradually reduced with the emergence of a dominant party leader. The centralization of power was achieved first by Ho Chi Minh who emerged as the major leader of a unified Vietnamese communist party in Hong Kong in 1931.[50] A similar trend which drastically reduced factionalism in the Chinese Communist Party occurred in 1935 when Mao seized firm control of the party organization after the Long March.[51] Factionalism and diverse articulation on party policy persisted the longest time in the Korean communist revolution where the emergence of a dominant party leader did not occur until after the Japanese surrender, and Kim Il-song with strong Soviet assistance consolidated his control over a single party organization just before the formation of a communist state in North Korea.[52]

By far the most important element in the political process in the communist-oriented indigenous response was the communist party. In essence the communist party *was* the political process in the three exiled communist revolutions. It was also one of the most significant fusional historical inputs in the emergence of the communist societies in China, Korea, and Vietnam. It was a foreign institution modeled on Leninist principles, including a small party elite and a hierarchical party structure held together by democratic centralism. Yet just as the communist ideology, especially its Marxist precepts, was modified considerably by indigenous values and behavior, so was Lenin's concept of the communist party altered by domestic values, institutions, and circumstances in the three Asian societies. The structure and goals of the communist party was perhaps changed the most by the traditional Confucian emphasis on a harmonious blending of different classes representing "the people" in an organic and stratified society. This effort involved some unexpected paradoxes. The communist parties in these emerging totalitarian polities stressed cooperation with partially like-minded groups while waging a vigorous revolutionary struggle. While propounding dogmatic revolutionary goals, they engaged skillfully in a form of "coalition-building" among diverse classes and groups in their pursuit of political power. The communist party thereby did not serve as the "vanguard of the working class." Nor was it the vanguard of the disgruntled peasantry. Instead the communist party was the vanguard of members from all groups and parties capable of being co-opted into a revolutionary struggle led by communist leaders against foreign "imperialism" and "indigenous feudalism."

The diversity of representation in the revolution led by the communist party served an important political and symbolic role. As already cited, the communist party itself had an upper leadership level composed of professional intellectual-revolutionaries and a lower rank and file level composed of peasants. Its membership also included representatives from "democratic" classes such as students and workers, and it included cooperative members from "bourgeoise" classes such as shopkeepers, industrialists, and landlords. It likewise gained added strength from cooperative non-communist political parties and groups through the use of the "united front" taught by Comintern agents and the model of the Bolshevik revolution in the Soviet Union.[53] A unique Asian modification to these forms of "interest aggregation" was a continuation of symbolic cooperation with non-communist groups and parties seeking the same broad societal goals. Even after the communist party achieved dominant power just before gaining complete national independence, it permitted most non-communist parties to continue to exist, although their political role was controlled and monitored by the communist party. These parties included the China Democratic League and the Revolutionary Committee of the Kuomintang in China,[54] the Democratic Independence Party and the Working People's Party in North Korea,[55] and the Democratic Party and the Socialist Party in North Vietnam.[56] The preservation of these non-communist political parties was markedly different from the communist revolutions in the Soviet Union and Eastern Europe. The presence of many of these non-communist organizations at the time of the seizure of power by the communist party constituted a capitalist element in the midst of a historical revolution against capitalism. Yet this ideological and tactical compromise was a clear indication that the communist party in each of these Asian societies was essentially the leader of a coalition of classes rather than a revolutionary vanguard of a single class. In explaining this role of the Chinese Communist Party, Professor Fairbank has declared: "One of Mao's departures from Marxism-Leninism is to assert that the Party leads China's regeneration not only on behalf of the proletariat but also on behalf of a coalition of major classes — in effect, the whole people."[57]

The most significant deviation by the communist party in China, Korea, and Vietnam from Leninist party doctrine, however, was the use of peasants as the dominant revolutionary force. This was a distinct East Asian innovation which made the communist party in these three societies drastically different from its counterpart in the Soviet Union or in Western industrialized societies. The reason for this vastly modified and extended organizational structure in these three emerging totalitarian societies was the fact that only in China, Korea, and Vietnam was the communist party able to build its revolutionary organization on the powerful force of peasant nationalism. Only in these societies did large numbers of disgruntled peasants gain sufficient political consciousness and engage in organized military action over an extended period of time against foreign oppression. Only in these societies was the harshness of foreign rule so severe as to foment this kind of populist militancy in the indigenous response. Mao Tse-tung has described this revolutionary fervor among the peasantry in China as follows:

> The rise of the present peasant movement is a colossal event. In a very short time, in China's central, southern, and northern

provinces, several hundred million peasants will rise like a tornado or tempest, a force so extraordinarily swift and violent that no power, however great, will be able to suppress it. They will break all trammels that now bind them and rush forward along the road to liberation. They will send all imperialists, warlords, corrupt officials, local bullies and bad gentry to their graves.[58]

This phenomena involved another paradox in the communist revolutions in that the most radical and revolutionary political leadership in the indigenous response anywhere in Asia gained political power through the sacrifices of the most traditional and conservative social class. As stated by Scalapino and Lee regarding the communist revolution in Korea, "the Communists were quite prepared to use traditional means to reach radical ends."[59] Yet the peasantry in each society was initially aroused to this monumental historical role, not by the indigenous communist party, but by the brutalities perpetrated by foreign rulers. In effect, it was the Japanese in China and Korea, and the French and Japanese in Vietnam who indirectly made the communist party into an awesome and formidable revolutionary organization.

Some variations occurred in the timing and methods by which the leaders of the communist parties came into positions of influence and power. Yet the members of these small revolutionary elites had many common characteristics. Virtually all came from "middle class" backgrounds in which their fathers were either relatively prosperous peasants or aspirants for low level positions in the traditional bureaucracy. Many were the sons of Confucian scholars. Most of them received relatively high levels of education largely through their own efforts or foreign assistance at several educational institutions and at scattered periods of time. Many also came from economically deprived regions of their societies which had a tradition of rebelliousness against the central political authority. Most Chinese communist leaders were born and raised in the central Yangtze River valley where many uprisings against imperial rule had begun.[60] Most Vietnamese communist leaders came from the provinces of northern Annam which had intermittently served as the major source of political dissidents throughout much of Vietnamese history.[61] The family backgrounds of the communist party leaders in Korea were more varied because of the geographically diversified locations of the communist party organizations, yet the party leaders who assumed control of North Korea with Soviet assistance after World War II were from remote Manchurian border provinces which had long been havens of political opponents of the traditional regimes in both China and Korea.[62] This rural, peasant-oriented background of most communist party leaders contrasted sharply with the more urban, professional- or commercial-oriented background of the non-communist nationalist leaders in these societies.

The members of the communist party elites developed considerable intellectual ability, although few were deep thinkers or brilliant scholars. In spite of the fact that they came mostly from rural backgrounds, they were sufficiently "Westernized" to reject their own traditional culture and to seek desperately the modernization and independence of their own society. They were distressed by the abuses imposed on their country by the Western powers, and their intense determination to abolish this foreign control made them into political activists. They soon became social revolutionaries as well as militant nationalists. Their alienation from the status quo was so strong that they wanted to go beyond the removal of foreign domination and create a "new" society. In the process of political maturation they became leaders with unmitigated ambition, energy, and zeal.

One of the most salient uniformities among the communist party elites was their acquisition of important leadership roles at a very youthful age. Mao Tse-tung was only 25 years old when he joined the Chinese Communist Party in 1921, and he and Chu Teh became the leaders of the rural-based faction of the Party after 1927 when both were in their early 30's. Ho Chi Minh likewise was in his late 20's when he joined the French Socialist Party after World War I just as its radical faction was splitting off to form the French Communist Party. Ho was in his 30's and 40's between the two world wars when he organized the bulk of the Vietnamese communist party organization in southern China, Southeast Asia, and eventually inside Vietnam. Perhaps most remarkable in this context was the example of Kim Il-song who joined a communist youth group in Manchuria in 1926 when he was 14 years old. Kim joined a branch of the Korean Communist Party five years later, and at the age of 19 he took over the leadership of a small band of Korean dissidents which waged guerrilla warfare against the Japanese. Kim was only 33 years old in 1945 when he started his drive for control of the new communist state which the Soviets helped to establish in North Korea.

The youthfulness of the communist party leaders in the three emerging totalitarian polities enhanced their revolutionary zeal and gave added vigor to the communist revolutions. The young age of the party leadership combined with their rural background gave the communist party elites many advantages over the more elderly non-communist nationalist leaders from urban environments.[63] The communist leaders, in brief, were more rugged than their nationalist opponents, more ruthless and unrestrained in their power, and more effective in the role labeled by Professor North as a "specialist on violence."[64]

The Governmental Process

The governmental process was either nonexistent or weak during most of the communist-oriented indigenous response in China, Korea, and Vietnam. The official governments in each of these societies were, in effect, the "enemy," i.e. the Chinese Nationalists and Japanese military forces in China, the Japanese colonial regime in Korea, and the French colonial regime and Japanese military occupation in Vietnam. The strenuous demands of waging an ideological revolution against these domestic and/or foreign opponents usually precluded the opportunity for the communist leaders to set up official organs to conduct the normal functions of government. As previously cited, the communist elites prior to national independence were engaged almost entirely in party-building and revolution-building; they had few opportunities to promote state-building or official institution-building.

The primary exceptions to this general feature of the exiled communist revolutions were the soviet system and the assertion of communist party leaders as *government* leaders at the end of World War II. The first form of governmental rule, the soviet system, was used only in China and Vietnam for relatively brief periods of time, and it had a limited institutional effect only in China. The second form of governmental authority was very important in all three emerging communist societies in the transition from the exiled revolution to the formation of independent totalitarian states.

The soviet system consisted of communist party control and a modicum of governmental functions in small rural areas detached from the authority of the established central government. The first soviets in China were formed in 1927 by Mao Tse-tung, Chu Teh, and small communist military forces in the Ching Kang Shan mountains on the borders of Hunan and Kiangsi provinces.[65] In this remote territory the rural-oriented faction of the Chinese Communist Party performed some government functions such as the collection of taxes, the implementation of land reform, the establishment of elementary and adult schools, the recruitment of military personnel, and the enforcement of social reforms such as the prohibition of opium-smoking, gambling, and sex discrimination.[66] From this modest beginning of governmental authority, the Chinese communists expanded their control over larger areas in the central provinces, and in November 1931 they proclaimed the formation of the "Chinese Soviet Republic" at Juichin in Kiangsi province. Yet by 1934 the "Republic" ceased to exercise effective authority in the central region due to the annihilation campaigns waged by the Chinese Nationalists. After the Long March, Mao and his followers expanded the soviet system in Shensi and several adjoining provinces. In this area more extensive governmental functions were conducted by the Chinese communist party until the end of World War II, although in this second phase of the revolution much of the official authority was based on military commands such as the Eighth Route Army and the New Fourth Army.[67]

The soviet system was also attempted in 1930-1931 during a time of severe hunger and unrest among peasants in central Vietnam. The Nghe-An soviets, following the example of the Chinese communists, attacked the armed forces of the central government and sought to set up a secure rural revolutionary base.[68] Yet the terrain was unsuitable for extended guerrilla warfare and the French colonial troops crushed the Nghe-An soviets within a few months.

The second form of official authority consisted of communist party leaders assuming a role as *government* leaders in the brief but crucial period during and after World War II. An important factor expanding the official status of communist party leaders was the need to deal with foreign governments in reestablishing political authority following the Japanese surrender. This broadening of governmental authority occurred in China as Mao Tse-tung and other Chinese communist leaders conducted important negotiations with government officials from the United States, the Soviet Union, and a few European powers from 1945 to 1949. A similar tendency took place in Korea as Kim Il-song received strong official support from the Soviet military authorities from 1945 to 1948. And increasing recognition as a government leader was bestowed on Ho Chi Minh as he sought to establish the Democratic Republic of Vietnam in 1945–1946 and as the communist revolution in Vietnam intensified its vigor and scope from 1950 to 1954.

It is important to reemphasize that it was not a foregone conclusion at the beginning of these brief post-war periods that the communist elites would emerge victorious as the government leaders of a sovereign nation-state. As cited previously, the communist party leaders had many advantages over their nationalist opponents, but their assumption of governmental power over a portion of national territory was assisted by many unplanned international events over which they had no control. Mao's final success, for example, was greatly enhanced by Chiang Kai-shek's inability to provide dynamic and imaginative leadership at a crucial time, by the intermittent disagreements and conflicting policies between the Chinese Nationalists and the United States, and by Chiang Kai-shek's refusal to accept advice from foreign military strategists to consolidate his power south of the Yangtze River rather than gamble on risky military operations against the Chinese communists in Manchuria. The transition from a party to a governmental status by the communist leaders in Vietnam was aided in even greater degree to unpredictable foreign developments. Ho Chi Minh's quest for dominant government control was enhanced by such factors as the brief occupation of northern Vietnam by Chinese Nationalist troops in 1945–1946 which brought many non-communist nationalists to the surface followed by the total withdrawal of the Chinese forces which enabled the communists to eliminate many of their nationalist rivals. Ho's official role was likewise strengthened by the decision of the French government to conduct the early post-war negotiations with him in France where he gained international recognition as the dominant "nationalist" leader of his country, and by the decision of the Eisenhower administration in 1954 not to intervene in Indochina and accept the formation of a communist state in North Vietnam. Even in North Korea where the Soviet military authorities immediately supported Kim Il-song for the top government position, many unexpected international events facilitated Kim's ascension to power such as the prolonged conflict between the "old" Korean communists and the United States military authorities in South Korea which gave Kim valuable time to consolidate his power, and by the decision of the United States to acquiesce to Soviet demands for a partitioned Korea in a part of the world where American power was decidedly superior to Soviet power.

All other governmental institutions in the three truncated totalitarian states were subordinate to the dominant control of the communist party. The formal governmental apparatus was outlined and legitimized by party documents or constitutions hastily drafted during the final stages of gaining political power. The Chinese communists established the People's Republic of China using the *Common Program* and the *Organic Law* to define the broad principles and structure of their new government.[69] The new states in North Korea and North Vietnam were based on constitutions previously drafted by the communist party leaders.[70] In each polity, the governmental organization was designed to implement the policies of the communist party. Each level of government was structured to extend "democratic centralism" from the communist party to a tightly centralized official bureaucracy. Legislative and judicial organs exerted no independent institutional controls and were controlled by party-executive authority. An elaborate system of local government likewise extended party controls to all rural areas.

Unlike the political systems analyzed in the two preceding chapters, the outputs or official policies of the three emerging totalitarian states were relatively undeveloped in both domestic and foreign affairs at the time of independence and sovereignty. In spite of the numerous goals defined rather rigidly by the communist ideology, many policies of the new governments were vague and ambiguous. The intensity and scope of the revolution had caused the communist elites to know much about what they were against; it did not give them much opportunity to determine what they were for.

Yet a few policies in domestic and foreign affairs were apparent at the time of national independence. In domestic policy the new communist governments planned to eliminate all vestiges of imperialism, capitalism, and feudalism, a course of action which in a short time enabled the ruling regime to remove any significant form of foreign or indigenous political opposition. They likewise planned to conduct sweeping economic and social changes, including the nationalization of all industry, extensive land reform, and government ownership of all communication, transportation, and educational facilities. The implementation of specific aspects of these policies was greatly affected by the fact that the government leaders in each communist state had been life-long professional revolutionaries. With the partial exception of the Chinese communists, they had no experience in administering policies of a government which was not at war with a determined ideological enemy. They had not yet confronted the inevitable conflict between politicians and administrators in the formulation of public policy. They had not yet engaged in serious debate within their own party ranks whether to continue the ideological struggle against imperialism abroad or to concentrate on more mundane problems of internal economic and social development.

The foreign policy of the emerging communist governments was somewhat more focused and precise than domestic policy. All three communist states intended to maintain close relations with the Soviet Union as an ideological and diplomatic ally and as a model of economic and social development. They also planned to maintain close diplomatic relations with each other, although in keeping with tradition and because of physical and population size, North Korea and North Vietnam looked in some degree to Communist China as an ideological and economic model. All three communist states established diplomatic relations with communist governments in Eastern Europe. Communist China and North Vietnam likewise exchanged diplomatic relations with several non-aligned nations such as India, Burma, and Indonesia since the nationalist leaders in these emerging non-communist societies had given moral support to their revolutions against Western "imperialism." A major element of the foreign policy of all three communist governments was bitter hostility toward the United States as the leader of the Western capitalist powers. Equally important was the policy of "national liberation" in the truncated non-communist society in adjoining or nearby national territory, a policy which reinforced animosity toward the United States for its role of protecting the non-communist states in Taiwan, South Korea, and South Vietnam.

The leaders of the three communist governments had more experience in foreign policy than domestic policy since their rise to power had involved important support from foreign governments. Yet in foreign policy they were also generally inexperienced. Like some of the nationalist leaders in the emerging quasi-democracies in South and Southeast Asia, they were somewhat naive and approached foreign policy in its early stages in terms of universal ideals and humanitarian goals. They actually knew very little about modern industrialized societies and the impact of modern military technology on the global balance of power. They knew little about many political and legal aspects of modern international diplomacy. Perhaps most important, they knew little about the impact of time on upgrading national interests and downgrading political ideologies.

Chapter 13

The Truncated Authoritarian Polities

The two non-communist societies which emerged in the southern sectors of the truncated territories in Korea and Vietnam developed distinct forms of authoritarianism. Although there were some significant differences in the final admixtures, many of the traditional and Western historical inputs which contributed to the highly centralized polities in the communist-dominated territories of these societies also enhanced the evolution of highly centralized polities in the non-communist territories. These factors included secular-oriented values, behavior, and institutions induced over a period of many centuries by Confucian cultural systems and class structures.[1] Authoritarianism in South Korea and South Vietnam was also bolstered by memories of grandeur from former empires or great traditions which immediately preceded foreign colonial rule, a factor which acquired special importance in these new societies devoid of an elaborate revolutionary ideology (such as the communist ideology in North Korea and North Vietnam) and seeking desperately to establish some historical links to the pre-colonial past. Each of these societies, like its northern competitor, was also a *dominant-ethnic* society comprising essentially a single racial and linguistic community with a highly uniform culture.[2]

Common Western influences which oriented the indigenous response in these two polities toward their own form of authoritarianism were the low-transferable political and administrative structures maintaining French or Japanese colonial rule, and the intensive efforts by foreign colonial authorities to transmit their own culture to the colonized society. The combination of these highly oppressive and disruptive policies produced similar types of nationalism over the same sequences from the end of the nineteenth century until the achievement of national independence. The strong nationalism and anti-colonial sentiment which affected the political systems in South Korea and South Vietnam were likewise aroused by a high degree of harshness in both colonization processes.[3] Yet the kind of nationalism which developed in the two non-communist societies was much more diversified than in the two communist societies. In some ways it resembled the different forms of nationalism in the six quasi-democracies in South and Southeast Asia. Some nationalism in Korea and Vietnam prior to World War II was militant, but some was moderate and conservative. A small minority of indigenous nationals even collaborated with the foreign colonial rulers and had a vested interest in the preservation of the colonial system. Most forms of nationalism which shaped the polities of South Korea and South Vietnam consequently supported limited political goals. Unlike the inveterate militant nationalism which molded the totalitarian polities in North Korea and North Vietnam, the prevailing nationalism in the two non-communist sectors sought only the end of foreign colonial rule and opposed the revival of the traditional political order. Beyond these goals it wanted no further major changes. The predominant form of non-communist nationalism was strongly opposed to a drastic social restratification and redistribution of wealth as espoused by the communist-oriented revolutions.

One of the most significant fusional historical inputs in the indigenous response influencing the formation of these two authoritarian political systems was the "exiled movement." As cited previously, this movement differed from the exiled revolutions which played a major role in the establishment of the communist polities in North Korea and North Vietnam.[4] The exiled movements consisted of the common goals and actions of Korean and Vietnamese nationalists living in foreign countries until the final stages of the colonization process. Their primary purpose was to keep alive the spirit of nationalism and to seek foreign support for the nationalist cause. Their leaders and organizations were scattered over a larger and more diversified global area than in the communist-oriented revolutions. The Korean exiled movement had the bulk of its supporters in China, Hawaii, and the United States, while the Vietnamese exiled movement received support at various times in China, Japan, France, Thailand, and the United States.[5] These dispersed centers of international support made the exiled nationalist movements more fragmented and differentiated than their communist counterparts. In contrast to the extensive assistance of the Soviet Union to the communist revolutions in Korea and Vietnam over a period of several decades, the aid from foreign countries to the two exiled nationalist movements was little more than moral and vocal support until the extensive aid program from the United States only two or three years prior to national independence. The exiled nationalist movements also never developed a permanent organized capacity to engage in military or subversive operations against foreign or domestic opponents as did the communist parties seeking power in Korea and Vietnam. The exiled nationalist movements were shaped much more by the personalities of strong nationalist leaders in contrast to the strong revolutionary leaders, revolutionary ideology, and Soviet assistance which bolstered the communist exiled revolutions. Yet in spite of these weaknesses, the exiled nationalist movements provided the bulk of the political leadership in the southern sectors of the truncated polities at the crucial time when Korea and Vietnam were partitioned by the major powers, and as the United States became the prime source of external support for the preservation of these two non-communist societies.

DOMESTIC ENVIRONMENT

The loss of political independence by the peoples of Korea and Vietnam and the extensive foreign exploitation of their natural resources in many respects caused a cultural reaction to be the major element of the indigenous response. At least in the early years of foreign rule, the cultural heritage was the only common possession of the colonized populations that could not be taken away by the foreign colonial power. Yet as the colonization process developed over a period of several decades, the large foreign disruption of the indigenous culture aroused a complex and varied reaction. At one extreme, the ethnocentrism and orthodoxy engrained by many centuries of Confucianism induced an intensive racial, linguistic, and cultural pride. It resisted the appeal of many foreign influences and wanted no major changes in traditional behavior. This highly conservative reaction gradually produced a growing sense of cultural patriotism and a propensity for indigenous-led cultural and social change. Somewhat paradoxically, the militant aspects of this emerging trend were utilized by the Korean and Vietnamese communist parties to strengthen their ideological demands for a "new" national culture.

Yet the dominant cultural elements of the indigenous response developed into an increasingly differentiated array of traditional and modern values and behavior. Prior to World War I the cultural legacy of the defunct Yi dynasty in Korea and the symbolism of the declining imperial system in Vietnam still retained considerable influence and vigor. During the 1920's traditionalism in both colonized societies continued to be strong, yet a growing awareness of modern technological and social advances in rapidly industrializing nations such as France and Japan brought in larger doses of a more "advanced" foreign culture. From the early 1930's until the Japanese surrender, the dominant urban culture became heavily imbued with foreign influences. Assimilation, both forced and voluntary, reached an all-time high.[6] The accelerated blending of foreign and domestic cultures was not consistent or linear. Between the two world wars there were several bitter reactions against the growing inroads of foreign cultural influences and renewed efforts to retain traditional institutions and customs. A resurgence of cultural patriotism erupted just after the atomic bombs fell on Hiroshima and Nagasaki and the initial indigenous struggles began toward some form of self-government. The prevailing mood in these early euphoric months in Korea and Vietnam was to throw off the yoke of cultural "imperialism" and reassert the vitality and unity of the indigenous culture. The possible renaissance of an unencumbered indigenous culture was a major factor causing large numbers of indigenous people in both societies to oppose the partitioning of non-communist and communist sectors. The strong desire for cultural unity was a significant influence causing Syngman Rhee and most nationalist leaders in South Korea to oppose the Moscow Agreement in 1945 for a four-power trusteeship over the entire peninsula for five years which they claimed would perpetuate foreign rule and be a prelude to a communist take-over.[7] A similar reaction occurred among nationalist leaders in South Vietnam opposing the partitioning of their country at the Geneva conference in 1954 as the French began the process of turning over the responsibility for its survival to the United States.[8]

Yet on the eve of national independence the cultural environment in the territories which became South Korea and South Vietnam was increasingly unsuitable for the emergence of a unified national culture. Cultural pluralism was growing rather than declining as sizeable numbers of influential indigenous returnees came back to their native land after many years in foreign exile, and as swarms of indigenous migrants fleeing the oppression of the communist-dominated sectors poured across the boundaries at the 38th and 17th parallels just before the establishment of these two new national societies. Even in many rural areas of South Korea and South Vietnam there were numerous subcultures. The ensuing cultural malaise during these very brief formative periods had little sense of a nation-wide political orientation or purpose. Henderson has referred to these conflicting cultural and social cross-currents during this time in South Korea as "forces of chaos."[9] Buttinger has likewise described the influences of numerous religious and "feudal" groups in South Vietnam at the same time as major contributors to "chaotic political conditions."[10] The drastic action of partitioning these recently liberated colonized societies after several decades of harsh colonial rule merely added another psychological burden to a widespread feeling of cultural shock and dismay.

In spite of the relatively high transformative social policies of French and Japanese colonial rule, their three-tiered educational systems actually brought modern knowledge to only a small number of indigenous persons.[11] Although new school buildings were erected in almost every province in the colonized societies, the bulk of the local populace was essentially untouched by Western-oriented learning. By the end of colonial rule in both societies a majority of children of primary school age were receiving little or no formal education and almost 50% of the total population was illiterate.[12] Institutions of higher education enrolled only a small fraction of the eligible students. In Korea in 1941 there were 9,565 Korean students in all colleges and technical schools, and at the same time in Vietnam there were 3000 Vietnamese students in higher level educational institutions. Only one university had been constructed in each colonized society, the Keijo Imperial University in Korea and the University of Hanoi in Vietnam. Private schools operated mostly by Christian missionaries enrolled sizeable numbers of indigenous students in both societies at the pre-university level. One of the most significant elements of these foreign-sponsored educational systems was the opportunity for indigenous students to attend universities in the colonial power. Yet these channels were also opened to only small numbers of indigenous students. In 1936 some 6000 Korean students were enrolled in high schools, colleges, and universities in Japan.[13] During the decade of the 1930's approximately 100 Vietnamese students were sent annually to universities in France at public expense, and a slightly larger number studied at French universities each year with private means.[14]

The participation of indigenous students in these partially modernizing educational systems resulted in various reactions. Some of these overlapped with the different cultural responses previously cited, and virtually all of them shaped new forms of political thought. As mentioned in Chapter Twelve, the communist-oriented revolutions in Korea and Vietnam had their beginnings in the disillusionment and frustrations among indigenous intellectuals at institutions of higher education inside the colonized society or in the territories of the colonial power following World War I. Yet a majority of indigenous students at these modern learning centers did not adhere to the communist ideology. Instead they were influenced by many currents of world thought, including various forms of Christianity, capitalism, democracy, socialism, nihilism, and fascism.

The mingling of these foreign doctrines produced three reactions which contrasted sharply with the attitudes of militant radicals joining the indigenous communist parties. One response was an urban orientation which gradually separated the emerging educated class from the rural peasants. By World War I the non-Marxist educated groups were, in effect, cut off from their traditional village roots. A second response was the formation of new group loyalties based on school and university ties. Friendships made from membership in alumni associations and "old boy" contacts supplemented traditional bounds of filial piety. A third response was an individual and collective identity crisis which found some solace in a general espousal of nationalism but actually had little specific content or purpose. The demise of the traditional culture left these educated urban nationalists psychologically adrift. Unlike the indigenous communists who turned to Marxism-Leninism and "found themselves" in an organized movement opposing foreign colonial rule, they had no new ideology or value-system to replace the vacuum left by the decay of Confucianism. By the time of national independence many non-Marxist nationalists were still groping and despondent. This reaction among educated Koreans has been described by Henderson as follows:

> The comparative unity of ideas and beliefs that Yi Confucianism had sustained was shattered. The intellectual climate of the state changed rapidly. Ruled by a power that brooked no participation from ordinary Koreans and by means and laws disagreeable to the subjects, the prevailing intellectual attitude toward government became cynical, often revolutionary, nihilistic. No ground for a political belief to unite, motivate, and sustain a nation and its people, even should independence come, was given.... Bitterness and despair accompanied the expansion of intellectual horizons....[15]

As previously explained, most economic changes during the colonization process in Korea and Vietnam benefitted the colonial powers much more than the local people. At the end of the colonial period the vast majority of the indigenous population remained in subsistence agricultural roles either as small landholding peasants or dispossessed rural workers. Foreign enterprises owned virtually all of the industrial, commercial, and mining facilities, and foreigners owned and operated most of the large-scale rural enterprises such as the French-owned rubber plantations in Cochin China. Indigenous resentment against this severe and widespread economic exploitation was a major psychological factor utilized by the communist parties in both societies to bolster their revolutions.

Yet other aspects of the indigenous response in the colonial economy contributed to a conservative and rightest orientation in the southern territories of these truncated societies at the time of national independence. During the period of colonial rule a small indigenous landlord and entrepreneurial class had emerged. The indigenous landlords in Korea came from the remnants of the traditional *yangban* and from high officials who collaborated with the Japanese or were co-opted by them as the colonization process began. Large tracts of land were transferred to this original indigenous landowning class (and approximately 1000 Japanese landlords) through arbitrary and complex registration procedures imposed by Japanese colonial authorities on illiterate peasants.[16] A small Korean industrial and commercial class engaged largely in rice and food processing also developed in many urban areas. A similar development occurred in Vietnam where some 2000 indigenous landlords acquired vast landholdings by the end of World War II.[17] Some members of this landlord class had obtained land during the migrations of sizeable numbers of Vietnamese into the fertile delta regions of Cochin China just prior to French colonial rule, although virtually all of the Vietnamese landlords acquired a secure and legal title to their landholdings during French colonial rule. A small Vietnamese urban bourgeoise likewise began to evolve in large cities such as Hanoi, Hue, and Saigon after the rapid industrial and commercial development of World War I.[18] By 1945 these small indigenous upper and middle classes in both colonized societies had considerable vested interests in the colonial economy. Not all of their members were collaborators with the foreign colonial regime, and in the pre-1945 period many had supported gradual reforms toward some kind of self-government.

The partitioning of Korea and Vietnam into communist and non-communist sectors had a drastic impact on many members of these previously favored economic classes. The formation of communist governments in the northern territories caused many members of the landowning and business classes to flee to the southern sector. These newly dispossessed migrants sought as quickly as possible to start a new life, often with some assistance from family members living in the south, but also with some expectation of benefits from the emerging non-communist government. Their intense fear and hatred of the communist state in the north contributed to a militant anti-communism. Many migrants from the north also sought desperately to obtain new economic roles commensurate with their former status, a motive which gave support to the conservative and rightist policies of the new political elites led by Syngman Rhee and Ngo Dinh Diem.

In the southern sector of these truncated societies the small indigenous landlord and business class was much less affected by the partitioning, and many of these relatively affluent persons began to acquire considerable political influence as the non-communist governments were established. In South Korea virtually all Japanese-owned agricultural lands were sold by the United States Military Government at very fair prices to Korean tenant peasants just prior to the national election for the first popularly-elected government. This action served to reduce pro-communist sympathies in the southern sector and it won widespread rural support for the conservative leadership of Syngman Rhee increasingly supported by the United States.[19] Just prior to the formal establishment of the Republic of Korea, the American military authorities also transferred control of Japanese-owned urban real estate to the newly-formed government of President Rhee who in turn sold this property under very favorable conditions to his followers who included many members of the landlord and business class.[20] By the time of national independence these rural and urban groups were strong supporters of the Rhee regime and exercised a growing power in the newly-elected National Assembly.

A conservative base underlying the non-communist government in South Vietnam developed in a somewhat different manner from that in South Korea, but by the time of national independence it was exerting similar political influences. French landlords did not return to the rural areas after World War II and the bulk of their land was transferred to the government of South Vietnam just prior to national independence.[21] Vietnamese landlords were also reluctant to live in rural areas due to intermittent guerrilla warfare. Large areas of fertile land in the southern sector were consequently occupied and cultivated by small-scale peasants and former rural tenants without official registration or title. Appeals from these rural cultivators for land reform and legal ownership were resisted by absentee landlords residing in the urban areas who gained the cooperation of the Vietnamese bureaucracy still closely allied to the rural gentry.[22] The conservative influence of the indigenous landlord class caused the government of Ngo Dinh Diem to delay official steps toward land reform until after national independence. Diem's regime also received strong conservative backing from approximately 900,000 Roman Catholic refugees who fled North Vietnam at the time of partition and were given special official assistance in their resettlement in the south. Diem sought both moral and political support from these northern refugees, and he appointed many sympathetic followers from the northern and central provinces to important positions in his new government.[23]

One of the most significant economic factors promoting a strong conservative orientation in the new governments of South Korea and South Vietnam was the massive aid program hastily organized by the United States to prevent these two truncated societies from falling under communist control.[24] The partitioning of Korea and Vietnam placed the bulk of the industrial facilities constructed during the colonial period in the communist sectors and the major agricultural lands in the non-communist sectors. The division of these formerly unified colonized societies thereby caused them to become highly dependent on American assistance for their industrial development as well as their national survival.

The American aid programs in both societies were designed for the long-range economic advancement of the entire indigenous population and a special effort was made in their implementation to alleviate some of the hardships of the lower income people. Yet in their initial stages, they actually strengthened the influence of the inchoate indigenous bureaucracy trained by the former colonial power and still attached to the Confucian standard of perpetuating the prestige of the bureaucracy rather than the welfare of the people. The early American aid programs also enhanced the status and influence of the relatively small number of educated persons, some of whom were in positions of growing power and wealth. The rapid inflation and economic uncertainty of the turbulent pre-independence period made these meagerly trained and inexperienced civil servants highly susceptible to bribery and corrupt practices from private vested interests. A major paradox in the American effort to promote the rapid economic development in these two truncated societies was the unique indigenous response during the final two or three years of the colonial era which revived in modified form some significant political elements of the traditional pre-Western society.

THE POLITICAL SYSTEM

The development of politically relevant fusional historical inputs in the political systems of the two truncated authoritarian societies were influenced largely by two goals: 1) the struggle to end foreign control over the entire colonized society, and 2) the struggle to prevent the expansion of communist control from the northern sector over the non-communist society in the southern sector. The first objective involved the effort of the indigenous nationalist movement to resist the intensive political and cultural penetration by the foreign-imposed colonization process from its early years until the end of World War II. The second goal caused the hasty and desperate effort to erect a political and governmental apparatus capable of withstanding the communist threat in the very short period of two or three years just prior to the formal establishment of national independence. The combination of these two endeavors produced a very distinct and unique political system. Unlike the communist polities in the northern sectors, they had no established ideology or model, foreign or domestic, to guide them in forming a stable government in a society suddenly partitioned by the decisions of major international powers. Instead the two truncated authoritarian polities were forced to rely heavily on the advice, instructions, and material support of a new international power, the United States, adjusting to new and awesome responsibilities in a drastically different and more dangerous international environment. These conditions produced a normative process with a highly defensive and personalistic political ideology, and a diversified and fluid political culture. They also induced a political process dominated by a single political leader pursuing the role of a "savior" of a beleaguered society cut off abruptly from a large portion of its own countrymen through an unexpected historical accident. The governmental process was accordingly shaped by the emergence of strong executive-dominated institutions utilizing the limited official structures and trained personnel left behind by the former colonial power and new governmental institutions modeled ostensibly along Western democratic lines.

Normative Process

The indigenous response in Korea and Vietnam produced a diversity of political values and norms. The harshness of foreign colonial rule aroused a militant reaction among a minority of indigenous people, largely within the small official and intellectual class, who started the communist revolutions which developed into the two totalitarian polities as already explained. Other indigenous reactions induced different political ideas, including various forms of nationalism, democracy, capitalism, socialism, and, at the very end, a unique concept of personalism.

The earliest form of nationalism in Korea and Vietnam was produced largely by the foreign threat to the traditional cultural ethnocentrism and the time-honored status of the Confucian scholarly-bureaucratic class. It was also a reaction caused by a desperate effort to preserve the prestige and memory of the imperial great tradition. The early intervention by French and Japanese military forces did not create an ethnic or racial self-awareness among the indigenous people. Instead it gave this native force a target as well as a channel to express itself in defending traditional values and institutions.

The initial form of nationalism in both colonized societies was not a form of nationalism as understood by large numbers of people in the West. It has been labeled by Duiker as "proto-nationalism."[25] It consisted largely of a vague form of patriotism and a loosely defined loyalty to the traditional society. It was espoused most vehemently by disgruntled members of the official class who reacted with a crude and reckless xenophobia aimed at the complete removal of foreign domination. This sentiment took concrete form in Vietnam in the Can Vuong movement from 1884 to 1896 which sought to restore the young emperor, Ham Nghi, to the throne and to expel French colonial authority.[26] Armed resistance to the French won strong support from some members of the traditional bureaucracy and landlord class as well as from sizeable numbers of peasants. The movement advocated no modern reforms and appealed entirely to traditional loyalties. It relied on traditional military weapons, and it was readily crushed by French colonial troops. A similar response occurred in Korea in the Tonghak rebellion which sought to replace the declining Yi dynasty with a new "kingdom" led by an ambitious religious leader (Choi Bok-sool), some discontented officials, and masses of peasants from 1893 to 1895.[27] Only extensive intervention by Japanese military forces finally quelled this local insurrection against a weakening indigenous dynasty. Another outburst of anti-foreign violence took place just after the formation of the Japanese protectorate in Korea in 1906. This insurgency by "Righteous Armies" swept over several provinces for almost two years before harsh suppressive measures by Japanese troops finally brought it to an end.

Proto-nationalism failed in its objective to halt the early expansion of colonial rule, yet it established a symbol of local resistance against foreign domination that inspired future indigenous leaders. It likewise vividly revealed many outmoded characteristics of the traditional society in dealing with industrialized colonial powers such as France and Japan, and it served as a painful reminder of the urgent need for a mastery of modern science and technology by the indigenous society. Duiker has declared that the memory of the Can Voung movement in Vietnam "was destined to live on as a symbol of Vietnamese resistance to outside control that would nurture the patriots of the future."[28] And in describing the early outbreaks of nationalistic sympathies in Korea, Lee has stated that "the Korean nationalist movement up to 1910 was still in the category of 'traditional nationalism' and its leaders were intent on maintaining the *status quo*. Their loyalty was to the existing political forms, the emperor, and rule by the literati class. Yet at the same time there were evidences . . . of 'modern nationalism'."[29]

A distinct form of militant nationalism emerged as more Western political ideas penetrated both colonized societies and foreign colonial rule became firmly entrenched. The development of this fusional historical input began in Vietnam after 1900 and in Korea following World War

I. It comprised a harsh anti-foreign sentiment caused by a deep-seated racial and cultural pride increasingly agitated by the imposition of foreign domination. This radical type of nationalism assumed a high level of intensity and a powerful racial and cultural overtone because of the planned efforts by the foreign colonial power to reduce or destroy the influence of the indigenous culture. It did not want to restore the traditional society, yet at the same time it sought to preserve some elements of traditional behavior.

Militant nationalism in Korea and Vietnam was also deeply affected by the Western concepts of the nation-state, national equality, and national progress. It urgently wanted the indigenous society to become a free and independent nation and a respected sovereign member of the modern international community. The advocates of this activist form of nationalism were mostly members of the small official and intellectual class with a general conservative political orientation in contrast to the militant nationalists who were attracted to Marxism-Leninism and participated in the communist revolutions. Non-communist militant nationalists were likewise opposed to the kind of class warfare advocated by the communist ideology, and they refused to link indigenous anti-foreign movements to the international apparatus controlled by the Soviet Union. Their dominant goal was the removal of all types of foreign control, an objective so important that it could be justifiably pursued by the use of violence.

Militant nationalism took form in occasional overt protests and acts of resistance against the colonial power. In Korea this latent collective hostility was seen in the March First Movement in 1919 in which the early post-war idealism and deep frustration over the stringency of Japanese colonial rule touched off a massive non-violent demonstration led by Korean religious leaders, intellectuals, and students.[30] A similar outburst of indigenous defiance occurred in 1929 when Korean students engaged in an organized strike and committed acts of violence against Japanese security forces to protest the mistreatment of a Korean school girl by a Japanese national. In Vietnam, the Thai Nguyen uprising was led by a small group of indigenous insurgents who killed more than one hundred French officials and soldiers from August to December 1917.[31] About a decade later a small group of revolutionaries active in the nationalist party, the Viet Nam Quoc Dan Dang (VNQDD), staged a short revolt at a military outpost in Yen Bay in the northern provinces while seeking to foment a mutiny among indigenous troops. These acts of violence were ruthlessly suppressed by the security forces of the colonial power, and they invariably resulted in the execution or imprisonment of many nationalist leaders. The small groups of militant nationalists who escaped these suppressive counter-measures and remained inside the colonized society were forced to operate clandestinely and were prevented from establishing an organized nationwide movement.

A simultaneous form of militant nationalism was foreign exile by activist leaders who symbolized the intense indigenous opposition to foreign colonial rule and appealed for foreign assistance against the oppression of the colonial power. With very few exceptions, this was the only open form of militant nationalism outside the communist revolutions that could be expressed on a permanent basis. One of its early adherents was Syngman Rhee who left Korea in 1904 as Japanese colonial rule was being established.[32] Rhee went to the United States for advanced education, and by the 1920's he was among some 6000 exiled Korean nationals seeking support for the cause of Korean independence. In 1919 approximately 700 Korean exiles in Shanghai formed a "Provisional Government" to publicize internationally the dramatic March First demonstration inside Korea and the continual demand of the Korean people for national self-determination. The most famous Vietnamese political exile was Phan Boi Chau who fled to Japan in 1905 after failing several times in open resistance against French colonial authority.[33] For almost two decades Phan assisted in educating Vietnamese students in Japan and in planning organized resistance against French rule inside Vietnam. His efforts were aborted by imprisonment in China and his arrest by French authorities in Shanghai in 1925. Small groups of Vietnamese nationalists active in plotting organized resistance against the French remained in southern China until World War II.[34]

The predominant type of nationalism in Korea and Vietnam during the indigenous response was a unique form of moderate nationalism. For the overwhelming majority of the native population who remained in the colonized society and wished to preserve their personal and family security, it was the only kind of nationalism which could be openly manifested on a continual basis. Like militant nationalism, this fusional historical input combined traditional and Western values which aroused a collective pride among the indigenous people, yet it produced an evolutionary, rather than a revolutionary, approach by mixing some of the traditional emphasis on harmony and order with the Western stress on efficiency and stability. Moderate nationalism sought the same long-range goals as militant nationalism by endeavoring to preserve the indigenous culture and to end foreign colonial domination. However, it tempered this pursuit with the more reasonable understanding that such a goal was not attainable in the short-run by scattered acts of violence and that many internal and external changes would be required before it could be fulfilled. It was aware of many shortcomings in the traditional society, especially the orthodox Confucian dogmatism and parochialism which had sapped the creativity of the native people for many centuries To cope with its own outmoded past, it advocated extensive borrowings from the culture of the foreign colonial power, especially its science and technology, which it considered vital in preparing for the vaguely defined future time when conditions could be favorable for the achievement of national independence.

Moderate nationalism was confined largely to urban areas where it won adherents from a diverse array of indigenous persons, including those who collaborated actively with foreign colonial authorities yet who could never separate themselves from their own past and local identity. It also affected the larger indigenous urban class which avoided extensive personal contacts with foreign colonial officials, and quietly and passively sought to preserve its own ethnic and collective self-awareness. The political norms induced by this kind of moderate nationalism were thereby part of a relatively subtle and subdued native reaction to the most oppressive kind of colonial rule in Asia. These norms required enormous patience, forbearance, humility, and hope in striving to learn more about the processes of modernization and at the same time to strengthen the social consciousness of the indigenous people.

Cultural nationalism was the most significant manifestation of moderate nationalism in these two colonized societies. It comprised a growing desire of the indigenous people to display aspects of their own culture which were not usually suppressed by the colonial authorities, and at the same time to embark on new patterns of shared behavior which could depict marked differences between the cultures of the native populace and the colonial power. This non-violent nationalist reaction was different in many respects in Korea where the indigenous people were reacting against the intrusion of another Asian culture which they felt was inferior in many ways to their own in contrast to the politically-motivated cultural response of the Vietnamese people which was aroused by the intervention of a Western culture that was totally new and considered by many to be more "advanced."[35] Yet in both colonized societies a subtle patriotic undertone influenced a collective effort by the native urban people to maintain a coherent cultural identity. This trend resulted in increasing cultural pluralism, yet it constituted the primary method of peacefully and continually protesting against the intensive cultural incursions by the foreign colonial power. It also was the major form of indigenous nationalism within the colonized society which had some opportunity to expand and flourish.

Cultural nationalism in Korea induced a strong desire by increasing numbers of indigenous persons to participate and excel in modern education. Henderson has stated: "Koreans, indeed, took their frustrations over impotence and leaderlessness out in these years [beginning in the early twentieth century] very largely on education and were swept with a nationwide conviction that only through it could they assert national pride."[36] Education was closely related to Christianity which became perhaps the predominant means of expressing a "peaceful" form of nationalism during the Japanese colonial period. The Christian churches in Korea not only served as a significant media for indigenous nationalism; they also elevated sizeable numbers of persons from traditional lower classes into leadership roles. Also important were the channels of journalism and literature which were intermittently suppressed by Japanese censors, but which gradually aroused a stronger national consciousness among an increasingly educated urban population. With ingenious subtlety, Korean writers employed newspapers and literary journals to spread ideas which engendered a growing sense of national identity and self-confidence. A prominent Korean author, Yi Kwang-su, write a series of essays in a magazine called *Kaebyok* (Creation) in 1921 advocating stringent self-improvement measures by the Korean people before national independence could become feasible.[37] Three Korean-language newspapers, the *Tong-A Ilbo,* the *Choson Ilbo,* and the *Sidae Ilbo* survived until 1940, and they served as powerful shapers of indigenous nationalist sentiment. Regarding this role of journalism and literature, Henderson has stated:

> The function of these newspapers — and of a few magazines like Yi Kwang-su's *Kaebyok* (Creation) — in maintaining national consciousness was great. Despite censorship, they were important forums of public opinion, though demanding an astute reading between the lines. Less obviously, they were important intermediary institutions serving as magnets and meeting houses for those in the nationalist movement.[38]

Cultural nationalism in Vietnam was expressed almost entirely in literary form, especially in journalism and poetry. It served the dual role of spreading patriotic sentiment and a much wider use of the indigenous script, *quoc-ngu*. More than its counterpart in Korea, it sought explicitly to combine traditional and Western values. An early Vietnamese writer who contributed to this trend was Phan Chu Trinh who both praised and criticized the French and Vietnamese cultures in an effort to create a "new Vietnam."[39] From 1906 to 1907 Phan operated the Free School of Hanoi (Dong Kinh Nghia Thuc) to introduce Vietnamese youth to a synthesis of Western knowledge and traditional values.[40] After the closure of his school, a period of imprisonment, and a ten-year exile in

France, he wrote numerous essays and poems on various themes relating modernization to Vietnamese progress and freedom. Another prolific writer in the indigenous literary movement was Nguyen Van Vinh who published several magazines and newspapers from 1907 to 1920 in both French and *quoc-ngu* which disseminated a highly progressive and reformist message. Nguyen's influence was one of the most important in expanding the use of the Vietnamese script and a knowledge of French culture into the intensely Confucianized provinces in northern Vietnam.

Perhaps the most important contributor to this literary aspect of Vietnamese cultural nationalism was Pham Quynh.[41] At the suggestion of a high-ranking French security official, Pham and another Vietnamese editor in 1917 founded the journal, *Nam Phong* (Wind from the South), which became the most penetrating indigenous publication during French colonial rule. Until its end in 1934, *Nam Phong* provided its readers with Pham's analyses of both Western and Eastern thought relevant to Vietnam's quest for modernization and eventual freedom. At different times the journal was traditional, conservative, progressive, liberal, pro-French, and nationalistic. On a much broader scale it sought to revive the blending of Occidental and Oriental cultures initiated in 1906 by Phan Chu Trinh in the Free School of Hanoi. Regarding Pham's impact on Vietnamese literature prior to 1945, Duiker has declared:

> The crux of Pham Quynh's thought was thus how best to preserve what was of value in traditional Vietnamese culture while at the same time absorbing what was useful from the outside world. And the answer... lay in a mixture of conservatism and progress, in a careful selection of values from East and West to achieve a harmonization *(trung dung)* of contrasting cultures. Only thus could society both retain its roots and keep up with environmental changes.[42]

A final form of nationalism in the indigenous response which exerted an enormous influence in the formation of the political systems in South Korea and South Vietnam was a type of personal nationalism. This concept of nationalism had its roots in the traditional institution of the emperor and consisted of a latent popular loyalty to this highest ranking dynastic official who both symbolized the unity of the people and served as their political leader. Personal nationalism was derived in part from the Confucian "mandate of heaven" which legitimized and, in some degree, humanized the exercise of political power. The personalized loyalty engendered by this traditional value declined more rapidly in Korea where the imperial dynasty was completely abolished by the Japanese colonial system than in Vietnam where a facade of the traditional imperial system was retained by the French colonial authorities. Yet in both colonized societies the emerging nationalist senti-ment sought at times to give special prominence and appeal to strong indigenous leaders who managed to voice a genuine nationalist sentiment and at the same time avoided the wrath and suppression of the foreign colonial regime. Such persons were few in number, and many who tried to maintain this tenuous mid-position either were eventually co-opted into various forms of collaboration by the colonial authorities or imprisoned for endangering the stability of colonial rule. Indigenous personalities also became important as the nationalist movement inside and outside these colonized societies prior to 1945 intermittently split into competing factions.

The personalistic mode of nationalism assumed paramount importance after World War II when these two societies were partitioned and the communist "war of national liberation" in the northern sector was directed at the non-communist society in the south. As previously explained, the confusion and cultural malaise during the hasty formation of both South Korea and South Vietnam lacked a sense of political direc-tion and consensus. The different forms of nationalism in the non-com-munist sectors produced a vast array of leaders, factions, and parties competing actively for political power. Within this disorganized turbulence one view which gradually gained considerable popular sup-port was the need for a powerful leader who could bring some unity and order to these fledgling polities in this critical historical period and symbolize their determination to remain free from totalitarian control. This growing demand for strong political leadership had important cul-tural overtones. In addition to its intense opposition to communist political ideology, it opposed the policy of the communist regimes in the northern sectors to abolish traditional institutions and create a "new" national culture. Perhaps the most broadly supported political opinion within South Korea and South Vietnam in this important formative period was the desire to preserve as much as possible of the traditional culture.

In some respects the emergence of this form of personal nationalism revived certain political norms and modes of behavior of the early "proto-nationalism" which had sought to prevent the initial imposition of foreign colonial rule. It no longer advocated a blind loyalty to the imperial dynasty or a reckless military reaction against a more modernized foreign power. Instead it was now a response against totalitarian domination by a communist regime composed of indigenous political leaders. Most important, this form of personal nationalism created a political milieu favorable to the rise of a "savior" or "super-patriot" who could command widespread popular appeal and stand above the unstable political conditions of the time in order to preserve a free and independent non-communist society. This condition in turn strengthened the trend toward a highly centralized and authoritarian political system capable of withstanding the military and subversive threats from the communist sectors in the north. It contributed greatly to the establishment of a strong and personalized leadership by Syngman Rhee in South Korea and Ngo Dinh Diem in South Vietnam.

The values of Western democracy also influenced several aspects of the indigenous response in these two developing societies. While the individualistic and liberal ethos of democratic ideology introduced totally new ideas and modes of behavior during the early stages of the colonization process, they gradually won acceptance among some intellectuals as Confucianism declined. Democratic norms in many ways bolstered the nationalist movement. The idea of popular sovereignty fostered the concept of national self-determination. The stress on individual rights aroused a growing sympathy for some legal protection of basic human freedoms. Yet until 1945 all democratic theorizing was done in a vacuum. It was predicated on *a priori* assumptions which had no opportunity of being tested. It often led to naivete and confusion regarding the dignity and equality of the individual and the dignity and equality of the nation-state. Phan Boi Chau in Vietnam, for example, repeated much of the eclectic and self-contradictory principles of Sun Yat-sen which joined an appeal for the dignity of the indigenous people with a determination to establish a unified nation with "one heart" and "one strength."[43] More confusing and awesome was the political doctrine of *Personalism* which was embraced by Ngo Dinh Diem and others in Vietnam during the final years of French colonial rule. This theory espoused many references to individual dignity and human rights, yet its dominant theme was the need for an all-embracing state to protect the security of the society and to promote social and economic progress prior to any significant political freedoms.[44] Regarding the untested democratic ideals advocated by Korean moderates, Lee has stated:

> Intellectual and non-intellectual nationalists alike borrowed the liberal slogans of the West and shouted demands for self-determination, the equality of man, and democracy in politics, but these were imported ideas. Korea had been a deeply conservative nation. Ideals may change, but deep-rooted habits and behavior do not change so rapidly. Reform-oriented nationalists were greatly hindered by this fact.[45]

Democracy assumed a special importance as strong political leadership began to emerge in South Korea and South Vietnam after World War II and new governments were formed to oppose the nearby communist threats. Highly centralized institutions to implement the authoritarian rule of new anti-communist leaders incorporated much of the letter but a modicum of the spirit of constitutional government. A democratic facade for a new form of rightist elitism was employed for several reasons. The makers of these two newly independent republics realized that democracy was again in vogue in the aftermath of World War II and they wanted their new political system to appear modern and progressive. They wanted to depict the sharp contrast between the non-communist society in the southern sector and the totalitarian polities in the north. After a long experience under foreign colonial rule, they needed some democratic trappings to claim their status of national equality with other members of the international community. And perhaps most important, they needed some democratic borrowings to retain the support of the United States, just beginning to assert its new role as the leader of the "Free World" and the only major power capable of containing communist expansion on a global scale.

In spite of the extensive economic exploitation of Korea and Vietnam by foreign colonial rule, the idea of capitalism also became firmly implanted in the emerging pattern of political norms. Only a few indigenous persons in both colonized societies benefitted from the capitalist system during the colonization process, but as already explained many members of this wealthy minority retained control of their property during the transition from colonial status to independent nationhood. Some indigenous landlords and urban entrepreneurs actually increased their property holdings and acquired a growing political influence by the time of national independence. The desire of the vast peasant class in both societies was likewise directed toward legal possession of their own private plots of land. In South Vietnam the large French-owned rubber plantations were maintained intact and encouraged by the newly-independent government to expand their production. As in the six quasi-democracies and the three bureaucratic polities in Asia previously analyzed, the concept of capitalism did not become an explicit "ideology" in the emerging value-systems of South Korea or South Vietnam. Yet a subtle orientation toward private enterprise and a limited governmental role in economic affairs became increasingly powerful among a large majority of the populace. A capitalist-oriented polity also received a strong impetus in both of these truncated authoritarian societies as the United States became the primary source of foreign economic aid and many of the early assistance programs stressed private enterprise.

Various forms of socialism were advocated in both colonized societies by indigenous intellectuals, students, and a few labor leaders from the early period of foreign colonial rule.[46] Most of these leftist sympathies favored some kind of Fabian-type doctrine advocating a sizeable governmental role in the redistribution of wealth and the curtailment of economic and social inequality. As in the three bureaucratic polities in Nationalist China, Japan, and Thailand, socialist ideas circulated in a hostile environment during most of the colonization process in Korea and Vietnam. The Japanese and French colonial authorities suppressed left-wing ideas due to their strong "anti-imperialist" overtones. A similar enmity toward socialism was maintained by the new rightist indigenous leaders in South Korea and South Vietnam due to the close relationship (in their minds) between socialism and communism.

A significant characteristic of the political culture in the early indigenous response was a sullen and resentful submissiveness. It comprised a political attitude aroused by the desire to avoid punitive measures from the colonial authorities and at the same time to promote some self-awareness and self-respect among the indigenous people. Political orientations became increasingly fluid and diversified as the colonization process developed in spite of the very narrow limits within which a modicum of indigenous political participation took place. It was this condition which caused the primary form of the indigenous response to be different types of *cultural* participation.[47] This diversity contained a common disrespect and hostility toward political authority, and it produced a propensity to evade many governmental regulations. Like the exiled communist revolutions, the political culture inside Korea and Vietnam manifested its own kinds of opportunism.

These trends shaped the political culture which emerged after World War II in the truncated societies in the southern sectors. Much of the opportunism and hostility toward political authority remained in spite of the achievement of national independence. After waiting several decades for national freedom many people in the newly-independent republics of South Korea and South Vietnam also discovered that they did not trust each other. The struggle to develop some kind of political consensus and establish a new political system while confronting a nearby communist threat likewise produced a widespread sense of insecurity and suspicion. Some moderate leaders were suspected of collaboration with the former colonial power. Some liberal spokesmen with socialist tendencies were suspected of communist sympathies. Some persons with families living in the northern sectors were suspected of divided loyalties. In numerous ways the political culture, like the political ideology, contributed to an environment conducive to the rise of a strong personal leader.

Political Process

Indigenous participation in the politics of the colonization process in Korea and Vietnam was extremely limited and intermittent. Colonial policy was made largely by the government of the foreign colonial power and political activity within these two colonized societies was dominated almost entirely by foreign administrators and entrepreneurs. The communication and articulation of political interests by indigenous persons was confined largely to moderate nationalists and collaborators. Local political organizations of modest size did develop from time to time, but they were carefully monitored and frequently suppressed by foreign colonial authorities. As previously explained, various national leaders emerged during the period of colonial rule with diverse appeals for social reforms and eventual liberation, but no indigenous political leadership capable of seeking the formation of an independent government appeared until the surrender of Imperial Japan and the rapid post-war transition to national independence. The sudden release of foreign oppression and the quick upsurge of pluralistic political forces in Korea and Vietnam immediately after 1945 contributed to the development of highly centralized and authoritarian forms of government in the southern sectors of these formerly colonized societies.

Political communication in this type of emerging polity was affected in considerable degree by the modern communication system established by the foreign colonial power. This modern media enabled indigenous political thinkers and activists for the first time in their history to have a rapid means of contacting a nation-wide audience. News about occasional political demonstrations and outbreaks of indigenous violence against colonial authority was quickly disseminated to the local populace. As already cited, the press in Korea and literary publications in Vietnam were especially powerful means of arousing and sustaining a form of cultural nationalism during the colonial period. The growing literacy among the indigenous people and the increasing use of the indigenous script served to augment the impact of politically-oriented messages from the pens of nationalist thinkers and leaders advocating various forms of "self-strengthening" as a prerequisite for eventual independence.

An important supplementary channel of political communication consisted of the personal contacts between indigenous nationalists both inside and outside the colonized society. This face-to-face method confined the dissemination of political information to small groups and resulted in highly diversified patterns of political awareness and opinion, yet it was a method of political communication difficult to suppress by the colonial authorities. Personal contacts among indigenous intellectuals and students at institutions of higher education as well as among workers at their places of employment likewise served as important conduits of political information. At times of partial relaxation by the colonial regime, indigenous lecturers in both societies traveled in provincial areas and explained aspects of nationalism and modern development to sizeable numbers of rural villagers. In the 1920's and 1930's speaking tours by Korean students educated in Japan aided in spreading nationalist sentiment in many rural provinces, while a similar influence was made by Western-educated members of the scholarly-gentry class in Vietnam.[48] Very important were the personal contacts between nationalist leaders and groups inside the two colonized societies and exiled nationalist movements in foreign lands. This channel of political communication bolstered hope and perseverance among local nationalists by spreading information on increasing international tension during the 1930's and the possible demise of Japanese and French colonial rule through pending adversities in major international conflicts.

Indigenous participation in interest groups and political parties in this type of emerging polity tended also to be restricted and sporadic. Both kinds of political organizations exerted essentially the same political role. While some indigenous groups labeled themselves as "political parties," they consisted actually of political organizations with a small active membership usually espousing a fairly specific objective and goal. The highly regimented form of colonial rule precluded the formation of political parties seeking significant indigenous participation in the policy-making process of the colonized society. Only during periods of partial diminution of colonial authority could moderates and conservatives among the local populace organize in some degree to pursue common goals with any chance of influencing colonial policy. Other titles used by politically active groups were "leagues," "societies," "movements," "committees, and "fronts." They engaged primarily in interest articulation rather than interest aggregation. Only after the Japanese surrender in August 1945 and the transition toward national independence did they initiate efforts at coalition-building and a serious endeavor to get their own leaders into important positions in the newly-independent governments.

Interest groups and political parties in these two developing societies were of four kinds: (1) reformist, (2) noncommunist radical, (3) religious, and (4) economic. Some overlapping occurred in the roles performed by these different fusional historical inputs, yet each had a fairly distinct influence in the evolving political life of these colonized societies.

Reformist groups and parties were essentially the overt organized manifestation of moderate nationalism. They combined in varying degrees traditional values of harmony, moderation, and order with Western ideas of democracy, progress, and representative government. Their leaders were gradualists who realized that national independence was a distant goal and they consequently stressed different methods of self-improvement for the immediate future. These loosely organized groups were basically anti-colonial yet they sought to avoid extremist actions in an effort to maintain a non-violent method in seeking eventual self-rule. At times some members of these "middle-road" groups undertook a more radical and strident reaction to the harsh form of colonial rule, and some of these activists joined the ranks of the communist party or the non-communist radicals. However, the primary role of the reformist groups during the colonial period was to seek tactical changes in specific aspects of colonial policy and in some degree to assist an evolutionary approach to national independence.

Interest groups of this kind in Korea exerted their largest influence during the 1920's when Japanese colonial rule was somewhat less severe than in its initial stages and in the more militant period from 1931 to the end of World War II. In 1922 a small group of upper-class Koreans established the Preparation Committee for the Establishment of the People's University in order to raise funds from the indigenous populace for the construction of a modern university. This effort was abortive due to the limited financial response of Koreans, but the efforts of this group prodded the Japanese colonial regime to erect Keiji Imperial University. Shortly thereafter the Society for the Encouragement of Native Products set up branches in villages throughout the country to promote the purchase of Korean-made goods and to boycott Japanese and Chinese shops. The Korean provisional government established in China at various times included moderate factions whose primary goal was to strengthen modern attitudes and knowledge inside Korea as a prelude to national independence.[49]

Organized political groups in Vietnam with very few exceptions were active only in Cochin China where the French maintained a direct form of colonial rule. Indigenous political organizations were generally forbidden in the protectorates of Annam and Tonkin. Most of the reformist organizations in the southern sector of the colonized society were closely intertwined with the nationalist movement and many consisted of loosely organized followers of influential writers and journalists, some of whom have already been explained. One of the earliest interest groups was the Free School of Hanoi organized in 1907 by Phan Chu Trinh whose influence on the indigenous response in Vietnam has been labeled by Duiker as "the Reformist Approach."[50] During the 1920's Bui Quang Chieu, a French-educated journalist established his own French-language newspaper in Saigon and simultaneously launched the Constitutionalist Party consisting mostly of middle and upper class Vietnamese who agitated at first for a reduction of Chinese and French influence in the colonial economy and later for limited political reforms.[51] A similar party active at the same time was The Hopes of Youth founded by another French-educated writer, Nguyen An Ninh, who established a French-language journal in Saigon called the *Cracked Bell (Cloche Féleè)*. This organization and publication won a wide appeal among young people in the southern provinces by focusing on a "spiritual" and "moral" revival in addition to fostering a stronger political and national sentiment. During the few tense years preceding national independence when the French attempted to suppress the Viet Minh and retain some kind of control through Emperor Bao Dai, the Great Vietnam Civil Servants Party composed largely of middle and upper class government officials managed to exert a modest political influence and at the same time evade liquidation by the communist insurgents.[52] At this time Ngo Dinh Diem established a small political party in the central and southern provinces called the National Extremist Movement largely among Roman Catholics to resist both the communists and the French.[53]

The non-communist radical groups, like the indigenous communist parties, tended to operate clandestinely inside the colonized society and openly in foreign countries. These political organizations were initially led by persons near the upper levels of the traditional ruling elite who reacted to foreign colonial rule with a combination of intense cultural pride and the Western concept of nationalism. Their political response was emotional, militant, and conservative. As previously cited, they vigorously opposed the communist-oriented revolutions due to their heavy dependence on the Soviet Union and the Marxist-Leninist ideology. They were xenophobic and anxious to remove all traces of foreign domination, yet they opposed a drastic change of many traditional values and a major restratification of the traditional class structure. Like the reformists they wanted to retain some aspects of the traditional culture, and like the communists they were prone to use violence. In times of severe suppression by the colonial power, many radical nationalists became convinced of the need for some form of external support in the pursuit of national independence, and some of these intensely disgruntled activists joined the indigenous communist party. When circumstances were favorable, radical nationalists were also willing to join in "united fronts" with both communist and reformist groups in opposing colonial rule. Yet in spite of their strong nationalist orientation, the non-communist radicals failed to establish stable nation-wide organizations. Instead these groups were frequently plagued by factional disputes among competing leaders, many of whom lost contact with their organizations after lengthy periods of imprisonment for their militant nationalist activities.

Non-communist radicals inside Korea were poorly organized throughout the colonial period. The rigid security measures of the Japanese police confined most of the radical and militant response among the indigenous people to the communists and their front organizations. The major organizational achievement of the radical nationalists was their role in the national coalition called the New Staff Society *(Shinkan-hai)* formed from 1927 to 1931 in cooperation with the communists and some reformist and religious groups.[54] This political organization set up labor, youth, and peasant branches in the colonized society, and according to Lee, it "served as the opposition party to the government."[55] The New Staff Society obviously did not seek a significant role in the government of the colonized society, but it did become temporarily a nation-wide organization expressing indigenous grievances against colonial rule. Many of these grievances took violent forms. Radical nationalists in the Society assisted the widespread student strikes in 1929–1930, and they were active in anti-Chinese riots in 1931.

The major organizations of Korean radical nationalists were the militantly conservative factions in the exiled nationalist movement. One of these groups was the Korean Independence Party led by Kim Koo in China during the 1930's.[56] Kim and his party revived the Korean provisional government in Shanghai in 1937 and aided in organizing a small Korean military force which assisted the Chinese Nationalists in military operations against the Japanese occupation. The most influential party of non-communist radicals in the Korean exiled nationalist movement, however, was the Friends Association *(Dongji-hai)* organized by Syngman Rhee in Hawaii in 1921.[57] This tightly organized group dedicated to the personal leadership of Syngman Rhee supported his diplomatic agitation on behalf of Korean independence in China, Europe, and the United States from 1932 until the end of World War II. The Friends Association at times cooperated with other Korean parties and groups within the exiled nationalist movement, but Rhee's organization tended to be the most militant and active. It exerted a significant role in assisting its leader to become the first president of the newly-formed Republic of Korea in 1948.

Unlike Korea, the radical nationalists in Vietnam were much stronger inside the colonized society than abroad. The only significant organized group of this kind outside Vietnam was the Modernization Society founded in 1904 by Phan Boi Chau who went into exile in Japan to promote organized resistance against the French. Almost a decade later Phan launched a similar organization in Canton called the Restoration Society which was modeled along the same lines as the Kuomintang and sought active assistance from the Chinese Nationalists.[58] This organization got to the stage of establishing a small Restoration Army composed of young Vietnamese studying in China who sought to wage a total revolution against French colonialism in Vietnam and actually plotted the assassinations of several French officials and Vietnamese collaborators. Yet the major non-communist radical party prior to independence was the Vietnamese Nationalist Party *(Viet Nam Quoc Dan Dang* — VNQDD) formed in 1927 by a group of intellectuals seeking the violent overthrow of French colonialism.[59] The VNQDD, like the Restoration Society, was organized like the Kuomintang and its membership consisted of students, soldiers, lower level civil servants, and small businessmen. This radical nationalist organization engaged in selected armed attacks against French officials and government installations, and in 1930 it staged the abortive uprising at the Yen Bay military outpost. The harsh suppression of this brief indigenous insurgency by French security forces in effect crushed organized resistance activities by non-communist radicals until World War II. Some radical nationalists were active in the Viet Minh led by Ho Chi Minh during the war in the common struggle against the French and the Japanese. Yet after the war the VNQDD became a leading opponent of the communists in the final struggle among indigenous political groups to replace French rule. In 1947 the VNQDD joined a coalition with the Cao Dai, Hoa Hao, and other non-communist organizations to support a government independent of communist control.[60]

Religious groups in Korea and Vietnam were based on a variety of sacred teachings which the colonial regimes were never able to suppress. These groups were consequently able to operate more openly on a continual basis than other indigenous organizations. Their membership was also more widespread and diversified. In addition to their religious mission they engaged in numerous political activities and made some of the most significant contributions to the nationalist movement. Their political role overlapped most readily with the non-violent approach of the reformist parties and groups, yet some of their members undertook actions which at times were as militant as those espoused by the communists and the radical nationalists.

The Christians in Korea, especially the Protestants, were among the first indigenous groups to support an organized resistance movement against Japanese colonialism, and they exerted a major influence on the March First Movement which erupted in 1919. The indigenous religious movement, *Chondokyo,* which combined elements of Confucianism, Christianity, Buddhism, and shamanism and won a large following among lower economic and social classes also gave strong organizational support to anti-Japanese resistance. Large numbers of members in both religious groups were arrested by Japanese security forces in the suppression of the March First Movement.[61] Each of these religious groups comprising approximately eight per cent of the indigenous population likewise continued to exert intermittent political influences through their own organizations of young people, workers, peasants, women, and students.

The major politically-oriented religious groups in Vietnam were the Cao Dai and the Hoa Hao.[62] Like the *Chondokyo* in Korea, the Cao Dai was a syncretic religious movement which numbered about 2,000,000 followers by the post-World War II period. Cao Dai adherents lived in all parts of Vietnam, although their major concentration was in the southern provinces between Saigon and the Cambodian border. The Hoa Hao was a more loosely organized Buddhist sect numbering approximately 1,500,000 followers who resided mostly in the southwestern provinces in the Mekong River delta. Both of these religious groups were populist in character and headed by spiritual leaders with little formal education.[62] They became increasingly active in opposing French colonial rule in the 1930's and cooperated with the Japanese during World War II to gain protection from French oppression. Following the Japanese surrender their leaders joined briefly with Ho Chi Minh and the communists in resisting the return of French colonial rule, yet after 1947 both religious groups broke with the communists and cooperated with the French in the transitional political reforms leading toward national independence. The Cao Dai and the Hoa Hao were the only non-communist organizations with any sizeable popular support during this unstable period, and they had representatives in every cabinet formed by Bao Dai from 1949 to 1954. Just prior to national independence, the Roman Catholics in the southern provinces, augmented in size by the growing influx of refugees from North Vietnam, began to organize their own political groups to support the emerging leadership of Ngo Dinh Diem.

The economic groups in both colonized societies were the most unstructured and amorphous indigenous groups during the colonial period. They consisted essentially of indigenous landlords and urban entrepreneurs who collaborated and/or cooperated in varying degrees with the foreign colonial regime. Their primary goal was to maintain their favored economic and social status which they pursued through personal contacts with the colonial authorities and election to the few seats for indigenous representatives on advisory councils. After the

Japanese surrender this wealthy privileged group became one of the chief targets of the communists and many members in this group, especially those residing in the northern provinces, did not survive the transition from colonial rule to national independence. Yet the landlords and urban entrepreneurs who retained their property holdings in the southern sectors soon realized that the newly-formed non-communist republics would be protected by the United States and they quickly asserted a new and powerful influence through personal contacts and financial support to political leaders and parties in the new governments.

Although interest groups and political parties in this type of evolving polity exercised very limited influence on colonial policy, they did serve as important training grounds for the large number of political parties and groups which developed very rapidly in the early post-independence period. On a very limited scale they provided experience to indigenous leaders in organizing popular support to pursue a common political goal. They likewise comprised the organizational channels which contributed to the political polarization in these two formerly colonized societies as they became partitioned into communist and non-communist sectors. The four types of political organizations analyzed above quickly aligned themselves into moderate and rightist coalitions in the increasing competition with the communists and among themselves for the major offices in the new governments.

The reformist and religious groups became the nuclei of political parties tending toward a moderate political orientation. In South Korea their major organization was the Democratic Independence Party led by Kim Kiusic and Ahn Chai-hong; in South Vietnam they consisted of the loose coalition including the Cao Dai, Hoa Hao, some Roman Catholic groups, and some moderate factions formerly attached to the VNQDD. These middle-road groupings were the most vocal in seeking the inclusion of all indigenous parties in the first independent government. They made the strongest appeals to the Americans to assist in the formation of a genuine representative form of government. They were the most reluctant to accept the partition of their society on ideological grounds by the major foreign powers.[64] By the time of independence the political influence of these moderate parties had declined rapidly due to their limited popular support and their weak organizational structure. They lacked skills in clandestine political action and were unable to compete with the violence and terror used by both the communists and the rightists in the final struggle for political power. Most moderate leaders in both emerging societies retired from politics when the new governments were formed in the southern sectors under strong authoritarian leadership.

The conservative political parties which developed in these two former colonized societies received much of their organized support from the non-communist radicals and the upper class economic groups of the colonial period. Young militant nationalists comprised most of the rank and file membership in these parties, while wealthy landlords and businessmen provided much of their financial support. In South Korea these rightist parties included the Korean Democratic Party headed by Song Chin-woo, the National Society for the Rapid Realization of Korean Independence led by Syngman Rhee, and the Korean Independence Party led by Kim Koo.[65] In South Vietnam the conservative parties were the remnants of the militant factions of the VNQDD, the Personalist Labor Revolutionary Party organized hastily during the final months prior to national independence by Ngo Dinh Nhu, Ngo Dinh Diem's brother, and the National Revolutionary Movement established at the time of Diem's assumption to power to support his personal leadership.[66] These rightist parties emerged victorious over the moderates because of their militancy and willingness to use violence. Yet they were decidedly inferior in political strength to the communists. They had virtually no popular support outside of a few urban areas, and they lacked organizational unity and discipline. They quickly developed some skills in clandestine political action against both the communists and the moderates, but they were no match for the capabilities in subversion and intrigue acquired by the communists from their revolutionary activities over a period of many years. Without external support the rightist parties also would likely have been defeated. The major influence which strengthened them just prior to national independence and preserved their role in post-independence politics was the policy of the United States to protect the security of South Korea and South Vietnam against communist aggression.

The political leadership in these polities bolstered by the personal form of nationalism was the most important fusional historical input in the emerging political process. It blended both traditional and Western behavior in a manner unique in Asia due to the fact that the harsh form of colonial rule and the communist revolutionary actions made the non-communist response essentially leaderless. As already explained, numerous non-communist leaders did emerge during the colonial period, but none of these leaders at the time of establishing new governments had any administrative experience and very few had any significant popular support. The political leadership consequently had to be literally created in a very short time-span to cope with the staggering problems of these truncated non-totalitarian societies. The political leadership also had to be made from the dual demands of the recently liberated indigenous population and the foreign policy of the United States. This bifurcated process produced a type of political leadership which was not like any of the political elites elsewhere in Asia. Instead, the highly diversified needs to bring some unity to an extremely fragmented and demoralized society, to remain independent of communist control, to preserve aspects of the traditional culture, and to provide a "savior" for a beleaguered people induced a type of leadership which concentrated virtually all political power in a single person. In South Korea this person was Syngman Rhee; in South Vietnam it was Ngo Dinh Diem.

There were numerous differences in the personal background, experience, and temperament of Syngman Rhee and Ngo Dinh Diem which affected their rise to positions of political power. While both men were born into traditional upper class families, Rhee did not become a Christian until he was a young man while Diem's family had been devout Roman Catholics for more than two centuries.[67] To depict their bitter opposition to foreign colonial rule both men went into long periods of political exile. Yet Rhee left his native country as an unknown youth in 1904 for travel, education, and agitation on behalf of Korean independence in the United States, Europe, and China, and he did not return to Korean soil until 1945; Diem instead went into a self-imposed exile inside Vietnam after resigning from a government post in 1933 until he traveled to Japan, the United States, and Europe in search of foreign support from 1950 to 1954. Rhee received a very prestigious modern education at George Washington, Harvard, and Princeton universities in the United States, while Diem obtained a strong traditional training at an administrative school in Hue operated by his own father for the sons of upper class officials followed by a brief period of study at the School for Law and Administration managed by the French in Hanoi. During his long stay abroad, Rhee was very active in leading his own nationalist organization, serving as the principal of a Korean school, and seeking foreign support for Korean independence, yet he had no governmental experience prior to the formation of the Republic of Korea.[68] Diem in contrast had served with distinction as a provincial governor in central Vietnam from 1929 to 1933, and for a short time he held an appointment made by Emperor Bao Dai as the Minister of Interior until he resigned in protest against French colonial domination.[69] By the post-World War II era Rhee was recognized as an eminent nationalist leader to large numbers of Koreans both inside and outside his country, while Diem was known mostly to small numbers of Vietnamese and French officials. Rhee was a gregarious extrovert who married an Austrian woman while traveling in Europe, yet he had no children or family of his own to assist him in his political career. Diem was a shy and retiring bachelor who relied heavily on his own brothers, in-laws, and numerous relatives to aid him in exercising his political power.

In spite of these contrasting characteristics, the elevation of Rhee and Diem to positions of political power in this type of authoritarian polity was due to several important similar factors.

One of these factors was a reputation as a genuine nationalist leader accompanied by convincing evidence of intensive anti-colonial resistance. The top political role as a "super-patriot" and a "savior" in these newly-truncated societies could not tolerate anyone with a background involving collaboration with the former colonial regime. Popular resentment toward the harsh form of colonial rule was so widespread and deepseated that no one tainted with a reputation of cooperating with former colonial authorities was qualified to hold the highest political office. In spite of the fact that many former collaborators in both societies soon held important governmental positions, especially in the army and the police, stability in the top political post was possible only for a person with a long and convincing anti-colonialist record. It is largely due to this condition that the new political leaders in both of these emerging polities came from a lengthy period of political exile. Physical detachment from the political process of the former colonized society induced an image of nationalist and anti-colonialist "purity," an attribute which placed them far above many active nationalist leaders inside the society who were suspected of cooperating at various times with the former colonial regime. This factor greatly enhanced the political stature of Syngman Rhee. During his foreign exile spanning four decades he denounced Japanese colonialism with unrestrained vigor, and on numerous occasions he appealed to foreign governments and major international conferences for support for the cause of Korean independence. According to Henderson, by 1945 Rhee's "anti-Japanese record was unassailable."[70] Diem's anti-colonialist background was also lengthy and impressive. At the young age of thirty-two he resigned a prestigious post in the colonial bureaucracy to protest against French colonial rule, and he remained aloof from any personal contact with the French colonial regime until after World War II. He was offered the position of Premier in the first government set up by the French in 1949, yet he refused to accept this post since France was not granting full independence to Vietnam. Even after the fall of Dienbienphu in May 1954 when the French were desperately seeking to leave Vietnam, Diem again refused the Premiership because the colonial rulers wanted to retain control of the armed forces.[71] Only when the final independence agreements were negotiated a month later which granted complete political freedom to Vietnam did he agree to serve as the top leader of the Vietnamese government. By this time he had acquired a remarkably unstained and unimpeachable anti-colonialist record.

A second factor which strengthened the quest of Rhee and Diem for political leadership was their militant anti-communism. This quality was urgently needed as the former colonized societies were partitioned along ideological as well as geographical lines. Political leadership in South Korea and South Vietnam required persons with a near-fanatical opposition to the communist regimes in the northern sectors. In considerable degree this militant anti-communism was merely an extension of militant anti-colonialism. In the aftermath of World War II both Rhee and Diem bitterly resisted the imposition of a foreign ideology and a foreign political system on their societies even under indigenous sponsorship, just as they had long resisted the imposition of foreign colonial rule. Their anti-communism was derived in some degree from their Christian backgrounds, and it received added impetus from ideological convictions and personal opposition to communism during their period of political exile. Although Rhee was seldom personally active in the leadership of the Korean provisional government in China, he strongly opposed efforts by some nationalists within this organization to cooperate with the Korean communists in opposing Japanese colonial rule.[72] More convincing were his vigorous anti-communist zeal and maneuverings after his return to Korea in 1945. Diem's anti-communism developed during his long period of political exile from his personal contacts with other militant nationalists who also opposed the communist approach to national independence.[73] His opposition to communism was further strengthened when his older brother was murdered by the Viet Minh and he was captured and imprisoned himself by Ho Chi Minh's guerrillas just after World War II. Diem's unyielding opposition to communism was vividly revealed when he refused an offer by Ho Chi Minh to serve in a top ministerial post in the first government of the Democratic Republic of Vietnam.

A third and crucial factor in the assumption of Rhee and Diem to positions of political power was the near-total leadership vacuum at the time of establishing these two non-communist polities. This void at the top of the emerging political process placed considerable discretion in the final choice of political leadership in the hands of the Americans who were accepting the responsibility for the future security of these new national societies. Yet in effect the Americans had very few if any real choices. In many respects the selection of the new political leadership in both South Korea and South Vietnam was shaped by the former colonial powers who had suppressed non-communist nationalists during the colonial period and by the ideological partitioning of these former colonized societies after World War II. The basic goal of early American policy was to assist the few indigenous leaders available at this important formative time and help them establish some form of constitutional democracy.

This objective was pursued for over two years in South Korea by the United States military occupation which supported the moderate interim government controlled by the Democratic Independence Party that was headed by Kim Kuisic and Ahn Chai-hong. Yet these moderate leaders refused to cooperate in the national elections sponsored by the United States and the United Nations in May 1948 for the formation of a new government since these elections resulted in the permanent partitioning of Korea. Thereafter the United States had no realistic choice other than supporting the authoritarian rule of Syngman Rhee. The new Korean leader had created many critics in the United States government over a period of many years because of his uncompromising stubborness, yet he also had many friends at the top levels of the United States military establishment, including General Douglas MacArthur and, after 1947, Lt. General John Hodges, the American military commander in South Korea.[74] The selection of political leadership in South Vietnam just before its independence was even more restricted than in South Korea. The United States government had virtually no contact with the few non-communist Vietnamese leaders until Diem began his foreign exile and visited the United States in 1950.[75] His contacts in Washington D.C. aroused little enthusiasm among top American government officials, including staunch opponents of communist expansion such as Secretaries of State Dean Acheson and John Foster Dulles. Yet Diem had many influential friends in the United States, including Cardinal Francis Spellman, Senator John F. Kennedy, Senator Mike Mansfield, Congressman Walter Judd, and Justice William O. Douglas. In the end the United States government gave its strong support to rightist leaders such as Diem and Rhee as they assumed the top roles in guiding the early destiny of their newly-independent societies. In its own interests, the United States needed to bolster strong anti-communist leaders in these emerging polities who were recognized as genuine nationalists and had some chance of creating order and stability in extremely vulnerable strategic locations. In undertaking this policy, the United States became a major source of political legitimacy at the highest level of political process.

Governmental Process

The low transferable political and administrative structures combined with the harsh forms of Japanese and French colonial rule precluded any significant indigenous participation in official governmental institutions in these two colonized societies. As previously cited, the only indigenous participation in the policy-making process was the election of a few upper class indigenous representatives to various advisory councils and the very limited admission of indigenous persons to middle and lower levels of the civil bureaucracy. Near the end of colonial rule sizeable numbers of indigenous personnel were also brought into the armed forces. Yet no non-communist leader served as a government official until the formation of the truncated societies in South Korea and South Vietnam.

The formal organs of government created at the time Syngman Rhee and Ngo Dinh Diem acquired political power served a special purpose since both men had been selected as leaders of a new *government,* not because they were the leaders of a popular and well-organized political party. At the beginning of their tenure as dominant political leaders they consequently had to rely almost entirely on official governmental institutions to exercise their political authority. This was in marked contrast to the communist elites in the northern sectors whose power rested on their control of highly disciplined party organizations. While the governmental process in North Korea and North Vietnam became a facade for totalitarian party control, the governmental process in South Korea and South Vietnam became the major instrument for a highly personalized authoritarian rule.

The constitutional frameworks which defined the new governmental process in the two authoritarian polities was a fusional historical input embodying much traditional content and, paradoxically, considerable aspects of the highly centralized political systems of the former colonial powers. The official governmental organization and procedures in both societies contained very few elements of Western democracy. The constitution in South Korea was modeled in many respects after the Meiji constitution in Japan, and the constitution in South Vietnam showed many French influences.[76] The new constitutional documents were hastily drafted by small committees appointed by Rhee and Diem who had little knowledge of constitutional forms of government. Both drafting committees used the services of American constitutional experts, but their role in shaping the final document was marginal.[77] Rhee and Diem exerted the primary influence in the wording of these constitutions which were overwhelmingly approved by legislative bodies controlled by their followers.

The provisions in the constitutions elaborating civil rights and explaining the nature of the state gave the strongest appearances of constitutionalism and individual freedom. In each case sovereignty was vested in the "people," and the state was described as a "democracy" with "a republican form of government." Individual rights included equality before the law, the right of private property, the right to hold public office, and the freedom of speech, press, religion, and assembly. These rights, however, were legal rights, rather than constitutional rights, and they could be amended or restricted at any time by law.

The fundamental government structure defined by the constitution was a strong presidential system with a weak legislature and an ambiguous role for the judiciary.[78] The President in both governmental processes was granted extensive powers over economic, administrative, social, diplomatic, and military affairs. He was given special powers in the budgetary process as well as broad emergency authority in the very likely event of civil strife, international threats, or other forms of national crises. The constitution of South Vietnam even gave the President the power to suspend civil rights and other individual freedoms during the first legislative term.[79] These constitutional provisions, in effect, established in both societies what Duncanson has labeled a "dictatorship in law."[80]

The legislative bodies in both truncated polities were directly elected by the people and given powers to approve laws and international agreements. The representatives were granted special freedoms from arrest and imprisonment while serving in the national legislature, and in South Korea the National Assembly had the added powers to initiate impeachment proceedings against the President, Cabinet, judges, and other high officials whenever they "violated in the exercise of their duties, provisions of this Constitution or other laws." Yet the powers of these legislative bodies were carefully proscribed. Their deliberative sessions were limited to one each year in South Korea and to two three-month sessions a year in South Vietnam. Their action on pending legislation and financial bills could be blocked by Presidential veto which was extremely difficult to override by large weighted majorities in the legislature. The President in South Vietnam was given the special authority to spend funds in his proposed budget if it was not approved by December 31 of each year.

The judiciary was allegedly established as an "independent" branch of government in both constitutions, yet several provisions greatly qualified the autonomy of the courts and made their role tenuous and vague in checking executive authority and protecting individual rights. The President was granted extensive power in the appointment of judicial officials, and the salaries and status of the judiciary were subject to laws over which the executive branch exercised the dominant role. The independence of the courts in South Korea was further compromised by the provisions for a constitutional committee empowered to judge the constitutionality of any law or executive action which was composed of members from the executive, legislative, and judicial branches, yet the judicial members were a minority. A similar diminution of judicial autonomy occurred in South Vietnam by provisions for a Constitutional Court composed of "a chairman appointed by the President with the consent of the National Assembly; four high-ranking judges or lawyers appointed by the President; [and] four Deputies elected by the National Assembly" to "decide the constitutionality of laws, orders in council, and administrative regulations."[81]

As in the emerging communist regimes in the northern sectors, the official policies or outputs of the new governments in South Korea and South Vietnam were undeveloped and untested. The absence of a previous governmental process under indigenous control prevented any large number of detailed proposals regarding post-independence domestic and foreign affairs. Like their communist opponents, Rhee and Diem were much more specific about what their new governments were against than what they were for.

Yet a few policies were implied or becoming apparent at the time of national independence. In domestic affairs the major policy espoused by both governments was the broad goal to save the society from communist control which in turn justified a high priority to internal security and stability. This objective caused both anti-communist regimes to use rigorous measures in suppressing persons and groups voicing criticism of the new political leadership. It made the control of the army and the police the first prerequisites of Rhee and Diem in consolidating their power. It prevented the evolution of a loyal political opposition and discouraged constructive criticism at a time when some sense of popular participation in these newly-independent governments was most urgently needed. Both non-communist regimes also proposed significant economic and social changes, but these desperately needed changes were greatly hampered in their initial stages by inefficiency, corruption, and personal favoritism in the organization of administrative departments and agencies.

The foreign policy of both truncated authoritarian polities was heavily shaped by the critical need to retain the close cooperation of the United States. The very survival of these newly-formed societies depended on this achievement. Yet unlike the communist regimes in the north, the governments of South Korea and South Vietnam did not look to their major-power ally as both a supporter of national security and domestic development and an ideological mentor. While Rhee and Diem urgently sought American military, diplomatic, and economic aid, they had little more than contempt for the democratic values and institutions of the

United States. In order to balance their heavy reliance on American assistance, both leaders established prompt diplomatic relations with other anti-communist authoritarian governments in Asia, including Nationalist China and Thailand, as well as with other Western powers such as Great Britain, France, and West Germany. Both governments avoided official contacts with non-aligned nations such as India, Burma, and Indonesia. They espoused a deep-seated animosity toward the Soviet Union and Communist China as leaders of the Communist bloc, and they gave the highest diplomatic priority to resisting the "war of national liberation" against their own people and territory waged by the communist regimes in the north.

Chapter 14

The Hybrid Polity

The vast island archipelago ruled by the Netherlands until 1949 developed into a national polity which was in a classification of its own. The assimilation of traditional and Western influences in the indigenous response in no other society in Asia was like it. Fusional historical inputs in nearby societies such as India, Burma, Malaya, and the Philippines were also highly pluralistic and differentiated, yet the quality and the scope of diversity in the political values, behavior, and institutions of the new nation-state called the Republic of Indonesia were markedly unlike those in any other Oriental society emerging from Western domination. It is for this reason that I have labeled Indonesia a "hybrid" polity. This term refers to a society and political system characterized by an unusually high degree of heterogeneity in origin, development, and composition in both the pre-Western era *and* the period of the Western impact. It is a composite polity blending or seeking to blend significantly dissimilar cultures and behavior.

Numerous aspects of the pre-Western historical development of Indonesia contributed to a profoundly compounded cultural and political system. It was the only emerging society in Asia formed by the intermittent amalgamations of three major religions, Hinduism, Buddhism, and Islam.[1] It is the only example in the region of what I have defined as a "mixed-penetrated" society, in this case a society shaped by large influences of the "consumatory" dogmatism of Islam and the "instrumental" eclecticism of Hinduism and Buddhism.[2] The vast geographical size of the archipelago further intensified divisions in the political roles of these diverse religious traditions. The dogmatism and orthodoxy of Islam became much more deeply entrenched in western portions of the archipelago such as Sumatra and Western Java, while the eclecticism and pluralism of Hindu-Buddhist norms retained much strength in Eastern Java, the Moluccas, and Lesser Sunda islands. The hierarchical class structure in many areas also incorporated elements of different religious behavior. The Hindu-oriented aristocracy *(prijaji)* maintained a significant social and political role in many regions, while the sultan, *ulama,* and a strong merchant orientation were powerful in areas where Islam was predominant. Some elements of Islamic law were absorbed into the emerging society, yet many legal norms were based on Hindu *adat* law.

The polity in Indonesia was derived from a *dominant-ethnic society* composed almost entirely of people from the Malay race, however as in the Philippines this common racial origin was fragmented by regional and parochial loyalties oriented toward specific island communities.[3] Yet unlike the Philippines, this insular regionalism in Indonesia was compounded by strong memories of the power and grandeur of great traditions such as Srivijaya, Sailendra, and Majapahit, and numerous middle traditions such as Atjeh, Makassar, Ternate, Mataram, Bantam, Djokjakarta, and Surabaja. Considerable pluralism was likewise imparted to many traditional political values and modes of behavior by their different time-spans prior to the Western impact. According to some of my previous estimates the religious eclecticism of Hinduism and Buddhism, for example, had existed in Indonesia for 973 years prior to Dutch colonial rule, while the religious dogmatism of Islam was practiced in the archipelago for only 173 years.[4] The great tradition of Srivijaya had lasted for 548 years and had been defunct for 481 years when the Western impact began, while the middle tradition of Mataram had endured for 173 years and it was declining but still intact when the Dutch first arrived. The differences in the durations of these and other traditional historical inputs augmented the multiplicity of significant political values and institutions.

Dutch colonial rule exerted a new dimension of divisiveness in the island society, and in many ways it exacerbated deep-seated differences between traditional historical inputs. The intensive economic-oriented form of Dutch colonial domination also imparted the least number of unifying and integrating influences to the indigenous response of any Western colonial power in Asia. This uni-dimensional type of foreign rule augmented the diversification of the emerging Indonesian polity in many ways. The local populace responded to the intensive exploitation of their natural resources by different means and in different time-periods as Dutch colonial administrators and private entrepreneurs expanded their control over the archipelago in a staggered and piece-meal manner. The eclectic-pragmatic concept of colonial rule based on "cultural relativism" erected major social and intellectual barriers between the Dutch colonial regime and the small partially Westernized indigenous elite. The absence of a suitable cultural milieu and some kind of psychological guidance for the new modernizing upper class in effect preserved and often aggravated important differences within its ranks. In contrast to the high-transferable political and administrative structures of colonial rule by which the British and the Americans in their colonized societies provided some open and official channels for the new indigenous leadership to begin the process of nation-building, the Dutch in Indonesia moved essentially in the opposite direction. Much like the French in Vietnam they established low-transferable political and administrative structures which blocked any serious attempt by indigenous leaders to develop a common political consensus and experience.

The Dutch added other schisms in Indonesian society by pursuing a high transformative economic policy and a low transformative social policy. The heterogeneity caused by these divergent economic and social influences was heightened by varying responses of the indigenous population to a colonial rule which oscilated between paternalistic humanitarianism and harsh suppression. Pre-Western divisions based on geography and class structure were also increased by differences in the indigenous reactions to "divide and rule" policies used by Dutch colonial administrators over the longest time-period of any Western colonial power in Asia as well as by the indigenous response to the very brief but shattering Japanese military occupation during World War II. Significant differences in the developing society and political system in Indonesia were likewise caused by the high level of military violence in the final stages of colonial rule.[5]

DOMESTIC ENVIRONMENT

The indigenous reaction to the secularizing impact of Dutch colonial rule resulted in significant changes in religious values and behavior which in turn formed deeper cleavages in the emerging society. Some of these cleavages took place within Islam which had already spread to a large majority of the population; new cleavages occurred between Islam and Hindu-Buddhist (largely Javanese) behavior. These religious divisions assumed increasing importance due to the economic-oriented colonial policy of the Dutch which made no major conscious efforts to interfere with the indigenous culture. On the contrary, many aspects of Dutch colonialism sought to bolster the indigenous culture which augmented many of its internal differences. The result was that no single group affected by religious changes became politically dominant as in several other Asian societies. The indigenous reaction to Dutch rule, in effect, made it impossible for Islam alone to assume a pre-eminent political role in spite of the fact that it embraced approximately 90% of the population. Instead several religious movements became significant fusional historical inputs in the developing hybrid polity.

The major divisions within Islam which emerged during Dutch colonial rule were the orthodox and reformist. Some overlapping occurred in these two branches of the massive Moslem community, yet each upheld many distinctive values and behavior.

Orthodox Islam in the archipelago was significantly different from that in the Middle East. One eminent scholar has even referred to a form of "Indonesian Islam" due to its extensive blending with Hinduism in India from where it originally came and with Hinduism and Buddhism as it spread over the island society.[6] Yet within the emerging Indonesian society this variant of Islam upheld much of the traditional teachings of the Koran and opposed many non-Islamic concepts and modes of behavior. Orthodox Islam adhered to a strict monotheism, an equality of all believers, and a close relationship between religious doctrine and social and political affairs. Loyal followers of the Prophet were expected to give unmitigated obedience to the *ulama* (or *kijaji*); they were likewise obligated to send their children to the *pondok* or traditional Moslem schools.[7] The orthodox Moslem in Indonesia embraced the *santri* religious mode opposed to pre-Islamic behavior including polytheism, mysticism, and the caste system. The *santri* believed fervently in the idea of a pure and unified Islamic community *(ummat)* of devout followers. According to Professor Geertz:

> What concerns the *santris* is Islamic doctrine, and most especially the moral and social interpretation of it. They seem especially interested, particularly the urban "modernist" *santris,* in apologetics: the defense of Islam as a superior ethical code for modern man, as a workable social doctrine for modern society, and as a fertile source of values for modern culture.[8]

Although it condemned many Western values, orthodox Islam was strengthened by the Dutch colonial regime as it enabled increasing numbers of indigenous Moslems to travel to the Middle East after the mid-nineteenth century for the holy pilgrimage and religious training. Modern transportation facilities provided by the Dutch increased the number of Indonesians making the annual *hadj* from about 2000 in 1850, to 7500 to 1900, to 52,000 in 1926–7.[9] Personal exposure to the original source of Islam tended to augment the orthodoxy of this branch of the Islamic movement in Indonesia and to direct it away from its earlier intermingling with Hinduism and Buddhism. The Dutch provided additional favors to the followers of orthodox Islam in the 1920's as they opposed the reformist Moslems who comprised the bulk of the nationalists agitating against Dutch colonial rule.[10]

The reformist Islamic movement began early in the twentieth century and contained more Western and fewer traditional ingredients than its orthodox counterpart. In many ways this form of modernizing Islam was a major element of the indigenous response to the Ethical Policy, especially its broadened educational opportunities, inaugurated by the Dutch in 1901.[11] This indigenous religious orientation was shaped heavily by the movement espousing Modern Islamic Thought which started in Egypt at the end of the nineteenth century and sought to combine the social and political norms of Islam with Western science and technology. It vehemently rejected the superstitions often espoused by Islamic practices as well as the rigid conservatism of orthodox Moslems. It opposed rote learning in the *pondok* schools and the confinement of writing lessons to the Arabic script. Reformist Moslems established their own schools called *madrasah* which taught secular subjects such as math, geography, history, and Latin characters, and often included the formal education of women. Their number increased from almost none in 1900 to 12,000 schools with 1,500,000 students at the time of national independence.[12] Reformist Islam soon became a growing movement which wanted to be part Western and part traditional. This religious trend was also assisted in its early years by the Dutch who facilitated travel for Indonesians to the Middle East. While orthodox Moslems from the archipelago reinforced their conservative religious beliefs by visits to Mecca, many reformist Moslems had increasing contacts with the leaders of Modern Islamic Thought at Al-Azhar University in Cairo.[13] The Dutch likewise indirectly aided the reformist Islamic movement by serving as a target of the growing nationalist sentiment among modernizing Moslems and by refraining from interference with the rapid growth of *madrasah* schools.

The increasing split between orthodox and reformist Islam was accompanied by a more pervasive conflict between diverse indigenous reactions to the teachings of the Koran and Hindu-Buddhist behavior which retained much strength and in some areas was strengthened by the policies of the Dutch colonial regime. The *prijaji* was the major factor which preserved many Hindu-Buddhist values and indirectly contributed to these religious schisms. This native aristocracy which emerged from the remnants of the Mataram kingdom in central Java was incorporated into the highly exploitative system used by the Dutch to obtain valuable food products and raw materials from rural villagers. This form of indirect colonial rule which was firmly established in the Culture System in 1830 converted the *prijaji* into a widespread bureaucratic class responsible for the collection of prescribed quantities of cash crops.[14]

The *prijaji* received many privileges from the Dutch colonial regime for their services and their positions were made hereditary. Yet they gradually lost the respect and protective role they formerly had from the rural villagers who saw them, as explained by one historian, "as the extended arm of the colonial government."[15]

The *prijaji* were removed from positions of power at the end of Dutch colonial rule when a new class of nationalist leaders assumed control of the newly-independent government shortly after World War II. However, for over a century this indigenous upper class competed with the *santri* tradition of orthodox Islam, and in spite of their declining stature they assisted in maintaining many Hindu-Buddhist influences, including important decision-making customs of the village communities.[16] The practice of *musjawarat* involved the right of all villagers to engage in community deliberations, and the concept of *mufakat* was the unanimous decision of these deliberations which, according to one source, was "the essence of social relations and community action."[17] Also important was the idea of *gotong rojong*. Much like the consensus-making tradition in pre-Western India, this mode of behavior embodied a communal loyalty and sense of responsibility among the members of a rural village which emerged from *mufakat* or the final agreement after extensive discussion and compromise. The *prijaji* likewise aided in maintaining the widespread system of Hindu-oriented *adat* law which the Dutch eventually incorporated into their legal system for the island society.[18] Political influences derived from these and other Hindu-Buddhist values caused some unifying tendencies within broader areas of the complex and diversified indigenous response. In some degree they promoted an idea of an indigenous society extending beyond each of the three dominant religious movements. As will be seen, they exerted a considerable effect on the modernizing nationalist leadership which established the Republic of Indonesia at the end of Dutch colonial rule.

A fusional historical input which also induced some integrating influences in the indigenous response was the emergence of a three-tiered linguistic system. As in the six Asian quasi-democracies formed by British and American colonial rule, the politics in Indonesia was deeply affected by: (1) the language of the Western colonial power, (2) a "national" language, and (3) numerous local languages and dialects.[19] The integrative effect came from the Dutch language and the new national language called *Bahasa Indonesia;* strong divisive influences continued to come from the provincial and communal languages.

The Dutch language in Indonesia exerted a similar modernizing effect on a small minority of indigenous persons, much like the English language was doing in India, Pakistan, Ceylon, Malaya, Burma, and the

Philippines. It was a necessary communication channel for admission into the middle and upper levels of the bureaucracy. Dutch was also the language of modern education which opened the minds of indigenous people to the expanding knowledge of the West, including liberal and progressive ideas of government and politics. Yet unlike the British and Americans, the Dutch frequently restricted the use of their own language in their colonized society. In the early years this practice was due largely to the widespread use of the Indonesian language by Dutch officials and entrepreneurs, and to a superior attitude of the Dutch claiming that the use of their own language by local people was, what one source has labeled, "a sign of arrogance."[20] In the 1930's the Dutch colonial regime officially restricted the use of the Dutch language as small numbers of educated Indonesians became more aggressive in the bureaucracy and in promoting nationalism. However, the use of Dutch at other times was fostered by the colonial authorities, especially during the relatively idealist period of the Ethical Policy from 1900 to 1930. The growing demand of indigenous persons for a knowledge of the Dutch language caused colonial officials to imitate aspects of the infiltration policy advocated almost a century earlier by Lord Macaulay in India.[21] The increasing use of Dutch did not induce as many fragmenting forces among diverse "sub-national" groups and leaders as the spread of English did in the emerging quasi-democracies. This was due to the fact that a knowledge of Dutch was much more confined in the archipelago than was the unrestricted use of English in the British and American colonies. Yet the Dutch language did exert a powerful divisive influence in separating the small modernizing elite from the broad masses of their own people. Dutch was also a significant factor in exacerbating the schism between orthodox and reformist Islam.

The restrictions on the use of the Dutch language during most of the colonial era caused the dominant Indonesian language to become a second *lingua franca* in the archipelago. This highly eclectic language comprising what Professor Kahin has called a "bazaar Malay" had been disseminated in the islands by foreign and indigenous merchants for several centuries,[22] and in major coastal enclaves it was spoken by numerous communal groups, including Sumatrans, Javanese, Balinese, Buginese, Makassarese, Dayaks, Chinese, and Arabs. During the nineteenth century the Dutch colonial authorities purposely encouraged the use of this language to facilitate communications with indigenous people throughout the entire island society. This policy was readily adopted by educated native leaders after 1908 to promote a common cultural and political identity.[23] In 1926 this language was formally called *Indonesian* for the first time, and it quickly became a potent instrument in the expanding nationalist movement. The Dutch soon resorted to official restrictions on the use of the Indonesian language as well as of Dutch in an effort to stem the spread of nationalism. Yet the Japanese military occupation during World War II aided enormously in spreading this indigenous language to all areas of the archipelago and to all levels of government, commerce, and education.[24] *Bahasa Indonesia* became even stronger during the military struggle against the Dutch after the war. By this time it had become a powerful unifying influence because in many ways it too was a "foreign" language. Except for a small area in Sumatra from where it originated, the Indonesian language belonged to no single group or island community. Numerous foreign and local terms had been incorporated into its structure and morphology. It thereby had many advantages in becoming a genuine "national" language acceptable to the sensitivities of provincial groups with their own languages and dialects. Unlike any of the six quasi-democracies in South and Southeast Asia, Indonesia alone possessed a fairly well established national language at the time of national independence.

Yet in spite of two *lingua franca,* the third tier of the linguistic pattern embraced by far the largest number of indigenous people. Knowledge of Dutch and *Bahasa Indonesia* in 1949 was confined primarily to urban areas, and these two languages were spoken by a very small minority of the total population. Most people spoke only a provincial language or dialect. The multiplicity of languages continued to be a powerful fragmenting force.

The low transformative social policy of the Dutch restricted the exposure of modern education to a very small minority of the indigenous people. Yet as in other Asian colonized societies, the same profound reaction among progressive native people was exerted by the modest channels of Western education. One source has judged that the Dutch schools for indigenous students, in spite of their paucity, were "perhaps the most important single institution in twentieth-century Indies history."[25] In considerable degree the indigenous response to the meager modern educational opportunities was a function of traditional cultural and religious values. Members of the orthodox Islamic movement with its high degree of religious dogmatism and the fusion of religion and politics either resisted or responded slowly to Western education. The advocates of reformist Islam, conversely, with their high degree of religious eclecticism and psychological pluralism reacted more favorably to modern knowledge and learning. A similar receptivity tended to come from the Hindu-Buddhist tradition fostered considerably by the *prijaji* aristocratic class. A large majority of the Indonesians who first reached the top levels of the educational institutions established by the Dutch in the archipelago or who obtained an advanced education at a university in the Netherlands were younger members of the *prijaji* class.

As elsewhere in the region, the major political influence within the indigenous response to modern education, especially in its upper levels, was the formation of a small modernizing indigenous elite propounding its own forms of nationalism. This effect was not planned or intended by the Dutch who wanted only a sufficient number of local persons for low and middle level positions in the colonial bureaucracy.[26] Yet the expanding indigenous exposure to Western ideas such as equality, progress, democracy, individual rights, and national self-determination engendered a growing anti-colonial sentiment and a stronger desire for national independence. Some aspects of the new educational process overlapped with the more widespread use of the Dutch language and produced many similar unifying influences. It imparted a common intellectual experience and a new value-system to small educated minorities in different parts of the archipelago; it likewise started the process of creating a new "national" identity. Modern education, in effect, began the conversion of Sumatrans, Javanese, Balinese, and other islanders into Indonesians.

Modern education, however, induced many more divisive than integrative effects, and it contributed markedly to a hybrid-type polity. As the only channel of upward social mobility available to indigenous persons after 1900, it created a new middle and upper class and it broadened the differences between orthodox and reformist Moslems. It started a social leveling process which elevated the role of Western-educated school teachers and reduced the stature of the *ulama* and *santri*.[27] Indigenous participation in the Dutch schools also created a new urban sub-culture with numerous educated youth increasingly frustrated by the lack of satisfying employment. Probably most significant in a political context, Western education, like the language of the Western colonial power, separated this new elite from its own people and the roots of its own culture. This perplexing class division was well described by Soetan Sjahrir, one of the nationalist leaders, who wrote from a Dutch prison in 1934 as follows:

> Am I perhaps estranged from my people? Why am I vexed by the things that fill their lives, and to which they are so attached? Why are the things that contain beauty for them and arouse their gentler emotions only senseless and displeasing for me?... We intellectuals here are much closer to Europe and America than we are to the Boroboedoer or Mahabharata or to the primitive Islamic culture of Java and Sumatra. Which is our basis: the

West, or the rudiments of feudal culture that are still found in our Eastern society?[28]

Indigenous thinkers such as Sjahrir sought to synthesize Eastern and Western thought which in turn aroused an early vision of an independent national society combining traditional and modern values. Their Dutch education gave them high aspirations and great hopes for the future, but it provided a woefully inadequate number of educated leaders for the post-independence era. The institutions of higher education were designed for the needs of the colonial bureaucracy and had trained only a few thousand Indonesians in law, medicine, and engineering. They did not provide education in vitally important subjects such as administration, economics, and agriculture for the future leadership of a nation-state with almost 80,000,000 people.

The fragmenting effect of the plural economy established by the Dutch was another factor in the domestic environment which promoted the evolution of a hybrid polity. In some respects the politically-relevant pluralistic influences induced by the highly diversified economic operations of Dutch and other Western entrepreneurs in the archipelago were similar to the fragmenting influences caused by the economic impact of the British in their colonized societies. Yet the divisiveness caused by Dutch colonial rule in Indonesia was much more extensive than the British counterpart since a much larger proportion of the indigenous population was affected by foreign economic exploitation than in the British colonies.[29] The Dutch created much more commercialized agriculture than did the British, and more like the French in Vietnam, the Dutch allowed fewer indigenous people to remain in subsistence agriculture. They gave greater favors to the Chinese in the commercial sector and hampered the development of an indigenous business class more than any other Western colonial power. They likewise caused the small industrial sector to be entirely in Western or Chinese control.

The diversification of the indigenous populace caused by commercial agriculture did not assume major political significance until the Ethical Policy in the early twentieth century. Prior to this time the forced production and delivery of export crops by rural villagers preserved the dominant status of the indigenous aristocracy employed in administrative roles by the Dutch colonial regime. The social and economic status of the peasant was also maintained by the Agrarian Law of 1870 which prohibited the sale of land by Indonesians to aliens.[30] Yet class stratification began to change as the Dutch introduced new crops and relied more on private enterprise after 1900. The rural economy became increasingly affected by the vagaries of international trade which, in spite of the altruistic intentions of some Dutch colonial officials, caused many hardships for large numbers of rural villagers. This development also tended to politicize many provincial areas. Rural discontent became one of several economic grievances which supported the emergence of nationalism, a trend which reached significant proportions in the 1930's when the depression caused many peasants to lease their land to Chinese merchants or money-lenders. Rural unrest was largely scattered and disorganized, but it formed a predisposing force which was readily aroused by urban nationalists during the Japanese occupation and the military struggle against the Dutch after the war.[31] This economic change, however, did not create a large indigenous landlord class as in Vietnam, Korea, and the Philippines. Instead it precluded the formation of a strong wealthy landed class with rightist or conservative economic interests as the new nation-state achieved its independence. The only conservative economic classes were the *prijaji* and the Chinese, both of whom were removed from positions of power in the early post-independence era. This development also made some form of socialism the dominant economic doctrine in the emerging political ideology.

The domination of commerce and the small industrial sector by Dutch and Chinese entrepreneurs provided the major economic grievances which produced a particular type of urban nationalism. Discrimination against the very small indigenous business class was widespread and rampant. Dutch shipping companies manipulated their freight rates on raw materials produced by Indonesian enterprises and took exorbitant profits. They imported cheap manufactured textiles which ruined the native weaving industry and enabled Chinese merchants to monopolize the profitable *batik* trade.[32] The Chinese likewise replaced Indonesian merchants in lucrative enterprises such as the distribution and sale of rice, tapioca, and kapok.[33] This preponderance of the Dutch and Chinese in commerce and industry deprived the emerging society of a sizeable and modernizing indigenous business class. It was a major factor confining the new national leadership almost entirely to political activists and middle-level civil servants detached from any significant indigenous business class. It also affected the role of religion in the developing political system as the small indigenous business class was largely Islamic. Animosity against foreign economic discrimination within this native class consequently exacerbated the splits between orthodox Islam, reformist Islam, and the Hindu-Buddhist tradition. Each group had a different approach to modernization and opposing the Dutch colonial regime. Traditional Moslem entrepreneurs remained deeply attached to the quest for religious purity and the *pondok* schools; they organized along religious lines in opposing Dutch and Chinese interference with their traditional economic roles. The reformist Moslems and children of the *prijaji* eagerly pursued a Western education and modern skills; they sought to eventually replace the Dutch and the Chinese by gaining administrative experience and political independence. The conflicts between these diverse indigenous groups became increasingly complex and sensitive when the Japanese removed the Chinese and the Dutch from their dominant economic and administrative positions during World War II and assisted the small indigenous merchant class in gaining a much larger role in the national economy.

THE POLITICAL SYSTEM

Politically relevant fusional historical inputs in the indigenous response were formed by the struggle against an intensely economic-motivated form of colonial rule maintained by one of the smallest Western European nations over the largest society in Southeast Asia. As in the six quasi-democracies, this quest involved the need to create a new form of indigenous government after a lengthy historical gap *between* the period of the pre-Western traditional society and the new era of national independence. Yet unlike the national societies emerging from British and American colonial rule, the new polity in Indonesia contained several important traditional forces which had been uninterrupted and were actually strengthened by the unidimensional economic policy of Dutch rule. The new political system had also developed in a belated and haphazard manner which made no indigenous political party or group predominant at the time of national independence. Some unity was quickly achieved by the small group of nationalist leaders who came to the fore during the Japanese occupation and waged the military campaign against the Dutch for national independence, but this tiny inexperienced elite represented widely divergent segments of the emerging national society. The indigenous response, in effect, engendered a normative process composed of markedly different political ideologies and a highly fluid and variegated political culture. The political process consisted of both cooperative and competitive interrelationships between several powerful political parties and groups, and at the time of national independence it was controlled by a coalition leadership relying heavily on the personality and symbolism of a single national spokesman selected by his peers in this crucial historical period because of his oratorical skills.. Indigenous participation in the governmental process, as in Korea and Vietnam, did not occur on any sizeable or influential scale until the final stages of foreign colonial rule and the initial stages of establishing an independent nation-state. In this process new government structures and administrative organizations were shaped largely by sudden changes and power vacuums in the surrounding international environment.

Normative Process

The predominant element in the indigenous political ideology, as elsewhere in Asia, was nationalism. In the Indonesian archipelago it was a fusional historical input induced by the response of both religious and secular movements to the Western concept of the nation-state. It was also shaped by the near-total absence of indigenous participation in the formulation and implementation of colonial policy. Except at the very end of colonial rule, nation-building was completely detached from state-building. While a common opposition to Dutch colonialism provided a modicum of unity to the pluralistic indigenous groups, nationalism likewise increased many of the differences between these groups. Dissimilarities in education and economic interests aroused various ideas of communal loyalty. Different degrees of militancy were affected by modifications in the degree of harshness of Dutch colonial rule which ranged from severe repression of indigenous political thought and action to stolid paternalism. Dutch suppression was never imposed long enough to force nationalist groups to remain underground and gain skills in clandestine organization (as in the communist revolutions in Korea and Vietnam), yet it was never sufficiently benign to allow nationalist groups to seek mass organization and participation on a permanent basis. According to one historian: "The history of organized nationalism in Indonesia is a history of a multiplicity of societies able to enter loose alliances from time to time, but more frequently drawing apart from each other, splitting and regrouping."[34] Nationalism accordingly served as another impetus to an emerging hybrid polity as no single form of nationalist thought became pre-eminent.

A form of conservative nationalism developed among orthodox Moslems who sought to assimilate the teachings of the Koran with the Western idea of national self-determination. The intensity of this particular form of religious nationalist sentiment varied from docility to fanaticism. It grew out of the religious fervor of the nineteenth century which caused scattered "holy wars" against the Dutch and sought a purification of Islam in the archipelago. It was more opposed to the threat of Christianity brought by the Dutch than their political and economic domination. These pan-Islamic eruptions were suppressed by the colonial regime and this transnational religious loyalty declined during the early years of the twentieth century due to the rise of reformist Islam. Yet conservative nationalism revived in the 1920's with the formation of the *Nahdatul Ulama,* a rural-based organization of Moslem scholars and prosperous *hadji* seeking to preserve orthodox Islam.[35] The gradual development of economic and social modernization in some rural areas tended to reduce the cleavages between the nationalist views of orthodox and reformist Moslems, yet a basic division within the dominant religion continued into the post-independence era. The major idea motivating the nationalism of orthodox Islam was the fusion of religion and politics seeking to inculcate the values of the Koran into the policies of government. By the end of Dutch colonial rule, this kind of conservative nationalism no longer upheld strong pan-Islamic goals; instead its major objective was the establishment of an Islamic state capable of promoting "pure" Islam throughout the archipelago. In effect, it placed Islam above politics.[36] It wanted a sovereign nation-state unencumbered by the syncretism of pre-Islamic indigenous thought, the proselytism of Christianity, or the agnosticism of Western liberalism.

The indigenous response also embodied two forms of militant nationalism, one religious and the other Marxist. The religious element came from the reformist Islamic movement which initiated the nationalist reaction against Dutch colonial rule. This trend was started by economic and cultural grievances which caused modernizing Moslem merchants in Java in 1912 to form the first nationalist organization, the *Sarekat Islam,* to oppose Chinese and Dutch discrimination in the *batik* trade.[37] Yet the major motivation behind this form of militant nationalism was political. It was an indigenous reaction to the "imperialism" of Dutch colonial rule and the early nationalism of Sun Yat-sen spreading among the local Chinese communities. It was shaped by Modern Islamic Thought which found one of its most receptive fields in Indonesia. While this form of nationalism retained a strong religious orientation, it introduced many secular influences which imparted an enormous impact on nationalist thought throughout the archipelago. Professor Kahin has declared: "It was the nationalistic, anti-imperialist, and socialistically inclined program of this movement [*Sarekat Islam*], rather than the ideas of Pan-Islam, which was the "epidemic" that attacked so considerable a part of the Indonesian population."[38] In contrast to the orthodox Moslems, the nationalism of reformist Islam separated politics from religion. It openly advocated major reforms of Dutch colonialism and it sought to arouse a national consciousness among all Indonesians, including the peasantry. For this reason it was the form of Islamic nationalism most rigorously opposed by the colonial authorities which in turn tended to increase its militancy. Militant nationalism among modernizing Moslems sought the formation of a sovereign nation-state eliminating the superstitions and corruption of orthodox Islam and assimilating the pursuit of modern knowledge in science, technology, European history, and Western culture. It advocated a type of Islamic socialism stressing social justice and welfare, and it incorporated into its doctrine some aspects of Western political thought, including representative government and individual rights. Militant nationalism within the expanding ranks of reformist Moslems drew its leadership and membership from all indigenous classes and thereby suffered almost at the outset from numerous schisms and divisions.[39] Yet in spite of its heterogeneity and instability, it spawned new forms of nationalism and began the warning to the Dutch that their colonial rule would no longer go unchallenged by the indigenous people.

The Marxist form of militant nationalism in Indonesia, as in China, Korea, and Vietnam, started as a reaction among radical intellectuals against the extreme harshness of foreign political and economic domination.[40] The originators of this radical movement, however, were Dutch, not Indonesians, a factor which compromised some of its early nationalist content. When this movement became organized under the leadership of the communist party in 1920 it joined the Comintern controlled by the Soviet Union and became even more involved in transnational loyalties and influences. Nevertheless, Marxism found a receptive audience among frustrated indigenous intellectuals due to the extensive economic exploitation imposed by the Dutch and Chinese and what they saw as antithetical contradictions in this form of Western "capitalism." A form of radical nationalism more extreme than that of the reformist Moslems also came from the ready acceptance of Lenin's concept of Western "imperialism" as the highest stage of capitalism.[41] In effect, the militant anti-imperialism espoused by Marxism-Leninism became the basic principle upholding militant nationalism by Marxist advocates in Indonesia. It was the first form of nationalism to advocate complete independence and the total abolition of Dutch colonial rule. Yet in spite of this radical political doctrine, militant Marxist nationalism was frequently weakened by the inability of communist party leaders to adapt Marxism-Leninism to the highly eclectic intellectual and cultural elements in Indonesian society, especially the complexities of its strong religious life. The ranks of militant Marxism were consequently often divided over the application of communist doctrine to changing social and economic conditions in the archipelago, including varying degrees of cooperation or hostility with non-Marxist forms of indigenous nationalism. Yet the militant nationalism of the Marxist movement contributed what one historian has labeled "an element of toughness and rigor" into Indonesian nationalism. This source has further declared:

> It [Indonesian Marxism] provided a recognition of the role of force in human affairs, a conviction that the Dutch would prove unable to make concessions that would inevitably conflict with their clear economic interest, and a consequent awareness of the need for struggle. These elements underlay the noncooperative sectors of organized nationalism.[42]

Moderate nationalism in Indonesia, unlike its counterparts in most of South and Southeast Asia, developed *after* the emergence of both religious and Marxist forms of nationalism. Yet it was the form of indigenous nationalism which had the largest content of Western political thought and was most influenced by indigenous returnees who had obtained an advanced education in the Western colonial power (such as Mohammed Hatta and Soetan Sjahrir) or by indigenous intellectuals who had received an extensive Western education in the colonized society (such as Sukarno). In some respects moderate nationalism in the archipelago was like that in the six quasi-democracies emerging from Anglo-American colonial rule; it sought basically a gradual transition from colonial status to independent nationhood through non-violent means and peaceful negotiations with the Western colonial power. Yet this kind of nationalism was never given a chance to develop along moderate lines under Dutch colonial rule. Most moderate nationalist leaders were frequently imprisoned by the Dutch after the late 1920's and released by the Japanese in 1941. In spite of these harsh measures, a gradualist and reformist orientation persisted in this nationalist movement by stressing education, social welfare, and journalism until major advances toward complete independence were pursued during the Japanese occupation and after World War II.

Moderate nationalism was the most eclectic of the four forms of indigenous nationalism. It embodied both complementary and conflicting ideas which gave it a distinctly vague, general, and idealistic sense of direction. Its leaders were largely nominal Moslems who adhered to a modicum of Islamic behavior, but who were also influenced by Marxism and socialism.[43] This form of nationalism was secular and pragmatic, yet it also included many elements of the Hindu-Buddhist tradition, especially the values of *gotong-rojong* and *mufakat* which were used to incorporate all indigenous ideas and interests into the fabric of a new nation-state. This unique combination of traditional and Western influences was seen in the promulgation of *Pantja Sila* by Sukarno in

August 1945 when he proclaimed the formation of the Republic of Indonesia. *Pantja Sila* was a new composite of five principles which have been labeled by Kahin as "the philosophical foundation of an independent Indonesia."[44] The five principles were nationalism, internationalism or humanitarianism, representative government, social prosperity or social justice, and belief in one God. Moderate nationalism in the archipelago was likewise greatly influenced by the doctrines of various Western thinkers such as Locke, Jefferson, Rousseau, Mazzini, and Sorel as well as Asian nationalists such as Sun Yat-sen, Gandhi, and the Meiji reformers in Japan. The concept of the nation-state was used by moderate nationalists to originate the idea of an *Indonesian* nation incorporating people from all segments of the island society and using an *Indonesian* national language as a common means of communication.[45]

The economic exploitation imposed by the Dutch and Chinese stigmatized capitalism among all emerging indigenous groups and it never attained a significant role in the political ideology. In many respects capitalism was the "enemy" which made various forms of socialism acceptable to all Indonesian political movements and intermittently gave them some motivation for cooperation. Traditional values such as *gotong-rojong* and *mufakat* also clashed with the individualism and aggressiveness of the capitalist system.[46] This development in the normative process of the emerging polity compromised some aspects of the growing emphasis on individual and group freedom. It also implied an active governmental role in economic and social affairs after independence and a heavy reliance by the small but expanding indigenous business class on government support and regulations.

The emerging political culture was shaped by the interaction of the different elements of the political ideology with a large amorphous rural population and a very small and highly diversified leadership class. Much like South Korea and South Vietnam, the political culture developed very late in the colonization process due to the harsh suppression of indigenous political action by the foreign colonial power. Most shared patterns of behavior involved in this important fusional historical input surfaced only during the few years just prior to the formal termination of Dutch colonial rule.

At the mass level the bulk of the indigenous population had no experience in organized political action. With the exception of the orthodox Moslems, the Dutch prevented organizational contacts between the new elite and rural villagers. Traditional values in the countryside consequently remained strong. Yet the village population of the archipelago had relatively few "parochials" totally detached from involvement with governmental authority.[47] Instead there were large numbers of "subjects" in the rural villages whose lives had been significantly affected by the high-transformative economic policies of the Dutch. The primary collective force among this vast dispersed peasantry was a nascent nationalism caused by the growing resentment against foreign rule and foreign intervention. This attitude had been gradually gaining strength over a period of many decades, and it reached unprecedented potential during the Japanese military occupation and the military campaign against the Dutch.[48]

The primary characteristic of the political culture, however, as elsewhere in the region, was the distinct behavioral patterns within the new political elite. This leadership group in Indonesia was very likely the smallest modernizing elite in Asia. Professor Feith has estimated it to number between 200 to 500 persons at the time of national independence.[49] At the same time it was one of the most diversified political elites in the entire region. It was held together by the growing influence of nationalism and a common opposition to the Dutch, but its leaders represented various indigenous movements with markedly deep-seated differences. Some of these differences overlapped with the religious and nationalist movements already explained. Other differences were related to ethnic and social dissimilarities. All differences were affected by variegated blendings of traditional and Western influences.

A major contrast in the emerging political culture was that between what one source has defined as "functional" and "political" elements of the new leadership class.[50] The functional attitude was a bureaucratic attitude which came from the small number of Indonesian leaders who had been employed in the colonial civil service. These persons supported many goals of the nationalist movement, but they were primarily attached to an efficient administrative apparatus and gradual changes in the status quo. According to Van Niel: "These men were not inclined to take idealist excursions; they were practical administrators."[51] The "political" group, on the other hand, were active nationalists oriented more toward political action and direct confrontation against the Dutch. They were not militant revolutionaries, but they were more inclined than the functional group to disrupt the status quo and seek major economic and social reforms. Another dissimilarity in the emerging political culture was more related to ethnic and religious differences. This contrast has been described as the division between "the Javanese-aristocratic and the Islamic-entrepreneurial" political cultures.[52] Both forms of indigenous political behavior had long been shaped by traditional and Western historical inputs. According to Feith, the Javanese-aristocratic political style "was born of state organization in the wet-rice-agriculture-based inland empires of Java, of shallow Islamization, and of a long period of intensive Dutch impact, which produced enormous densities of population, a hollowing out of the structures of social integration, and an incapacitation of entrepreneurship."[53] It was more anti-Dutch, less anti-Chinese, more nativist, and more socialistic than its Islamic counterpart. In contrast, the Islamic-entrepreneurial political culture had its roots in the widely dispersed maritime communities along the coasts of Sumatra, northern Java, Kalimantan, and Sulawesi. Its adherents were much more influenced by Islam and included members of numerous ethnic groups. This form of political behavior was also more oriented toward the individualism, competition, and modern economic innovations evolving from Western capitalist societies. These diverse political cultures, in turn, contributed greatly to a hybrid-type polity. Each form of political behavior provided a different view of the new national society and different versions of the role of its government.

Political Process

The indigenous response produced a political process which was partially like that in the six quasi-democracies developing under British and American colonial rule. Considerable diversity existed within the new political leadership, and there was a wide intellectual and cultural gap between the new national elite and the mass of rural people. Yet the prohibition of popular political participation by the Dutch colonial regime as well as long periods of imprisonment of the nationalist leaders precluded prolonged efforts to aggregate indigenous political groups. The political process in Indonesia thereby acquired many characteristics of the emerging polities in Korea and Vietnam. The communication and articulation of indigenous political interests usually remained indirect and subdued. Indigenous political organizations of modest size did evolve, but they were carefully monitored and occasionally suppressed by the Dutch. The release of national leaders by the Japanese in 1941 and the partial freedom to mobilize portions of the Indonesian people during World War II contributed to a significant indigenous role in governmental affairs for the first time since the beginning of Dutch colonial rule. The military struggle against the Dutch after the war strengthened the trend toward a highly fluid and pluralistic political process. Some aspects of this trend favored the development of a democratic political system; some aspects favored the formation of a distinct type of authoritarianism.

Indigenous participation in political communications varied with changes in Dutch colonial policy. During periods of relative relaxation of police powers the dissemination of political information and opinion by Indonesian thinkers and leaders took place largely through the overt mass media such as the vernacular press and radio.[54] This means of communication was small at first, but by the end of the military conflict against the Dutch, the press, for example, was reaching an estimated readership of 1,000,000 to 1,500,000 people.[55] One of the most effective channels of political communication was the institutions of higher education which were already engaged in spreading both the Dutch and Indonesian languages.[56] In periods of political suppression, politically conscious Indonesians turned to cultural and social activities much like indigenous leaders in the colonized societies in Korea and Vietnam. These efforts involved the familiar "self-strengthening" endeavors in areas such as education, public health, and social welfare to spread modernizing influences in preparation for eventual independence.[57] This indirect and subtle form of political communication also took place in the fields of journalism and literature. During the 1930's the literary publication, *Pudjangga Baru,* aided in spreading modern ideas by a new group of national writers. It also helped in fostering a revival of Indonesian art, including notable advances by writers such as Charil Anwar who developed a new form of poetry in *Bahasa Indonesia.*[58] These two styles of indigenous political communications, open and indirect, reinforced each other. They assisted in promoting nationalism and the idea of progress. They likewise aided in supplying some unity among the leaders of different religious, economic, and ethnic groups within the emerging national elite.

Interest groups in this kind of polity became active shortly after 1900 and represented a vast variety of organized indigenous opinion. Their membership tended to be relatively small which usually made them acceptable to the Dutch colonial regime. Most of them combined economic and social motivations. They expressed a collective solidarity and at times sought some kind of favorable action by the colonial authorities. Yet their primary long-range role was to support the nationalist organizations led by major political parties. The labor movement, for example, began with the organization of the Union of Railway and Tramway Personnel in 1908.[59] Labor unions spread rapidly thereafter and soon formed an important base for militant political parties. Western-educated members of the *prijaji* aristocratic class during the same year organized the *Budi Utomo* in an effort to combine traditional values with a new national identity. The leaders of this organization established special schools and looked to Indian thinkers such as Gandhi and Tagore for guidance in amalgamating Hindu and Western behavior.[60] A group of Eurasians in 1912 joined with a small number of

Indonesian intellectuals and formed the National Indies Party to represent members of the indigenous middle class who planned to reside permanently in Indonesia. This organization was quickly suppressed by the colonial regime, but a radical faction within its membership soon assisted in organizing Marxist groups which eventually merged into the communist party.[61] Student groups were established in Holland and Indonesia, and they gradually exerted a growing political role. In 1922 Indonesian students in the Netherlands organized the Indonesian Union which joined five years later with the Bandung Study Club led by Sukarno in creating the Indonesian Nationalist Party. Women's groups likewise began forming in 1912. A leading organization called *Putri Merdeka* (Independent Women) for many years devoted the bulk of its efforts to education, but in 1928 a federation of women's organizations began participating in the struggle for national independence.[62]

The role of political parties in the indigenous response overlapped with the efforts of many interest groups in arousing a stronger national consciousness. Political parties, in effect, grew from the early political probings of one or more interest groups. Yet the political parties which were active in the 1920's and again after the Japanese occupation exerted several distinct influences. They served as what Soedjatmoko has called "the main vehicles of growing national awareness."[63] Within the limits of time and organizational scope imposed by the Dutch, the political parties were the primary indigenous means of inculcating a sense of national and political identity among wide segments of the Indonesian people. They went beyond interest articulation and engaged actively in interest aggregation by including numerous smaller groups within the ranks of their loose organizations. All political parties likewise combined nationalism with a specific religious or secular doctrine and thereby contributed to the deep splits within the emerging hybrid polity. In many respects the political parties began functioning like large interest groups seeking certain particular goals but also arousing stronger demands for national independence. Their growing size produced a threat to the colonial system and caused the Dutch to suppress them. Their size and influence at the time of national independence also produced a fusional historical input of profound importance in the form of the only multiparty system in Asia.

The *Nahdatul Ulama* (Council of Moslem Teachers — NU) was formed in 1926 to represent the orthodox Islamic movement as it split from the modern and reformist *Sarekat Islam*.[64] The formation of the NU as a primarily religious organization enabled it to avoid the Dutch suppression of political parties prior to World War II. It was merged during the Japanese occupation with other Moslem groups into the

Masjumi (Council of Indonesian Moslem Associations), and it participated in the military struggle for independence after the war. Yet orthodox Moslem leaders were highly dissatisfied with the mass Islamic organizations created after 1941, and just prior to national independence they broke away and formed their own party, the Indonesian Islamic Association Party (PSII).

The development of political organizations by the reformist Islamic movement began with the formation of the *Sarekat Islam* in 1912 by Javanese merchants to counteract Dutch and Chinese economic competition. Yet this organization quickly assumed a wide political goal and attracted the largest mass following by any indigenous party during Dutch rule.[65] A closely related organization representing reformist Moslems was the *Muhammadiyah* also founded in 1912. The *Muhammadiyah* had a widely dispersed middle-class and peasant-based membership, and its major activity was the promotion of modern schools. In contrast to the *Sarekat Islam* organized almost entirely in Java, the *Muhammadiyah* stressed Islamic goals rather than Javanese interests, and it thereby gained considerable strength in the outer islands. It was the dominant group within the *Masjumi* formed by the Japanese during the war, and at the time of national independence it was the largest political party in the archipelago.

The *Partai Kommunis Indonesia* (PKI) had its roots in the small radical socialist group, the Indies Social Democratic Association, started by the Dutch communist, Hendrik Sneevliet, in Java in 1914. Like communist parties elsewhere in Asia, it consisted at first of Marxist-oriented intellectuals who sought to penetrate the small trade union movement. In May 1920 several capable Indonesian leaders such as Semaoen and Darsono joined the Dutch radicals and formed the PKI.[66] It was the first communist party organized in Asia. Much like the tactic of the Chinese communists seeking to infiltrate the much larger organization of the *Kuomintang,* the PKI sought to penetrate the *Sarekat Islam* and gain control over its massive militant movement. This effort was blocked by Sarekat leaders who ousted communist members from their ranks in 1921. The PKI soon became the most disciplined political party in the archipelago, but it too suffered from numerous divisions engendered by the eclectic and pluralistic culture. Splits within the party organization caused small factions to engage occasionally in hastily planned acts of violence which were quickly crushed and caused enormous setbacks to the party. In 1926 a small band of PKI cadre staged a military attack against government buildings in Batavia and several other cities in Java with the hope of sparking a popular uprising. Yet this move was suppressed by Dutch military forces within a few days, and Dutch counter-measures against the party stopped virtually all organizational activities until World War II. Another coup was attempted by a faction of PKI leaders in 1948 against the new republic during the military campaign against the Dutch. This action was defeated by loyal army troops within a few weeks, and the PKI entered the post-independence period the following year greatly weakened by a reputation of opportunism and treachery.

Moderate nationalism found its organizational spokesman in the Indonesian Nationalist Party (PNI) created by Sukarno and other Dutch-educated intellectuals in 1927.[67] This party was the most widely acclaimed political organization prior to the end of Dutch rule, and it combined within its ranks the support of other political parties and groups. During its very brief overt activity from 1927 to 1929 it followed many of the same coalition-building tactics of the Congress Party in India and the Nacionalista Party in the Philippines.[68] The PNI membership consisted mostly of younger *prijaji,* civil servants, and a number of peasants, and it was the only political party to have some sizeable popular support in both rural and urban areas.[69] Its goals, like its brand of nationalism, were fairly vague. They stressed the broad objectives of national unity and a socialist-oriented economy. In spite of its modern leadership, the PNI was the political party most attached to Hindu-Buddhist traditions, including the consensus-making approach of *gotong-rojong* and *mufakat.* Although its leaders had been imprisoned most of the time since 1929, it quickly regrouped at the end of the Japanese occupation and sought a wide appeal as the party most closely attached to Sukarno.

In addition to the four political parties cited above, the emerging party system had numerous smaller parties, groups, associations, etc. In the new parliament of 236 members established at the time of independence, there were a total of 22 political organizations represented, many with some kind of *national* constituency.[70] The size of party representation varied from 49 members in the Masjumi to 2 members in a small faction called the Peasant Group.[71] The strong desire of each party to exert an influence in the post-independence government and the absence of any majority party created a powerful demand for a coalition approach to politics and a wide sharing of political power. This unique development of Western-style political parties blended very well with traditional values such as *gotong-rojong* and *mufakat* stressing broad-based consensus and compromise in decision-making. In many respects this developing multi-party system was ideal for some form of parliamentary democracy; it militated against authoritarian rule. Yet other counteracting influences at the time of independence posed a significant potential threat to democracy. The wide dispersal of power made the political process extremely fluid and unstable. At the end of the struggle against the Dutch, Sukarno was showing some signs of becoming a charasmatic leader, and somewhat like General deGaulle in France, he gave indications of seeking a political role above all political parties in order to serve as the leader of all the people. No national elections had ever been held prior to independence, and no party had any verifiable measurement of its popular support. Some political parties were less influenced than others by the traditional stress on consensus-making and pushed strongly for their particular interests. Very important, a new military leadership was beginning to emerge with markedly different political views from the civilian politicians who provided the leadership of the highly fragmented multi-party system.

The political leadership, as elsewhere in Asia, was the most significant element in the emerging political process. Most of the indigenous leaders were closely attached to different political parties, but some of the political maneuvering and exercise of political power was detached from political organizations. This development contributed much to an elitist and oligarchical political leadership. As in South Korea and South Vietnam, the political elite in Indonesia also came into positions of power during a very short period of time. The sudden removal of Dutch colonial rule by the Japanese and the intense military struggle by Indonesians against the Dutch after the war rapidly thrust indigenous leaders into governmental posts of broad authority. There was little time to establish stable or institutionalized power relationships in the hasty moves to gain national independence. And more than in any other polity in Asia, the political leadership in Indonesia at the time of national independence was a collective leadership reflecting the enormous diversity and pluralism of a new national society.

Several common characteristics provided some unity within the new political elite. Except for the top spokesmen of the orthodox Islamic organizations, the political leaders were largely the sons of the *prijaji* aristocratic class which provided some uniform values and behavior. All were Western-educated, either at institutions of higher education in Holland or in Indonesia, prior to World War II. One scholar has shown that 91% of the members of the first national parliament, 94% of the members in the first cabinets, and 100% of the indigenous members of the colonial civil service had obtained an advanced Western education.[72] Virtually all members of the Indonesia elite were youthful; most were in their 30's and early 40's when they assumed important governmental positions. The political leadership was totally devoid of entrepreneurs or businessmen with practical experience in commerce or industry.

Yet the emerging political elite, as partially explained before, was deeply divided at the time of national independence. Some of the intra-elite competition was caused by the differences between the "political" activist and the "functional" administrator approach to government and politics. Some was caused by ideological differences between various political parties. Some was caused by strong personalities seeking greater authority in an intense struggle for power. Many splits just prior to independence were also caused by the development of an indigenous military force and a growing political role by army officers. In 1946, for example, the communist leader, Tan Malaka, organized a coup supported by a portion of the army to seize the first cabinet headed by Sjahrir and supported by Sukarno. This effort was prevented when Tan Malaka was arrested by the government, although he was later released by a sympathetic military commander who for a time had kidnapped the Prime Minister.[73] Some of the bitter infighting within the political elite also revealed a blatant opportunism and disregard of future consequences as shown in occasional alliances between right-wing orthodox Moslems and left-wing communists against moderate leaders among reformist Moslems and secular nationalists. These extreme forms of political instability augured poorly for the quality of government in the post-independence period and indicating a growing need for some kind of strong leadership. These conditions caused one author to declare: "Indonesia's most pressing trouble, in these circumstances is, perhaps, not the danger of personal or minority dictatorship, but the absence of genuine leadership supported by adequate power."[74]

Governmental Process

The low transferable political and administrative structures combined with the harsh form of Dutch colonial rule obviated any significant indigenous role in the governmental process prior to national independence. Yet due to the vacillating repression imposed by the Dutch and the unique manner in which it was removed from the archipelago, Indonesians were able to participate in a modest but growing degree in some formal offices and institutions of government. The development of this fusional historical input came in three stages. The first stage involved the election of a few indigenous leaders to seats in advisory legislative bodies such as the Volksraad and provincial and local councils established by the Dutch colonial regime after 1900. A somewhat larger area of indigenous participation during the same period was employment at the middle and lower levels of the colonial bureaucracy. The second stage came with the Japanese occupation when the shortage of Japanese military personnel and the exigencies of the war effort enabled Indonesian leaders such as Sukarno and Hatta to gain admission to increasingly important official positions. By the end of the war they had acquired valuable administrative experience as well as a much higher degree of political self-confidence. The third stage was the formation of the Republic of Indonesia and several official institutions created by the provisional constitution in August-September 1945 in order to symbolize the end of foreign colonial rule. This hastily formed government was forced to wage a bitter military struggle during the next four years against the Dutch, and it did not exercise effective control over much territory in the archipelago. On one occasion the entire official leadership of the new republic was captured by Dutch military forces, although these persons were soon released to resume negotiations for independence with the Dutch government due to international pressures.[75]

In addition to its symbolic role to the international community, the provisional constitution of 1945 provided legitimacy to the political leadership of the new republic. However, it did not define accurately the allocations of authority within a sovereign government. It gave some organization and ranking to the new leadership, but it did not clarify important power relationships between executive and legislative jurisdiction. In considerable degree the provisional constitution legitimized the wide dispersal and fragmentation of power which existed among political leaders and groups at the end of the Japanese occupation. The top position of President was given to Sukarno due to his earlier role as a nationalist leader, his long imprisonment, wartime role, and oratorical skills in arousing support from the Indonesian people.[76] Just before independence Sukarno began asserting some of the mystical powers embodied in the traditional village leadership role in seeking good fortune for the people and interceding against social adversities. As previously explained, he also began using certain traditional values such as *mufakat* and *gotong-rojong*. The post of Vice-President was acquired by Mohammed Hatta who in many ways supplemented and balanced the leadership role of Sukarno. Hatta was educated in Holland and trained as an economist. He was a devout Moslem from Sumatra, a moderate, pragmatist, and development-oriented. Like Sukarno, he had obtained a wide popular appeal due to this lengthy imprisonment by the Dutch and his wartime role with the Japanese. The governmental roles exerted by Hatta and Sukarno were called for a time a *"dwi-tunggal"* or a "duumvirate."[77] Soetan Sjahrir served as Prime Minister and played a key role in the first government established by the provisional constitution. Sjahrir had also been educated in Holland and was incarcerated for many years by the Dutch colonial regime. He led an underground movement during the Japanese occupation, and his wartime experience was useful in the military campaign against the Dutch.

These and other leaders of the first government aided Sukarno in appointing the first legislative body called the Central National Commitee composed of representatives from the major political parties and groups. This body at first had 135 members and was later increased to 236 members. The first provisional constitution provided many features of a presidential-type system as the President was given authority to appoint the Prime Minister and members of the Cabinet, initiate most legislation, and exercise broad emergency powers (which were frequently used from 1945 to 1949). Yet some significant elements of the parliamentary system were also incorporated into the first indigenous government. The Central National Committee was authorized to enact all laws and to hold the Prime Minister and Cabinet responsible for the administration of governmental affairs. This ambiguity in the authority of the executive and legislative branches was not resolved in the abortive federal constitution set up by the Dutch as they left in 1949, or in the second provisional constitution restoring a unitary form of government a few months after the Dutch recognition of Indonesian independence. The second provisional constitution actually increased the parliamentary features of the governmental process by granting greater authority to the Cabinet and the legislative body and reducing the President largely to a ceremonial role. This development was certain to cause major conflicts in post-independence governments.

In addition to the modicum of constitutionalism in the emerging governmental process, the indigenous response in this part of the new political system also included the development of the military as a growing political force. The formation of this "institutional interest group" within the formal structures of the government or what I have earlier referred to as "military politicians" was part of the indigenous reaction to the Japanese occupation and the military struggle against the Dutch for national independence.[78] With the exception of the three bureaucratic polities in Nationalist China, Japan, and Thailand, this phenomena made Indonesia one of the few polities in Asia where military leaders exerted an independent political role prior to national independence. This development in Indonesia was more like that in Japan where military officers *shared* political power with civilian politicians at the end of the period of Western intervention, rather than where military officers dominated politics as in Nationalist China and Thailand. This condition was another factor contributing to a hybrid polity.

The Indonesian military leadership, like the civilian political elite, was diversified and fragmented. This characteristic was due to the piece-meal manner in which the armed forces were expanded. A very small group of Indonesian officers were trained by the Dutch prior to World War II, most of whom were trusted Christians recruited from the large Christian communities in the eastern islands of the archipelago.[79] A much larger group of Indonesian officers was recruited and trained by the Japanese from 1943 to 1945, and many military leaders who played a major role in post-independence politics began their official careers during this period. These officers included Generals Nasution, Sudirman, Jani, Sarbini, and Suharto. A third group of military officers assumed important positions in the government during the military campaign against the Dutch from 1945 to 1949.

Military officers became involved in government and politics about the same time as most of the civilian politicians. The Japanese occupation gave these young men who had no advanced Western-oriented education an opportunity to achieve positions of increasing power. They were greatly influenced by the Japanese military stress on a "fighting spirit," and they immediately began to challenge the role of civilian leaders as the organized struggle began against the Dutch.[80] This trend prevented any serious attempt by civilian government leaders to assert effective controls over the armed forces. In the ensuing political controversies, the military leaders, like the political parties, cooperated with any group or faction which assisted the pursuit of their goals. The military, for example, joined with the communists in opposing civilian political leaders (such as Hatta and Sjahrir) who were seeking a negotiated settlement with the Dutch. At other times the military cooperated with orthodox Islamic leaders against the Western-educated nationalists in seeking to spread their influence into rural areas.[81] Yet the Indonesian officers corps was greatly divided at the time of national independence. The staggered expansion of the armed forces and the intermittent role of international diplomacy in the termination of Dutch colonial rule prevented the military leadership from forging a unified organization or political influence.

As in South Korea and South Vietnam, the policies of the new government in Indonesia were largely undeveloped and untried. The belated indigenous role in the governmental process precluded the formulation of many specific goals in domestic and foreign affairs for the post-independence era. Like the communist and authoritarian governments in China, Korea, and Vietnam reacting against harsh forms of foreign domination, the emerging government in Indonesia was much more knowledgeable on what it was against than what it was for.

A general objective in domestic affairs was to construct a socialist-type economy and a welfare state that would eventually abolish the inequities imposed by the Dutch and Chinese. The modest administrative experience of many Indonesian leaders and the total absence of a powerful indigenous entrepreneurial class meant the government would play the major role in promoting economic and social development. In 1947 the Sjahrir regime drafted the Kasimo Plan to increase the production of food by land reclamation, new irrigation projects, improved agricultural technology, and the resettlement of excessive population in Java to the outer islands.[82] Yet this and other official plans at the time of national independence faced enormous obstacles due to the lack of qualified administrative personnel and meager financial resources. In many respects the combination of traditional and Western influences on the archipelago oriented the new government away from economic problem-solving and involved it in the more urgent task of preserving some form of national unity in a highly pluralistic society.

The foreign policy of the new government was shaped by the long period of harsh colonial suppression and the bitter struggle for national independence. A strong antipathy toward the Dutch and a somewhat lesser suspicion of its American and European allies directed Indonesia away from any strong attachment to the Western bloc. At the same time a strong fear of both domestic and foreign communists prevented the emerging government from seeking close relations with the Soviet Union, Communist China, or other communist nations. The desire to be friendly with "both sides" in the international community combined with the intense fervor of Indonesian nationalism caused a foreign policy seeking its own form of "non-alignment" or "neutralism." Upon attaining independence Indonesia promptly exchanged diplomatic relations with major Western and communist powers, and at the same time drew closer to other non-aligned nations such as India and Burma. It likewise followed the example of many other newly-independent nations and sought an active role in the peace-keeping activities of the United Nations.

Chapter 15

The Dynastic Polities

The indigenous response in the two French protectorates of Cambodia and Laos contained the largest degree of traditional influences and the least amount of Western values of any national society emerging in Asia. The combination of indigenous and Western behavior likewise induced the lowest level of cultural secularization and political participation. The traditional orientation in this kind of polity was similar in many respects to that in the princely states in the Indian sub-continent which remained virtually untouched by the Western impact. The pre-Western elitist legacy in these isolated societies sought to retain political authority in a very small and privileged class. The dynastic quality came from the pursuit of dominant political and administrative power by the royal family and leading members of the aristocracy.

The formation of this type of polity in Cambodia and Laos was due primarily to the minor interactions between the Theravada Buddhist cultural systems in both societies and the low transferable political and administrative structures of French colonial rule. They were also shaped by the low transformative economic and social policies administered by the French.[1] As previously explained, the French colonial regime in Indochina largely ignored Cambodia and Laos and used these two societies mainly as buffer states between Thailand and British Burma and their important economic and cultural interests in Vietnam. The French made no attempt to extend *mission civilisatrice* to Cambodia and Laos; they likewise did not apply their unitary-doctrinaire concept of colonial rule. Instead they formed very small governmental and non-governmental linkages in both colonized societies. The French exercised a low degree of harshness in the colonization process, and both societies experienced relatively low levels of violence in the final stages of colonial rule.

Religious norms in this kind of polity remained largely intact.[2] These values included religious progressivism and political apathy which maintained a deep attachment to traditional behavior such as merit-making, monastic training, and a strong reverence for the Buddhist priesthood. Religious eclecticism and psychological pluralism preserved an easy-going individualsm which inhibited any significant development of achievement values or a propensity to change. A sense of fatalism and determinism continued to pervade the collective social consciousness which prevented any important moves toward political modernization. Just prior to World War II the French actually aided in strengthening Buddhism in both societies which increased traditional loyalties and fostered closer cultural bonds between the monarchy and the vast rural peasantry.[3]

The languages of the dominant ethnic groups were closely related to the Theravada Buddhist cultural systems, and they also assisted in preserving traditional values and behavior. The spoken language in this type of society was the predominant means of communication; the written language was used only by the small urban elites and the Sangha. A "folk" language prevailed in the little traditions in rural areas, and the traditional "court" language of the royalty and aristocracy was preserved by the leading families. Neither the spoken nor written forms of the indigenous language were altered by the French colonial regime. However, the increasing use of the French language by the indigenous upper class was a significant fusional historical input. As in other colonized societies in Asia, it added another barrier to admission into the social and political elite, and it increased the separation between the urban and rural classes. The French language increasingly influenced the indigenous elite toward Western culture which resulted in a mixed lifestyle that oriented the upper class away from some forms of traditional behavior.

Language caused both integrative and fragmenting influences. The language of the dominant ethnic group became the "national" language, and it served as a unifying channel within this major social and political group. The Cambodian language exerted a powerful centralizing influence among the Cambodian (Khmer) people who constituted more than 90% of the population of the new national society, and in Laos the language likewise unified the Lao people inhabiting the fertile lowlands adjoining the Mekong River. Yet this common linguistic group in Laos

comprised slightly less than 50% of the entire population, and the re-
mainder consisted of tribal groups or "remote peasants" residing in the
mountainous terrain. The diversity of spoken and unwritten languages
among these small groups of mountain tribesmen kept them socially and
politically divided. The Lao language also exerted a divisive influence in
the newly-emerging national society in Laos as it oriented large numbers
of Lao people toward the much larger Lao population residing in the
northeastern provinces of Thailand.[4] In effect, the widespread use of
spoken and unwritten languages in both Cambodia and Laos at the time
of national independence prevented these societies from having "mass"
communication systems. Political information and opinion was confined
largely to the small urban elites.

The educational system consisted essentially of the monastic training
provided in village temples which received only minimal modernizing
changes from Western sources and served essentially to maintain the
traditional cultural system. The major fusional historical input in the
realm of education was the admission of a very small portion of
indigenous youth into the few educational facilities established by the
French colonial regime. No schools of any significance were established by indigenous persons prior to national independence. A meager
French-styled educational structure in Cambodia consisted of approximately 500 primary schools enrolling 100,000 students, five
secondary schools with less than 2000 students, and a small teachers
training college, vocational school, and several specialized schools.[5] The
only institution of "higher" education was The National Institute of
Legal, Political, and Economic Studies in Phnom Penh which provided
part-time training to about 250 civil servants. Most upper class
Cambodians received advanced education in Vietnam or France. Similar
but more rudimentary educational facilities existed in Laos in 1953 where
primary schools enrolled only 15,000 to 20,000 students and four
secondary schools enrolled less than 700 students. The only institution of
higher education was the Pavie College in Vientiane.[6] Virtually all upper
class Lao received advanced education in France.

The dominant characteristic of the economy was subsistence agriculture consisting of wet-rice production by rural villagers on small
privately-owned plots of land. The intense agricultural attachment of the
peasants in this kind of society was closely intertwined with traditional
cultural values and behavior. One source has described this pervasive
attitude in Laos as follows:

> There can be no doubt that the people of Laos are at present
> overwhelmingly oriented toward the soil. The qualities that go to

make up the rural agricultural way of life would probably rank high in the Lao scale of values. Within this way of life land is of primary importance and attachment to the land is undoubtedly one of the outstanding characteristics of the rural Laotian today.[7]

Unlike peasants in China, Japan, and India, the rural villagers in Cambodia and Laos had little desire to acquire more land than they could cultivate themselves. Tenant farming and landless peasants were rare. This proclivity to self-sufficient agriculture was shared by more than 95% of the peasants in Laos and some 90% of the peasants in Cambodia. A small commercial sector in Cambodia exported a modest rice surplus each year to Vietnam and France, but this more advanced economic activity had no major political significance. The Lao economy produced no rice surplus, and instead it was often required to import rice from Thailand. The powerful agricultural tradition among indigenous peasants inhibited their movement into non-agricultural economic roles. The only feasible employment alternative for an indigenous peasant was a position in the civil service which held the highest respect and prestige. Yet this kind of livelihood required something beyond a secondary education and was extremely rare for a rural villager. The deep love of the soil and strong rural customs also prevented the use of personal savings for higher economic and social standards. If not in debt, a typical peasant would use any surplus income in religious merit-making or the enjoyment of periodic village festivals. In effect, the combination of traditional economic roles and traditional religious norms precluded the development of modernizing values and behavior.

Another characteristic of the economy in the two dynastic polities was foreign domination of the small commercial sector. The potentially important development of an indigenous business class generating demands for economic and political reforms was thereby aborted. Commerce was dominated by French, Chinese, or Vietnamese entrepreneurs during most of the French colonial period, although in the final stages a predominant commercial role was acquired by the Chinese.[8] French enterprise thereafter was largely confined to the export of rubber from Cambodia and the export of tin and gold from Laos. Until the time of national independence the Cambodian economy exported slightly more goods than it imported giving it a favorable balance of trade. Laos, however, by 1953 was exporting less than $1,000,000 each year mostly in the form of tin concentrates, and it was importing $10,000,000 - $12,000,000 in food and manufactured goods. Under French colonial rule this deficit was made up by surplus income acquired in the other Indochina colonies.

At the time of national independence, however, this adverse trade relationship in Laos induced a major demand on the new government to acquire sufficient foreign financial assistance to maintain the nation's economic and administrative viability. This condition created a major external linkage involving extensive foreign intervention in Laotian national affairs.

THE POLITICAL SYSTEM

As already cited, the amalgamation of traditional and Western historical inputs in the dynastic polities was shaped primarily by the strong influence of traditional values and behavior. The preservation of the royalty and aristocracy by the French prevented any significant disruptive gap between the pre-Western traditional societies and the era of national independence. Many prerogatives of the traditional ruling elite were consequently kept intact, and some powers of the royal family were actually strengthened by French colonial rule. The political system at the time of national independence thereby consisted mostly of the political values and relationships within the traditional ruling class. Other classes and groups were largely excluded from positions of power because of the intense apathy and deference to authority engendered largely by traditional religious norms.

Normative Process

Pre-independence nationalism in this type of emerging polity comprised a fusional historical input combining a vague indigenous religious and racial pride and the Western concept of national equality. It was also motivated by a latent but growing desire to end foreign domination and to assert the right of national self-determination.[9] This attitude was restricted to the small traditional elites residing in urban areas. In addition to its opposition to the continuation of Western colonial rule, pre-independence nationalism in Cambodia and Laos manifested a suspicion of former regional enemies such as Thailand and the two Vietnams.[10] It likewise contained an anti-Chinese and anti-Vietnamese bias in domestic affairs. A new national pride derived considerable strength from an effort to revive memories of former great traditions and middle traditions of the pre-Western period. This influence was stronger in Cambodia than in Laos since research by French scholars had supplied much reliable historical data on the extensive power and influence of the Khmer empire from the eighth to the fifteenth centuries. In Laos the vision of past grandeur was weaker since it was confined to the Kingdom of Lan Xang from the fourteenth to the seventeenth centuries and several relatively brief middle traditions.

Militant nationalism tended to be more Western and less traditional than moderate nationalism. It supplemented the Western idea of national equality with Western concepts of secular progress and the propensity to make rapid social and political change. It also downgraded the values of gentleness, apathy, and deference in the traditional cultural system. This form of nationalism espoused the achievement of national independence promptly after the removal of the Japanese military occupation and prior to the reestablishment of French colonial rule at the end of World War II. It advocated the use of violence against French domination in seeking national independence. It contained some overtones of republicanism and the termination of the institution of the monarchy. This form of nationalism in Cambodia was most vividly depicted by Son Ngoc Thanh who established the first Cambodian-language newspaper in Phnom Penh criticizing French colonial rule and who agitated against French domination during and after World War II.[11] Son's ideas won considerable popularity, but his nationalist sentiments were mitigated by his extremism, his birthplace in Cochin China, and his Vietnamese parentage. Militant nationalism couched in Marxist-Leninist terminology was likewise advocated in Cambodia by Vietnamese communists just prior to national independence. This ideology temporarily attracted some followers among Cambodian dissidents, but it was severely weakened by its foreign source. Militant nationalism in Laos was expressed in the rightist sentiments of Prince Phetsarath and the *Lao Issara* (Free Lao) movement advocating the immediate termination of French colonial rule following World War II. A more intense militancy was espoused by the Communist-oriented doctrine of Prince Souphannouvong and the *Pathet Lao* organization seeking an end of French colonialism and "imperialism."[12] Militant nationalism in this kind of normative process was considerably weakened by its conflict with the moderate and pacifistic values deeply engrained in the Theravada Buddhist cultural system as well as the widespread tendency to preserve the traditional class structure, especially the monarchy. Militant nationalism was likewise harmed by its unrealistic effort to seek the forcible overthrow of French colonial rule with either nonexistent or extremely weak indigenous military forces.

Moderate nationalism acquired the dominant status in the national normative process in this type of polity at the time of independence. It was less Western and more traditional in content and style than militant nationalism. It sought limited changes largely through the initiative of the traditional ruling elite and by gradual and non-violent means. It manifested some aspects of "traditional nationalism" as defined by Professor Carlton Hayes in which the national political ideology was based on "historic rights," "aristocratic" and "evolutionary, if not reactionary" values, and a doctrine which "tended to regard sovereignty as plural and sought to reconcile loyalty to the nation state with continuing loyalty to class and locality...."[13] It wanted the complete termination of Western domination, but this motive was mellowed by a recognition of the achievements and benefits bestowed by French colonial rule. In Cambodia and Laos moderate nationalism contained considerable respect and appreciation for the modest but initial technological innovations started by the French as well as the termination of internal strife through a unified and stable administrative system. This form of nationalism also acknowledged the role of French power and influence in protecting these societies from regional enemies in Thailand and Vietnam, and it hoped to gain national independence in a manner which would continue French protection and assistance in an uncertain future. Moderate nationalism in Cambodia was advocated by King Sihanouk, Prince Monireth, and many other leading members of the royal family. Sihanouk adhered to this concept throughout eight years of increasing domestic pressure and intense negotiations with the French in achieving national independence.[14] In Laos this form of nationalism was upheld by King Sisavang Vong, Prince Souvanna Phouma, Prince Boun Oum, and many other traditional leaders.[15] Moderate nationalism in both societies was bolstered by the values of restraint and non-violence in the Theravada Buddhist cultural system. It also gained strength by a realistic and pragmatic approach in dealing with the French during the final years of colonial rule. Instead of resorting to the arduous path of seeking a military victory over French colonialism, it won predominant support by relying on persuasion and diplomacy in the quest for national independence.

The political culture in this kind of polity consisted of the political attitudes and behavior of various factions within the emerging traditional elite. This fusional historical input was shaped by the effort of each aspiring faction to combine its own interests with the vague goals of a new nationhood. Nationalism consequently aided in affecting the scope and methods of the political culture. It assisted in centralizing new patterns of political behavior in Cambodia among factions based solely on personalities within a single emerging elite. The conflict between the reassertion of traditional prerogatives of the monarchy and the goals of a few competing anti-monarchial groups was both intensified and mitigated by the common effort to pursue national independence. Cambodian political culture thereby became highly focused in one political arena or milieu. Political culture in Laos involved more fragmented behavioral patterns based on both personalities and geographic interests. Nationalism affected these patterns of behavior in requiring compromise and accomodation by traditional leaders representing provincial loyalties and seeking maximum benefits within a new national consensus. In effect, Laotian political culture comprised new attitudes and modes of behavior among the traditional leaders of several former middle traditions who were required to govern a new national society.

Political Process

As elsewhere in Asia, the emerging political process constituted a pattern of relationships which confined active participation in decision-making to a small minority of the indigenous population. In the two dynastic polities, the communication, articulation, and aggregation of political interests and the final selection of official policies was limited to a sharply delineated royal and aristocratic class. This evolving political process interacted closely with the normative process in maintaining dominant political power in the control of traditional leaders.

Political communication consisted of the distribution of information and opinion to an extremely small audience in the few urban areas of both colonized societies. A modest press in Cambodia in 1953 consisted of a few private newspapers printed in the French, Chinese, and Cambodian languages with a combined circulation of less than 12,000 readers.[16] Printed information in Laos was disseminated to a few thousand people by small newspapers and mimeographed pages in the French and Laotian languages.[17] The press in both colonized societies was owned or controlled by prominent political leaders or aspiring political parties. Four small radio stations in Cambodia and a single radio station in Laos broadcast several hours each day to a very modest urban audience. The bulk of the information and opinions channeled in this part of the emerging political process came from foreign sources and indigenous political leaders. Information or opinions criticizing the new political elite was usually distributed by personal contacts or through a small portion of the local press. No political information or opinion was transmitted by intellectuals outside the indigenous political leadership or by institutions of higher education. This primitive mode of political communication fostered considerable fluidity in the maneuvering among competing factions within the traditional leadership just prior to national independence. It hampered efforts by these leaders to reach sizeable numbers of people and build some kind of political organization. It indirectly encouraged a new form of "palace politics."

Interest articulation consisted mostly of protests made by disgruntled leaders who hastily formed loosely disciplined political organizations during the demise of French colonial rule. The major bond within these early interest groups was a similar approach to the achievement of national independence. Each group espoused its own form of nationalism and placed no significant emphasis on economic or social issues. The protests made by these groups tended toward some form of anomic political action ranging from overt demonstration to organized guerrilla warfare.

In Cambodia the major group protesting the gradual movement toward national independence was the *Khmer Issarak* (Free Cambodia) consisting of followers of the militant nationalist, Son Ngoc Thanh. The arrest and exile of Son by the French in 1946 caused many of his supporters to engage in guerrilla warfare against French security forces in the northern and western provinces while other adherents sought diplomatic support from the government in Thailand. A general amnesty the following year caused many members of the Khmer Issarak to surrender to the Cambodian government and form a political party.[18] Scattered remnants of this dissident movement continued armed attacks against government forces, and some insurgents received assistance from the communists in Vietnam. A much smaller and less violent dissident group in Laos known as the *Lao Issara* was formed by Prince Phetsarath in 1945 to oppose the pro-French policies of King Sisavang Vong and other traditional leaders.[19] The Lao Issara controlled the government in Luang Prabang until the return of the French in 1946 when most of its leaders fled into exile in Thailand. The establishment of Laos as a semi-independent associated state in the French Indochina Union in 1949 caused the Lao Issara organization in Thailand to dissolve and most of its members returned to Laos. A larger protest group in Laos consisted of the *Pathet Lao* formed by Prince Souphanouvong who maintained a militant opposition to any form of French colonial rule after World War II and the conciliatory policies of the moderate Laotian leaders.[20] Prior to national independence Souphanouvong and the Pathet Lao paramilitary forces controlled large areas in the northern and eastern provinces with considerable assistance from the communists in Vietnam. The combination of this internal rivalry and the international negotiations at the Geneva conference leading to national independence required Laos to maintain a neutral foreign policy and to integrate Pathet Lao military units with the armed forces of the Royal Laotian government.

The refusal of Souphanouvong and the Pathet Lao to implement this treaty agreement contributed to a national society separated partially by ideology and partially by an intra-elitist (and intra-family) struggle for power. The role of these dissident "interest groups" in both Cambodia and Laos also generated a form of political behavior which subsequently encouraged the use of violence by small disgruntled groups whenever their demands were not achieved by gradual and non-violent means.

Political parties in both Cambodia and Laos were closely related to the dissident interest groups. They consisted of small personal followings organized either by disgruntled leaders seeking a favorable position in a newly-independent government or by traditional leaders already in positions of power who wanted to preserve their favorable political status. Like the interest groups, they bolstered the power of aspiring political leaders. The major difference between political parties and interest groups was the non-violent and overt approach to political power by electoral and parliamentary means. Political parties engaged in little interest aggregation or coalition-building seeking a wider popular appeal. They became extremely fluid and fragile organizations as their leaders and members shifted readily from party to party and as some political parties quickly dissolved.

In Cambodia three political parties were formed just after World War II to obtain seats in the Consultative Assembly which drafted the first constitution. Each of these political parties was launched by a member of the traditional elite. Prince Norodom Montana organized the Democratic Progressive Party seeking a gradual movement toward national independence and a constitutional monarchy.[21] Prince Norodom Norindeth started the Liberal Party advocating national independence and the continuation of close cooperation with France. Prince Sisowath Youtevong formed the liberal-oriented Democrat Party with young French-educated followers and the "leftist" adherents of Son Ngoc Thanh pursuing a strong legislature and genuine parliamentary rule. The initial electoral success of the Democrat Party enabled it to play a dominant role in drafting the first constitution and to emerge as the major opposition to King Sihanouk. This political party, however, declined in power as national independence approached and Sihanouk gained self-confidence in asserting many traditional prerogatives of the absolute monarchy.

Political parties in Laos were also largely instruments of aspiring members of the traditional elite. The Independent Party was launched by Phoui Sananikone at the time of the return of the French in 1946 and the flight of the Lao Issara leadership into exile in Thailand.[22] Prince Souvana Phouma and Katay Sasorith formed the National Progressive

Party in 1949 following the dissolution of the Lao Issara in Thailand and the return of its leaders to Laos. A small Democratic Party and National Union Party were also organized by leading members of the aristocracy in the early 1950's. The erratic maneuvering among these early political parties served essentially to enhance the power of the traditional leadership class.

As elsewhere in Asia, political leadership was the dominant element in the political process and was also closely related to the political culture. In Cambodia the political leadership developed into a singular personalized form due to the politization of the monarchy.[23] This political figure was King Norodom Sihanouk who assumed an increasingly secure power position during the final two years of French colonial rule. The young monarch combined certain traditional and Western characteristics and was himself an important fusional historical input which provided the basis for a charismatic form of political leadership. Educated in French schools in Phnom Penh and Saigon and selected by French colonial administrators and the Cambodian Council of the Throne at the age of eighteen as the reigning monarch from among several more experienced contenders (including his own father and uncle), Sihanouk gradually asserted the traditional powers of the absolute monarchy until he was the dominant political leader at the time of national independence.[24] A collective political leadership emerged in Laos from the politization of the aristocracy. The persons comprising this ruling group included the leading royal princes and members of prominent provincial families. They also comprised an important fusional historical input combining traditional and Western influences. The reigning monarch, King Sisavang Vong, had received one year of education in France, and the three leading princes, Phetsarath, Souvanna Phouma and Souphanouvong, were educated at French universities in law or engineering.[25] In the formation of an independent government during the final years of French colonial rule, the political leadership of Souvanna Phouma was enhanced because his mother was of royal lineage. The political leadership of Souphanouvong was harmed by the fact that his mother was a commoner and he had married a Vietnamese woman. Except for Souphanouvong, the emerging collective political leadership in Laos was held together by common racial and religious bonds and the need for sufficient unity in governing a newly-independent national society. Yet within this ruling political elite numerous divisions and conflicts were caused by provincial and kinship loyalties.

Governmental Process

The low level of exposure of Cambodia and Laos to French influences and the strong traditional orientation in these two colonized societies prevented a significant indigenous role in the governmental process until the major reforms began in 1949 which transferred some official juris-diction to indigenous control. Thereafter emerging indigenous leaders began to fill increasingly important government positions. Constitutions were promulgated which became largely an official facade for an elitist political process preserving the privileged status of a traditional ruling class. They served primarily as symbols of approaching national independence rather than instruments of limited governmental authority.

The introductions of the new constitutional frameworks elaborated the traditional duties of the people more than any modern civil rights. They also perpetuated dynastic authority by detailed provisions defining royal succession and prerogatives. This traditional usage was formally institutionalized in the Cambodian constitution by limiting the monarchy to male descendants of King Ang Duong and stipulating that future monarchs would be selected by the reigning monarch or the Council of the Throne.[26] Dynastic rule in Laos was fostered by the constitutional provisions restricting the monarchy to male descendants of King Sisavang Vong, and the numerous articles upholding the person of the king as "sacred and inviolable," requiring the king to be the "protector" of the state religion of Buddhism, providing the king with considerable titular and appointive powers, and making him the theoretical source of all executive, legislative, and judicial powers.[27]

In spite of the elaborate provisions defining many traditional prerogatives of the king, a mode of dynastic rule markedly different from the pre-Western era was envisioned in these constitutional frame-works. The intention of the framers was to create a constitutional role in which the monarch would reign but not rule. Additional institutionalized structures of government were established so other traditional leaders could actually control the political affairs of the new national society. This form of "Westernized" and "parliamentary" dynastic rule was quickly established in Laos due to the weak political position of the king and the strong political power wielded by princely politicians and prominent provincial families. This form of dynastic government did not evolve in Cambodia where the strong political position of King Sihanouk enabled him to assert the titular powers of the monarchy and claim that other organs of the newly-established government (the cabinet and National Assembly) were not effectively exercising their "delegated" powers. The ensuing struggle between Sihanouk using his traditional ceremonial powers and anti-monarchial opponents upholding the limited powers of a constitutional monarchy was instrumental in causing Sihanouk to abdicate from the monarchy and form his own mass political organization, the *Sangkum Reastr Niyum* (People's Socialist Community), immediately after national independence.[28]

The council of ministers or cabinet in these parliamentary constitutional frameworks assisted in maintaining these different forms of dynastic rule.[29] In Laos the cabinet became the chief governmental organ of the ruling princes and aristocrats who began distributing power and portfolios among their own ranks according to shifting alignments of political influence. The appointive power and ceremonial role of the monarchy merely sanctioned these intermittent cabinet changes among leading political personalities. The cabinet in Cambodia likewise consisted of prominent traditional leaders, yet it exercised an administrative rather than an executive role just prior to national independence. Although the cabinet was collectively responsible to the National Assembly, the absence of coherent and disciplined political parties in the legislative body enhanced the capacity of King Sihanouk to block legislative opposition and make all major political decisions. Top administrative posts were distributed to trusted relatives and personal aides by the monarchy in Cambodia and by the cabinet in Laos during the final stages of French colonial rule, a trend which reinforced dynastic authority in these two societies. Employment in the new indigenous civil service was legally opened to any citizen with proper professional qualifications, yet the educational and experience prerequisites for these administrative positions also limited admission in the bureaucracy to members of the traditional ruling families.

The legislative bodies created by the constitutional frameworks were totally alien political institutions. These representative structures offered the greatest potential to modernize some elements in these strongly traditional polities. Yet these Westernized "democratic" bodies, modeled after the legislatures of the Third and Fourth Republics in France, were organized officially and non-officially to prevent any major threat to the continuation of dynastic rule. One method for achieving this purpose was the constitutional provisions for an upper house possessing only advisory powers, but with sufficient prestige to exert considerable undefined influence and authority. The Council of the Kingdom in Cambodia consisting of 24 persons at least 40 years of age was appointed from the royal family, provincial elites, the professions, and the civil service.[30] This highly conservative body was designed to check legislative opposition to the emerging traditional elite. A smaller twelve-member King's Council consisting of six members appointed by the king and six members appointed by the National Assembly was incorporated in the constitution in Laos to achieve a similar purpose.[31]

The lower house in these new constitutional frameworks comprised the major institutionalized channel for direct and popular participation in the governmental process. The National Assembly in both societies was fully elected and possessed the constitutional authority to change cabinets by a vote of no-confidence. Yet these Western-styled legislative bodies did little to restrain the perpetuation of dynastic rule. The lower house in Cambodia contained some political opponents of King Sihanouk, but it was greatly weakened prior to national independence by the constitutional authority of the king or the cabinet to dissolve this popularly elected body. The National Assembly in Laos was a weak and servile legislative body from the outset due to the large number of traditional leaders (and government supporters) among the elected representatives. The legislatures in both societies were likewise reduced in influence during the final years of Western colonial rule since the only real issue was the form and timing of national independence. They thereby acquired no meaningful experience in law-making or in checking the administration of national affairs by the executive authority.

The judiciary in these societies, like the lower house legislative bodies, offered some potential for checking the trend toward dynastic rule.[32] An independent and professional court system could conceivably have upheld an institutional obstacle to arbitrary executive power. Some efforts were made in this direction during the final years of French colonial rule in Cambodia. A few French jurists and French-educated Cambodian lawyers were employed in the courts by the newly-emerging government, and the administration of justice for a brief period utilized fair and objective standards. Yet this trend was reduced by the time of national independence through the constitutional authority of the chief of state to commute judicial sentences, an authority used intermittently by Sihanouk to enhance his expanding power. The judiciary in Laos had few trained judges and lawyers at the time of national independence and a small legal staff was largely engaged in the codification of laws.

Finally, these two dynastic polities were deeply affected by the official policies administered by indigenous leaders at the time of national independence. The chief characteristics of the policies in this kind of governmental process were little or no development of domestic policies and a highly formulated and articulated foreign policy. In both Cambodia and Laos the new political elites were preparing several economic and social plans to improve the post-independence national society, yet these domestic programs were extremely meager and vague. They depended heavily on foreign assistance and were designed to enhance the prestige and power of the indigenous political leadership as much as to help the people. In sharp contrast, the tradition-oriented leadership had definite and strong views on issues of foreign policy based on their own personal interests. This policy in Cambodia consisted of a broad consensus within the ruling dynastic elite to retain good relations with France, but at the same time to adhere to a policy of non-alignment in international politics.[33] In Laos a diversity of interests induced a fragmented foreign policy shaped by the personal relationships of different members of the emerging elite with specific foreign powers. These policies ranged from pro-French and pro-American to pro-Peking and pro-North Vietnamese.[34] In both societies the prevalence of internal splits within the ruling elites linked to specific external threats provided little opportunity for popular participation in some form of constitutional democracy and instead it aided the continuation of authoritarianism and dynastic rule after national independence.

Chapter 16

Terminal Analysis of Fusional Historical Inputs

The application of politically relevant terminal factors is required in assessing the final modifications of fusional historical inputs as they became the basic ingredients or elements of a new political system at the time of national independence or complete national sovereignty. As in Parts One and Two, this methodological tool provides important supplementary variables in comparative political analysis.[1] In the case of fusional historical inputs, it involves an assessment of the indigenous response to the specific terminal factors which affected the final stages of Western historical inputs.

The terminal factors which affected the final stages of fusional historical inputs in Asian societies are the following:

1. *The Duration of Discrete Fusional Historical Inputs in the Indigenous Response of the Colonization Process or the Unequal Treaty Process:* This analysis involves the measurement of the time-span of specific politically relevant values, modes of behavior, and institutions in the emerging national society, especially the specific elements of the new polity as they were formed by the interaction of traditional and Western historical inputs. A complete analysis of these time factors for each emerging national society in Asia would require a vast and complex array of the estimated or exact dates of the origin and duration of each specific fusional historical input. Such an analysis is not possible in an exploratory work of this kind, and only a few illustrative examples of this chronologically-oriented terminal factor can be presented here. Table XX comprises a comparison of the estimated or exact date of the origin of various fusional historical inputs and their duration in years in different Asian societies. The dates of achieving national independence or complete national sovereignty are shown in parentheses under the name of each Asian society. The estimated or exact dates of the origin of each fusional historical input are shown in parentheses in the table under the duration of each fusional historical input measured in years.

The duration of specific fusional historical inputs in the emerging societies in Asia shown in Table XX reveals some interesting aspects of this important terminal factor. Common characteristics of the time-span of several fusional historical inputs in Nationalist China, Japan, and Thailand indicate some of the reasons why the polities in these semi-independent societies developed toward centralization and authoritarianism. The relatively brief durations of democratic values in the political ideology (5-31 years), interest groups (18-23 years), political parties (17-23 years), and a modernizing legislature (5-15 years), tended to weaken any trend toward some form of constitutional government. In these same societies the much longer period of indigenous involvement in a modernizing executive (30-82 years) and a modernizing administration (28-53 years) contributed to the formation of a non-democratic "bureaucratic polity." Conversely, similar characteristics in the duration of significant fusional historical inputs in India, Burma, Malaya, and the Philippines assisted the evolution of constitutional democracy in these emerging national societies. These inputs included a relatively lengthy duration of an indigenous experience with democratic values (6-51 years), interest groups (11-36 years), and political parties (6-62 years). Within these emerging political systems the duration of other significant elements also enhanced the development of democratic government, including indigenous participation in a constitutional framework (4-39 years), and a fairly balanced time-span of the indigenous response in a modernizing legislature and a modernizing executive and administration.

Major characteristics of the durations of fusional historical inputs in the authoritarian and totalitarian societies which emerged from harsh forms of foreign domination or from little exposure to Western influences are the fairly lengthy exposure in most of these societies to Western democratic values (22-47 years) and similar durations of the existence of interest groups and political parties (25-47 years). Yet the most common characteristic in these non-democratic societies is the very brief time-span of indigenous participation in various forms of constitutionalism (4-9 years) and modernizing institutions (4-13 years).

2. *The Indigenous Response to the Size of Western Linkages in the Colonization Process:*[2] Large Western governmental linkages which tended to resist a negotiated and peaceful transition to national independence during the final stages of the colonization process induced a reaction of increasing hostility from indigenous nationalist leaders. This response generated a strong desire among the emerging indigenous elite to remove all "remnants" of Western colonialism. It reinforced militant nationalism and the use of violence in seeking the termination of Western domination. It also provided a salient issue which favored the formation of a large indigenous communist party. In many cases this kind of indigenous response comprised a natural and emotional reaction

Table XX. A comparison of the estimated or exact date of origin of selected fusional historical inputs in emerging Asian societies and their duration.

EMERGING NATIONAL SOCIETIES

FUSIONAL HISTORICAL INPUTS	Nationalist China (1943)	Japan (1898)	Thailand (1937)	India (1947)	Burma (1948)	Malya (1957)	Philippines (1946)
Political Ideology							
Differentiated Nationalism	23 (1920)	23 (1875)	17 (1920)	47 (1900)	28 (1920)	11 (1946)	51 (1895)
Constitutional Democracy	31 (1912)	18 (1880)	5 (1932)	28 (1919)	27 (1921)	6 (1951)	45 (1901)
Socialism	13 (1930)	8 (1890)	5 (1932)	27 (1920)	27 (1921)	27 (1930)	16 (1930)
Interest Groups	23 (1920)	18 (1880)	—	27 (1920)	28 (1920)	11 (1946)	36 (1910)
Political Parties	23 (1920)	17 (1880)	—	62 (1885)	27 (1921)	6 (1951)	39 (1907)
Constitutional Framework	15 (1928)	9 (1889)	5 (1932)	38 (1909)	13 (1935)	4 (1953)	39 (1907)
Modernizing Executive	31 (1912)	30 (1868)	82 (1855)	28* (1919)	13 (1935)	4 (1953)	31 (1915)
Modernizing Administration	53 (1890)	28 (1870)	45 (1892)	57 (1890)	28 (1920)	37 (1930)	45 (1901)
Modernizing Legislature	15 (1928)	9 (1889)	5 (1932)	38 (1909)	11 (1937)	4 (1953)	39 (1907)
Modernizing Judiciary	23 (1920)	18 (1880)	45 (1892)	27 (1920)	27 (1920)	22 (1935)	45 (1901)

*Indigenous participation in modernizing executive in India done largely at the provincial level.

which produced many grievances and issues detrimental to the non-violent development of the emerging national society. The muted resistance and spirit of accomodation of sizeable Western non-governmental linkages, on the other hand, generated considerable good-will and sympathy toward these Western groups among the indigenous political leadership at the time of national independence. This reaction strengthened moderate nationalism and conservative nationalism. It enabled most of these non-governmental linkages to remain in the newly-independent national society. These phenomena were seen in the contrasting indigenous responses in the emerging democratic societies in India, Burma, Malaya, and the Philippines and in the emerging authoritarian or totalitarian polities in Indonesia, Korea, and Vietnam.

EMERGING NATIONAL SOCIETIES

Communist China (1949)	South Korea (1948)	North Korea (1948)	South Vietnam (1954)	North Vietnam (1954)	Indo- nesia (1949)	Cam- bodia 1953)	Laos (1953)
—	(28) 1920	—	(47) 1907	—	(41) 1908	(17) 1936	(8) 1945
—	(16) 1920	—	(34) 1920	—	(22) 1927	(4) 1949	(4) 1949
—	(28) 1920	—	(34) 1920	—	(29) 1920	—	—
—	(28) 1920	—	(47) 1907	—	(41) 1908	(8) 1945	(8) 1945
(28) 1921	—	(27) 1921	(47) 1907	(25) 1929	(37) 1912	(8) 1945	(8) 1945
—	—	—	—	(9) 1945	(4) 1945	(4) 1949	(4) 1949
(13) 1935	(3) 1945	(3) 1945	(5) 1949	(9) 1945	(4) 1945	(4) 1949	(4) 1949
(13) 1935	(3) 1945	(3) 1945	(5) 1949	(0) 1945	(4) 1945	(4) 1949	(4) 1949
—	(3) 1945	(3) 1945	(5) 1949	(9) 1949	(4) 1945	(4) 1949	(4) 1949
—	(3) 1945	(3) 1945	(5) 1949	(9) 1949	(4) 1945	(4) 1949	(4) 1949

The large governmental linkages in the French, Dutch, and Japanese colonial systems induced widespread hostility and militant forms of nationalism, while the much smaller British and American non-governmental linkages contributed to considerable good-will and moderate and conservative types of nationalism.

3. *The Indigenous Response to the Size, Economic Role, and Duration of Regional Alien Communities:*[3] The emerging political leadership tended to resent the lack of cooperation from large regional alien communities during the final stages in the struggle for national independence. They also feared these groups might wield excessive political influence after the termination of colonial rule. Nationalist leaders were likewise apprehensive of Western colonial administrators bestowing special privileges on these groups at the time of granting

national independence. Fewer fears were generated in the indigenous nationalist leadership by relatively small regional alien communities during the final stages of Western colonial rule. New political leaders exhibited confidence that they would be able to control these modest alien groups. These contrasting phenomena were seen in the strong nationalist feelings of Burmese political leaders toward the large Indian community in Burma and the more muted nationalism directed at the much smaller Chinese community. In Malaya the situation was reversed. Malay nationalism was directed primarily at the large Chinese community; it was much less intense toward the relatively small Indian community. Filipino nationalism was only modestly affected by the relatively small Chinese community, while nationalism in Indonesia was greatly intensified by the presence of an urban minority of almost 2,000,000 Chinese.

The economic role of the regional alien community likewise influenced nationalist attitudes as Western colonial rule came to an end. Indigenous nationalism was directed more strongly at regional alien groups engaged in economic roles which could exercise significant political power after national independence than at economic roles which exerted little or no political influence. Indigenous nationalism was consequently aimed primarily at regional aliens employed in entrepreneurial roles; it was less intense against regional aliens working in skilled or unskilled labor. This phenomenon was significant in Indonesia and Malaya where indigenous nationalism was directed more intensely at the Chinese business class than toward Chinese skilled or unskilled workers. Nationalism in Burma was likewise aimed much more at Indian merchants and money-lenders than at Indians engaged in any kind of laboring role.

The intensity of nationalist attitudes among indigenous nationalist leaders was also shaped by the duration of these alien communities in the emerging national society. This terminal factor was closely related to the time-span of the economic role of the regional alien community cited above.

4. *The Indigenous Response to the Degree of Harshness of the Western Colonial Process or the Unequal Treaty Process:* The varying degrees of harshness in the colonization process and the unequal treaty process shaped many political values, modes of behavior, and institutions. A low degree of harshness by Western powers tended to generate a similar response by indigenous nationalist leaders. It encouraged a moderate reaction. The nationalist movement was confined primarily to urban areas and it remained relatively small. It exhibited little or no inclination to use physical force or violence to terminate Western colonial rule. Nationalist leadership in the colonized societies consisted

almost entirely of civilians, primarily lawyers and professional persons, who gained recognition and prestige for their political skills and negotiating ability in obtaining national independence from the Western colonial powers. These leaders were directly involved with Western colonial authorities in drafting mutually acceptable constitutional frameworks for the emerging national society. Some important leaders in the three semi-independent societies were also civilians, largely members of upper-class families, who also won recognition and prestige for their diplomatic skills and negotiating ability in obtaining the abolition of the unequal treaties with Western powers. Many Western historical inputs in both types of society affected by a low degree of harshness continued to be accepted by the indigenous leadership and populace, and they were transferred relatively intact to completely independent or sovereign national societies.

A high degree of harshness in the colonization process or the unequal treaty process, conversely, induced a similar reaction among the indigenous populace. It encouraged the use of violence in the pursuit of national independence and promoted militant forms of nationalism. It produced a nationalist movement which was active in both urban and rural areas. Nationalist leaders in the colonized societies were civilians, yet they developed skills in political maneuver, intrigue, and guerrilla warfare to retain their leadership of the nationalist movements. The violent struggle against Western colonial rule generated large irregular military forces as well as national martyrs and heroes. It helped create the psychological environment and personal sacrifices conducive to the emergence of charismatic nationalist leaders such as Sukarno and Ho Chi Minh. A high degree of harshness in colonized societies also produced relatively large indigenous communist parties which used Western imperialism as the major issue to recruit new party members. Just prior to national independence most indigenous communist leaders also opposed the compromises and concessions granted by the emerging nationalist leaders to the departing Western colonial power. Political leadership in the semi-independent society of China affected by a high degree of harshness consisted of the military leaders of the Chinese Nationalist regime and the party-military leaders of the Chinese Communist movement. Both of these Chinese political organizations used the extensive interference of Western powers under the unequal treaties as a major issue in augmenting their membership and power. Many Western linkages in China were tarnished by the severity of Western diplomatic and military intrusions, and many Western influences were rejected by the Chinese Nationalists as they established their regime on Taiwan and by the Chinese Communists as they gained control of the mainland.

436   The Indigenous Response

5. *The Indigenous Response to the Degree of Military Violence in the Final Stages of the Colonization Process or the Unequal Treaty Process:* A low degree of military violence during the final stages of Western domination induced few if any changes in the emerging political systems. This phenomenon in Ceylon, Korea, Laos, and Cambodia caused no significant expansion of the indigenous nationalist movements, and it preserved the stature of emerging political leaders. Little or no military action precluded the participation of large numbers of indigenous persons in the military defeat of Imperialist Japan or the Western colonial power. It engendered no significant disruption in rural areas. It caused little or no damage to technical or educational facilities capable of assisting economic and social modernization after the achievement of national independence.

A high degree of military violence in the final stages of the Western impact, conversely, induced a variety of political influences. It accelerated the process of nation-building and tended to politicize both urban and rural areas. It increased popular participation in the indigenous nationalist movement and created the opportunity for the emergence of young military heroes such as Aung San in Burma and Ramon Magsaysay in the Philippines seeking important roles in the future political leadership of their emerging national societies. The war against Imperialist Japan temporarily elevated the political stature of Chiang Kai-shek. The wartime achievements of these and other nationalist leaders increased affection and support among their followers.

At the same time, a high degree of military violence induced numerous influences detrimental to the future unity and stability of these emerging national societies. Wartime destruction strengthened a deep-seated fatalism fostered by traditional values in the indigenous cultural system which in turn weakened many rational and humanitarian influences previously implanted by Western historical inputs. Intensive military action brutalized political behavior and reduced respect for human life. It promoted a view that the external world and the domestic society are governed largely by physical forces in which the strong prevail over the weak. This attitude caused widespread alienation and generated increasing rivalry in the struggle for political power. It intensified many grievances between rivaling ethnic, economic, and social groups. A high degree of military violence likewise caused the dispersal of large quantities of small arms among the urban and rural populace which increased a propensity toward violence and anomic political action. Widespread military activity also inflicted physical damage to economic and educational facilities which hampered early modernization efforts in these newly-emerging national societies.

A high degree of military destruction in China induced several new influences in the final stages of the unequal treaty process. The exigencies of World War II caused the United States and Great Britain to abolish their special treaty privileges in 1943 which enhanced Chinese nationalist sentiment in areas outside Japanese control and elevated China's international stature. Yet the widespread understanding among Chinese Nationalist leaders that this action was taken by the two major Western powers only to bolster China's wartime role rather than to recognize its internal judicial and administrative modernization continued to foster anti-Western feelings in the Chinese government and people which in turn hampered the continuation of many Western historical inputs.

A high degree of military violence by Imperialist Japan and Nationalist China engendered new influences in the final stages of several colonization processes in Southeast Asia. Japanese atrocities in Burma, the Philippines, and Malaya throughout World War II, as well as looting by Chinese troops in Burma and northern Vietnam aided in shattering the myth or desirability of Asian unity. These impositions by two major Asian powers also revived some respect for the relative moderation and enlightenment of certain aspects of Western colonial rule. Japanese brutalities engendered intense popular animosity in China and Southeast Asia. They created the issue of post-independence reparations, and hindered the post-war revival of natural trade relations between a highly industrialized society and nearby sources of raw materials. Japanese military occupation of these societies likewise severed relations between the indigenous communist parties and the Soviet Union. Local communist leaders were consequently required to rely on their own initiative and resources throughout the war. Their organizations became increasingly disciplined and unified in the bitter guerrilla warfare against Japanese occupation forces, and they tended to acquire superior military skills and organizational techniques compared to the much larger but less disciplined nationalist insurgent groups. Indigenous communist parties in Burma, Malaya, and the Philippines were therefore primed for violence in the early post-war period, either against the Western colonial power or against the newly-independent national government.

6. *The Indigenous Response to the Psychological, Political, and Economic Effect of World War II on the Attitude of Western Colonial Powers Toward Granting National Independence to Colonized Societies:* The effect of World War II in strengthening the attitude of Western colonial powers to transfer sovereignty promptly to indigenous political leadership enabled most of the previously established Western historical inputs to remain intact. This phenomenon occurred in the American and

British colonial systems. By promoting the rapid transfer of national independence to the Philippines, the United States was required to terminate only its governmental linkage comprising a few remaining colonial administrators. Important non-governmental linkages such as American entrepreneurs and American missionaries remained sizeable and strong. A large American community continued to reside in the newly-independent Republic of the Philippines. A similar attitude by Great Britain caused only the removal of governmental linkages of colonial administrators and some colonial military forces from the newly-independent national societies in South and Southeast Asia. Large non-governmental linkages continued to function as during the pre-independence era. A large British community remained in all of these former colonies.

World War II induced an opposite propensity in the Netherlands and France, and it strengthened the determination of these two Western colonial powers to resist the efforts of indigenous political leaders to achieve national independence. This policy in Indonesia generated additional hostility toward Dutch colonial rule and stigmatized virtually all Dutch linkages in the eyes of the Indonesian leaders and people. When the Netherlands was finally forced to grant independence to its former colony, most Dutch entrepreneurs and missionaries left the newly-independent society. The few Dutch non-governmental linkages which remained in Indonesia operated in a hostile and uncertain environment. Almost all Eurasians went to Holland, and the Dutch community in the Republic of Indonesia rapidly declined. The French adhered to a similar policy and generated widespread animosity toward virtually all French linkages in Vietnam. Most of these colonial groups were also removed at the time of national independence. Only a few French entrepreneurs, missionaries, teachers, and scholars remained in the newly-independent society in South Vietnam; except for a small diplomatic mission, all French linkages were removed from the communist society in North Vietnam.

Conclusion

In spite of some fairly elaborate terminology, chronologies, and typologies presented in this study, its basic methodology is relatively simple. It consists essentially of the isolation, classification, and explanation of politically relevant historical factors — labeled here as *historical inputs* — during the chronological development from their origin until they became a part of a newly independent national society. These historical inputs have been broadly defined as interrelated values, modes of behavior, and institutions which emerged, disappeared, survived, or blended with other historical inputs as they passed through various stages of political history. Numerous concepts and analytical tools have been presented by which these historical inputs can be measured and assessed in some degree in their evolution into the normative, political, and governmental processes of the seventeen emerging polities in the region of Asia.

The study has also included my own form of macro-linkage-analysis designed to explain the cross-societal interactions between external influences and internal factors in the development of a "penetrated political system." This effort has entailed the analysis of politically-relevant historical inputs in the context of their total human and geopolitical environment which, as previously cited, has tried to present the "big picture" of government and politics. The work has gone beyond the country-by-country approach and focused on primary similarities and differences within and between various types of political systems in Asia. This endeavor in turn has sought to make these parts of the newly-independent polities in the region more clear and understandable. Some of the analysis has involved fairly precise calculations of historical data (such as the duration in years of various terminal factors), but much of the quantification effort has evolved fairly broad and comparative measurements (such as the high-low continua used in the terminal analyses and the analysis of the colonization and unequal treaty processes).[1] Elsewhere the research has consisted largely of "broad brush" historical coverage and my own explanations and interpretations. I have made no attempt to elaborate in detail the many interesting ramifications suggested by much of the historical data and analysis. This is a task for future research by new and experienced scholars alike who are interested in the role of history on contemporary political systems.

Part Three of this study dealing with the indigenous response is of special significance to the field of comparative politics. The fusional historical inputs derived from both traditional and Western sources analyzed in this section comprise politically relevant ingredients, elements, factors, or "roots" of independent or sovereign national societies. It is at this point where the comparative analysis of political history used in this book is linked to empirical political theory. Political history obviously did not stop on the day of achieving national independence or complete national sovereignty; political developments continued to be affected by the inexorable force of time. Yet the chronological development of the political system in a specific phase of political history did stop as the polity acquired a totally new form and developed in a new environment. Thereafter different relationships between external and internal factors became involved in the development of the political system. As explained in the Introduction, it is at this point where I would differentiate between the *Westernization* and *modernization* of Asian societies.[2] Westernization, in brief, was a historical impact derived from either the total political control of an indigenous society through colonial rule or the partial political control through the unequal treaty process by Western nations (or in the special case of Japan after 1898, by a technologically advanced nation). This impact on indigenous societies ended at the time of achieving national independence or complete national sovereignty. Modernization obviously overlaps with Westernization, but it is a much more complex process. It consists of the diverse interactions in the development of *independent* societies as they have been shaped by new external influences, including official aid programs of the Western and communist power blocs since the beginning of the Cold War, multinational corporations, regional organizations (such as the Association for Southeast Asian Nations), and the political and technical bodies of the United Nations. Very important, modernization involves increasing increments of indigenously-induced mastery over both human and physical obstacles to national development. It is a condition of an organized society in which one of the most crucial issues for people individually and collectively, as Apter points out, is the vital element of *choice*.[3] Many important aspects of the early phases of this "self-strengthening" process have been discussed and analyzed in Part Three dealing with the response of different Asian societies to either Western colonial rule or the Western-imposed unequal treaties.

The analytical framework presented in this study makes it possible to measure in some degree the traditional, Western, and amalgamated content of the fusional historical inputs of independent Asian societies. These inputs are an important aspect of what Professor Easton has called "situational data" which is necessary for a more precise and reliable method of political analysis.[4] This method makes possible a higher level of order in a complex mass of historical data as well as a more accurate mode of explaining political tendencies and trends. The accuracy of this method of analysis obviously has many limitations since many factors affecting human phenomena are themselves in a process of change and are subject to numerous unforeseen forces. Organized polities are always subject to human will and some freedom of choice in their collective actions. At the same time, certain predictions of political developments based on systematic historical research can be made. Professors Almond and Powell have stated:

> The processes of political change are extremely complex and rest
> upon a very large number of interacting factors. Yet, the hope
> for prediction and, indeed, for any kind of reasonably
> parsimonious explanation, lies in the fact that every system is the
> prisoner of its past. The way in which a system faced certain
> types of problems, and the nature of its present characteristics as
> they bear the mark of those efforts, limit and constrain the
> alternatives which lie before it. History does not, of course,
> determine the future, but it may well limit or foreclose certain
> alternatives.[5]

Some explanatory capacity of my analytical framework can be gained by utilizing a form of *longitudinal political analysis*.[6] This method consists of positing reasoned judgments based on the accumulated or aggregated combination of all politically relevant fusional historical inputs in each national society at the time of its independence or sovereignty. It consists, in brief, of blending or merging all political factors and assessing their role in the functioning of the entire polity. This method would require an evaluation of political values, modes of behavior, and institutions as they evolved through the era of the traditional society and the period of colonial rule or the unequal treaties, and as they were affected by relevant terminal factors. It would show with some degree of accuracy the nature of these historical inputs as they formed the normative, political, and governmental processes of a new political system. This analytical procedure would include appropriate quantitative data, but it would rely considerably on qualitative judgments and interpretations.

Such a process of analysis would obviously be extremely lengthy and complicated. Some of its explanations would always be subject to controversy and conflicting interpretations due to new historical data. Yet longitudinal political analysis could give the political scientist a more accurate knowledge of the historical environment or historical foundation of a new political system than is now possible. It could delineate the salient variables in the political landscape at the beginning of a new national society. It could provide some understanding of the inter-relationships between complementary and competitive political forces in any modernizing nation-state. This effort, for example, could shed more light on the basic factors which have contributed to the preservation of constitutional democracy in some Asian societies since the termination of Western colonial rule. It could also provide better knowledge of important historical inputs which have bolstered authoritarian influences in the period of the independent or sovereign national society. These assessments are extremely complex and involve many factors besides the historical, but the conceptual tools presented in this study can provide useful qualitative and quantitative explanations regarding these perennial academic and practical problems.

I will illustrate this method of longitudinal political analysis with the case of India where the persistence of constitutional democracy since August 1947 has amazed many political scientists and political observers. The continuation of "the world's largest democracy" with its ancient religions, abject poverty, and manifold social problems since national independence has aroused widespread interest. Many observers have attributed this accomplishment to such factors as the political skills of Jawaharlal Nehru, the colonial "legacy" of the British, and the ethnic and cultural pluralism in the Indian sub-continent. Many political analysts have also predicted the end of democracy in India and the emergence of an authoritarian political system as attempted by Mrs. Indira Gandhi from 1975 to 1977.

Table XXI below shows the aggregation of politically relevant values, modes of behavior, and institutions comprising the traditional, Western, and fusional historical inputs in the historical environment in India which tended to strengthen democracy at the time of its national independence.

Table XXI. An illustration of longitudinal political analysis showing an aggregation of politically relevant values, modes of behavior, and institutions comprising aspects of traditional, Western, and fusional historical inputs in India which strengthened constitutional democracy at the time of its national independence.

VALUES — TRADITIONAL HISTORICAL INPUTS — shaped by military invasions, foreign traders, foreign communities, high-exposure strategic location, increasing population size, pluralistic population composition.

Religious Eclecticism — Psychological Pluralism: individual tolerance, moderation, consensus; duration of 4257 years.

VALUES — WESTERN HISTORICAL INPUTS — Shaped by economic type of British colonial aggrandizement, eclectic-pragmatic concept of British colonial rule, high-transferable political and administrative structures maintaining British colonial rule, high-transformative economic and social policies in the colonized society.

Concept of the Nation-State: secularism, achievement, change, social mobilization; duration of approximately 90 years.

Concept of Progress: secularism, achievement, change; duration of approximately 190 years.

Concept of Equality: individualism, achievement, change; duration of approximately 90 years.

Modernization: secularism, universalism, achievement, change; duration of approximately 190 years.

Ideological Pluralism: diversity, tolerance, consensus; duration of approximately 90 years.

Moderate Nationalism: individual freedom, national freedom, tolerance, consensus; duration of approximately 60 years.

Liberal and Leftist Ideologies: economic egalitarianism, social welfare, change; duration of 27 years.

VALUES — FUSIONAL HISTORICAL INPUTS — shaped by indigenous response to small British governmental linkages and large non-governmental linkages, the absence of sizeable regional alien communities, the low degree of harshness of British colonial rule, the moderate response to the strong desire of Great Britain to grant national independence shortly after World War II, the militant anti-Pakistani orientation and national unity caused by the high degree of violence at the time of partition.

Progressive Norms in Urban Areas: eclecticism, secularism, experimentation, assimilation; duration of 97 years.

Differentiated Nationalism: pluralism, tolerance, consensus; duration of approximately 62 years.

Table XXI Cont'd.

Constitutional Democracy: limited government, political freedom,
civil rights, political participation; duration of 28 years.
Socialism: economic egalitarianism, social welfare, political
participation; duration of 27 years.

MODES OF BEHAVIOR — TRADITIONAL HISTORICAL INPUTS
Separation of Religion and Politics: functional differentiation,
tolerance, compromise, consensus; duration of 2957 years.
High Adaptability to Foreign-induced Change: tolerance,
assimilation, consensus; duration of 4257 years.
*Low Degree of Cohesiveness within the Hierarchical Class
Structure of Great and Middle Traditions:* tolerance, compromise,
consensus; duration of approximately 2700 years.
*Low Degree of Cohesiveness of the Societal Structure of Great
and Middle Traditions:* tolerance, ethnic and cultural pluralism;
duration of approximately 2700 years.

MODES OF BEHAVIOR — WESTERN HISTORICAL INPUTS
Expanded Cultural Pluralism: individual freedom, tolerance,
compromise, consensus; duration of approximately 190 years.
Modern Urbanization: universalism, achievement, secularism,
change; duration of 90 years.
Spread of English Language: universalism, secularism, Western
liberalism; duration of 190 years.
Humanitarian Reforms: individual dignity, tolerance, change;
duration of 190 years.
Promotion or Performance of Scholarly Research: cultural pride,
self-confidence, change; duration of 117 years.
Increased Sub-system Differentiation: secularism, achievement,
change; duration of 190 years.
Modernizing Indigenous Entreprenurial Class: secularism,
achievement, change; duration of approximately 67 years.
Urban and Rural Proletariat: secularism, economic security;
duration of approximately 47 years.

MODES OF BEHAVIOR — FUSIONAL HISTORICAL INPUTS
English Language in Urban Areas: universalism, secularism,
achievement, change, social mobilization; duration of 117 years.
Ethnic Culture: pluralism, tolerance, consensus; duration of 190
years.
Modern Education: achievement, change, pluralism, social

Table XXI Cont'd.

mobilization; duration of 112 years.

Modern Commerce: urbanization, secularism, achievement, change; duration of 190 years.

Modern Industry: urbanization, secularism, achievement, change; duration of 57 years.

Urban Political Culture: universalism, secularism, pluralism, consensus; duration of 90 years.

Modern Political Communication: secularism, achievement, pluralism, political participation; duration of 47 years.

Interest Groups: secularism, pluralism, consensus; duration of 27 years.

Dominant Political Party System: pluralism, political competition, political participation; duration of 62 years.

Civilian Political Leadership: moderation, pluralism, consensus; duration of 38 years.

INSTITUTIONS — TRADITIONAL HISTORICAL INPUTS

Numerous Middle Traditions: ethnic and cultural pluralism, particularism; duration of those intact at time of Western impact ranging from 83 years to approximately 400 years; duration of many defunct middle traditions ranging from 100 years to 600 years; duration between their demise and date of initial encounter of subsequent traditional society with Western impact ranging from 50 years to 4000 years.

Few Defunct Great Traditions: memories of cultural grandeur and achievement, collective pride, self-confidence; duration ranging from 147 years to 325 years — duration between their demise and initial encounter of subsequent traditional society with Western impact ranging from 50 years to 1942 years.

INSTITUTIONS — WESTERN HISTORICAL INPUTS

Western-oriented Institutions of Higher Education: achievement, universalism, secularism, change; duration of approximately 167 years.

Rationalized Indigenous Bureaucracy: secularism, achievement, stability, social mobilization; duration of approximately 60 years.

Constitution Democracy: limited government, civil rights, political freedom, duration of 90 years.

Modernized Indigenous Military Forces: secularism, achievement, stability, security; duration of 117 years.

Modern Mass Media: secularism, achievement, change, social mobilization; duration of 127 years.

Table XXI Cont'd.

INSTITUTIONS — FUSIONAL HISTORICAL INPUTS
  *Declining Traditional Class Structure: secularism, achievement,
  change; duration of 190 years.
  *Modernizing Transitional Class Structure: secularism,
  achievement, change, consensus; duration of 97 years.
  *Constitutional Framework: limited allocations of governmental
  authority, political participation; duration of 38 years.
  *Modernizing Executive: national unity, consensus, achievement,
  change; duration of 28 years.
  *Modernizing Administration: national unity, stability, achievement,
  change; duration of 57 years.
  *Modernizing Legislature: political representation, political
  participation, pluralism, social mobilization; duration of 38 years.
  *Modernizing Judiciary: limited government, civil rights, political
  freedom; duration of 27 years.

The accumulative effect of reinforcing tendencies in similar politically
relevant characteristics as shown in Table XXI provide a reasonably
good basis on which to predict that the historical environment of the
Indian political system would foster many democratic values, modes of
behavior, and institutions in the post-independence era. Salient
democratic characteristics of varying durations which acquired strength
and influence from the concatenation of traditional, Western, and
fusional historical inputs include pluralism, tolerance, moderation, consensus, secularism, achievement, change, political freedom, and political
participation. These democratic qualities were especially significant in
their role in key elements of the newly-independent Indian polity such as
the urban political culture, free political communications, British-
educated civilian political leadership, and rationalized bureaucracy.

At the same time, it is important in predicting the continuation of
strong democratic influences in the Indian political system after August
1947 to cite the many authoritarian characteristics in the historical
environment at that time which can also be assessed by using
longitudinal political analysis. It is not necessary to make a complete
analysis of these factors here and a brief illustration of their
accumulative historical effect should suffice. Some salient characteristics
generated by traditional, Western, and fusional historical inputs which
oriented the Indian political system toward authoritarianism include the
following: dogmatism, pietism, a disdain for secular affairs, and a high
capacity for suffering induced by the value of religious idealism-political

apathy for a duration of 3257 years; a sense of inertia in secular affairs and a high capacity for suffering induced by fatalism-historical determinism for a duration of 4257 years; a growing indigenous desire for national unity and national security induced by the concept of the nation-state for a duration of 62 years; ascription, particularism, inequality, and human degradation induced by the caste system for 2957 years; inertia, ascription, and political apathy among the preponderance of the population dwelling in little traditions for a duration of 4257 years. Some values included in the longitudinal political analysis of democratic influences in the historical environment of the Indian polity also strengthened certain authoritarian tendencies including modernization, achievement, and change which induced an intense indigenous desire to "catch-up" with Western nations in economic and social standards by a highly centralized and efficient political system. Some institutions in the historical environment of India which promoted democracy thereby had the potential of enhancing authoritarian political rule, including the bureaucracy, the armed forces, and the police which upheld the responsibility for preserving progress and unity in the newly-independent national society.

In addition to the predictive capability of longitudinal political analysis, a more systematic methodology using historical data can be employed in other areas of comparative politics. One of these areas is political development. This aspect of the discipline of political science is relatively new and much more thought and research will be required before a genuine scientific approach can be made in assessing different levels and sequences of political development. Yet some consensus among political scientists already exists that three criteria of political development are equality, capacity, and differentiation.[7] A major conclusion of my study is that each of these criteria is closely related to the traditional, Western, and fusional historical inputs used in my own analytical framework and that these historical factors can be more accurately assessed than in the past.

The concept of equality in Asian societies is one of the major Western historical inputs originally disseminated by the colonization process or the unequal treaty process. This distinctly Western value penetrated more deeply into colonized societies where the colonization process utilized high transferable political and administrative structures and high transformative economic and social policies. This phenomena was most advanced in the colonized societies under British or American colonial rule. The idea of equality was applied to both the emerging nation-state and to the individual. Equality was less intense in colonial systems with low transferable political and administrative structures under Dutch,

French, or Japanese colonial rule. In the semi-independent societies, the idea of equality was confined largely to the nation-state during the unequal treaty process and it was not widely applied to the individual. Equality was consequently more advanced in the political systems in India, Pakistan, Ceylon, Burma, Malaya, and the Philippines than in Nationalist China, Japan, Thailand, Vietnam, or Indonesia.

The capacity of the political system is closely related to the skills of the political elite and the bureaucracy in managing the outputs or official policies related to the economy and the entire society. As shown in this study, the capacity to cope with the physical and human environment was a function of specific fusional historical inputs in the indigenous response, especially religious or doctrinal norms, the political culture, the political leadership, and the executive-administrative structures in the governmental process. The highest degree of capacity among the emerging polities in Asia was achieved in the bureaucratic polities in Nationalist China, Japan, and Thailand with their spreading urban secular culture, an increasingly military-dominated class structure, a progressive and bureaucratic political culture, a military-oriented political leadership, and rationalized administrative structures. A similar assessment of political capacity would show somewhat less advancement in the quasi-democracies in India, Pakistan, Ceylon, Burma, Malaya, and the Philippines where more emphasis was placed on democratic procedures and individual freedom.

The quality of differentiation is also affected by many historical inputs, especially the degree of eclecticism in traditional cultural values, the degree of transferability of political and administrative structures in the colonization process or the degree of demonstration effect of Western official missions in the unequal treaty process, and the political ideology and political leadership in the indigenous response. The highest level of differentiation was achieved in the six quasi-democracies with their high assimilative capability, specialized political organizations, and a democratic and pluralistic ethos seeking a consensus on political issues from numerous groups and governmental institutions. Political differentiation was considerably less in all other emerging societies in the region with their more centralized political and administrative structures.

The different levels of development in equality, capacity, and differentiation in these and other Asian societies at their moment of independence are consequently inextricably involved with their political history. A more accurate measurement of relevant historical factors can provide some basis for explaining post-independence advances and retrogressions according to these three criteria. Any theory of political development must therefore include an analysis of political history.

According to Professor Pye, "In the last analysis the problems of political development revolve around the relationships between the political culture, the authoritative structures, and the general political process."[8] Each of the three political elements cited by Pye are essential parts of the normative, governmental, and political processes in my own analytical framework of an emerging national society.

Another area in comparative politics where a more accurate and orderly use of historical data can be effectively employed is in area studies. This aspect of political science, as in other social sciences, has made little if any progress in utilizing a common approach to the role of history with some kind of precision. Professor Robert Ward referred to this problem in his presidential address to the annual meeting of the American Political Science Association in 1973 when he cited the three "shared characteristics" of area specialists as a concern for language, culture, and history. He described the historical factor and its related role in area specialization as follows:

> A final characteristic that area specialists tend to share is a high regard for the importance and relevance of history as a determinant of political outcomes. This is really a subcategory and a consequence of their concern with the cultural context of politics. One does not study culture in a historical vacuum. The same should be true of politics. It is a conceit born of the Enlightenment and reinforced by certain trends in current social science theorizing that political attitudes, behavior, or institutions can be explained or understood in terms that do not involve a substantial historical element.
>
> This set of characteristics — a concern with language, with culture, and with history — is really all the "theoretical" or "methodological" baggage that area specialists possess in common. I personally do not find it a very impressive endowment.... [It] is basically commonsensical, wholly predictable, and... inevitable given the nature of their professional subject-matter. It is certainly not of an order of complexity, precision, interrelatedness, or pretentiousness that would justify labeling it as a methodology or even a technique.[9]

The analytical framework presented in this study may be useful in some degree in meeting this important need for a historical methodology suitable for area studies. While it utilizes historical data only from Asian societies, it can with some modifications be applied to other regions. The analysis of sacred-oriented traditional societies as presented in Chapter

One, for example, can be applied to emerging political systems in the Middle East such as Turkey, Iran, Iraq, Syria, Jordan, Egypt, and Saudi Arabia which were also built on sacred-oriented cultural systems and have many values, modes of behavior, and institutions derived from one or more religions. The pre-Western class structures in these Middle Eastern societies were hierarchical and sacred-oriented as in South and Southeast Asia. All had powerful traditional historical inputs from one or more great traditions of long duration and relatively few traditional historical inputs from middle traditions. All were shaped by factors used in my methodology of macro-linkage-analysis, especially military invasions, foreign missionaries, foreign traders, and indigenous returnees. Most were subjected to the Western impact in the form of indirect colonial rule in which the urban centers were heavily influenced by both governmental and non-governmental linkages from the West while other sectors of the society remained untouched by Western historical inputs.

The historical role in the emerging political systems in sub-Sahara Africa can be analyzed in a manner similar to the atomized-animist traditional society in the Philippines with a near-total absence of great or middle traditions prior to the Western impact. The developing nations in this region were shaped almost entirely by a direct form of Western colonial rule motivated by what I have labeled an economic type of aggrandizement for a relatively brief duration. Western historical inputs in Africa were transmitted to the colonized society largely through the Western linkages of colonial administrators, entrepreneurs, and Christian missionaries. The indigenous response took place primarily among Christian converts and it occurred almost entirely in a very brief period of ten to fifteen years prior to achieving national independence.

The polities in Latin America were likewise shaped almost entirely by the Western impact and the indigenous response in spite of the culturally impressive but politically fragile pre-Western empires of the Mayas, Incas, and Aztecs. In many respects the formation of the political systems of Latin America was also like that in the Philippines in which the dominant pre-Western political experience was confined to the village culture of numerous and scattered little traditions. The historical analysis of these emerging national societies during the important period of the Western impact and the indigenous response can be assessed in considerable detail by using many conceptual tools presented in this study.

With further development and greater sophistication in historically-oriented political models, I see no reason why historical research on the developed polities of Europe cannot contribute to a more orderly and accurate method of political analysis. Many aspects of the analytical framework presented in this study may already be applicable to the political systems of this important region. Pre-industrial European societies resembled many aspects of the sacred-oriented traditional societies in South and Southeast Asia. All had hierarchical class structures with a priestly class exerting a significant political role. Important traditional historical inputs were shaped by both great and middle traditions. Except for Great Britain where modern industrialization began, the "Western impact" in most emerging European societies consisted of the spread of science and technology with all its political and social consequences. This dissemination can be analyzed fairly well with the historical methodology used in this study, especially the spread of politically relevant historical inputs through governmental linkages such as diplomats and national military forces and non-governmental linkages such as entrepreneurs and indigenous returnees. The indigenous response in each European society can be viewed as the domestic reaction to modern industrialization; it can be measured in some degree as politically relevant values, modes of behavior, and institutions used in my model of an emerging national society. The termination of these fusional historical inputs could be made at the time of the economic "take-off" of these societies when, according to Professor Walt Rostow, their political development had achieved the necessary "building of an effective centralized national state" and economic growth had become a "normal condition."[10]

Finally, a more systematic analysis of historical factors can be useful to government policy-makers. A more precise understanding of history can provide some basis for better knowledge and prediction in this intensely precarious "art of the possible." Many non-historical factors are obviously important in the selection of foreign policy alternatives, yet a more accurate and thorough understanding of the traditional, Western, and fusional content of historical elements in contemporary political systems can improve the quality of foreign policy decisions. Along this line Professor Black has stated:

> The role of historical analysis as a guide to the future is essentially one of determining the dimensions of the problems that are likely to engage policy. The pitfalls of the historical perspective as a guide to policy are many... [Yet at] the very least, an understanding of history should help one to ascertain those changes that are likely to take place regardless of policy, those that are likely to be achieved — if at all — only at enormous human cost, and the range of choices within which policy can operate on the basis of acceptable costs.[11]

452 Westernization of Asia

The methodology presented in this book has analyzed many historical factors in the political systems of Asia which have been of great concern to foreign policy-makers since these societies became independent or completely sovereign and which will continue to be of major significance in the future. It has shown, for example, many of the historical factors explaining why some nations in Asia have upheld the primacy of foreign policy while others have focused largely on domestic affairs. It has shown many historical factors explaining why moderate nationalism is dominant in some Asian societies and a form of militant nationalism is ascendant in others. The contemporary role of other historical inputs are also of major interest to government policy-makers, including the strength of achievement values which affects economic development, the pre-independence activities of major political parties which have shaped their post-independence influence, and the pre-independence experience of modernizing bureaucracies which has affected the stability of entire national societies.

This study is only a modest start in the crucial area relating history to diplomacy and foreign-policy making. Yet, hopefully it can stimulate similar efforts by other scholars and contribute in some degree to peace and progress in Asia and other regions of the world.

Notes

Introduction

1. Hans Kohn, *Orient and Occident* (New York: The John Day Company, 1934).
2. Ibid., p. v.
3. Maurice Zinkin, *Asia and the West* (New York: Institute of Pacific Relations, 1953).
4. K.M. Panikkar, *Asia and Western Dominance* (London: George Allen and Unwin Ltd., 1953).
5. Donald F. Lach, *Asia in the Making of Europe* (Chicago: The University of Chicago Press, 1965).
6. Some of the major works on political development and political modernization are Gabriel Almond and James S. Coleman, eds., *The Politics of the Developing Areas* (Princeton: Princeton University Press, 1960); Gabriel Almond and G. B. Powell, Jr., *Comparative Politics: A Developmental Approach* (Boston: Little, Brown and Company, 1966); Samuel H. Beer, *Modern Political Development* (New York: Random House, Inc., 1974); David E. Apter, *The Politics of Modernization* (Chicago: The University of Chicago Press, 1965); A.F.K. Organski, *The Stages of Political Development* (New York: Alfred A. Knopf, 1965); Cyril E. Black, *The Dynamics of Modernization* (New York: Harper and Row, 1966); Lucian W. Pye, *Aspects of Political Development* (Boston: Little, Brown and Company, 1966); Lucian W. Pye and Sidney Verba, eds., *Political Culture and Political Development* (Princeton: Princeton University Press, 1965); Donald E. Smith, *Religion and Political Development* (Boston: Little, Brown and Company, 1970); S.N. Eisenstadt, *Modernization: Protest and Change* (Englewood Cliffs, N.J.: Prentice-Hall, Inc., 1966); Edward Shils, *Political Development in the New States* (The Hague: Mouton, 1962); Daniel Lerner, *The Passing of Traditional Society* (Glencoe, Illinois: Free Press, 1963); Joseph Lapalombara and Myron Weiner, eds., *Political Parties and Political Development* (Princeton: Princeton University Press, 1966); Samuel P. Huntington, *Political Order in Changing Societies* (New Haven, Conn.: Yale University Press, 1968); Clifford Geertz, ed., *Old Societies and New States* (Glencoe, Illinois: Free Press, 1963).

7. Samuel P. Huntington, "The Change to Change," *Comparative Politics* (April 1971), p. 313.

8. George F.W. Young, "Civis Americanus sum: Are we, too, to 'decline and fall'?" *The University of Chicago Magazine* (Spring 1975), pp. 20–1. For an explanation of civilizations as the basic unit of historical analysis see D.C. Somervell's abridgement of Volumes I–VI of Arnold J. Toynbee, *A Study of History* (London: Oxford University Press, 1946), Chaps. I, II.

9. See David Easton, "An Approach to the Analysis of Political Systems," *World Politics* (April 1957), pp. 383–408; *A Framework for Political Analysis* (Englewood Cliffs, New Jersey: Prentice-Hall, Inc., 1965), pp. 112–7; *A Systems Analysis of Political Life* (New York: John Wiley and Sons, Inc., 1965), Parts Two and Three.

10. Gabriel A. Almond and G. Bingham Powell, Jr., *Comparative Politics: A Developmental Approach* (Boston: Little, Brown and Company, 1966), p. 169.

11. Throughout this study the shorter terminology, "the indigenous response," will be used rather than the longer term, "the indigenous response to the Western impact." It will refer to the phenomena of Asian societies and peoples responding and reacting to the impact of Western influences. See Rajni Kothari, *Politics in India* (Boston: Little, Brown and Company, 1970), pp. 44–50; Vincent A. Smith, *The Oxford History of India* (London: Oxford University Press, 1958), pp. 729–39; John K. Fairbank, Edwin O. Reischauer, and Albert M. Craig, *East Asia: The Modern Transformation* (Boston: Houghton Mifflin Company, 1965), pp. 179–243, 313–407; John Bastin and Harry J. Benda, *A History of Modern Southeast Asia* (Englewood Cliffs, N.J.: Prentice-Hall, Inc., 1968), pp. 67–152.

Part One: The Traditional Society

1. Cyril E. Black, "Foreign Area Studies: Emergent Changes and Trends," in Fred W. Riggs, ed., *International Studies: Present Status and Future Prospects* (Monograph 12 in a series sponsored by The American Academy of Political and Social Science, Philadelphia, October 1971), p. 8.

2. Donald Eugene Smith, *Religion and Political Development* (Boston: Little, Brown and Company, 1970), p. 5.

3. Several qualifications are involved in the classification of the atomized animist cultural system in the Philippines in the sacred-oriented category. Actually, all cultural systems in Asia had a strong animistic orientation which underlay their "higher" religions or doctrines. Also, animist beliefs were essentially focused on surrounding physical objects and hence had a significant secular quality. Yet animist beliefs in the Philippines were the only "religious" or "sacred" values in an area which

was untouched by any of the major religions or philosophies of Asia. It was the only cultural system in Asia devoid of any centralized political authority and it consisted of hundreds of small autonomous village communities. For these and other reasons I have called it an "atomized animist" cultural system and placed it in the sacred-oriented classification.

4. At this point it may be useful to explain that all Confucian cultural systems had some religious elements. China, Korea, and Vietnam were influenced in their early development by Mahayana Buddhism and Taoism. Japan experienced strong religious influences from Shinto, Taoism, and various forms of Buddhism. The predominant orientation of these cultural systems on the eve of the Western impact, however, was secular and this-worldly.

5. Robert Redfield, *Peasant Society and Culture* (Chicago: University of Chicago Press, 1956), p. 27.

6. Ibid., p. 41.

7. Gideon Sjoberg, "Folk and 'Feudal' Societies," *The American Journal of Sociology* (November 1952), pp. 231-9.

8. My use of the term middle tradition has some theoretical shortcomings since it also often had one or more intermediate levels of administrative authority between the central political elite and the little traditions in rural villages. Yet I have employed this concept to overcome some of the analytical deficiencies in the oversimplified two-level approach of Redfield. The use of the middle tradition does provide some basis for a more realistic empirical framework for analyzing the societal structure of the traditional society.

Chapter 1. Sacred-Oriented Traditional Societies

1. For an explanation of politically relevant elements of Hinduism see A. L. Basham, *The Wonder That Was India* (London: Sidgwick and Jackson, 1954), Chapter IV; Percival Spear, *India: A Modern History* (Ann Arbor: The University of Michigan Press, 1972), Chapter II; Amaury De Riencourt, *The Soul of India* (New York: Harper and Brothers, 1960), Chapters III, IV, VII; William T. de Bary, ed., *Sources of Indian Tradition* (New York: Columbia University Press, 1958), Chapters IX–XIII.

2. Norman D. Palmer, *The Indian Political System* (New York: Houghton Mifflin Company, 1971), Second Edition, pp. 16-8.

3. Rajni Kothari, *Politics in India* (Boston: Little, Brown and Company, 1970), pp. 266-8. See also De Riencourt, op. cit., pp. 106-17.

4. Vincent A. Smith, *The Oxford History of India* (London: Oxford University Press, 1958), pp. 61-70.

5. Kothari, op. cit., p. 23. In some historical works the term *"varna"* has also been translated as "class" rather than "caste." Both terms refer

to the extended kinship grouping of early Hindu society. See Spear, op. cit., p. 41; de Bary, op. cit., pp. 224–8; Bashram, op. cit., pp. 148–51; De Riencourt, op. cit., pp. 95–103.

6. Vincent Smith, op. cit., p. 62.

7. Donald Eugene Smith, *Religion and Political Development* (Boston: Little, Brown and Company, 1970), p. 37.

8. S. N. Eisenstadt, *The Political Systems of Empires* (New York: The Free Press of Glencoe, 1963), p. 62.

9. See Bashram, op. cit., pp. 81–93; De Riencourt, op. cit., pp. 77–89.

10. Lucian W. Pye, *Politics, Personality, and Nation-Building: Burma's Search for Identity* (New Haven: Yale University Press, 1962), p. 73.

11. Ibid., p. 77.

12. Palmer, op. cit., pp. 167–9.

13. Robert Redfield, *Peasant Society and Culture* (Chicago: University of Chicago Press, 1956), p. 61.

14. For a detailed interpretation of politically relevant elements of Buddhism see Edward J. Thomas, *The History of Buddhist Thought* (New York: Barnes and Noble, Inc., 1933), Chapters VI–X; Helmuth von Glasenapp, *Buddhism: A Non-Theistic Religion* (London: George Allen and Unwin Ltd., 1970), Chapters 2, 3; Ananda K. Coomaraswamy, *Buddha and the Gospel of Buddhism* (New York: Harper and Row, Publishers, 1964), Chapters I–V.

15. G. Coedes, *The Indianized States of Southeast Asia* (Honolulu: East-West Center Press, 1968), pp. 14–35.

16. Donald Smith, op. cit., pp. 43–4.

17. W. Howard Wriggins, *Ceylon: Dilemmas of a New Nation* (Princeton: Princeton University Press, 1960), p. 182.

18. See Kemal A. Faruki, *The Evolution of Islamic Constitutional Theory and Practice* (Karachi: National Publishing House Ltd., 1971); W. Montgomery Watt, *Islamic Philosophy and Theology* (Edinburgh: Edinburgh University Press, 1962); Ilse Lichtenstadter, *Islam and the Modern Age* (New York: Bookman Associates, 1958), Chapters II, III, VIII; Erwin I. J. Rosenthal, *Islam in the Modern National State* (London: Cambridge University Press, 1965), Chapter 2; Murray T. Titus, *Indian Islam: A Religious History of Islam in India* (London: Oxford University Press, 1930); Clifford Geertz, *Islam Observed: Religious Developments in Morocco and Indonesia* (New Haven: Yale University Press, 1968.

19. See Vincent Smith, op. cit., pp. 232–80; D. G. E. Hall, *A History of South-east Asia* (London: Macmillan and Company, Ltd., 1955), pp. 176–85; John F. Cady, *Southeast Asia: Its Historical Development* (New York: McGraw-Hill Book Company, 1964), Chapter 8; Brian Harrison, *South-east Asia: A Short History* (New York: St. Martin's Press, 1967), Chapter VI.

20. David Joel Steinberg, ed., *In Search of Southeast Asia* (New York: Praeger Publishers, Inc., 1971), p. 74.

21. John H. Kautsky, ed., *Political Change in Underdeveloped Countries* (New York: John Wiley and Sons, Inc., 1962), p. 17.
22. Donald Smith, op. cit., p. 66.
23. Vincent Smith, op. cit., p. 359.
24. For a description of early Filipino society see Teodoro A. Agoncillo and Oscar M. Alfonso, *A Short History of the Filipino People* (Quezon City: University of the Philippines, 1960), Chapters II, III; Gregorio F. Zaide, *Philippine Political and Cultural History* (Manila: Philippine Education Company, 1957), Vol. I, Chapters II-VI.
25. Onofre D. Corpuz, *The Philippines* (Englewood Cliffs, New Jersey: Prentice-Hall, Inc., 1965), pp. 22-3.
26. William McCord, *The Springtime of Freedom* (New York: Oxford University Press, 1965), p. 27.
27. Agoncillo and Alfonso, op. cit., pp. 23-30.
28. Jean Grossholz, *Politics in the Philippines* (Boston: Little, Brown and Company, 1965), p. 17.
29. Zaide, op. cit., pp. 57-9.

Chapter 2: Secular-Oriented Traditional Societies

1. For a historical background on political elements of Confucianism see Edwin O. Reischauer and John K. Fairback, *East Asia: The Great Tradition* (Boston: Houghton Mifflin Company, 1958), Chapter III; William T. de Bary, ed., *Sources of Chinese Tradition* (New York: Columbia University Press, 1960), Chapters VI-IX; Amaury De Riencourt, *The Soul of China* (New York: Coward-McCann, Inc., 1958), Chapters 2-5; Kenneth S. Latourette, *The Chinese: Their History and Culture* (New York: The Macmillan Company, 1946), Chapters II, III; Owen and Eleanor Lattimore, *China: A Short History* (New York: W. W. Norton & Company, 1944).
2. Reischauer and Fairbanks, op. cit., p. 70.
3. See William E. Henthorn, *A History of Korea* (New York: The Free Press, 1971), Chapters 4, 5; Shannon McCune, *Korea's Heritage: A Regional and Social Geography* (Rutland Vermont: Charles E. Tuttle Company, 1956), Chapters 3, 4; Bong-youn Choy, *Korea: A History* (Rutland, Vermont: Charles E. Tuttle Company, 1971), Chapters 2-4; Gregory Henderson, *Korea: The Politics of the Vortex* (Cambridge: Harvard University Press, 1968), Chapters 2, 3; Joseph Buttinger, *The Smaller Dragon: A Political History of Vietnam* (New York: Frederick A. Praeger, 1958), Chapters I-III; Ellen J. Hammer, *Vietnam: Yesterday and Today* (New York: Holt, Rinehart and Winston, Inc., 1966), pp. 54-102; Dennis J. Duncanson, *Government and Revolution in Vietnam* (New York: Oxford University Press, 1968), Chapter 2.

4. Dun J. Li, *The Ageless Chinese: A History* (New York: Charles Scribner's Sons, 1971), p. 148.
5. Reischauer and Fairbank, op. cit., pp. 82–97; Latourette, op. cit., pp. 88–98.
6. Paul M. A. Linebarger, Djang Chu, and Ardath W. Burks, *Far Eastern Governments and Politics* (Princeton, New Jersey: D. Van Nostrand Company, Inc., 1954), p. 39.
7. Reischauer and Fairbank, op. cit., p. 81.
8. Ibid., p. 426–34.
9. Cited in John K. Fairbank, *The United States and China* (Cambridge, Massachusetts: Harvard University Press, 1971), p. 21.
10. Linebarger, Chu, and Burks, op. cit., p. 9.
11. Reischauer and Fairbank, op. cit., pp. 85–133.
12. Henthorn, op. cit., pp. 34–52; Choy, op. cit., pp. 21–9.
13. Buttinger, op. cit., pp. 129–76; Duncanson, op. cit., pp. 39–54.
14. For a description of politically relevant aspects of pre-Western history in Japan see Reischauer and Fairbank, op. cit., Chapters 11, 12: William T. de Bary, ed., *Sources of Japanese Tradition* (New York: Columbia University Press, 1958), Chapters III–V; George B. Sansom, *A History of Japan to 1334* (Stanford: Stanford University Press, 1958), Chapters II–IV; Katsuro Hara, *An Introduction to the History of Japan* (New York: G. P. Putnam's Sons, 1920), Chapters III–VI; John Whitney Hall, *Japan: From Prehistory to Modern Times* (New York: Delacorte Press, 1968), Chapters 2–5.
15. Reischauer and Fairbank, op. cit., pp. 541–2.
16. See Edwin O. Reischauer, *The United States and Japan* (Cambridge, Massachusetts: Harvard University Press, 1954), pp. 129–32.
17. G. B. Sansom, *The Western World and Japan* (New York: Alfred A. Knopf, 1965), pp. 183–6.
18. Reischauer, op. cit., pp. 133–41.
19. Mikiso Hane, *Japan: A Historical Survey* (New York: Charles Scribner's Sons, 1972), pp. 152–65.
20. Sansom, op. cit., p. 169.
21. Reischauer, op. cit., p. 136–7.
22. Sansom, op. cit., p. 182.
23. Hane, op. cit., pp. 166–8.
24. Reischauer, op. cit., pp. 156–63.
25. John Whitney Hall, "Japan" in Robert E. Ward and Dankwart A. Rustow, *Political Modernization in Japan and Turkey* (Princeton, New Jersey: Princeton University Press, 1964), p. 19.
26. Sansom, op. cit., p. 181.
27. Hane, op. cit., p. 159.

Chapter 3: The External Environment and Linkages

1. James N. Rosenau, ed., *Linkage Politics: Essays on the Convergence of National and International Systems* (New York: The Free Press, 1969), p. 45.
2. James N. Rosenau, "Pre-theories and Theories of Foreign Policy," in R. Barry Farrell, ed., *Approaches to Comparative and International Politics* (Evanston, Illinois: Northwestern University Press, 1966), p. 20.
3. Vincent A. Smith, *The Oxford History of India* (London: Oxford University Press, 1958), Chaptes 1-3; Radhakamal Mukerjee, *A History of Indian Civilization* (Bombay: Hind Kitabs Ltd., 1956), Chapters VIII-XI.
4. Hinduism and Buddhism (after Asoka) extended their influences in India and elsewhere in Asia by voluntaristic and nonmilitant means. Islam spread to Southeast Asia in a similar manner. Confucianism, on the other hand, relied on military conquest during two major cultural expansions to Vietnam (221 B.C.-939 A.D.) and to Korea (during the Han, Yuan, and Ching dynasties). At other times, Imperial China upheld the view that its culture was to be envied by societies living away from its borders and to be absorbed by societies living near its borders. It never sought to spread Confucianism like a religion. This all-embracing cultural outlook was a major reason it succumbed to Indian influences in Southeast Asia (excluding Vietnam). According to De Riencourt: "Indian Civilization respected the political autonomy of its colonies and the cultural freedom of all its units, and, on the whole, worked through peaceful penetration. The Chinese, on the other hand, proceeded by conquest, assimilation and absorption into the all-encompassing Chinese Civilization — the 'only' Civilization in the eyes of the arrogant Sons of Han." (Amaury De Riencourt, *The Soul of India,* [New York: Harper & Brothers, 1960], p. 161.)
5. D. G. E. Hall, *A History of South-East Asia* (London: Macmillan & Co. Ltd., 1955), Chapters 3, 4; John F. Cady, *Southeast Asia: Its Historical Development* (New York: McGraw-Hill Book Company, 1964), Chapter 4; Lucian W. Pye, "Southeast Asia," in Gabriel A. Almond and James S. Coleman, eds., *The Politics of the Developing Areas* (Princeton: Princeton University Press, 1960), pp. 70-3.
6. Edwin O. Reischauer and John K. Fairbank, *East Asia: The Great Tradition* (Boston: Houghton Mifflin Company, 1958), Chapters 4, 7, 8; Kenneth S. Latourette, *The Chinese: Their History and Culture* (New York: The Macmillan Company, 1946), Chapters IV, VII, IX; Dun J. Li., *The Ageless Chinese* (New York: Charles Scribner's Sons, 1971), Chapters IV, VIII, X.
7. Joseph Buttinger, *The Smaller Dragon: A Political History of Vietnam* (New York: Frederick A. Praeger, 1958), pp. 92-110.

8. Hall, op. cit., Chapter 2; Brian Harrison, *South-East Asia: A Short History* (New York: St. Martin's Press, 1967), Chapters III–V.

9. G. Coedes, *The Making of South East Asia* (Berkeley: University of California Press, 1966), p. 52.

10. Latourette, op. cit., pp. 126–38.

11. Bong-youn Choy, *Korea: A History* (Rutland, Vermont: Charles E. Tuttle Company, 1971), pp. 21–9.

12. Hall, op. cit., Chapter 10; Cady, op. cit., Chapter 8; Kenneth P. Landon, *Southeast Asia: Crossroads of Religions* (Chicago: The University of Chicago Press, 1949), pp. 140–7.

13. S. N. Eisenstadt, *The Political Systems of Empires* (New York: The Free Press, 1963), p. 184.

14. Rhoads Murphey, "Traditionalism and Colonialism: Changing Urban Roles in Asia," *The Journal of Asian Studies* (November, 1969), p. 68.

15. Coedes, op. cit., p. 39.

16. Paul M. A. Linebarger, Djang Chu, and Ardath Burks, *Far Eastern Governments and Politics: China and Japan* (New York: D. Van Nostrand Company, 1956), pp. 89–91.

17. Wolfgang Franke, *China and the West* (New York: Harper and Row, 1967), pp. 22–7.

18. Herbert Feith, "Indonesia," in George M. Kahin, ed., *Governments and Politics of Southeast Asia* (Ithaca: Cornell University Press, 1964), Second Edition, pp. 184–6.

19. Harold C. Hinton, "China," in George M. Kahin, ed., *Major Governments of Asia* (Ithaca: Cornell University Press, 1963), Second Edition, pp. 14–5.

20. Harrison, op. cit., p. 20; Reischauer and Fairbank, op. cit., pp. 146–8.

21. Shannon McCune, *Korea's Heritage: A Regional and Social Geography* (Rutland, Vermont: Charles E. Tuttle Company, 1956), p. 27; Reischauer and Fairbank, op. cit., pp. 411–4.

22. Landon, op. cit., p. 68.

23. W. A. R. Wood, *A History of Siam* (Bangkok: The Siam Barnakich Press, 1933), Chapters 6–8.

24. Victor Purcell, *The Chinese in Southeast Asia* (London: Oxford University Press, 1965), Chapters 2–4.

25. Hall, op. cit., pp. 173–4, 272–4, 436–7.

26. Sir Percival Griffiths, *Modern India* (London: Ernest Benn Limited, 1957), p. 43.

27. Wood, op. cit., pp. 159–61.

Chapter 4: Terminal Analysis of Traditional Historical Inputs

1. David E. Apter, *The Politics of Modernization* (Chicago: University of Chicago Press, 1965), pp. 85–94.

2. The comparisons of politically relevant characteristics depicted in the continuum in this and subsequent chapters are based on my own readings
   of Asian political history as well as on my own observations and intui-
   tion. They are not based on any "scientific" or quantitative mode of
   analysis. Many scholars will disagree with specific characteristics presented in these continua. Yet they are primarily suggestive and
   intended to arouse further interest and research in this method of comparative political analysis.
3. John H. Kautsky, ed., *Political Change in Underdeveloped Countries*
   (New York: John Wiley and Sons, Inc., 1962), p. 18.
4. Brian Harrison, *South-East Asia: A Short History* (London: MacMillan &
   Company, Ltd. 1954), pp. 106–15.
5. D. G. E. Hall, *A History of Southeast Asia* (London: MacMillan and
   Company, Ltd., 1955), pp. 478–89.
6. In almost all Asian traditional societies a legendary and/or "foundational"
   period preceded the dates selected here for the date of origin when reasonably reliable historical evidence or records began to appear. Also, in
   most traditional societies in Asia there were two distinct yet overlapping periods when they encountered the Western impact. The first
   period consisted essentially of small numbers of Western explorers,
   missionaries, traders, or commercial enterprises operating in a private
   or semi-private capacity during the preindustrial era in Europe. The
   second period consisted of a much broader array of Western influences
   after the beginning of the industrial age in Europe which were usually
   supported by the political, economic, and military power of their home
   governments. These different aspects of the Western impact will be discussed and analyzed in considerable detail in Part II. Generally, the
   beginning of the second period of the Western impact in the eighteenth
   and nineteenth centuries will be used here to designate the time of the
   initial major encounter between the traditional societies in Asia and the
   Western impact.
7. The dates used in all duration tables explaining this fifth terminal factor
   have been taken from numerous books on Asian history. However,
   most of the chronological data has been obtained from the following
   sources: Vincent A. Smith, *The Oxford History of India* (London:
   Oxford University Press, 1958); D. G. E. Hall, *A History of Southeast
   Asia* (London: Macmillan and Co. Ltd., 1955); John F. Cady, *Southeast Asia: Its Historical Development* (New York: McGraw-Hill Book
   Company, 1964); Edwin O. Reischauer and John K. Fairbank, *East
   Asia: The Great Tradition* (Boston: Houghton Mifflin Company,
   1958).
8. The traditional society in the Philippines has been excluded from Table VI
   since it consisted only of little traditions prior to the Western impact
   and had little if any documented indigenous collective consciousness of
   its own origin.

Part Two: The Western Impact

1. Cf., pp. xx–xxii above.
2. Karl W. Deutsch, "The Growth of Nations: Some Recurrent Patterns of Political and Social Integration," *World Politics* (January 1953), pp. 169–72, 189–94, reprinted in Arend Lijphart, ed., *World Politics* (Boston: Allyn and Bacon, Inc., 1971), Second Edition, pp. 100–1.
3. Ibid., p. 101.
4. G. B. Sansom, *The Western World and Japan* (New York: Alfred A. Knopf, 1965), p. 9.
5. See Sansom, op. cit., Chap. 2; K. M. Panikkar, *Asia and Western Dominance* (London: George Allen and Unwin, Ltd., 1959), Part VIII; and Donald F. Lach, *Asia and the Making of Europe* (Chicago: University of Chicago Press, 1965).
6. Brian Harrison, *Southeast Asia: A Short History* (London: Macmillan and Co., Ltd., 1954), p. 69.

Chapter 5: The Colonization Process

1. Considerable controversy exists among students of Russian history regarding the degree of "Westernization" of pre-Bolshevik Russian society. Throughout the Tzarist era the Russian people underwent many historical experiences that were not shared by Western societies, including detachment from the mainstream of the Judeo-Christian tradition, the Renaissance, the Reformation, and the Enlightenment. The "Tartar yoke" was imposed for two centuries on the Russian people which contributed to a political culture containing a high degree of autocracy, ruthlessness, and xenophobia. Yet the basic orientation of Russian (and later Soviet) society has always been toward the Western community of nations. Professor Jesse D. Clarkson has stated: "The late appearance of Russia on the historical scene and the conditions of the environment in which Russians lived profoundly affected Russia's evolution, but the main lines of her history were the same as those of the West. Strongly individual as Russia's history has been, Russia's kinship is to Europe, not to "Asia." (*A History of Russia,* New York: Random House, 1961, p. 6.)
2. Brian Harrison, *Southeast Asia: A Short History* (London: Macmillan and Co., Ltd., 1954), pp. 64–71.
3. John F. Cady, *Southeast Asia: Its Historical Development* (New York: McGraw-Hill Company, 1964), p. 173.
4. Mary E. Townsend, *The Rise and Fall of Germany's Colonial Empire* (New York: The Macmillan Company, 1930), pp. 178–80.
5. David J. Dallin, *The Rise of Russia in Asia* (New Haven: Yale University Press, 1949), pp. 15–17; John K. Fairbank, Edwin O. Reischauer, and

Albert M. Craig, *East Asia: The Modern Transformation* (Boston: Houghton Mifflin Company, 1965), pp. 43–52.

6. Amaury De Riencourt, *The Soul of India* (New York: Harper and Brothers, 1960), pp. 200–2.

7. D. G. E. Hall, *A History of South-East Asia* (London: Macmillan and Company, 1955), Chapter 14.

8. Harrison, op. cit., Chapter XIII; Cady, op. cit., Chapter 14.

9. A question arises regarding the "Western" content of the Japanese impact, as in the case of the degree of Westernization imparted by Tzarist Russia (and the Soviet Union). The view upheld in this study is that Japan extended an impact containing certain technological, economic, and social elements which it had learned from the West. At the same time, most political and cultural aspects of the Japanese colonization process remained intensely Asian.

10. Edwin O. Reischauer, *Japan: Past and Present* (New York: Alfred A. Knopf, 1964), Chapters XI, XII; David H. James, *The Rise and Fall of the Japanese Empire* (London: George Allen & Unwin, Ltd., 1951), Chapters VI–XII.

11. Hugh Borton, *Japan's Modern Century* (New York: The Ronald Press, 1970), Chapters 17, 18.

12. See David J. Dallin, *Soviet Russia and the Far East* (New Haven: Yale University Press, 1948), Chapters I–III; and Charles B. McLane, *Soviet Strategies in Southeast Asia* (Princeton: Princeton University Press, 1966), Chapter I.

13. Cady, op. cit., Chapter 11; John Bastin, ed., *The Emergence of Modern Southeast Asia: 1511–1957* (Englewood Cliffs, N.J.: Prentice-Hall, Inc., 1967), pp. 36–42; Gregorio F. Zaide, *Philippine Political and Cultural History* (Manila: Philippine Education Company, 1957), Chapters XII, XIII.

14. Cady, op. cit., pp. 421–3; Hall, op. cit., Chapters 34, 35.

15. Cf. pp. 72–96, above.

16. Hall, op. cit., Chapter 12; Cady, op. cit., Chapter 9; Harrison, op. cit., Chapter 8; Bastin, op. cit., pp. 8–24.

17. India produced the most wealth of any Western colony in Asia. See De Riencourt, op. cit., Chapters XII, XIII; K. M. Panikkar, *Asia and Western Dominance* (London: George Allen & Unwin, Ltd., 1953), pp. 111–28.

18. Willard H. Elsbree, *Japan's Role in Southeast Asian Nationalist Movements: 1940 to 1945* (Cambridge: Harvard University Press, 1953), p. 15.

19. Hall, op. cit., Chapters 14–16; Cady, op. cit., Chapter 10; Harrison, op. cit., Chapters IX, X; Bastin, op. cit., pp. 25–42.

20. Quoted in Townsend, op. cit., p. 56.

21. Dallin, op. cit., pp. 16–7.

22. Quoted in Beatrice Pitney Lamb, *India: A World in Transition* (New York: Frederick A. Praeger, Inc., 1968), p. 194.

23. Lucian Pye, "The Politics of Southeast Asia," in Gabriel A. Almond and James S. Coleman, eds., *The Politics of the Developing Areas* (Princeton: Princeton University Press, 1960), p. 93.

24. Ibid.

25. Quoted in Dean Worcester, *The Philippines, Past and Present* (New York: MacMillan and Company, 1930), Appendix III.

26. Rupert Emerson, *From Empire to Nation* (Cambridge: Harvard University Press, 1960), pp. 69-70.

27. Cady, op. cit., p. 566.

28. George E. Taylor, *The Philippines and the United States* (New York: Frederick A. Praeger, 1964), Chapter 3: Primo L. Tonko, *The Government of the Republic of the Philippines* (Quezon City: R. P. Garcia Publishing Company, 1965), Chapters II-IV; Vincent A. Pacis, *Philippine Government and Politics* (Quezon City: Bustamante Press, 1963), Chapters IV, V.

29. Vincent A. Smith, *The Oxford History of India* (London: Oxford University Press, 1958), pp. 762-838; Sir Percival Griffiths, *The British Impact on India* (London: MacDonald, 1952), Chapters 33, 34.

30. Dallin, op. cit., p. 106.

31. This analysis excludes consideration of the political and administrative structures used in the dynastic colonial system of Portugal and the "East India" companies of the Netherlands, Great Britain, and France during the mercantilist period of the first phase of the Western impact. These early Western structures lacked the modern characteristics which became increasingly incorporated in the political systems of many Western societies during the nineteenth and twentieth centuries, and they exerted few permanent influences in the formation of a new historical environment. The analysis likewise excludes consideration of the low-transferable political and administrative structures established by Germany during its brief colonial rule in Asia which had no significant effect on the formation of a new historical environment in several Asian societies.

32. Onofre D. Corpuz, *The Philippines* (Englewood Cliffs, New Jersey: Prentice-Hall, Inc., 1965), pp. 24-9.

33. Hall, op. cit., pp. 490-2.

34. Cady, op. cit., pp. 530-1.

35. Dennis J. Duncanson, *Government and Revolution in Vietnam* (New York: Oxford University Press, 1968), pp. 72-103; Ellen J. Hammer, *The Struggle for Indochina* (Stanford: Stanford University Press, 1954), pp. 63-93; Joseph Buttinger, *Vietnam: A Dragon Embattled* (New York: Frederick A. Praeger, 1967), Chapters I, IV.

36. Hugh Borton, *Japan's Modern Century* (New York: The Ronald Press Company, 1970), Chapters, 12, 13; Cady, op. cit., Chapter 25.

37. *The Japan Year Book 1943-1944,* The Foreign Affairs Association of Japan, The Nippon Times Press, 1943, pp. 899-900.

38. George M. Kahin, *Nationalism and Revolution in Indonesia* (Ithaca, New York: Cornell University Press, 1952), Chapter 4; Harry J. Benda, *The Crescent and the Rising Sun* (The Hague: W. van Hoeve Ltd., 1958), Chapters 7, 8.
39. Cady, op. cit., pp. 362-3.
40. Hall, op. cit., pp. 492-3.
41. Ibid., p. 661.
42. Cady, op. cit., pp. 419-25.
43. Duncanson, op. cit., pp. 103-17.
44. Cady, op. cit., p. 548.
45. Taylor, op. cit., Chapter 4.
46. Garel A. Grunder and William E. Livezey, *The Philippines and the United States* (Norman: University of Oklahoma Press, 1951), Chapter VII.
47. Cady, op. cit., p. 481.
48. Hall, op. cit., pp. 654-58.
49. Sir Percival Griffiths, *Modern India* (London: Ernest Benn Ltd., 1962), Third Edition, p. 60.
50. Buttinger, op. cit., pp. 89-94.
51. Taylor, op. cit., pp. 72-6.
52. Joseph R. Hayden, *The Philippines: A Study in National Development* (New York: The Macmillan Company, 1942), Chapter XXI.
53. Cady, op. cit., pp. 573-4.

Chapter 6. The Unequal Treaty Process

1. See John K. Fairbank, Edwin O. Reischauer, and Albert M. Craig, *East Asia: The Modern Transformation* (Boston: Houghton Mifflin Company, 1965), pp. 144-55, 204-11; D. G. E. Hall, *A History of Southeast Asia* (London: Macmillan and Company Ltd., 1955), pp. 578-83.
2. Wolfgang Franke, *China and the West* (New York: Harper and Row, 1967), pp. 66-76; Hugh Borton, *Japan's Modern Century* (New York: The Ronald Press, 1970), pp. 30-72.
3. H. G. W. Woodhead, et al., *Occidental Interpretations of the Far Eastern Problem* (Chicago: University of Chicago Press, 1926), p. 90. Spain, which maintained a colonial system in the Philippines until 1898, also had an unequal treaty with China.
4. See Kenneth S. Latourette, *The Chinese: Their History and Culture* (New York: The Macmillan Company, 1946), pp. 380-94; Dun J. Li, *The Ageless Chinese* (New York: Charles Scribner's Sons, 1971), pp. 407-34.
5. Wesley R. Fishel, *The End of Extraterritoriality in China* (Berkeley and Los Angeles: University of California Press, 1952), p. 232. See also Fairbank, Reischauer, and Craig, op. cit., pp. 145-8; John F. Cady, *Southeast Asia: Its Historical Development* (New York: McGraw-Hill Book Company, 1964), pp. 344-8.

6. Fishel, op. cit., pp. 16–7.

7. Westel W. Willoughby, *Foreign Rights and Interests in China* (Baltimore: The Johns Hopkins Press, 1920), pp. 35–41.

8. Fishel, op. cit., pp. 18–25; Willoughby, op. cit., pp. 51–64.

9. Edith E. Ware, *Business and Politics in the Far East* (New Haven: Yale University Press, 1932), p. 12.

10. The two exceptions were the French official mission in Japan and the United States official mission in Thailand. Germany and Russia maintained sizeable official missions in China and Thailand prior to World War I, yet their unequal treaties were terminated abruptly through the adversities of the war and their long-run demonstrative effect was minimal.

11. Harley F. Macnair and Donald F. Lach, *Modern Far Eastern International Relations* (New York: D. Van Nostrand Company, Inc., 1950), p. 45.

12. W. G. Beasley, *The Modern History of Japan* (London: Weidenfeld and Nicolson, 1963), pp. 76–87.

13. Cady, op. cit., p. 345.

14. Walter F. Vella, *The Impact of the West on Government in Thailand* (Berkeley and Los Angeles: University of California Press, 1955), p. 343.

15. Wolfgang Franke, *China and the West* (New York: Harper and Row, Publishers, 1967), pp. 76–7.

16. Beasley, op. cit., p. 138.

17. Hall, op. cit., Chap. 37.

18. Macnair and Lach, op. cit., pp. 40–1. Through the most-favored nation clause a similar move was made by the British official mission in Thailand to extend extraterritorial privileges to British Asian subjects (Indian, Burmese, Ceylonese, Chinese, etc.), yet on a more limited scale than the French.

19. Frank C. Darling, "The Evolution of Law in Thailand," *The Review of Politics* (April 1970), pp. 208–9.

20. Macnair and Lach, op. cit., pp. 45–8.

21. Beasley, op. cit., p. 139.

22. Frank C. Darling, *Thailand and the United States* (Washington, D.C.: Public Affairs Press, 1965), pp. 16–7.

23. Francis B. Sayre, "The Passing of Extraterritoriality in Siam," American Council, Institute of Pacific Relations, 1928, p. 4.

24. Macnair and Lach, op. cit., p. 55.

25. Beasley, op. cit., p. 62.

26. Franke, op. cit., p. 134.

27. Vella, op. cit., p. 343.

Chapter 7: Governmental Linkages

1. Cf. Figure IX, p. 104, and Figure XIII, p. 147, above.
2. Cf. pp. 61-2.
3. Cf. pp. 63-71.
4. See Rupert Emerson, *From Empire to Nation* (Cambridge, Massachusetts: Harvard University Press, 1960), Chap. 10; and Mostafa Rejai and Cynthia H. Enloe, "Nation-States and State-Nations," *International Studies Quarterly* (June, 1969), pp. 145-8.
5. For a brief general discussion of the historical evolution of the concept of the nation-state by Western colonial powers see Lucian W. Pye, *Aspects of Political Development* (Boston: Little, Brown and Company, 1966), pp. 6-19. See also Emerson, op. cit., Chaps. 2, 3.
6. Edmund S. Glenn, "The Two Faces of Nationalism," *Comparative Political Systems* (October, 1970) pp. 352-3.
7. Karl W. Deutsch, "The Growth of Nation: Some Recurrent Patterns of Political and Social Integration," *World Politics* (January, 1953), pp. 169-70; Karl W. Deutsch, "Social Mobilization and Political Development," *American Political Science Review* (September, 1961).
8. Rejai and Enloe, op. cit., p. 151.
9. The society created in the Philippines by Western colonial administrators is difficult to classify in these categories since it contains a preponderant majority of people of Malay stock. However, it probably fits more closely to the consensual-ethnic society classification since its major social divisions consist of differences among the Tagalog, Ilocano, Cebuano, Moro, and other sub-national groups.
10. Rhoads Murphey, "Traditionalism and Colonialism: Changing Urban Roles in Asia," *The Journal of Asian Studies* (November, 1969), pp. 83-4.
11. One notable exception in Asia was the transfer of the British colonial capital in India from Calcutta to Delhi in 1911 to legitimize British colonial rule on the site of the capital of the defunct Mogul Empire.
12. Daniel Lerner, *The Passing of Traditional Society* (Glencoe, Illinois: The Free Press, 1958), pp. 47-52.
13. Sir Percival Griffiths, *Modern India* (London: Ernest Benn Ltd., 1957), p. 78.
14. Emerson, op. cit., p. 133. See also Karl W. Deutsch, *Nationalism and Social Communication* (Cambridge: M.I.T. Press, 1953), Chap. 6.
15. Griffiths, op. cit., p. 54.
16. Joseph R. Hayden, *The Philippines: A Study in National Development* (New York: The Macmillan Company, 1942), p. 535.
17. David J. Steinberg, ed., *In Search of Southeast Asia* (New York: Praeger Publishers, Inc., 1971), p. 180.
18. John F. Cady, *Southeast Asia: Its Historical Influence* (New York: McGraw-Hill Book Company, 1964), p. 318.

19. This general assessment must be qualified by the fact that Japanese officials exerted some functions of high-transferable political and administrative structures in Southeast Asia during World War II, although this influence consisted largely of accelerating developments in these structures already created by the Western colonial powers.
20. Sir Percival Griffiths, *The British Impact on India* (London: MacDonald, 1952), Sections II, III.
21. George E. Taylor, *The Philippines and the United States* (New York: Frederick A. Praeger, 1964), Chapter 3.
22. Griffiths, op. cit., pp. 151–3; Cady, op. cit., pp. 474–7.
23. Gabriel A. Almond and G. Bingham Powell, Jr., *Comparative Politics: A Developmental Approach* (Boston: Little, Brown and Company, 1966), pp. 259–99.
24. K. M. Panikkar, *Asia and Western Dominance* (London: George Allen and Unwin, Ltd., 1953), pp. 197–202.
25. For example see Jawaharlal Nehru, *Toward Freedom* (Boston: Beacon Press, 1958), pp. 244–50.
26. V. P. Menon, *The Story of the Integration of the Indian States* (New York: The Macmillan Company, 1956), pp. 9–19; D. G. E. Hall, *A History of Southeast Asia* (London: Macmillan and Company, Ltd., 1955), Chapter 29.
27. M. K. Gandhi, *Gandhi's Autobiography* (Washington, D.C.: Public Affairs Press, 1960), pp. 11–7.
28. Brian Harrison, *Southeast Asia: A Short History* (London: Macmillan and Company, Ltd., 1954), pp. 64–71.
29. For a description of the deployment and influence of British security forces in India, see Griffiths, *The British Impact in India,* pp. 196–215.
30. Panikkar, op. cit., p. 29.
31. Griffiths, *The British Impact in India,* p. 64.
32. Hayden, op. cit., Chap. 29.
33. Garel A. Grunder and William E. Livezey, *The Philippines and the United States* (Norman: University of Oklahoma Press, 1951), pp. 234–41.
34. Gregory Henderson, *Korea: The Politics of the Vortex* (Cambridge: Harvard University Press, 1968), pp. 106–10.
35. Vincent A. Smith, *The Oxford History of India* (London: Oxford University Press, 1958), pp. 621–32.
36. Frank N. Trager, *Burma: From Kingdom to Republic* (New York: Frederick A. Praeger, Publishers, 1966), pp. 132–3.
37. J. M. Gullick, *Malaysia* (New York: Frederick A. Praeger, Publishers, 1969), pp. 57–64, 196–205.
38. A good example was the Boxer Rebellion in China in 1900. See John K. Fairbank, Edwin O. Reischauer, and Albert M. Craig, *East Asia: The Modern Transformation* (Boston: Houghton Mifflin Company, 1965), pp. 394–404.
39. Mikiso Hane, *Japan: A Historical Survey* (New York: Charles Scribner's Sons, 1972), pp. 245–74.

40. Cady, op. cit., pp. 501-5.
41. Significant published studies by early Western diplomatic officials included *The Commentaries of the Great Affonso D'Albuquerque, Second Viceroy of India* (translated from Portuguese into English, 1875-1884) by the famous Portuguese explorer, *Journal of an Embassy from the Governor of India to the Courts of Siam and Cochin China* (1828), by John Crawfurd, the British envoy who led a diplomatic mission to Thailand and Vietnam, *Embassy to the Eastern Courts of Cochin China, Siam, and Muscat* (1837), by Edmund Roberts, who led the first American diplomatic mission to Asia, and *The Kingdom and People of Siam* (1857), by Sir John Bowring, who negotiated the first unequal treaty with the king of Thailand.
42. The books by Thomas Meadows exerted an interesting feedback into Western influence elsewhere in Asia. Meadow's writings on the traditional civil service system in China played an important role in the adoption of some of the Chinese procedures and practices by the British civil service in India, Burma, Ceylon, and Malaya.
43. Hugh Borton, *Japan's Modern Century* (New York: The Ronald Press, 1970), pp. 206-8.
44. See Hane, op. cit., p. 276; Walter F. Vella, *The Impact of the West on Government in Thailand* (Berkeley: University of California Press, 1955), p. 348.
45. See Edwin O. Reischauer, *Japan: Past and Present* (New York: Alfred A. Knopf, 1964), pp. 114-24.
46. Hall, op. cit., pp. 598-612.
47. Fairbank, Reischauer, and Craig, op. cit., p. 336; Cady, op. cit., p. 499.
48. Examples of these writings include *Diplomatic Memoirs* (1909) and *American Diplomacy in the Orient* (1926) by John W. Foster who served as an American envoy to several diplomatic posts in Latin America and Europe as well as an adviser to the government of China; *Five Years in Siam; from 1891 to 1896* (1898) by H. Warington Smyth, a British educator, who served as an adviser to the Thai government; and *Siam: Treaties with Foreign Powers, 1920-1927* (1928) by Francis B. Sayre who served as a foreign affairs adviser to the Thai government and played an instrumental role in terminating its unequal treaties with all Western nations.
49. Fairbank, Reischauer, and Craig, op. cit., p. 671.
50. Charles B. McLane, *Soviet Strategies in Southeast Asia* (Princeton, New Jersey: Princeton University Press, 1966), pp. 27, 88. Sneevliet also played a significant role in assisting the formation of the Chinese Communist Party in Shanghai in 1921.
51. The direct role of the Soviet government in the outbreak of the Communist insurgency in Malaya and elsewhere in Southeast Asia following the Calcutta conference in 1948 is not clear. The emergence of these subversive movements, however, coincided with ideological and political goals espoused by the Soviet Union since the early 1920's.

Chapter 8: Nongovernmental Linkages

1. John F. Fairbank, Edwin O. Reischauer, and Albert M. Craig, *East Asia: The Modern Transformation* (Boston: Houghton Mifflin Company, 1965), pp. 66–79.
2. Rupert Emerson, *From Empire to Nation* (Cambridge: Harvard University Press, 1960), p. 182.
3. Max Weber, *The Protestant Ethic and the Spirit of Capitalism* (New York: Charles Schribner's Sons, 1930), Chapters 2 & 4; David C. McClelland, *The Achieving Society* (Princeton, New Jersey: D. Van Nostrand Company, Inc., 1961), Chapter 2. It is interesting (and unfortunate) that in Chapter 9 entitled "Sources of n Achievement" in McClelland's important study there is no consideration of the role of Western entrepreneurs imparting this significant value to non-Western societies.
4. See J. S. Furnivall, *Colonial Policy and Practice* (New York: New York University Press, 1956).
5. Rhoads Murphey, "Traditionalism and Colonialism: Changing Urban Roles in Asia," *The Journal of Asian Studies* (November, 1969), p. 69.
6. G. B. Sansom, *The Western World and Japan* (New York: Alfred A. Knopf, 1965), pp. 145–6.
7. Sir Percival Griffiths, *Modern India* (London: Ernest Benn Ltd., 1957), pp. 76–7.
8. Quoted in David J. Steinberg, ed., *In Search of Southeast Asia* (New York: Praeger Publishers, Inc., 1971), p. 258.
9. See Sir Percival Griffiths, *The British Impact on India* (London: MacDonald, 1952), Section IV; Furnivall, op. cit., Chapter 2; James Ingram, *Economic Change in Thailand Since 1850* (Stanford: Stanford University Press, 1955), Chapters 2–7.
10. For example see Jawaharlal Nehru, *Toward Freedom* (Boston: Beacon Press, 1958), pp. 275–85.
11. M. K. Gandhi, *Gandhi's Autobiography* (Washington, D.C.: Public Affairs Press, 1960), pp. 494–514.
12. See Fairbank, Reischauer, and Craig, op. cit., pp. 30–43, 152–3; Vincent Smith, *The Oxford History of India* (London: Oxford University Press, 1958), pp. 724–8.
13. A notable exception during this period, already cited, was the proselyting work of Roman Catholic missionaries in the Philippines who were assisted in some degree by the administrative and military power of the Spanish government.
14. Wolfgang Franke, *China and the West* (New York: Harper and Row, Publishers, 1967), pp. 35–6.
15. Amaury De Riencourt, *The Soul of China* (New York: Coward-McCann, Inc., 1958), pp. 138–52.

16. Kenneth S. Latourette, *The Chinese: Their History and Culture* (New York: The Macmillan Company, 1946), pp. 369–71.

17. K. M. Panikkar, *Asia and Western Dominance* (London: George Allen and Unwin, Ltd., 1953), p. 314.

18. See H. G. E. Woodhead, *Occidental Interpretations of the Far Eastern Problem* (Chicago: University of Chicago Press, 1926), p. 126.

19. Akira Iriye, *Across the Pacific: An Inner History of American-East Asian Relations* (New York: Harcourt, Brace and World, Inc., 1967), pp. 18–21.

20. Robert N. Bellah, ed., *Religion and Progress in Modern Asia* (New York: The Free Press, 1965), p. 195.

21. John F. Cady, *Southeast Asia: Its Historical Development* (New York: McGraw-Hill Book Company, 1964), pp. 370–3.

22. Franke, op. cit., pp. 128–131.

23. Charles H. Haskins, *The Rise of Universities* (Ithaca: Cornell University Press, 1957), pp. 1–2.

24. Fairbank, Reischauer, and Craig, op. cit., pp. 615–9; Smith, op. cit., pp. 717–22.

25. Latourette, op. cit. p. 369.

26. Panikkar, op. cit., p. 293.

27. Quoted in Kenneth E. Wells, *History of Protestant Work in Thailand 1958* (Bangkok: Church of Christ in Thailand, 1958), p. 61.

28. Fairbank, Reischauer, and Craig, op. cit., p. 360.

29. Frank N. Trager, *Burma: From Kingdom to Republic* (New York: Frederick A. Praeger, 1966), pp. 363–4.

30. Dennis J. Duncanson, *Government and Revolution in Vietnam* (New York: Oxford University Press, 1968), pp. 66–7.

31. Griffiths, op. cit. , pp. 57–8.

32. Martin F. Herz, *A Short History of Cambodia* (London: Stevens and Sons, Ltd., 1958), pp. 62–3.

33. See Nehru, op. cit., pp. 269–75.

34. Griffiths, *Modern India,* pp. 57–62, 87–92.

35. The classification and analysis of the influence of indigenous returnees constitutes a major theoretical problem since this particular linkage was intimately involved in both the Western impact and the indigenous response (which will be described and analyzed in Part III). The assessment of this specific penetration is included here since it was inextricably interlinked with the colonization and unequal treaty processes, and it directly affected the secularizing historical factors imparted by Western nations.

36. Cf. pp. 68–9, above.

37. David G. Marr, *Vietnamese Anticolonialism: 1885–1925* (Berkeley: University of California Press, 1971), p. 229.

38. Emerson, op. cit., p. 199.

39. For example see Nehru, op. cit., pp. 30–9.

40. Duncanson, op. cit., pp. 122–3.

41. Dorothy Woodman, *The Republic of Indonesia* (London: The Cresset Press, 1955), pp. 160-6.
42. For examples of this very important political trend in Asia see Benjiman I. Schwarz, *Chinese Communism and the Rise of Mao* (Cambridge: Harvard University Press, 1958), Chapter I; George M. Kahin, *Nationalism and Revolution in Indonesia* (Ithaca, New York: Cornell University Press, 1952), pp. 46-53; Vella, op. cit. pp. 360-5.
43. Woodman, op. cit., pp. 150-2.
44. Gandhi, op. cit., pp. 127-68.
45. Marr, op. cit., pp. 257-77.
46. See D. Mackenzie Brown, *The Nationalist Movement: Indian Political Thought from Ranade to Bhave* (Berkeley: University of California Press, 1961), Chapters VII-XI; Fairbank, Reischauer, and Craig, op. cit. pp. 658-72.
47. The linkage comprising Eurasians, like that of the indigenous returnees, constitutes another theoretical problem since it was intimately involved in both the Western impact and the indigenous response (to be analyzed in Part III). It is included in this classification of non-governmental linkages since it was a significant penetration into several colonial systems, and it assisted in shaping some of the secular influences caused by Western colonial powers.
48. For an assessment of the diversity of the Eurasian class in a former Western colony see C. H. Crabb, *Malaya's Eurasians — An Opinion* (Singapore: Eastern Universities Press Ltd., 1960). See also V. R. Gaikwad, *The Anglo-Indians: A Study in the Problems and Processes Involved in Emotional and Cultural Integration* (New York: Asia Publishing House, 1968).
49. For example see George E. Taylor, *The Philippines and the United States* (New York: Frederick A. Praeger, Publishers, 1964), p. 38.
50. Rajni Kothari, *Politics in India* (Boston: Little, Brown and Company, 1970), pp. 105-6; W. Howard Wriggins, *Ceylon: Dilemmas of a New Nation* (Princeton: Princeton University Press, 1960), pp. 23-4.
51. The classification of foreign communities as the final non-governmental linkage involved in both the colonization and unequal treaty processes creates another theoretical problem since all foreign communities contained varying numbers of Western government officials. Yet the non-governmental classification seems most appropriate since Western officials usually comprised a small minority of the foreign communities, and the influences induced by the Western communities were caused primarily by their collective life styles and modes of behavior irrespective of official or non-official status.
52. Cf. pp. 70-1, above.
53. Fairbank, Reischauer, and Craig, op. cit., pp. 340-2; Walter F. Vella, *The Impact of the West on Government in Thailand* (Berkeley: University of California Press, 1955), pp. 342-4.

54. For a brief description of this attitude in India see Panikkar, op. cit., pp. 116-8.
55. See Victor Purcell, *The Chinese in Southeast Asia* (London: Oxford University Press, 1965), Part I.
56. For a description of relevant aspects of this assimilation process in Thailand see Richard J. Coughlin, *Double Identity: The Chinese in Modern Thailand* (Hong Kong: Hong Kong University Press, 1960), pp. 74-91.
57. Emerson, op. cit., p. 49.
58. See Norman D. Palmer, *The Indian Political System* (Boston: Houghton Mifflin Company, 1971), pp. 50-8; Garel A. Grunder and William E. Livezey, *The Philippines and the United States* (Norman: University of Oklahoma Press, 1951), Chapter V.
59. Panikkar, op. cit., p. 117.
60. Griffiths, *The British Impact on India,* op. cit., Chapter 34.
61. Grunder and Livezey, op. cit., Chapters 9, 10.

Chapter 9: Terminal Analysis of Western Historical Inputs

1. See Myron Weiner, "South Asia," in Gabriel A. Almond and James S. Coleman, eds., *The Politics of the Developing Areas* (Princeton: Princeton University Press, 1960), pp. 163-4.
2. Cf. pp. 82-96, above.
3. See Table VII.
4. This terminal factor applies only to the colonized societies.
5. For an explanation of this tendency among the large governmental linkages in Vietnam see Dennis J. Duncanson, *Government and Revolution in Vietnam* (New York: Oxford University Press, 1968), pp. 91-103.
6. This terminal factor also applies only to colonized societies.
7. See Victor Purcell, *The Chinese in Southeast Asia* (London: Oxford University Press, 1951), Chapters 8, 19, 22, 35, 49, 55.
8. The Dutch began imprisoning Sukarno and other leaders of the Indonesian Nationalist Party in 1929. See George M. Kahin, *Nationalism and Revolution in Indonesia* (Ithaca, New York: Cornell University Press, 1952), pp. 90-100.
9. See Joseph Buttinger, *Vietnam: A Dragon Embattled* (New York: Frederick A. Praeger, Publishers, 1967), pp. 196-226.
10. Bong-youn Choy, *Korea: A History* (Rutland, Vermont: Charles E. Tuttle Company, 1971), pp. 173-8.
11. This terminal factor exerted no influence in the abolition of Japanese colonial rule in Korea. The terms of the Japanese surrender gave no choice to the Japanese government for the future status of Korea, and all authority for Korean internal affairs was immediately transferred to the Allied powers. All Japanese linkages in Korea were removed in the early post-war period.
12. Kahin, op. cit., Chapters VII, VIII.

13. See Ellen J. Hammer, *The Struggle for Indochina* (Stanford: Stanford University Press, 1954), pp. 110–27.

Part Three: The Indigenous Response

1. The term "response" has been used much more frequently by historians than by political scientists in assessing the reaction within Asian societies to the Western impact. An exception to this practice has been Rajni Kothari in this book, *Politics in India* (Boston: Little, Brown and Company, 1970), pp. 44–50. His analysis, however, is extremely brief and is limited primarily to an explanation of several political trends among the Indian populace during the period of British colonial rule. In contrast, many historians have focused sizeable portions of their studies on specific domestic reactions to Western influences. For example, see John K. Fairbank, Edwin O. Reischauer, and Albert M. Craig, *East Asia: The Modern Transformation* (Boston: Houghton Mifflin Company, 1965), pp. 179–243, 313–407; Vincent A. Smith, *The Oxford History of India* (London: Oxford University Press, 1958), pp. 729–39; John Bastin and Harry J. Benda, *A History of Modern Southeast Asia* (Englewood Cliffs, N.J.: Prentice-Hall, Inc., 1968), pp. 67–152; Harry J. Benda and John Larkin, *The World of Southeast Asia: Selected Historical Readings* (New York: Harper and Row, Publishers, 1967), Part IV; Paul H. Clyde and Burton F. Beers, *The Far East: A History of Western Impacts and Eastern Responses, 1830–1975* (Englewood Cliffs, N.J.: Prentice-Hall, Inc., 1975). As cited in the Introduction to this study, these portions of excellent historical writings provide much significant data for political research, but they have limited utility in political analysis. They do not contain a sufficient focus on politically relevant values, institutions, and modes of behavior, nor do they use a suitable analytical framework for explaining the relationships of these political factors to each other and to other elements of the society.
2. K. M. Panikkar, *Asia and Western Dominance* (London: George Allen and Unwin Ltd., 1959), p. 237.
3. See Chapters Seven and Eight, especially pp. 220–9.
4. Joungwon Alexander Kim, "The Politics of Predevelopment," *Comparative Politics* (January 1973), pp. 211–35.
5. Numerous sources could be cited which analyze traditional, transitional, and modernizing factors in the political systems of non-Western societies. Some of these works have been cited previously in this study. Basic books in this field are Gabriel A. Almond and James S. Coleman, eds., *The Politics of the Developing Areas* (Princeton: Princeton University Press, 1960) and the seven Studies in Political Development published under the auspices of Committee on Comparative Politics of

the Social Science Research Council by Princeton University Press.
Other important books are Gabriel A. Almond and G. Bingham
Powell, Jr., *Comparative Politics: A Developmental Approach*
(Boston: Little Brown and Company, 1966); David A. Apter, *The Politics of Modernization* (Chicago: The University of Chicago Press,
1965); Samuel P. Huntington, *Political Order in Changing Societies*
(New Haven: Yale University Press, 1968); Clifford Geertz, ed., *Old
Societies and New States* (New York: The Free Press, 1963); Daniel
Lerner, *The Passing of Traditional Society* (New York: The Free Press,
1958); Fred W. Riggs, *Administration in Developing Countries*
(Boston: Houghton Mifflin Company, 1964); C. E. Black, *The
Dynamics of Modernization* (New York: Harper and Row, Publishers,
1966); David E. Apter, *Some Conceptual Approaches to the Study of
Modernization* (Englewood Cliffs, New Jersey: Prentice-Hall, Inc.,
1968); and Lloyd I. Rudolph and Susanne Hoeber Rudolph, *The
Modernity of Tradition: Political Development in India* (Chicago: The
University of Chicago Press, 1967).

6. For a scholarly analysis of important elements in the early urbanization of
Asian societies see Ashish Bose, *Studies in India's Urbanization
1901–1971* (Bombay: Tata McGraw-Hill Publishing Company Ltd.,
1973); T. G. McGee, *The Southeast Asian City* (New York: Frederick
A. Praeger, Publishers, 1967); Gerald Breese, *Urbanization in Newly
Developing Countries* (Englewood Cliffs, N.J.: Prentice-Hall, Inc.,
1966).

7. For an assessment of basic aspects of nationalism in Asia see Hans Kohn,
The Age of Nationalism: The First Era of Global History (New York:
Harper and Brothers, Publishers, 1962); William L. Holland, ed.,
Asian Nationalism and the West (New York: The Macmillan Company,
1953); Joseph Kennedy, *Asian Nationalism in the Twentieth Century*
(New York: St. Martin's Press, 1968); Rupert Emerson, *From Empire
to Nation* (Cambridge: Harvard University Press, 1960).

8. See Lester R. Brown, *In the Human Interest* (New York: W. W. Norton
and Company, Inc., 1974); William Petersen, *Population* (London: The
Macmillan Company, 1969), Second Edition; Alfred Sauvy, *General
Theory of Population* (New York: Basic Books, Inc., 1969), Part Two;
Neil W. Chamberlain, *Beyond Malthus: Population and Power* (New
York: Basic Books, Inc., 1970).

9. Almond and Powell, op. cit., pp. 24–5.

10. For a full explanation of these two empirical theories see David Easton,
A Framework for Political Analysis (Englewood Cliffs, N.J.: Prentice-
Hall, Inc., 1965); David Easton, *A Systems Analysis of Political Life*
(New York: John Wiley and Sons, 1965), Almond and Powell, op. cit.

11. Easton, *A Framework for Political Analysis,* p. 56.

12. Almond and Powell, op. cit., p. 18.

13. For an elaborate definition and analysis of political culture see Almond
and Powell, op. cit., pp. 50–72. See also Gabriel A. Almond and Sid-

ney Verba, *The Civic Culture* (Boston: Little, Brown and Company, 1965); Lucian W. Pye and Sidney Verba, eds., *Political Culture and Political Development* (Princeton: Princeton University Press, 1965); and Young C. Kim, "The Concept of Political Culture in Comparative Politics," *Journal of Politics* (May 1964), pp. 313–36.

14. For more elaborate definitions of political communication, interest articulation, and interest aggregation see Almond and Powell, op. cit., Chapters VII, IV, V. See also Lucian W. Pye, ed., *Communications and Political Development* (Princeton: Princeton University Press, 1963); and Joseph LaPalombara and Myron Weiner, eds., *Political Parties and Political Development* (Princeton: Princeton University Press, 1966).

15. Cf. pp. xxi-xxii.

Chapter 10: The Quasi-Democracies

1. Cf. pp. 165–6.
2. This response was most prevalent among indigenous Christians, Eurasians, and indigenous returnees.
3. For a scholarly study showing the continuity rather than the conflict between aspects of traditional and modern behavior see Lloyd I. Rudolph and Susanne Hoeber Rudolph, *The Modernity of Tradition: Political Development in India* (Chicago: The University of Chicago Press, 1967).
4. Jawaharlal Nehru, *The Discovery of India* (New York: The John Day Company, 1946), p. 38.
5. Guy Hunter, *South-East Asia: Race, Culture, and Nation* (New York: Oxford University Press, 1966), p. 119.
6. D. S. Sarma, *The Renaissance of Hinduism,* quoted in Griffiths, op. cit., p. 61.
7. James S. Coleman, ed., *Education and Political Development* (Princeton: Princeton University Press, 1965), p. 38.
8. See Edward Shils, "The Intellectuals in the Political Development of the New States," *World Politics* (April 1960), pp. 329–68.
9. Stephen N. Hay, *Asian Ideas of East and West: Tagore and His Critics in Japan, China, and India* (Cambridge: Harvard University Press, 1970), p. 312.
10. Rupert Emerson, *From Empire to Nation* (Cambridge: Harvard University Press, 1960), p. 170.
11. David J. Steinberg, ed., *In Search of Southeast Asia* (New York: Praeger Publishers, 1971), p. 205.
12. For a description of this rural development in Burma see J. S. Furnivall, *Colonial Policy and Practice* (New York: New York University Press, 1956), pp. 84–94. Another group of landlords in Burma was a class of Indian moneylenders who also acquired land from the foreclosure of debts by small insolvent landowners.

13. John F. Cady, *A History of Modern Burma* (Ithaca: Cornell University Press, 1958), pp. 303–7; George E. Taylor, *The Philippines and the United States* (New York: Frederick A. Praeger, Publisher, 1964), pp. 84–5.
14. Sir Percival Griffiths, *The British Impact in India* (London: MacDonald 1952), pp. 428–39.
15. See Victor Purcell, *The Chinese in Southeast Asia* (London: Oxford University Press, 1965), pp. 69–75, 329–40, 542–51.
16. For a description of this trend in India see Griffiths, op. cit., pp. 440–52.
17. This requirement contrasted markedly with the need to remove partial foreign controls and the continuity between the traditional society and the status of complete national sovereignty in Nationalist China, Japan, and Thailand which were shaped by the unequal treaty process. Additional comparisons between the indigenous response in these different types of societies emerging from Western domination will be made in Chapter Eleven.
18. For a scholarly discussion of the admixture of these traditional and Western values in colonized societies see Emerson, op. cit., Chapter X.
19. For an explanation of this phenomenon in India see Myron Weiner, "South Asia," in Gabriel A. Almond and James S. Colemen, eds., *The Politics of the Developing Areas* (Princeton: Princeton University Press, 1960), p. 168.
20. Daniel Lerner, *The Passing of Traditional Society* (New York: The Free Press, 1958), p. 47.
21. For explanations of this kind of nationalism in three of these societies see Rajni Kothari, *Politics in India* (Boston: Little, Brown and Company, 1970), pp. 50–61; Frank N. Trager, *Burma: From Kingdom to Republic* (New York: Frederick A. Praeger, Publishers, 1966), Chapter 3; Onofre D. Corpuz, *The Philippines* (Englewood Cliffs, N.J.: Prentice-Hall, Inc., 1965), pp. 65–71.
22. Jawaharlal Nehru, *Toward Freedom* (Boston: Beacon Press, 1958), p. 234.
23. For a detailed explanation of this aspect of nationalism see Werner Levi, *The Challenge of World Politics in South and Southeast Asia* (Englewood Cliffs, N.J.: Prentice-Hall, Inc., 1968), Chapter II.
24. The attempt by armed dissidents in Kashmir to break away from India and join Pakistan at the time of partition was a similar phenomena of ethnic nationalism, although the Muslim insurgents did not seek at that time the establishment of an independent nation-state.
25. Emerson, op. cit., p. 228.
26. J. M. Gullick, *Malaysia* (New York: Frederick A. Praeger, Publishers, 1969), pp. 124–34.
27. See Kothari, op. cit., pp. 86–92; Trager, op. cit., pp. 150–2.
28. Nehru voiced this opinion while writing his autobiography in prison. See Jawaharlal Nehru, *Toward Freedom* (Boston: Beacon Press, 1958), pp. 348–51.

29. Harry J. Benda, "Reflections on Asian Communism," in Tilman, op. cit., p. 266.
30. Only in the Philippines did this type of political system witness the spread of communism to peasant organizations, although this development was led by urban-based intellectuals. See Charles B. McLane, *Soviet Strategies in Southeast Asia* (Princeton: Princeton University Press, 1966), pp. 165–88.
31. Lucian W. Pye, *Aspects of Political Development* (Boston: Little, Brown and Company, 1966), pp. 104–12.
32. Alvin Rabushka and Kenneth A. Shepsle, *Politics in Plural Societies: A Theory of Democratic Instability* (Columbus, Ohio: Merrill Press, 1972), pp. 74–97.
33. The term "bargaining political culture" was coined by Professor Jean Grossholz in her study, *Politics in the Philippines* (Boston: Little, Brown and Company, 1964), pp. 157–9. She defined its "key elements" as "the highly personal and reciprocal nature of authority; the tendency to see all relationships as a matter of power; the expectation that all action in favor of another created a credit, to be drawn as needed; the use of manipulative language; and the pakiusap practice of using middlemen in sensitive negotiations." (p. 159)
The term "bargaining political culture" is also used by Kothari, op. cit., pp. 263–4. It is my own thesis that a bargaining political culture developed in all six of the quasi-democracies.
34. See Gabriel A. Almond and G. Bingham Powell, Jr., *Comparative Politics: A Developmental Approach* (Boston: Little, Brown and Company, 1966), p. 53.
35. For a discussion of this mode of political behavior in the Philippines, see Corpuz, op. cit., pp. 93–100.
36. For an explanation of this form of political communications see Elihu Katz, "The Two-Step Flow of Communication: An Up-To-Date Report on an Hypothesis," *Public Opinion Quarterly* (Spring, 1957), pp. 61–78; Elihu Katz and Paul F. Lazarfield, *Personal Influence* (New York: The Free Press of Glencoe, 1955).
37. For a discussion of this phenomenon in India see Sir Percival Griffiths, *Modern India* (London: Ernest Benn Ltd., 1957), pp. 67–72.
38. For a description of this development in India, Pakistan, and Ceylon see Weiner, op. cit., pp. 185–7.
39. Lucian W. Pye, *Politics, Personality, and Nation Building: Burma's Search for Identity* (New Haven: Yale University Press, 1962), p. 26.
40. W. Howard Wriggins, *Ceylon: Dilemmas of a New Nation* (Princeton: Princeton University Press, 1960), p. 151.
41. Almond and Powell, op. cit., pp. 75–8.
42. Joseph LaPalombara and Myron Weiner, eds., *Political Parties and Political Development* (Princeton: Princeton University Press, 1966), p. 3.

43. A partial exception to this phenomena occurred in Pakistan and the Philippines. No small opposition parties existed in Pakistan at the time of partition and independence. A large number of Filipino politicians in the Nacionalista Party broke away and formed the Liberal Party at the time of national independence to campaign for the first elected President and Congress in the new republic. This development has often been labeled as the beginning of a "two-party system." Instead, the similarities between the members and policies of the two political parties, the extensive party-switching, and the inability of third parties to gain power manifested many of the same characteristics of a dominant party system. Professor Onofre Corpuz has stated: "The two-party system in the Philippines was in fact two parties in name only, and it was more accurate to refer to it as a 'one-and-a-half' party system. Normally there was a large majority party looming over a minority that could not be completely ignored because of its legal status, but that was impotent." See Corpuz, op. cit., p. 95.

44. It is interesting to note that only in this kind of political system were left-wing political parties able to operate openly in the indigenous response of emerging national societies in Asia. The only exception was the brief period of overt political activity by the Chinese Communist Party from 1921 to 1927.

45. For scholarly analysis of this phenomenon in India see Myron Weiner, *Party Building in a New Nation: The Indian National Congress* (Chicago: The University of Chicago Press, 1967), pp. 30–4; Stanley A. Kochanek, *The Congress Party of India: The Dynamics of One-Party Democracy* (Princeton: Princeton University Press, 1968), Chapter XIII.

46. LaPalombara and Weiner, op. cit., p. 14.

47. James MacGregor Burns, "Wellsprings of Political Leadership," *The American Political Science Review* (March 1977), p. 267.

48. See Grossholz, op. cit., p. 109.

49. Norman D. Palmer, *The Indian Political System* (Boston: Houghton Mifflin Company, 1971), p. 53.

50. Taylor, op. cit., p. 61.

51. This method of sharing executive powers in India was confined only to the provincial governments. See Palmer, op. cit., pp. 56–7.

52. Cf. pp. 171–2.

53. Palmer, op. cit., p. 50.

54. Griffiths, op. cit., p. 195.

55. Taylor, op. cit., pp. 57–63.

56. Garel A. Grunder and William E. Livezey, *The Philippines and the United States* (Norman: University of Oklahoma Press, 1951), p. 160.

57. For a discussion of many aspects of this conflict see Henry F. Goodnow, *The Civil Service of Pakistan* (New Haven: Yale University Press, 1964), pp. 3–19.

58. Amos Perlmutter, "The Presidential Political Center and Foreign Policy: A Critique of the Revisionist and Bureaucratic-Political Orientations," *World Politics* (October 1974), p. 93.
59. John F. Cady, *A History of Modern Burma* (Ithaca: Cornell University Press, 1958), pp. 559–65.
60. R. S. Milne, *Government and Politics in Malaysia* (Boston: Houghton Mifflin Company, 1967), pp. 34–41.
61. Grunder and Livezey, op. cit., Chapter XIII.
62. For a brief explanation of this important influence in India see Griffiths, op. cit., pp. 152–3.
63. For a scholarly analysis of pre-independence attitudes of indigenous political leaders toward foreign affairs see Werner Levi, "The Elitist Nature of New Asia's Foreign Policy," *Asian Survey* (November 1967), pp. 762–75.
64. Nehru has discussed his views on this aspect of British-Indian relations in his autobiography. See Nehru, op. cit., pp. 260–85.

Chapter 11: The Bureaucratic Polities

1. See Fred W. Riggs, *Thailand: The Modernization of a Bureaucratic Polity* (Honolulu: East-West Center Press, 1966).
2. Ibid., p. 378.
3. Ssu-yu Ten and John K. Fairbank, eds., *China's Response to the West* (Cambridge: Harvard University Press, 1961), p. 46. See also John K. Fairbank, *The United States and China* (Cambridge: Harvard University Press, 1971), Third Edition, Chapters 6–8; Wolfgang Franke, *China and the West* (New York: Harper and Row, Publishers, 1967), Chapters V–VII.
4. Herbert Passin, "Japan" in James S. Coleman, ed., *Education and Political Development* (Princeton: Princeton University Press, 1965), pp. 272–3.
5. Fairbank, op. cit., p. 188.
6. Walter F. Vella, *The Impact of the West on Government in Thailand* (Berkeley: University of California Press, 1955), pp. 348–9.
7. Mikiso Hane, *Japan: A Historical Survey* (New York: Charles Scribner's Sons, 1972), pp. 289–91.
8. Quoted in G. B. Sansom, *The Western World and Japan* (New York: Alfred A. Knopf, 1965), p. 459.
9. Riggs, op. cit., Chapters IV, V.
10. See Carsun Chang, *The Third Force in China* (New York: Bookman Associates, Inc., 1952).
11. Rong Syamananda, *A History of Thailand* (Bangkok: Thai Watana Panich Co., Ltd., 1973), pp. 162–3.
12. For detailed analyses of the modern economic development of Japan see William W. Lockwood, *The Economic Development of Japan* (Prince-

ton: Princeton University Press, 1954); E. Herbert Norman, *Japan's Emergence as a Modern State* (New York: Institute of Pacific Relations, 1940); William W. Lockwood, ed., *The State and Economic Enterprise in Japan* (Princeton: Princeton University Press, 1965), Chapters I–IX.

13. Hane, op. cit., pp. 278–9.
14. James R. Townsend, *Politics in China* (Boston: Little, Brown and Company, 1974), pp. 50–1.
15. James C. Ingram, *Economic Change in Thailand Since 1850* (Stanford: Stanford University Press, 1955), Chapter 10.
16. Ibid., Chapter 4.
17. E. Sydney Crawcour, "The Tokugawa Heritage," in Lockwood, ed., op. cit., p. 44.
18. Lockwood, op. cit., pp. 12–25.
19. Norman, op. cit., pp. 111–4.
20. Fairbank, op. cit., p. 224.
21. Townsend, op. cit., pp. 49–50.
22. Alexander Eckstein, "The Economic Heritage," in Alexander Eckstein, Walter Galenson, and Ta-chung Liu, eds., *Economic Trends in Communist China* (Chicago: Aldine Press, Inc., 1968), pp. 64–7.
23. Ingram, op. cit., pp. 98–105.
24. David A. Wilson, *Politics in Thailand* (Ithaca: Cornell University Press, 1962), pp. 44–5.
25. Cf. pp. 268–9.
26. Mostafa Rejai and Cynthia H. Enloe, "Nation-States and State-Nations," *International Studies Quarterly* (June 1969), pp. 149–50.
27. Hans Kohn, *The Idea of Nationalism: A Study in Its Origin and Background* (New York: The Macmillan Company, 1944), pp. 18–9.
28. Fairbank, op. cit., p. 89.
29. Reischauer, op. cit., pp. 112–3.
30. Wilson, op. cit., p. 82.
31. See John K. Fairbank, Edwin O. Reischauer, and Albert M. Craig, *East Asia: The Modern Transformation* (Boston: Houghton Mifflin Company, 1965), pp. 394–404, 665–9.
32. Sun Yat-sen, *San Min Chu I: The Three Principles of the People* (Taipei: China Cultural Service, 1953), p. 31.
33. Hane, op. cit., p. 323.
34. Quoted in Vella, op. cit., p. 352.
35. Professor David Apter posits the hypothesis that science is also an ideology characteristic of modernizing societies. See David E. Apter, *The Politics of Modernization* (Chicago: University of Chicago Press, 1965), pp. 319–54. This assessment would consequently entail the inclusion of science as an ideology in the indigenous response in Japan. In my view science does not comprise an ideology that lends itself to political analysis in the same context as nationalism, constitutional democracy, capitalism, socialism, and communism. Instead science is a

specific methodology or research technique which seeks exact knowledge and fundamental laws in virtually every aspect of a modernizing
society.
36. Emerson, op. cit., pp. 254–5.
37. For a discussion of this phenomena in Japan see Hane, op. cit., pp.
378–81. Another good example was the bitter opposition of the conservatives in Thailand to the socialist-oriented economic plan proposed
by Pridi Phanomyong in 1933. See Vella, op. cit., pp. 374–7.
38. See David A. Wilson, "Thailand and Marxism," in Frank N. Trager,
Marxism in Southeast Asia (Stanford, Stanford University Press,
1959), pp. 58–101.
39. See Benjamin I. Schwartz, *Chinese Communism and the Rise of Mao*
(Cambridge: Harvard University Press, 1958), Chapters XII, XIII.
40. Gabriel A. Almond and G. Bingham Powell, Jr., *Comparative Politics: A
Developmental Approach* (Boston: Little, Brown and Company, 1966),
p. 53.
41. Fairbank, Reischauer, and Craig, op. cit., pp. 701–4.
42. Hane, op. cit., p. 318.
43. Almond and Powell, op. cit., pp. 74–8.
44. Hane, op. cit., p. 361.
45. Fairbank, op. cit., p. 260.
46. Hane, op. cit., p. 268.
47. Almond and Powell, op. cit., p. 77.
48. Fairbank, Reischauer, and Craig, op. cit., pp. 683–701.
49. Hugh Borton, *Japan's Modern Century* (New York: The Ronald Press,
1970), pp. 165–8.
50. See Frank C. Darling, *Thailand and the United States* (Washington,
D.C.: Public Affairs Press, 1965), pp. 26–32.
51. Vella, op. cit., pp. 382–6.
52. James R. Townsend, *Politics in China* (Boston: Little, Brown and Company, 1974), p. 37.
53. Vella, op. cit., p. 378.

Chapter 12: The Truncated Totalitarian Polities

1. The use of the term "truncated" to describe and analyze the formation of
the People's Republic of China differs slightly in a geopolitical context
from its application to North Korea and North Vietnam. In each case
it refers to the communist sector which developed on the territory of
the same traditional society as an adjoining or nearby non-communist
sector. Yet the truncated status of the "two Koreas" and the "two
Vietnams" involved the division of a formerly unified society along
politically defined and highly controversial boundaries at specific
latitudinal parallels chosen by the leaders of major world powers at
international conferences outside of Asia. The truncated status of the

"two Chinas," conversely, consisted of the division of the former traditional society along a natural water barrier between the mainland and Taiwan due to the final outcome of a civil war.

2. Cf. pp. 36–9., above.
3. See Figure XV, p. 243.
4. See Benjamin I. Schwartz, *Chinese Communism and the Rise of Mao* (Cambridge: Harvard University Press, 1958), pp. 17–8; Jacques Guillermaz, *A History of the Chinese Communist Party, 1921–1949* (New York: Random House, 1972), Chap. 3.
5. See Chong-sik Lee, *The Politics of Korean Nationalism* (Berkeley: University of California Press, 1963), Chap. 7; Robert A. Scalapino and Chong-sik Lee, *Communism in Korea* (Berkeley: University of California Press, 1972), Vol. I, pp. 9–16; Gregory Henderson, *Korea: The Politics of the Vortex* (Cambridge: Harvard University Press, 1968), pp. 80–8.
6. See Hoang Van Chi, *From Colonialism to Communism: A Case History of North Vietnam* (New York: Frederick A. Praeger, Publisher, 1964), pp. 29–47; Joseph Buttinger, *Vietnam: A Dragon Embattled* (New York: Frederick A. Praeger, Publisher, 1967), pp. 209–26; Robert F. Turner, *Vietnamese Communism: Its Origin and Development* (Stanford: Hoover Institution Press, 1975), Chaps. 1, 2; William J. Duiker, *The Rise of Nationalism in Vietnam, 1900–1941* (Ithaca: Cornell University Press, 1976), Chap. 11.
7. In the next chapter dealing with the development of South Korea and South Vietnam I will use the term "exiled movements" to designate the scattered nationalist organizations of Koreans and Vietnamese in foreign countries which shaped the formation of these two non-communist truncated societies. These exiled nationalist groups did *not* develop a sustained military or subversive capacity during their years in exile, and the primary source of power supporting their national survival after independence was that provided by the United States.
8. Guillermaz, op. cit., Chaps. 17–22; Lyman P. Van Slyke, *The Chinese Communist Movement* (Stanford: Stanford University Press, 1968), pp. 24–33.
9. Scalapino and Lee, op. cit., Chaps. 1–3; Dae-sook Suh, *The Korean Communist Movement, 1918–1948* (Princeton: Princeton University Press, 1967), Chaps. 1, 2, 6, 7, 8.
10. Hoang Van Chi, op. cit., Chaps. *2–5.*
11. Buttinger, op. cit., pp. 744–54.
12. Cf., pp. 38–9.
13. John King Fairbank, *The United States and China* (Cambridge: Harvard University Press, 1971), Third Edition, p. 61.
14. See Lee, op. cit., Chap. 1; Henderson, op. cit. pp. 19–35.
15. Hoang Van Chi, op. cit., pp. 6–8; Dennis J. Duncanson, *Government and Revolution in Vietnam* (New York: Oxford University Press, 1968), pp. 45–64; David G. Marr, *Vietnamese Anticolonialism*

1885–1925 (Berkeley: University of California Press, 1971), Chap. 1; Virginia Thompson, *French Indochina* (New York: Octagon Books, Inc., 1968), pp. 25–57; Duiker, op. cit., pp. 21–6.

16. Mao Tse-tung, *Selected Works of Mao Tse-tung* (Bombay, India: People's Publishing House, Ltd., 1954), Vol. 3, p. 107.
17. Cf., p. 44 above.
18. Schwarz, op. cit., pp. 10–26.
19. See Guillermaz, op. cit., pp. 54–6; Suh, op. cit., pp. 135–8; Buttinger, op. cit., pp. 203–4.
20. James R. Townsend, *Politics in China* (Boston: Little, Brown and Company, 1974), p. 51.
21. Henderson, op. cit., p. 77.
22. Ibid.
23. Buttinger, op. cit., p. 167.
24. Ibid., pp. 175–6.
25. Ibid., pp. 174–5.
26. Guillermaz, op. cit., pp. 42–5.
27. Henderson, op. cit., p. 96
28. Ibid., p. 97.
29. Buttinger, op. cit., p. 194.
30. Buttinger, op. cit., p. 195.
31. I have borrowed the term "peasant nationalism" from the excellent study of this form of nationalism in China by Chalmer Johnson. See his book, *Peasant Nationalism and Communist Power* (Stanford: Stanford University Press, 1962).
32. Ibid., p. 5.
33. Scalapino and Lee, op. cit., p. 139.
34. Duiker, op. cit., pp. 217–29.
35. Bernard B. Fall, *The Viet-Minh Regime* (New York: Institute of Pacific Relations, 1957), pp. 16–7.
36. For a scholarly discussion of the influence of Marxism on early revolutionary thinkers in these three societies see Townsend, op. cit., pp. 64–7; Stuart R. Schram, *The Political Thought of Mao Tse-tung* (New York: Frederick A. Praeger, Publishers, 1969), Chap. 2; Scalapino and Lee, op. cit., pp. 61–4; Milton Sacks, "Marxism in Viet Nam," in Frank N. Trager, ed., *Marxism in Southeast Asia* (Stanford: Stanford University Press, 1959), pp. 107–11.
37. Duiker, op. cit., p. 290.
38. Ho Chi Minh, *On Revolution: Selected Writings, 1920–1966,* edited by Bernard B. Fall (New York: Frederick A. Praeger, Publisher, 1967), pp. 6–10.
39. Vladimir Lenin, *Theses and Statutes of the III Communist International,* Communist International, 1920, p. 68.
40. See Mao Tse-tung, op. cit., p. 109.
41. For a description of the "socialist revolution" which abolished French colonial rule and established the communist system in North Vietnam

see Le Duan, *The Vietnamese Revolution: Fundamental Problems, Essential Tasks* (Hanoi: Foreign Languages Publishing House, 1970), pp. 85–101.

42. Cf., p. 307.
43. George Vernadsky, *A History of Russia* (New Haven: Yale University Press, 1951), p. 56.
44. For a description of the role exerted by these political agents see Robert C. North, *Moscow and Chinese Communists* (Stanford: Stanford University Press, 1963), pp. 87–9, 149–50; David J. Dallin, *Soviet Russia and the Far East* (New Haven: Yale University Press, 1948), pp. 106, 112; Suh, op. cit., pp. 33–5.
45. See Edgar Snow, *Red Star Over China* (New York: Random House, Inc., 1944), p. 153.
46. Ibid., p. 160–1.
47. Suh, op. cit., pp. 15, 48, 67.
48. Scalapino and Lee, op. cit., p. 206.
49. Sacks, op. cit., p. 109.
50. Hoang Van Chi, op. cit., p. 49.
51. Guillermaz, op. cit., pp. 340–65.
52. Scalapino and Lee, op. cit., pp. 340–65.
53. See Van Slyke, op. cit., pp. 34–65; Suh, op. cit., pp. 85–95; Turner, op. cit., pp. 23–8.
54. Wen Shih, "Political Parties in Communist China," *Asian Survey* (March 1963), p. 158.
55. Scalapino and Lee, op. cit., pp. 701–2.
56. Hoang Van Chi, op. cit., pp. 69–70.
57. John K. Fairbank, "The People's Middle Kingdom," *Foreign Affairs* (July 1966), p. 583.
58. Mao Tse-tung, *Selected Works* (New York: International Publishers, 1954), pp. 21–2.
59. Scalapino and Lee, op. cit., p. 230.
60. Robert C. North, *Kuomintang and Chinese Communist Elites* (Stanford: Stanford University Press, 1952), pp. 65–72.
61. Duncanson, op. cit., pp. 141–2. Ho Chi Minh was born and raised in Nghe An province which was the native province of famous rebels such as Le Loi and the Tay Son brothers. Nghe An was also the site of the peasant uprising in 1930–31 which took several months to quell by the French colonial regime.
62. Scalapino and Lee, op. cit., pp. 230–1.
63. For a good assessment of this factor regarding the contrasting leadership capacities of the Chinese communists and the Chinese nationalists see Fairbank, op. cit., p. 260.
64. North, op. cit., p. 55.
65. Schwartz, op. cit., p. 102.
66. Guillermaz, op. cit., p. 170.

67. For a good description of the Shensi soviets see Snow, op. cit., pp. 219-51.
68. Hoang Van Chi, op. cit., pp. 49-51.
69. Fairbank, op. cit., pp. 328-9.
70. Scalapino and Lee, op. cit., pp. 372-3; Bernard B. Fall, *The Two Vietnams* (New York: Frederick A. Praeger, Publishers, 1963), pp. 131-3.

Chapter 13: The Truncated Authoritarian Polities

1. Cf. pp. 349-50, above.
2. South Vietnam, like North Vietnam, was a partial exception to this classification. It had some minorities, including Chinese nationals, in many urban areas, and Cambodians, Chams, and mountain tribesmen living along portions of its national boundaries. Yet at the time of national independence in the mid-1950's approximately 90% of the population in South Vietnam was ethnically Vietnamese.
3. See Figure XV, p. 243.
4. Cf. footnote 7, p. 483.
5. Chong-sik Lee, *The Politics of Korean Nationalism* (Berkeley: University of California Press, 1963), pp. 129-55, 167-70; William J. Duiker, *The Rise of Nationalism in Vietnam* (Ithaca: Cornell University Press, 1976), pp. 38-45, 65-72; Bernard B. Fall, *The Two Vietnams* (New York: Frederick A. Praeger, Publisher, 1963), pp. 242-5.
6. Lee, op. cit., p. 238; Duiker, op. cit., pp. 179-80.
7. Bong-youn Choy, *Korea: A History* (Rutland, Vermont: Charles E. Tuttle Company, 1971), pp. 208-11.
8. Joseph Buttinger, *Vietnam: A Dragon Embattled* (New York: Frederick A. Praeger, Publishers, 1967), Vol. II, pp. 834-42.
9. Gregory Henderson, *Korea: The Politics of the Vortex* (Cambridge: Harvard University Press, 1968), p. 113.
10. Buttinger, op. cit., pp. 851-9.
11. Cf. pp. 167-8, 143.
12. Henderson, op. cit., p. 89; Dennis J. Duncanson, *Government and Revolution in Vietnam* (New York: Oxford University Press, 1968), p. 105.
13. Henderson, ibid.
14. Duncanson, op. cit., p. 106.
15. Henderson, op. cit., p. 91.
16. See Choy, op. cit., pp. 153-7.
17. Buttinger, op. cit., p. 855.
18. Duiker, op. cit., pp. 103-5.
19. Henderson, op. cit., p. 156.
20. Richard C. Allen, *Korea's Syngman Rhee: An Unauthorized Portrait* (Rutland, Vermont: Charles E. Tuttle Company, 1960), pp. 104-5.
21. Duncanson, op. cit., pp. 243-4.
22. Buttinger, op. cit., pp. 855-6.

23. Robert Scigliano, *South Vietnam: Nation Under Stress* (Boston: Houghton Mifflin Company, 1964), pp. 50-5.

24. For an explanation of the early American aid programs in these truncated societies see Robert T. Oliver, *Syngman Rhee: The Man Behind the Myth* (New York: Dodd Mead and Company, 1954), pp. 280-93; and John D. Montgomery, *The Politics of Foreign Aid: American Experience in Southeast Asia* (New York: Frederick A. Praeger, Publisher, 1962), pp. 20-5, 44-8.

25. Duiker, op. cit., p. 287.

26. David G. Marr, *Vietnamese Anticolonialism* (Berkeley: University of California Press, 1971), Chap. 3.

27. Choy, op. cit., pp. 127-32.

28. Duiker, op. cit., p. 30.

29. Lee, op. cit., p. 85.

30. Ibid, pp. 111-26.

31. Marr, op. cit., pp. 76-8.

32. Oliver, op. cit., pp. 76-8.

33. Duiker, op. cit., pp. 31-47.

34. Ellen J. Hammer, *The Struggle for Indochina* (Stanford: Stanford University Press, 1954), pp. 23-4.

35. It is important to stress here that most modernizing Koreans had great respect for Japanese technological advances, while they reacted with intense hostility to the forced intrusion on nontechnical aspects of Japanese culture.

36. Henderson, op. cit., p. 88.

37. Lee, op. cit., p. 240.

38. Henderson, op. cit., p. 93.

39. Duiker, op. cit., p. 55.

40. Marr, op. cit., Chap. 7.

41. Ibid., pp. 213-4.

42. Duiker, op. cit., p. 121.

43. Marr, op. cit., p. 149.

44. See Fall, op. cit., pp. 246-9.

45. Lee, op. cit., p. 278.

46. See Choi, op. cit., pp. 190-4; Duiker, op. cit., pp. 82-7.

47. Cf. pp. 307, 336, above.

48. Lee, op. cit., p. 242; Marr, op. cit., p. 187.

49. Choy, op. cit., pp. 186-90.

50. Duiker, op. cit., Chap. 3.

51. For a detailed analysis of the rise and influence of the Constitutionalist Party see R. B. Smith, "Bui Quang Chieu and the Constitutionalist Party in French Cochinchina, 1917-1930," *Modern Asian Studies* (April 1969), pp. 131-50.

52. Scigliano, op. cit., p. 74.

53. Fall, *The Two Vietnams,* pp. 241-2.

54. Choy, op. cit., pp. 184-5.

55. Lee, op. cit., p. 253.
56. Choy, op. cit., pp. 189–90.
57. Ibid.
58. Marr, op. cit., pp. 216–19.
59. Scigliano, op. cit., p. 71.
60. Chester A. Bain, *Vietnam: The Roots of Conflict* (Englewood Cliffs, New Jersey: Prentice-Hall, Inc., 1967), p. 114.
61. Spencer J. Palmer, *Korea and Christianity* (Seoul: Hollym Corporation Publishers, 1967), pp. 65–6.
62. Bernard B. Fall, "The Political Religious Sects of Vietnam," *Pacific Affairs* (September 1955), pp. 235–53.
63. Scigliano, op. cit., p. 19.
64. Choy, op. cit., pp. 223–4; Buttinger, op. cit., pp. 834–42.
65. Choy, op. cit., pp. 221–3.
66. Scigliano, op. cit., pp. 75–8.
67. Allen, op. cit., p. 34; Fall, op. cit., p. 235.
68. Oliver, op. cit., Chaps. VI–XII.
69. Duncanson, op. cit., p. 211.
70. Henderson, op. cit., p. 151.
71. Fall, op. cit., p. 243.
72. Lee, op. cit., pp. 151–5.
73. Fall, op. cit., pp. 239–40.
74. Henderson, op. cit., pp. 152–3.
75. Buttinger, op. cit., pp. 846–51.
76. See Paul S. Dull, "South Korean Constitution," *Far Eastern Survey* (September 8, 1948), p. 207; Scigliano, op. cit., pp. 34–9.
77. The American specialist in South Korea was Professor Paul S. Dull, and the American expert in South Vietnam was Professor J. A. C. Grant. See Dull, ibid.; J. A. C. Grant, "The Vietnamese Constitution of 1956," *American Political Science Review* (June, 1958), pp. 437–63.
78. The constitution of South Korea established the office of a Premier or Prime Minister, but due to Rhee's influence this position was not designed as the chief of government in a normal parliamentary system. Instead the Premier was merely an administrative head of the Cabinet, or as described by Rhee "an assistant to the president, who will be the real executive head. . . ." Quoted in Oliver, op. cit., p. 272.
79. Article 98.
80. Duncanson, op. cit., p. 228.
81. Articles 85 and 86.

Chapter 14: The Hybrid Polity

1. These three religions were also involved in the political development of the Indian subcontinent, although Buddhism never became firmly implanted in India even though it was the land of its origin. Buddhism

exerted a significant political influence only during the reign of Asoka in the third century B.C., and it declined as an organized religious movement after 600 A.D. As already cited, Hinduism and Islam were the two dominant religions shaping the politics of the Indian states, yet in the subcontinent there was relatively little assimilation or fusion between these two diverse religious systems which significantly affected their political development.

2. Cf. pp. 73-4, above.

3. Cf. pp. 165-6, above.

4. Cf. pp. 84-90, above.

5. Cf. pp. 243-5, above.

6. Harry J. Benda, *The Crescent and the Rising Sun* (The Hague: W. van Hoeve Ltd., 1958), Part One.

7. See Clifford Geertz, *The Religion of Java* (Glencoe, Illinois: The Free Press, 1960), pp. 177-90.

8. Ibid., p. 127.

9. Clifford Geertz, "Modernization in a Muslim Society: The Indonesian Case," in Robert O. Tilman, ed., *Man, State, and Society in Contemporary Southeast Asia* (New York: Praeger Publishers, 1969), p. 204.

10. Benda, op. cit., pp. 61-99.

11. Robert Van Niel, *The Emergence of the Modern Indonesian Elite* (The Hague: W. van Hoeve Ltd., 1960), Chap. II.

12. Geertz, op. cit., p. 207.

13. Ibid., p. 204.

14. W. F. Wertheim, *Indonesian Society in Transition* (The Hague: W. van Hoeve Ltd., 1959), pp. 61-6.

15. Benda, op. cit., p. 16.

16. The rural tradition in Indonesia was heavily intermixed with Islamic behavior and was called the *abangan* tradition. For a detailed description of the behavior of this element of the cultural system see Geertz, op. cit., pp. 121-30.

17. Jeanne S. Mintz, "Marxism in Indonesia," in Frank N. Trager (ed.), *Marxism in Southeast Asia* (Stanford: Stanford University Press, 1959), pp. 172-3.

18. Bruce Grant, *Indonesia* (London: Melbourne University Press, 1964), pp. 99-100.

19. Cf. pp. 262-3, above.

20. Bernard H. M. Vlekke, *Nusantara: A History of Indonesia* (The Hague: W. van Hoeve Ltd., 1959), p. 382.

21. Indicative of this policy was the following statement by Dr. C. J. Nieuwenhuis, a Dutch educational expert, early in the twentieth century: "If we want to promote Indonesian unity, let us begin first with the highest social classes, with the elite; and then, as the British did in India and the French in Annam, we must institute a language which can represent international culture fully as the general medium for social intercourse. In Indonesia this language will have to be Dutch."

Quoted in S. Takdir Alisjahbana, *Indonesia: Social and Cultural Revolution* (London: Oxford University Press, 1966), p. 62.

22. George McTurnan Kahin, *Nationalism and Revolution in Indonesia* (Ithaca: Cornell University Press, 1952), p. 97.
23. Alisjahbana, op. cit., pp. 63–9.
24. Dorothy Woodman, *The Republic of Indonesia* (London: The Cresset Press, 1955), pp. 297–300.
25. David Joel Steinberg, ed., *In Search of Southeast Asia* (New York: Praeger Publishers, 1971), p. 292.
26. Alisjabana, op. cit., pp. 27–9.
27. J. D. Legge, *Indonesia* (Englewood Cliffs, New Jersey: Prentice-Hall, Inc., 1964), pp. 9–11.
28. Soetan Sjahrir, *Out of Exile* (New York: The John Day Company, 1949), pp. 66–7.
29. For a detailed comparison of economic aspects of Dutch colonial rule in Indonesia and British colonial rule in Burma see J. S. Furnivall, *Colonial Policy and Practice* (New York: New York University Press, 1956), pp. 251–75.
30. Vlekke, op. cit., pp. 306–7.
31. Malcolm Caldwell, *Indonesia* (London: Oxford University Press, 1968), p. 62.
32. Wertheim, op. cit., p. 94. *Batik* is Indonesian-designed cloth.
33. Caldwell, op. cit., p. 64.
34. Legge, op. cit., p. 127.
35. Benda, op. cit., pp. 50–2. *Hadji* are Moslem males who have made the pilgrimage to Mecca.
36. The primacy of Islam over secular political thought is depicted in the following passage from a speech by a leading orthodox Moslem shortly after national independence criticizing Sukarno for stressing the idea of a national state in the highly eclectic political doctrine, *Panja Sila,* declared at the time of national independence: "They [Indonesian revolutionary fighters] fought and sacrificed themselves—those who died to become Martyrs no less than those who still live and stand upright, the Holy War fighters of our time—for one idealism, for one ideal inspired by the goal and purpose of their lives: to devote themselves to God, praise be to Him the Most High, by upholding His Word and by expecting merely His grace. They fought to place Islam in the life of our society and state. They fought to establish the Sovereignty and the Law of Islam." From a speech entitled "We are Moving towards a Republic of Indonesia Based on Islam," by K. H. Muhammad Isa Anshari in 1957, quoted in Harry J. Benda and John A. Larkin, *The World of Southeast Asia: Selected Historical Readings* (New York: Harper and Row, Publishers, 1967), p. 252.
37. Jeanne S. Mintz, *Mohammed, Marx, and Marhaen: The Roots of Indonesian Socialism* (New York: Frederick A. Praeger, Publishers), p. 21.
38. Kahin, op. cit., p. 48.

39. Caldwell, op. cit., p. 66.
40. For a detailed explanation of the origin of Marxism and communism in Indonesia, see Jeanne S. Mintz, "Marxism in Indonesia," in Frank N. Trager, ed., *Marxism in Southeast Asia* (Stanford: Stanford University Press, 1959), pp. 176–80.
41. Kahin, op. cit., p. 51.
42. Legge, op. cit., p. 121.
43. Jeanne S. Mintz, *Mohammed, Marx, and Marhaen,* Chaps. 3–6.
44. Kahin, op. cit., p. 122.
45. Steinberg, op. cit., pp. 296–7.
46. Caldwell, op. cit., pp. 67–8.
47. Cf. p. 277, above.
48. Kahin, op. cit., p. 129.
49. Herbert Feith, *The Decline of Constitutional Democracy in Indonesia* (Ithaca: Cornell University Press, 1962), p. 108.
50. For a detailed analysis of this dichotomy in Indonesian political culture prior to national independence see Van Niel, op. cit., Chap. 4.
51. Ibid., p. 242.
52. Feith, op. cit., pp. 31–2.
53. Ibid.
54. Kahin, op. cit., p. 41.
55. Thom Kerstiens, *The New Elite in Asia and Africa* (New York: Frederick A. Praeger, Publishers, 1966), p. 194.
56. Alisjahbana, op. cit., pp. 63–6.
57. For a brief description of the influential "wild schools" started by Indonesians during this period see Steinberg, op. cit., p. 299.
58. Caldwell, op. cit., p. 74.
59. Kerstiens, op. cit., pp. 187–8.
60. Vlekke, op. cit., pp. 348–9.
61. Kahin, op. cit., p. 70.
62. Woodman, op. cit., p. 159.
63. Soedjatmoko, "The Role of Political Parties in Indonesia," in Philip W. Thayer, ed., *Nationalism and Progress in Free Asia* (Baltimore: The Johns Hopkins Press, 1956), p. 130.
64. Van Niel, op. cit., p. 217.
65. Steinberg, op. cit., pp. 294–5.
66. Kahin, op. cit., p. 74.
67. Ibid., p. 90.
68. It is interesting at this point to speculate that if the PNI had not been suppressed by the Dutch at this time, it may have entered the period of national independence as the leader of a dominant party system similar to that developing in the relatively free political environment maintained by British and American colonial rule. The divisions between the political parties in Indonesia were deep, and the time duration between 1929 and 1945 was relatively short. Nevertheless, the PNI in a free pollitical environment would almost certainly have made some progress

in building an integrated and unified national party organization.
69. Kerstiens, op. cit., p. 145.
70. Feith, op. cit., p. 122.
71. Ibid., p. 128.
72. Soelaeman Soemardi, "Some Aspects of the Social Origin of the Indonesian Political Decision-Makers," *Transactions of the Third World Congress of Sociology* (London: 1956) cited in Legge, op. cit., p. 109.
73. Guy J. Pauker, "The Military in Indonesia," in John J. Johnson, ed., *The Role of the Military in Underdeveloped Countries* (Princeton: Princeton University Press, 1962), pp. 203-5.
74. Legge, op. cit., p. 12.
75. Kahin, op. cit., pp. 332-45.
76. C. L. M. Penders, *The Life and Times of Sukarno* (Rutherford, New Jersey: Fairleigh Dickinson University Press, 1974), Chaps. II-V.
77. Benjamin Higgins, *Indonesia: The Crisis of the Millstones* (New York: D. Van Nostrand Company, Inc., 1963), p. 80.
78. Cf. pp. 312-3.
79. Pauker, op. cit., p. 188.
80. Ibid., pp. 198-99.
81. Wertheim, op. cit., p. 167.
82. Higgins, op. cit., p. 29.

Chapter 15: The Dynastic Polities

1. Cf. Table XIV, p. 145.
2. See David J. Steinberg, *et al.*, *Cambodia: Its People, Its Society, Its Culture* (New Haven, Connecticut: Human Area Files Press, 1959), pp. 68-74; Frank M. LeBar and Adrienne Suddard, eds., *Laos: Its People, Its Society, Its Culture* (New Haven, Connecticut: Human Area Files Press, 1960), pp. 49-54.
3. David J. Steinberg, ed., *In Search of Southeast Asia* (New York: Praeger Publishers, 1971), pp. 328-33.
4. Joel M. Halpern, *Economy and Society of Laos,* Monograph Series No. 5, Southeast Asia Studies, Yale University, 1964, pp. 8-9.
5. Steinberg, *Cambodia,* pp. 252-6.
6. LeBar and Suddard, op. cit., pp. 82-6.
7. Ibid., p. 198.
8. Halpern, op. cit., pp. 16-7.
9. See John P. Armstrong, *Sihanouk Speaks* (New York: Walker and Company, 1964), Chap. 3; Sisouk Na Champassak, *Storm Over Laos* (New York: Frederick A. Praeger, Publisher, 1961), Chap. 2.
10. Roger M. Smith, *Cambodia's Foreign Policy* (Ithaca: Cornell University Press, 1965), pp. 140-2, 153-72; Joel M. Halpern, *Government, Politics, and Social Structure in Laos,* Monograph Series No. 4, Southeast Asia Studies, Yale University, 1964, pp. 25-8.

11. Michael Leifer, *Cambodia: The Search for Security* (New York: Frederick A. Praeger, Publishers, 1967), p. 26.
12. Sisouk, op. cit., pp. 21-9.
13. Carlton J. H. Hayes, *The Historical Evolution of Modern Nationalism* (New York: Richard R. Smith, Inc., 1931), pp. 110-1.
14. Martin F. Herz, *A Short History of Cambodia* (New York: Frederick A. Praeger, Publishers, 1958), pp. 77-95.
15. Arthur J. Dommen, *Conflict in Laos: The Politics of Neutralization* (Frederick A. Praeger, Publishers, 1964), pp. 18-30.
16. Steinberg, *Cambodia,* op. cit., p. 143.
17. LeBar and Suddard, op. cit., p. 138.
18. Herz, op. cit., pp. 77-8.
19. Dommen, op. cit., Chap. 2.
20. Ibid., pp. 70-83.
21. Roger M. Smith, "Cambodia," in George M. Kahin, ed., *Governments and Politics of Southeast Asia* (Ithaca: Cornell University Press, 1964), p. 610.
22. LeBar and Suddard, op. cit., pp. 104-8.
23. Leifer, op. cit., pp. 43-55.
24. Armstrong, op. cit., pp. 40-51.
25. Steinberg, *In Search of Southeast Asia,* p. 330.
26. Steinberg, *Cambodia,* pp. 122-5.
27. LeBar and Suddard, op. cit., p. 121.
28. Armstrong, op. cit., pp. 19-25.
29. Steinberg, *Cambodia,* pp. 125-8; LeBar and Suddard, op. cit., pp. 122-4.
30. Steinberg, *Cambodia,* pp. 128-30.
31. LeBar and Suddard, op. cit., pp. 124-6.
32. Steinberg, *Cambodia,* pp. 130-2; LeBar and Suddard, op. cit., pp. 126-7.
33. See Smith, op. cit., Chap. III.
34. See Dommen, op. cit., Chaps. 3-5.

Chapter 16: Terminal Analysis of Fusional Historical Inputs

1. Cf. Chaps. Four and Nine.
2. This terminal factor applies only to the colonized societies.
3. This terminal factor also applies only to the colonized societies.

Conclusion

1. For a strong indictment of the overuse of quantification in historical analysis see Jacques Barzun, *Clio and the Doctors: Psycho-History, Quanto-History, and History* (Chicago: The University of Chicago Press, 1974).
2. For an excellent explanation of important aspects of Westernization and modernization see David E. Apter, *The Politics of Modernization*

(Chicago: The University of Chicago Press, 1965), Chap. 2.

3. *Ibid.,* pp. 9–12.

4. David Easton, *The Political System: An Inquiry into the State of Political Science* (New York: Alfred A. Knopf, Inc., 1971), Second Edition, p. 194.

5. Gabriel A. Almond and G. Bingham Powell, Jr., *Comparative Politics: A Developmental Approach* (Boston: Little, Brown and Company, 1966), p. 301.

6. For a brief discussion of the comparative advantages of longitudinal and cross-societal analysis in political research see John V. Gillespie, "An Introduction to Macro-Cross-National Research," in John V. Gillespie and Betty A. Nesvold, eds., *Macro-Quantitative Analysis* (Beverly Hills, California: Sage Publications, 1971), p. 23.

7. See Lucian W. Pye, *Aspects of Political Development* (Boston: Little, Brown and Company, 1966), pp. 45–8.

8. *Ibid.,* p. 48. An analysis of historical data will also be necessary in assessing the crises and sequences of political development presented in the seventh volume in the series of Studies in Political Development published by the Committee on Comparative Politics of the Social Science Research Council. According to this study these crises are the identity crisis, the legitimacy crisis, the participation crisis, the penetration crisis, and the distribution crisis. See Leonard Binder, et al., *Crises and Sequences in Political Development* (Princeton: Princeton University Press, 1971).

9. Robert E. Ward, "Culture and the Comparative Study of Politics, or the Constipated Dialectic," *The American Political Science Review* (March, 1974), pp. 193–4. This article is the presidential address delivered at the Sixty-Ninth Annual Meeting of the American Political Science Association, New Orleans, Louisiana (September 6, 1973).

10. W. W. Rostow, *The Stages of Economic Growth* (New York: Cambridge University Press, 1960), p. 7.

11. C. E. Black, *The Dynamics of Modernization: A Study in Comparative History* (New York: Harper and Row, Publishers, 1966), pp. 158–9.

Index